AF605958

The Backcountry Venture

The Carolina Backcountry Venture

Tradition, Capital, and Circumstance in the Development of Camden and the Wateree Valley, 1740–1810

Kenneth E. Lewis

The University of South Carolina Press

Published by the University of South Carolina Press
Columbia, South Carolina 29208

www.sc.edu/uscpress

Manufactured in the United States of America

25 24 23 22 21 20 19 18 17
10 9 8 7 6 5 4 3 2 1

Library of Congress Cataloging-in-Publication Data
can be found at http://catalog.loc.gov/.

ISBN 978-1-61117-744-2 (cloth)
ISBN 978-1-61117-745-9 (ebook)

To the memory of Stephen I. Thompson, teacher, mentor, and friend, whose work inspired my interest in colonization and its impact on those involved in the processes of change associated with it

Contents

List of Illustrations

Preface

It is hard to know where to start to describe a work that has occupied my life for the past forty years. I have not been immersed in it continuously during this time, but it has never been far away. I became acquainted with Camden in the fall of 1974, shortly after I joined the staff of the Institute of Archaeology and Anthropology at the University of South Carolina. The site of the eighteenth-century town had been the subject of several archaeological projects sponsored by the Camden District Heritage Foundation in the 1960s, research aimed primarily at locating the fortifications constructed there during the American Revolutionary War. By the time I arrived, the town site was administered by the Camden Historical Commission, a local administrative unit created by the legislature to operate and develop it as a historical park. Seeking to expand its knowledge of the early settlement, the Commission turned to the Institute to initiate archaeological work designed to explore the town that had been one of the earliest European communities in South Carolina's backcountry.

I had recently completed graduate studies at the University of Oklahoma in which my work focused on the expansion of agricultural societies and their adaptation to conditions encountered on the frontier. As one of the earliest European settlements in South Carolina's interior, Camden seemed to offer an excellent opportunity to investigate the development of a colonial community and the response of its residents to the conditions they encountered. Camden was also an ideal situation in which to examine the role of archaeology in historical research. The late 1960s and early 1970s were a time of debate among archaeologists, and questions had been raised regarding the field's disciplinary orientation as well as the importance of material culture in the study of societies that produced a written record. Many still believed that archaeology could be employed only to support the more complete information revealed by documents. But the then-"new" archaeology promised an alternate way of examining behavior through an examination of its material remains and emphasized the processes, or regularities, that underlay the actions of people. By investigating the residue of past activities, archaeologists believed they could discern patterns that reflected the processes that shaped the world of the past. Already, archaeologists such as Jim Deetz had demonstrated that the popularity of objects followed regular curves over time, and Stanley South had employed statistical methods to discern historic occupation dates from the relative frequencies of ceramic fragments. Processual archaeologists had begun to explore the processes that underlay past change and the factors that influenced it. Surely the site of Camden held material evidence that could speak to its history and to the development of the backcountry as well.

The key to Camden's past was understanding its role in the colonization of South Carolina's interior. The process of settlement expansion created frontiers, these transitory zones in which immigrant societies settled, interacted with Native peoples, overcame the temporary isolation of distance, and established a production base that eventually enabled them to become a part of a larger parent state. South Carolina's experience in the eighteenth century was certainly distinctive, yet it also shared much with other frontiers. A comparative approach to the frontier had intrigued me as a graduate student at the University of Oklahoma, where I worked with Stephen I. Thompson, a cultural anthropologist whose ethnographic work focused on modern colonization in South America and the adaptive changes that influenced immigrant societies on the frontier. Steve had studied with Julian Steward and Joseph B. Casagrande, two of the leading postwar American anthropologists, whose comparative perspective and understanding of human ecology contributed to his view of the frontier as a widespread experience. This approach had broad implications for explaining the histories of colonial regions, and I felt that examining Camden through the comparative framework of frontier studies would benefit my comprehension of the town's distinctive development and assist in the design of archaeological research aimed at exploring the nature of this community and the world in which it existed.

Central to the study of Camden are the twin themes of continuity and change. As immigrants from Europe of other parts of British colonial America, residents of the backcountry carried with them the capitalist economic orientation of their homelands and maintained cultural traditions that guided the region's development. These formed the basis for their adaptations to the conditions encountered on the edge of settlement, circumstances that shaped the economy and society of the frontier and guided its transition. But the broader currents of politics and war also impacted the new communities and interrupted the processes that incorporated the backcountry into the society of Atlantic America. My research sought to examine the development of the region through the microcosm of one such community to reveal a complete and accurate picture of Camden's history and the forces that shaped it.

As my inquiry proceeded over the years, I became increasingly interested in the scale at which to observe change. While the grand scale represented by processes of agricultural colonization helped explain the outlines of the backcountry's evolution, the nature of its details required a more narrow approach aimed at determining just how changes had occurred and how they had manifested themselves on the level of frontier communities and the households that composed them. Such an approach allowed me to explore more clearly the relations between the newcomers and indigenous peoples as well as those between the ethnically diverse immigrants themselves. More recently, studies of the interaction between individuals and their societies have focused on the role of agency in the emergence of social and economic structures. This level of analysis led me to investigate the activities of key persons and those with whom they interacted to create a viable economy in the backcountry and promote the region's commercial growth. The scale of observation has helped guide my research, both historical and archaeological, and helped me understand the relevance of smaller actions and events to the larger processes that shaped the region's development.

The traumatic events of the American Revolution interrupted Camden's growth as a community in a terrible way. This brief but significant episode brought a harsh military occupation and a bitter civil war to the backcountry and nearly destroyed all that had preceded it. Perhaps because a tour in Vietnam was barely four years in my past, I was sensitive to the situation the war created. On the one hand, it placed a British garrison at Camden far from home in what must have seemed a wilderness and embroiled it in a partisan conflict in which the losers awaited an unpleasant fate. At the same time, the pervasiveness of the conflict polarized the region's population, forcing South Carolinians to take sides in a struggle that threatened the very existence of the society and economy so recently and tenuously formed on the periphery of European settlement. It was not hard to comprehend its impact on those who had cast their fortunes with the rebellious state as well as those who had opposed it. The war did not create or destroy the backcountry, and it was more than the fortifications around an occupied town. Occurring at a defining moment in Camden's history, it influenced not only its future but also the interpretation of its past.

My involvement with Camden and the backcountry has been a long road that involved many people over the years. Certainly none of the research there would have been possible without the work of those individuals and organizations concerned with preserving and maintaining the site of the eighteenth-century town. The Camden District Heritage Foundation, founded by Richard and Margaret Lloyd in 1967, provided the impetus for preserving the town site and was instrumental in raising funds to support the historical park, called Historic Camden, and conduct research there. Two years later, the state legislature created the Camden Historical Commission as a local administrative entity to operate and develop the site, which later became an affiliated unit of the National Park Service. In 2000 the Commission and the Foundation merged to form the Historic Camden Foundation, which currently administers the historical park.

Many people and organizations have contributed to the success of the research at Camden. Historic Camden has been the sponsoring agency, and the directors with whom I have worked exhibited great foresight in recognizing the importance of archaeology in developing this important site. Both Hope Cooper, under whose directorship my work in 1974–1977 and 1981 took place, and Joanna Craig, who played a crucial role in the archaeological research in the 1990s, were instrumental in securing support for the major projects and, together with their staffs, provided assistance throughout the investigations and were of inestimable help in coordinating the support of other agencies. Shirley Ransom, who assisted Ms. Cooper, also worked tirelessly to ensure the success the success of our endeavors. I also wish to thank former director Stephen Smith for his support and encouragement of the research. Without the backing of the Camden Historical Commission and the Camden District Heritage Foundation, the archaeological projects could never have taken place. In particular, I want to thank Dick Lloyd for his continuing active support and John K. DeLoach Jr. and Lanning P. Risher for their interest in my work.

During the course of my research, I have worked with many scholars who have contributed to the success of this endeavor. Several individuals at the University of South Carolina stand out. They include Jo Anne McCormick, who carried out documentary research in cooperation with the 1974–1975 project, organizing and compiling a great deal of primary information useful then as well as years later. More recently, Carolyn B. Lewis provided much-appreciated assistance with the additional archival research necessary to complete this study. Keith Krawczynski helped assemble plats and land records in the 1990s to provide a first look at the evolving settlement patterning in the Wateree Valley. I enjoyed many useful conversations with George Terry, historian of the lowcountry and later administrator at the USC. H. Roy Merrens also provided a helpful geographical perspective on the region. Always helpful was advice given by Charles F. Kovacik and John J. Winberry of the Department of Geography, whose knowledge of South Carolina's history always emphasized the relevance of space to all things. I also benefited from discussions with historians Charles Joyner and Peter Wood, whose work has provided many insights into African American society in colonial South Carolina. Conversations with scholars of the Shenandoah Valley frontier, geographer Robert D. Mitchell, and historian Warren R. Hofstra, helped expand my understanding of the dynamics of colonial expansion in the Southern backcountry.

From the beginning, the South Carolina Institute of Archaeology and Anthropology at USC has been a part of my research at Camden. Robert L. Stephenson directed the Institute during the time of the initial archaeological projects in the 1970s and was particularly supportive of my work there. His successor, Bruce Rippeteau, continued SCIAA's commitment to archaeology at Camden by generously providing specialized field equipment for the projects conducted in the 1990s. The success of an archaeological project owes much to the enterprise of the field supervisors, whose efforts and insights often go unmentioned and unappreciated. Without the assistance of Michael O. Hartley and Frank Krist, the results of the 1974–1975 and the 1996–1997 projects would have been greatly diminished, and I thank them both for their efforts. I conducted the analyses of archaeological materials recovered in the early projects at the Institute and wish to thank Jacqueline Carter for her efforts in processing and recording these data. Robert N. Strickland, who carried out earlier excavations at Camden, provided information crucial to later analyses conducted by W. Thomas Langhorne Jr. and myself. My later work required access to the records of all previous projects at Camden, a task greatly facilitated by the hard work and concern of SCIAA collections manager Sharon Pekrul and research associate Tommy Charles. Darby Erd produced the excellent illustrations of the Kershaw House. The Consortium for Archaeological Research at Michigan State University provided laboratory space for Frank Krist, Leslie Riegler, Andrew S. Farry, and Kevin Nichols, who conducted the analysis of materials collected in the later investigations. Cindy Davis-Fusel went beyond the call of duty to provide photographs of contemporary structures at Camden.

Over the years my work has benefited from conversations with a number of archaeologists at USC whose knowledge and insights often helped me see what I might otherwise have overlooked. Stanley South has been a continuing influence on my work at Camden and elsewhere. As perhaps the most profound innovator in historical archaeology in the 1970s and certainly its greatest proponent, Stan offered encouragement that gave me the confidence to explore change on a broad scale and to use new methods to discover and examine the processes that shaped Camden and the backcountry. At SCIAA, Mark J. Brooks, director of its Savannah River Archaeological Research Program, was constantly supportive, and he and Adam King vetted my knowledge of the state's prehistory. The directors of two

South Carolina archaeological consulting firms provided information helpful in spatial analyses, and I wish to thank Carl Steen, of the Diachronic Research Foundation, and Michael Trinkley, of the Chicora Foundation. I also appreciate all that I learned in conversations and interactions with those involved in historical and archaeological research relating to the state during the past four decades, including David Anderson, Ron Anthony, Stephen G. Baker, Richard D. Brooks, Cort A. Calk, Richard F. Carrillo, Charles Cobb, David Colin Crass, Chester DePratter, Roy Dickens, Lesley M. Drucker, Leland G. Ferguson, Patrick Garrow, Stanton W. Green, Michael Harmon, Michael O. Hartley, Stephanie Holschlag, John H. House, Lisa Hudgins, Susan Jackson, J. W. Joseph, Chris Judge, Pelham Lyles, James Michie, Sue Mullins Moore, Nena Powell Rice, Michael J. Rodeffer, Elizabeth Reitz, James D. Scurry, Theresa Singleton, Katherine Singley, Russell Skowronek, Steven D. Smith, Linda France Stine, Roy Stine, Gail Wagner, Thomas Wheaton, and Martha Zierden.

Recent archaeological investigations by R. P. Stephen Davis Jr. and Brett H. Riggs of the Research Laboratories of Archaeology at the University of North Carolina, Chapel Hill, have revealed exciting new information on the Catawba people and their role in the economy of the upper Wateree Valley. Excavations at numerous village sites occupied during the late colonial and early federal periods have yielded material items that shed much light on the adaptations of these resourceful Native people. Catawba ceramics were a recognizable item of exchange at Camden and remained a staple of trade in later years. Archaeology has been crucial in understanding the larger context of this artifact's development, and Davis and Riggs have willingly shared their research with me.

My research at Camden has involved many individuals who have assisted me in numerous ways. I wish to thank Kershaw family scholar Frank K. Babbitt, whose insatiable quest for information relating to Joseph Kershaw made available sources otherwise not available. Charles Baxley, editor of *Southern Campaigns of the American Revolution,* and Michael G. Scoggins, research director of the Southern Revolutionary War Institute, helped me sort out the details of the conflict in the backcountry. Martha Daniels, curator of the Mulberry Plantation Archives, assisted me by providing details of John Chesnut's early life, as well as a portrait of Chesnut. Camden historian Joan Inabinet helped clear up a nagging mystery concerning the early Methodist Church. I also want to thank Marge and Jim Faber for first bringing Phinehas Thornton's letter by to my attention.

This work could never have been complete without the help of those entrusted with the archival materials on which our knowledge of the past rests. They include Robert McIntosh of the South Carolina Department of Archives and History; E. L. Inabinet, Allen H. Stokes, Sam Fore, and Graham Duncan of the South Caroliniana Library at the University of South Carolina; J. Mitchell Reams and Neal Martin of the James A. Rogers Library at Francis Marion University; John White of the Southern History Collections at the University of North Carolina, Chapel Hill; Harry Miller of the Wisconsin Historical Society; Katherine Richardson of the Camden Archives and Museum; the staff of the William L. Clements Library at the University of Michigan; and the staffs of the Clerk of Court and Probate Judge in Kershaw County and Lancaster County, South Carolina.

Writing is a complicated process of combining ideas and information in a form that is not only accurate but also understandable to readers. I am forever grateful to those who read and critiqued the manuscript versions of this book. Carolyn B. Lewis has always been my most valuable critic. Her perusal of the entire manuscript resulted in comments and suggestions that helped me work out many rough spots, and this study benefited greatly from her review. Woody Bowden, a retired English teacher, student of Southern history, and one on my oldest friends, offered many helpful suggestions that made the text flow more smoothly. Charles Baxley's knowledge of the American Revolution in the South ensured the completeness and accuracy of my discussions of the war in South Carolina. Discussions with Helen Perlstein Pollard helped me unravel the mysteries surrounding the emergence of complex societies, Lynne Goldstein enhanced my knowledge of Jewish community structure, and conversations with Margaret Holman about a variety of topics were always enlightening. I also wish to thank the two anonymous reviewers at the University of South Carolina Press. Illustrations are crucial to a study of regional change, and I am indebted to those who produced the artwork accompanying this study. The maps, plans, and other line art are the work of Christopher Valvano and Joshua Schnell. I want to thank Kathy McGlynn for helping me prepare the electronic copy of this manuscript for publication and Alex Moore of the University of South Carolina Press for his support during the publication process.

In this study I have attempted to combine sources of knowledge from several disciplines to examine the historical question of how and why a region developed as it did. As an anthropologist who deals with complex, literate societies through both the written and the material records they leave behind, I feel I must acknowledge those who have given me insights helpful in guiding the scope and direction of my work. At the University of Florida, Solon Kimball introduced me to the idea of community, a concept he helped pioneer in anthropology. Functionalist in orientation, his community study approach focuses on human activities, the interactions and relationships of those involved in them, as well as their patterning in time and space. This approach has obvious implications for an examination of groups within an expanding immigrant society, whose structure derives from the interactions of their members and whose evolution is shaped by the success of their adaptive behavior. Throughout my work at Camden, I have employed the notion of community as an organizing element to explain its development as a frontier settlement and to interpret the nature and meaning of its material remains.

Wisdom from others has helped shape the orientation of my work as well. William E. Carter's insistence that to be anthropology, archaeology must examine questions of behavior drew me away from culture history. Similarly, Robert E. Bell's admonition that historical archaeology must tell us something more than documents made me think beyond the written record. Delineating the material manifestations of behavior rests on archaeological methodology grounded in theory and capable of explaining the larger behavioral context of objects. Processual archaeology offers a logic that emphasizes the links between past activities and the material record they leave behind. Rich Pailes drew my attention to the potential of archeology as a powerful tool to examine human behavior and helped me explore questions beyond the scope of culture history. Stanley South insisted that historical archaeologists employ such sound methodology and derive their conclusions on the basis of clear and demonstrable links between material patterning and the behavior that produced it. The construction of bridging arguments tying the nature of Camden's evolution to the form, content, and distribution of its archaeological remains was crucial to examining the historical processes that shaped South Carolina's backcountry. The strength of my conclusions owes much to the logical soundness of Stan's approach.

Because Steve Thompson's research in colonization inspired my interest in frontier studies, I cannot close without mentioning a strange twist that connected him to this study in an unexpected way. Not long after I had finished the first season's archaeological field work at Camden, I presented the results at one of the annual Frontier Symposia held at the University of Oklahoma. At a party one evening Steve mentioned that one of his ancestors had lived in North Carolina and had fought in the American Revolution. Corp. Murdoch McLeod had served with Lt. Col. John Hamilton's Royal North Carolina Regiment, a unit that was active in the Southern Campaign of 1780–1781. As part of Lt. Gen. Charles Earl Cornwallis's command, it participated in the British victory at the Battle of Camden and subsequently became part of the Camden garrison. Under the command of Lt. Col. Francis Lord Rawdon, this force was charged with the unenviable tasks of occupying and pacifying a large portion of South Carolina's backcountry. Murdoch McLeod's residence at Camden was not a happy time. Indeed, it may well have been the worst year of his life. At war's end he and other Loyalists suffered the further indignity of being deported to Nova Scotia, yet he and his family persisted. Steve and Murdoch are gone now. But perhaps, somewhere in the Great Beyond, they are sitting down with a cold beer, swapping tales, and laughing their heads off at the follies of those who study the frontier.

Chapter 1

"So Great a Change in a Small Community"

Five days before Christmas in 1850, Phinehas Thornton began a letter to his niece Clarissa Martin in Philadelphia. After many years of separation, she had come back into his life through a chance meeting with a mutual friend who had boarded with her while traveling with his daughter the previous summer. During their stay, Mrs. Martin inquired about the branch of her family that had settled in South Carolina, with whom she and her northern relatives had lost contact. She asked particularly about her "Uncle Thornton," whom she had not seen since childhood. Phinehas Thornton seemed surprised and pleased by her interest and expressed regret for the many years that passed since he had communicated with his sister's children. Aware of his failing health, he was anxious to pass on details about the lives of her southern relatives. He was now seventy-one and one of the few survivors of the generation that had witnessed the family's diaspora at the end of the previous century.[1]

Phinehas Thornton's move to Camden, situated on the Wateree River in north-central South Carolina, was part of the wider migration of northerners to the state following the American Revolution. Their arrival coincided with the emergence of the backcountry, as the interior was generally known, as a commercial agricultural region. Born in New Jersey in 1779, he came to Camden in 1793 to join his parents and several siblings who had previously settled there.[2] Eleven years later he married Elizabeth Williams of Raynham, Massachusetts, who accompanied him to his adopted home. Thornton soon joined Camden's growing retail establishment, first as a partner of his brother-in-law Dan Carpenter and then as an independent merchant, operating a general store not far from the town market. In 1820 he became the postmaster of Camden, a post he held for twenty-three years, until ill health forced him to resign his position.[3] Now in retirement, he looked back over his nearly six decades there as one of the oldest surviving members of a family that included five generations. Though he was always a man of modest means, Thornton's choice of career placed him literally in the center of Camden and at the heart of the town's affairs. His roles as storekeeper, town postmaster, and leader in the Methodist Church brought him into contact with the influential as well as with ordinary citizens. As one whose life was intertwined with the affairs of the community, he possessed a unique perspective on the town and its evolving role in South Carolina's interior.[4]

During his lifetime Phinehas Thornton observed events and changes that affected his family as well as the broad transformations that affected the larger world in which he lived. The Camden he initially encountered in the closing years of the eighteenth century had only recently emerged from its frontier past and the chaos of the American Revolution, and the people and places there represented a tangible link to the seminal period of its development. Over the next six decades, however, both the early town and many of its residents had vanished. "There are not more than five or six persons a living now, and there is but two buildings now standing that was here when I came," he wrote; "there is a new generation and a new town sprung up in that time."[5] Camden's rapid and profound transition following the Revolution was undeniable to one whose lifetime had spanned this time of recovery and economic growth. But Camden's development did not begin in the closing years of the eighteenth century. Rather, this period witnessed the closing movement of a much broader pageant in which the settlement had played a central role, a performance whose drama and complexity fascinated contemporary observers as well as later chroniclers of South Carolina's history.

Camden's antebellum expansion was the product of a larger process of evolutionary change whose roots lay in the historical milieu of British colonization and the expansion of European settlement into the interior. This experience significantly altered the backcountry, transforming the land and affecting the lives of its aboriginal and immigrant inhabitants, and set the stage for the town's rise to prominence. Almost from its inception as a focus of frontier settlement in the middle years of the eighteenth century, its site at the mouth of Pine Tree Creek played a key role in the economic and social life of the Wateree Valley. As a center of agricultural production and trade in the interior and the focus of political and administrative authority on the frontier, the locale became the axis around which the region's early history revolved.[6] Camden's emergence there was distinctive and extraordinary and begs for an explanation. Why did central traits manifest themselves here and not elsewhere? Why did they assume the form that they did? And how did Camden's rise shape the region around it? It is tempting to attribute the course of Camden's past to the colorful and dramatic events associated with the European settlement of South Carolina's interior, the exotic adventure of the deerskin trade, the tragedy of the Cherokee War, the melodramatic violence of the Regulator movement, and the internecine viciousness and destruction of the American Revolution in the backcountry. Did these remarkable occurrences and the seemingly larger-than-life individuals who inhabited the world of the frontier mold history in their image? One cannot deny that any or all of these factors influenced the course of Camden's development. Certainly exceptional events occurred and involved many of Camden's inhabitants and often affected them profoundly. On the other hand, all of these influences operated within the broader historical framework of South Carolina's participation in the greater Atlantic world of the eighteenth century. As a part of this larger phenomenon, distinctive developments in South Carolina were both a local adaptive response to particular circumstances encountered here and a manifestation of broader processes that governed British colonization on the eastern seaboard of North America. To understand Camden's rise, we must look beyond its immediate surroundings and consider the broader processes that brought it into being and affected the actions of the individuals who settled the backcountry.

Contexts of Colonization

The colonization of South Carolina's interior was a consequence of the global expansion of Europe, a process propelled by capitalist economic motives that encouraged nation-states to increase home production and enlarge markets by extending their overseas dominions into peripheral regions where resources and labor costs were relatively lower.[7] British colonization of North America's eastern seaboard was a manifestation of this process in that it brought valuable resources under the control of the home country through the occupation of new lands. Successful colonization required resettling people, creating a production base, and establishing a stable economy and society at the outer edge of Britain's political sphere of influence. South Carolina's success as a producer of specialized agricultural commodities for an export market depended on the ability of its new inhabitants to transplant complex European social, political, and economic institutions to a place where they did not previously exist.[8] How they accomplished this affected the form of colonization and had far-reaching consequences for the nature and form of the settlements that arose to support it.

As an element in the greater process of colonial expansion, the Wateree Valley and its inhabitants shared an experience comparable to that of settlers in other agricultural colonies. Comparative cross-cultural studies have identified similarities that describe the structure of frontier settlement and its change over time as the areas they occupied became an integral part of stable economies. They emphasize that individual frontier settlements are components of larger systems and may be studied in light of the roles they played in the evolution of the larger region in which they were situated. Camden's links to a broader process of change can provide valuable clues to its development. At the same time, recognizing the function of the settlement and the larger system allows us to use the town's experience to explore regional phenomena. In many ways Camden represents the history of the backcountry in microcosm.[9]

Explaining Camden's remarkable past requires an understanding of how a wider process of change played out in the context of the South Carolina's interior during the eighteenth century. How did agricultural expansion in the context of the backcountry influence the region's particular growth and direct the form and nature of its settlement? As a frontier, South Carolina's interior had much in common with Great Britain's other North American provinces, but the circumstances of its geography and the order of its settlement also made it distinctive. Situated to the south of the longer-established colonies, its peripheral position placed it near lands claimed by Spain and adjacent to territories controlled by powerful Native societies. Because the province was settled later than its neighbors, its position in time also affected the direction of its development.

Settlement of the backcountry was tied closely with South Carolina's economy. Colonization occurred first in coastal lowcountry and followed the West Indian pattern of specialized commercial plantation farming based on enslaved labor, the nature of which fostered distinctive economic, social, and political institutions that created and molded the region's character. Because the lowcountry produced great wealth, its perceived vulnerability prompted the subsequent colonization of the interior. Expansion into the backcountry dispersed a diverse pioneer population over a vast land where they encountered challenges different from those presented by the coastal region. Here immigrants developed economic and social arrangements capable of sustaining them on the periphery of settlement, organizing and administering an undeveloped region, and building a production base capable of supporting growth and fostering the backcountry's incorporation within the expanding commercial economy of British America and, later, the nascent United States. Here factors particular to the backcountry influenced the region's development and conditioned its transition into a mature agricultural region, a process that affected both the character and the appearance of its settlements.

Levels of Observation

Investigations of the influence of general processes and particular factors on the backcountry's early development are complicated by the fact that they often manifested themselves differently at various levels of observation. Conditions associated with the time and location of British colonization affected the structure of regional society in its entirety as well as the elements that composed it. Pioneers entered a new world in which they encountered an unfamiliar environment and a multiethnic milieu, the nature of which shaped their settlements, the links connecting them, and all other elements that made up the cultural landscape of the interior. Collectively these settlements formed an integrated regional system composed of disparate but interrelated components. All were involved in the larger process of change, but not in the same way. The function of immigrant settlements varied, they shared unequal access to resources and trade, and their inhabitants met unique threats and opportunities that enhanced or diminished their potential for success in the new country.

Although the backcountry's new residents lived in an area under the nominal control of the crown, it lacked the presence of a central authority and the formal administrative structure necessary to integrate economic, political, and social activities within the region. As in other newly settled areas, members of pioneer households devised indigenous measures to provide for their security and created the linkages that helped them persist and establish a base for production and trade. Those with mutually beneficial economic and social interests formed rural communities that reflected their common needs.[10] In place of the formal organizational structures found in longer-settled areas, they developed arrangements that laid a foundation for more conventional economic, social, and political institutions that transformed the backcountry and facilitated its integration within the larger commercial economy. The appearance of these community institutions was central to Camden's emergence as a central place and may be observed in individual settlements as well as over the province as a whole. These different but complementary scales of observation offer the strength of two levels of analysis.

A Broad Scale of Analysis

A wider approach examines the nature of regionwide institutions within the larger context in which they operated and views their development from the perspective of the province as a whole. Contemporary observers and long-term residents recognized that Camden's early rise to prominence was tied to its position in wider networks of production and trade and that greater outside forces had shaped the great changes they had witnessed during their lifetimes.[11] The structure of the pioneer economy in the South Carolina backcountry grew out of conditions encountered at the periphery of European expansion and changed as the region was subsequently incorporated within the larger colonial world. Broad-scale analyses of societal-level strategies help define the impact of wider conditions on the economic and social milieu of pioneer communities.

A wider approach derives strength from its ability to define institutions in a general way and observe their nature on a comparative basis. For example, if we seek to explain the arrangements by which backcountry residents produced crops and goods, how they modified them for use or transport, and how they moved them to consumers, we must first investigate the nature of the regional economic institutions of production, processing, shipping, and marketing. On a broad scale, the organization of backcountry trade may be viewed as an outcome of the larger setting of the provincial and Atlantic economies and its characteristics explored by comparing them to trade in similar regions elsewhere. The impact of larger events, such as the Cherokee War, were felt throughout the backcountry and provided a context that prompted coordinated indigenous political action. This level of analysis can reveal the effect of regional arrangements, be they networks of trade or administrative institutions, on the composition of individual communities and the nature of their activities and identify evolutionary trends that provide a context in which to examine the impact of change in the Wateree Valley. A broad-scale approach also facilitates the investigation of the social impact of wider forces, such as evangelical religion or the significance of the militia or the Regulator movement, as political institutions in shaping the region and its settlement. Such a "system-centered" view further recognizes that the outcomes of early strategies affected existing resources and social arrangements and effectively altered the conditions around which new strategies would be designed. Although a regional scope provides a context in which to model Camden's development, it limits the extent to which it can explain the form and precise direction of change. To examine these phenomena, we must employ a closer level of analysis.

Narrowing the Scale of Analysis

A more restricted scale of analysis, in contrast, assesses community institutions from the viewpoint of the individuals and households involved. The strength of this perspective lies in the detail its sources provide about activities that constituted community institutions and how they were carried out. The particular view offered by those involved in such activities also allows us to observe the adaptive nature of community institutions, examine their changes over time, and investigate their role in shaping regional variation. Nowhere is this better illustrated than in the account of Sarah Thompson Alexander, another long-term Camden resident. Writing in 1850, she looked over the events that had affected South Carolina over the preceding half century but viewed them through the lens of the community in which she lived. "Change is the irrecoverable decree of all beneath the sun," she wrote, "but in no small place perhaps do you see so great a change in a small community as here." Although Mrs. Alexander accepted the existence of larger forces in Camden's past, she also recognized that specific individuals and the institutions they created had affected the direction of change. Recalling the rise of the Methodist Church, she carefully portrayed it not as an organic development imposed from outside but rather as the result of actions taken by particular people in pursuit of distinct goals.[12]

A narrow scale of analysis is particularly useful in exploring economic questions concerning production, processing, and shipping in the backcountry. Instead of looking at these solely in a broad regional context that emphasizes general influences such as crops and market demand, a narrower view focuses on how people organized community-level institutions to carry out those economic activities. The records of individuals and households that participated in the churches, assemblies, courts, fairs, markets, militia units, and other indigenous organizations of the backcountry, chronicled their development, and how they operated within frontier communities.[13]

Emphasizing a narrow scale of analysis also recognizes that adaptations by individuals and small groups played a significant role in directing change. To understand their significance, we must first consider *how* they articulated with larger entities and *why* they were important to their structure and operation. In the backcountry, as in frontiers elsewhere, societal institutions did not appear full-blown and imposed from above but rather were created by individuals who recognized needs and possessed the labor and resources to provide them. Successfully establishing pioneer institutions depended on the ability of individuals to negotiate social alliances necessary to organize groups capable of carrying out specific activities. In this sense, this process of interaction shaped community institutions, whose form was largely contingent upon the actions of human actors as agents of change. In a developing society, rapid change continually altered conditions and necessitated constant innovation. Larger external forces underlay the settlement of the backcountry, but the course of Camden's development was also affected by the cumulative actions of individuals and cannot be explained without reference to them.[14]

This study of Camden focuses on its rise the focus of the creation of the backcountry's central economic institutions. Survival on the frontier depended on a society's ability to establish a subsistence base that allowed it to achieve a level of security and begin to generate wealth. Growth depended on viable economic institutions, the nature of which holds the key to understanding the backcountry's development and the society it created. A "subject-centered" analysis will explore institution building from the perspective of those involved and examine how they employed resources and structured social relationships to help them persist and enhance their prospects for success. The economic strategies individuals implemented over time guided the course of backcountry history, and an understanding of these strategies helps explain their actions of in wider cultural context.

Directions of Inquiry

Any study of eighteenth-century South Carolina covers well-trodden ground, and the question inevitably arises as to what insights this work hopes to contribute to our knowledge of the state's colonial past. Certainly the major figures, events, and places involved have been examined and are well known to those familiar with the period. The expansion of settlement into the backcountry, the development of an agricultural economy, the Revolutionary War, and the emerging plantation economy are all topics explored by scholars who have sought to describe, interpret, and explain events that transpired and explore their broader impact on what followed.[15] Although this book deals with familiar territory, my intent is not to rehash the works of others. Rather, I seek to employ available information, both written and material, to examine what I believe was the key process that guided the direction, form, and nature of settlement in South Carolina's interior. Agricultural expansion, arising in the larger context of the European world economy and its insatiable appetite for resources, was the engine that drove inland colonization. But, while continental in scope, it was carried out by individual people obliged to cope with the particular circumstances encountered in a distinctive regional setting. Neither a monolithic force directed from the outside nor the collective action of colonists acting independent of larger influences, colonization incorporated elements of both. The roots of South Carolina's colonization lay in the capitalist world system, but the manifestation of this process reflected the manner in which its players adapted the system's needs to a fluid regional situation complicated by a multitude of sometimes unanticipated factors. Only by addressing the dual nature of colonization will its structure emerge.

Chapter 2 sets the stage for our study by reviewing the circumstances of South Carolina's colonization in the larger context of European expansion and the British experience in North America. It examines the occupation of the southern Atlantic seaboard and the development of the economic, political, and social institutions that overcame the difficulties inherent in establishing a new colony along the Carolina coast and facilitated successful settlement and the creation of a viable agricultural export economy. Colonists transposed a Caribbean model of plantation farming based on specialty crops and enslaved labor, a strategy that accelerated the growth of commercial production and allowed the accumulation of great individual wealth, conditions that underlay the establishment of a stable administrative organization in the province. But the colony's perilous geographical position, together with the demographic disparities that accompanied its plantation economy, left the province vulnerable.

Efforts to alleviate threats to the rich coastal colony led officials to mandate an expansion of small farm settlement into South Carolina's interior, a process explored in Chapters 3, 4, and 5. This movement differed markedly from those encountered by earlier immigrants to the coastal area. The backcountry's new inhabitants had to adapt to conditions of physical and economic isolation, poor transportation, undercapitalization, an absence of integrating institutions, and the uncertainties posed by external threats in order to survive and persist in a region that remained tenuously linked to the larger Atlantic world and that lacked an adequate economic and administrative infrastructure. To ensure success under such conditions, immigrants developed strategies of regionally based social cooperation that encouraged internal production, promoted exchange, and provided security. These arrangements fostered interdependence among settlers and incorporated both immigrants and indigenous peoples in the emerging regional economy. Far from being an insurmountable challenge, the situation in the backcountry offered the opportunity to enlarge South Carolina's commercial economy. Entrepreneurial individuals fashioned new strategies to expand trade through networks of alliances, stimulate agricultural production, and encourage the growth of the social, religious, and political institutions necessary to form rural communities on the frontier and organize a regional economy. Settlement in the central interior centered on Fredericksburg Township in the Wateree River Valley, and by the 1750s Pine Tree Hill had emerged as the center of regional trade. Its rise as a focus of activity established a precedent for the role it would play in the rise of the backcountry.

Chapters 6, 7, and 8 examine the backcountry's economic and political consolidation in the decade prior to the American Revolution. This period witnessed an influx of capital and expertise that underwrote the shift to wheat and indigo as cash crops for export by providing the infrastructure for processing and transportation necessary to support this transition. Shifts in the volume of production and an increasing orientation toward export markets restructured trade and drew the backcountry closer to the economy of the Atlantic world. The period also saw the beginning of the backcountry's formal integration into the administrative structure of the province, a development that set the stage for the region's rising importance in the closing years of the century.

The growth of commercial mercantile activity at Pine Tree Hill was dominated by Joseph Kershaw and his associates. With access to lowcountry capital and connections, Kershaw built an infrastructure in the interior, but his success derived from his networks of personal alliances, which overcame the social diversity of the backcountry and created a complex support structure for the production, collection, and redistribution of goods and produce. A successful commercial economy depended on formal social and political institutions to ensure the security necessary for its efficient operation. To this end, residents worked to establish administrative and judicial districts in the backcountry, and the resulting stability they brought encouraged investment in large-scale, specialized commercial agriculture. This period marked the beginning of a shift toward plantation production with an increasing reliance on slave labor, changes that altered the region's economy and demography. Now a prosperous settlement at the center of the backcountry's increasingly complex economy, Pine Tree Hill took the name Camden in 1768.

The American Revolution in the southern backcountry had a stifling impact on regional development at all levels. Simmering political differences began to divide its residents but remained beneath the surface until the British invasion and occupation of the interior in 1780 polarized its population and launched a bitter civil war. The conflict devastated the countryside and tore apart communities. It interrupted agricultural production, disrupted trade, destroyed settlements, and dislocated their residents. Chapters 9 and 10 explore the impact of this conflict on the backcountry and particularly at Camden. Occupied and fortified by the British army, the town became a military base, and two important battles and several skirmishes took place nearby. The army's presence divided the local population, reordering personal and business relationships, and existing networks served to structure militias on both sides. But their bonds also crossed the political rifts that divided the backcountry's residents. The war left few with their property and fortunes intact; many residents suffered devastating personal setbacks as they saw stores, mills, and plantations destroyed. Later, those on the losing side faced the confiscation of their estates and political exile. In the end, the waste generated by the violence and its aftermath delayed the transition begun in the prewar period and slowed the course of future development for the backcountry and those who lived there.

The remaining chapters examine Camden's recovery in the postwar period and its subsequent fluorescence in the new century. The years following the Revolution brought both continuity and change. Although part of a now independent United States, South Carolina remained enmeshed in the larger world economy and responded to its role as a supplier of raw commodities for export markets. Strong demand for rice permitted rapid recovery of the lowcountry economy; however, debts and losses arising from the war and the cost of rebuilding a devastated infrastructure, coupled with diminished markets for older crops, delayed economic recovery in the interior. The adoption of cotton agriculture in the early nineteenth century restored the backcountry's economic viability and encouraged the spread of large-scale production based on unfree labor. Agricultural prosperity also promoted the expansion of retail trade and the formal institutions that supported it. At the center of a region increasingly integrated within the national economy, Camden arose from the ashes of the Revolution to become a substantial county seat in South Carolina's interior. Although the antebellum town faced economic competition posed by the rise of rival towns and newly opened western territories, its diminished position could not erase the glories of its past. Pivotal roles in opening the backcountry to trade and the conflict for independence ensured that Camden would always occupy a unique position among the settlements of the region.

When Phinehas Thornton and Sarah Alexander looked back upon the changes that had occurred during their lives, they recalled not only experiences particular to themselves but also the changes that constituted the broader process that accompanied Camden's transition from a frontier settlement to an integral element in the larger commercial economy. This process operated at the scale of individuals as well as that of the larger society in which they lived, and an awareness of the nature of the links between them is crucial to investigating the dramatic and far-reaching changes that shaped the South Carolina backcountry. Understanding the process that created Camden demands that we examine the events and forces that shaped the past of this extraordinary place at the multiple levels on which they occurred.

Chapter 2

"More Valuable to the Mother Country Than Any Other Province"

The Economic Basis for Colonial Growth

The year 1760 marked a turning point in the career of Henry Laurens. One of South Carolina's most prosperous merchants, Laurens had amassed a fortune dealing in commodities flowing between the colony's entrepôt of Charleston and England, Africa, and the West Indies. Laurens invested his profits in planting, and his success as a producer as well as a trader had made him one of the province's wealthiest men. In the fall of that year he traveled far into the interior of South Carolina as a lieutenant colonel in the provincial militia on an expedition against the Cherokees on the frontier. Through his journey Laurens gained familiarity with large portions of the backcountry, and he became acquainted with many of its inhabitants. He spent time in the central region of the Congarees, campaigned in the mountains on the northern boundary of the province, and visited the Moravian colony of Wachovia in nearby North Carolina seeking recruits. When he returned to Charleston the following year, Henry Laurens had broadened his economic perspective considerably (Fig. 2.1).[1]

His experience as a merchant made Laurens aware of the extensive opportunities the region had to offer those with the resources and insight to take advantage of them. The short stay in Wachovia convinced him that the industrious inhabitants of this recently settled region in the backcountry constituted a favorable market for retail trade. In 1761 he approached the elders of the Moravian community, offering them lucrative terms to shift their business from other outlets to Charleston. His endeavor led to the incorporation of these remote settlements within the market sphere of South Carolina's principal port.[2] Laurens's labors to capture the Moravian trade mirrored his efforts to extend his activities elsewhere in the interior. His success reflected his business acumen but also bore witness to the expansion of commercial exchange into the South Carolina backcountry in the second half of the eighteenth century. This process marked the passing of the frontier and the beginning of the region's incorporation into the larger Atlantic economy. The growth of the interior economy involved commodity production as well as exchange, and before the end of the decade Laurens and others were actively purchasing large tracts in the interior in anticipation of their rising value as plantation lands.[3] The changing role of the backcountry was already evident in 1763 when Laurens revealed to one of his most important mercantile

2.1 Henry Laurens was a successful merchant and planter and one of the wealthiest men in South Carolina. Familiar with the backcountry through his military service, he promoted the expansion of trade into the interior. Prominent in the public affairs of the province, Laurens later played a central role in the movement for independence. Courtesy of Library of Congress, Washington, District of Columbia.

associates in London that "we now have a large field for Trade opening . . . & a vast number of people setling down upon our frontier Lands." As the expansion of large-scale production buoyed land sales in the interior, it increased demand for enslaved labor and imported supplies and provided an excellent and reliable market for the merchants who imported them.[4]

The experiences of Henry Laurens illustrate wider changes that accompanied the growth of settlement in colonial South Carolina after 1750. These developments were, of course, shaped by a multitude of distinctive factors unique to the time and place in which they occurred. But broader influences affected the expansion of the colony, providing the impetus for change and establishing the structure within which it occurred. Although political motives certainly played a role in this phenomenon, economic factors overwhelmingly guided settlement in the backcountry. These forces underlay British colonization in North America and directed its spread on the southern Atlantic seaboard, where it promoted successful commercial agriculture in South Carolina's lowcountry. They constituted a process that arose with the emergence of a capitalist economy in Europe and accompanied the subsequent growth of a powerful global system centered in the nation-states of that continent. The expansion of Europe led to the creation of the modern world and influenced the economies of colonial areas everywhere.

The Global Context of the Atlantic Economy

The wealth and prominence of Henry Laurens and others derived from colonial South Carolina's highly successful role as a producer of specialized agricultural commodities for an export market. Less than a century after its founding, the province was among the most productive of Britain's North American colonies as well as one of the richest, and it developed more rapidly than others along the Atlantic seaboard. Following an inauspicious beginning in the late seventeenth century, South Carolina's settlers established a staple economy based on crops that were well suited to the area's distinctive coastal environment and transformed this low, flat region of forests, marshes, savannas, and swamps into a veritable agricultural factory. Known as the lowcountry, the area became home to literally thousands of residents of African and European descent and gave rise to highly prosperous plantations situated along its numerous navigable waterways. Although the bulk of production and much of the population remained rural, the results of the settlers' efforts were gathered, processed, stored, managed, and traded from a central metropolis that dominated the colony and served as its principal port. Why did such a distinctive economy develop, and how could it have come about so quickly? The answer is, in part, linked to the resources at hand, for they provided the basis for production. But their exploitation as a source of wealth depended on broader factors that supplied the impetus and wherewithal to develop them. To understand the ascendency of the lowcountry, we must examine its role in a larger context.[5]

The landing of English colonists at Albemarle Point near the mouth of the Ashley River in 1670 formally extended British sovereignty southward along the Atlantic coast of North America. Although the settlement's presence challenged Spanish territorial claims in the region, its primary purpose was as much economic as political. South Carolina's initial colonists came overwhelmingly from the British colonies in the West Indies, where the commercial production of sugar had already created a thriving export economy and a distinctive creole society. Indeed, Barbados was the richest, most highly developed, and most populous of all England's American colonies. The lucrative nature of plantation agriculture on Barbados brought wealth to entrepreneurs and encouraged its extension to other Caribbean islands and the adjacent mainland (Fig. 2.2). Eager to enlarge their economic domain, many Barbadians migrated to South Carolina, not because they had been failures in the Caribbean but rather because no unimproved arable remained in the sugar islands. The movement of West Indian planters to the mainland helped set the course for South Carolina's development and effectively made it the colony of a colony.[6]

The economy in which the founders of the Carolina colony participated was one that promoted growth to capture and control resources, and its specialized production required participation in a complex network of global scope. It derived from British America's involvement in the capitalist world economy, a system that accompanied the expansion of Europe in the fifteenth century and that ushered in a market-based economy that eventually extended its boundaries to encompass the entire world. This new economy incorporated a capitalist mode of production as its primary organizing principle and included a multiplicity of political systems within its scope. As a system of production based on wage labor, a free market, and the private appropriation of profit, capitalism had as its prime

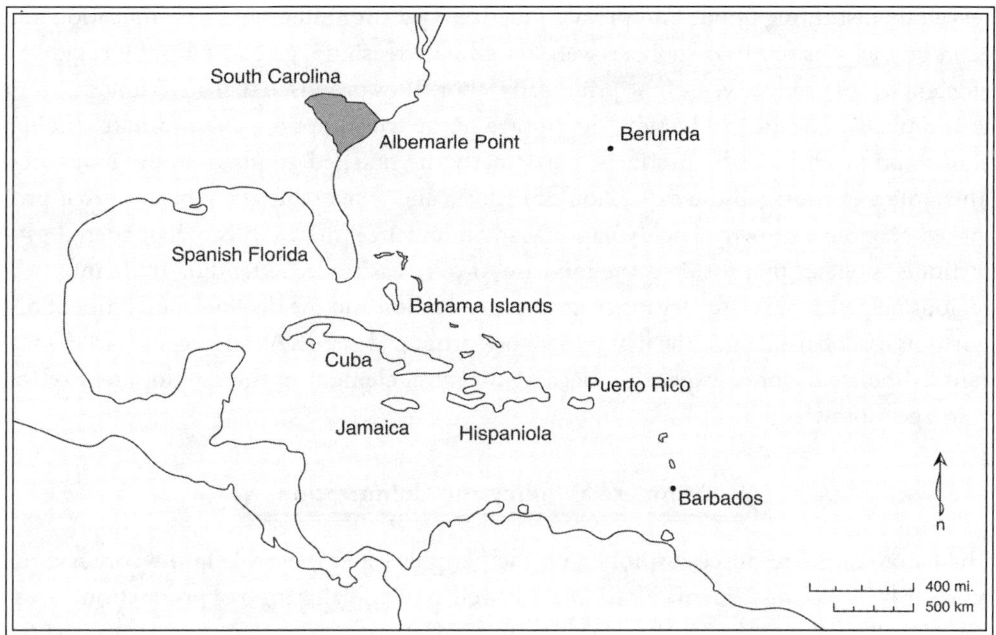

2.2 South Carolina and its neighbors at the beginning of the eighteenth century. Author's original map.

mover the potential of unlimited accumulation of capital. Operating in an arena too large for any single political entity to control, capitalists gained a structurally based freedom of maneuver that allowed them to enlarge their activities and acquire surpluses across national boundaries. As a result, production became increasingly directed away from goods meant for domestic trade and toward those intended for long-distance exchange. At the same time, a greater demand arose for all goods, favoring expanded production to accommodate the system's enlargement and giving rise to the institutionalized arrangements that defined the nature of this capitalist world economy.[7]

Closely related to this form of organization was the *axial division of labor,* in which unequal exchange became a major mechanism of surplus transfer and concentration. In other words, capitalists employed geography to separate the functional elements of the system so that the production of essential but lower-ranking goods (those for which labor was less well rewarded) was placed in *peripheral areas,* physically separated from the *core states* situated at the system's center. Because it was easier to move capital and merchandise than labor over great distances and across political boundaries, this arrangement reduced costs to producers. At the same time, the political security provided by the core states protected their accumulated capital. Exchange within the world economy was characterized by a system of vertical specialization that brought raw materials from the periphery to the core and moved manufactures and services in the opposite direction.[8]

Capitalist economic expansion reflected the principles of *mercantilism,* a set of assumptions grounded in the notion that a state's economic and political interests were best served by instituting public and private practices that promoted political unification and economic expansion. These policies were aimed at increasing aggregate output through the efficient use of productive factors, principally labor. They proposed that governments work to stimulate domestic production, discourage home consumption, and promote external consumption of domestic products, particularly the finished goods of home industries. This policy encouraged the expansion of exports and a favorable trade balance that promoted economic growth. Highly nationalistic in practice, mercantilism engendered protectionist policies that fostered the increase of overseas trade. Extending trade into new regions helped avoid crises arising from overproduction and the decline of investment opportunities, and it enlarged the market for core-produced goods. As an integral part of mercantilist policy, colonial expansion became a central element in the development of the world economy.[9]

Commercial Policy and Colonization

The nature of the resources exploited on the periphery and their role in the core nation's economy shaped the form of colonization as well as the organization of production. Those colonies that produced agricultural staples for export grew crops that were *noncompetitive* with those grown in the homeland. Because conditions conducive to their cultivation were often found in environments distinctly different from those found in Europe, staple colonies tended to be situated overseas. Exploitative plantation agriculture dominated these colonies, although their economies also relied on mining, timbering, ranching, and trading with Native peoples. The scale and specialized character of plantations also affected their nature. Large-scale plantations that produced specialized, labor-intensive, exotic crops, such as rice, sugar, or cotton, required a substantial advanced investment by wealthy promoters, who anticipated a large return on their investment, and the organization and administration of the colonies in which they were situated demanded a high level of managerial and technical skill.[10] Producing commodities almost solely for a global market tied the colonial economy closely to mercantile interests at the core and reduced the colony's insularity from homeland political and financial institutions. Authorities in the mother country paid close attention to affairs in the colony and often attempted to manipulate activities there directly, restricting opportunities for indigenous economic diversification. Shaped by these forces, immigrant settlement usually took the form of enclaves where change came largely in response to the development of more efficient production technologies or shifts in market demand. As integral suppliers of raw materials, such *cosmopolitan* colonies were the most economically valuable colonial regions.[11]

Colonization also occurred in temperate regions suitable for staples similar to those raised at home, but here the much lower market return on investment failed to attract the substantial amounts of capital capable of financing more profitable ventures. Colonies producing *competitive* staples instead relied on the migration of labor from the parent state and adopted a different scale of production. Large numbers of immigrants of more moderate means established family farms that required a much lower capital outlay to provide an efficient scale of production. The difference in the marginal value of products created an incentive for settlers to migrate voluntarily to these colonies, although land shortages, unemployment, persecution, famine, and war also helped populate these colonies. In their role as resettlement territories for excess homeland population, such colonies established a political presence on the periphery that might not otherwise justify their expense. If placed in strategic areas, settlement colonies could also protect core state interests from international rivals, pirates, Native peoples, and internal insurrections and might provide valuable commodities to the homeland and its other colonies.[12]

The production of competitive goods had implications for a colony's organization as well as its historical trajectory. Its diversified economy and weak commercial relations with the core state encouraged subsistence as well as surplus production. Colonists directed a substantial portion of exchange inward and invested surpluses in a regional infrastructure to facilitate the collection, processing, and marketing of produce at a local level. Funds that might have left the colony were instead invested in real assets there. A regionally focused colonial economy adapted to local conditions encouraged the development of indigenous social and political institutions that further decreased the number of interacting links between homeland and colony. The relative isolation from homeland influence freed such colonies from complete dependence on the core state and encouraged residents to take a more active part in determining the direction of development. Such *insular* colonies came to be characterized by pervasive social and political changes unrelated to their economic role in the world system. Institutions created to stabilize a society facing the insecurities found on the periphery fostered a distinct colonial identity and could exacerbate conflicts between colonial and homeland interests.[13]

Colonization in South Carolina

In the course of a hundred years, both of these types of colonization appeared in South Carolina. Each played a crucial, yet distinctive, role in the settlement of the province, and both shaped the course of its commercial agricultural development. The circumstances that gave rise to cosmopolitan and insular colonization were partly historical and reflected the development of Britain's North American colonies as a part of its overseas expansion. South Carolina was a structural element of the world economy; however, the form of its colonization was also influenced by the organization of capitalist production, the mechanisms by which it operated, and the mercantilist notions that enmeshed the policies of nation states in this process. Becoming a viable component in the world economy required colonists to establish production on the periphery. This entailed an organization that employed a mode of labor control suitable to accomplish this on a scale large enough to yield a product whose exchange was sufficiently remunerative to make it an integral element of a commodity chain anchored in the European core. South Carolina's settlers attempted to develop a production base centered on a marketable staple, but they did so in a distinctive and alien environment whose amenability was uncertain and that presented conditions that demanded substantial adaptations. The newcomers had to identify and develop specific crops suitable to the region and profitable enough to justify substantial investment and be transportable over long distances to homeland markets. Accomplishing this ensured South Carolina's success, but a cosmopolitan colony in the lowcountry brought with it conditions that dramatically shaped further settlement in the province.

Despite the lowcountry's economic growth, it soon became clear that the region could not exist on its own. South Carolina's history became a tale of two separate but interconnected regions. The coastal region was home to a vibrant capitalist agricultural economy that thrived on the production of noncompetitive staples and that grew to depend on a single staple produced by coerced labor. But it lay exposed and potentially vulnerable to foreign rivals and powerful Native societies. To stabilize the British presence in the southern colonies, secure the lowcountry, and counterbalance excesses that grew out of its extreme economic specialization, colonial authorities encouraged settlement of the interior. Although part of the same province, the backcountry lay remote from the coastal zone, and isolation from markets prevented it from following the lowcountry's path to immediate commercial success. As an insular colony, the backcountry's economic development took a different trajectory, but the region remained dependent on the earlier colony and looked to it for the institutional support necessary to consolidate the interior and bring about commercial exchange with external markets. The histories of both regions were irrevocably intertwined and cannot be investigated separately. The lowcountry and its economy cast a long shadow over the interior, and the course taken in settling the backcountry must be seen in this broader context.

Adaptations to the Lowcountry Environment

Britain's global network of market-driven production and trade guided the development of South Carolina's economy, but the direction of the region's growth also reflected its geographical context. To be successful, colonization had to accommodate the requirements of large-scale commercial production and long-distance marketing within the particular physiographic conditions encountered along the Carolina coast. Settlers' adaptations shaped the form of production as well as the political institutions created to administer the region and the societal structures that emerged there. Ecological constraints restricted the initial colony largely to the narrow confines of the coast throughout the colonial period; however, the colony's early presence, its direct overland links to the interior, and the overwhelming power of its wealth extended the lowcountry's influence far beyond its boundaries. Its seminal importance calls attention to the rise of its commercial economy.

The founders of the Carolina venture sought a location on the North American mainland where they could replicate the successful Caribbean pattern of producing noncompetitive staples on a grand scale. They settled on the Outer Coastal Plain of North America, a land whose nearly featureless topography reflected its sedimentary origins. Rising and falling sea levels during the Pleistocene Epoch modified this landform with numerous terraces that complicated the lower courses of the many rivers passing through it. Along the southern coast lay remnant islands and barrier islands formed by the erosion of the mainland and modified by marine processes. The broad Santee Delta marked the beginning of a wide, unbroken coastal strand that extended as far as present-day North Carolina.[14] Like the islands, the new colony was accessible by sea and possessed a warm, moderate climate. Early observers found the coastal region favorable for agriculture, and their reports encouraged settlement as soon as conditions permitted.[15] Within the first few decades of its existence,

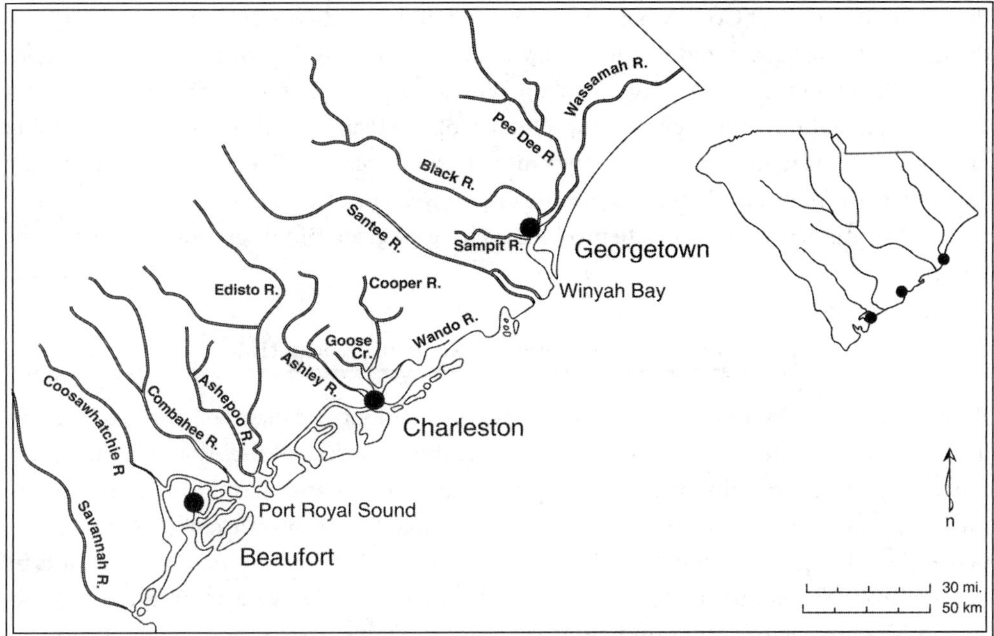

2.3 The geographical setting of settlement the South Carolina lowcountry during the early eighteenth century. Author's original map.

the area's new residents acquired the resources and labor necessary to transform the lowcountry into an exemplary mercantilist colony.[16]

The commercial orientation of the Carolina venture, together with the character of the new environment, shaped the patterning of settlement in the lowcountry. The Lords Proprietors, who possessed administrative authority under the colonial charter, hoped to control development and political stability by concentrating settlement, but, despite their intentions and careful planning, perceptions of agricultural efficiency guided the form of land occupancy.[17] Seeking to enter commercial production, colonists sought the highest-quality lands and gravitated to the "deepest and most fertile soils" found in the bottom lands that spread along coastal streams and rivers.[18] They intended to duplicate the success of colonial agriculture in Barbados by emulating the island model. This involved expanding production rapidly through large-scale plantation farming employing unfree labor. Although settlers initially brought few slaves with them, most intended to eventually possess large estates and sought lands upon which to situate them.[19]

Immigrant planters settled on higher elevations along the coastal rivers and streams that provided easy means of travel and transport (Fig. 2.3). They first took up lands along the Ashley River in 1670 and then moved up the Cooper and Wando Rivers and along Goose Creek, creating a pattern of dispersed settlement. Charleston, laid out at the harbor at the confluence of the Ashley and Cooper in 1680, became the urban center of the Carolina colony.[20] By the beginning of the eighteenth century, plantation settlement encompassed the Stono, Edisto, and Coosawhatchie Rivers and in the next two decades spread north to the mouth of the Santee and south to the vicinity of Port Royal. Two new ports, Beaufort, on Port Royal Sound, and Georgetown, on Winyah Bay, arose as secondary urban foci for the rural plantation settlements of the Outer Coastal Plain.[21] Although a high mortality rate from malaria made the lowcountry a more perilous place to live than any other part of British North America, planters found the region well suited for large-scale staple agriculture and continued to concentrate production here even after immigration penetrated the interior.[22]

Achieving a Commercial Scale of Production

Both the Proprietors' need for a return on their investment and planters' hopes of increasing their wealth rested on their ability to market the resources of the Atlantic seaboard in the larger world economy, and their entrepreneurial intent and desire to engage in commercial production would transform the newly occupied areas into an active element of the periphery.[23] Despite the commercial motives that underlay their venture, early attempts by South Carolina's colonists to develop viable export commodities were not immediately successful. The Proprietors' attempts to find a marketable staple led to experiments with ginger, silk, grape vines, olives, indigo, tobacco, cotton, hemp, flax, dates, almonds, and other European crops, but all were impractical or could not compete successfully with the exports of other colonies. In light of these failures, South Carolinians sought other products for trade.[24]

Several early strategies to generate wealth met with limited success, and each affected the colony's development in both the short and the long term. The first involved livestock raising, an endeavor well suited to the frontier, where investment capital was limited and labor remained in short supply, but access to unlimited land allowed colonists to expand their operation at little expense. Shipped overland to Charleston, Carolina beef found a lucrative market in the British West Indies. Crucial to the success of livestock raising were a knowledge of its management and experience in its practice. Colonists immigrating to South Carolina from Highland Britain and enslaved Africans from Senegambia brought knowledge of Old World cattle-raising traditions. In South Carolina, a syncretistic tradition of large-scale livestock raising evolved that proved extremely adaptive to the conditions encountered in the lowcountry during the early decades of colonization.[25]

South Carolinians also turned to lumber and naval stores, a marketable commodity to a nation whose power and overseas trade was carried in wooden ships. Facing shortages of naval stores from traditional Baltic sources, Parliament enacted a bounty to encourage their production in England's American colonies. The abundant pine forests of the Coastal Plain provided exports of pitch and tar used in shipbuilding and supplied the West Indies with lumber, shingles, and staves for barrels and hogsheads. Although South Carolina became the major producer of naval stores in the first quarter of the eighteenth century, a falling market, continued European competition, and a growing desire by planters to commit labor to more profitable agricultural activities led to their rapid decline in South Carolina.[26]

Trade with Native peoples for slaves and deerskins became the early colony's most significant form of commerce. Initiated by the Lords Proprietors, the Indian trade generated profits through arrangements with external groups that supplied products and captives that could then be turned into capital and labor. This economic relationship grew out of the political instability among Native peoples. European contact brought epidemic diseases that decimated aboriginal populations, and competition over access to imported goods fostered endemic intertribal warfare that dislocated aboriginal groups.[27] The trade expanded South Carolina's geographical presence rapidly, but the lack of effective regulation led to widespread abuse by traders and gave rise to violent and widespread resistance to the new colony. An organized conspiracy arose among the Yamassees, Creeks, Choctaws, Cherokees, and other Southeastern groups with whom the Carolinians traded and boiled over in the Yamassee War, a conflict that nearly destroyed the colony in 1715. South Carolina's victory removed an immediate threat and gave the colony possession of new lands that enlarged its territory, but the Indians' defeat also marked the decline of the slave trade.[28] The exchange of deerskins soon resumed, however; it remained an important part of the colonial economy and provided South Carolina with its first staple product, one that accounted for perhaps half the value of the colony's exports to Britain. Its substantial capital contribution established Charleston as the focus of economic activity in the colony and its central port. Despite the friction the trade continued to generate with indigenous peoples, its success allowed South Carolina to grow both economically and spatially and set the stage for its emergence as a commercial colony.[29]

The Rise of Commercial Agriculture in the Lowcountry

By the mid-eighteenth century, South Carolina's leading newspaper proclaimed with confidence that "Rice [is] Our Staple Article of Export."[30] This was true in terms of both its value and the volume of its harvest. Rising on the shoulders of the colony's early economic ventures, plantation agriculture changed South Carolina's economy dramatically by introducing a renewable and highly marketable commodity at a time when conditions in the core began to favor the production of New World dietary items for consumption in Europe. As the expanding economies of northern Europe raised the real income of consumers and increased their demand for new products, war and weather calamities disturbed the grain supply and led to critical shortages on the continent, increasing the demand for imported foodstuffs. The time was right for South Carolina's development as a supplier of noncompetitive commodities.[31] Within thirty years of its founding, the lowcountry economy centered on rice, a grain whose value brought its planters great and immediate wealth and established their dominant role in South Carolina's development. The particular requirements of rice cultivation created a distinctive landscape and influenced the region's relationship to the rest of the province.

The first half of the eighteenth century witnessed the rise of rice as South Carolina's dominant crop. Although shortages of labor and capital delayed the crop's early development, colonists rapidly developed varieties and cultivation methods, built up seed rice, prepared lands, and obtained workers to cultivate rice on a large scale.[32] Output expanded in the 1720s when growing demand for rice and an abrupt decline in the naval stores trade shifted attention to the new crop.[33] As the number of planters increased, changes in the organization of trade and shipping and improvements in techniques of rice production lowered planters' production costs and increased the volume of rice available for market.[34]

The explosion of production, however, also caused prices to fall, requiring that planters develop greater efficiencies to maintain profitability. Rice planters achieved this by cultivating and processing rice in greater quantities and enlarging their labor force. Such economies of scale were further enhanced by more effective land use and the introduction of innovative technology. Rice growing became synonymous with large-scale plantation agriculture in the lowcountry.[35]

The nature of rice growing created South Carolina's colonial landscape. To carry out production on an industrial scale, planters modified the techniques and organization of rice growing to increase efficiency and minimize costs. Cultivation of the crop evolved rapidly in the lowcountry as planters innovated and drew heavily on the knowledge and experience of an enslaved West African labor force whose members were familiar with rice agriculture. Rice growing shifted from upland field cultivation without irrigation to methods that took advantage of field flooding. Planters first developed small, impounded inland fields along freshwater streams and then turned to large fields that utilized the tidal action of large coastal rivers for irrigation. Although the technology of tidal rice field construction, with its elaborate system of dikes, canals, and trunks, required a considerable investment, its increased efficiency returned large dividends by lowering costs of production. The success of tidal field cultivation changed the scale of rice growing in the lowcountry, and its distribution defined the zone of staple production in the lowcountry. Planters favored the lower portions of the region's coastal rivers and gravitated to the Savannah, Combahee, Ashepoo, and Edisto, along the southern coast, and the Cooper River, near Charleston. Farther north, amenable conditions prevailed on the Santee, Sampit, Black, Pee Dee, and Waccamaw Rivers nearer the port of Georgetown (Fig. 2.3).[36]

The success of rice as a commercial crop opened the door to the development of indigo as a second staple. The indigo plant produced a deep-blue dye that was integral to the manufacture of fabrics by Britain's expanding textiles industry, and the need for a reliable supply in time of war encouraged its cultivation in the colonies. Its high return on capital investment quickly made indigo a lucrative staple despite its late introduction. Planters initially concentrated production in the lowcountry, where they raised indigo on the higher lands behind the rice fields throughout the lowcountry from the Savannah River to north of Georgetown. Indigo could also be cultivated above the lower riverine areas of the coast, and its potential as a money crop had implications for the expansion of commercial agriculture into South Carolina's interior.[37]

Large-scale commercial agriculture altered the economy and society in the lowcountry. The efficiencies offered by economies of scale favored the success of large, specialized plantations, whose owners invested their profits in expanded staple production at the expense of diversified farming. Smaller planters, facing competition from larger planters and a decline in the market for naval stores, saw their role in the economy increasingly shrink as the income gap between the two groups widened. This disparity further reduced opportunities for those who lacked the capital to become large rice growers and helped marginalize others who pursued alternative economic activities in what was fast becoming a specialized commercial agricultural region. The growth of rice production established a viable and permanent economic base in the lowcountry, and this highly profitable export commodity brought a favorable balance of trade that tied South Carolina's economy firmly to England,

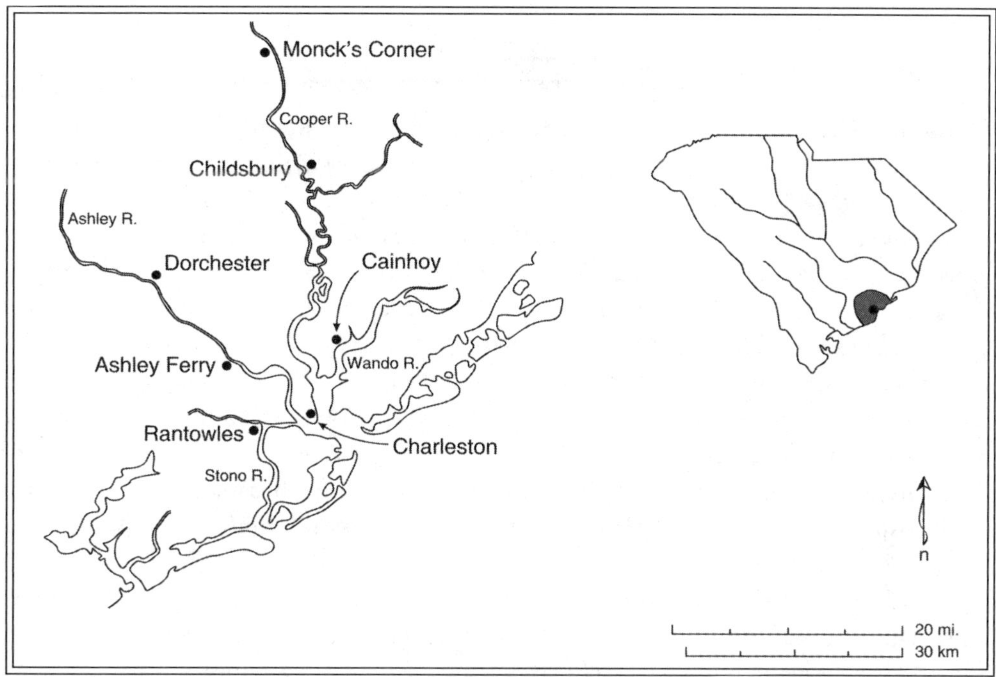

2.4 Principal nucleated settlements in the vicinity of the Charleston in the early eighteenth century. Author's original map.

Europe, and the West Indies. At the same time, it increased the colony's dependency and created extreme variations in wealth and a marked demographic shift as enslaved people of African descent increasingly outnumbered Europeans.[38]

The structure of rice production influenced the nature and patterning of settlement in the lowcountry. This distinctive arrangement grew in large part out of the organization of large-scale agriculture. Rice was grown only within a relatively limited area, frequently at sites accessible by navigable water. The crop could be milled on the plantation and shipped by water or land without an elaborate processing infrastructure and its associated network of settlements. Indigo too was processed by growers and transported directly to market. The dispersed arrangement of rice and indigo plantations in the coastal region placed most of its population in scattered rural enclaves. The distribution of plantation communities also discouraged a level of market interaction sufficient to promote the growth of towns and inhibited their appearance in the lowcountry.[39] Small nucleated settlements usually appeared at strategic locations where roads intersected major waterways. They housed facilities required by planters transporting produce to coastal ports and accommodated the periodic economic and social needs of shippers, travelers, and local elite residents (Fig. 2.4). Ashley Ferry Town and Dorchester on the Ashley, Cainhoy on the Wando, Childsbury and Moncks Corner on the Cooper, and Rantowles on the Stono all grew up within a thirty-mile radius of Charleston, but none of these transshipment points became significant markets, and most contained only a few structures.[40]

The Metropolis of the Province

Charleston arose as the central port for the lowcountry, the conduit through which shipping and commerce passed between Great Britain and South Carolina. Founded ten years after the initial settlement on Albemarle Point, the city had always been the colony's principal connection with the world, and its precedence gave it an advantage beyond that provided by geography alone. Situated on a peninsula at the confluence of two coastal rivers, the settlement and its harbor were easily defended, and adjacent waterways provided direct access to the surrounding coastal region. Despite the fact that it did not lie on any of the great rivers, Charleston was well situated to become the point for overland expansion into the interior. Early on, its role as the hub of the Indian trade made Charleston the focus for economic activity and a funnel for trade and immigrant settlement. Lying at the center of an extensive overland trail network stretching far inland, the city became the mart of southern British North America, the principal outlet for its overseas commerce, and the home of those who conducted it.

Charleston dominated South Carolina's lowcountry. It became home to wealthy planters seeking to avoid the unhealthiness of the surrounding countryside, as well as merchants and others engaged in business, making it both a focus of export commerce and a magnet for import trade. The city's central commercial role provided the impetus for modifying the natural landscape to create a "second nature" composed of "improvements" such as settlements, fields, roads, ferries, river landings, and other new elements conducive to commercial trade and agricultural production. The altered landscape of South Carolina's lowcountry reinforced Charleston's economic position but also made it the social and cultural hub of the region. Although plantation agriculture dispersed the coastal region's European population, the city unified the province's elites, who intermingled there and intermarried, producing a tightly knit community whose members shared values and interests. Charleston's second nature ensured its dominance of the lowcountry and made it the major metropolitan center for the southern colonies.[41]

As South Carolina's central settlement, Charleston was the logical choice for its capital. Under Proprietary rule it was the seat of the governor and the proprietors' representatives and, later, the Assembly. When the colony passed under the authority of the Crown and the Board of Trade, the executive, legislative, and judicial functions remained there, and Charleston became the seat of a growing bureaucracy of agencies that oversaw taxation, customs, admiralty law, the survey and transfer of land, and the activities of the military and the Church of England. In addition to being the focus of mercantile and planting interests, Charleston, with its concentration of civil and religious functions, became the center of the province's increasingly complex administrative infrastructure as well. The centralization of public offices strengthened the city's role as a center of regional self-government. Throughout the colonial period and beyond, the city dominated political and social life in South Carolina.[42]

South Carolina possessed two secondary ports in the eighteenth century, but neither challenged Charleston's dominance. Georgetown lay in a protected location on Winyah Bay, at the mouth of the Pee Dee River and close to the mouth of the great Santee, and its location allowed it to become a regional center for the northern rice-producing region. Draining a large portion of the interior, these two river systems provided direct access to the backcountry. A bar and shallow harbor, however, prevented Georgetown from becoming a deep-water port, and it failed to attract the mercantile activity of its neighbor to the south. As a result, Georgetown became a depot where produce from the surrounding area was collected for forwarding to Charleston.[43] South Carolina's proximity to Spanish Florida discouraged colonization along its southern coast, and permanent settlement of the region came only after the 1715 Yamassee War. Beaufort, on the island of Port Royal, grew slowly in the following years. Its situation and large, deep harbor facilitated its role as a collection point for local trade by water, and it became a regional center for rice and indigo production; however, it lacked direct access to a great river, and its island location hampered overland access. Because of these deficiencies, Beaufort remained a small settlement throughout the colonial period.[44]

The economy of South Carolina's lowcountry not only ensured the permanence of the colony but also set the course for its future growth. By the third decade of the eighteenth century, production had coalesced around rice and indigo as commercial staples. The success of these two export crops tied South Carolina to Great Britain in a dependent relationship typical of cosmopolitan colonization, one that brought great wealth and enlarged production. But this arrangement also stifled change and perpetuated economic, political, and social arrangements that supported plantation agriculture. South Carolina's expansion occurred in this context, and Europeans immigrating to the interior did so in a milieu created by institutional mechanisms developed in the lowcountry. These influenced the nature of backcountry settlement, subsistence, and production and shaped the region's entry into the wider Atlantic economy.

Administrative Growth in a Colonial Environment

The specialized nature of plantation agriculture molded the structure of society in South Carolina and influenced the administrative system that governed the province. Public institutions that arose in the coastal region were extended to the frontier, and their character profoundly affected development in the backcountry. South Carolina's government evolved in response to the intentions of home-country interests, the reaction of colonial residents, and the requirements of an expanding agricultural economy. The resulting institutions were well adapted to conditions of the lowcountry and the needs of those who dominated its society, but these factors also gave the colony a distinctive political character that hampered the management of a rapidly developing province. Why did things turn out the way they did?

Perhaps the most distinctive characteristic of South Carolina's administration was its concentration of power in political institutions designed to function at the level of the colony as a whole to the neglect of local interests. This pattern came about in response to the rise of a viable commercial staple economy dependent on a crop confined largely to the Outer Coastal Plain. The requirements of trade and marketing focused exchange almost exclusively on the port of Charleston, and the volume of this activity and the wealth it generated resulted in the city's rapid emergence as an urban center and the entrepôt of the province. Most of South Carolina's European inhabitants lived in this city and made it the social, political, and religious focus of the province and the obvious choice as a center of government. This demographic pattern and Charleston's central role allowed the city to dominate the political life of the lowcountry and discouraged the development of local administrative institutions.[45] But other historical factors also influenced the development of South Carolina's distinctive form of government.

The conflict between the colony's early leaders and the Proprietors over the implementation of the Fundamental Constitutions exerted a particularly strong influence on the political structure of the province. As the colony's charter, this document prescribed an administrative organization capable of managing affairs at all levels. Resistance by South Carolinians to the extension of Proprietary authority, however, hampered the implementation of the Fundamental Constitutions and encouraged the rise of the legislative Assembly to oppose the governor and his Council. This body represented the interests of those residing in all parts of the province. Because control of the Assembly was critical to managing policy affecting the colony as a whole, competition for power and authority at the central level led to the neglect of the province's four counties, and they never acquired an administrative function or operated as units of local government.[46]

The Assembly's struggle for political control outlasted the Proprietary period and continued to dominate South Carolina's political scene following the shift to a royal administration in 1721.[47] The legislature's success derived from its members' ability to adopt unified positions representing provincial concerns. Propelled by common economic interests and the dominating cultural influence of Charleston, its members increasingly shared a feeling of community that blunted internal antagonisms and encouraged unity among them. Drawn from the colony's elite, members of the Assembly adopted a political ideology that vested the responsibility of power in the hands of those whose economic prosperity demonstrated possession of the qualities necessary to govern. Elitist in its assumptions, this ideology also stressed the obligation of those in power to their constituents and fostered the notion that agreement among the people's representatives was necessary for success in their struggle against executive power. Solidarity enhanced the perception of the Assembly's fundamental political importance in the colony's administration; as an active legislature whose growing power challenged the prerogatives of an appointed governor and a Council, it served as a united front against outside domination.[48]

But the Assembly also reached beyond its function as the colony's legislative body and assumed responsibility for internal administration as well. Its control over the appointment of civil officers who received their salaries from the public treasury allowed the legislature to influence the provincial treasurer, the comptroller, and the commissioners of Indian affairs, as well as those in other administrative departments. The Assembly expanded its responsibility at the local level through appointed commissions whose members were changed with carrying out specific functions, such as maintaining public roads, improving river navigation, and managing local needs, and these bodies were responsible to the legislature for their activities. In the absence of a municipal government, such commissions managed the city of Charleston, regulating commerce, public safety, and other aspects of urban life. Because the Assembly also held the provincial purse strings, it controlled the expenditure of funds for public improvements, and inhabitants throughout the province submitted petitions and requests directly to this body.[49]

Although the Assembly dominated local government, the governor controlled one institution that played a limited role in regulating society in the lowcountry. Appointed as administrative officials in each county, justices of the peace could assess fines for legal infractions, decide suits for debt, determine cases involving fraud and damages for small amounts, and grant licenses for tavern keepers and peddlers. Their greatest authority, however, grew out of the need to regulate the system of slavery on which the lowcountry's economy rested. With the assistance of freeholders, justices possessed the power to try offenses of blacks held in bondage, including capital cases, and to pronounce sentences on those found guilty. But, here also, circumstances kept power concentrated in the capital. Although the county courts, presided over by justices of the peace, attempted to adjudicate civil suits, a legislative act permitting plaintiffs to choose the site of the trials effectively destroyed their authority. Because the merchants who filed most of the suits preferred to have them tried in Charleston, outlying county courts found little business. As long as the colony's population was concentrated in the lowcountry, the Charleston courts accommodated the interests of most South Carolinians; however, subsequent expansion would strain this legal system beyond its limits.[50]

In the absence of local government, the institutions of the established Church of England oversaw everyday activities across the province. South Carolina followed the Barbadian pattern of creating parishes as administrative units of manageable size to supervise both civil and ecclesiastical activities of its inhabitants. Ten initial parishes were delineated in 1706, but the spread of the colonial population along the coastal plain and into the interior later required the addition of thirteen more. Within each parish, an elected vestry was responsible for maintaining church properties, administering parish schools, and supervising the care of the poor, as well as occasionally serving as an investigatory body. Each parish also supported two churchwardens, whose duties were largely civil. These officials managed elections within the parishes, and in the unincorporated city of Charleston they also oversaw the operation of the hospital and orphanage. Together with the appointed commissions, South Carolina's parish institutions helped maintain order and administer to local needs.[51]

These distinctive institutions established a pattern of administration well adapted to geographic and economic conditions in South Carolina's lowcountry. The ease of communication and transportation in a relatively small coastal region tied the port and population center of Charleston to its limited hinterland and facilitated centralized management by those representing the colony's chief economic interests. The common concerns of the planters and merchants who formed the colonial elite fostered an ideology that emphasized public service and ensured the participation of the wealthiest residents at all levels of government. The shared interests of legislators in the provincial Assembly, appointed commissioners, parish churchwardens, members of the vestries, and justices of the peace permitted the smooth operation of a government whose functions mirrored their needs. As long as these conditions prevailed, this form of administration proved adequate; however, the structure of a provincial government created to manage cosmopolitan colonization in the lowcountry produced a rigidity that limited its ability to accommodate the changes inherent in such growth. Rapid territorial expansion placed new demands on South Carolina's political system, and its inadequacies created the need for indigenous institutions to govern backcountry settlement.

A Mature Colony with Growing Pains

By the third decade of the eighteenth century, the province of South Carolina had become a viable part of Great Britain's American empire. Settlement had spread across the fertile coastal region and had begun to penetrate portions of the interior. Commercial staple crops dominated a vibrant agricultural economy that brought riches to the region and made it an important trading partner for home-country merchants and a major consumer of British goods. The capital of Charleston lay in the center of the province and at the apex of its economy. As the metropolis of the southern colonies, the city was Carolina's entrepôt and the hub of its domestic affairs. Charleston was home to an administration that had become increasingly responsive to the colony's interests despite its close ties to the Crown. A powerful provincial Assembly and its functionaries protected commercial production and trade from the excesses of imperial power and managed provincial affairs on the one hand; however, their dominance of South Carolina's government at all levels stifled the development of local institutions and set a precedent for elite control in all political matters. Its structure would be severely strained by the requirements of administering a rapidly expanding colony.

The economic success of the lowcountry guaranteed the colony's wealth but also increased its vulnerability on two counts. As the southernmost of Britain's North American colonies, its existence threatened Spanish territorial claims in Florida, and the activities of Carolinian traders disrupted Spain's influence in the region. British interaction with Native peoples also extended west toward French Louisiana. Although these peripheral areas lay beyond the bounds of the coastal lowcountry, their security became increasingly important to the colony's well-being, if not its existence. South Carolina's mode of agricultural production was critically significant to the colony's economic survival, but its composition held the seeds of discord. Intensive plantation agriculture, employing unfree labor, resulted in a largely rural pattern of settlement and ensured that Europeans remained a minority subject to potential revolt. Although plantation farming and the Indian trade brought wealth to the colony, the nature of the provincial economy increased the threat of both external and internal instability, challenges that generated an official response that changed the composition of the colony and dramatically altered the direction of its growth.

Concerns for the safety and stability of the valuable lowcountry economy weighed heavily on Britain's Board of Trade, the official body that administered the country's overseas colonies, and demanded a permanent solution. When South Carolina's newly appointed royal governor arrived in 1730, he brought a bold plan to solve the colony's vulnerability by implementing a radical scheme to enlarge the colony by resettling new immigrants in the interior. An influx of Europeans would at once provide a militia to defend the frontier and counterbalance the lowcountry's growing African population. The Assembly enthusiastically approved Gov. Robert Johnson's effort to encourage inland settlement and subsidize immigration to the newly opened lands.

The "Township Plan" of 1730 occurred at an auspicious time. Rising demand for and fewer restrictions on South Carolina's exports increased the demand for new agricultural lands, unavailable for more than a decade. At the same time, the strategic placement of the interior townships, together with plans to establish the neighboring colony of Georgia, promised to improve security for the region as a whole.[52] Intended to solve the dilemma created by the lowcountry's commercial success, the new colonizing scheme dramatically altered the course of South Carolina's development by introducing extensive settlement of the backcountry. In its ethnic composition, economy, society, and political organization, the interior contrasted markedly with the lowcountry, and these differences created two distinct regions. Although their interests were often at odds with one another, they remained linked as interdependent elements of a single system.

Chapter 3

"That Remote Part of the Province"

Expansion into the Interior

The year 1733 had been an eventful one for James de St. Julien, a man of many talents and considerable experience. A planter and stock raiser in St. Johns Berkeley Parish, he possessed an estate of at least 3,800 acres, but St. Julien was no stranger to the frontier. Both he and his brother Peter had been active early in the Indian trade, and their location astride the Cherokee Path afforded them access to the central interior as well as the upper Savannah River region.[1] As one of the colony's more influential traders, James de St. Julien had only the previous year been called upon to assist in expanding the British colonial presence southward along the Atlantic coast. Lowcountry residents welcomed the protection offered by the settlement of Georgia between their province and Spanish Florida and endeavored to support the success of this recently chartered colony. Aware of the importance of maintaining friendly alliances with Native peoples in the region, South Carolina's governor and Council turned to St. Julien, whose prestige among the resident Creeks would ameliorate potential misunderstanding and hostility. In late January they dispatched him to Port Royal Island to assure the new colony's leader, James Oglethorpe, of South Carolina's cooperation and to assist him in his dealings with Georgia's aboriginal inhabitants.[2]

St. Julien's role in the initial success of Oglethorpe's venture likely led to his undertaking another important mission before the close of the year. Commissioned by South Carolina to carry out the survey of a new interior township for the settlement of European immigrants, he found himself in a country well beyond the fringes of European settlement and control. Though distant from the lowcountry, Fredericksburg Township lay astride overland routes that made it a gateway to the northern reaches of the province as well as the lands beyond. But more important was its proximity to the Wateree River, a feature that dominated its landscape and demarcated the township's western boundary. As the region's principal physiographic feature, this watercourse had always shaped the human presence in the land that it traversed.

The Wateree River enters the South Carolina backcountry as the Catawba, flowing from its origins in the mountainous Blue Ridge of North Carolina across the rolling hills of the Piedmont on its way to the sea. It follows a relatively straight course through the descending topography, growing in size as tributaries draining the broad uplands feed into it. As it reaches the Sandhills, the Wateree leaves the resistant crystalline geology that

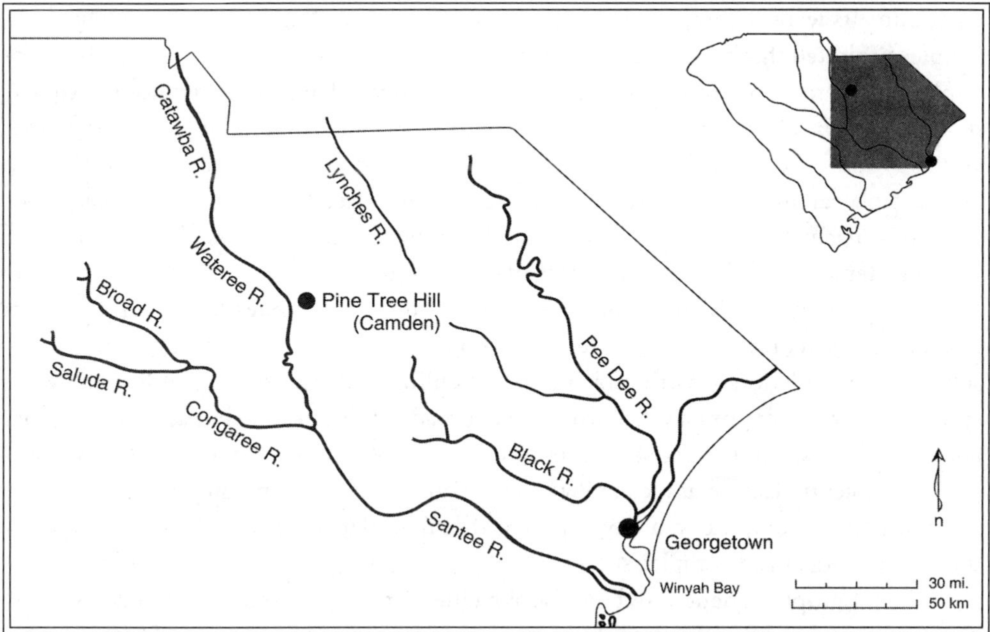

3.1 The Wateree River and other major watercourses in eastern South Carolina. Author's original map.

underlies the interior and drops more rapidly as it encounters the softer rocks of the Coastal Plain. Here, at the Fall Line, the river begins its journey across South Carolina's widest landform, where it forms wide, lazy meanders through swamps and forested lowlands. Farther along, it joins the Congaree to become the Santee, combining two of the interior's major river systems as it passes through the lowcountry toward the Atlantic. Just as the drainage of the Congaree unites the lands of western South Carolina, the Wateree binds together a wide swath of the central interior and connects it to the world beyond. From time immemorial the great river has been inseparable from the region's history. Flowing through the heart of the backcountry, it carries the soul of its past (Fig. 3.1).

The Wateree Valley became a focus of European immigration in the eighteenth century, but the human presence in the region surrounding it has a much deeper past.[3] Archaeology has revealed material evidence of an occupation extending back as far as 12,500 years to the Pleistocene-Holocene transition, a period that witnessed climatic improvement and a change in vegetation. South Carolina was still dominated by homogenous boreal forests and highly mobile Paleoindian groups that subsisted by broad-spectrum foraging as well as by hunting a wide variety of animals, including the large Pleistocene mammals that remained in the closing years of the Ice Age.[4] Moderation of the cooler, moister climate initiated dramatic changes in the regional environment, however, and by 7500 B.C. the boreal vegetation was replaced by deciduous forest. The warmer, drier climate brought the appearance of mixed oak and pine woodland that evolved into the modern forest vegetation dominated by pine after 5000 B.C. Although rich, the resources of these mixed forest environments were geographically diverse and seasonal, and mobile groups of aboriginal peoples exploited this broad subsistence base by adapting a generalized strategy based on hunting, gathering, and foraging. This way of life, known to archaeologists as the Archaic, persisted on the Piedmont and upper Coastal Plain from about 8000 to 1000 B.C., then gradually transitioned into one in which intensive collecting and small-scale horticulture began to play an increasingly greater role. This gradual alteration of the aboriginal subsistence base ushered in the Woodland cultural tradition, which witnessed a movement toward greater social and political complexity. The shift from a reliance on collecting to a greater dependence on food production was based on native domesticates, supplemented by maize and cucurbits ultimately derived from Mesoamerica. These changes encouraged substantial population growth and supported cultural innovations, including the widespread production of pottery, the formation of broader communities living in large, permanent settlements, and the construction of monumental architecture in the form of earthworks. The centralization associated with the Woodland Period in South Carolina implies increased social complexity, a development that underlay the rise of large, fully agricultural, highly organized complex societies that persisted well into the seventeenth century.[5]

When Europeans penetrated the Carolina interior, they encountered the descendants of sophisticated polities that had dominated the Southeast for centuries. These societies, called Mississippian, arose out of the Woodland base about A.D. 800 and were characterized by changes that accompanied a shift to maize agriculture. Dependency on food production as a major subsistence strategy encouraged Mississippian groups to seek the most suitable environments for this endeavor.[6] Gravitating to the fertile floodplains of major rivers, they took advantage of the well-drained, easily tilled soils for garden plots as well as the protein resources offered by fish and waterfowl in the channel remnants and oxbow lakes. A reliance on agriculture offered a dependable food supply capable of supporting population growth and the development of complex political and economic structures. Anthropologists have identified societies organized on the basis of ranked hierarchical leadership that facilitated the management of production, the redistribution of surpluses, and the coordination of social activities, as chiefdoms. Dramatic changes in the patterning of settlement accompanied the appearance of chiefdoms in the Mississippian, as expanding populations became increasingly concentrated. Settlements began to form regional systems, centered on a large, paramount town containing temple mounds, ball courts, and other architecture devoted to sacred as well as secular administrative activities. Tied economically and politically to these centers, smaller satellite communities of varying size and importance spread along the floodplains of the region's major rivers and formed a distinctive regional landscape.[7]

The first European observers of the Carolina interior encountered large towns built by these complex societies. At the height of the Mississippian, between 1250 and 1300, settlements containing ceremonial mounds existed along major rivers from southern North Carolina to northern Georgia, and their number continued to increase over the next century and a half. Beginning about 1450, residents abandoned the numerous mound centers in the Savannah River Valley as well as those along the Broad and Saluda Rivers, resulting in a dramatic shift in the patterning of aboriginal settlement. In less than a century the focus of occupation shifted west to the Oconee River in Georgia and east to the Wateree Valley.

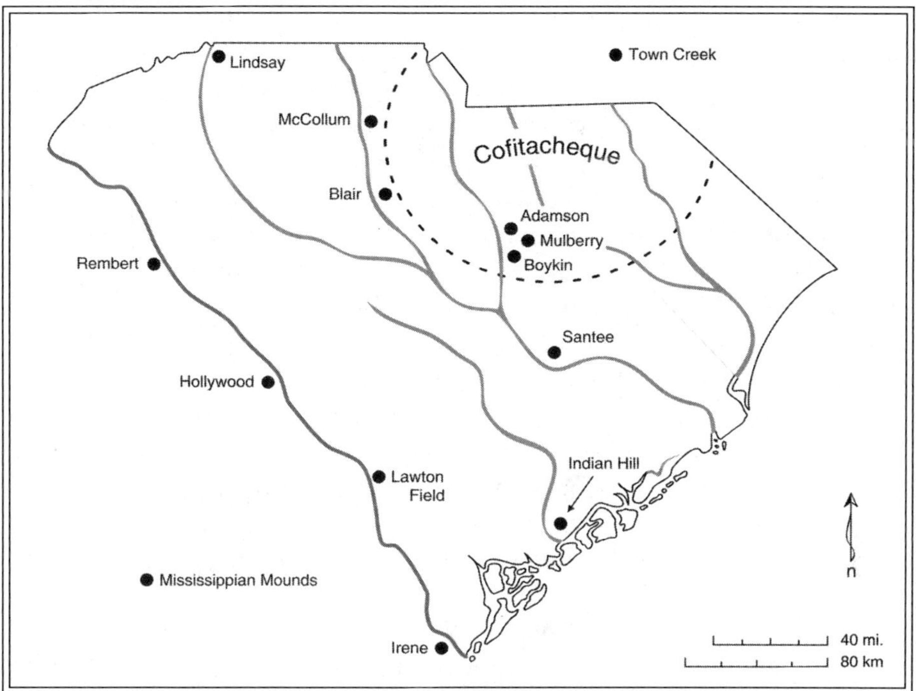

3.2 The location of Cofitacheque and the extent of its associated territory in the sixteenth century shown in relation to other Mississippian mounds. Author's original map adapted from Leland G. Ferguson, "Archaeological Investigations at the Mulberry Site," *South Carolina Institute of Archaeology and Anthropology, Notebook* 6, nos. 3–4 (1974): 60.

When the Spanish explorer Hernando de Soto traveled north from the Gulf of Mexico, he encountered the towns of Ocute and Cofitacheque in these two respective locations (Fig. 3.2).[8]

The principal town of Cofitacheque was situated on the east side of the Wateree just south of present-day Camden at the Mulberry site. A substantial village existed at Mulberry, and both it and the Adamson site, not far upriver, contain mounds.[9] Cofitacheque's territory comprised a substantial portion of northeastern South Carolina but may also have extended from the Atlantic coast to the North Carolina border and included all of the peoples in the Pee Dee-Yadkin River drainage, the Santee and Wateree/Catawba River Valleys, and the lower portion of the Broad River (Fig. 3.2).[10] As the central figure in a geographically extensive polity, Cofitacheque's leader assumed the political, religious, and economic authority associated with a paramount chief who stood at the apex of a ranked, kin-based social structure. Contemporary observers noted that Cofitacheque dominated a number of smaller polities from which it drew tribute and that its chieftains exhibited distinctive characteristics that reflected their high status and set them off from others. In addition to facing limits imposed by restrictions on their behavior and consumption and the use of a distinctive court dialect, they were carried on litters and received overtly deferential treatment.[11]

Although in decline, Cofitacheque was a functioning chiefdom at the time of initial European contact and remained a recognizable polity for perhaps a century and a half (Fig. 3.3). Sporadic visits by Spanish explorers reported its existence as early as 1540, when Hernando de Soto encountered its central settlement on the Wateree, but the Spanish left no permanent presence in the interior. Juan Pardo's expedition from the Santa Elena colony on the Carolina coast passed through the chiefdom two decades later, and Pedro de Torres reached Cofitacheque from St. Augustine in 1628. Spanish influence in the Southeast began to wane in the seventeenth century, and the establishment of a permanent English settlement at Albemarle Point in 1670 marked the presence of a new power with different interests. Within a few months of the colony's founding, Henry Woodward traveled to Cofitacheque and convinced the chieftain to visit Charleston in return. The relationship with the newcomers lasted only a few years, however, and after 1681 references to Cofitacheque vanish from English records. When John Lawson ventured into the Wateree Valley in 1701, he found that the ancient chiefdom no longer existed as a political entity. Instead he encountered several groups of agricultural peoples whose names and locations imply that they were elements of the same groups that Spanish explorers had encountered as Cofitacheque a century and a half earlier.[12]

As the new century began, residents of the polities that once made up the Cofitacheque chiefdom began to experience the unhappy consequences of English colonization. In the Carolina colony, the destructive impact of the broader European presence on the eastern seaboard soon engulfed aboriginal societies as they became increasingly enmeshed in and dependent on participation in the Indian trade. During the first decades of the colony's existence, the dislocation of Native peoples and accompanying internecine warfare, coupled with the introduction of alien diseases and environmental stress brought on by drought, combined to decimate most of the coastal groups and bring them under the control of the English, who began shifting their attention to more distant peoples farther west. As the most active thrust of the trade expanded along the Savannah River and the tributaries of the Congaree, the aboriginal peoples in the upper Wateree Valley remained remote from intensive colonist contact. As with the Cherokees and Creeks to the west, distance mitigated the impact of the Indian trade on the northern peoples. In contrast to Native groups on the Coastal Plain, those that had constituted the northern portion of Cofitacheque remained unpacified and culturally distinct. Comprising the Esaws, Waxhaws, Catawbas, and Sugarees, they formed a confederacy known collectively as the Esaws.[13]

The Yamassee War of 1715 united nearly all of the aboriginal peoples against the South Carolina colony in a massive general uprising, the outcome of which dramatically rearranged the political landscape of the region. Although their geographic situation shielded the northern Indians from the intense contact that triggered the conflict, exploitation and abuse by traders and unkept promises by the colonial government drew them into the coalition. Initial Native successes threatened the existence of the colony, but within two years the rebellion collapsed, with devastating effect on those groups in the lowcountry. But the war exposed the military weakness of South Carolina's government and its inability to control the interior, and it forced officials to reassess the colony's relationship with the more distant Native peoples.[14] The Cherokees and Creeks remained strong on the northwestern frontier, and intact aboriginal groups still occupied the upper Wateree. As a persistent

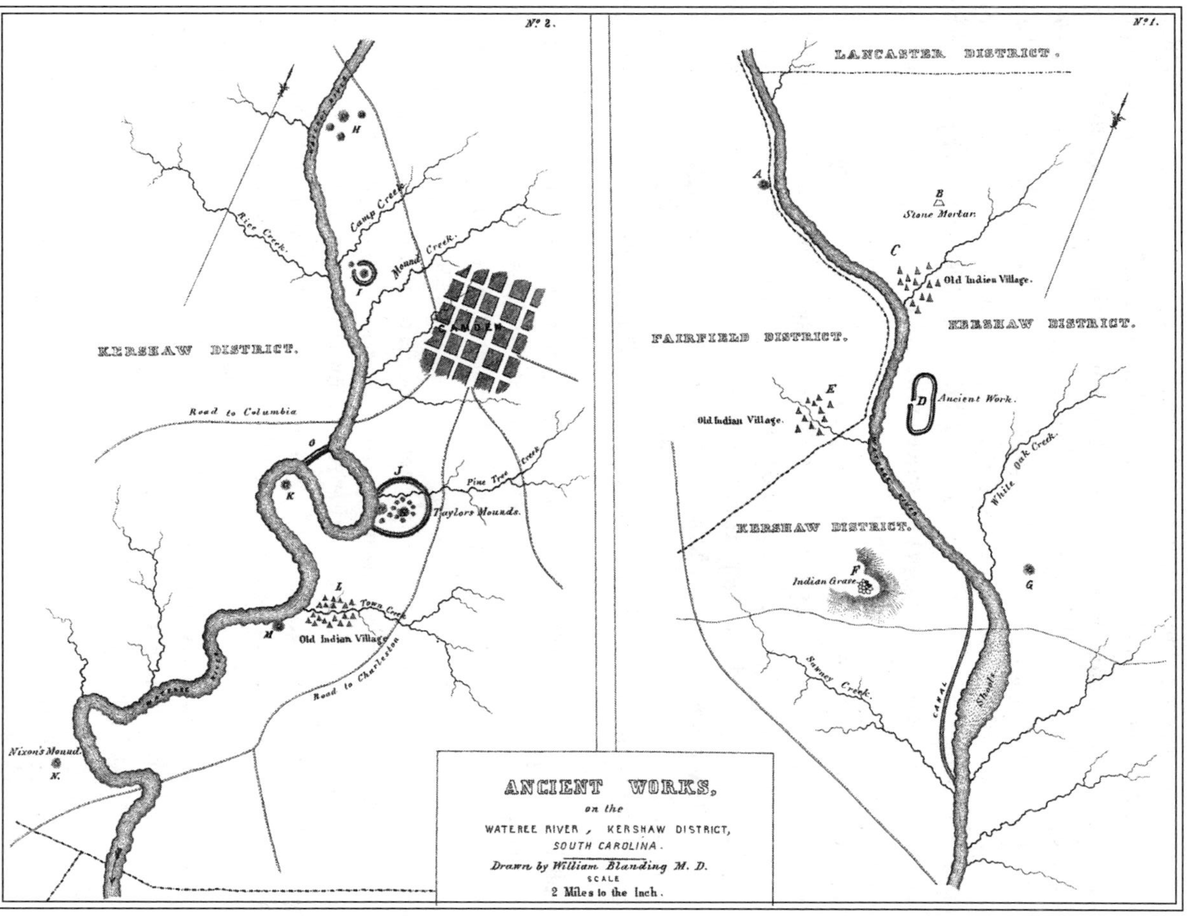

3.3 Dr. William Blanding's map of the Wateree Mounds in the 1840s. Source: Ephraim G. Squier and E. H. Davis, *Ancient Monuments of the Mississippi Valley* (Cincinnati: J. A. and W. P. James, 1848), Plate XXXVII, 105–108.

Native presence on their traditional estate, the Catawbas became a magnet for the decimated remnants of societies that had once belonged to the Cofitacheque chiefdom, as well as others. Survivors of the once numerous Congarees and Santees gravitated to the upper Wateree Valley, as did the Waterees, Sugarees, Cheraws, Enos, Chowans, Yamassees, Pee Dees, Saponies, and Cussas. There, through a process of consolidation born of shared experience and purpose that overcame differences in ethnicity and language, they achieved a new collective identity as the Catawba Nation. As the successor to earlier polities, the Catawbas maintained a viable aboriginal presence in the Wateree Valley and emerged as a significant factor in its historical development.[15]

The postwar Catawba coalescence brought greater economic and political ties with the province of South Carolina. Already involved in the larger trade in deerskins, the Catawbas had come to accept European technology and the dependency it entailed, and the cessation of hostilities provided an opportunity to open ties to colonial suppliers. Because the Catawbas' situation in the upper Wateree Valley offered access to Virginia as well as to Charleston, South Carolinians now had to compete for their trade. Anxious to avoid earlier problems, South Carolina attempted to regulate trade by creating a public monopoly of the under the auspices of the Assembly. Initially trade was conducted at two garrisoned factories established in 1716 on the Savannah River and at the Congarees. The latter factory, called Fort Congaree, served the Catawba towns. Exchange expanded in the hands of licensed traders, bringing an increased dependence that shifted the locations of the Catawba settlements closer to the trading paths. By midcentury all were located along the Catawba River within two or three miles of one another.[16] The Catawbas realized that a trading arrangement that relied on a finite resource such as deerskins could not last indefinitely and initiated a political strategy that drew them closer into the colonial orbit. Again taking advantage of their location, Catawba leaders argued persuasively that proximity to the frontiers in both Carolinas and Virginia situated them ideally to protect the colonies from attack by the French or their Indian allies. Always wary of external threats, South Carolina's leaders welcomed the Catawbas' headmen in Charleston and offered to support their people with weapons, ammunition, clothing, supplies, and gifts in exchange for their services as guardians.[17]

By the second quarter of the eighteenth century, the Catawbas had adapted to a world forever changed by the European presence. Survivors of the political upheaval that had destroyed the old Mississippian order as well as diseases and a devastating colonial war that had decimated their lowcountry brethren, they now found themselves drawn into in a global economic system governed by international trade and political alliances beyond their control. As the northern guardians of the South Carolina colony, they controlled the territory and resources of a homeland that still lay beyond the reach of coastal settlement; however, the forces of change that had already so altered their lives were part of a larger process that had only begun to run its course. Colonial leaders saw the Catawba presence as only a stopgap in controlling the broader backcountry frontier. South Carolina's vast interior was about to play a central role in a wider imperial scheme intended to secure the southern colony by settling European immigrants in its outer regions. When the newcomers arrived from afar, they too encountered a new world, but not an empty one. They were but the latest occupants of an ancient land.

The Township Plan and Inland Settlement

The passing of colonial administration to Crown control in 1729 brought a dramatic shift in the patterning of European settlement in South Carolina. When Robert Johnson arrived as royal governor, he carried a set of instructions from the Board of Trade to overcome the colony's military and civil vulnerabilities by altering the composition of its population. A planter and former governor under the Proprietary regime, Johnson was familiar with the situation in the colony and, in concert with London merchants, proposed to the Board that the current cost of maintaining the lowcountry's security be alleviated by situating Protestant immigrants from Europe in the interior. Their numbers would offset those of the disproportionately large enslaved African population in the coastal region and provide the wherewithal to put down slave revolts, while a militia formed of small resident landholders in the backcountry would defend the colony from potentially hostile Native groups as well as outside threats from the Spanish and French. The new immigration policy reflected a marked shift away from recruiting colonists on the basis of their value to the existing economy and instead emphasized their role in expanding and securing its territory. This endeavor required careful planning, and Johnson's instructions spelled out a specific scheme to attract immigrants and locate them in the most advantageous manner.[18]

The Township Plan was a powerful influence on the distribution of population in the interior. Its authors sought to occupy the region by laying out rectangular township tracts of twenty thousand acres adjacent to major rivers. Most of the township was to be surveyed as farmland, except for 250 to 300 acres reserved for a nucleated town center. As an incentive to settle, the instructions proposed that resident immigrants who cultivated their holding receive a lot within the town as well as a tract of fifty acres for each member of the grantee's household. Indentured servants who served out their agreements could also take up land in the townships. As an added inducement, the payment of quitrents on these lands was waived for ten years. To further assist the new immigrants, most of whom had limited means, the instructions authorized the governor to request that the Assembly subsidize the costs of transportation and settlement. The legislature imposed a tax on imported slaves to establish a fund to cover the expense of surveying the townships, paying the passage of poor European Protestants to South Carolina and supplying them with provisions as well as tools and equipment for farm making. Although its uneven level of support failed to eliminate all hardships, the province continued to subsidize immigration throughout the colonial period.[19]

Grants of land in South Carolina's interior came with the expectation that new inhabitants would form a militia to defend the area they occupied. Militias played a significant and continuing role in protecting and maintaining order in the colony, and all males between sixteen and sixty years of age were obliged to bear arms in its defense. These units helped the colony resist a Spanish invasion in 1706 and Indian attacks during the Yamassee War, and the militia's duties in policing the lowcountry's burgeoning African population provided reassurance in the face of rising fears of slave insurrections. As the colony expanded, the militia's central role required additional manpower to face the specter of wider external threats, and the inclusion of backcountry immigrants was crucial to protecting the frontier in time of emergency.[20]

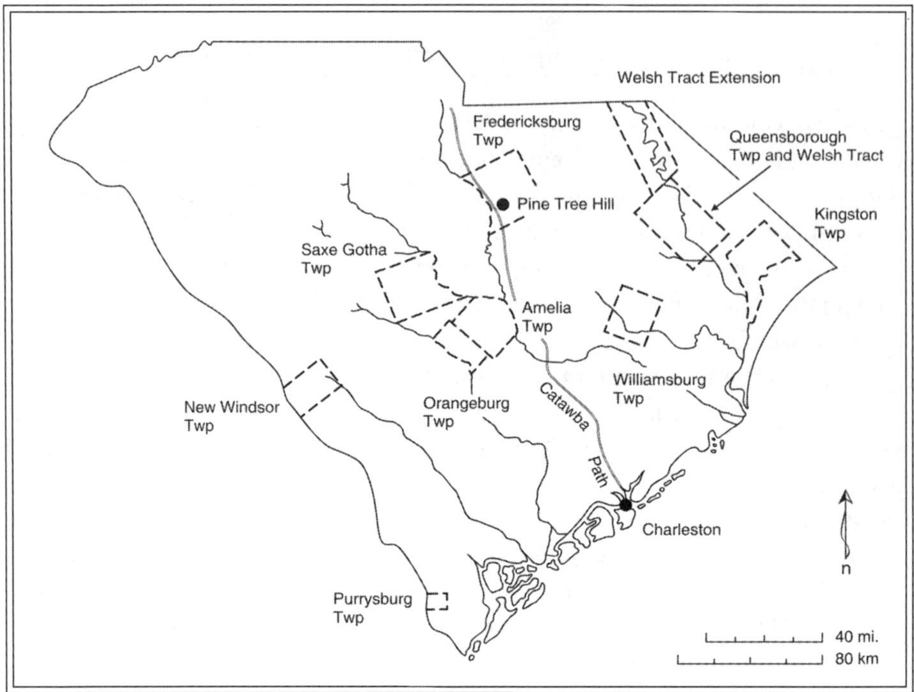

3.4 The townships established in 1731 in response to Gov. Johnson's plan to settle the interior. Fredericksburg Township on the Wateree River was the farthest inland and did not attract immigrants for nearly a decade. Author's original map adapted from Julian J. Petty, *The Growth and Distribution of Population in South Car*olina (Columbia: South Carolina State Planning Board, 1943; reprint ed., Spartanburg, SC: The Reprint Co., 1973), 38.

To implement orderly interior growth, Johnson's instructions specified that eleven townships be established along the major rivers from the Waccamaw in the north to the Altamaha in the south (Fig. 3.4). Georgia's creation as a separate province in 1732 removed the two southernmost townships from South Carolina's jurisdiction, but the nine remaining tracts were laid out in the province between 1731 and 1735, all situated on the Coastal Plain at varying distances as far inland as the Fall Line. The earliest was surveyed on the lower Savannah in 1732. Purrysburg Township was the culmination of a nearly decade-long effort by its founder, Jean Pierre Purry, a Swiss entrepreneur who hoped to establish a European colony in what he perceived to be an ideal environment. Its first immigrants arrived in 1733, and soon a small nucleated settlement developed there.[21]

In addition to Purrysburg, four other townships were created in the western portion of the province. Farther up the Savannah, New Windsor was laid out in 1735 at the site of Fort Moore, the factory established for the western Indian trade in 1716. Attracting both English and Swiss immigrants, the township grew slowly in its first decade and stagnated following the establishment of Augusta as a regional trade center in neighboring Georgia. Legislation also created Orangeburg and Amelia as adjacent townships facing the North Edisto and Santee Rivers, respectively. Opened to settlement in 1735, they attracted German and Swiss immigrants, who arrived through the port of Charleston. Two years earlier, surveyors had laid out Saxe Gotha Township at the confluence of the Broad and Saluda Rivers, where the principal overland route from Charleston passed through the Congarees on the way to the Cherokee nation. The presence of Fort Congaree had drawn settlers to the area quite early, but after Saxe Gotha's lands were opened to settlement in 1735, large numbers of Germans flocked there to become the dominant ethnic group in a region that came to be called the "Dutch Fork."[22]

In eastern South Carolina, four additional townships appeared. Williamsburg was laid out on the Black River in 1731 and became home to Irish Protestants, who congregated in a section known as the King's Tree. The province surveyed two other townships, Kingston on the Waccamaw and Queensborough just above the confluence of the Pee Dee and Lynches Rivers, but newcomers perceived their poorly drained soils and swampy terrain to be unsuitable for agriculture and neither attracted substantial settlement; however, in 1737 Welsh immigrants from Pennsylvania successfully petitioned to have Queensborough Township extended farther up the Pee Dee. Known as the Welsh Tract, the new area stretched all the way to the North Carolina line and opened the upper Pee Dee drainage to settlement. The region accommodated large numbers of immigrants, including many who arrived overland from the northern colonies.[23]

The provincial government situated the last of the eastern townships at the point where Pine Tree Creek emptied into the Wateree River just above the Fall Line. Like Saxe Gotha, Fredericksburg Township lay on a major overland thoroughfare into the interior. The road to the Catawba Nation, which branched off the Cherokee trading path at the head of the Santee, passed through the new township and linked it to Charleston. Farther inland, the Catawba Path connected with the principal route to the northern colonies. Fredericksburg formed a gateway into the northern backcountry, and its situation gave it strategic significance in the development of the wider region. Surveyors laid out the township in 1734, but the province issued no grants for land there for three more years. Nevertheless, immigrants soon began settling along the Wateree.[24]

Although Fredericksburg and the other townships established a British presence in the interior of the province, they did not immediately re-create the society from which they emerged. The Township Act was enacted to serve the interests of the lowcountry, and, while it offered opportunities to work as small farmers and artisans to the immigrants who resettled there, it provided them less than adequate support. Distant from the older settled area and linked to it by a road network created earlier to serve the Indian trade, Fredericksburg was relatively isolated and unable to guarantee immigrants' political or economic integration. The provincial government seemed unable to manage interior settlement or support its growth, leaving these matters largely to those whose interests lay in the backcountry's development. New residents faced the tasks of forging communities, maintaining civil authority, and creating an economy in a sparsely settled region lacking an infrastructure of production and transportation. They would have to accomplish all of these to transform the backcountry and lay the foundation for an integrated commercial economy and a politically unified state.[25]

The dramatic changes that took place in South Carolina's backcountry during this crucial period grew out of the region's role as an insular frontier on the periphery of an expanding world economy. Broad patterns of population expansion, transportation systems development, and shifting settlement function reflect regularities tied to the structure of colonization in South Carolina's interior.[26] The scope of this approach, however, is often too wide to reveal how changes actually occurred, what specific factors caused them, and why things took the particular form they did. To answer such specific questions, we must examine the backcountry and the processes that shaped it on a much narrower scale, one that incorporates historical circumstances particular to the time and place of settlement and addresses the impact of individual agency on the development of the economic and political strategies that transformed the backcountry from a frontier into an integral part of a larger state.

Fredericksburg on the Wateree

In December 1733 James de St. Julian began to survey the new township on the Wateree River. Employed by the provincial Council to produce a plat of Fredericksburg, he spent the next two months traversing and recording details of the territory specified in the Township Act. His plat portrayed a large, diagonally oriented tract situated on the east side of the river, extending from a point just above Sanders Creek on the north, northeast as far as Little Lynches River, southeast past the headwaters of the Black River, and southwest to rejoin the Wateree near the mouth of Rafting Creek. Pine Tree Creek emptied into the great river approximately halfway between the township's northern and southern boundaries and marked the location of the proposed town site, a rectangle through which the Catawba Path passed on its northward route paralleling the Wateree (Fig. 3.5). St. Julian's plat recorded information about the nature of the township's land and its resources, and the formal delineation of its legal boundaries imposed social order on an area of wilderness. This document offered colonial officials the prospect of directing immigration to the Wateree Valley, but the absence of a systematic plan to populate the region left the course of settlement to pioneers, whose interpretation of the landscape shaped their decisions about where to settle.[27]

Topography played an important role in decisions of where to settle (Fig. 3.6). Pioneers initially lacked the means and the experience with large-scale agriculture necessary to develop the bottomlands cultivated by commercial producers of the lowcountry and instead sought out smaller tracts more amenable to grain and mixed farming. They avoided the lower, wetter Coastal Zone in favor of higher and better drained lands in the interior. Immediately adjacent to the coast, advances and retreats of the sea during the Pleistocene Epoch had formed the flat, often wet, and almost featureless topography of the Outer Coastal Plain. Its low terraces and coastal features, the winding and often contorted patterns of its rivers, and the swamp-like appearance of the distinctive Carolina bays deterred agricultural development and added to the less than enthusiastic perception of the region common among the residents of townships situated there. Proceeding inland, pioneers encountered the rolling hills of the Inner Coastal Plain. Its uneven surface merges with the hilly topography of the Sandhills, a narrow, discontinuous physiographic region that crosses South Carolina in a band from northeast to southwest. The Sandhills mark the ancient shoreline of the Atlantic Ocean, and the action of waves has reworked the sand and

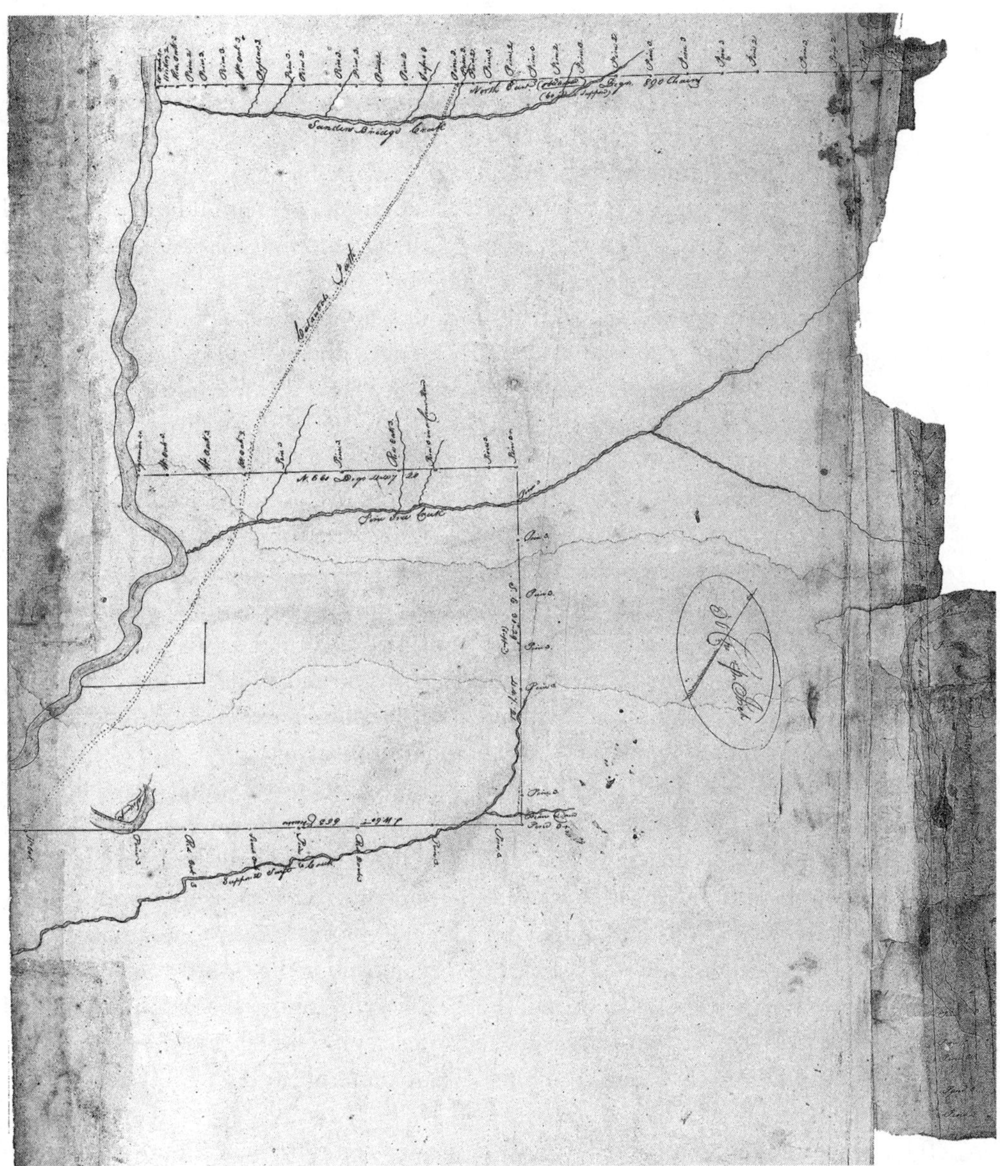

3.5 Plan of the Town of Fredericksburg on Wateree River, by James de St. Julian. This fragmentary document shows the north and east lines of the township as well as the Wateree River and its principal tributaries. Pine Tree Creek runs through the center of the township and the tract set aside for a nucleated settlement. Sanders Creek lies near the northern boundary, and Swift Creek enters the Wateree farther south. Little Lynches River is partially visible along the township's eastern line. The Catawba Path, leading to the Indian settlements upriver, traverses the township from south to north. Notations of the species of trees encountered on the survey lines provide clues to the native vegetation of the region. Courtesy of South Carolina Department of Archives and History, Surveyor General's Office, Copies of Plats and Plans, 1728–1800, p. 47 (2 February 1734).

clay sediments deposited there to form its distinctive topography. Within this region lies the Fall Line, a geological boundary zone where the resistant crystalline rocks of the interior abut the more easily eroded sedimentary rocks of the Coastal Plain. Here uneven erosion created rock outcrops and rapids along the rivers. Below the Fall Line, swamplands often surround the meandering rivers.[28]

Topography, and the processes that created it, produced the soils of the Sandhills and the Inner Coastal Plain. The sandy textured Entisols that predominate here afford excellent drainage, but rapid leaching results in a low retention of nutrients and organic material. Formed from marine deposited sediments, the soils' varying proportions of quartz and kaolinitic clay affects their fertility and suitability for agriculture. The sandier soils tend to be droughty and poorly suited for crops, but those with a higher loam content are useful as farmland. Unlike upland Entisols, those in stream and river flood plains form on sediments washed down from the Piedmont. Here silty loam soils in riverine environments contain rich flood deposits well suited to crops, but their situation makes them subject to flooding, and farming them requires dikes and other flood-control structures (Fig. 3.6).[29]

Vegetation reflects both soils and topography, and it guided the newcomers' assessment of the interior lands' potential for grain agriculture. The Piedmont and much of the Coastal Plain lie within the Oak-Pine Forest Region, a floral formation that covers most of the southeastern United States east of the Appalachians. Prior to European colonization, white, scarlet, and black oaks and southern red hickories dominated the hardwood forests, although yellow poplar, red maple, and blackgum intermixed with pines also occurred in some areas. On sandier and drier soils, longleaf pines with an oak understory persisted from an earlier successional stage as a subclimax forest, and on the poorest soils scrubby oaks predominated. Differences in drainage also produced considerable variation in forest types. The floodplains of the great rivers and their major tributaries, whose bottomlands flood for considerable periods but remain dry much of the year, were home to hardwood communities. The great brownwater swamps that extend along the Congaree and Wateree Rivers contained red gum, cottonwood, white ash, elm, sycamore, hackberry, white and red oak, and maple.[30] The occurrence of hardwood forests, pine subclimax forests, and bottomland hardwood forests influenced colonists' evaluations of land suitability in the backcountry.

The Europeans who immigrated to South Carolina's interior townships did not locate randomly. As farmers, they chose land carefully on the basis of physical attributes that reflected its suitability for production, and these perceptions shaped the direction of settlement. By the second quarter of the eighteenth century, colonists interpreted South Carolina's environment on the basis of previous knowledge and recent experience. They relied on information acquired firsthand in the New World by naturalists such as Mark Catesby, who associated topography, soil, and vegetation with the quality and fertility of land. His *Natural History,* first published in 1731, distinguished the "flat, sandy country" of the Outer Coastal Plain from the hilly topography farther inland, where the presence of "oak and hiccory lands" indicated fertility second only to the rich "rice lands" of the lowcountry. Immune from inundation, these elevated lands and their mixed sand and loam soils were suited to raising grain, pulse, roots, and herbage and yielded valuable timber. In addition, he noted the presence of pine barrens that contained soils of "light sterril sand" capable of

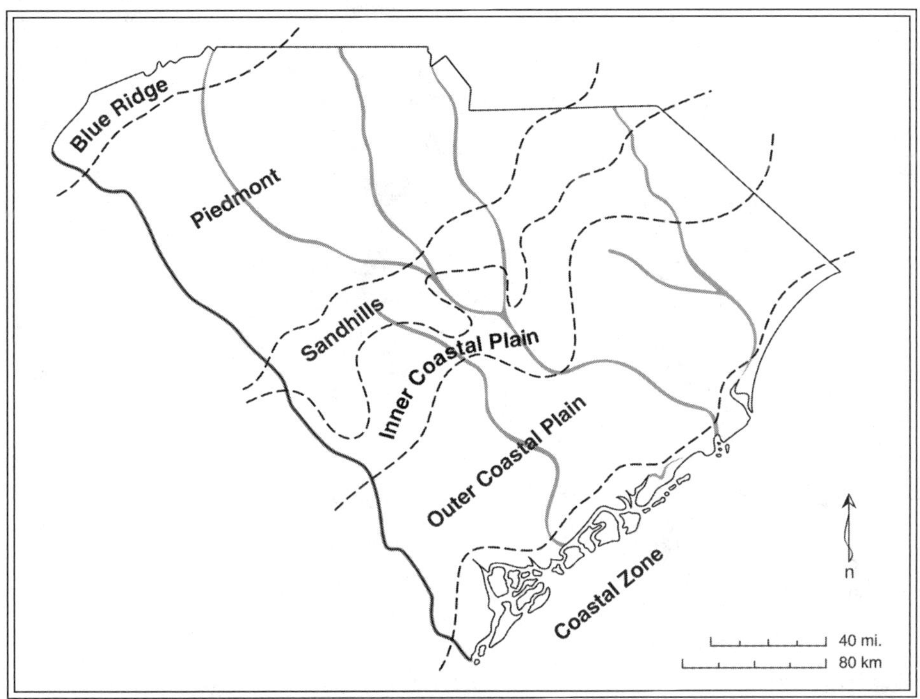

3.6 The major landform regions of South Carolina. Author's original map adapted from Charles F. Kovacik and John J. Winberry, *A Geography* (Boulder, Col.: Westview Press, 1987), 6.

supporting only conifers and scrubby oaks, as well as low, wet environments adjacent to large rivers, whose "vast burden of mighty trees" indicated the most fertile soil of any in the country. Despite their richness, their vulnerability to regular inundation lessened the agricultural value of river lands and made them less attractive to pioneers.[31] Others agreed with Catesby that a combination of deciduous forests and high topography produced land suitable for grain and other crops, "rich land," "good soil," and "rich, red loamy land," where "everything planted grows well and yields much fruit."[32] They also concurred with his assessment of the poor quality of the sandy pineland soils but recognized the commercial value of the trees that grew there as a source of lumber, turpentine, and pitch. Riverine lowlands presented a paradox for newcomers who could initially undertake the expense of bringing their potentially valuable soils under cultivation. A developing perception that associated malaria and other diseases with low, wet environments further deterred their settlement.[33]

As immigrants occupied the backcountry, experience revealed the advantages of the more inland townships for small-farm agriculture. Often they rated the topography and soils in the townships on the Outer Coastal Plain as less desirable and "less fertile and valuable than those . . . which lie remote from the sea."[34] Settlers in Williamsburg Township, for example, complained to the Assembly that they had found no land suitable for grain growing in this flat, wet region, contrasting its qualities with those in the "Wateree Township," where the soils resembled those of the "Northern Colonies, where the greatest quantities

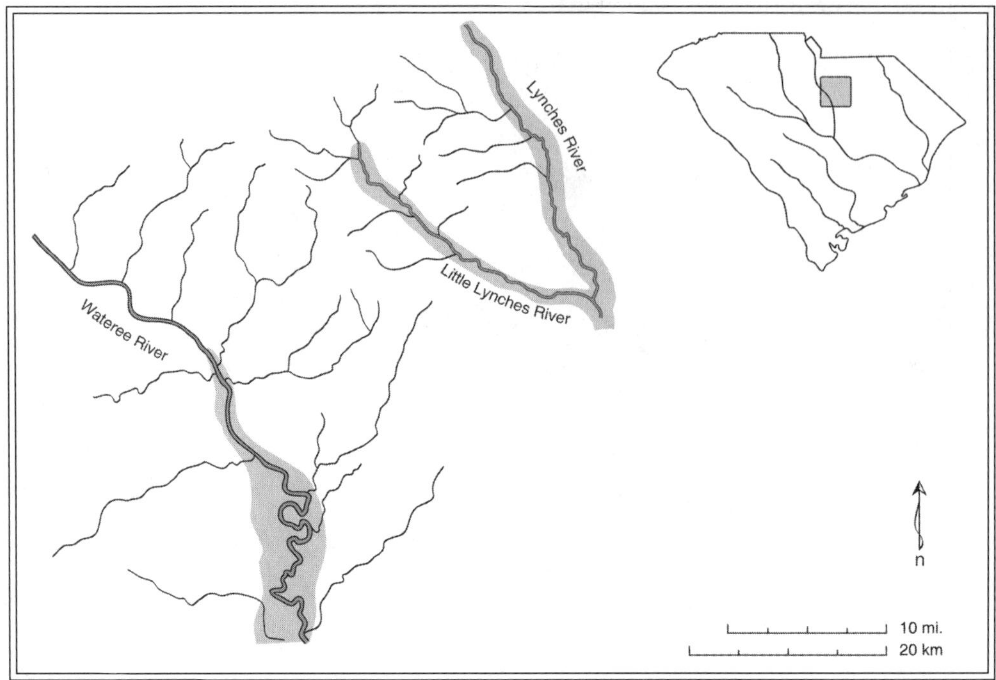

3.7 Floodplains along the Wateree and Lynches Rivers in the vicinity of Fredericksburg Township. Author's original map adapted from Cleaveland J. Mitchell Jr., *Soil Survey of Kershaw County Area, South Carolina,* U.S. Department of Agriculture, Soil Conservation Service, in cooperation with the South Carolina Experiment Station and the South Carolina Land Resources Conservation Commission (Washington, D.C.: Government Printing Office, 1989).

of grain were produced."[35] A preference for favorable farming environments led settlers to direct their attention toward the townships in the Inner Coastal Plain, Sandhills, and Piedmont. An official survey emphasized the high quality of these lands, singling out the presence of "champion land exceeding good for the corn and all other grain" on the upper Savannah, Saluda, Wateree, and Pee Dee Rivers.[36]

The success of agricultural colonization depended on environmental factors, the interpretation of which played a significant role in the distribution of settlement in Fredericksburg Township. As James de St. Julian's survey party walked the length and breadth of the township's boundaries in the winter of 1734, their lines exposed a cross section of the environments on the east side of the Wateree River. St. Julian's plat documented the presence of hardwood forests of sycamore, white and red oaks, and tupelo in the river and stream valleys (Fig. 3.7). Swamps along Lynches River and an oxbow of the Wateree and a "cane run" on Pine Tree Creek comprised additional wetlands. Later observers noted the area's many watercourses that formed "deep creeks and impassible morasses . . . covered with heavy timber and thick underbrush."[37] Farther inland, the surveyors encountered upland forest dominated by white oak, red oak, and poplar and finally the pinelands that occupied much of the high ground between the Wateree and Lynches Rivers to the east.[38] Here infrequent exposure to fire from natural causes as well as deliberate burning by Native peoples to clear lands for hunting maintained large areas of longleaf pine subclimax forest, consisting of extensive areas of "open pine wood . . . destitute of brush wood."[39] Scrubby oak communities grew on the poorest sandy soils of the least desirable lands.[40]

The newly surveyed township possessed an environment whose rolling topography and mixed forest vegetation offered desirable environments for immigrating small farmers. Certainly the Catawba Path provided direct access to the high, forested lands paralleling the river, from which settlement might later spread into surrounding areas. But the colonists who came to the Waterees, as the area was called, understood that their survival and persistence depended on more than simply the quality of the land they occupied. Success on the frontier required them to employ environmental resources in a manner conducive to developing an infrastructure that would sustain them and provide a basis for their eventual entry into the larger Atlantic economy.

Chapter 4

"Those Townships Being the Frontier Places"

Strategies for Settling the Backcountry

In the late spring of 1752 a group of distressed inhabitants in the Wateree Valley addressed a petition to the governor, the Council, and the Assembly of the province. Eager to enter commercial farming, the petitioners spoke of the fertility of the land and its capacity to yield wheat, barley, oats, rice, and peas, as well as flax, hemp, and other crops. Their success in stock raising further supplied them with butter, cheese, pork, beef, and tallow. But, despite the fecundity of the new land and its adaptability to familiar crops, circumstances that went along with settlement discouraged them "from raising any larger quantities than what is sufficient for home consumption." Largely separated from outside markets by distance and inadequate transportation, the residents of Fredericksburg and the other inland townships appealed to the colonial government for aid in overcoming the difficulties that arose from their situation and shaped the distinctive nature of the backcountry economy. For more than a decade, both inhabitants of the backcountry and lowcountry officials had recognized the region's potential role as a supplier of grain and other cash crops to the coastal region. The production of these commodities, at the time imported from the northern colonies, offered pioneer farmers a potential entre to commercial agriculture. But the cost of clearing watercourses, building roads, establishing ferries, and taking the other steps necessary to connect the coastal settlements with the interior prevented the realization of this goal. Despite their aspirations, immigrant farmers on the Wateree remained economically isolated and adapted by restricting the geographical scope of exchange.[1]

Immigrants to the South Carolina backcountry faced the paradox inherent in colonization: the need to establish an economy in the absence of the infrastructural elements necessary to support the institutions on which a stable political and social environment depended. Surviving and persisting in a new country in conditions far different from those they knew in longer settled places required that they overcome the difficulties of relocating to an unfamiliar area and establish a production base from scratch. Their journey into the interior took them far from home and situated them physically beyond the limits of the traditional social and economic institutions on which they had always depended. To succeed as agriculturists and build a viable production base on the frontier, pioneer settlers had to organize their society using the limited resources available.

In the years following the implementation of the Township Act, the provincial government endeavored to attract immigrants to the interior by providing support for them to resettle on the frontier. In addition to granting European Protestants passage, conveying land, supplies, and provisions to settlers, and exempting them from quitrents and other taxes, the Assembly supplied information about the region, subsidized the survey of tracts, furnished ministers to the townships, worked to curtail absentee ownership, reserved lands for specific groups, limited terms of indentured servitude, extended tax relief, and provided direct aid raised by subscription.[2] These efforts successfully accomplished the initial task of populating the frontiers of the province, enticing large numbers of people to leave their homes in England, Ireland, Wales, Scotland, France, Germany, Switzerland, and other parts of British North America to relocate in the Carolina backcountry.[3]

Despite the government's expenditures and careful planning, these efforts did little to support and sustain the newcomers once they arrived. Maintaining a viable pioneer society demanded more than furnishing the wherewithal for basic subsistence. All of the immigrants came from established market-oriented societies governed by broad economic, social, and political institutions that enmeshed individuals and families in larger communities that linked rural populations and focused their activities on urban centers. Although state authority did not impose itself directly on kin-based household organization, households operated within a broader milieu of state institutions that governed basic societal interests of defense, governance, law, economics, and religion. These institutions were operationalized through a formal infrastructure whose elements ensured security and stability, organized and regulated activities, and supported agriculture, manufacturing, and trade.[4] South Carolina lacked the resources to establish such an infrastructure in the distant backcountry, where the relative isolation of dispersed settlement and a low level of available capital assets thwarted the imposition of the colony's larger institutions. The cost of establishing facilities for producing, processing, transporting, and marketing agricultural staples in a peripheral area mitigated the government's ability to immediately provide these services. It also deterred colonial officials' attempts to provide mechanisms capable of administrating the vast territories undergoing settlement, ensuring their security, or imposing mechanisms for social integration. These conditions had broad implications for the development of Fredericksburg Township and the backcountry.[5]

Although most immigrants came to South Carolina's interior intending to continue their lives as farmers, merchants, or artisans who operated within a commercial economy, conditions in the new country made it impossible for them to immediately re-create traditional patterns of production and exchange.[6] Colonists initially overcame their circumstances of isolation by creating an inward-directed economy with an emphasis on regional self-sufficiency. The structure of this economy encouraged diverse production, promoted local reinvestment of surpluses, and stimulated the growth of indigenous institutions that organized the frontier region and provided a basis for its eventual transformation and integration within the greater milieu. This process accounts broadly for the changes that occurred in the South Carolina backcountry, but understanding the mechanisms that generated these new institutions is crucial in explaining the region's development. Such mechanisms often operated on a narrow scale and are reflected in the specific adaptations pioneers made to succeed in new country.

The Difficulty of Access

To survive and endure in the backcountry, newcomers coped with conditions inherent to the periphery of the larger Atlantic world. Chief among the impediments to development was difficulty of access. Living more than a hundred miles inland in the rolling Sandhills, the new residents of Fredericksburg Township found themselves far from Charleston and only tenuously connected with the lowcountry. In deliberately placing the townships on major rivers, officials presumed that their locations would be approachable by water and that residents might travel by river to and within the areas of new settlement. Unfortunately, these watercourses often proved difficult routes for travel and transportation. Although generally navigable below the Fall Line, most were obstructed by rafts formed by fallen trees and other vegetation, and none of the rivers provided direct access to the entrepôt.[7] Water transport on the vast Santee drainage was particularly hindered by the nature and location of the river's mouth. Unlike that of other major rivers, the Santee's discharge did not form a natural harbor but emptied directly into the Atlantic Ocean through a wide, swampy delta situated between Charleston and Georgetown. The depth of the bay into which it flowed required the use of shallow-draft boats that had then to navigate the fifty miles to the capital along a route only sporadically protected from the open sea by barrier islands. This risky passage limited the usefulness of the Santee River as a transportation route for bulk shipping.[8]

Overland travel benefited from the presence of preexisting routes created to facilitate exchange among aboriginal peoples or to serve the deerskin trade (Fig. 4.1). By the early years of the eighteenth century a dendritic system of trails, centered on Charleston, extended far into the interior. Passing northward from the entrepôt along the Santee, the "Old Road to the North" forked, with its western branch following the Congaree drainage into the Cherokee country. The eastern branch crossed the Santee below its confluence with the Wateree and paralleled the latter's eastern bank northward. Farther inland, the Catawba Path intersected routes running along the foothills of the Appalachians to western North Carolina and Virginia and to the colonies to the north.[9] As a network of penetration routes, the trails became potential trade corridors. Their form influenced the distribution of future interior settlement and promoted the colony's principal port as the mart for the newly opened backcountry.[10] But trade and settlement required a transportation system capable of moving bulk goods over long distances.

Land access routes to the interior proved adequate for immigration, but their inability to handle substantial bulk goods traffic prevented substantial trade and shut off the region from the lowcountry markets. The primitive nature of interior roads, together with the myriad rivers and streams that traversed the province, severely hindered the development of overland trade and thwarted settlers' ability to enter commercial markets. Throughout the years of early settlement, requests for assistance from the Assembly centered on the difficulties encountered with rivers and swamps along the routes to Charleston. Residents of Fredericksburg, recognizing the isolation of settlers on the north side of the Santee, pointed out that "carrying their cattle and other commodities to market [without] hardships and

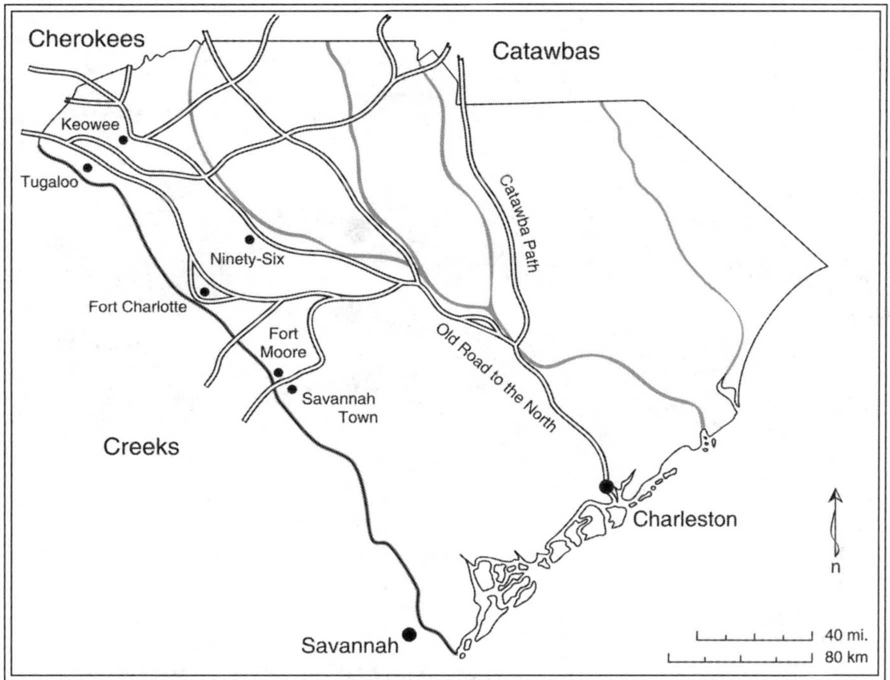

4.1 Principal Indian trade routes in eighteenth-century South Carolina. Author's original map adapted from William E. Myer, "Trail System of the Southeastern United States in the Early Colonial Period," in "Indian Trails of the Southeast," *Annual Report of the Bureau of American Ethnology* 42 (1928): Plate 15.

inconvenience" required not only good roads but also causeways over the swamps, as well as bridges and ferries at river crossings too deep or dangerous to ford (Fig. 4.2).[11]

Although the restricted capacity of long-distance transport precluded new residents of the backcountry from immediately participating in outside markets, conditions in the early settlement period did not bring complete isolation. Obstructed rivers and poor roads failed to cut off colonists from other settlements and force them into self-sufficiency. Despite lacking the means to carry out production and trade on a commercial scale, backcountry households were never entirely self-reliant. Newly arrived immigrants brought with them agricultural skills as well as the supplies, equipment, and domestic animals needed to begin life in the new country. Many also possessed specialized skills needed to operate mills and tanneries and make and repair tools and other items needed to sustain life on the frontier. Pioneers also imported a variety of goods. Their continual need for household utensils and ceramic vessels, agricultural implements, tools, machinery, implements, and other finished goods to replace those worn out or broken precluded complete self-sufficiency and obliged colonists to raise a surplus for exchange with the outside as well as within large but regionally restricted frontier markets. Such "communal self-sufficiency" typically bound residents of the periphery, both immigrants and aboriginals, in an extensive system of local exchange

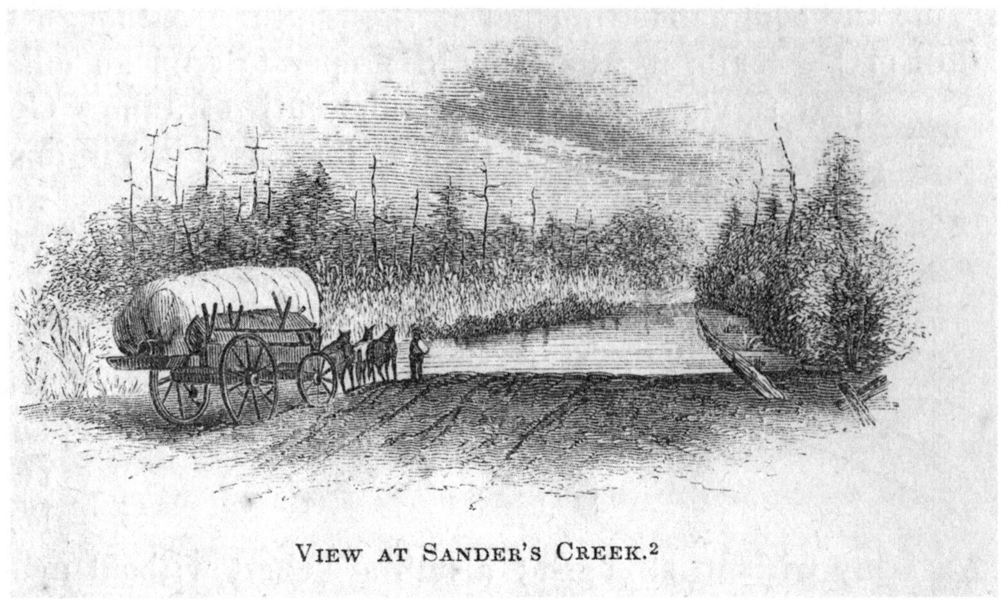

4.2 Overland travel in eighteenth-century South Carolina. The drawing depicts the ford where the Catawba Path crossed Sanders Creek in northern Fredericksburg Township. Source: Benjamin J. Lossing, *Pictorial Field Book of the American Revolution in the South,* Vol. 2 (New York: Harper & Bros., 1852), 461.

of goods and labor that sustained a substantial home market for farm products and locally made items as well as occasional products suitable for export.[12] This adaptive process involved several strategies; all had precedents, and none were mutually exclusive.

Alternate Strategies of Subsistence

The long human presence in South Carolina's backcountry shaped the landscape encountered by colonists. Complex Native societies that had occupied its lands, hunted its forests, and farmed its soils left their mark in the subclimax woodlands, old fields, and systems of trails the linked points in the interior. More recently, trade and warfare had subjugated and scattered many aboriginal peoples and restructured interior routes that connected their settlements and those of the Europeans. The early experience of colonization acquainted Europeans with the nature of the countryside and its resources, but the size and extent of the inland territories and their remoteness from the lowcountry made the interior an alien environment to those who came to settle there. To claim the new land and reshape it in their own image, European colonists first had to establish themselves. To survive and persist, they exploited the region's resources directly by hunting and indirectly through herding and agriculture.

Perhaps the most direct survival strategy was hunting. Although most of the nations from which South Carolina's immigrants came denied hunting to commoners, it remained part of the mixed subsistence strategies practiced in marginal areas of Europe and Native America and quickly spread among European settlers in the New World.[13] Hunters ranged far into the interior to exploit the region's abundant native species, particularly deer, although elk, bear, and turkeys were also sought. Although they preceded agricultural pioneers, hunters often remained in settled areas. Many emerged from the Indian trade, but the strategy also drew others from the new settlements. In many cases, hunting remained an important adjunct to agriculture for pioneer households during the settlement period, when the lengthy and arduous tasks of farm making consumed nearly all of the colonists' time. Hunting also constituted an alternative strategy for those unwilling or unable to enter agriculture. South Carolinians, as well as their neighbors in North Carolina and Georgia, observed mobile groups of people who subsisted by hunting, and some colonists in permanent settlements relied on hunting as their only source of food. Traveling west from the Wateree River in the 1760s, Charles Woodmason encountered poor settlers whose survival depended heavily on game.[14] In addition to its destructive effect on animal populations, extensive hunting, especially if carried out at night with the aid of fire, became increasingly dangerous as the density of settlement increased. By the 1770s, the great damage done by such "vagrant" hunters had made them a great nuisance in Cheraws District on the Pee Dee River.[15]

Livestock raising, being both land and labor extensive, was an effective adaptation to frontier conditions and became an important component of the backcountry economy, producing foodstuff for consumption as well as trade. Stock raising had been a successful early strategy in the lowcountry and was ideally suited to the conditions on the poorly settled frontier. Here it provided newly arrived colonists with a means of realizing a return with a minimum of investment. Backcountry operators benefited from the availability of vast lands over which the province granted them use rights, as well as from an absence of competition for their use, and they soon assembled extensive herds.[16] As independent ventures or investments by lowcountry planters, stock raising centered on isolated cowpens. These settlements usually consisted of a homestead of several hundred acres with cattle enclosures and hog shelters, together with dwellings for the operators and enslaved laborers and fenced fields for provision crops.[17] Livestock raising shifted to the Inner Coastal Plain after 1730 and by midcentury had spread into neighboring North Carolina and Georgia and later into the Piedmont (Fig. 4.3).

Perhaps the most profound impact of livestock raising was that it created a surplus product that was immediately available for export from the backcountry.[18] Unlike crops that required land clearing and that had to be harvested, processed, and shipped, cattle and hogs could be raised with a minimum of investment and driven to outside markets. The initial impetus for livestock raising in the lowcountry was to obtain an export product for trade with the West Indies, and by the second quarter of the eighteenth century the range of markets had expanded to include North American urban centers. Livestock became the backcountry's earliest export product, and raisers drove cattle over interior routes to northern markets in Philadelphia and New York, as well as to Charleston, Savannah, and St. Augustine.[19]

Although well adapted to frontier conditions, livestock raising could not compete with agriculture and always remained a marginal activity in South Carolina. Cattle and hogs

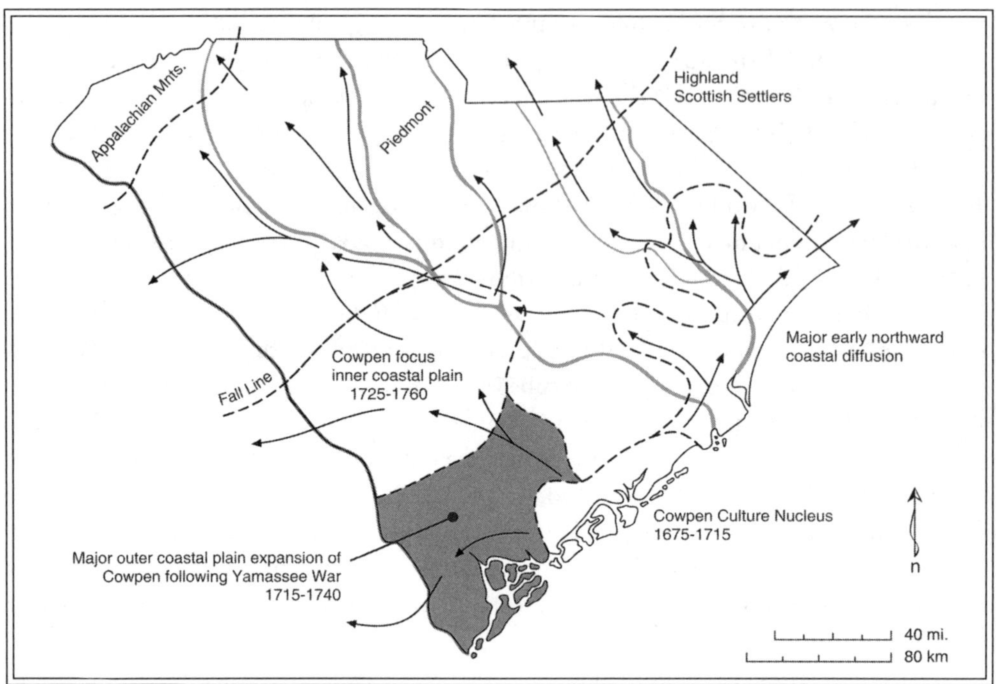

4.3 The expansion of livestock raising in colonial South Carolina during the eighteenth century. Author's original map adapted from Terry G. Jordan, *North American Cattle Ranching Frontiers: Origin, Diffusion, and Differentiation* (Albuquerque: University of New Mexico Press, 1993), 111.

required considerable territory for forage, and the land-extensive nature of herding brought returns that were inherently less than those derived from more land-intensive uses such as crop growing. Without competition for land, livestock raising remained a lucrative activity and thrived; however, the expansion of farming in the interior brought greater rivalry for land, and livestock ranges became increasingly centered on the less desirable areas of the Coastal Plain west of Orangeburg. Cowpens stretched from the Edisto Forks through the upper Coosawahatchie and Salkehatchie drainages to the Savannah River and later spread above the Fall Line into the drainages of the Wateree, Congaree, and Saluda Rivers into the Piedmont (Fig. 4.3). Growing competition for land, together with losses resulting from epidemic disease, precipitated a decline in livestock raising after midcentury. Livestock raising remained a viable strategy in the backcountry even after the American Revolution but played a diminished role in South Carolina's agricultural economy.[20]

Agriculture on the Frontier

Pioneer settlers to South Carolina came largely from rural villages in Europe, where most of them had made a living in farming or activities related to it, and immigrated to America with the intent of continuing a familiar way of life amid the more bountiful resources offered by the new country. In the backcountry, however, they had to adapt traditional agriculture, like other economic endeavors, to the conditions they encountered in a peripheral region, where their tenuous physical links to the distant outside world restricted trade and minimized the influence of larger markets. Without a cash market for their crops and with limited access to imported finished items, settlers found that nearly all surpluses of food and goods had to circulate within a limited area, where regional trade supplied the needs of resident colonists as well as new immigrants to the frontier. Circumstances redirected the structure of traditional farming to accommodate a noncapitalist market. Agriculture in a commercial economy was a family enterprise in which farmers grew crops for cash, participated in larger markets, and consumed finished goods made elsewhere. It centered around *simple commodity production,* an arrangement in which kinship affected the role of labor and its relationship to the ownership and means of production. Unlike a factory, the family farm did not possess class divisions separating owners and laborers. In the factory, owners controlled the means of production. Labor had no role in decision making and remained subject to the owner's interests. But on family farms, the owner's household members performed labor, and additional temporary help came from other farm households. Wages did not serve as a means to create social division within farm households but instead were a means of redistributing capital within and between households and served to finance the establishment of new farms and to overcome labor discrepancies among existing farm households. Simple commodity production provided a stability that protected farmers from the vicissitudes of a capitalist economy. Its structure also incorporated a flexibility that allowed households to accommodate conditions encountered on the periphery of settlement.[21]

On the frontier, farm households adapted simple commodity production to the constraining conditions imposed by their new situation. A limited market and the difficulties associated with external trade, as well as scarce capital and a perennial shortage of labor, restricted the production of a surplus. Even if it existed, surplus produce could generate no accumulated wealth in the absence of commercial markets. Rather than impinging on the structure of simple commodity production, these circumstances redirected its cooperative structure to different ends. Although limited opportunities left farmers with an uncertain market for their produce, individual households were not self-sufficient and had to direct some of their efforts toward exchange with others. To accomplish this, frontier agriculturists adopted a *household mode of production,* an initial arrangement directed toward producing and distributing goods on the basis of need rather than price. A product's use value to consumers overrode its value as a commodity, and exchange served to meet the economic needs of the larger pioneer community. By creating and maintaining ties among frontier households, trade served a socially integrative function beyond its economic role. These ties enmeshed immigrant agriculturists in a web of mutual exchange of goods and services, which served to tie them together in a web of mutual obligation. Farm households diversified crop production to deal with uncertain demand for foodstuffs, and those with relevant skills milled grain, repaired tools and implements, tanned hides, and manufactured furniture and other household items for their neighbors. Specialized production appeared early and accompanied regional exchange. By increasing the variety of goods available to settlers, the varied contributions of the colonists were crucial to supporting settlements and creating the economic structure of a farming region.[22]

This is not to say that backcountry farmers remained immune to the influences of the larger capitalist marketplace. Despite their attenuated ties with the market, they assigned values to the goods and services exchanged in transactions that reflected the pervasive reliance on money. Cash-poor colonists accustomed to a market economy continued to express exchange values of products in monetary units, but cash equivalents served as a means of comparison and did not actually turn goods or labor into money. Rather, they helped each party in a transaction ensure that he or she received something whose worth was equal to the worth of that given. Recording transactions in cash values, a process sometimes called money barter, also allowed settlers to keep track of exchange over time to accommodate varying production schedules and provided credit for those with few resources. Cash equivalencies facilitated exchange among backcountry farmers, herdsmen, and hunters and provided a basis for storekeepers, traders, innkeepers, craft workers, and others to supply limited services and imported finished goods. Gov. William Bull was correct when he stated that "our internal commerce is carried on by credit or barter, especially between the backsettlers and Charlestown." The direct exchange of goods with comparable use value, without the mediation of money, discouraged the transformation of products and services into a universal equivalent for the purpose of maximizing monetary surpluses. As long as these circumstances persisted, they inhibited capital formation and mitigated the penetration of a capitalist economy.[23]

The economic conditions associated with frontier settlement affected not only the organization of agricultural production but also its scale and range. In order to survive and persist under conditions of semi-isolation, poverty, and uncertainty, pioneer farmers sought to maximize their flexibility to allocate resources differentially toward multiple ends. Despite immigrants' desire to enter market production, the precariousness of frontier farming encouraged them to ensure that their own needs were met first. By following a strategy of "composite farming," they channeled their efforts to sustain the farm household and produce surpluses or specialized goods for trade. Neighboring households exchanged goods among themselves directly but also made sales outside their immediate community to storekeepers, hunters, livestock drovers, traders, millers, and others who constituted their limited links to a larger world.[24] Composite farmers found it safest to avoid specialization and instead to generalize production around diverse crops that had proven to be well adapted as initial cultigens.

Corn, or maize, was a versatile plant whose characteristics made it an ideal pioneer crop. In widespread use by Native agricultural peoples in the Americas long before the coming of the Europeans, it was quickly adopted by the newcomers. Corn was widely available and familiar to South Carolinians. Planters cultivated it extensively as a subsistence crop in the lowcountry and believed it to be well adapted to interior soils, and it accompanied the earliest settlers to the interior. Immigrants used a digging stick or hoe to plant this native crop amid the stumps and roots of newly cleared land, and it yielded an early return. Planted in April, corn ripened in October and could be harvested through the end of the year. "Its easy culture, great increase, and above all its strong nourishment" led early observers, such as the naturalist Mark Catesby, to recommend it as a food that could be processed with minimal equipment, transported and stored easily, and prepared in a variety of ways as pone, mush, or hominy. Indeed, cornbread constituted a major dietary component of many backcountry pioneer households. Because it was planted in widely separated hills, corn could be grown in combination with other American and European food crops, including squash, pumpkins, watermelons, cucumbers, peas, sweet potatoes, beans, Irish potatoes, turnips, and other garden vegetables.[25]

European grains also made an early appearance in the backcountry. Farmers grew small quantities of rye, oats, and barley, but demand for them remained low in the regional economy. Wheat, however, showed great promise both as a subsistence and a commercial crop. A substantial market for flour had always existed in the lowcountry, and that region's dependence on wheat imported from the northern colonies led authorities to seek an indigenous source. The perception that interior lands were best suited for this grain raised hopes that the newly opened lands in the backcountry might profitably be placed in cultivation. Although a bounty passed by the Assembly in 1745 encouraged the production of flour made from South Carolina, the limited capacity for processing wheat in the backcountry and the expense and difficulty of shipping it over long distances discouraged farmers from raising this crop for export. Nevertheless, they produced substantial surpluses by the 1750s.[26]

Grain and fruit also constituted the basis for distilled and fermented alcohol, products that were widely consumed in the eighteenth century and whose easy transport made them valuable in trade. Many settlers cultivated fruit orchards of peach, pear, and apple trees for subsistence,[27] but as Gov. James Glen reported in 1748, "the people in the new townships make very good spirits from grain and other materials, and, as this will come cheaper, so it may supply the place of rum amongst the Indians and Negroes." In addition to making distilled spirits for trade, they supplied a substantial regional market with brandy, rum, and whiskey through frontier taverns and stores.[28] A regional market for beer and wine also existed, but brewing was more complicated than distilling, and a lack of capital to establish breweries discouraged at least one early attempt in Saxe Gotha Township. Despite initial legislative support and the extraordinary effort of its backers, a scheme to develop viticulture among the French Huguenot settlements on the Savannah River also failed.[29]

In additional to grain, settlers grew products for other purposes. An early attempt to promote a commercial crop on the South Carolina frontier centered on the cultivation of indigo, a plant valuable in the production of dye. To encourage indigo in its North American colonies, the British Parliament offered a bounty in 1749, and South Carolina's Assembly promoted indigo growing by offering seed to backcountry settlers. Indigo reputedly required little labor to produce, and its relatively small bulk made it relatively easy to transport, making it seem an ideal frontier crop. Its processing, however, was a complicated and delicate matter that required specialized skills and equipment. This placed indigo making beyond the means of initial settlers and delayed its production, like that of other cash crops, until conditions changed in the backcountry.[30] Nonedible fibers, such as hemp, used in rope making, and flax for cloth also appeared on frontier farms but found a largely home market despite bounties for their export.[31]

Although distance and the costs of processing and transportation continued to restrict interaction between the backcountry producers and the world economy, larger forces of evolutionary change continued to influence the region's growth. It is one thing to observe the transition to commercial agriculture at this broad level as a consequence of a wider process of economic expansion, but this does little to explain how change actually took place. To comprehend the transformation of the backcountry, we must investigate this phenomenon on the narrower scale of the elements upon which the frontier economy operated. This entails another look at how the structure of society accommodated production and exchange on the frontier and how it formed the basis for the region's social and political organization during the initial settlement period.

The Organization of Production on the Frontier

As the primary unit of subsistence and production on the frontier, the family farm constituted the basis for structuring economy and society in the backcountry. In the pre-industrial European society from which immigrants came, the family was central to the scale of almost all activity. Most work was organized and carried out within the family, and its structure provided the means for organizing production. Linked by kinship ties that defined their membership as well as their roles, households included the conjugal family unit as well as more remote relatives and outsiders, including servants or slaves. The farming household provided the setting for work and organized the labor of its members. It served as a vehicle for the management and redistribution of pooled farm income that ensured the security and survival of the group and the success of its endeavors. As such, the household was ideally suited to function as the principal economic institution in a region dependent on simple commodity production.[32]

In spite of its traditional economic significance in postmedieval Europe, the family-based household did not exist or operate in a vacuum. Households and the communities they constituted were enmeshed in larger, permanent institutions that integrated them with the broader world in which they existed. The church, courts, parliaments, governmental agencies, schools, and markets brought larger groups of people together to facilitate exchange, disseminate information, regulate behavior, and exact obligations to the state. Although the specialized nature and episodic occurrence of these institutions distinguished them from the everyday continuity of household activities, the existence of such wider entities provided a necessary context in which to carry out the functions of a nation-state.[33] Institutions linked households to communities, which in early eighteenth-century England were still largely rural. Socially stratified by class, community organization revolved around the wealth, occupation, or inherited status of individuals and was structured around civil and ecclesiastical institutions at the village level. These included formal and informal administrative bodies, manorial courts, assemblies, and guilds that established and oversaw rules regulating and ensuring conformity in personal behavior, rules of husbandry and agricultural practice, customs of tenure and inheritance, and the structure of trade.[34] On a broader scale, villages fell within the scope of the parish, which formed the basic unit of local government. Originally units of ecclesiastical jurisdiction charged with regulating activities outside the scope of the manorial courts, parishes became an extension of the state after the Reformation. The county, or shire, was the next larger administrative unit. As with the parish, its officials served as agents of the Crown and were responsible for collecting taxes, regulating wages, and punishing some crimes.[35] By the time colonization in South Carolina's backcountry began, economic changes had already begun to alter the order of life in postmedieval Britain, creating conditions that encouraged migration to the New World colonies. Although many were dissatisfied with changing circumstances in their homeland, immigrants to the interior were nevertheless accustomed to a social environment shaped by familiar cultural institutions that integrated the roles of households at multiple levels. The absence of these larger state institutions presented an immediate challenge to settlers. To re-create a functioning society in the new country, households adapted by assuming a much broader role.

Economic realities in the backcountry affected the structure of pioneer society. Even at midcentury, the region was barely under the control of South Carolina's colonial authorities and lacked a functioning administrative system and the infrastructure necessary to support large scale, organized exchange. Their absence deterred the development of commodified markets and restricted production largely to levels that could be absorbed by the local community. Although frontier households operated in an attenuated political and economic environment, their inhabitants remained subjects of the colonial state and were not isolated from the demands it made on them. Pioneer residents received title to their property from the state and, in turn, owed its government obligations in the form of militia service and quitrents. As members of a technologically complex society, they also depended on imported finished goods. The need to obtain manufactured items such as tools, plows, utensils, weapons, gunpowder, and other articles necessary for survival on the frontier forced pioneers to produce something for exchange.[36] The need to maintain a surplus to supply the demands of government officials, merchants, and other outside powerholders linked the regional economies of the backcountry to the larger state and required that households address the necessity of producing a surplus as part of their economic adaptation.

Of Peasants and Economically Marginal Societies

Lying at the edge of colonial expansion, far from South Carolina's center of power and tied only tangentially to its economy, frontier agricultural households constituted a society whose economy was marginal from the larger whole. As such, it shared structural similarities with traditional *peasant* societies. These communities of rural agricultural producers maintain ties to urban markets but, because of geographical isolation, economic constraints, and political restrictions, exist as a separate class segment of the larger population. In general, peasant societies remain subservient to outside elites, but, because their members retain effective control over cultivation through land ownership or other means, they preserve a degree of independence. As with frontier farmers, market restraints oblige peasant societies to focus their production on maintaining household needs rather than on creating a surplus for reinvestment. Unlike that of a commercial farmer who raises specialized crops and participates in a market economy, the paramount goal of a peasant farmer is the maintenance of the subsistence of his household and its social status within a narrow range of peasant households. Each household must produce crop surpluses as a means of obtaining money to purchase the goods and services it requires to exist and sustain its social position; however, peasants do not see agriculture as a business enterprise in which the factors of production are redirected toward maximal returns rather than minimum risk and whose product is invested in amortizing and expanding the operation.[37]

The economy of traditional peasant societies represents an adaptation to the conditions in which their members live, but their situation is not immutable if the obstacles to commercial farming are removed. This change involves a major shift in the institutional context in which they operate. Peasant households can transition from household to market production only when they are able to free themselves of the economic and political tributary obligations to their overlords or when the introduction of capitalist industry offers alternative employment that frees up enough land to allow farmers to amass the resources needed to produce specialized crops on a commercial scale.[38] Frontier farmers were, of course, not subject to the political and economic restrictions that deter peasants from entering into commercial production, but geographical isolation imposed similar economic conditions that kept them out of wider markets and obliged them to adopt a comparable strategy until the situation changed. Because the backcountry economy was an adaptive response to its residents' existence as an economically marginal society, a comparison of its structure to that of peasant societies can offer analogies useful in understanding the early growth of this region.[39]

In peasant societies, production is directed toward the security and persistence of the household as an economic unit. A household's success depends on its ability to provide for subsistence. Obviously it must take care of its members' caloric needs as well as furnish seed for crops, livestock feed, clothing, and other expendable goods and supply the wherewithal to buy and repair tools, keep up buildings, and acquire tools and utensils. But the state, merchants, and other outside powerholders extract a share of household production, and each household must have resources to carry out these responsibilities. The household must also maintain a "ceremonial fund" to fulfill obligations of sociability and responsibility to family, friends and neighbors. The last of these is particularly important because, together with external demands, the cost of underwriting social relations has the potential to easily exceed the household's resources allocated for subsistence and replacement.[40] Why is this so?

The need to possess a fund of resources for social obligations reflects the importance of interhousehold ties, but the rituals the fund supports also have broader implications for the organization of the wider peasant community. Larger than the individual households that compose it, the community serves as the context within which occur the interactions on which the community's survival depends. In the absence of broader institutions, households depend on reciprocity, the sharing and communal management of resources, and cooperative labor to ensure their continuity. Because the rituals that link households are public formalities, they hold the potential of becoming more elaborate, and this tendency requires households to intensify production to meet the cost of the expected reciprocity. The necessity of household interdependency thus creates a tension with the independent subsistence-related interests of each household, and the potential discord resulting from it must be ameliorated. Peasant households avoid conflict by developing instrumentalities of power that control the settings in which people interact with others. Resting on the hegemony of shared cultural meanings and practices, these mechanisms govern the means by which individuals circumscribe the actions of others within specific settings and produce institutional constraints that regulate behavior.[41] How do such instrumentalities arise?

Anthropologists who have analyzed politically decentralized societies have observed that the mechanisms by which households ameliorate the tensions inherent in potentially conflicting demands between households take the form of rituals that transform surplus goods and labor into socially productive relations. Established through negotiation, rituals serve as integrative mechanisms that legitimize these social demands and mediate opposing interests in the absence of central authority. Rituals serve a political role in that they help maintain the distinctness of households and keep them from being subsumed in a larger entity. They also establish an ongoing opposition between households as givers and receivers of delayed reciprocity. This is illustrated by the ritual of marriage, which strengthens and legitimizes social demands between households. Marriage plays a key role among independent peasant households that depend on one another for the labor necessary to accomplish tasks involved in production because it ties their members together through a relationship that entails ceremonial requirements. In the absence of an overriding authority to regulate the exchange of labor necessary for agricultural production and other tasks, affinal ties facilitate the movement of workers between households. Such ties provide assistance for planting, harvesting, and processing of crops, and they ensure that each household will have access to other resources during times of need. Networks of relationships deriving from marriage, as well as links formed by friendship and acquaintance, enmesh households in a web of ritualized reciprocity that preserves their distinctness within the larger community, while ensuring that each has access to the resources necessary to sustain itself and to provide for its future.[42]

Although rituals such as marriage are symbolic acts underlain by an institutionally distinct sacred structure, interactions associated with friendship and acquaintance consist only of repetitive prescribed behavior whose formalized, conventionalized, and stylized nature permits people to maintain their society in equilibrium. These rituals reflect a common belief system about how the world should be and how people should act in it. Such beliefs can encompass production and exchange and the proper manner in which they are carried out. In the absence of formal institutions, rituals associated with these economic functions perform an integrative role in negotiating exchange and reconciling conflicting interests within a community of independent households, resulting in the formation of a *ritual economy.* Ritual economies organize household production and regulate politics in societies lacking commoditized markets and institutions for central control. By nature, ritual economies resist development into more complex forms because the attachments and obligations maintained by households already consume their surpluses. For such change to occur, economic and political influences must be sufficient to overcome the perception that ritualized relationships are necessary for household survival.[43]

As economically marginal societies, the structure of peasant communities must be understood in the context of the systems of social relations that link such "little communities" and their members to one another and to the outside world. These systems revolve around activities that help define community structure. One kind of social relations links people who belong to groups of progressively larger size. They consist of territorially based connections, ranging from personal relationships between individuals through broader ties based on kinship and neighborhood to more formal relations that extend outside the community.

Such systems exist within and reach beyond the community to facilitate interaction among people and to bind the society together at multiple levels. Activities of the market form a second system of social relations that tie the regional household economy to that of the greater society. They involve traders who remain part of the communities from which they come but who can range far beyond its boundaries, engaging in activities different from those of local producers and associating with distant outsiders. Because economic activities associated with markets may occur only irregularly at impermanent and changing sites, a trader's influence on community social and political structure is limited. Both hierarchical social relations and those associated with markets create networks that constitute systems that are countrywide in scope. Such networks knit together peasant communities and connect them with the outside world. Social and economic networks integrate the settlements of a region through the various connections of their inhabitants, and the nature of their ties defines the networks' structure. These networks form the basis for regional integration and constitute the medium by which little communities interact with the larger world.[44]

The structure of peasant societies, organized around household production, is a viable adaptation to conditions similar to those imposed by the semi-isolation of the frontier. An emphasis on the household as the central unit of production and a reliance on ritualized reciprocity as a mechanism for ameliorating the tensions associated with exchange provide the basis for a social structure capable of integrating society where formal political institutions are lacking, and ensure a level of security in the absence of central authority. Peasant societies maintain ties beyond the household through informal institutions that employ kinship and association to bind communities and to link them to the outside world. The networks of interaction that integrate economically marginal societies offer a flexibility that allows their members to extend social relations over wide areas and maintain the level of exchange necessary to support a regional economy. Although British colonial America lacked the political institutions found in peasant societies, the conditions that prevented frontier farmers from entering commercial agriculture mimicked the economic insulation of these traditional societies and obliged them to develop similar strategies to survive and succeed. These strategies would hardly have been alien to South Carolina's immigrants because most of them came from peasant backgrounds in England and Europe. Indeed, the mechanisms that would allow them to persevere in the new country had precedents in their past.[45]

Chapter 5

"The Great Inconveniences of People in Those Remote Places"

Forging a Regional Economy

The circumstances of initial settlement shaped the nature of production and trade on the Wateree Valley frontier. Although the small size of the area's population restricted the volume of production, the primitive state of agricultural development also meant that farmers could barely accommodate demand. Continual immigration and natural increase created a constantly expanding market, but the chronic shortage of labor on the frontier affected the rate at which land could be cleared, fenced, and placed in cultivation. Indeed, residents of nearby Saxe Gotha Township complained that the tasks involved in farm making and producing a surplus sufficient to feed a growing population were so demanding as to leave them no time for any public obligations.[1] High local demand and limited production capacity ensured that most crops and livestock raised by pioneer households were consumed in the region, a situation that favored diversified agriculture and minimized surpluses available for external sales.

The nature of exchange also affected the structure of frontier society. Immigrants to the South Carolina backcountry usually settled in *communities of accretion,* composed of residents who might have had no previous connections with one another. As is common in regions undergoing rapid immigrant settlement, these rural communities lacked the network of social, political, and religious ties that traditionally provided systems of mutual support and assistance and formed the basis for the community's organization. Although former ties of association and kinship, as well as common origin, ethnicity, and religion, helped bond some newcomers, their communities generally lacked a sense of unity and coherence, and their members could not replicate the society from which they came. In the place of old ties, settlers had to develop new linkages in response to the conditions they encountered. The new residents of Fredericksburg and the other interior townships relied on exchange between households as the medium out of which to organize society in the South Carolina backcountry.[2]

Trade on the frontier required mechanisms to ensure the cooperation necessary to facilitate the redistribution of surplus products. Informal local markets oversaw the exchange of goods and services between members of a widely scattered population, but these tended to be episodic, unscheduled, and largely unsupervised. The success of such markets depended on safeguards that protected against abusive market practices.[3] These structures arose through the ritual of repetitive, formalized behavior, which encouraged market participants to exchange goods and services according to need rather than to achieve profit. As in the peasant societies from which most settlers came, the need to supply household subsistence, a desire to maintain community solidarity, and the lack of opportunities to invest profits discouraged the accumulation of wealth beyond that needed to pay for goods and services that could be obtained through obligatory means from the individuals who provided them.[4] Although some might profit from exchange, the chief function of local markets was to supply provisions necessary for daily life to a dispersed population that lacked other retailing opportunities. These frontier markets differed markedly from the officially sanctioned fairs in the lowcountry, which were highly organized institutions that generated a high volume exchange. Such fairs were meeting places of professional merchants who bought and sold goods for profit to wider markets.[5] In the first half of the eighteenth century, fairs in South Carolina appeared only in lowcountry crossroad centers such as Ashley Ferry, Dorchester, and Childsbury (Fig. 2.4), where a high flow of traffic in export commodities encouraged the development of retail trade.[6] In the local markets of the backcountry, the nature and volume of exchange discouraged the emergence of a merchant class. But such markets were not unorganized.

The Organization of Backcountry Exchange

Although backcountry residents remained largely insulated from the lowcountry's commercial economy, their adoption of a monetary standard for the exchange of goods and services allowed them to employ mechanisms of credit to maintain accounts between suppliers and recipients in the local markets. Credit allowed the periodic settlement of accounts between households and facilitated trade in produce and labor. Arrangements based on credit also helped them acquire imported items and finished goods or specialized services. In contrast to the prevailing system in the lowcountry, where formal institutions eased the flow of credit in commoditized markets, credit in the interior depended on mechanisms organized at the household level and housed in facilities that operated on that scale.[7]

Exchange facilities played a crucial role in creating the frontier economy of the South Carolina backcountry by providing the means to redistribute the diverse goods and services provided by immigrants and maintaining a tenuous economic link to the outside world. Because of their role in converting raw agricultural products into a usable form, mills became focal points of activity, and their ability to draw settlers from a wide area made them a crucial element in expediting interhousehold exchange in a region lacking formal trading institutions. Gristmills ground locally produced grain into flour and meal for use by farmers and their neighbors, and saw mills turned trees into the lumber necessary to construct houses and farm buildings (Fig. 5.1). Stores often grew up associated with mills, offering settlers an outlet for produce as well as a source of ironware, ceramics, and other imported items. In South Carolina, mills became early centers of trade, an activity that elsewhere gravitated to taverns and ironworks as well.[8] Here individual craftspeople who relocated to South Carolina's interior townships exchanged their wares for the produce of

5.1 A water-powered grain mill in the South Carolina Backcountry. This nineteenth-century mill with its overshot wheel is typical of those constructed during the previous century to process grain for local consumption and later export. Courtesy of South Caroliniana Library, University of South Carolina, Columbia, South Carolina.

others. Among them were newly arrived blacksmiths, carpenters, coopers, weavers, and tailors who practiced their trades at home in the new country.[9]

Mills accompanied the flow of immigration into the backcountry and shaped the distribution of early settlement in the Wateree Valley. These relatively complex machines required an investment by operators to acquire their machinery and carry out construction. Conditions encountered on the frontier presented millers with the difficult task of amassing the capital and resources necessary to place the facility in operation. They found limited assistance from a provincial sinking fund that included a bounty for those who established mills in the inland townships.[10] To collect the bounty, individuals had to demonstrate that a residential population that required such a facility already existed. Consequently, early mills very likely accompanied new settlement, and their locations should reveal its movement into the Wateree Valley.

Settlers in Fredericksburg Township built mills on its major streams soon after the lands were opened to settlement (Fig. 5.2). Enterprising individuals gathered the endorsements of resident households and petitioned the Assembly for funds to construct mills.[11] Although immigration occurred slowly, within seven years of the first land grants in 1737 a sufficient number of settlers had arrived to support the construction of mills on tributaries on the east side of the Wateree. Charles Ratcliffe, who received a grant of 250 acres in 1743,

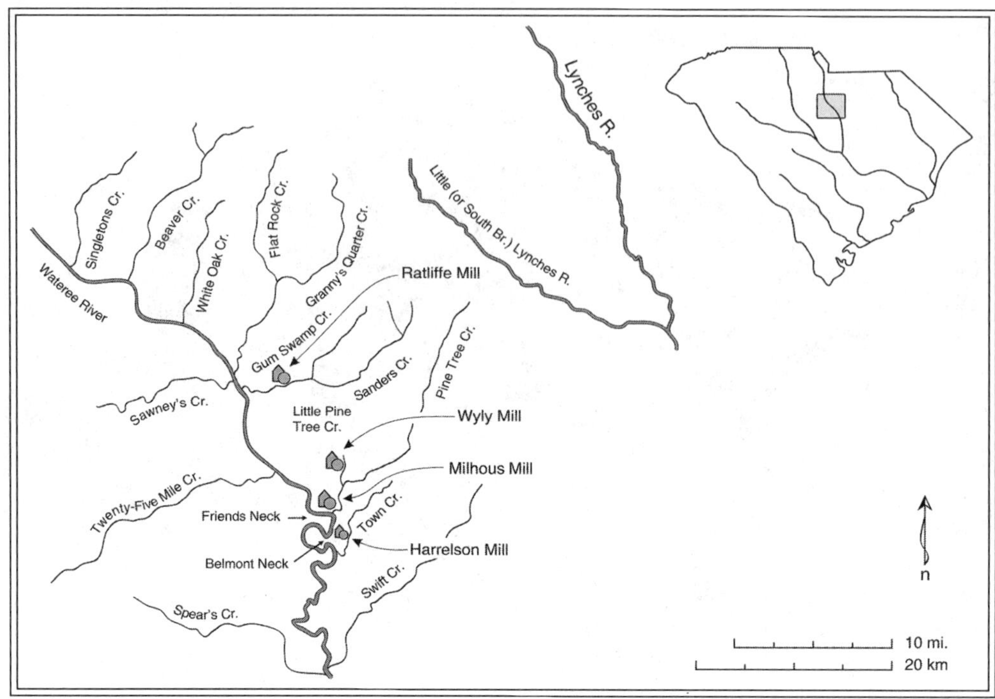

5.2 Locations of early mills erected along streams of the Wateree Valley in the vicinity of Fredericksburg Township. Author's original map.

and Paul Herrelson, who claimed 450 acres two years later, requested funds for mills to serve at least three dozen households. Soon Harrelson's mill was in operation on Town Creek, and a mill dam straddled Sanders Creek on Ratliffe's tract farther to the north. Robert Milhous, who arrived in Fredericksburg Township in 1751, acquired several parcels on Pine Tree Creek and built a saw and gristmill there. William Ferrell purchased one of Milhous's tracts from his heirs in 1758 and operated a mill there. Farther upstream, settlers erected sawmills and gristmills on Little Pine Tree Creek during the 1750s. By 1760 additional mills situated to the east on the tributaries of Lynches River also contributed to the region's agricultural economy.[12] Mills constituted the earliest physical infrastructure of exchange among pioneer residents on the Wateree Valley and reflected the emergence of a regional economy. Mills were points of exchange as well as facilities to process and redistribute produce, and their presence promoted the integration of a diverse frontier community and established the larger social context upon which the growth of commerce depended.

The pioneer population grew with the Wateree Valley's development. Initial European settlement expanded slowly in the 1730s but began to accelerate rapidly a decade later. The earliest arrivals included individuals who had engaged in the Indian trade as well as family groups that immigrated from the outside. The population of the Wateree drainage grew tenfold between 1745 and 1750 and nearly tripled in the succeeding five years. Some of the later settlers had previously lived in Williamsburg, Orangeburg, and Amelia Townships and the Congarees, while others were lowcountry planters seeking opportunities in the interior.

The following decade brought increased overland movement from the north, as a substantial number of settlers fleeing the hostilities of the Seven Years' War poured into the South Carolina backcountry from the frontiers of North Carolina, Virginia, and Pennsylvania. The period also witnessed immigration directly from Europe, as families from Ireland and England, as well as Germany, arrived in the region. By 1760 pioneer settlement totaled more than four thousand and extended well up the Wateree Valley.[13]

The economy of the backcountry rested upon the interdependency of households, and its structure was regulated by the organization of the community of which they were a part, as well as by the mechanisms that controlled the settings in which interaction occurred. Most immigrants to the Wateree Valley arrived as families or small kin groups. Their diverse origins, background, and interests prevented the formation of a community whose members had ascribed roles and relationships. To create a functioning society here, immigrants had to negotiate mechanisms of interaction that ameliorated tensions arising from the competing interests of households and to legitimize the social relations between them. Peasant societies shared marketing constraints in common with those of the frontier and used mechanisms that regulated the exchange of household surpluses in a ritualized context. The formalized, conventionalized, and stylized behaviors that characterized such ritual economies lent themselves to an immigrant society that lacked the formal organization of a covenanted community and provided the mechanisms that governed exchange in South Carolina as they did elsewhere in the early southern backcountry.[14] The cultural elements that formed its ritual economy were drawn from the social organization of the immigrant society.

Kinship and Households

Relations among frontier households revolved around two institutions that had always been key elements of social structure in rural Europe. Perhaps the most pervasive of these was kinship, through which people defined and organized their family members as well as wider groups of people linked by blood and affinity. Among most western European immigrants, the notion of family also referred to a set of kinfolk as well as an assemblage of co-residents. This concept recognized the *household,* a spatial unit composed of people related genetically or by common purpose and united under a patriarchal head, as the principal unit of identity and production. In colonial British America, households remained independent economic units whose members lived together.[15] Most settlers came to South Carolina's backcountry as members of previously existing households or those that formed later in America. As a result of different economic circumstances, household size and composition varied considerably and included nuclear families as well as larger extended units that included apprentices, servants, and slaves. The size of tracts granted to settlers in Fredericksburg Township and on adjacent lands west of the river reflected the variety of immigrant households.[16] Under the terms of the Township Act, the number of persons in an applicant's household determined the amount of land conveyed. Entitled to fifty acres for themselves as well as for each family member and servant, an immigrant petitioned the governor and the Provincial Council for a survey warrant and arranged to have the tract surveyed and platted. When the governor returned the signed plat, ownership of the land passed to the petitioner. These applications, plats, and grants provide specific details regarding the pioneer households on the Wateree Valley frontier.[17]

Documents relating to land acquisition reveal the composition of immigrant households during the early years of its settlement in the Wateree Valley. Records indicate that households in the 1740s and 1750s varied considerably, and those as small as a single immigrant and groups of nearly a dozen people received land. But most were not extensive. During the first decade and a half of settlement, 180 of the 184 initial grants registered for lands in this region included 550 or fewer acres, and 165 were smaller than 350 acres (Tables 5.1, 5.2). Most grants were relatively small. Those for 100, 150, 200, and 300 acres dominated the last group, indicating that nearly 90 percent of the households contained two to six members. These incoming households were comparable in size to those living in the Welsh Tract and its extension lying just to the east, another area then undergoing settlement.[18] In the midst of these modest parcels, one anomalously large grant of 2,500 acres was made to an absentee owner, James Michie, a planter and member of South Carolina's lowcountry elite. His immense wealth and ownership of slaves contrasted with the assets of other immigrants and allowed him to acquire large backcountry tracts for speculation.[19] In general, household size provides a rough image of the pioneer population, but these numbers still leave many questions regarding its composition unanswered.

Land petitions are a source of information about the composition of immigrant households in the Wateree Valley. Some reveal only household size. Mark Catterton's petition, for example, tell us that he received two hundred acres in Fredericksburg Township for his family of four in 1743. The following year the Council issued a warrant to accommodate Oliver Mehaffey's three-member household for 150 acres on Grannys Quarter Creek.[20] Other petitions, however, give more information. They confirm that most households were based on kinship and usually comprised nuclear families of varying size. Some, like those of Thomas Bryan, who filed for one hundred acres in Fredericksburg Township in December 1743, and John Bennett, who acquired a similar size tract on Pine Tree Creek five years later, were composed of couples without children. Other settlers, such as John Hudson and William Kelly, brought families with eight and nine children, respectively, to their lands in Fredericksburg.[21] Households sometimes included additional family members as well. Roger Padgett brought his two younger sisters with his own family, Daniel Bready migrated from Virginia with his brother and his "very infirm" mother, and his fellow Virginian Charles Ghent's "aged" parents accompanied Ghent to the frontier.[22] Petitions filed by survivors recorded the form of partial family groups resulting from the loss of members either before or during settlement. Elizabeth Bearfoot and her four children received the land warrant requested earlier by her late husband, and Anthony Duesto's amended claim reflected his family's recent loss of three of its nine members. Similarly, the widowed Anne Duyett successfully petitioned for the land on which she and her five children lived.[23]

Colonial households also included those bound to them in service. Legally obligated to work for fixed terms to pay off debts, fourteen indentured servants accompanied eight of the new families to the Wateree Valley (Table 5.3). Most of these households incorporated a single "white servant," but several brought more with them to the frontier. Quaker families immigrating directly from Ireland came with the largest numbers of bound servants. Josiah Tomlinson and his four children transported four indentured servants, and five

Table 5.1. Households Receiving Grants in Fredericksburg Township and the Wateree Valley, 1739–1756

Name	*Date of Warrant*	*Vol. & Page*	*Household Size*	*Tract Size*	*Servants, Slaves*
Rattray, Alexander	7-6-1739	I:139	[10]	500	0
Catterton, Mark	10-5-1743	I:173	4	200	0
Bryan, Thomas	12-5-1743	1:173	2	100	0
Sheldon, John	3-6-1743/4	I:183–184	4	200	0
Gray, William	10-5-1744	I:196	[7]	350	0
Black, John	10-5-1744	I:196	[8]	400	0
Radcliffe, Charles	10-5-1744	I:198	1	50	0
Branham, Richard	10-5-1744	I:197	[4]	200	0
Summerford, Jeffrey	11-29-1744	I:201	4	200	0
Mehaffey, Oliver	11-29-1744	I:201	3	150	0
Herrelson, Paul	11-29-1744	I:201	9	450	0
Wright, Anthony	1-31-1745/6	I:240	9	450	0
Williams, John	3-14-1744/5	I:216, II:17	7	350	0
Gibson, Luke	1-31-1745/6	I:240	2	150	1
McKennie, Benjamin	11-20-1746	I:260	9	600	3
Swinney, John	11-20-1746	I:260	6	300	0
Duyett, Anne (widow)	11-20-1746	I:258	3	300	0
Hope, John	11-20-1746	I:259	5	400	3
McConnell, John	6-14-1747	I:282	5	250	0
McDaniel, Daniel	11-21-1747	I:300	3	300	3
Jones, Thomas	1-13-1747/8	I:302	3	200	1
Payne, William	1-22-1747/8	I:303	6	300	0
Gibson, Roger	1-23-1747/8	I:305	2	500	8
Hudson, John	1-30-1747/8	I:307	10	500	0
Gibson, Luke	3-9-1747/8	I:312	-	100	-
McDaniel, Daniel	6-9-1748	I:316	0	500	10
Kelly, William	6-10-1748	I:317	11	550	0
Rogers, Robert	6-10-1748	I:317	6	350	1
McCormick, Thomas	1-18-1748/9	II:7	9	450	0
Hudson, John	1-18-1748/9	II:7	-	200	-
Neilson, Samuel	1-24-1748/9	II:9	?	850	?
Leadon, Thomas	1-24-1748/9	II:10	4	200	0
Rork, Bryan (bricklayer)	1-24-1748/9	II:10	5	250	0
Bready, Daniel	1-24-1748/9	II:10–11	3	150	0
Todd, John	1-24-1748/9	II:11	3	300	3
McCormick, Patrick	1-24-1748/9	II:11	6	300	0
Malloy, Edward	1-24-1748/9	II:12	6	[300]	0
Arledge, John	2-2-1748/9	II:13	7	350	0
Gregory, Richard	2-2-1748/9	II:13	6	300	0

Table 5.1. *(continued)*

Name	*Date of Warrant*	*Vol. & Page*	*Household Size*	*Tract Size*	*Servants, Slaves*
Padgett, Roger	2-2-1748/9	II:14	6	300	0
Newitt, William	2-6-1748/9	II:16	6	300	0
Collins, John	2-6-1748/9	II:17	7	350	0
Michie, James	2-16-1748/9	II:19	0	2,500	50
Sheldon, John	2-16-1748/9	II:20	4	200	0
Seawright, William	2-16-1748/9	II:20	0	150	3
Rattray, Alexander	2-23-1748/9	II:21	2	500	8
Bearfoot, George	3-16-1748/9	II:26	4	300	2
Bacott, Samuel	3-16-1748/9	II:27	6	1,000	14
McKinnie, John	3-16-1748/9	II:27	9	450	0
Duesto, Anthony	3-16-1748/9	II:28	6	300	0
Bennett, John	3-16-1748/9	II:28	2	100	0
Laffite, John	5-2-1749	II:40	2	150	1
Senior, George	5-2-1749	II:40	6	400	2
Elliott, Thomas	7-4-1749	II:49	1	50	0
Pinson, Thomas	8-1-1749	II:54	3	150	0
Giles, Knowles	8-1-1749	II:55	2	250	3
Pinson, Isaac	8-1-1749	II:55	4	200	0
Buxton, Samuel	8-2-1749	II:56	1	50	0
Ghent, Charles	9-6-1749	II:64	3	150	0
Gibson, John	9-6-1749	II:64	3	150	0
Maddox, John	9-6-1749	II:66	6	300	0
Black, John	10-3-1749	II:73	2	100	0
Pain, John	10-3-1749	II:72	10	500	0
Guess, William	10-4-1749	II:79	3	150	0
Harper, Thomas	10-4-1749	II:81	1	50	0
Mehaffy, Oliver	10-19-1749	II:84	2	150	1
Sanders, George	10-19-1749	II:84	0	300	6
Branan, Michael	10-19-1749	II:86	3	150	0
Lindsey, Charles	11-7-1749	II:89	6	300	0
Ragland, John	11-8-1749	II:94	3	200	1
Mitchel, Alexander	8-6-1751	II:210	1	50	0
Scott, William	10-1-1751	II:217	3	750	-
Tomlinson, Josiah	10-25-1751	II:220	5	450	4
Wyly, Samuel	10-25-1751	II:219	2	250	3
Griggs, Samuel	11-5-1751	II:224	4	200	0
Milhous, Robert	11-6-1751	II:231	2	350	5
Russell, Samuel	11-6-1751	II:231	2	200	2
McDaniel, Daniel	12-3-1751	II:238	5	400	3
Edwards, William Newitt	12-3-1751	II:239	2	150	1
Toland, Bryan	12-3-1751	II:240	2	150	1

Name	Date of Warrant	Vol. & Page	Household Size	Tract Size	Servants, Slaves
Anderson, David	1-7-1752	II:243	1	300	5
Pines, John Frederick	3-6-1752	III:18	[2]	100	0
Milhous, Robert	5-5-1752	III:36	6	300	0
McGirt, James	5-5-1752	III:33	0	350	7
Moon, Thomas	7-7-1752	III:50	2	100	0
Downing, Moses	7-7-1752	III:49	4	200	0
Kelly, Timothy	8-4-1752	III:58	3	150	0
Rattray, Alexander	8-4-1752	III:58	0	50	1
Brown, William	8-4-1752	III:55	3	150	0
Canty, John	8-4-1752	III:55	0	150	3
McCormick, Patrick	8-4-1752	III:56	2	100	0
Adamson, James	10-3-1752	III:78	4	200	0
Lee, John	11-7-1752	III:110	3	200	1
Wyly, Samuel	12-5-1752	III:130	6	300	0
Neilson, Jared	2-6-1753	III:172	1	350	6
Landgroalen, Magdalena	3-23-1753	IV:274	[3]	150	0
Kirkland, Richard	6-5-1753	III:39	5	350	2
Joos, John	1-1-1754	IV:6	1	50	0
Courson, David	1-15-1754	IV:12	[7]	350	0
Mehaffey, Oliver	10-1-1754	IV:80	[4]	200	0
Jones, George	12-7-1754	IV:102–103	3	150	0
Watson, Archibald	12-7-1754	IV:102–103	4	200	0
Jessop, John	12-7-1754	IV:102–103	2	100	0
Wyly, Samuel	9-3-1754	IV:109	[6]	300	?
Pain, Joseph	2-4-1755	IV:118	3	150	0
Hope, John	4-1-1755	IV:134	5	250	0
Tomlinson, Josiah	10-21-1755	IV:190	2	100	0
Melone, Cornelius	10-21-1755	IV:196–197	2	100	0
Wyly, Samuel	12-5-1755	IV:216	0	300	6
McKewn, James	1-6-1756	IV:233	3	150	0
John Dixson	1-6-1756	IV:240	6	300	0
McKennie, Benjamin	4-6-1756	IV:264	[4]	200	0

accompanied Robert Milhous and his family. The household of Samuel Wyly, who would play a central role in the region's development, contained three persons in debt bondage.[24] Documents are silent on the identity of most bound servants, and we know little about their origin or situations. Some, perhaps, were poor immigrants who arrived destitute and had to sell themselves or their children for a period of years to pay their passage. Charleston newspapers of the 1740s and 1750s regularly advertised the sale of men, women, and children, many of whom were skilled tradesmen, artificers, farm workers, and domestic servants and most of whom came from Germany and the British Isles.[25] Others indentured

Table 5.2. Land Grants in the Wateree Valley by Size, 1739–1757

Size of Grants	*Number of Grants in Fredericksburg Twp.*	*Number of Grants West of the Wateree River*	*Total Number of Grants*
50	9	8	17
100	18	12	30
150	22	6	28
200	15	15	30
250	6	8	14
300	17	12	29
350	9	8	17
400	4	0	4
450	3	0	3
500	3	3	6
550	1	1	2
600	1	0	1
700	0	1	1
1,000	0	1	1
2,500	0	1	1
Totals	108	76	184

themselves prior to immigration. Cornelius Melone and his wife, for example, accompanied Samuel Wyly's family from Ireland and worked out their four-year indentures in South Carolina. Upon completion of their service, they successfully applied for a hundred-acre tract on Twenty-five Mile Creek, certified by Wyly as deputy surveyor.[26] Like the Melones, most of those who worked under indentures intended to eventually become landowners under the provisions of the Township Act. Not all poor immigrants followed this strategy. Some who lacked the financial wherewithal to begin farm making on the frontier sought assistance from the provincial Assembly, which amended the Township Fund to provide support for such indigents. At least three settlers on the Wateree benefited from the provisions of this legislation.[27]

Enslaved Africans composed another segment of the unfree labor brought to the Wateree Valley, but only a relatively small proportion of immigrants held others in bondage (see Table 5.4). Of the 184 documented households on the Wateree, 27 included slaves. Bondsmen represented a substantial investment, and their numbers are likely to reflect the relative wealth of settlers as well as their relative status among their peers.[28] Samuel Bacot, a lowcountry planter from Goose Creek in Berkeley County, became the area's largest resident slave owner. He, his wife, Rebecca, and their four children settled west of the Wateree with fourteen unfree laborers.[29] Roger Gibson and Alexander Rattray each brought eight slaves to their newly acquired lands in the late 1740s. A successful planter in Williamsburg Township, Gibson apparently invested the fruits of his earlier enterprise in a larger holding on the frontier, where his skill as a blacksmith made him a valuable member of the community. Rattray was a gentleman from Charleston who had previously purchased land on the

Table 5.3. Number of Indentured Servants in Wateree Valley Households

Number of Servants/Household	*Number of Households*	*Total Number of Servants*
1	5	5
2	1	2
3	1	3
4	1	4
Totals	8	14

Wateree, and his wealth and early presence there may have enhanced his status among later settlers. As a mark of their high standing, both men were captains of local militia companies.[30] Absentee owner James Michie's fifty slaves reflected his previous wealth. Several others who possessed multiple slaves were also planters with previous experience in South Carolina. George Sanders, Jared Neilson, and David Anderson migrated from the vicinity of Black River in Prince Fredericks Parish.[31] Most of the slave owners in the Wateree Valley possessed far less wealth and had fewer bondsmen in their households. Eighteen households, two-thirds of those with enslaved members, included three or fewer unfree members, and half of these counted only a single slave.

As in most interior frontier regions in the eastern woodlands, the initial demography of the Wateree Valley was characterized by youth and by small households that lacked the presence of an older generation. The number of small acreages granted also reflects the composition of the immigrant population. Most households comprised families of two adults

Table 5.4. Number of Slaves in Wateree Valley Households

Number of Slaves/Household	*Number of Households*	*Total Number of Slaves*
1	9	9
2	1	2
3	8	24
4	0	0
5	1	5
6	3	18
7	1	7
8	2	16
9	0	0
10	1	10
11	0	0
12	0	0
13	0	0
14	1	14
Totals	28	105

and three or four children, a size typical of those settling on the frontier in British North America. The relatively small size of these biological family units implies that many of the initial households represented very young families, including some that were still childless. Indeed, the sizable number of tracts of one hundred or fewer acres suggests that many grants were made to couples or to individual pioneers seeking to begin families in the backcountry. Households in the region had yet to attain the much larger size that sprang from natural growth in subsequent years.[32]

Although lacking the experience gained from time spent in older settled regions, young families on the frontier employ kinship, and the ritual obligations associated with the relationships it created, as an important element to bind together communities of accretion. As an organizing element that extends beyond the level of the individual household, kinship provides a basis for linking multiple households for common purposes. Settlers on small-farm frontiers realize the advantages of maintaining a larger kin group to provide the mutual support and assistance necessary to establish farms and other enterprises in unfamiliar surroundings. Shared labor is integral to the organization of farm activities, and interaction among kin forms the basis for simple commodity production. Kin groups provide security and protection for members, assisting those who suffer economic or personal calamity and caring for one another in times of crisis. Consequently, immigrants to the frontier often find it advantageous to migrate with relatives. Sometimes they settle in proximity to one another in kin-based geographical clusters.[33] But what role did clusters based on ties of blood or marriage play in the early settlement of this portion of the South Carolina frontier?

A number of those migrating to the Wateree Valley possessed prior blood ties. Several groups of early settlers shared surnames. Some were relatives, but the relationships of others are less clear. For example, at least nine individuals named Kirkland acquired land in various parts of the region between 1753 and 1755. They included John Kirkland and his sons, Moses and William, but their relationship to Edward, Joseph, Richard, and Robert Kirkland is uncertain.[34] Thomas McCormick and Patrick McCormick acquired two tracts in Fredericksburg Township within one week's time in January 1748, and Robert Seawright and William Seawright were both granted warrants for land in Belmont Neck on the same day in 1737. Although their ties are unspecified, the dates of their arrival and the proximity of their holdings imply that they were close male relatives, perhaps brothers or cousins.[35] Four individuals with the surname Gibson took up lands west of the river. Roger, mentioned earlier, received his large tract south of Belmont Neck in 1747, while John settled much farther south in the vicinity of Spears Creek two years later.[36] Luke Gibson and Susanah Gibson acquired adjacent tracts between Buck Creek and Mill Creek, also in 1749. The proximity of their claims implies that they were relatives, perhaps siblings, and their location next to the lands of Luke's uncle, Anthony Wright, suggests a kin-based settlement cluster.[37]

A number of Quaker families migrated to the Wateree Valley in the 1750s, and many of their members intermarried. One of the most prominent was that of the aforementioned miller Robert Milhous, who acquired 350 acres in Friends Neck in 1751 and a mill site on Pine Tree Creek across the river the following year. In 1757 his sons Samuel and Henry received three hundred acres nearby opposite Belmont Neck, and his son John bought lands originally granted to George Senior.[38] Other kinsmen included John and Robert Belton, who settled west of the Wateree, as did Timothy, Samuel, and Walter Kelly and James and John Adamson.[39] Marriage ties among first-generation immigrants further strengthened these relationships by creating affinal linkages between families. For example, two brothers, Joshua English and Robert English, who immigrated with their family in 1754, married Elizabeth and Mary Adamson, daughters of James Adamson, who had arrived two years earlier. The union between their sister Mary English and John Belton linked their families, and Hannah Belton's marriage to Samuel Kelly established ties between these kin groups.[40] The intermarriage of pioneer Quaker families reflected a trend among the wider population as the region began to fill and those coming of age sought to establish themselves as farmers in a country abounding in natural resources.

Ties of blood and affinity provided pioneer households with the means to accomplish the cooperative tasks necessary to survive and persist on the frontier. Links between families helped establish networks of mutual assistance essential to farm making in the Wateree Valley. Clearing land, building fences, planting and harvesting crops, and erecting houses and farm buildings in a new and potentially hostile country were monumental tasks, often demanding assistance beyond the household. The communal labor involved in the regular seasonal round of farm work required cooperation that kin-based linkages would certainly facilitate. As in peasant communities, kin ties helped create a structure within which to organize production and exchange of labor and goods, and the relationships they established were integral to the ritual economy. But kinship was not the only unifying thread in the new land.

Religion: Creating Ties That Bind

As a functioning aspect of culture, religion has always played a significant role in maintaining the life of communities. It serves to integrate the behavior of individuals in society, guide them through crises, define their values, and provide a basis for ethics. Religion not only explains and gives meaning to the world; it also provides sacred authority and explanation for the present social order and the place of the individual in it. Maintaining a sense of individual identity and belonging is central to people in all societies but is crucial to those frontier settlers who formed dispersed communities of accretion in which traditional social ties were often absent. Religion offered a powerful force for social cohesion in the South Carolina backcountry, and membership in a denomination provided solidarity that increased the chances for success in the new land.[41]

Although immigrants to the backcountry shared a common European origin, their cultural backgrounds and experiences were not the same, and their views of the world were far from uniform. The backers of the township plan believed that a common Protestant faith would ensure the loyalty of immigrants on South Carolina's frontier, but many belonged to a variety of nonconforming Protestant denominations. Their arrival, together with the rise of evangelical sects inspired by the Great Awakening, ensured religious diversity among the colonial population of the interior. Initial settlers to the new townships included French Huguenots, German Lutherans from Baden, Würtemberg, and the Rhineland, German- and French-speaking Swiss, Scots-Irish Presbyterians, and Welsh Baptists, drawn largely from elsewhere in Britain's American colonies, and Irish Quakers, as well as settlers adhering to the Church of England.[42]

By the 1740s evangelism had spread throughout the backcountry, strongly influencing the orientation of Presbyterian, Regular and Separate Baptist, Congregationalist, and Lutheran churches and shifting the religious orientation of the region's settlers dramatically away from the established church. Although collective migration by people of common origin allowed particular denominations to prevail in some areas, the continual arrival of new settlers to take up lands within and outside the townships maintained the spiritual heterogeneity of the frontier population. Despite the doctrinal differences that separated evangelical churches, all shared a belief system that stressed the participation of the individual in the religious experience, a feature that allowed them to become an integrating institution well adapted to the conditions encountered by the members of a pioneer society. Church membership helped settlers form networks that bound new residents economically as well as spiritually and assisted them to overcome the isolation of the frontier and organize a regional economy.[43]

The diversity of the Wateree Valley's population affected the growth of religious organizations there. Lacking the dominant ethnic element found in many of the townships, residents included people who had migrated from the lowcountry and from other townships, particularly Williamsburg, as well as those who traveled south from Pennsylvania, Virginia, and the northern colonies and others who had come directly from Europe.[44] This ethnic smorgasbord of Scots-Irish, Scots, English, Germans, Irish, and relocated colonists represented a number of Protestant denominations that the Anglican missionary Charles Woodmason described as "a mixed medley of religions [as] . . . anywhere to be found."[45] Few had arrived as members of organized churches, and some who came from other frontier regions appear never to have belonged to any denomination. On the other hand, the majority of immigrants came from areas where traditional religious institutions existed, and they probably would have participated in them had ecclesiastical structures been present in the backcountry. Despite its support of an established church, South Carolina's government made little effort to introduce religious institutions in the backcountry. The Assembly provided funding for an Anglican minister to preach in the Waterees in 1756 and established St. Mark's Parish as an ecclesiastical and political unit encompassing a large portion of the central interior the following year. But more than a decade passed before the post was filled, and the proposed church and parsonage were not constructed. Organized religion grew slowly during the early decades of settlement, and only a small fraction of the frontier population belonged to organized congregations. Even as late as the 1760s, Baptist and Presbyterian itinerants, known for their aggressive proselytizing, were still in the process of establishing formal churches in the region.[46] Only a small group of Irish Quakers, who settled between Sawneys and Swift Creeks, successfully organized a religious institution.

Unlike other newcomers to the Wateree Valley, the Quakers came from Ireland together. At least twenty settlers from the Dublin Monthly Meeting and the Edenderry Monthly Meeting removed to South Carolina in 1751. Although they did not emigrate as an organized community, they espoused a common faith whose value system rejected formal religious structures and emphasized the equality of the individual, the importance of behavior as an expression of Christian virtue, and the central role of the household. Its members interacted through the medium of the meeting.[47] Quakers in the Wateree Valley formed the Fredericksburg Meeting, which met regularly under the leadership of Robert Milhous and Samuel Wyly. The meeting served an important integrative function by maintaining contact among members' households, establishing a medium for interacting with traveling Friends, and providing support for the new setters scattered across the region. Comfortable with ethnic and religious pluralism, the Quakers were accepting of and interacted easily with outsiders, and, as in the middle colonies, their meetings were attended by non-Quakers as well.[48] Indeed, their emphasis on commitment to the church and public discipline made their teachings compatible with those of contemporary Baptist and Methodist denominations.[49] The Fredericksburg Monthly Meeting played a central role among Friends in the Wateree Valley during the settlement period as immigration swelled the number of Quakers in South Carolina. Only later, as changing conditions accompanying the close of colonization altered the composition of the region's population, did the meeting decline in importance as an institution. Although the subsequent period saw the Quaker community on the Wateree wither through outmigration and assimilation, its presence as an integrative institution during the initial decade of settlement contributed significantly to the success of this process.[50]

Religion provided a mechanism for social and economic integration, linking households of common faith in a system of mutual interaction and support. Such organizations incorporated both kin and nonkin households in a wider network of ritualized ties that extended across the region and maintained important links with the outside. Religious organizations also introduced a structured organization that oversaw the activities of their members and helped coordinate their activities. In the absence of civil officials with political authority, leaders arose from the immigrant households to assist newcomers and visitors and to manage critical elements of early production. It was probably no accident that the two prominent Quaker households also established the earliest mills and stores in the Wateree Valley. Control of processing facilities helped structure the exchange of goods and services and provided the basis for organizing trade on a wider scale. A regional economy based on ritualized relationships associated with ties of kinship and religion served the interests of an isolated backcountry through a series of loosely organized relationships among households. Such a system was extremely flexible with regard to its ability to expand to incorporate new elements or shed existing ones. These adaptive characteristics made the region attractive to larger capitalists who possessed the means to underwrite the production and transportation expenses necessary to support export trade and who sought to incorporate new territories.

Samuel Wyly: A Man for All Seasons

Although connections based on kin and faith undoubtedly served as a basis for interaction in the Wateree Valley, the regional economy depended on institutions rooted in the household. Their success rested on the ability of members to establish ties and to organize the resources and people required to carry out production and exchange. Not surprisingly, the person who assumed a principal role here came from one of the area's prominent Quaker households. Ambitious to succeed economically in what must have seemed an arena of boundless opportunities, Samuel Wyly sought success in multiple directions, and his activities were central to the economic development of the region. Wyly was born in Ireland in 1722 and, following his marriage to Dinah Milhouse in the 1740s, resided with his family in Timahoe in County Kildare. Dinah and their three children, John, William, and Robert, accompanied Wyly to South Carolina in October 1751. They arrived in Fredericksburg Township the following year, settling on lands purchased near Pine Tree Creek. Together with Robert Milhous, he assumed a position of leadership in the Fredericksburg Meeting, taking an active role in the organization's activities and maintaining regular correspondence with its parent London Yearly Meeting. Following Milhous's death in 1755, Wyly became the Meeting's most influential member, holding various positions in the Quaker community. In 1759 he conveyed to the Meeting four acres near his Pine Tree Creek land for a meetinghouse and cemetery. Situating the essential facilities of the Society there established his holdings as a focus of activity in the Wateree Valley.[51]

Samuel Wyly's growing economic role in the Wateree Valley paralleled his importance in the Society of Friends. Eager to become a successful planter and entrepreneur, Wyly expanded his land ownership in Fredericksburg Township, acquiring a grant for one hundred acres on Sanders Creek and two larger tracts farther east on Lynches River. He soon focused his attention on Pine Tree Creek, however, and began to concentrate his holdings there. By the mid-1750s he had bought out the grants of several early settlers east of the Wateree. These lands, near the site of Wright's Ferry, provided direct overland access from the river to the Catawba Path and formed the core of a larger tract that included a substantial grant of 650 acres and mill sites on Little Pine Tree Creek (Fig. 5.3). The proceeds from his holdings provided the wherewithal to accumulate land through purchase as well as headright warrants, which he acquired as he added enslaved servants to assist him in his new enterprises. Wyly located his residence plantation, called Mount Pleasant, on this estate and established other business activities along the roads and watercourses that passed through it.[52]

Samuel Wyly's economic enterprises centered on agriculture and trade. Before 1761 he dammed Little Pine Tree Creek and constructed grist- and sawmills there. The mills gave him an important role in regional grain and lumber production, and the traffic they generated placed him at the center of trade. Wyly followed the practice of many frontier mill operators and operated a store at a location called Pine Tree, near the point where the Catawba Path crossed the creek of the same name.[53] His facility accommodated crops and other regional products for exchange as well as imported goods for trade. He also used it to store provisions and finished goods purchased by the provincial government for the Catawbas. But, despite Wyly's efforts, the region's isolation and its lack of capital and the economic constraints it placed on customers continued to limit the widespread accumulation of liquid wealth and fostered the continuation of an economy based on reciprocity, in which merchants functioned as agents of credit who facilitated the ritualized redistribution of goods and services. Only when conditions changed to overcome these impediments would trade become profitable enough for merchants to engage in it as their sole livelihood.[54]

The location of Wyly's businesses shaped the economic geography of colonial settlement in the Wateree Valley. Their proximity to Robert Milhous's grist- and sawmills on Pine Tree Creek established the locale as a center for milling for early residents on the river.

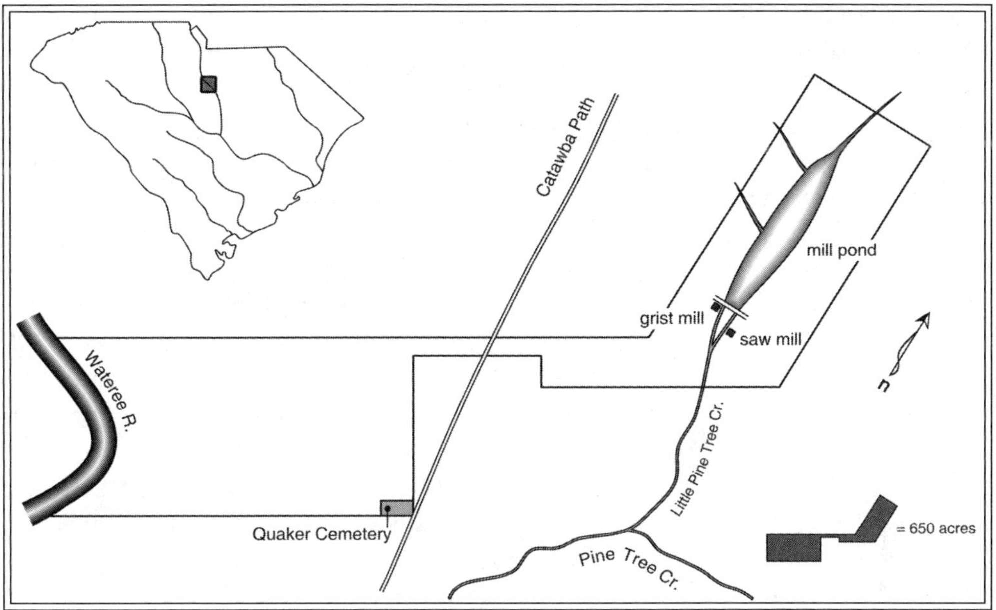

5.3 Samuel Wyly's landholdings in the vicinity of Pine Tree Creek. The land he donated to the Society of Friends for a meetinghouse and cemetery lay adjacent to the Catawba Path, and his mills and pond dominated Little Pine Tree Creek. Author's original map.

Its proximity to the Catawba Path encouraged its growth as a focal point for exchange, and it soon became the hub of the regional economy. Wyly's economic activities expanded well beyond those of a successful farmer, and his influence stretched far outside the Quaker community.

Aware that the nature of a regional economy would always restrict production and limit the commercial success of plantation farming in the Wateree Valley, Samuel Wyly turned his attention to several alternative activities that opened new business opportunities. He held several provincial public offices that offered their holders limited authority in the interior. Appointed a justice of the peace for Craven County, a large district encompassing roughly the northeastern half of the province, Wyly could adjudicate cases of debt, fraudulent sales of grain, and damage to agricultural property, and he could also grant licenses to tavern keepers and peddlers.[55] Justices also played a political role, given their authority to call residents together to hunt for suspected criminals. In their capacity as arbiters of justice, they periodically presided over court days, events that drew crowds and served as socially integrating activities that enhanced the officeholder's standing in the community.[56] As a deputy surveyor, Wyly was the indispensable official responsible for surveying lands and preparing plats for parcels granted and transferred. His duties made him familiar with the territory and its inhabitants, including the resident Catawba people, who were important military allies of the province and prominent participants in the regional economy.[57]

His public offices brought Wyly into regular contact with the world outside the Wateree Valley, and his interactions there enhanced his political and economic roles. Like other backcountry justices of the peace and deputy surveyors, he regularly traveled to Charleston to meet with superiors, and his connections undoubtedly led to his appointment as an agent to the Catawbas. As an official representative of the governor, Wyly delivered provisions and supplies to the Indians and conveyed information and intelligence between the provincial government and its Native clients.[58] He also acted as a contracting agent to provide support for Gov. William Henry Lyttelton's military expedition against the Catawba's old enemies, the Cherokees. Wyly played an important role in developing transportation routes to the northern backcountry through his participation in commissions charged with opening roads to the Catawba Nation and the Pee Dee Valley and clearing obstructions on the Wateree.[59] Shortly before his death, in 1768, Samuel Wyly was elected as a representative to the Assembly from St. Mark's Parish, one of the three large administrative districts in the backcountry. He declined to serve because, as a Quaker, he could not take the required oaths.[60]

Samuel Wyly became a leading figure in the frontier community on the Wateree. His role in the Society of Friends and his success as a farmer and mill operator made him instrumental to the development of agricultural production and regional exchange. Wyly's public offices established his political presence as a representative of the provincial government in the backcountry. But the inability of the colonial regime to project its authority inland through effective political institutions restricted his public role, just as the regional economy limited his ability to produce and market the surpluses necessary to generate wealth. In spite of his extensive personal linkages, his efforts could not overcome the isolation of distance, and he lacked the investment capital necessary to organize production on a commercial scale. This in no way minimized the importance of Wyly's network of contacts in integrating the Wateree Valley. As a system based on the interaction of households, the existence of the regional economy depended on the continual flow of information Wyly's network allowed between them and those outside the area. Of particular importance was the link to the Native peoples of the region.

The Catawba Exchange

The aboriginal presence in the Wateree Valley cast a long shadow over more recent European settlement. At the time colonization in Fredericksburg Township began, in the 1740s, this ancient land was home to Native peoples whose world had been substantially altered by the impact of disease, war, and European expansion (Fig. 5.4). The resident Catawba people were largely a nation of refugees from dislocated upland groups that had coalesced in response to proximity, common experience, and shared concerns.[61] Situated on South Carolina's northeastern frontier, they had long been active in the trade for deerskins and slaves. More recently, the Catawbas had become valuable allies protecting the province from potential threats on the frontier.[62] As such, they found themselves enmeshed in a complex economic and political relationship with a provincial government that provided them with increasing amounts of goods and services in return for their loyalty. Their precarious political position made the Catawbas vulnerable, and continuous warfare with neighboring peoples produced a level of instability. Declining game resources and substantial population losses from a smallpox epidemic in 1738 combined to disrupt traditional

5.4 Sketch of a Catawba warrior, perhaps Capt. Redhead, accompanying a letter of introduction by Joseph Kershaw. Courtesy of South Caroliniana Library, University of South Carolina, Columbia, South Carolina.

patterns of agriculture and subsistence. Their uncertain state and their growing need for European technology brought an increasing reliance on supplies and gifts from the outside, enhancing their dependence on state largesse and drawing them closer within the colonial world. Subsumed by the expansion of South Carolina, the Indians' fate depended on their ability to find a place in the new order.[63]

The Catawbas' experience mirrored a process of identity formation often encountered on the periphery of European expansion in the New World. Caught in the drive by British colonial interests to acquire land and resources, Native peoples of the Carolinas responded to the accompanying violence and the decimation of their populations by forging a new identity that allowed them to accommodate to the circumstances in which they found themselves. Despite their origins as separate groups that spoke a variety of languages, they recognized the economic and political advantages of unity for their survival and persistence. As the expansion of European settlement threatened the Catawbas' subsistence base, the social process that produced their derived identity helped them negotiate a new economic relationship with the province.[64]

The Catawbas' new role altered the nature of exchange. It differed from the earlier trade in that it involved the direct transfer of gifts and supplies by provincial agents to Native leaders, who often visited Charleston to confer directly with colonial officials. This arrangement no longer calculated exchange on the basis of units of comparable value, nor did it presume to generate a profit for the province. Rather, the transfer of presents symbolized a desire to create a stable relationship between two peoples whose past had been uneven and whose future was uncertain. The ceremonial aspect of the Catawba exchange, together with the regularity of its occurrence, made it a ritual intended to maintain peaceful coexistence on the frontier. In this sense, it became another component of a regional economy organized around availability and need.

Although managed by the provincial government and paid for with public funds, the Catawba exchange depended on agents to distribute the array of gifts that included corn, sugar, rum, and other provisions; hats, boots, and clothing of all sorts; firearms, flints, bullets, and powder; as well as travel, board, entertainment, and medical expenses of visiting Indian delegations. Accounts for expenses related to the Catawbas' welfare, subsistence, and role in defending the backcountry became an integral part of the provincial budget in the 1740s and 1750s.[65] Although decisions regarding presents and services lay in the hands of lowcountry officials, their implementation depended on independent merchants and other vendors. The commissary general relied on Charleston merchants such as Alexander Rigg to purchase "trading guns," or Thomas Brown, an Indian trader in the Pee Dee country, to supply provisions, or Archibald Campbell, a storekeeper at the Congarees, to bury several Catawbas who had died while traveling to the capital.[66] Unlike Indian traders of an earlier time, agents lacked the ability to control the trade, nor could they manipulate it to their own ends. Nevertheless, many profited from their participation, either directly or through advantages derived from their role as provisioners. Already a central figure in the region, Samuel Wyly acted as an agent to the Catawbas and expanded his network to include the Catawba leaders, in particular Hagler, who had become *Eractasswa,* or chief, in 1750. Hagler, an enterprising individual who developed crucial ties with colonial officials, led the Catawbas for the next dozen years and played a key role in maintaining their cultural integrity in the face of European contact.

For frontier entrepreneurs like Samuel Wyly, public purchases of provisions opened commercial avenues outside the regional economy and, with them, the prospect of accumulating wealth for investment. Supplying the Indians created an increased demand for corn, which in turn provided an incentive to enlarge production. The certificates that Wyly received as payment for corn delivered constituted a direct transfer of money or credit that could be used to purchase land or imported goods and supplies for his own use or exchange. Or such income might pass into the hands of local farmers on whom he depended to fill orders. Sometimes the amount of produce required was beyond the capacity of backcountry farmers, and Wyly was pressed to turn to outside subcontractors to fill the order. When he could not complete Gov. Lyttelton's request for nine hundred bushels of corn, Wyly had to pass the order on to the Charleston merchant Solomon Milner and to John Narney, a Colleton County planter.[67] Even so, Wyly still received commissions for purchasing, storing, transporting, and distributing such produce and goods, as well as for relaying information to and from the Catawbas.[68] These remunerations provided the capital needed for constructing and maintaining the physical infrastructure to carry out trading activities. Facilities for storage and transportation were also integral to milling and farming, and Wyly invested heavily in the land, equipment, and labor needed to expand these ventures. By the close of the 1750s, his plantation and mills were well established, as was his growing mercantile business. As one of the few residents of the backcountry who possessed the financial wherewithal and the external connections to acquire goods on credit, Wyly began to enlarge his operations and may have operated an inn in addition to his store.[69] These developments solidified his position in the regional economy of the frontier, but in themselves they were insufficient to overcome the effects of the region's physical isolation. The infrastructural elements Wyly introduced, however, provided one of the key elements necessary for change. And the Catawbas remained an important factor in this equation.

Absorbed by the expansion of South Carolina, the Catawbas found their identity threatened on multiple fronts. By the middle decade of the eighteenth century, their involvement in the political affairs of the province and their growing dependency on its largess had become a mixed blessing. On one hand, their political position as protectors of the frontier allowed them to bargain for their services, a practice that yielded a bounty of material wealth. Indeed, Hagler's ability to convince officials that continued support was in the province's best interest enabled him to sustain his people through times of great change.[70] On the other hand, the Catawbas' abandonment of traditional subsistence patterns left them less able to provide for themselves and vulnerable to the demands of outsiders. As time passed, the situation worsened. European immigrants defied official restrictions and occupied old agricultural fields, competed for traditional hunting lands, and trespassed on ancient burial grounds. Despite a ban on the survey of lands surrounding their towns and Samuel Wyly's efforts of to enforce it, settlers continued to encroach on the Catawba estate, altering the land with fields, buildings, fences, roads, and bridges.[71] Competition for resources led to conflict between Indians and settlers and often resulted in raids or other forms of theft. On several occasions, escalating tensions resulted in more violent crimes, including murder.[72]

Although they were allies of South Carolina, the Catawbas' close association with the province did not protect them from outside dangers. On the northern edge of the province, they lay exposed to attack from their traditional enemies. Persistent warfare with the Six Nations and French-allied Indians in the west reduced the Catawbas' numbers and occasionally threatened their political structure. A 1749 raid, for example, killed nearly all the Catawba leaders who were returning home from a visit to Charleston. Hostilities increased in intensity with the rising level of frontier violence that accompanied the outbreak of the Seven Years' War, in 1756.[73] Regular attrition from conflict, however, did not compare to the catastrophic losses from epidemic diseases to which the Catawbas lacked immunity. In 1738 a smallpox epidemic struck the Indians of South Carolina's interior and killed nearly half of the Catawbas' estimated population of 2,300. In the next two decades their numbers recovered to around 1,600, but in the summer of 1759 a second, more devastating visitation of the disease occurred. Originating among the Chickasaws in French Louisiana, smallpox spread east to the Cherokees and the Catawbas.[74] From there it moved on to the European frontier settlements and the lowcountry, eventually reaching as far as Bermuda. Although it took a toll on European and African populations, smallpox was particularly devastating among Native peoples, carrying off at least half the Catawbas. By the close of 1759 only about 350 to 400 destitute members remained, having abandoned their towns and dispersed into the hinterlands along the Wateree (Fig. 5.5).[75] The smallpox epidemic brought the Catawbas to a crossroads. To maintain their cultural identity in their traditional homeland, they would have to adapt in the face of European expansion. Although decimated,

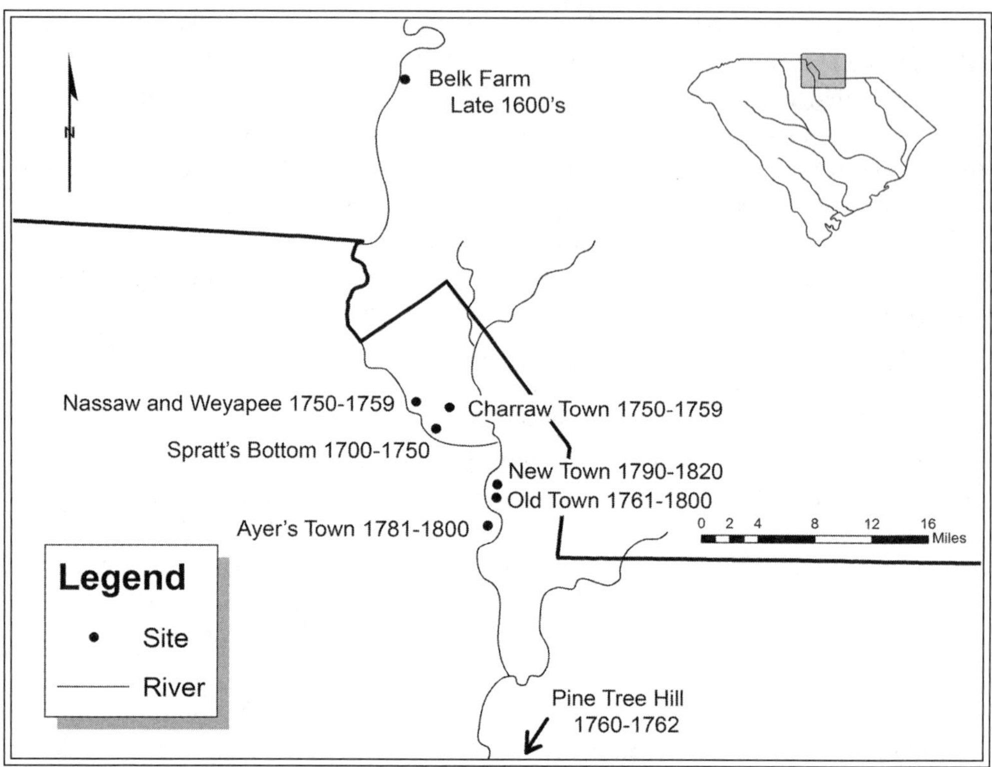

5.5 The Catawba settlements and reservation on the Catawba/Wateree River. Author's original map adapted from Steven G. Baker, "The Working Draft of: The Historic Catawba Peoples: Exploratory Perspectives in Ethnohistory and Archaeology" (Columbia: Office of Research, University of South Carolina, 1975), 114; Brett H. Riggs, "Temporal Trends in Native Ceramic Traditions of the Lower Catawba River Valley," *Southeastern Archaeology* 29 (2010):, 32.

they regrouped under Hagler's leadership and made plans that ensured their role as an integral part of the colonial economy.

By the 1750s the economy of the Catawbas reflected their position in the changing world of the frontier. Increasingly dependent upon Europeans for provisions, finished goods, tools, and weapons, as well as for intoxicating drink, they had become "neighbor-Indians" who not only received government supplies but also participated in the regional economy. They habitually engaged in informal, face-to-face exchange with Europeans for a wide range of goods and services. Not always mutually beneficial or necessarily friendly, this activity nevertheless resulted in the movement of goods, such as guns, ammunition, and blankets, as well as whiskey, corn, and other provisions between Natives and newcomers.[76] The informal interactions associated with such "frontier exchange" created a web of flexible and fluid interethnic relations that permitted each group to maintain its cultural traditions in spite of larger political changes.[77]

Adaptation to the conditions of European colonization altered the Catawbas' traditional way of life and brought dramatic change to some aspects of their culture. As elsewhere in the postcontact Southeast, hunting and warfare had become increasingly important as the means to participate in the trade for goods upon which Native people were becoming dependent. These activities, traditionally associated with men, came to dominate Catawba economic life in the eighteenth century but diminished significantly in response to the disappearance of game and to political manipulation by a British administration seeking to solidify alliances with Native groups against competing European enemies. At mid-century, Catawba males still clung to their roles as warriors and procurers of provisions and gifts from colonial officials. Leadership by collective consent remained in the hands of men, and astute chiefs like Hagler recognized the importance of sustaining such traditions. Still, their growing inability to contribute substantially to the Catawba subsistence made the economic importance of men increasingly uncertain and promoted the role of women as the principal carriers of the group's cultural traditions.[78]

In spite of the changes in Catawba society, women remained the traditional makers of pottery, an artifact that had always been an important component in the tribal economy. Long an integral component of material culture in Native America, ceramics represented a craft whose products displayed great variety. Because clay is an infinitely malleable material, aboriginal potters employed forms and decorative techniques that differed regionally and that presumably expressed cultural and ethnic continuity as well as diversity. Catawba pottery exhibited characteristics that reflected the cultural and historical heritage of its makers, and the structure of their society influenced its patterning. The Catawbas, like many other Southeastern groups, reckoned descent through the female line, that is, through the matrilineage. This arrangement facilitated the direct transmission of information among women from generation to generation and was a powerful thread for conservatism in the form and style of objects they created. Consequently, the wares made by Catawba women expressed not only their continuing craft role as potters but also cultural continuity through the persistence of traditional decorative styles and patterns during a time of upheaval.[79]

Archaeological sites once occupied by the Catawbas and their ancestors have yielded evidence of a remarkable continuity over time in the ceramics they made and used. Investigations at several sites in the Wateree Valley yielded pottery bearing the distinctive stylistic traits of the Lamar ceramic tradition, manufactured by Native peoples over a large portion of the Southeast from Mississippian times into the early historic period. Lamar ceramics exhibit distinctive characteristics, such as complicated stamped surface treatments, folded rims or appliqué rim strips on jars, and bold incised treatments on plain or burnished carinated bowls. Potters in Catawba towns continued to make Lamar forms during the time of European colonization. Archaeological remains at the sites of Nassaw and Weyapee (Fig. 5.5), two villages that were abandoned during the 1759 epidemic, indicate that a people that had already adopted guns, knives, metal ware, and glass bottles and that consumed beef as part of their diet still used these traditional ceramics.[80] The juxtaposition of Lamar wares with European-introduced items offers clear evidence of a dramatic conservatism that persisted among the Catawbas despite their participation in the regional frontier economy. In the wake of the smallpox epidemic that decimated the Catawbas and diminished their productive base and the expansion of a colonial agricultural economy that threatened to envelop their world, the Catawbas would draw upon the technological experience of their women to adapt to the economic challenges of dramatic change.[81]

Countering Threats to Dominion: The Militia

Although the province failed to establish viable social and political institutions in the backcountry, the need to defend the colony from hostile enemies required it to assert authority over the interior through the projection of force. To accomplish this, the inhabitants of the inland townships were organized into militia units. From the beginning, South Carolina's leaders sought to counter threats by mobilizing the male population as a military force. The militia played an important role in crushing Native peoples during the Yamassee War in 1715 and later took part in several expeditions against Spanish Florida. In a world in which Europeans were increasingly a minority, lowcountry leaders saw a strong, armed presence as necessary to guard against slave revolts. Organized to patrol areas with large enslaved populations, the militia served as a police force to catch and punish runaways and to inspect slave settlements on plantations for weapons and illegal practices. Legislative acts established and increasingly formalized such patrols, especially in the wake of the slave plots discovered in the 1720s and 1730s and the violent Stono Rebellion of 1739. The patrols employed a militia composed of companies that formed a regiment for Charleston and each of the four counties, all under the command of the governor. Regular musters, accompanied by inspections and drills, produced an effective organization to police the densely populated lowcountry as well as an easily mobilized military force that could be called out quickly in times of general crises throughout the province.[82]

The backcountry militia existed as the only officially organized body in the new frontier settlements. Drawn from the immigrants in the backcountry townships, it provided a reservoir of manpower to protect the region, over which South Carolina maintained only nominal control. Authorities anticipated that these militia companies existed largely to protect European settlements from unfriendly Indians as well as external threats, and ranger units added a mobile force to counter extraordinary threats that arose in the interior. In a region largely without plantation settlements, no need for formal slave patrols existed, and militia units on the Wateree, like those elsewhere on the frontier, remained largely exempt from such duties.[83]

The distribution and composition of militia companies reflected the nature of backcountry settlement. As the members of each unit had to be drawn from the area in which they lived, a company's creation depended on the presence of a sufficiently dense population. Sparse settlement of the vast interior understandably limited the number of militia companies, and unit locations reflected the distribution of people. The nature of the region's physical environment often determined the boundaries of frontier militia districts, with muster sites situated at central points that minimized the natural barriers men had to cross. Districts usually followed natural geographic divisions, with muster grounds along major watercourses. Five militia companies were organized in the vicinity of Fredericksburg Township. Situated on either side of the Wateree and on the branches of Lynches River, they contained about three hundred officers and men (Fig. 5.6).[84]

As an activity that often drew strangers together, the militia assumed a social role that extended far beyond establishing a military presence in the backcountry. Although created as a defensive force, militia units acted only sporadically in this role, and the periodic

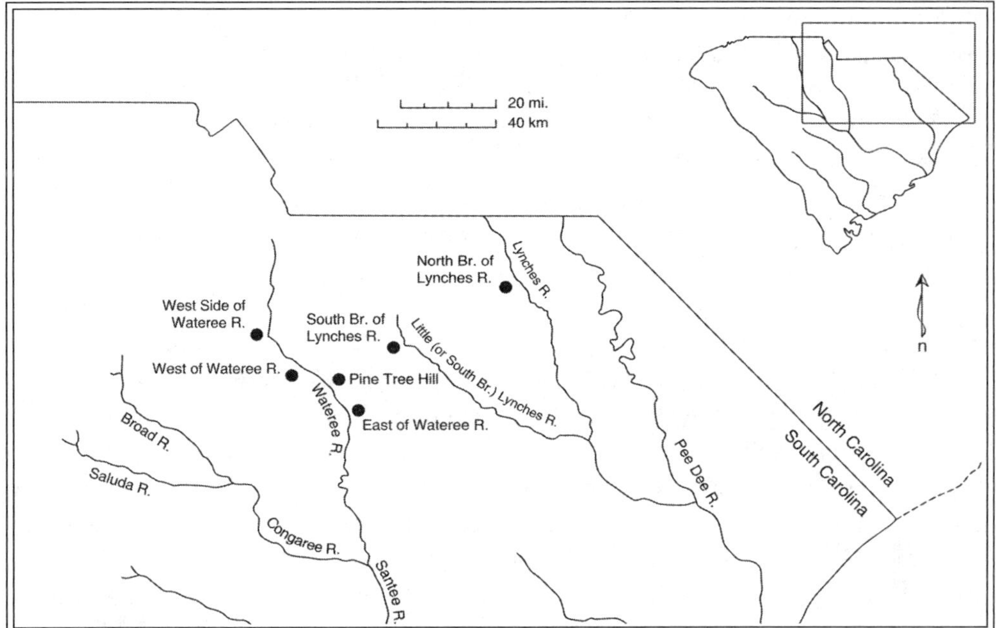

5.6 The five militia companies in the vicinity of Fredericksburg Township in 1757 drew their members from areas along the region's major rivers. Author's original map adapted from Julian J. Petty, *The Growth and Distribution of Population in South Carolina* (Columbia: South Carolina State Planning Board, 1943; reprint ed., Spartanburg, SC: The Reprint Co., 1973), 46, 217.

assembly of members took on other nonmilitary functions. Militia musters, conducted to carry out drills six times a year, became wider social occasions that brought the male residents, as well as many others, from a wide area together for common activities that involved more than training. Like the periodic courts held by justices of the peace, militia musters became opportunities for festivities that allowed people to gather for music making, shooting, dancing, reveling, drinking, political speaking, and other frivolities, activities that helped integrate the residents of the rural communities on the frontier. Serving under elected officers, who were usually selected on the basis of their standing in the community rather than military skills or experience, the militia organizations more likely reflected the social structure of the region from which its members came. Composed of conscripts under popular leaders, the militia was not always a well-trained or disciplined force. Its most important contribution may have been in establishing a precedent for cooperative activity between backcountry residents, forming ties that helped create indigenous institutions in the region.[85]

The Landscape of Frontier Settlement

By the close of the 1750s, nearly two decades of continuous European settlement had begun to transform the Wateree Valley, and the nature of the evolving frontier economy shaped the form, composition, and distribution of settlement. Newcomers occupied the land and displaced its aboriginal inhabitants, cleared forests, harnessed rivers as sources of power, opened routes of communication and trade, and altered the ancient landscape to make it suitable for grain agriculture. Although immigrants anticipated that commercial production would eventually replace the frontier economy and complete the region's incorporation into the wider Atlantic economy, they adapted to the conditions imposed by distance and isolation. Evidence for the patterning of settlement in the Wateree Valley reflects this accommodation, but it also records the changes that accompanied their efforts to transform the region as the process of frontier change unfolded.[86]

The landscape took form as immigrants began to occupy tracts on both sides of the great river. These lands presented colonial farmers with soils of varying potential on which to locate farms (Fig. 5.7). As the Wateree passed from the Piedmont, its course emerged from the sediments of granite and slate, traversed sandy and loamy soils of the Sandhills, and began its long journey across the loams and clays of the Coastal Plain. Here the topography changed from broad ridge tops and sharp side slopes to low, gently sloping lands below the Fall Line. The expanding flood plain of the Wateree formed ever more widening meanders on the flatter topography, and extensive wetlands and swamps lay along it and the nearby Lynches River. Some of these lowlands were suitable for grain and other crops, but susceptibility to inundation limited their appeal to pioneer farmers. The potential of the well-drained, loamy Piedmont soils was more promising, and only topography restrained their use. Although draughtiness and low nutrient-holding capacity made sandy soils less suitable for crops and small grains, the land's elevation made it preferable to richer lands that could flood when the river rose.[87]

Immigrants' limited resources and their perceptions of the landscape influenced the distribution of initial settlement. Most pioneers were small farmers whose lack of capital restricted their choice of lands to those that could be placed in cultivation rapidly without a large investment of labor. In the absence of markets, the higher costs of placing riverine lands in production could not justify the limited return, and newcomers avoided them. But their decision to locate farms on higher ground was also supported by a belief that associated low, wet floodplain lands and swamps with disease.[88] Most followed the example of Samuel Griggs, whose family of four located in the uplands, where they rapidly cleared a small portion of their tract to plant corn for subsistence and exchange.[89] Immigrants did not locate indiscriminately; however, their experience as farmers helped them judge the agricultural potential of soils and vegetation to identify desirable areas. Some did not hesitate to reject what they perceived to be inferior tracts in order to acquire those of suitable quality. When Thomas Leadon discovered that "no more good land was to be had" on the two hundred acres initially allotted to him on Pine Tree Creek, he applied for and received an equal amount in a more favorable location nearby.[90]

Pioneer farmers accommodated the semi-isolated conditions of initial colonization in the design and distribution of their landholdings. Although immigrant farmers were drawn to the higher, drier loamy soils of the rolling Sandhills, they also recognized that the river provided the most direct link between the points along its banks and therefore wished to acquire land on the water. Pioneers accomplished this by occupying linear tracts that stretched inland from the river's edge (Fig. 5.8). This arrangement provided shared access

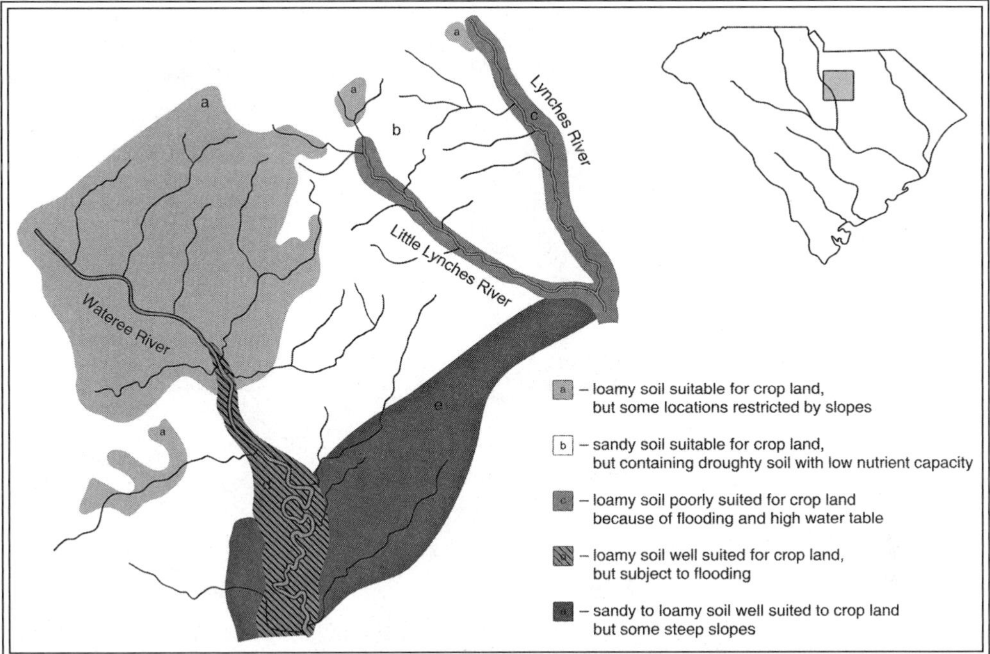

5.7 The Fall Line marked major changes in topography and the accompanying soil types, the distribution of which is clearly evident in the vicinity of Fredericksburg Township. Author's original map adapted from Cleveland J. Mitchell Jr., *Soil Survey of Kershaw County Area, South Carolinan* (Washington, D.C.: U.S. Department of Agriculture, Soil Conservation Service, in cooperation with the South Carolina Agricultural Experiment Station and the South Carolina Land Resources Conservation Commissio 1989).

to a common water route that facilitated communication and exchange with their neighbors and encompassed a variety of environments between the river and uplands. These long, narrow parcels, laid out perpendicular to the river, were reminiscent of the "long lots" employed extensively in French and British North America as well as in other parts of the New World. Settlers on the Wateree, like those in the Moravian colony of Wachovia in nearby North Carolina, recognized the advantage of the environmental diversity inherent in "long, narrow lots [that] secure[d] for each owner water, meadows, woods, etc." Long lots placed parallel to one another and perpendicular to the river also promoted a relatively compact pattern of settlement by situating residents relatively near one another. Such social proximity encouraged the formation of a rural community within which immigrant farmers could participate as producers and consumers in a regional frontier economy characterized by local exchange and constrained transportation.[91]

Unfortunately, documents identify few actual locations of early frontier settlements. Despite their graphic nature, most land plats were surveyed before the tracts were occupied and lack information about buildings, fences, and other improvements. Occasional plats were made later, however, and show the placement of structures as well as overland routes.

5.8 Initial settlers in the vicinity of Fredericksburg Township generally preferred long lots (shaded) that stretched inland from the Wateree River and encompassed a variety of land types. Author's original map adapted from Kenneth E. Lewis and Frank J. Krist Jr., "Settlement Expansion in Fredericksburg Township, South Carolina, 1740–1770," Report submitted to the Savannah River Archaeological Research Program, South Carolina Institute of Archaeology and Anthropology, University of South Carolina (1997), Part 5, 13.

Charles Ratcliff's tract on Town Creek contained both a mill and a mill pond, and Oliver Mehaffy's plat placed his house at the confluence of Grannys Quarter and Flat Rock Creeks. West of the Wateree, houses appeared on the tracts of Richard Singleton and Charles Lindsey. The plats also illustrated rectangular fields, one just behind Singleton's house and another near the intersection of two paths on the boundary of properties belonging to John Arledge and Richard Gregory.[92] The placement of structures also calls attention to the importance of topography. All were situated on high ground above the Wateree floodplain, yet close to the river.

The results of archaeological investigations in the Wateree Valley have identified several early colonial settlements situated near the documented locations of paths on both sides of the river. Although little evidence of these settlement remains above the surface, more than two and a half centuries of agricultural activity have not destroyed all buried remains of the region's past. Archaeological surveys have only begun to examine this vast area and have been largely limited to lands impacted by modern construction. Still, analyses of the ceramic artifact assemblages have revealed the presence of Europeans there prior to 1760.[93] Although these disturbed artifact scatters yielded no intact architectural remains, they indicate the locations of the habitations associated with them. Two lay on the east side of the river, on a high terrace rising about forty feet above the Wateree flood plain. Situated on properties granted to Bryan Rork and William Bready, these sites are likely associated with these two original grantees. West of the river and farther upstream, another site on James Ousley's land lay on a high terrace overlooking an Indian old field on the floodplain (Fig. 5.9).[94]

The pattern of initial settlement was also shaped by the routes of overland communication that tied the region together, and many initial immigrants located along the Catawba Path and other principal paths that physically integrated their pioneer community. Specific path destinations shown on surveys reveal the intricate network that linked the widely distributed immigrant farms in the Wateree Valley. The Rev. Woodmason noted that such "small paths, in many places grown up with grass or cover'd with leaves and indiscernible," formed the principal links between individual settlements.[95] These byways formed the myriad connections that linked the producers and consumers whose locations were the nodes of the regional economy. Many survey plats show paths to other settlers' farms. On Grannys Quarter Creek, paths connected Michael Branan's and Oliver Mehaffy's residences, and trails from each led to Thomas Maples's property lying immediately to the east.[96] A plat of Luke Gibson's tract west of the river reveals two routes south to Anthony Wright's farm on an adjacent property and a path north that passed through unoccupied lands to reach John Todd's property farther upriver (Fig. 5.9).[97] In a similar manner, southbound trails connected George Saunders with his neighbors William Harris and Thomas Jones, and the northern extension of one of these routes led to the residence of Thomas Crawford.[98] Although separated by distance from the outside, the residents of the region were not isolated from one another.

Paths in the Wateree Valley also led to more distant points. Plats sometimes identify routes labeled "up the river" and "down the river," but they often indicate more specific destinations. Several in Fredericksburg Township identify the Catawba Path leading to the Indian settlements farther upriver. Those of William Brown and John Furness specifically

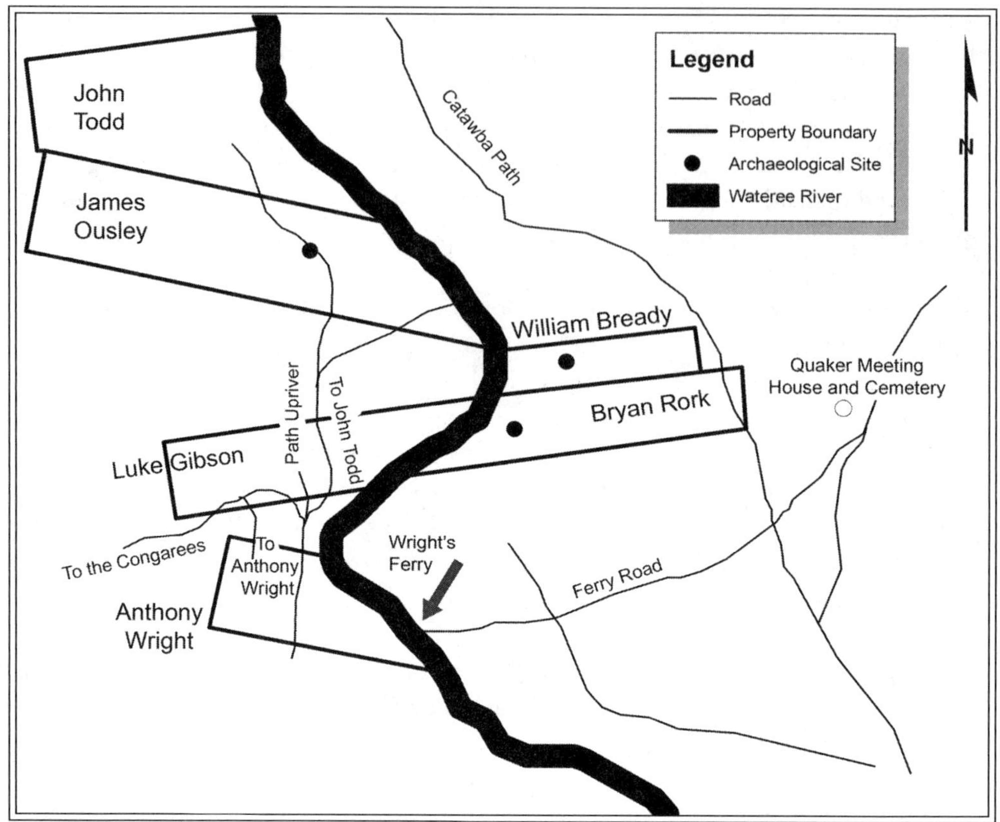

5.9 Evidence for early settlement and overland routes along the Wateree River in the vicinity of Fredericksburg Township. Archaeological sites, together with documented roads and paths, provide a partial picture of initial settlement and its connections. Author's original map.

testify to the road's downriver destination in the Santee settlements.[99] Paths also pointed to distant points. One passed southwest from Luke Gibson's property on the west bank to the Congaree and led to the settlements in Saxe Gotha Township (Fig. 5.9). Crossing the Congaree River at Joyner's Ferry, it joined routes leading west to Savannah Town, on the river of the same name, and those proceeding northwest to the Cherokee country. The Congarees also lay on the main route from Charleston. Proceeding inland from the coast via Goose Creek and Moncks Corner, it passed along the south side of the Santee, through Amelia Township, and offered the backcountry a direct connection to South Carolina's central port.[100]

The main road from Charleston also provided Fredericksburg Township with an overland link to the entrepôt, diverging near Amelia Township and reaching the Wateree settlements at several points along the river's course.[101] Proceeding north from this junction, it crossed the Santee River at Beard's Ferry and, as the Catawba Path, continued along the east bank of the Wateree River through Fredericksburg Township on its way to the Catawba nation.[102] Additional roads tied the Wateree settlements to those on Lynches River

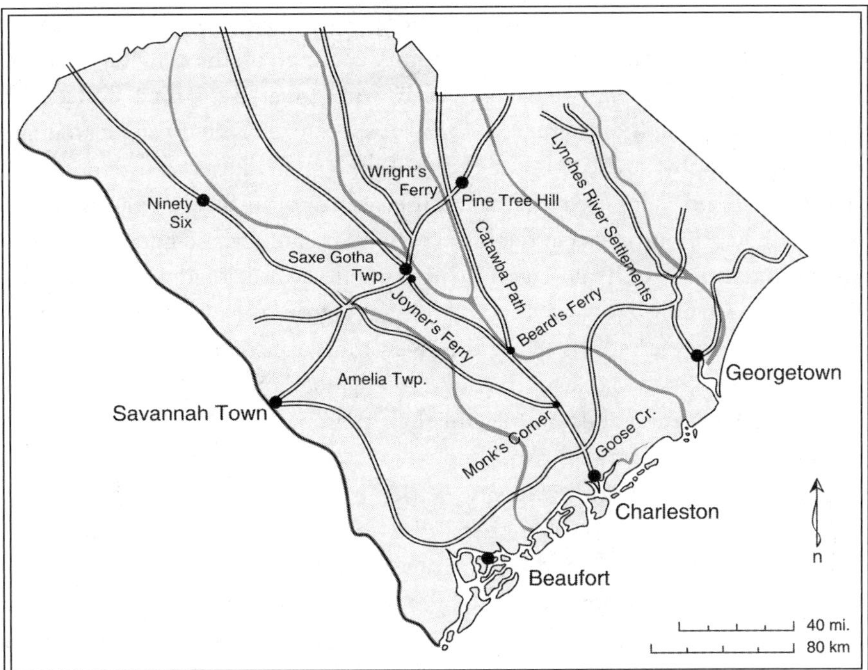

5.10 The network of principal overland transportation routes in South Carolina at mid-eighteenth century, showing major settlements and ferries. Author's original map.

to the east, as well as to the upper Pee Dee. By the 1750s a network of routes linked Charleston to the Wateree Valley and settlements across the backcountry. These routes of immigration were crucial in settling the interior, and the links they provided would be instrumental in incorporating the region into the larger commercial economy (Fig. 5.10).

The patterning of trade and communication routes strongly influenced the concentration of economic and social activity in the Wateree Valley. In the late 1750s the region's dispersed population still resided in the countryside, and no urban focus of retail and service activity had yet arisen.[103] Nevertheless, centralizing activities existed and began to gravitate toward a point on the Catawba Path where routes of internal movement converged. This spot lay on the east bank of the Wateree on the high terrace above the mouth of Pine Tree Creek, where the principal thoroughfare to Charleston bridged that stream and intersected a road leading to the river.[104] High ground on either side of the Wateree provided an ideal location for a ferry, and a west bank resident, Anthony Wright, established one there by 1754 (Fig. 5.9). Wright's Ferry, operated by his nephew Luke Gibson, was the principal link between the Fredericksburg settlements and the network of routes west of the river. The crossroads, known as "Pine Tree Hill," became the focus of routes east of the river and the destination of paths on both sides of the Wateree.[105]

The location was significant for other reasons as well. In addition to lying at an important intersection in the regional route network, it became, because of the presence of Robert Milhous's and Samuel Wyly's mills, the principal processing point for grain for the rural residents on both sides of the river. As such, it became a node that attracted other economic and social activities. The early Quaker community centered on the cemetery and meetinghouse near the road junction, and Samuel Wyly, who donated the tract, concentrated his trading and farming activities there. As a focus of specialized activity and a strategic point for integrating multiple functions in the region, Pine Tree Hill was on the verge of becoming a central place, a development that had implications for its future growth.

By the late 1750s, European settlement in the backcountry extended well beyond the township boundaries. The Great Wagon Road that followed the Piedmont from Pennsylvania to South Carolina brought Scots-Irish immigrants from the northern colonies into the upper Wateree drainage. Settling along the river, there called the Catawba, they formed rural communities in the Waxhaws. The newcomers relied on their ties of kinship and religion to develop to a regional economy, but their presence also brought European settlement even closer to the Catawba towns and encroached further on Indian lands. The area below Fredericksburg also saw increasing settlement from Williamsburg Township into the headwaters of the Black and Lynches Rivers, and immigration expanded east of the Santee Swamp above the mouth of the Wateree. This region, known as the High Hills of Santee, lay along the route from Fredericksburg to Charleston and attracted settlers mostly from the coast.[106] To the east of Fredericksburg, the opening of the Welsh Tract brought Europeans into the upper reaches of the Pee Dee. The region attracted Welsh settlers from eastern Pennsylvania, who traveled up the Pee Dee River from Georgetown to reach the fertile lowlands of the Welsh Neck, as well as immigrants from the South Carolina lowcountry and some Scots-Irish who traveled overland from the North.[107] Farther west, German immigrants dominated settlement in Orangeburg and Saxe Gotha Townships on the Congaree and formed a substantial portion of the new settlers who moved into Amelia Township on the Edisto and New Windsor Township on the Savannah. Their ethnic presence remained strong in these regions, reflected in the retention of language and customs and the prominence of the Lutheran Church.[108] An influx of Scots-Irish pioneers who settled outside the townships further swelled the population of western South Carolina. Their presence extended the range of European settlement in the interior, but colonization of the upper Savannah brought conflict with the resident Cherokees.[109]

All over the backcountry, immigrant groups opened farms, built mills, and created systems of trade like that in the Wateree Valley; yet the region remained isolated by distance and a lack of market access. The extension of settlement across the interior alone did not make it an integral part of the Atlantic economy. The next decade witnessed remarkable commercial growth and the appearance of an administrative structure that transformed the region. Broad processes shaped these changes, but the form they took was also a consequence of influences specific to this region. These events and the individuals who took part in them determined the course of development in the Wateree Valley.

Chapter 6

The Pine Tree Store

Commercial Expansion into the Backcountry

The late spring of 1748 found a young man recently arrived from England in the employ of John Ainslie, a Charleston merchant with whom he had shared the recent passage across the Atlantic. This was perhaps not an unusual situation for an enterprising immigrant in the commercial metropolis of Britain's southern colonies, but for Joseph Kershaw, a Yorkshire native, it was his "lucky step," an opportunity for financial success of which he intended to take full advantage (Fig. 6.1). It was not Kershaw's first experience in the commercial world. At the age of thirteen he had been apprenticed to John Royd, a London merchant banker and trader whose roots in Yorkshire likely provided the connection that permitted Kershaw to leave his rural birthplace of Baitings Gate, Soyland, near Ripponden in the West Riding, to expand his horizons in the nation's capital. During the seven years of his apprenticeship, Kershaw served as Royd's footman, a position that exposed him to the business of the East India trade and familiarized him with its workings and offered him entrée to the social circle of those engaged in commerce. Although Kershaw was apparently stifled in his efforts to rise in Royd's firm, his time there taught him the intricacies of overseas exchange and the organization of the shipping business. Undoubtedly it provided him with invaluable knowledge and the incentive to pursue mercantile trade as a means to attain wealth.[1]

During the following decade, Joseph Kershaw remained in Charleston, gaining experience in the mercantile trade and entry into a network of influential employers and their associates. As early as 1751 he became affiliated with an ironware and ship chandlery firm owned by the partnership of James Laurens and Jacob Motte. Laurens was a merchant like his wealthier brother Henry, but his business partner was also a politician and the public treasurer of the province. Jacob Motte's performance as public treasurer had recently come under public scrutiny, and his apparent ignorance of bookkeeping, his mixing of private and public accounts, and his late reporting and uneven collection of import duties led the Assembly to suspect him of misappropriating provincial funds. Following an extensive inquiry, Motte retained his position under the condition that he turn his estate over to a trust that included members of the governor's Council and other prominent persons until he had repaid the public funds that were missing under his care. Joseph Kershaw joined John Laurens, a trusted member of the Charleston business elite, as an official witness to this transaction. His inclusion in this select group indicates an acceptance of the newcomer

6.1 Joseph Kershaw, Ancrum, Lance & Loocock's agent in the backcountry, who established their store at Pine Tree Hill. Courtesy of Camden Archives, Camden, South Carolina.

into the business community, as did the appearance of his name as a witness to several land transactions involving Laurens and Motte.[2]

By 1754 Kershaw had cemented his relationship with the Laurens brothers. He became an associate of James Laurens & Co., acting as a sales agent for merchandise, but he also bought and sold provisions on his own through their store. This business link broadened to include an association with James's brother Henry, for whom Kershaw witnessed the purchase of Wambaw, a 1,250-acre plantation in St. James Santee Parish. This acquisition was especially significant in that it was Laurens's first plantation and marked the expansion of his economic strategy. But it demonstrated more than a shift from trade into commercial agriculture, for possession of land made him eligible for election to the Assembly and opened the door to a promising political career. Kershaw's success in making business connections furthered his ambitions as a merchant, but Laurens's example also made him aware of the multiple paths to wealth and power in the expanding colony.

Joseph Kershaw's association with the Laurens brothers and Motte led to a lucrative, though almost accidental, opportunity that helped the young merchant enter business on his own. This situation arose as a result of the desire of the Charleston merchants William Ancrum, Lambert Lance, and Aaron Loocock, who had recently formed a partnership, to establish a store in the backcountry. In 1757 the three men proposed to open a store among the settlements on the Wateree at Pine Tree Hill and approached Charles Woodmason to act as their resident agent. Like the partners, Woodmason had immigrated from England and settled as a planter in Prince Fredericks Parish on the lower Pee Dee River on tracts he acquired following his arrival in 1752. But his interests extended beyond agriculture. Recognizing the economic potential of the interior, he sought to avail himself of trading opportunities in the backcountry. His attempt to establish a store in the Congarees ended in disaster, however, when the Cherokees killed his agent, a Mr. Steele. This unfortunate event dramatically altered Woodmason's perception of the backcountry and his desire to participate in its economy. As long as Native societies remained strong in the interior, he sensed a danger in venturing beyond the relative safety of his lowcountry holdings and extending mercantile activities beyond his store on Black Mingo Creek.[3]

The offer to manage a store in the Waterees presented a dilemma to Woodmason. On one hand, it offered the potential of acquiring substantial wealth through the exploitation of an untapped market. Samuel Wyly, an entrepreneur who certainly understood the potential of opening the backcountry to commercial production and trade and recognized an opportunity for obtaining outside capital to finance it, met with him and made this point clear. Woodmason remained aware of the powerful Cherokee presence west of the Waterees. And his deep-seated fear of death at the hands of Indians made the proposal too risky in his mind. Despite Wyly's entreaties, Woodmason declined the offer. Upon learning of his decision, a fellow merchant, Jacob Motte, immediately rebuked him for his timidity. Despite his shortcomings in accounting, Motte's financial success did not arise from a failure to recognize profitable opportunities when they appeared, and this awareness was not lost on his employee Joseph Kershaw. Upon learning of Woodmason's reluctance, Kershaw approached him seeking his support in applying for the position. With Woodmason's permission and undoubtedly Motte's blessing, he became the agent for the partnership of Ancrum, Lance & Loocock in the Waterees and in the spring of 1758 set out to extend commercial trade to this portion of the South Carolina backcountry.[4]

The venture proposed by Ancrum, Lance & Loocock had implications far beyond opening the door to Joseph Kershaw's future. Its intent and scope promoted dramatic changes in the structure of the backcountry economy by introducing the conditions necessary to bring about the cultivation and processing of specialized crops on a scale sufficient for commercial production and to permit their sale on an export market. Accomplishing these tasks required an infrastructure that included the physical components to collect, mill, and transport produce, as well as the social and economic institutions to facilitate exchange between dispersed producers and distant coastal markets. As established Charleston merchants with resources at hand and access to credit, Ancrum, Lance & Loocock could assemble the capital to buy land, build structures to collect, house, process, and store goods and produce, hire the wagons to transport backcountry grain to Charleston and import finished wares into the interior, and pay employees engaged in the various phases of their business. Organizing the operation in the backcountry was another matter, one that entailed establishing institutional mechanisms of exchange to oversee the conduct of trade, as well as providing a stable and structured environment within which it could take place. The form they took would shape the course of the backcountry's development.

Financing Trade in the Backcountry

Establishing the infrastructure of trade depended on the availability of capital resources sufficient to cover the costs of creating and maintaining its physical elements. As colonial merchants, the partnership of Ancrum, Lance & Loocock operated in a financial world characterized by a chronic shortage of fixed capital. The operation of businesses and, more important, their expansion required working capital derived from loans or credit extended by others. In the absence of a viable banking system, credit gave merchants the means to acquire imported goods and backcountry produce and to develop an infrastructure for exchange. Just as the availability of credit facilitated the production and overseas trade of lowcountry agricultural commodities, it also provided the wherewithal to extend commercial exchange into the interior. But where did such credit come from?

Although no records of Ancrum, Lance & Loocock's commercial backcountry venture exist, their experience would have led them to follow the practices of other colonial mercantile firms in acquiring the capital necessary to launch a major expansion. Eighteenth-century metropolitan entrepreneurs had several means of raising capital. The most direct involved reinvesting on-hand resources of their own, but if these were unavailable they could resort to borrowing funds from others on bond, or they might rely on commercial credit from their suppliers.[5] Charleston merchants could have utilized all of these sources to finance the extension of trade; however, most relied heavily on their own resources. As well established and successful merchants, Ancrum, Lance & Loocock had presumably accumulated considerable capital in their individual and collective business dealings. Like other metropolitan merchants, they sought to employ their moderate fortunes as a source of additional income by reinvesting capital in various colonial ventures likely to bring a reasonable return. Indeed, merchants represented the largest group of investors in plantation mortgages, a lucrative local market for excess funds that became a primary source of developmental loans needed for agricultural expansion.[6]

The role of Charleston capital in promoting economic growth in the hinterland was not restricted to financing agriculture. Merchants such as Henry Laurens also invested in trade. Taking advantage of his visit to the Moravian community at Bethabara, North Carolina, he extended credit, underwritten by his personal wealth, to their store to acquire imported merchandise. Laurens's offer to his new business associates illustrates the mechanism by which such a backcountry venture was carried out. Operating as resident agents in the interior, the Moravian storekeepers received credit from Laurens for molasses, wine, hardware, and other finished goods shipped to them, all to be paid back within a specified time with deerskins, butter, and other backcountry products collected at the store and shipped by wagon to Charleston.[7] Credit from the Charleston merchant helped Moravian storekeepers enlarge their business by providing finished merchandise to sell at retail, but it also obliged them to market their produce through Laurens's firm. Once regular trade commenced, the need for credit encouraged the growth of backcountry production for an export market. Expanding trade also enhanced profits and the income of the merchant who managed it and compensated for the costs of managing the accounts.

Eighteenth-century merchants kept track of capital advanced to an agent by employing a recording system known as double-entry bookkeeping that allowed them to manage their accounts through the entry of debits (the accounts of those in debt to the merchant) and credits (the accounts of the creditors to whom the merchant was in debt) to record payments received and payments dispersed, respectively. Such an arrangement allowed an agent, as a customer, to maintain a running account into which commodities were deposited and on which the agent could draw credit for supplies. Accounts could be also used directly to subsidize production by giving a farmer or planter credit for a commodity not yet sold. Here the merchant acted as a commodity storage facility that maintained an account from which the producer could draw to purchase finished goods. A merchant could also use the account to advance credit to an agent via a bond before a commodity was delivered, an advantageous arrangement for a merchant establishing business in a distant, undeveloped area. In either case, the account was balanced when the merchant sold the commodity and remitted any differences.[8]

An example from the records of a later mercantile partnership headed by Joseph Kershaw illustrates how merchants managed a business at a distance. His firm's backcountry store recorded a number of distinct kinds of transactions in its account book. In January 1779 the partnership accumulated credits that included expenses of cash paid to acquire a variety of goods to be sold through the store as well as through a retail venture with two associates closer to Charleston. Additional funds were also needed for packing and transporting merchandise by land and water to the store and elsewhere as well as for the cost of handling and the cost of various business-related supplies. To balance these expenses, the partnership received income debited to it from individuals who paid accounts in full or in part to cancel their debts or the debts of others to the partnership. It also received cash paid by the store manager, Joseph Kershaw, to the partnership for goods he took for sale at Purrysburg, as well as for other sundries he purchased from them, and the store accepted further reimbursements by two individuals who joined the partnership in a retail venture. These transactions were balanced at the end of the month, with the excess debt carried over to the new month.[9]

An agent or other independent entity might also obtain operating capital by taking out a bond that placed him in debt to a lender with whom he might or might not have had business ties. Bonds provided a substantial advance of funds for a given period of time. Taking out a bond allowed an entrepreneur who needed to cover the initial costs of a venture the opportunity to acquire the necessary capital immediately. In exchange, the borrower reimbursed the lender for the use of the loan by paying interest in addition to the principal. Although this practice was intended as a legal arrangement formally obligating public parties, individuals often employed bonds as a means to shift funds among their friends, business partners, and associates. This practice introduced an informality that eased exchange in a world without formal financial institutions; however, its implementation frequently relied on trust and personal suasion that placed an additional burden on the lender. One such transaction involved the frontier trader Samuel Wyly, who took out a bond from the merchants William Ancrum and Aaron Loocock. At some point he fell into default on this loan, and, to prevent a lawsuit to recover the debt, Joseph Kershaw intervened for his friend and prevailed upon Henry Laurens to assume the obligation. Later, with the bond still unpaid, Laurens turned to Kershaw for assistance. Complaining of the difficulty in administering "these good-natured accounts for large sums & . . . acts of securityship," Laurens despaired of receiving prompt payment and seemed resigned to having the bond renewed for several more years.[10] While not without risk, issuing bonds among those with related business interests was a convenient means of extending credit in eighteenth-century South Carolina and one that facilitated commercial expansion into the interior.

Ancrum, Lance & Loocock relied on traditional financial mechanisms to provide the wherewithal for their Pine Tree Hill venture, yet the difficulties inherent in operating a business in a distant and undeveloped country also required that they be flexible and seek innovative arrangements to allow the flow of capital and credit in the absence of formal economic institutions. In such circumstances, the tradition of relying on informal transactions permeated exchanges and provided a basis for economic expansion on the frontier. Such arrangements not only involved the assumption of multiple financial functions by merchants but also emphasized the role of individual associations and social connections in the conduct of business. The success of their enterprise depended on the creation of a corporate structure based on personal ties, a strategy through which the partnership could acquire and integrate the resources necessary to construct the physical base for trade in the backcountry and, later, create an institutional structure to sustain its operation and support its growth.

The capital resources available to Charleston's mercantile community provided the flexibility needed to build an infrastructure of trade in the backcountry, but to succeed in this task the partners had first to acquire the resources with which to carry out the activities associated with collecting, processing, and shipping regional produce, as well as those involved in storing and distributing imported goods and, to a lesser extent, manufacturing and repairing goods locally. The two basic requirements for these business activities were land on which to erect facilities for conducting commercial trade and transportation between the Wateree Valley and Charleston.

Real Estate and Access

A successful mercantile operation on the backcountry frontier required physical infrastructure for its operations. To build it, the partners had first to acquire land for the stores, warehouses, processing facilities, and other buildings necessary to house its activities. Acquiring these parcels was also an investment strategy for those intent on promoting economic development in the interior. Over time, as external markets opened for frontier products, tracts obtained early usually rose in value. Real property acquired by grant or at low cost could yield future profits through sales as immigrants took up lands for farming and older residents expanded their operations. Ancrum, Lance & Loocock, as well as others with an interest in the firm, realized the potential of this opportunity and began taking up land in the Wateree Valley in the late 1750s.

The lands obtained by Ancrum, Lance & Loocock reflected both the needs of their business and the order in which they wished it to develop. The first step was to establish a base of operations for their production and processing facilities. Because access was central to trade, the company's properties had to be situated at the junction of crucial transportation routes. Therefore the parcels had to be located carefully. By the late 1750s the focus of European settlement in the Wateree Valley lay in the vicinity of Pine Tree Creek, where overland roads that supported immigration met routes that facilitated regional trade and communication with other settlements of the interior. The site was important to the Catawba trade and Samuel Wyly's budding frontier trading enterprises and to the location of his and Samuel Milhous's mills. Wyly's success at Pine Tree Creek undoubtedly encouraged Ancrum, Lance & Loocock to choose this location as the site of its Wateree store. The partners' backcountry venture offered a venue through which Wyly might expand the scope of his operations, and his involvement with their store from its inception was almost certainly not coincidental.

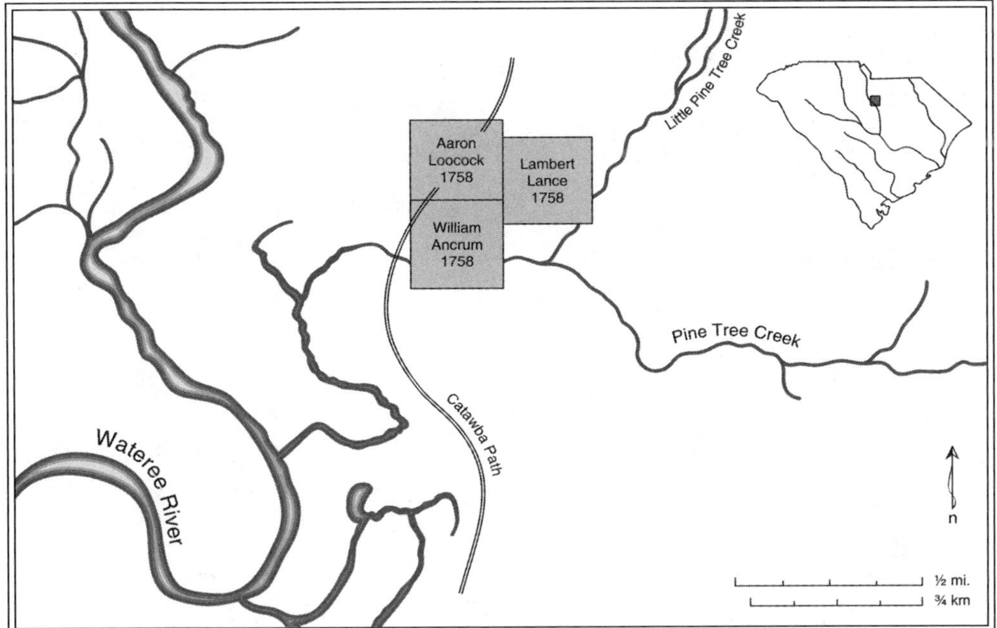

6.2 William Ancrum, Lambert Lance, and Aaron Loocock's initial land acquisitions at Pine Tree Hill in 1758. Author's original map.

The decision by Ancrum, Lance & Loocock to situate on Pine Tree Creek led to the firm's immediate acquisition of land in this vicinity. In the first year of the firm's operation, the province granted tracts of 150 acres to each of the three partners.[11] The earliest of these was the Pine Tree Hill tract granted to William Ancrum in June 1758. Lying just east of Samuel Wyly's lands, this named location occupied the high terrace over which the Catawba Path passed on its way along the eastern bank of the Wateree (Fig. 6.2). The western edge of Ancrum's property abutted the Quaker cemetery and the adjacent road that led to Wright's Ferry. The intersection of the ferry road with the Catawba Path nearby placed a key intersection of regional routes within the bounds of this property.

Ancrum, Lance & Loocock lost no time in exploiting the firm's holdings at Pine Tree Hill and soon established a presence there. Archaeological evidence of two early structures near the intersection of the Catawba Path and the ferry road testifies to the partners' immediate use of this location for their commercial activities (Fig. 6.3).[12] Intensive archaeological investigations at the sites of the structures in the 1990s revealed the time of their occupation and the nature of their use. The buildings were of earthfast construction, a technique that employed a series of posts anchored in the ground to support the structure's wooden framework. The spacing of the posts divided the structure into units called bays, and the number of bays determined the building's size. Derived from medieval roots in Europe, this form of architecture proved well adapted to the eastern woodlands, where abundant natural materials and ease of construction ensured its success. Earthfast architecture became

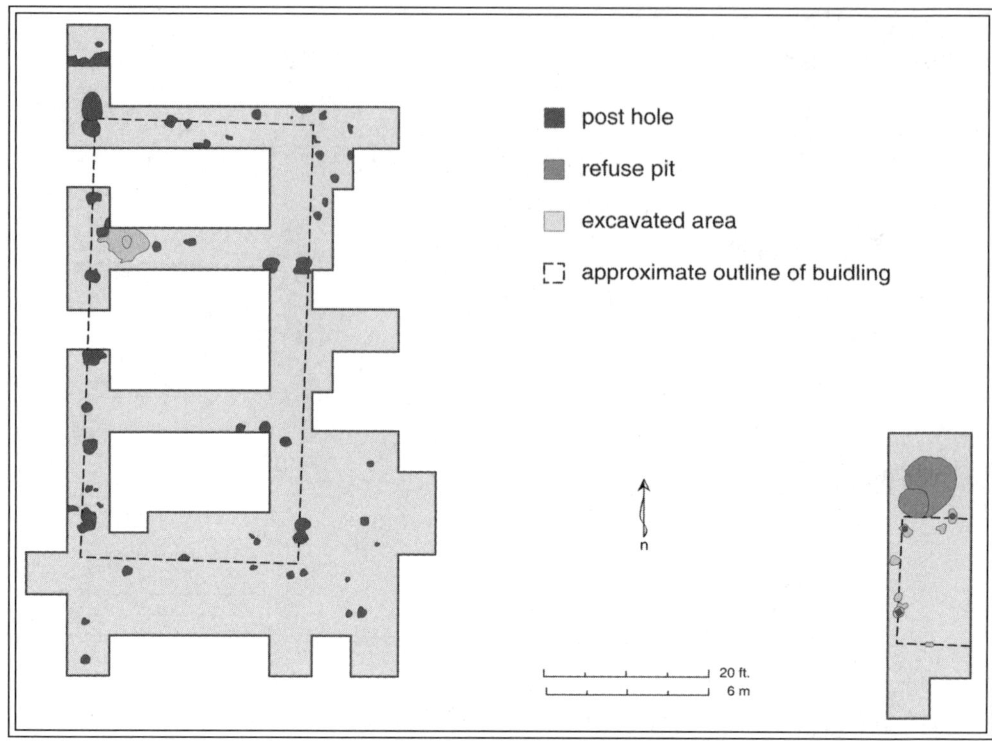

6.3 Plan of the two earthfast structures at Pine Tree Hill as revealed by post holes uncovered in archaeological excavations. The large building on the left was likely the store built for Ancrum, Lance & Loocock and later used by Kershaw & Co. Author's original map adapted from Kenneth E. Lewis, *Camden: Historical Archaeology in the South Carolina Backcountry* (Belmont, Calif.: Thomson Wadsworth, 2006).

firmly established in British North America, and pioneers in South Carolina's interior employed it widely in early frontier settlements (Fig. 6.4).[13]

The placement, contents, and construction of the two earthfast structures made them distinctive. Both shared a common angle of orientation of 6 degrees east of north, a 3-degree deviation from the grid upon which later buildings in the vicinity were laid out. This set them apart and is likely the result of their having been laid out together as a distinct settlement cluster. The assemblages of ceramic artifacts recovered at the sites of the structures provide evidence that they were the earliest erected there. British ceramics are among the most time-sensitive artifacts found on colonial sites. An analysis of those found here indicates that both buildings were erected no later than 1760. Thus they represent the earliest colonial occupation of the site.[14] The absence of brick in the earthfast buildings further distinguishes them from others and implies that they were constructed separately from them. The manufacture of brick required kilns that were typically not available during the initial settlement of the frontier, leading to the exclusive use of wood. In the Wateree Valley the earliest use of brick occurred in the 1760s, by which time Samuel Wyly was already well

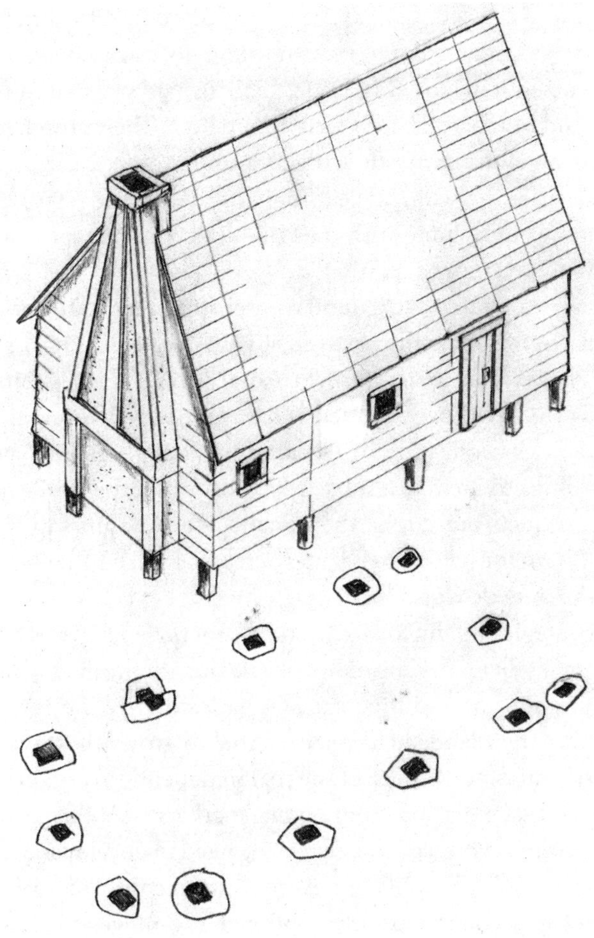

6.4 Architecture and archaeological plan of an earthfast structure typical of those constructed in the South Carolina backcountry in the mid-eighteenth century. The plan is shown directly below a drawing of the structure. It reveals a series of post holes, excavated to place the posts. One of the posts on the back of the building has been replaced, necessitating the excavation of a new post hole through the older one. On the left side of the structure, wooden posts supported a mud-plastered chimney like that on the small earthfast structure at Pine Tree Hill. Author's original drawing.

established there and Joseph Kershaw was already resident at Pine Tree Hill.[15] Architectural form also provided several clues to function. Both structures were composed of multiple bays, but they differed in size and form. The smaller building consisted of one or two bays, and, although partially obliterated by modern road construction, its remains indicate that it was seventeen feet wide. Its size and the presence of a wattle-and-daub chimney are typical of domestic dwellings. The second building was much larger and lacked a fireplace. Set on massive posts, it contained three large bays that provided a considerable unobstructed interior open space measuring fifty-four by twenty-eight feet (Fig. 6.3). Such a structure would have been suitable for receiving, processing, and storing bulk produce and merchandise and for other specialized activities associated with a trading venture. Its size and configuration, together with its lack of cellars and chimneys, are typical of stores and other public buildings.[16]

Objects associated with the two structures provide further evidence that the large earthfast structure was the Pine Tree Hill store and offer clues to the buildings' functions as well. Identifying the presence of storekeeping in the archaeological record is challenging because this specialized activity fails to leave extensive and conspicuous deposits of nonbiodegradable waste products like those generated by blacksmithing, pottery making, or other industrial activities. But specialized items used in trade, such as bale seals, used to secure bags of general merchandise, and iron barrel bands were found here. Their presence, together with a lower relative proportion of the domestic artifacts found at other buildings, points to the presence of goods in transit. The wide range of finished items recovered, although not found exclusively in stores, is in keeping with the building's commercial function and testifies to its role in the frontier economy.

The partners wisely chose the site for their backcountry enterprise. Ancrum's tract formed the nucleus of a larger parcel assembled by the partners at Pine Tree Hill (Fig. 6.2). Before the close of 1758 Lambert Lance received an adjacent 150-acre tract that encompassed the high terrace above Pine Tree Creek and extended as far as the fork dividing the branches of that stream. Aaron Loocock's acquisition of 150 acres just northwest of Pine Tree Hill extended the partners' holdings to include a substantial portion of the Catawba Path in this vicinity. Together the two tracts built upon the advantage of Ancrum's initial choice to locate at the intersection of two important overland routes that linked the focus of the earlier Quaker settlement to the outside world.[17]

To realize the advantages of a strategic trading location, the partners needed a transportation network capable of moving sufficient quantities of backcountry products and imported finished goods between the interior and the port of Charleston. By the 1750s, residents of the backcountry knew that their lands held the potential to grow wheat on a large scale and understood that successful development of the region depended on export sales of this crop. But they also realized that entry into commercial markets rested on critical transportation improvements.[18] Settlers expressed the increasing need to develop major trunk lines into the interior by petitioning the Assembly to clear routes and construct roads. Direct access to foodstuffs and other backcountry products offered advantages for lowcountry residents as well, because such internal movement reduced the colony's dependence on the northern provinces for provisions. The inherent value of this trade encouraged provincial investment in constructing and maintaining routes and feeder networks into the interior, a step that also furthered efforts to extend political control to the frontier.[19]

Internal improvements during the 1750s encouraged overland trade with the backcountry. With the introduction of large vehicles with iron-rimmed wheels pulled by teams of four or six horses, wagoners had the means to haul large cargoes over substantial distances on primitive roads. Their use brought a marked increase in traffic bearing backcountry produce to Charleston. So great were movements by wagon that they often wore out the bridges in the lowcountry parishes they traversed en route to the entrepôt. [20] Expanding trade brought growth in the infrastructure of transportation. Although still largely unimproved, recognized routes of trade and travel now penetrated the interior. Provincial almanacs described roads from Charleston to the middle Savannah River as well as to the central backcountry and carefully noted mileages and stops along the way. From the capital one might travel via Goose Creek to Moncks Corner and farther inland following the Congaree River to Saxe Gotha Township and the Congarees and beyond.[21] As we have seen, roads on both sides of the Wateree linked Pine Tree Hill to Charleston (Fig. 5.10). At the center of the road system in the Wateree Valley, Ancrum, Lance & Loocock's operation lay poised to become the focus of economic growth and consolidation of South Carolina's interior.

A key element in the operation of trade is regular and reliable communications between sources of production and markets. In the eighteenth century such interchange was largely conducted by mail. Letters containing instructions, accounts, bills of exchange, and other business correspondence were the lifeblood of overseas commerce, and merchants in major American ports such as Charleston depended on the mail to conduct exchange throughout the Atlantic world. To accommodate the needs of commercial interests, the British government established a regulated postal system that linked principal colonial centers with one another as well as with the home country.[22] By the second quarter of the century, official mail began passing overland directly between the North American provinces. South Carolina's Assembly established a sporadic postal service linking Charleston and Georgetown with the northern colonies via Cape Fear and Edenton in North Carolina in 1738, and by 1756 mails regularly moved over this route under the auspices of the colonial post office. Beyond the coastal post road, mail delivery depended upon private contractors who carried it to nearby settlements in the lowcountry.[23] Although the backcountry remained without official mail service until the 1790s, information and parcels traveled to and from points in the interior, connecting its residents to one another and the outside world. Private carriers linked points as distant as Bethabara in North Carolina directly to Charleston. From this port, land and water routes reached the northern colonies, and overseas mails provided direct connections with the British Isles and Europe. Because of its intermediate location, Pine Tree Hill assumed a key role in the exchange of information. By the early 1760s mail and packages originating in and destined for Bethabara, Salisbury, and other North Carolina settlements passed through Pine Tree Hill on the way to Charleston.[24] Pine Tree Hill's central location also facilitated the flow of mail from Charleston to settlements on the upper Pee Dee River.[25]

In 1758 South Carolina's backcountry lay on the threshold of transition. A substantial agricultural population now resided in the interior, and the routes by which they came opened the area to travel and communication. The regional economies that developed the Wateree Valley and elsewhere integrated frontier society and formed a basis for production on a scale limited only by restricted markets and the absence of an infrastructure capable of marketing backcountry goods to the outside world. The coming of Ancrum, Lance & Loocock's store to Pine Tree Hill provided the catalyst for change. Centrally situated with links to Charleston as well as other parts of the backcountry, it became the focus for economic transformation. But first two elements had to be in place—infrastructure for commercial production and institutions capable of integrating its components.

Building an Infrastructure of Production

The partners took a crucial step toward dominating regional trade by occupying a well-situated location on the upper Wateree, yet commercial success required more than the mere presence of facilities to gather and distribute goods passing into and out of the region. If they hoped to draw the backcountry into the larger Atlantic economy, they also needed a means to collect, process, and store bulk produce in sufficient quantities to justify export sales. Salable agricultural commodities would not only generate profits for the merchant who sold them in lowcountry markets but also serve as a basis for extending credit to frontier farmers, providing them the wherewithal to purchase imported tools, equipment, and other retail goods. Ancrum, Lance & Loocock realized that its operation required an infrastructure that extended beyond a store at Pine Tree Hill. Developing a commercial trade rested upon the partners' ability to establish the facilities necessary to acquire and market agricultural produce over long distances.

Frontier settlers raised crops that could be easily grown on newly cleared lands since they lacked the resources to clear large tracts or to modify land to accommodate specialized agriculture. Initially they turned to corn. This all-purpose subsistence crop found widespread acceptance in colonial America because its qualities allowed it to assume a unique role in the frontier economy. It could be processed with minimal equipment, and, as the basis for such staple foods as johnny cake, corn mush, hominy, and corn fritters, it was a mainstay of the farm diet. Corn was also a major component of animal feed and the main ingredient in the distilled alcoholic beverages widely consumed in colonial America. Despite corn's adaptability and its resistance to diseases that affected other grains, external demand was insufficient to justify its production as a commercial crop.[26]

Wheat quickly emerged as the cash crop of choice among backcountry farmers. Like corn, it was well adapted to frontier agriculture. But wheat required more extensive land clearing, was more difficult to harvest and thresh, and needed specialized facilities to process into flour. Nevertheless, it could be cultivated with limited labor and little capital investment on newly cleared land, and its production was well within the capability of a dispersed agricultural population. In addition, rising external demand for flour made the cultivation of wheat increasingly lucrative as an export crop.[27] South Carolina's lowcountry constituted a growing market for breadstuffs, and by mid-century the region imported considerable quantities of flour from the northern colonies. Recognizing the need to promote domestic production and the untapped agricultural potential of the backcountry, the provincial Assembly in 1744 offered a bounty on flour ground from South Carolina wheat and delivered to market in Charleston.[28] In spite of this encouragement, the lack of a processing and transportation infrastructure continued to frustrate settlers' attempts to enter export production.[29]

Settlers in the Wateree Valley and the Congarees planted wheat in increasing quantity during the 1750s, and many lowcountry observers believed that backcountry flour would equal the quantity of that imported.[30] Although resourceful immigrants like Samuel Wyly had erected mills, their limited output served few customers beyond residents of the immediate area. Inadequate facilities for processing also restricted their ability to meet sudden demands for excess flour. When Gov. William Lyttelton sought foodstuffs to supply his force marching against the Cherokees in 1759, for example, he was unable to acquire adequate flour and bread from the residents of the Congarees and was obliged to turn to the more distant settlements of the Yadkin Valley in North Carolina for provisions.[31] Backcountry farmers were capable of expanding production if demand increased and remained consistently strong. With access to coastal markets, the key to expanding production lay in establishing the infrastructure to acquire and process flour for shipment to Charleston.

The processing requirements of grain are directly tied to the size and composition of wheat-producing settlements. These encompass all the activities associated with the movement of harvested grain from the field to the places of its consumption. Such arrangements, called forward linkages, create the urban systems that emerge in frontier agricultural regions as they make the transition to commercial production. Crops, such as wheat, that are bulky, heavy, and perishable resulted in complex commodity flows and processing demands. These affected the nature of urban functions such as packaging, processing, and transportation services, as well as the provisioning and repair activities associated with freight shipment. Tobacco and rice, in contrast, were collected and processed largely on or near the plantations where they were raised and transported over relatively short distances directly to ports for overseas shipment. Wheat required centralized facilities for grain milling, grading, packing, and storage, as well as subsequent shipment over much greater distances to market. Central settlements housed specialized activities and services, and their concentration encouraged the growth of economic, social, and political functions associated with town life.[32] The scale of wheat production also affected the composition of the communities that grew up around processing centers. Because wheat was grown largely by small farmers, the income from its sale tended to be more widely distributed than it was in regions such as the lowcountry, where rice farming concentrated wealth in the hands of a small number of large landowners. More equitable income distribution created broader consumer demand that promoted the growth of retail businesses and increased the level of resident trade and services. As a result, wheat-growing regions became larger, more complex settlements that dominated the deep hinterlands.[33]

Ancrum, Lance & Loocock immediately sought to expand milling in the region. In the half dozen years after opening the initial store, the partners secured possession of key tracts controlling trade in the Wateree Valley and began to systematically acquire other properties critical to increasing grain processing. Milling was central to converting grain into a form that could be conveyed economically over long distances to coastal markets. The complex procedure of preparing wheat involved grinding the threshed grain into flour and then bolting it to sift it for fineness, a process that required specialized machinery. In the eighteenth century, flour mills depended on flowing water for power, and sites of abundant water power lying relatively close to Pine Tree Hill became desirable acquisitions for the partnership. Most mills employed an overshot water wheel that provided the most efficient operation; however, these had to be located on streams with descent adequate to provide a sufficient height of fall.[34] Several such sites could be found along Pine Tree Creek and its tributary Little Pine Tree Creek, where the streams passed from the higher ridges of the sand hills onto the floodplain of the Wateree River. Here Robert Milhous and Samuel Wyly had already erected mills in the vicinity of Pine Tree Hill, and the partners' presence there offered an opportunity to concentrate milling activity around this central location. Possession of the Pine Tree Creek drainage was crucial to controlling flour production in the Wateree Valley.

Within a short time the partners moved to expand and consolidate their individual holdings. Joseph Kershaw's knowledge undoubtedly influenced their choice of new tracts. As resident agent, he was intimately acquainted with the region and its resources and recognized how these might be incorporated into the company's operations. Kershaw's youth

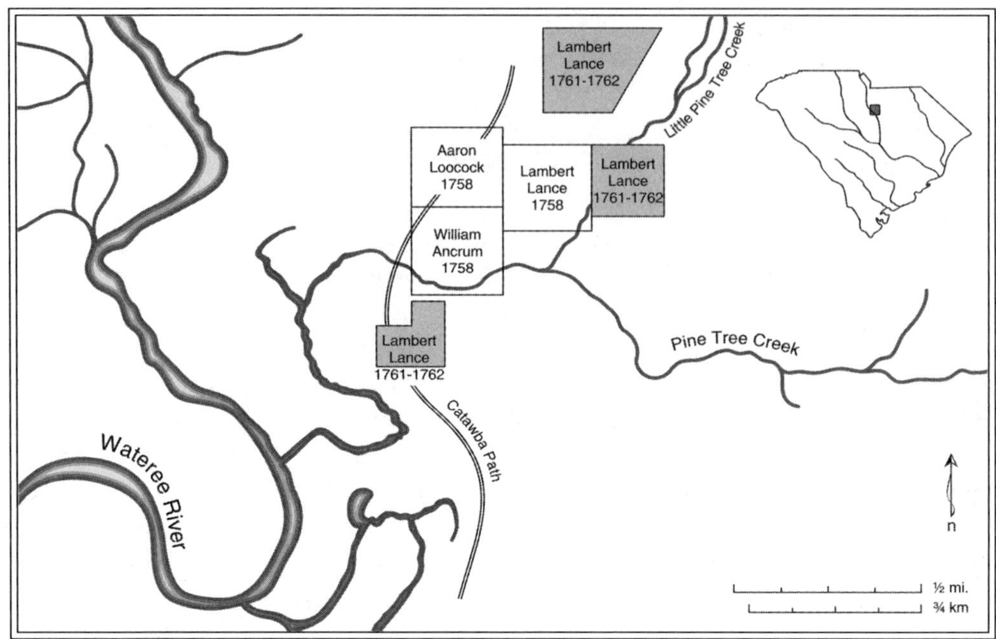

6.5 Additional tracts (shaded) acquired by Lambert Lance at Pine Tree Hill in 1761–1762. Author's original map.

in a part of Britain heavily dependent on water power for its textile industry made him aware of natural conditions favorable to mill placement, and he used his knowledge to select properties strategic to milling operations at Pine Tree Hill. In 1762 Lambert Lance acquired a grant for land on Little Pine Tree Creek adjacent to his previous holding and another parcel just north of Samuel Wyly's property. His third tract lay farther down Pine Tree Creek, just south of Ancrum's original Pine Tree Hill holding and just east of Robert Milhous's mill (Fig. 6.5).[35]

Kershaw also expanded his holdings dramatically during the early 1760s (Fig. 6.6). Through purchase, he gained ownership of two large tracts granted to John Black and William Gray. Their six hundred acres gave Kershaw control over the mouth and lower portion of Pine Tree Creek as well as access to the Wateree.[36] At the same time he acquired four properties that contained important mill sites. These included Robert Milhous's gristmill on Pine Tree Creek and Samuel Wyly's grist- and sawmills on Little Pine Tree Creek. The Wyly mills were situated on a substantial 467-acre tract recently assembled by the Quaker entrepreneur. It encompassed the extensive pond that provided the mills' water reserve and extended west adjacent to the three parcels belonging to Lambert Lance. It also bordered the north end of Aaron Loocock's 1758 property along the Catawba Path and another tract recently granted to Kershaw near Little Pine Tree Creek.[37] Farther south, below Friend's Neck, Kershaw purchased John McConnell's tract, a long, narrow property that stretched inland from the Wateree along Town Creek. He also acquired a parcel, originally granted to William Guess, that contained an existing mill dam and pond.[38] These purchases placed

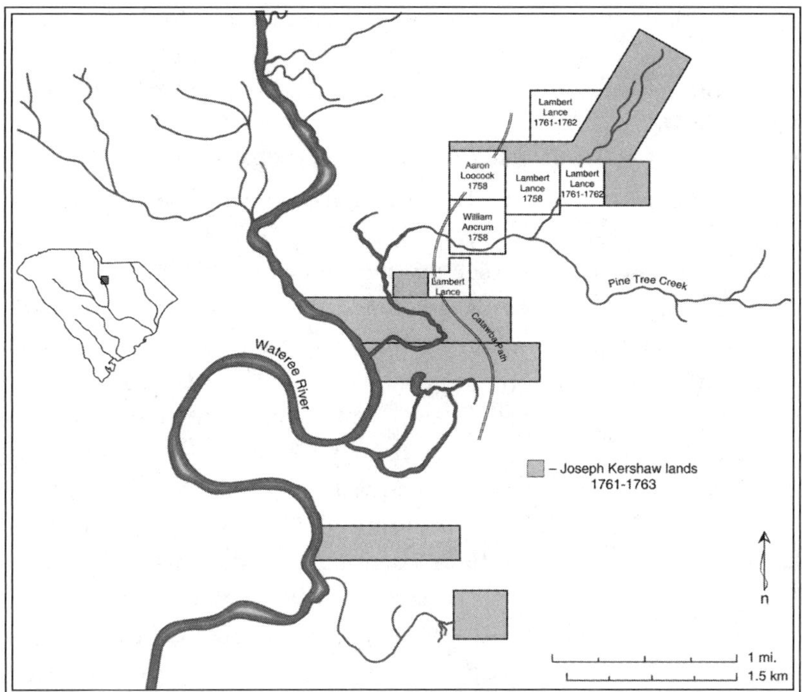

6.6 Tracts acquired by Joseph Kershaw at Pine Tree Hill and vicinity in 1761–1762. Author's original map.

Kershaw and the partners in a strategic position to corner flour production in the Wateree Valley. By 1763 they possessed three operating mills on Pine Tree Creek, and their ownership of its lower drainage offered additional waterpower opportunities for industrial growth. Potential mill sites on two other nearby streams also afforded openings for further expansion. Their holdings, which also encompassed the principal intersections of regional overland routes leading to both sides of the Wateree, provided Ancrum, Lance & Loocock with a base of operations on which to build production and trade in the backcountry.

The success of the Pine Tree Hill operation rested on the partners' ability to produce flour as a viable export commodity as soon as possible. As early as July 1760, less than two years after establishing the new store, Ancrum, Lance & Loocock advertised barrels of "fine Carolina flour, just arrived from Pine Tree Hill," for sale at the firm's Charleston store at prices comparable to those for flour imported from the North.[39] To accomplish this, the firm must have relied initially on existing mills to grind regional wheat. Joseph Kershaw likely worked out a cooperative agreement with Samuel Wyly, whose interest in developing the region had played such a crucial role in establishing the store. Wyly, who had recently enlarged his own operation to supply the Catawba trade, was eager to enter commercial production as a planter and would have seen cooperation with Kershaw as an opportunity to gain access to capital and resources useful in marketing his crops. The mill erected by Robert Milhous soon became available as well. The career of this man who had played such an important role in the Wateree Quaker community had been cut short by his unexpected death in 1755, and his heirs sold the greater part of the mill tract to William Farrell, an immigrant miller, three years later. Farrell subsequently joined or sold out to Kershaw, who soon acquired both properties to expand the partnership's milling operations at Pine Tree Hill.[40]

The alliance between Joseph Kershaw and Samuel Wyly sheds light on another aspect of export production in the backcountry—the transportation of bulk goods to and from the interior. Within two years of his arrival at Pine Tree Hill, Kershaw had apparently developed systematic overland trade between that location and Charleston by drawing on resident wagoners. As war with the Cherokees loomed in the late winter of 1760, Gov. William Henry Lyttelton made plans to mount another expedition against this powerful Indian nation. The anticipated line of march took the large force of regular troops and militia from Charleston through Moncks Corner, Eutaw, and the Congarees and required wagons to carry supplies and provisions. When advertising for contractors, the provincial government presumably favored those known to possess the resources to organize and coordinate long-distance transportation of goods and produce.[41] In designating Kershaw and Wyly as the agents for the Waterees, authorities recognized their demonstrated abilities as bulk traders as well as their central position as leaders in backcountry society.

Joseph Kershaw's role in trade led to his assuming a larger public role as a representative to South Carolina's aboriginal neighbors on the Wateree. Soon after his arrival, he cooperated with Samuel Wyly in several ventures among the Catawbas. In the spring of 1759 Kershaw became a supplier of provisions for the Indians and began carrying official correspondence to and from their settlements. The Catawbas' importance as provincial allies increased as the colony's relations with the Cherokees deteriorated in the late 1750s, and Kershaw assumed a greater share of Wyly's duties as government agent to these Native people. His importance as an intermediary grew in subsequent years and paralleled his emerging ascendance in the changing regional economy.[42]

Several factors influenced Joseph Kershaw's remarkable rise of as a principal figure in the South Carolina interior. Certainly his position as agent for the Charleston firm whose material wherewithal established a viable commercial enterprise in the backcountry was important. But alone it cannot explain how he reorganized the insular elements of a regional economy into a system that grew the substantial surplus of agricultural commodities that he then collected, processed, stored, and later transported over long distances to urban markets. It is noteworthy that he accomplished all these things in the absence of the formal institutions that usually structure economic change. In order to integrate this marginal society into the larger Atlantic economy of British North America, Kershaw and his associates had to overcome the perceptions that accompanied the rise of the ritual economy of the frontier, with its emphasis on obligations between households, limited production, and restricted social and economic ties with the outside world. Developing commercial trade required strategies to create new institutions capable of organizing social and economic interaction among backcountry residents. The strategies Joseph Kershaw employed to accomplish this help explain not only how he became a central figure in the rise of Pine Tree Hill but also why the settlement came to play a critical role of in the development of the backcountry.

Strategies for Economic Change in the Backcountry

Merchants who wish to conduct long-distance trade in the absence of formal economic institutions must develop alternate means to create and maintain cooperation among the parties involved. Such arrangements serve to overcome difficulties encountered as the scale of exchange is enlarged and the number of people engaged increases, even while the tempo of exchange remains discontinuous or episodic and information is often lacking among participants. Those involved in the long-distance trade of commercial agricultural commodities must minimize production and transaction costs in an economy characterized by specialization and division of labor, tasks that require cooperative arrangements that define and enforce exchange agreements among those involved in trade. These regulatory agreements benefit cooperating participants by controlling the production and transaction costs per exchange and increasing the potential level of gain through trade. The task of organizing long-distance trade and the new institutions that grow out of it is both political and economic in nature and must be understood in a context that includes both aspects of behavior.[43]

Establishment of a commercial economy in the South Carolina backcountry depended on an infrastructure to support production and trade, and the process that created it was tied inexorably to the development of this region. This development may be best examined through the perspective of political economy, a concept that recognizes the link between trade and the political milieu in which it occurs. It also acknowledges the context in which change occurs by emphasizing the connection between the circumstances distinct to the colonial region and those imposed by the larger world economy in which it evolved.[44] Studies of political economy often focus on the development of capitalism and the transition of traditional economies to capitalist production within a colonial context. By recognizing the existence of noncapitalist modes of production and their participation in the world economy, such studies make it possible to explore the distinctive nature of regional economies and their relationship to the larger system and its impact on their development over time. This is particularly helpful in examining change in formerly isolated frontier economies because the transition to capitalism transforms the social and political structure of colonial regions.[45]

Although studies of infrastructure building often emphasize the economic structure of colonial society in its entirety, they do not ignore the influence of the individuals who constituted it or their role in its development. Because the behavior of individuals defines and maintains a society's organization, their interactions make them agents of change. Thus, human agency, rather than the structure of the society in which it occurs, may be seen to precipitate cultural change and transformation. Individual behavior is, of course, not random because it occurs within structured contexts that are the products of past activity. The existing cultural structure influences present behavior and exerts pressures that set limits upon future conduct.[46] An awareness of the unity of structure and agency helps us observe and evaluate how individuals mold broader processes of change. Indigenous colonial institutions and the mechanisms by which they were generated reflected the actions of the individuals who brought them about, and agents like Joseph Kershaw are likely to have shaped the infrastructure of trade in the backcountry. Exploring the process by which institutions developed requires that we examine this phenomenon on the narrow scale on which individual agents operated. Although they acted within the structure of the frontier societies in which they lived, such individuals worked independently to integrate regional economies into that of the larger Atlantic world. Consequently, their actions heavily influenced the form of the resulting institutions.[47]

The substantial role of individuals made the development of frontier institutions inherently political and dynamic. This was especially so in British North America. Here entrepreneurs emerged from the milieu of societies characterized by inequality and hierarchical organization but whose increasingly capitalist orientation promoted flexibility and encouraged competition to achieve success. Individuals variously pursued wealth, status, or power within the wider norms of society by modifying existing institutions and developing innovative solutions to fit the changing conditions they encountered. Coming from such a background, these colonial entrepreneurs were well prepared for the challenges encountered in regions where formal institutional development was weak and ineffectual but where the benefits for cornering undeveloped markets were potentially large and rewarding.[48] Possessing the background, skills, and aptitude for business in an unstructured political environment, a man like Joseph Kershaw was ideally suited to build an infrastructure of trade in the absence of a preexisting framework.

But how did such an enterprising person go about organizing commercial exchange in the backcountry? Comparative studies of institution building in the absence of an effective higher authority have identified and assessed the actions of key individuals operating within the context of their communities and discovered that institution creation depended on strategies that were political in nature. To examine the appearance of complex institutions that arose without any form of centralized control, we may turn to recent discussions of self-organizing, complex adaptive systems. Within such systems, individual actions often seem unpredictable when viewed by themselves but result in recognizable and strikingly predictable patterning at the level of the society in which they occur. The phenomenon, known as "emergence," refers to the appearance of systemwide behavior as a result of local interaction, emphasizing the importance of the behavior of the system as a whole rather than the causal forces at work on its individual elements. In the South Carolina backcountry, the emergence of institutions was a result of the incompletely documented particular actions of individuals like Kershaw and his associates. When viewed collectively, however, their behavior followed a logic that produced a discernible structure that reflected strategies promoting the expansion of production and trade. How did these strategies emerge?[49]

Social cooperation lies at the core of institution building, and the success of settlement in the backcountry depended on the ability of individual agents such as Kershaw to develop strategies to encourage collaboration between producers and merchants and to avoid the mutually destructive outcomes inherent in their competitive quest for economic gain. To avert conflict, agents had to develop strategies of cooperation that allowed all parties to benefit. Although they often came from diverse backgrounds, residents of the backcountry shared cultural norms widespread in the emerging capitalist societies of western Europe.

These norms guided the behavior of those engaged in business and worked to establish long-term systemic stability while resident merchants pursued individual goals. Competitive maneuvering within a common cultural milieu increased the potential for change and promoted the development of new social institutions with familiar forms, institutions that emerged from the bottom up as a result of feedback between the actors and their social and natural environments.[50]

Joseph Kershaw's efforts to establish commercial agricultural production in the backcountry and to develop regular export trade with coastal mercantile interests accompanied his desire to acquire the wealth and prestige associated with success among merchants, a condition that might open the door to other forms of investment in the expanding colonial economy. To achieve his goals, Kershaw had to develop a cooperative strategy that permitted him to gain access to and to take advantage of the resources necessary to create a viable economy in a relatively isolated region characterized by limited production, low population density, and a poorly developed system of transportation and communications. Such a strategy was political in nature because it employed social power, that is, the capacity to control and manage the labor and activities of others to gain access to their benefits. Because economic strength was the medium through which to achieve power, this strategy involved controlling access to the most valuable economic resources. Although natural resources, such as land, were abundant in the backcountry, they remained largely undeveloped. Only when land occupied a strategic position relative to production or trade did it become a valuable economic resource. In a sparsely populated region, labor was a far more valuable commodity, and political success depended more heavily on strategies that linked people than on those that connected them to productive resources.

Several scholars have identified these as network strategies. Such strategies define relationships through marriage, trade partnerships, and alliances and result in broad systems of exchange that bind leaders and followers in networks of mutual support and competition. These relationships are personal but highly fluid in nature. The flexibility of network strategies has helped them play an important role historically in emerging heterarchical political organizations in nonstate societies that lack formal institutional structures. As opposed to hierarchical organizations, whose elements are subordinate to others and may be ranked, those in a heterarchical organization are unranked or possess the potential of being ranked in a number of different ways. There is no single permanent uppermost position. Network relationships build on the ties found in ritual economies and hold the potential to extend them to incorporate a greater number and variety of individuals over a wide area. Societies that are attempting to construct complex political institutions in the absence of existing central structures have often employed network strategies. Their use was particularly well suited to conditions encountered during the transitional period in the South Carolina backcountry.[51]

Joseph Kershaw relied on a network strategy to form a cooperative system that helped organize commercial exchange to transform the regional pioneer economy in the backcountry. Here human agency became the catalyst for creating a system of linkages between key components in the region, ties that coordinated the collection, processing, and transportation of produce and promoted the rise of social complexity. To accomplish this, Kershaw relied on his knowledge of the technical and organizational aspects of production and trade, his understanding of the nature of a frontier economy and the elements central to its operation, and his ability to develop means of manipulating them to his ends. During the years immediately following his arrival at Pine Tree Hill in 1758, he successfully began consolidating land holdings to establish a base that controlled processing sites and access to routes of internal and external trade. He facilitated this process through his own personal acquisitions as well as those of his employer, Ancrum, Lance & Loocock, and the apparent cooperation of the resident entrepreneur Samuel Wyly. To be financially successful, the operation depended on generating a high and consistent volume of trade, but the possession of the means to process, store, and transport produce did not by itself guarantee this end. Building a viable commercial enterprise at Pine Tree Hill required an effective structure within which to conduct exchange. In the absence of established institutions of trade, Kershaw had to create ties with elements of the rural communities of the Wateree Valley and beyond. The expansion of production and trade in the backcountry depended on his ability to forge a network of social links that extended beyond the immediate area of the store to incorporate the region's diverse inhabitants.

Shaping an Organization for Trade: The Catawba Connection

The initial success of the Pine Tree store was the result largely of Joseph Kershaw's incorporation of existing systems of regional trade acquired through the partners' purchase of existing mills and marked the first step in creating an economic network in the backcountry. By aligning himself with Samuel Wyly, Kershaw gained access not only to key elements of the processing infrastructure but also to local producers who used his facilities. As provincial agent and provisioner for the Catawba Nation, Wyly was involved in the acquisition, processing, and storage of foodstuffs and other provisions to supply these Native allies of the province, a task that also resulted in his building a network of suppliers. In addition, his position as deputy surveyor made him familiar with the land and inhabitants of the Wateree Valley, knowledge crucial to a merchant seeking agricultural produce for market. Wyly had also become a substantial landowner and planter who would have benefited from an expanded market for grain and who must have seen the new trading venture as providing entrée to commercial agriculture. At any rate, his association with Kershaw was profitable to both men in many ways and became the centerpiece of commercial trade in the central backcountry.

When the political situation on the frontier became unstable in 1759, the Catawbas' close relationship with Samuel Wyly drew them toward the new settlements in the Wateree Valley. Although the Seven Years' War initially spared South Carolina, growing animosity between English colonists and Cherokees in the western backcountry soon spilled over into open hostilities. Gov. William Lyttelton's mishandled negotiations with them, followed by his ineffectual expedition against the Cherokees in the fall of that year, led to an outbreak of widespread violence across the backcountry. With the exception of those gathered at fortified Ninety Six and isolated stockaded farms, colonists abandoned the country as far south as Orangeburg. Early in the new year provincial authorities attempted to wrest control of the frontier and hastily stockpiled supplies at the Congarees, Orangeburg, and Pine Tree Hill, but the defeat of a force of regular British troops in the summer of 1760 left colonial settlement in South Carolina's interior in jeopardy for another year.[52] A new expedition of regular troops under Lt. Col. James Grant and provincials commanded by Henry Laurens finally achieved success in 1761, defeating the Cherokees and laying waste to their towns. Facing an additional threat from Virginians and their Native allies to the north, the Cherokees sued for peace in the summer of that year. The outcome of the war weakened this powerful Indian nation but did not destroy it, and the Cherokees continued to occupy a strategic position on the frontier. Nevertheless, the pacification of the interior secured the country for European settlement, and this had clear implications for the future role of the Catawbas in the changing colonial world.[53]

South Carolina's war with the Cherokees brought their Catawba allies into conflict with a traditional enemy and drew them closer to the colony. In the spring of 1760, Gov. Lyttelton commissioned Wyly and Kershaw to engage the Catawbas to serve as couriers to isolated outposts in the Cherokee country and warriors in upcoming campaigns. In turn, the province supplied guns, blankets, clothing, and provisions for fifty warriors, including their leader, Hagler, who accompanied expeditions against the Cherokees.[54] Weakened by the recent smallpox epidemic, the Catawbas felt at risk on their traditional lands and sought the greater security of the British settlements. They pressed the governor to construct a fort to protect their families but in the meantime moved closer to Pine Tree Hill.[55] In July Superintendent of Indian Affairs Edmund Atkin, hoping to maintain the friendship of the colony's Indian allies, met with their representatives to conclude the Treaty of Pine Tree Hill. In exchange for earlier land claims, the Catawbas accepted a fifteen-mile square tract farther upriver at the confluence of Twelve Mile Creek and the Catawba River, where a fort would be constructed. South Carolina's success in the Cherokee War ensured physical security for the Catawbas, and legalizing ownership of their estate drew them toward the colonial economy, a role that soon enmeshed them in Kershaw's trading network at Pine Tree Hill.[56]

Perhaps the most dramatic consequence of the Catawbas' new situation was their involvement in the emerging regional economy of the Wateree Valley. As a people whose traditional subsistence base was virtually destroyed by the impact of European colonization and whose numbers were diminished by endemic warfare and disease, their survival became increasingly dependent on the newcomers who were now their neighbors. Still reeling from the impact of these calamities, Catawba survivors regrouped in the vicinity of Pine Tree Hill in 1760 and remained there for two years.[57] During that time they interacted intensively with neighboring settlers through trade, supplying Native-made products in exchange for supplies and finished goods. Although the Catawbas had long been trading partners with Europeans, the diminished availability of deerskins and other traditional forest products obliged the Indians to turn to other forms of merchandise for exchange. Such goods had to be not only within the Catawbas' technological capability but also in high demand in pioneer households.

Ceramics became the Catawbas' principal item in the trade with Europeans. Catawba women had a long tradition of producing fine wares and continued to make them throughout this period of crisis. This aspect of Catawba culture remained intact and ensured their economic viability despite the disruption of the traditional activities on which trade had depended. Archaeological evidence from settlement sites along the upper Wateree River testifies to the survival of ceramic manufacturing and to a remarkable change in both the scale of ceramic production and the form of the pottery itself (Fig. 6.7). Recent investigations at the site of Old Town, a settlement farther upriver to which the Catawbas returned in 1762, uncovered a large collection of ceramics that reveal that Catawba potters abandoned older traditional Lamar styles, characterized by decorated surfaces and traditional vessel forms, and replaced them with fine-bodied, temperless wares with plain, burnished, or polished surfaces. These new ceramics, called River Burnished wares by archaeologists, differed also in that vessels were now often made in the form of English pans, cups, flat-bottomed bowls, and plates, some of which were slipped or had painted designs. Many of the bowls and cups rested on footrings or pedestal bases similar to those found on European wares. Catawba ceramics changed dramatically within only a few years. [58]

The Catawbas' choice of this item for exchange was undoubtedly influenced by the demand for ceramics on the frontier. Like many other imported manufacture goods, ceramics were often in short supply in British America, and residents of more isolated interior regions often relied upon Native potters, who supplied wares used for cooking and eating. These were usually members of groups that, like the Catawbas, had been overrun by rapid European expansion and suffered significant economic impoverishment and cultural disorganization. Unlike more powerful inland groups, such as the Cherokees, whose physical separation gave them a flexibility that allowed them to maintain social and cultural continuity, the Catawbas' loss of their traditional means of subsistence made them dependent on the newcomers. One way of adapting to the new circumstances was to participate in the regional economy of the frontier by exchanging Native-made goods such as pottery.[59]

The Pine Tree Hill settlement lay close to the relocated Catawba village of 1760 and was ideally placed to participate in exchange with these Native people. Analysis of archaeological remains from foundations, construction pits, trash deposits, and other sealed features at the sites of early buildings attests to the extensive use of River Burnished ceramics. Catawba wares constituted more than 10 percent of the ceramics used by occupants of the two earthfast structures in the early years of their use, indicating a dependence on aboriginal ceramics to supplement those imported from Britain in the 1760s. The appearance of River Burnished wares at the store and its associated building may testify to the presence of laborers who lacked the means to acquire more expensive European wares. Vessel fragments appear to be pieces of bowls and globular jars that could have been used in specialized tasks like cooking but may well have seen use for storage, processing, and other domestic activities as well. The presence of River Burnished wares as a minority ceramic type in later archaeological contexts at Pine Tree Hill demonstrates the Catawbas' continued participation in the colonial economy on the Wateree after their removal in 1762. Ceramics had become a staple item of trade and would remain so well into the nineteenth century.[60]

Although the Wateree Valley's frontier settlements escaped the devastation the Cherokee War brought to western South Carolina, it nevertheless impacted the lives of their residents. On several occasions Cherokee war parties attacked isolated homesteads and killed or captured settlers living upriver from Pine Tree Hill. Reports of assaults on colonists at Fishing Creek and Hanging Rock, as well as the murders of others in the Waxhaws, including the family of a wagoner passing through Pine Tree Hill on his way to Charleston,

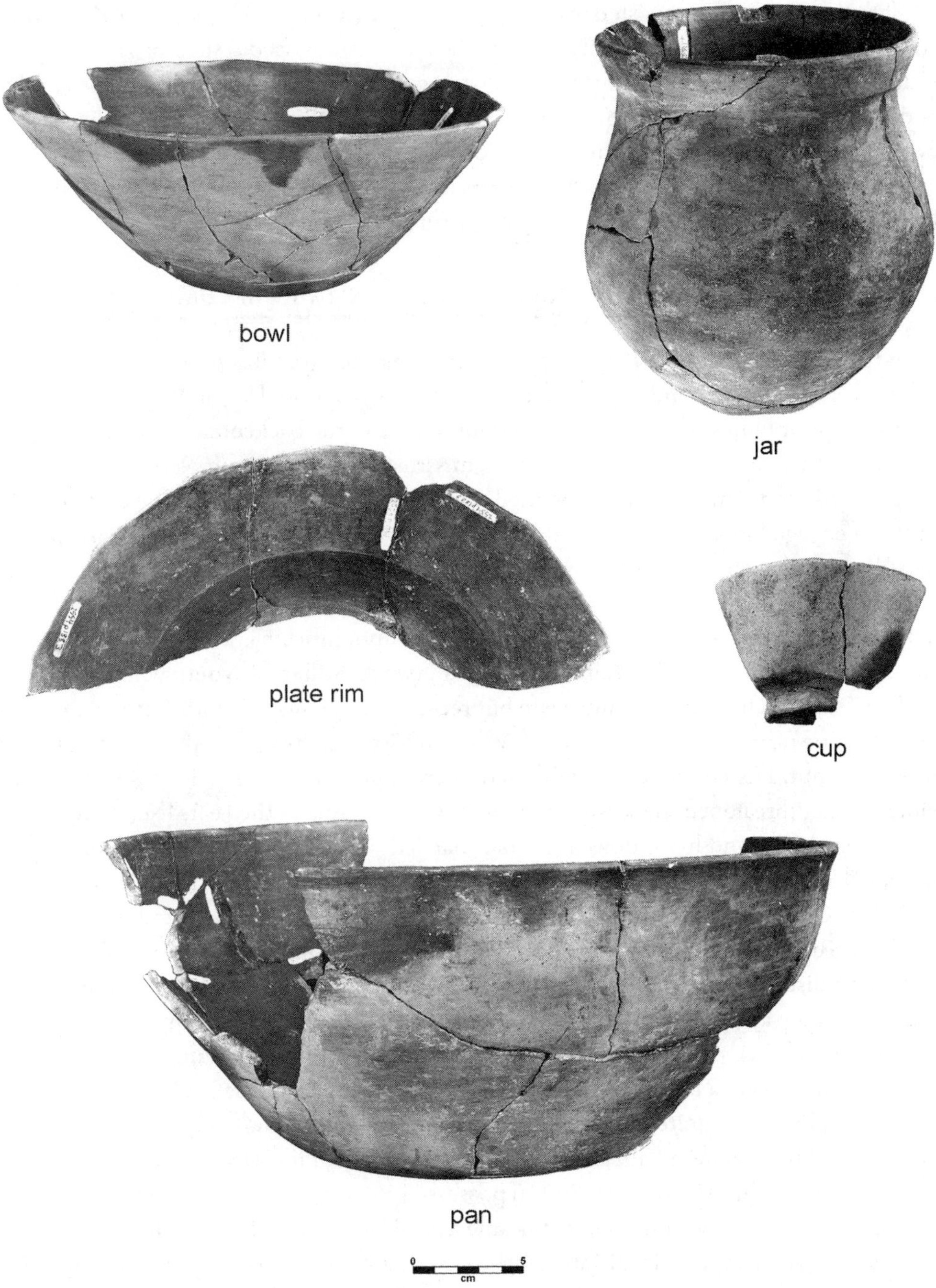

6.7 Catawba ceramics collected in archaeological excavations in York County, South Carolina. These fragments represent several types of vessels that parallel European forms. Courtesy of the South Carolina Department of Transportation and the Research Laboratories of Archaeology, University of North Carolina, Chapel Hill.

attest to the danger that persisted in the region. But the river formed a barrier that provided colonists some measure of security from western incursions, as did their proximity to the Catawbas, who were always eager to retaliate against their old enemies. The peace that ended the Cherokee War in 1761 generally terminated hostilities in South Carolina. However, the continuing colonial war brought occasional raids by northern Indians as late as 1763 and resulted in the deaths of Europeans as well as Catawbas, including Hagler, who had served so ably as their leader during those turbulent times.[61]

Shaping an Organization for Trade: A Network of Contacts

In spite of the disruptions that accompanied the Cherokee War, Joseph Kershaw expanded his network of contacts and formed critical alliances with several key individuals who provided important links to the immigrant communities in the backcountry. In a colonial society riven by ethnic and religious diversity, mistrust, and, often, animosity, the success of a regionwide economic venture depended on a strategy that encouraged the participation of those engaged in agricultural production. Kershaw created ties of association, kinship, and marriage that crosscut social divisions to establish relationships to serve as the basis for commercial growth.

John Chesnut entered Kershaw's sphere as an apprentice clerk at the Pine Tree Hill store and soon became a key individual in his network. Still in his youth when he arrived at Pine Tree Hill, he and his family were but recent immigrants to South Carolina. He was born on June 18, 1743, in the Shenandoah Valley of Virginia, the son of Alexander and Mary Ross Chesnut. His father, a surveyor, died in 1749, perhaps as a result of the increasing violence that threatened the western settlements of Virginia in the years leading up to the Seven Years' War, and his widowed mother married Jasper Sutton. The British disaster of Braddock's Defeat brought the dangers of the conflict closer in 1755 and prompted Jasper and Mary Chesnut Sutton and her three children to abandon their four-hundred-acre frontier farm. They retired first to Winchester, Virginia, and then moved south to Phifer's Creek, between Salisbury and Charlotte, North Carolina, and finally resettled in the Wateree Valley, where they acquired land in the vicinity of Fredericksburg Township.[62] In May 1762 Jasper Sutton received a grant for a hundred-acre tract he and his family had settled on Gum Swamp Creek, a branch of Sanders Creek. It was the first of seven holdings, totaling 1,500 acres, that he acquired in the vicinity of Sanders and Grannys Quarter Creeks. The parcel lay on the Catawba Path about seven miles north of Pine Tree Hill at a point where the road crossed this watercourse. Sutton possessed a strategic location for a public facility, and the tavern he erected on his farm became a local landmark.[63] Here as elsewhere on the frontier, taverns served as local gathering spots for area residents, and establishing a link with the family that owned such a facility extended Joseph Kershaw's social network to the pioneer settlements north of Pine Tree Hill.

John Chesnut proved to be a very capable apprentice and soon became a valuable asset to the company. His success and rapid advancement was mutually beneficial in that it provided him with a solid career and Kershaw with a trustworthy associate to help administer a rapidly expanding frontier enterprise operating with minimal outside assistance and lacking immediate oversight. Managing the collection, processing, and shipment of produce, be it flour or deerskins, required constant supervision. Having an additional set of skilled eyes and hands to troubleshoot milling, keep track of merchandise, arrange transportation, and preside over the books would certainly have made life less hectic for Ancrum, Lance & Loocock's agent at the Waterees and provided time for him to tend to business expansion. John Chesnut became a useful and necessary member of the Pine Tree Hill store operation, a role that tied his fate to that of the enterprise and those associated with it.

John Chesnut's presence at the store also had broader implications for the company. Like many newer immigrants to the region, he and his family were Presbyterians, an evangelical sect whose members formed a substantial portion of the backcountry's European population. Chesnut's family came as part of a great influx of new settlers migrating south along overland routes from North Carolina, Virginia, Pennsylvania, and Maryland. The newcomers concentrated their settlement above Pine Tree Hill and dominated the Waxhaws region.[64] Religion united the Scots-Irish Presbyterians, who soon formed organized churches. Responding to a call to the Waxhaws, the Rev. William Richardson relocated there in 1759 and before 1763 began an itinerancy that organized several congregations, including one at Fishing Creek on the Wateree. His success drew other Presbyterian ministers to the interior, and the number of churches rose steadily over the subsequent decade. A common religion bound immigrant households, reinforced ties of kinship and family, and played a key role in fostering social cohesion among neighbors on a frontier still lacking other formal integrating institutions.[65] Churches also helped define the bounds of the newly formed rural communities that formed the basis for agricultural production and exchange. Just as the Quaker meeting had helped support and organize the activities of early settlers on the Wateree, the Presbyterian congregations of the Waxhaws played a central role in sustaining their members upriver. Their participation was crucial to establishing commercial trade in the region, and Joseph Kershaw endeavored to include them in his network.

As an Anglican in a world dominated by dissenters and rent by religious factionalism, Joseph Kershaw found it particularly important to allay evangelicals' distrust of one who did not share their faith. Opposition to the established Church of England had many sources but generally grew out of conflicting belief systems. The tenets of evangelical religion that stressed conversion through rebirth, an individualistic and active participation in religious activities, and a reliance on the Bible as the ultimate authority conflicted with what its members saw as a conservative Church that relied on prescribed ritual ceremonialism rather than a conversion experience or submission to an ascetic discipline. In their minds, evangelical religion that promoted social activism and attention to the needs of their members contrasted sharply with an established Church that supported the status quo and seemed to show little concern for the needs of frontier residents. Perceiving the Church of England as dangerously complacent, they turned against its representatives in the backcountry.[66] Expanding business in the upper Wateree Valley required winning the trust of religious dissidents who resided there.

Joseph Kershaw's choice of John Chesnut as a responsible partner in the Pine Tree store gave him an important ally among a community of farmers whose cooperation was necessary. Charles Woodmason, the former merchant who returned to the backcountry in the 1760s as an Anglican itinerant, was well aware of the efficacy of this strategy. Woodmason recognized Chesnut's value to the enterprise even though he detested the Presbyterians who actively opposed his missionary efforts and despised Chesnut in particular. Perhaps musing on his earlier decision to decline the offer to operate the Wateree store, Woodmason gave Kershaw credit for having "faith and charity . . . much larger than I should have displayed had I settled at Pine Tree. For I hardly should have had that faith or that confidence in a poor beggar's brat or a herd of vile Presbyterians." But he also acknowledged the politically important role of the young employee, whom he envisioned to be "a spy on the Presbyterians, [who could] penetrate their secrets [and] attach them to Mr. K's interest, . . . and keep them steady to the plan chalked out by Mr. K."[67] The extent to which John Chesnut eavesdropped on the activities of his coreligionists may never be known, but he was almost certainly an important link to the Presbyterian community farther upriver, and his value as an emissary of the Pine Tree store cannot be underestimated.

The strong kin ties prevalent among the tightly knit Presbyterian colonists provided Kershaw with another key member of his business operation. Maintaining reliable and regular transportation among Pine Tree Hill, Charleston, and other locations was crucial to export trade, and its management had to be carefully coordinated with other store activities. By choosing John's younger brother James Chesnut as his chief wagon driver, Joseph Kershaw understood that James's loyalty to a family already enmeshed in his business would provide a trustworthy employee to supervise this important link to market. Placing a Chesnut kinsman in this role provided additional security for goods and produce en route to the store and must have eased Kershaw's mind regarding their safe arrival.[68]

In addition to his close association with Samuel Wyly, Joseph Kershaw extended his network to include others in the Quaker community near Pine Tree Hill. Among them was Zebulon Gaunt, a carpenter whose experience with milling made him a valuable asset to the company. Gaunt immigrated to the backcountry in 1762 and settled on two tracts on the Wateree sold to him by Kershaw the following year. These lay on the west side of the river just upriver from Wright's Ferry. Gaunt apparently came into Kershaw's employ about this time and over the next two decades managed his saw mills on Pine Tree Creek. His relative, millwright Nebo Gaunt, was also involved in Kershaw's enterprises. Zebulon Gaunt acquired another tract adjacent to Kershaw's and later operated the ferry that crossed the Wateree near the mouth of Pine Tree Creek to link the Fredericksburg settlements with those west of the river. Kershaw's ties to the Gaunts provided the expertise to build and maintain a viable milling operation at Pine Tree Hill, and provided access to a crucial regional transportation link in the Waterees.[69]

Joseph Kershaw's most personal link to the Quaker community came through his marriage to Sarah Mathis, the daughter of Daniel and Sophia Mathis, who settled 150 acres on Grannys Quarter Creek granted him in 1763. Like the Suttons' property on Gum Swamp Creek, this tract occupied a strategic position where the Catawba Path crossed a major watercourse north of Pine Tree Hill. Here the Mathises also maintained a tavern.[70] Although not large landowners, the Mathis family's public facility on a major interior artery leading to the settlements farther upriver gave Kershaw an additional opportunity to extend his network to producers below the Waxhaws. Marriage to Sarah Mathis increased the size of Kershaw's affinal family to include her three siblings, including her younger brother Samuel, who subsequently played a significant role in her husband's mercantile activities.[71]

The Moravian Connection in North Carolina

Founded as a planned, theocratic community of believers in the North Carolina interior in 1753, the Moravian settlements constituted a distinctive presence on the southern frontier. The Wachovia colony developed around the nucleated settlement of Bethabara, which became the focus of this centrally directed immigrant community. Bethabara contained Wachovia's principal religious, political, and economic institutions and was home to the administrators who governed the colony and represented its residents in the legislature. Here too resided the craftsmen and merchants whose activities generated profits to support the colony. Although the Moravian community strove to retain its spiritual and social separateness, from the beginning its residents interacted with outsiders in the region.[72] Indeed, Moravian leaders recognized that economic ties with the wider world were necessary to pay the costs of supporting the colony. The grist- and sawmills at Bethabara soon made it a regional center for flour and lumber production, and its store drew customers in need of manufactured goods. Craft specialists, including a doctor, a tailor, a tanner, a shoemaker, and a baker, as well as blacksmiths, carpenters, and others contributed to the community's income. The addition of a pottery in 1756 introduced the manufacture of a commodity with a potentially wide market in the backcountry.[73]

Just as the Catawba wares filled a need for ceramics in backcountry households, Moravian pottery found a ready market among frontier residents. Under the skilled management of Gottfried Aust, the Bethabara pottery turned out a substantial number of diverse products. Archaeological excavations at the site of his kilns uncovered a wide variety of often specialized wares used for the storage and preparation of food, as well as for eating, drinking, and other activities. They included fine tea wares, tobacco pipes, lamps, candleholders, and kiln furniture. Following an eastern European stylistic tradition, Aust's earthenwares were decorated with elaborate, colorful slipped designs and glazed.[74] The Moravian pottery were in widespread and constant demand among the residents of the Carolinas, drawing customers to the Bethabara store from as far away as the Wautauga settlements in present-day Tennessee.[75]

The Wachovia colony's desire to enter the larger Atlantic economy encouraged home production and extended the trade in ceramics into South Carolina. This development was the result in large part of the efforts of Henry Laurens, whose 1761 visit as a militia commander had made him aware of the potential business opportunities of trade. Although other ports were closer, none offered the variety of goods available in Charleston at comparable prices, and its merchants also paid higher prices for backcountry products. By 1762 South Carolina's entrepôt had become the Moravians' principal market. Wagon loads of deerskins, beaver pelts, tallow, butter, pottery, and medicinal herbs regularly traveled from Bethabara to Charleston by way of the Catawba Path, which passed through Pine Tree Hill.[76] The settlement's proximity to the principal overland route and the presence of Ancrum, Lance & Loocock's store fostered a secondary market for Moravian ceramics. During the 1760s, shipments of pottery from Bethabara arrived at the Pine Tree Hill store as well as at other destinations in the backcountry, and evidence of their use by residents is provided by the fragments of these wares recovered from archaeological deposits there.[77]

A Store at Pine Tree Hill

By the close of 1763 Ancrum, Lance & Loocock's Pine Tree Hill venture was firmly established. The partners and their agent had acquired land, set up processing facilities and recruited the people to manage them, developed long-distance transportation, and created an infrastructure of trade based on a network that linked the frontier store with producers in the region. Although dependent on the capital resources provided by the partners, the success of the store relied on the efforts of their agent, Joseph Kershaw, to develop a framework for trade in a region characterized by limited production and local exchange. To accomplish this, he employed a network strategy through which he extended social ties to the various elements of the rural pioneer population. Links with the early Quaker settlers at Pine Tree Hill and the communities of more recently arrived Presbyterian immigrants upriver helped him solicit the cooperation needed to acquire the surplus crops upon which export trade depended. Soon produce from pioneer farms began to flow southward to Pine Tree Hill. Six years after the store's founding, the Wateree Valley seemed poised to enter the commercial economy of the Atlantic seaboard.

Nowhere was the success of this endeavor more apparent than at its backcountry focus, the Pine Tree store. The sites of the two earthfast buildings on the Catawba Path have yielded artifacts that provide evidence of the extent to which the region had begun to participate in the larger Atlantic economy. Although their builders relied largely on available construction materials, they also made use of imported window glass, locks, fittings, nails, spikes, hinges, pintles, and other architectural hardware. Miscellaneous finished items, ranging from furniture fittings and music box parts to thimbles, dinnerware, and firearms, reveal the range of imported merchandise that passed through the store. Early deposits also provide direct evidence of trade. The excavated bale seals and barrel bands once enclosed sacks of merchandise and containers of goods destined for Pine Tree Hill or other points. Certainly backcountry flour was barreled and stored here prior to shipment.[78]

Ceramics accounted for a substantial portion of the imports at Pine Tree Hill, and the increasing volume of trade here corresponded with a revolution in the British pottery industry. By 1760 the production of traditional ceramics for expanding markets at home and abroad had resulted in a half-century of rapid growth, a phenomenon that brought great changes in the pottery's appearance and production. English potters experimented with innovative techniques and began to introduce molded cream-colored earthenwares that were highly fired, thin, and durable. These attractive ceramics satisfied the increasing demand for fine tablewares and were produced by factories in substantial quantities. Systematically developed, made in great quantity, and cleverly marketed by Josiah Wedgwood and others in the 1760s, creamwares rapidly supplanted the earlier ceramic types exported to British America and soon dominated the ceramic assemblages found on the sites of British colonial settlements everywhere.[79] Early sealed deposits at the Pine Tree Hill store contain small numbers of slipped earthenwares, salt-glazed stonewares, delftwares, and other earlier British ceramics, but creamwares dominate the contents of the larger archaeological assemblages from the 1760s and testify to the expansion of trade that occurred at the time of this ceramic revolution.[80]

The Pine Tree Hill store became a focus for trade in the backcountry. In the first few years of operation, it served as a collection point for locally milled grain as well as for deerskins and other frontier produce destined for coastal markets. Profits generated by its exports generated capital to expand operations and provided pioneer residents with credit to acquire imported finished goods, creating demand that broadened the market for them in the Wateree Valley. Supplying an expanding immigrant population offered an opportunity for the partners to increase their commercial success if they could find a way to enlarge the volume of business. Doing so involved more than increasing the flow of goods; expansion demanded that the company modify its operations to accommodate distribution on a broader geographical scale and at a greater level of complexity. This required changes in its organization. The system had begun to outgrow the capabilities of an initial framework that gave managerial control to the absentee partners in Charleston and left a single field agent in charge of implementing its actual operations. Joseph Kershaw's success in organizing and expanding the backcountry enterprise led the partners to grant him a greater role in its management. By 1763 newspaper advertisements recognized his ascendancy in the company by referring to the Pine Tree Hill store operation as Joseph Kershaw & Company to distinguish its operation from that of Ancrum, Lance & Loocock's Charleston establishment.[81] This change mirrored the need for a more extensive reorganization to accommodate growth. In order to maintain its integrity, the enterprise had to overcome the centrifugal tendency generated by its success. Expanding its network to acquire and manage trade on a much broader scale required a restructuring of the company to better integrate its loosely organized elements in a more formal arrangement. It needed to become a corporation.

Chapter 7

"Kershaw & Co's Store, . . . Where All Sorts of Produce Are Sold"

Consolidating Commercial Trade in the Backcountry

In mid-February 1770 the arrival of a packet boat from England carried long-awaited news that South Carolina's backcountry was finally to be incorporated within the political structure of the province. Among the incoming official correspondence was the royal confirmation of a legislative act to establish six judicial districts that encompassed the interior in a single administrative system. The new courts and jails, together with their associated officials, created a formal institution that dispersed legal authority heretofore concentrated in Charleston and provided a vehicle to implement governmental functions in the interior.[1] Although precipitated by a need for an authority to combat violent crime and provide order in the backcountry, the passage of the Circuit Court Act represented more than a response to individual attacks by banditti in the wilderness. Its infrastructure recognized the larger need to provide the stability necessary to develop commerce in the interior by creating a civil environment that protected agricultural producers, crafts people, merchants, and others whose business had become an integral part of the provincial economy.[2] The act was a formal recognition by the central government that the backcountry was no longer an isolated frontier.

The transition of the backcountry could not have taken place without the growing demand for grain that drew the region into the trade of the broader Atlantic world. In the early 1760s events in Europe dramatically expanded the overseas consumption of American grain, which before had seldom gone beyond the West Indies. A series of bad harvests in Great Britain brought acute shortages of provisions in Mediterranean countries, whose growing populations had become dependent on imported grain. Deficits in Spain, Portugal, and the Kingdom of Two Sicilies suddenly opened up a large new market for colonial wheat and flour. In response to a demand for breadstuffs from southern Europe, France, and even Great Britain, American grain production on newly settled lands, as well as in older farming regions, grew substantially during the following decade.[3] But exploiting this lucrative market required a considerable increase in the scale of production by farmers just emerging from the constraints of a regional economy.

By 1763 Ancrum, Lance & Loocock's Wateree venture had established a collection, processing, and transportation infrastructure capable of supporting wheat production in

South Carolina's interior. Employing a network strategy to incorporate nearby communities, Joseph Kershaw had begun constructing a broad economic and social network that linked them to the Pine Tree Hill store. The growth of wheat production in the Wateree Valley in the 1760s mirrored the widespread expansion of specialized grain farming across the backcountry of both Carolinas. This phenomenon brought urban functions to inland settlements, such as Cross Creek and Halifax in neighboring North Carolina. With the adoption of commercial agriculture, both grew as inland trading centers that linked the ports of Edenton and Wilmington, respectively, to producers in the interior.[4] Like Pine Tree Hill, both settlements drew trade from their expanding hinterlands and took on the role of central places. As components in the larger process that was transforming the southern backcountry, the evolution of these interior settlements reflects an alteration in economic strategies that permitted these frontier towns to encompass trade on a much broader scale. The organization of business at Pine Tree Hill was about to change.

The Partnership Evolves

Successful trade depended on effective communication between merchants and the producers and customers with whom they dealt. Ancrum, Lance & Loocock's hopes for commercial agriculture in the backcountry rested on the ability of their agent to develop and maintain regular working links with all the parties involved. But to expand business at Pine Tree Hill, the firm needed to effectively disseminate information and move goods over an even wider area. It accomplished this task by restructuring the firm to form a corporate group, one in which the individual members operated as representatives of the larger entity to which they brought expertise and resources. Such groups commonly arise to fulfill specialized functions in societies lacking central institutions and provide their members the autonomy, exclusivity, set procedures, and organization necessary to conduct business activities. Although they consist of multiple members, corporate groups present a united entity to the outside world.[5] How did such an organization benefit the expansion of the Pine Tree Hill venture?

Ancrum, Lance & Loocock and their resident agent formed an organization capable of extending and coordinating their activities over a hinterland extensive enough to make investment in an infrastructure worthwhile. A corporate trading concern offered advantages for broadening the scale of business in the backcountry. Like contemporary organizations in Europe, it drew strength from its size. Having a number of partners allowed the concern to reach a broader base of investors from whom to obtain sufficient capital to fund operations. Its external indivisibility combined the resources of its members, who shared the risks of business. In addition, it provided a formal organization whose members were bound by corporate decisions that regulated their activities and restricted the indebtedness they could incur. The partnership also provided operational flexibility in the sense that its collective interests could be represented by any of the individuals who constituted it.[6] As its agents, they might operate in Charleston or in Pine Tree Hill, the Waxhaws, or elsewhere in the backcountry where opportunities for business arose. A corporate group was useful in managing the pattern of growth established during the store's early years.

In January 1764 five individuals drew up a memorandum of agreement that forever altered the structure of trade in the South Carolina backcountry. Without dissolving the old concern, two of its original members, William Ancrum and Aaron Loocock, their former agent Joseph Kershaw, and two others formed a new partnership under Kershaw's leadership. The purpose of the organization was to create nothing less than a mercantile empire stretching from central South Carolina into its neighboring province to the north. The five members maintained equal interest as shareholders in a joint stock partnership that held land and goods collectively and conducted trade at several stores located at strategic sites in the interior. This cooperative venture was to exist for a period of ten years and four months, after which the holdings would be liquidated for the equal benefit of the partners.[7] The formation of this corporate group brought together a number of resources, the most important of which was the expertise of its new members. In selecting these partners, Ancrum and Loocock tapped individuals whose talents and experience promised the greatest success, leaving those with lesser abilities to the employ of smaller, less efficient concerns.[8] Remaining the dominant mercantile company in the backcountry was crucial as the region developed and drew additional traders and small storekeepers to compete for business. The firm's reorganization also shifted its management from Charleston to the backcountry. Although William Ancrum and Aaron Loocock remained in Charleston, the majority of the partners now resided in the interior, a move that recognized the importance of placing responsibility for decision making in the hands of those most familiar with local conditions.

Effective management of trade in a region undergoing transition required trustworthy and experienced leadership by those with a knowledge of the land and its inhabitants. Joseph Kershaw's choice as a new partner owed much to his previous five years' experience at Pine Tree Hill and his phenomenal success in developing the network on which the original venture in the Wateree Valley had come to depend. In recognition of his rising importance, the firm's Charleston office now conducted business under the name of Kershaw & Co. John Chesnut, whose talent and ambition had led him to become Kershaw's right hand, became the fourth partner. An important member of Joseph Kershaw's network, Chesnut brought his affiliation with the wider Scots-Irish Presbyterian community, which undoubtedly assisted in opening trade farther upriver.[9] Like his mentor's, John Chesnut's experience lay in organizing mercantile trade, and the firm's continued success in the backcountry depended on his expertise in managing the reorganized company In recognition of his wider role, the Pine Tree Hill store became Kershaw, Chesnut & Co., and the new business outlet upriver at Rocky Mount included his name as well.[10]

Joseph's brother Ely, a relative newcomer to the backcountry, became the fifth partner in the company. Born at the family's Yorkshire home in 1743, Ely was only five years old when his brother arrived in Charleston and must have come to South Carolina after Joseph was established as a merchant. Following in his older sibling's footsteps, Ely joined Joseph's household at Pine Tree Hill sometime before 1761. As an apprentice at the store, Ely apparently learned the business quickly, and his success as a merchant soon enhanced his social position in his adopted land. Three years later he was appointed tax inquirer and collector for St. Mark's Parish, an administrative unit encompassing the territory between the Pee Dee and Saluda Rivers.[11] Despite his initial association with the Rocky Mount store, Ely's role in the new partnership left him tied only tangentially with the settlements of the upper Wateree Valley. In the upcoming years he took on the much larger charge of opening trade with the residents of the Welsh Tract on the upper Pee Dee River at Cheraw Hill at a site to be called Chatham. Here, under the name of Ely Kershaw & Co., he extended business east beyond the borders of the province.[12]

As the partnership evolved, it reorganized its resources to underwrite the investment needed for a larger, more wide-ranging operation and shifted a significant portion of company management to operatives closer to sites of trade in the interior. The departure of Lambert Lance and the addition of new partners redistributed control of the firm's real assets among those who would manage it, and the manner in which this was carried out provides a picture of a business that has left very few other records. When Ancrum, Lance & Loocock and Joseph Kershaw formed the partnership of 1764, they consolidated their holdings of twenty-five tracts totaling 5,898 acres and divided the stock, consisting of sixteen shares, into equal portions of four shares each. Lambert Lance withdrew from the concern in August 1766, and William Ancrum and Aaron Loocock acquired his four shares "for certain considerations." Together they now owned six shares each, three-fourths of the firm's holdings. Joseph Kershaw possessed the remaining quarter (Table 7.1). In May of the following year the concern admitted two new partners, but not on an equal basis. The two additional members received a portion of only seventeen of the original twenty-five tracts. These seventeen parcels comprised 2,498 acres, or 42 percent of the total acreage owned. For the sum of £3,500 paid to both Ancrum and Loocock and £1,000 to Joseph Kershaw, Ely Kershaw and John Chesnut each acquired one-fifth interest in the seventeen tracts.[13] This gave each new partner control of less than 9 percent of the company's assets and made them, in effect, minor partners (Table 7.2).

Despite the uneven distribution of shares, the new partners nevertheless possessed considerable control over the company's most valuable assets. The seventeen tracts over which they together exercised a 40 percent interest contained the key components of the firm's infrastructure in the Wateree Valley. These included the Pine Tree Hill store as well as surrounding lands that controlled overland routes on both sides of the river. These communal lands also contained the valuable mill sites developed by Robert Milhous and Samuel Wyly along Pine Tree Creek, as well as sites for potential commercial development on the lower reaches of that watercourse. Although most of the seventeen properties were concentrated at Pine Tree Hill, possession of a twenty-acre parcel on the Congaree River gave the partnership control of Joyner's Ferry, near the fork of the Congaree and Wateree Rivers, a key link in the overland network route leading from the Congaree settlements to Charleston.[14] The tracts shared by the partners represented the developed portion of the company's real assets. The trade and processing activities carried out there generated profits that were the principal sources of investment revenue for maintaining and expanding the business. Although all of the partners held an interest in these core tracts and shared the income from these properties, the addition of the newer members reflected the firm's intent to expand by adding new properties to extend its business beyond the Wateree Valley.

Expanding Trade in the Backcountry: The Waxhaws

The partnership tied its economic future to the successful development of trade at Rocky Mount and the upper Pee Dee and placed the management of the new branch stores in the hands of the firm's newest members. Because their endeavors involved a corporate group,

Table 7.1. Tracts Constituting the 5,898 Acres of Land in the Possession of William Ancrum, Lambert Lance, Aaron Loocock, and Joseph Kershaw at the Time of the Redistribution in August 1766

350 acres on Pine Tree Creek granted to William Gray, Apr. 3, 1754, and purchased by Joseph Kershaw, April 29, 1761

100 acres on the fork of Pine Tree Creek granted to Joseph Kershaw, Dec. 5, 1761

100 acres at the Wateree River raft granted to Joseph Kershaw, Mar. 31, 1761

150 acres at Pine Tree Hill granted to Lambert Lance, June 4, 1759

100 acres at Pine Tree Hill granted to Lambert Lance, Dec. 5, 1761

100 acres at Twenty-Five Mile Creek granted to Lambert Lance, Mar. 31, 1761

150 acres at Pine Tree Hill granted to Aaron Loocock, June 4, 1759

150 acres at Pine Tree Hill granted to William Ancrum, Sept. 19, 1758

400 acres at Wateree Fork granted to Joseph Evans, Sept. 4, 1753 and purchased by Joseph Kershaw, Feb. 20, 1761

250 acres at Wateree Fork granted to Joseph Evans, Sept. 4, 1753 and purchased by Joseph Kershaw, Feb. 20, 1761

100 acres at Pine Bluff, Wateree granted to John Williams, Sept. 4, 1759

200 acres at Fredericksburgh Township granted to William Guess on May 15, 1751, and purchased by Joseph Kershaw, Aug. 1, 1763

50 acres at Pine Tree Mill granted to Robert Milhous on Mar. 14, 1757, and purchased by Joseph Kershaw, Jan. 25, 1762

20 acres, part of 400 acres called Joyner's Ferry, at the Congarees granted to Joseph Joyner on Apr. 3, 1761, and purchased by Joseph Kershaw, Mar. 1, 1761

497 acres at Little Pine Tree Mill, part of 650 acres granted to Samuel Wyly on Apr. 2, 1761, and purchased by Joseph Kershaw, Mar. 2, 1762

300 acres at Amelia Township granted to Thomas Winningham on Sept. 16, 1738, and purchased by Joseph Kershaw, Dec. 8, 1761

200 acres at the High Hills of Santee granted to William Harrison on July 4, 1759

50 acres at Twenty Five Mile Creek granted to Lambert Lance on Oct. 7, 1762

150 acres at Pine Tree Hill granted to Lambert Lance on Nov. 9, 1765

150 acres at Pine Tree Hill granted to Lambert Lance on Oct. 7, 1765

1,000 acres on Wateree Swamp granted to Ancrum, Lance, Loocock, and Joseph Kershaw on Oct. 20, 1763

1,000 acres on Wateree Swamp granted to Ancrum, Lance, Loocock, and Joseph Kershaw on Oct. 20, 1763

150 acres on Wateree Fork granted to Bryan Toland on Mar. 4, 1760, and purchased by Joseph Kershaw, Mar. 18, 1768

131 acres in Fredericksburgh Township granted to John Black on Oct. 4, 1749, and purchased by Joseph Kershaw, Jan. 28, 1762

50 acres at Wateree Fork granted to Lambert Lance on Oct. 25, 1764

5,898 acres total

Source: CBPR, Vol. F-3, 748.

Table 7.2. 17 Tracts Constituting 2,498 Acres of Land in the Possession of William Ancrum, Aaron Loocock, and Joseph Kershaw at the Time of the Redistribution of Lands to Include John Chesnut and Ely Kershaw in the Partnership, May 1767

350 acres on Pine Tree Creek purchased from William Serug and James McGirth, granted originally to William Gray, Apr. 3, 1754, and purchased by Joseph Kershaw, Apr. 29, 1761

131 acres in Fredericksburgh Township, part of 400 acres granted to John Black, Oct. 4, 1749, and purchased by Joseph Kershaw, Jan. 28, 1762

50 acres at Pine Tree Mill granted to Robert Milhous, Oct. 4, 1749, and purchased by Joseph Kershaw, Jan. 25, 1762

497 acres in Fredericksburgh Township, part of 650 acres granted to Samuel Wyly, Apr. 2, 1761, and purchased by Joseph Kershaw, Mar. 2, 1762

150 acres on Pine Tree Hill granted to William Ancrum, Sept. 19, 1758

20 acres, part of 300 acres called Joyners Ferry, at the Congarees, granted to Joseph Joyner, Jan. 9, 1752 and purchased by Joseph Kershaw, Mar. 1, 1761

150 acres on the south side of Wateree River, opposite the rafts, granted to Thomas Smith, Feb. 1, 1758

100 acres on west side of Wateree River granted to Joseph Kershaw, Mar. 31, 1761

100 acres on the fork of Pine Tree Creek granted to Joseph Kershaw, Dec. 5, 1761

150 acres in Fredericksburgh Township granted to Lambert Lance, June 4, 1759

100 acres on Little Pine Tree Creek granted to Lambert Lance, Dec. 5, 1761

150 acres on Pine Tree Creek granted to Lambert Lance, Nov. 9, 1762

150 acres in Fredericksburgh Township granted to Lambert Lance, Oct. 7, 1762

100 acres on Twenty Five Mile Creek granted to Lambert Lance on Mar. 31, 1761

50 acres on Twenty Five Mile Creek granted to Lambert Lance, Oct. 7, 1762

100 acres on Twenty Five Mile Creek granted to Henry Dongworth, Nov. 10, 1761, purchased by Joseph Kershaw

150 acres in Fredericksburgh Township granted to Aaron Loocock, Jun. 4, 1759

2,498 acres total

Source: CBPR, Vol. H-3, 22.

the ventures of Chesnut and the younger Kershaw drew on the collective wealth of the concern. Support came from profits generated by the partners' active participation in the land market in addition to those derived from trade. Ownership of land offered both territory on which to carry out operations and an investment that could generate capital or credit for business growth. Consequently, possession of real estate by any or all members of the corporate group ensured the others a resource that they could draw upon. Prior to the termination of the partnership in 1774, its members collectively acquired at least 2,100 acres and sold 650 acres in the backcountry.[15]

Although the partners' land dealings continued to reflect their interest in developing business in the vicinity of the original store, their pattern of acquisition clearly reveals a movement to expand the firm's activities beyond Pine Tree Hill. Over the ten years of the partnership's existence, its members gained possession of 1,500 acres farther up the Wateree Valley in a region known as the Waxhaws.[16] Encompassing portions of the Catawba River watershed in the undefined Piedmont borderlands of the Carolinas, the Waxhaws first attracted colonists around mid-century. After 1750 Scots-Irish settlers from Virginia and Pennsylvania began migrating southward along the Great Wagon Road that led along the foothills of the Appalachians, but the region also began to draw new immigrants directly from Europe. Hoping to attract additional residents to secure its hold on the interior, South Carolina changed its immigration policy in the 1760s, offering land, free passage, and other incentives to "poor Protestants" willing to occupy lands in the upper Wateree Valley. The new settlers, mostly poor farmers fleeing abusive landlords in northern Ireland, formed a distinctive population. Many shared ancestry as well as poverty, and their hard-line Presbyterianism set them apart from earlier residents. Unlike their predecessors, they came to the backcountry through Charleston and by the late 1760s constituted a separate element in the Waxhaws.[17] Although distinct from their more prosperous neighbors, the new pioneer farmers offered the partners a potential new market.

By the late 1760s, settlement growth justified opening commercial trade in the Waxhaws. Contemporary observers like Charles Woodmason found the region "surprisingly thick settled beyond any spot in England of its extent."[18] The extension of commercial agriculture to the Waxhaws offered trade and enhanced the investment value of lands in that region. Aware of the region's opportunities, several of the partners began accumulating property there. Aaron Loocock had previously received a large grant on Cane Creek, and Joseph Kershaw soon acquired land on Fishing Creek as well as additional property along the road to the Waxhaws (Table 7.3). The partners focused their efforts on Rocky Mount, an elevated location on the Wateree/Catawba River at its junction with Rocky Creek about twenty-six miles above Pine Tree Hill (Fig. 7.1). There they opened a store near a 250-acre tract on Cedar Creek that John Chesnut and Ely Kershaw purchased in 1765.[19]

The presence of a store upriver from Pine Tree Hill also allowed the partners to maintain contact with the Catawbas, who had removed north to their traditional homeland following the close of the Cherokee War in 1761. Their towns arose on lands reserved at the Waxhaw Old Fields by treaty the previous year. Reluctance on the part of South Carolina officials to formally set aside Indian lands in an area undergoing settlement delayed the survey of a promised reservation until 1763, when the Assembly commissioned Samuel Wyly to lay out the fifteen-square-mile tract (Fig. 5.5).[20] By then the Catawbas were no longer alone in the Waxhaws. Settlers migrating from the north had already begun to encroach on Catawba territory, exacerbating tensions between Natives and newcomers. Their status as

Table 7.3. Tracts Acquired by the Partners in the Waxhaws

Name	*Date*	*Acreage*	*Source*
Aaron Loocock	Oct. 20, 1763	1,000 acres on Cane Creek	CLG/CS, Vol. 11, 333
John Chesnut, Ely Kershaw	Oct. 9, 1765	250 acres on Cedar Creek	CBPR, Vol. E-3, 280
Joseph Kershaw	Dec. 13, 1771	250 acres on Fishing Creek	CPB, Vol. 17, 445

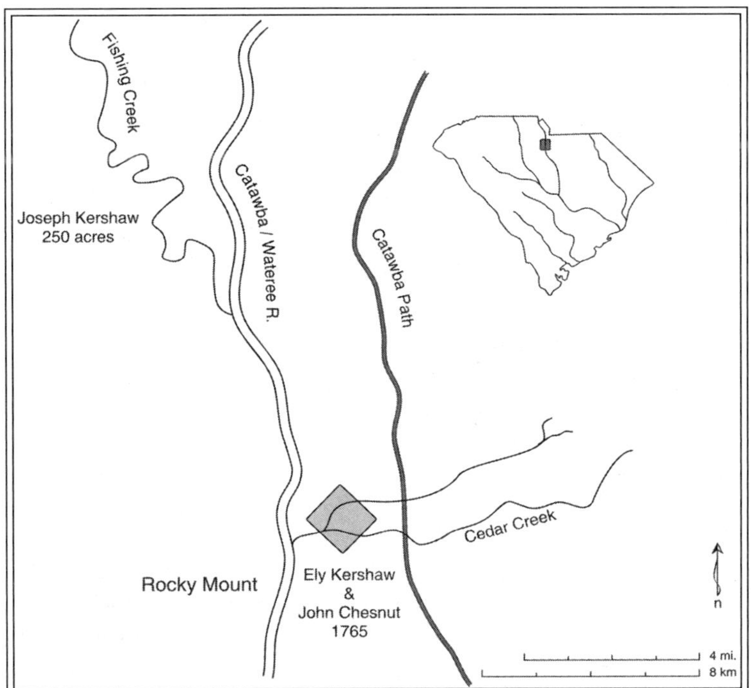

7.1 Lands acquired by the partnership at Rocky Mount and Vicinity in the Waxhaws. Author's original map.

reservation Indians made resistance difficult for a people who had become firmly enmeshed in the frontier economy and dependent on whites for subsistence as well as protection from both recent squatters and their traditional enemies. Catawbas not only traded pottery and other craft products but also assisted in recapturing runaway slaves. Many participated in religious services conducted by the Anglican itinerant Charles Woodmason.[21] Stable relations between the provincial government and the Catawbas depended on communication between parties, and Pine Tree Hill's principal merchant increasingly became the agent of provincial policy. By 1766 Joseph Kershaw had largely taken on Samuel Wyly's role as a buyer of deerskins and dispenser of goods on behalf of the state. Following Wyly's death in 1768, the merchant fully assumed his role as intermediary. Kershaw's official role in a region still without formal political organization reflected the partnership's central position as a social institution in the South Carolina interior, one now enhanced by its operation at Rocky Mount.[22]

The partners were not the first traders to enter the Waxhaws. Smaller merchants, such as John Moore, operated from his lands on Cane Creek as early as 1762, selling goods from the Moravian settlement of Bethabara and perhaps from Pine Tree Hill. John Walker, who amassed eight hundred acres on Rocky and Fishing Creeks and along the Catawba River, also ran a country store. Farther south, Thomas Wade conducted business at the point where the Catawba Path crossed Hanging Rock Creek. By the late 1760s James Patton, a prosperous farmer who with other family members owned several tracts on the Catawba

River, stocked his store with goods obtained from Kershaw & Co. Robert Crawford, an ambitious immigrant from Ireland, also conducted trade from his five-hundred-acre property on Waxhaw Creek. A leader in the Waxhaws community, Crawford became an important figure in Kershaw's economic network, a position mirrored in his later role in resisting British rule. None of these individuals were full-time storekeepers, and all lacked the capital and expertise to compete with Kershaw & Co. Indeed, Patten died in 1769 indebted to the partnership.[23] Unable to participate regularly in the international markets that supplied the partners and other larger wholesalers, they remained general retailers. The presence of the new store at Rocky Mount, far from curtailing their activities, encouraged the persistence of smaller traders as distributors for its ever increasing array of merchandise.[24]

Expanding Trade in the Backcountry: The Pee Dee

Farther east, the upper Pee Dee Valley offered an opportunity to tap the trade of settlements in this rapidly growing region. Laid out in 1737 for the benefit of Baptist immigrants from Pennsylvania, the Welsh Tract extended Queensboro Township to encompass lands along the Pee Dee River as far as twenty miles beyond South Carolina's line (Fig. 3.4). Immigrants began moving into the Welsh Tract in the 1740s, and its population grew rapidly with the addition of Presbyterian Scots-Irish refugees fleeing the violence of the Seven Years' War. Their presence added to the ethnic diversity of newcomers on the Pee Dee. The Welsh Baptists concentrated in the great bend of the Pee Dee just below its junction with Crooked Creek, an area that came to be known as the Welsh Neck. The colonial population of the Welsh Tract grew rapidly in the 1750s and 1760s, as settlement extended downriver as well as north past the Fall Line. By 1768 well over ten thousand people lived in the region.[25]

Although agricultural development in the upper Pee Dee Valley followed the familiar pattern of mixed farming, several factors encouraged the early appearance of commercial production. The navigability of the Pee Dee River linked interior settlements directly with the port of Georgetown. Unlike the Wateree, which had no direct connection with a port and was obstructed by a raft, the Pee Dee was open as far inland as the Fall Line at Cheraw Hill, allowing travel and trade along nearly its entire length. In addition, environmental conditions in the Pee Dee were amenable to the cultivation of indigo, a commodity made profitable by rapidly increasing demand in British markets as well as a bounty on its importation to the home country. The commercial production of indigo in the 1760s provided an impetus for external trade from the backcountry.[26] Business opportunities attracted several traders to the Welsh Tract, and by 1760 stores operated at various locations from Cashaway Neck north to the Fall Line above the Welsh Neck.[27]

The west bank of the river near Cheraw Hill became a focus of mercantile activity (Fig. 7.2). Lying near the head of navigation on the Pee Dee, it attracted a number of early stores to the vicinity of the mouths of Thompson Creek, Juniper Creek, and Huckleberry Branch. One was located just south of Cheraw Hill at a central point in the overland road network. Nicholas Rogers opened a store at the mouth of Thompson Creek just below its confluence with Juniper Creek on land he acquired in 1742. In 1757 an adjacent parcel came into the hands of Christopher Gadsden, an absentee Charleston merchant with business interests in Georgetown and the Pee Dee. Gadsden built another store there, which was operated by

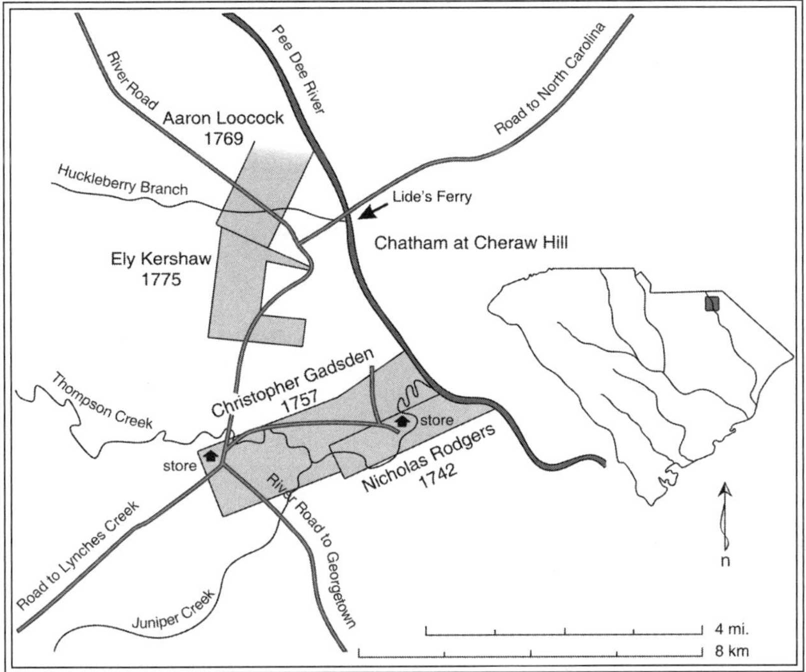

7.2 Lands acquired by the partnership at Cheraw Hill and vicinity, together with the locations of earlier stores and associated tracts on the Pee Dee River. Author's original map.

his agent for four years. Both tracts lay near a ferry crossing at the point where the road paralleling the river intersected the route to Lynches River.[28] This location allowed overland access to the Wateree Valley to the west as well as to Georgetown on the coast, and the ferry crossing linked them to settlements in North Carolina, including the growing center of trade at Cross Creek. Cheraw Hill controlled access to the upper Pee Dee Valley, an attractive location for a branch store.[29]

The partners gravitated to Cheraw Hill, acquiring a number of parcels along Juniper Creek and Huckleberry Branch near their confluence with the Pee Dee in the early 1770s. Owned both individually and collectively, these tracts gave them control of at least 1,300 acres that encompassed the junction of the roads that paralleled the river and led west through the Lynches Creek drainage to Pine Tree Hill (Table 7.4). Occupying the high bluff overlooking the river, their property also gave them direct access to Lide's ferry on the Pee Dee as well as to the settlements on nearby Thompson Creek.[30] This central location in the transportation network of the upper Pee Dee Valley offered Ely Kershaw & Co. an ideal site that the partners called "Chatham" when they opened a store there as early as 1769.[31]

As an extension of the partnership's operation at Pine Tree Hill, Ely Kershaw & Co.'s store had direct access to sources of supply. In addition to its overland ties with the Wateree Valley store, Cheraw Hill's location on a navigable river connecting it to Georgetown offered a second avenue of trade. The Chatham store received regular shipments of goods directly by wagon from the central warehouse at Pine Tree Hill, and cargoes from Georgetown

Table 7.4. Tracts Acquired by the Partners in the Vicinity of Cheraw Hill

Name	*Date of Acquisition*	*Acreage*	*Source*
Aaron Loocock	Oct. 31, 1769	250 Acres south side of Pee Dee River	CLG/CS, Vol. 19, 19
William Ancrum	Oct. 31, 1770	100 acres north side of Pee Dee	CPB, Vol. 13, 48
Ely Kershaw	May 12, 1770	150 acres on Juniper Creek	CPB, Vol. 11, 551
	July 20, 27, 1770	200 acres SW of Pee Dee River	CBPR, Vol. Z-4, 467
	July 30, 1775	300 acres on Huckleberry Creek	CPB, Vol. 17, 439
Aaron Loocock, William Ancrum, Joseph Kershaw, Ely Kershaw, John Chesnut	May 22, 1772	400 acres on Juniper Creek	CPB, Vol. 16, 406
Joseph Kershaw	Nov. 11, 1772	250 acres on Roads Branch on the road to Cheraws	CPB, Vol. 17, 443

merchants also arrived by boat. In return for exports of deerskins and indigo, a wide variety of finished goods passed through the store destined for frontier households. These included hardware, building materials, cloth and clothing, ceramics, spices, printed matter, alcohol, and foodstuffs.[32] The success of the Cheraw Hill operation is reflected in the growing number of smaller regional merchants in the 1770s. During that decade at least ten individuals operated stores on the upper Pee Dee drainage, including Joseph Wood, who opened a store and tavern near Thompson Creek in the early 1770s, and Thomas Elerbee, who maintained a store on a parcel adjacent to that of Nicholas Rogers.[33] As in the Waxhaws, smaller storekeepers became links in the partners' growing economic network in the upper Pee Dee Valley and drew emerging planters into an increasingly dependent relationship with Kershaw & Co.

Ely Kershaw's influence on the upper Pee Dee grew out of his position as manager of the Cheraw Hill store. Economic ascendancy brought with it an increased social and political presence as well, and his growing civic responsibilities reflected the emerging position of the newcomer in the society of the Welsh Tract. Here as elsewhere, religion played a key role in organization. Although the Welsh Neck Baptist Church emerged as the region's dominant religious institution, the Anglicans also established a presence at Cheraw Hill in the late 1760s. At the instigation of Charles Woodmason, residents successfully petitioned for the establishment of a separate parish on the upper Pee Dee, and in 1768 the Assembly created St. David's Parish, named in honor of its settlers' Welsh heritage. Although Anglicans accounted for only about a third of its inhabitants, they were the parish's wealthiest residents, and Ely Kershaw's membership in the Church of England placed him in this elite class.[34] As the region's leading merchant, he soon assumed an influential political role as well. In succeeding years he served as a vestryman, a church warden, and a collector of taxes for the parish as well as a commissioner to supervise building the court house and jail. In 1770 he donated land for St. David's Church and served as a commissioner to oversee its construction.[35]

Ties between religion and economics on the frontier enhanced Ely Kershaw's position in the wider society of the upper Pee Dee. Although the Anglican community to which he belonged remained a minority in the Welsh Tract, its members shared much with the Baptist elite of the region. As substantial landowners and slaveholders, they maintained common interests with the commercial producers of the Anglican and Baptist establishment in the lowcountry, and the Welsh Neck Church's membership in the Charleston Baptist Association reflected ties between members of this class. At Cheraw Hill, cooperation between the two denominations eventually took the form of sharing clergy with the Welsh Neck Church.[36] Cooperation between Anglicans and Baptists in the Welsh Tract helped Ely Kershaw create a network of ties formed through his position as merchant and church officer and extended the partnership's influence as a social institution in the upper Pee Dee Valley.

Ely Kershaw also established an important link to the emerging elite of the Wateree Valley through his marriage in 1769 to Mary Cantey. Mary was the daughter of Capt. John Cantey, a substantial backcountry landowner and descendant of a family whose lowcountry roots stretched back to the Barbadian migration of 1670.[37] John Cantey was established on the Santee in 1749, when he married Mary McGirt, the daughter of a plantation owner, James McGirt, and his wife, Priscilla. Three years later the McGirts shifted their residence to Fredericksburg Township. Cantey followed about a year later, acquiring property on Town Creek and at Pine Tree Hill. The gift of these tracts by Samuel Wyly and Joseph Kershaw in 1764 and 1765 implies that a relationship existed between the two merchants and Cantey, who was operating a tavern at Pine Tree Hill the following year. Ely Kershaw's marriage to Mary Cantey, whose sister Sarah wed Kershaw's partner John Chesnut in 1770, firmly tied Kershaw & Co. to two wealthy immigrant families with strong lowcountry ties.[38]

Incorporating the Canteys into the Kershaw network also established a link with the Richardsons, one of the most powerful planter families in the South Carolina backcountry. Richard Richardson was a political and civil leader and one of the largest landowners in Prince Fredericks Parish. He represented the region in the Assembly for nearly a decade in the 1750s and 1760s and held numerous regional and local offices. During the Cherokee War he rose to the rank of colonel and commanded a militia regiment in the Cherokee campaign. Richardson's ties to the Canteys and the McGirts derived from his marriage to John Cantey's sister Mary and from the service of his brothers-in-law John Cantey and James McGirt as officers in his regiment. John Cantey, his brother William, James McGirt, and Richard Richardson had previously worked together as commissioners to create St. Mark's Parish and to erect the parish church.[39] In the religiously diverse backcountry, their families' Anglican faith, derived from their lowcountry roots, as well as their wealth, set them apart from the majority of settlers. However, their elite status and political ties made them important allies for the partners in their efforts to stabilize and develop the region.

Expanding Trade in the Backcountry: The Congarees

Located at the confluence of the Broad and Saluda Rivers, the Congarees occupied a strategic position in the commerce of South Carolina's western backcountry. The region lay directly on the principal route connecting Charleston with the central interior. From the

Congarees the Cherokee Trading Path followed the Saluda to the trading settlement of Ninety Six before turning northwestward into Indian lands. Additional overland routes led west to the New Windsor settlements on the Savannah River, north up Broad River, and east to the Wateree Valley (Fig. 5.10).[40] Although Kershaw & Co. initially concentrated its efforts on developing commercial trade in the newly settled areas north and east of the Wateree Valley, it could not resist tapping the lucrative wealth of the rapidly growing western region as well.

Originally the nucleus of the German settlement in Saxe Gotha Township, the Congarees became a magnet for immigration in the years following the Cherokee War. Initial colonization centered on the garrison on the west bank of the Congaree River, but after 1748 settlement occurred along both sides of the river. Additional German settlers from the coast, as well as English and Scots-Irish migrating down the Great Wagon Road from the north, began to make their way to the forks of the Congaree and Wateree Rivers. They joined earlier colonists residing in the township lands west of the Congaree, and the area between the Saluda and Broad Rivers gained the name "Dutch Fork" from its German population. In the following two decades the area's population grew substantially, and settlement spread farther northwest along the Saluda. As elsewhere in the backcountry, agriculture developed around small-scale grain farming. Pioneer producers erected mills on streams leading into the major rivers, and by the 1760s a vibrant regional economy had emerged. The production of indigo prior to the American Revolution increased the area's potential for commercial development, a prospect that made the Congarees a viable area in which to extend trade.[41]

The prospect of trade in the Congarees led two of the partners to acquire several tracts at strategic locations in this rapidly growing region (Table 7.5). In 1768 Joseph Kershaw purchased two hundred acres from William Winchester on the Bush River, a tributary of the Saluda just above the forks of the Congaree. The following December he bought a three-hundred-acre parcel on Jackson's Creek, a stream that emptied into the Congaree River just below the forks. Major roads passed through these tracts, and their possession offered direct access to areas undergoing settlement in South Carolina's northwestern and central interior, in addition to the North Carolina frontier. The easterly route also provided another connection with the Waxhaws.[42] Three of the partners, William Ancrum, Aaron Loocock, and Joseph Kershaw, received a grant for an additional 350 acres on Cane Creek,

Table 7.5. Tracts Acquired by the Partners in the Vicinity of the Congarees

Name	*Date of Acquisition*	*Acreage*	*Source*
Joseph Kershaw	Jan. 15, 1768	200 acres at the fork of Broad and Saluda Rivers	CBPR, Vol. M-3, p. 419
Joseph Kershaw	Dec. 22, 1768	300 acres on Jackson's Creek	CBPR, Vol. Y-4, p. 186
John Chesnut	Dec. 29, 1772	100 acres and 1 town lot in Saxe Gotha	CBPR, Vol. V-5, p. 317
John Chesnut	Mar. 20, 1775	40 acres in Saxe Gotha	CBPR, Vol. W-5, p. 672

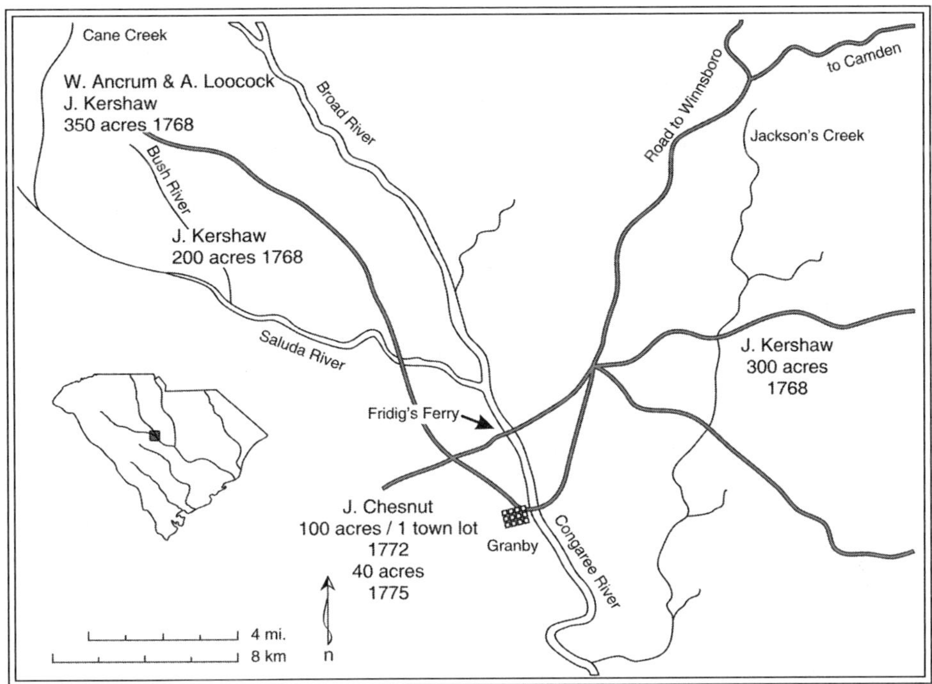

7.3 Lands acquired by the partnership in the Congarees and vicinity near the forks of the Congaree River. Author's original map.

a tributary farther up the Saluda. The proximity of this parcel to the trading settlement of Ninety Six and to the lands of John Savage, a prominent storekeeper and planter there, implies an interest in extending the firm's economic influence into the western backcountry as well.[43] Although there is no evidence to suggest that any of these locations were exploited by the partners for business, a fourth acquisition would give the concern an important economic advantage in the region.

When John Chesnut purchased a small property lying adjacent to Fridig's Ferry in 1772, the partners acquired control of a strategic location that allowed them to capture the trade of the Congarees (Fig. 7.3). The tract was situated on the west side of the river where a small settlement had grown up along the road between the site of the Congaree fort of 1715 and a newer fort erected in 1750. Located just below the confluence of the Broad and Saluda rivers at the shoals of the Congaree, Fridig's Ferry lay at the head of navigation and offered the northernmost crossing of that river and the shortest path between Pine Tree Hill and the Congarees. The intersection of the Charleston road and those leading to the Cherokee country and the western settlements on the Savannah River also lay here. Following the establishment of a public ferry there in 1754, the location became a major crossroads for backcountry traffic and a focus of activity along the river. Chesnut's subsequent procurement of an additional forty acres at the confluence of Mill and Congaree Creeks further expanded the company's presence at this hub of regional trade and transportation.[44]

Within two years of purchasing the Fridig's Ferry property, John Chesnut opened a store there under the name of John Chesnut & Co. The settlement around the store became known as Granby, named for the Marquis of Granby, an advocate of colonial rights.[45] Chesnut's Granby store gave the partners access to a wide area of the western South Carolina backcountry that was rapidly filling with new settlers following the Cherokee War. To stabilize the region and encourage immigration, the provincial government organized several new townships along the Savannah and its tributaries. Boonesborough Township on Long Cane Creek attracted Scots-Irish colonists from Virginia and North Carolina. German settlers moved into Londonborough Township on Hard Labor Creek, and Hillsborough Township on Little River had become home to French Huguenots. All soon spread beyond the boundaries of the townships and joined the dispersed, multiethnic creole population of the backcountry.[46]

In contrast to the situation in the Waxhaws and the Pee Dee Valley, hostile interactions with powerful Native groups deterred settlement in western South Carolina and limited the partners' success in that portion of the province. By the 1750s pioneer colonization had spread up the Savannah and into the upper Saluda and Broad River drainages, bypassing Ninety Six, long a focus of the extensive trade with the Cherokees in the interior. Lying adjacent to the Indian lands, the new settlements bore the brunt of hostilities when conflict erupted in 1760. The Cherokee War devastated the region, and Europeans abandoned of most of the territory beyond the Congarees and above Augusta. The war deterred immigration to South Carolina's western frontier even after its close, and agricultural colonization languished in New Windsor Township and elsewhere in the region.[47]

The Indian trade continued to be profitable there, and its economic dominance discouraged mercantile investment in commercial agriculture in western South Carolina. Nevertheless, the persistent immigrant market supported small traders on the frontier. Influential merchants such as Robert Goudey still catered largely to the Indian traders, but others began to serve pioneer farmers. Merchants, including John Tobler at Savannah Town and Audeon St. John, succeeded earlier storekeepers at the Congarees and established businesses that catered primarily to new settlers.[48] John Chesnut may well have intended to make his new store at the Congarees a base for regional trade by incorporating existing smaller merchants into the company's network.

The rise of Augusta as a focus of the Creek Indian trade in Georgia complicated matters by introducing a second source of imported goods into the western backcountry. On the Georgia side of the Savannah River, Augusta maintained direct ties by land and water to the coastal port of Savannah, which was fast becoming a rival to Charleston.[49] When the frontier on the upper Savannah expanded in the 1760s, Augusta's location and immediate access to an Atlantic port allowed it to become the principal supplier for Georgia and western South Carolina. The settlement's influential economic role was evident to a contemporary visitor, William Bartram, who remarked that, "without a competitor, [Augusta] commands the trade and commerce of vast and fruitful regions above it, and from every side to a great distance."[50] The merchants of Pine Tree Hill entered the Congarees after consolidating business in the northern backcountry, but by this time Augusta's growth as a center of inland trade posed a challenge that threatened the limits of their enterprise.

Consolidating the Center: The Store at Pine Tree Hill

As the focus of Kershaw & Co.'s business empire, Pine Tree Hill assumed a special role that made its form and function distinctive in the South Carolina backcountry. At the center of a wide network of trade, it was the principal node through which imported goods and information entered a broader system, and it was the collection point to which produce, deerskins, and other raw commodities of the interior flowed on the way to outside markets. By the mid-1770s the store served customers across much of South Carolina's interior and portions of neighboring North Carolina as well.[51] But the role of the store at Pine Tree Hill was more than that of a mere conduit for commodities. It also served as the clearinghouse for the company's far-flung subsidiary stores, which relied on the central facility to coordinate shipping and receiving and to provide accounting services for them as well as for various other businesses the partners controlled. In effect, the store functioned as a financial institution that managed the credit of its backcountry subsidiaries and their accounts with customers and introduced an organizational structure that facilitated change in the South Carolina interior.

Possessing the financial wherewithal and physical infrastructure to conduct exchange on a broad scale, the Pine Tree store became the agent for introducing a commercial economy in the backcountry. Its success depended on the firm's ability to provide credit to generate the capital farmers required to expand agricultural production and to develop manufacturing, repair, maintenance, and processing facilities to support export commodity trade. As in the lowcountry, limited alternative sources of capital placed merchants in the role of creditors who served as middlemen between producers and buyers. Without real competition, they virtually controlled the flow of exchange in the regions they served. Merchants stored grain, tobacco, indigo, and other crops for their clients and customers, to whom they could then issue credit for the commodities held. Such credit, in turn, allowed farmers, storekeepers, artisans, tradespersons, and others to purchase the firm's imported manufactured goods. To facilitate the process of exchange, merchants maintained journals of transactions with entries that recorded the monetary values of produce and merchandise received, stored, and shipped, as well as amounts loaned, owed on debts, and paid for services such as shipping and maintenance on facilities. All of these transactions relied on recorded credit and could be carried out without the need for large amounts of cash.[52] It was an ideal arrangement for a region without financial or other administrative institutions. Through the availability of credit, backcountry residents obtained not only the means to acquire imported manufactured goods but also the ability to invest in specialized economic activities on the frontier.

The account books of the Pine Tree Hill store furnish the best picture of its organization through their detailed listing of the concern's operation during the mid-1770s.[53] This journal reveals several types of transactions that illustrate the role of the store as a retail outlet for a variety of customers as well as the major wholesale distributor for the subsidiary stores at Pine Tree Hill, Rocky Mount, Chatham, and Granby. The transactions recorded funds moving into and out of the store's accounts. In the former category were payments received by the store for goods and services sold on accounts, collectively called sundries debited to the store, as well as payments received by the store for debts and payments administered by the store to settle accounts between other parties.

Most common entries involved the retail sales of merchandise. Several transactions that took place in February 1775 illustrate direct purchases of sundries on account. Joseph Kershaw's Sowerby plantation, likely named after its owner's birthplace, bought a pair of "Negro shoes" and four pairs of plow lines worth £2.2.6. A sawmill owned by James McGirt, whose family had by then joined the Canteys in the Wateree Valley, also purchased tools and supplies from the Pine Tree Hill store, ordering a dozen assorted files, the same number of gimlets, two pitching axes, a joiner's hatchet, three chisels, a jug, one thousand tenpenny nails, a tin pan, two mugs, two spoons, rum, barreled pork, and other items for a total of £30.[54] In the same month, Luke Gibson bought coarse fabric osnaburgs, checked cloth, calico, thread, buckles, handkerchiefs, and plow lines worth £22.14.3, and Abigail Gibson acquired a scarlet cardinal, a fashionable hooded cloak. Isabella Reed spent a total of £2.9.9 for household supplies, including vest buttons, buckram, silk, train oil, and a quart of rum, purchased on several visits to the store. Zebulon Gaunt, manager of Kershaw's saw mills, also bought clothing materials, sugar, rum, and other sundries over the course of the month. The variety and volume of merchandise purchased from the store illustrates the extent to which manufactured imports had entered the backcountry by the 1770s to fill the diverse needs of its residents.

The store also acted as a middleman to maintain balances between customers who held accounts there. In this capacity it received payments from individuals that were then debited to accounts of others. Most entries, such as the store's receipt of £5 from Jesse Williams to be placed in the account of John Belton in December 1774, did not mention specific services; however, others recorded more particular information. For example, in the same month the store credited £8.15.0 from Joseph Kershaw's account to that of Jasper Sutton to pay for an order of homespun that John Chesnut's father had supplied to Abner Petty. The store further transferred £3.5 from William Ancrum's account to that of a Mr. Summerford for recapturing an escaped horse. Sometimes the ledger recorded payments to the store by the trading concerns that it served. It noted, for example, the transfer of credit by Kershaw, Chesnut & Co., the resident concern at Pine Tree Hill, to a Mr. Branson for work "done on the meat house" in February 1775. Other entries simply recorded payments made by customers on their accounts without reference to particular purchases or debts.

On the other side of the ledger were payments debited by the store to others. These were usually assigned to the accounts of farmers for crops, livestock, or other products taken in by the store for later sale. Usually the payments were recorded as debits to cash or to an individual. When John Adkins supplied twenty hogs to the store at the end of November 1774, the ledger indicated the transfer of £56 to his account. It noted Arthur B. Ross's receipt for beeswax, tallow, and deerskins, both dressed and "hairy," two months later, as well as the company's payment of £11.19.6 to Thomas Griffin the previous December for the balance due on the indigo and indigo seed the company had purchased from him. The ledger often recorded transfers of funds by the stores operated by members of the partnership to the private accounts of individuals or from individuals to the stores. It noted, for example, the payment of £38.10.0 by Kershaw, Chesnut & Co. to cover the cost of shipping seven hogsheads of tobacco to Charleston by boat in April 1775. Five months earlier it indicated the receipt of funds by Kershaw, Chesnut & Co. from James Arnett to be credited to his account at the Rocky Mount store. These payments on account facilitated complex financial transactions across great distances and provided backcountry residents with the flexibility required to expand production for export markets and the financial wherewithal to enter commercial agriculture.

One of the most important functions of the central store at Pine Tree Hill was the coordination of transfers of credit and goods between it and the subsidiary stores operated by the partners. By the mid-1770s the store was a hive of activity, receiving goods from Charleston and redistributing them among the far-flung backcountry stores. Its distributive role was recorded in entries made on the first of February 1775, when the store consigned large orders of goods worth £4,811.15.10 to Chatham and Granby. Delivered overland by wagon, they included a variety of items, including cloth of many types, thread, buttons, and finished clothing for men and women, as well as writing implements, paper, blank books, Bibles, and religious texts. Tools, implements, and equipment for both general and specialized tasks constituted a second category of goods. Whipsaws, chisels, sadler's hammers, files, gouges, and grindstones flowed from the storehouse at Pine Tree Hill to the stores at Chatham and Granby, and smaller consignments went to nearby Rocky Mount. The ledgers recorded numerous transactions for merchandise as well as balances due on the costs of for shipping between stores. For example, the Granby store debited £35.14.2 3/4 to the Chatham store in December 1774 for sundries consisting mostly of cloth. Most of these cargoes included of finished goods, relatively compact and easily shipped overland by wagon. Carried in barrels, casks, or bales of bagged general merchandise, such items could be conveniently transported to this central location on the Wateree, where they could be accounted for, stored, and distributed to customers or subsidiary stores on demand. Archaeological excavations at the site of the Pine Tree Hill store have yielded bale seals and fragments of barrel bands, the material remains of shipping containers discarded at the central point of regional trade.[55]

The Pine Tree Hill store managed the shipment of imported merchandise as well and charged the accounts of subsidiary stores for the transport of goods from Charleston. The ledgers illustrate the movement of merchandise into and out of this central storehouse. On their journey inland, an undertaking referred to as "up carriage," and, later, between other stores, imported items moved via hired transport. Records of shipments often specified their carriers, such as Charles Ogilvie, who brought supplies to Pine Tree Hill; John Fields, who carried goods from there to the Chatham store; a Mr. Coaker, who delivered them to the Congarees; and Ely Kershaw's wagon, which hauled a cask of shot from Pine Tree Hill to Chatham.

Transferring cargoes of backcountry produce to the coast, or "down carriage," employed additional means of transport. Flour, the major export crop, was shipped overland to market in Charleston; however, more recently introduced agricultural commodities, such as tobacco and indigo, were too heavy and bulky to move easily by wagon.[56] The navigable Pee Dee River gave the Cheraw Hill store direct access to the entrepôt via Georgetown, and the removal of the Wateree raft provided Pine Tree Hill access to the Santee drainage. Above its confluence with the Wateree, the Congaree's open waters extended inland to reach the

Dutch Fork. Settlers on the Pee Dee began planting indigo in the 1760s, and Ely Kershaw & Co. began shipping it downriver by boat before the end of the decade. Tobacco production in the backcountry also expanded in the 1760s, and growers exported it in quantities sufficient to demand the appointment of inspectors in the Congarees, Cheraw Hill, and Pine Tree Hill in 1768. As early as 1766 Kershaw, Chesnut & Co. maintained boats for the carriage of tobacco from Pine Tree Hill to the mouth of the Santee and along the coast to Charleston.[57] Whether an individual store transported produce itself or arranged for its delivery to market, the profits generated were credited to the store's account and recorded in its ledger as payment for merchandise shipped and debited to them.

A reliable and regular mail service played an essential role in integrating the economy of the province and maintaining the regular movement of goods throughout the Backcountry. In the absence of an official post, the movement of mail to the backcountry relied on merchants, travelers, and other private carriers. By the 1760s, Pine Tree Hill had assumed a central role in mail distribution, and letters and packages from recipients and senders across the northern portion of the province regularly passed through the store. The Catawba Path became a preferred overland route to North Carolina, and its branches also reached the settlements on the upper Pee Dee. By the time of the American Revolution a regular fortnightly post connected them with the entrepôt. Additional routes tied the region with Augusta, on the Savannah River.[58]

The store ledger also recorded the continued participation of the Catawba Indians in commerce at Pine Tree Hill. Acting as the governor's representative in various negotiations, Joseph Kershaw maintained contact with the Catawbas, conveying grievances regarding settlers on Indian lands, arranging for the care and protection of their delegations en route to the capital, and requesting gifts and compensation for services.[59] As a merchant, he was also the Catawbas' principal supplier of goods through the Charleston-based concern of Kershaw & Co. His accounts reveal expenses incurred in providing flour, butter, bread, cheese, rum, wine, cloth, leather breeches, shoes and boots, and china, as well as fees for services such as postage for letters delivered and the cost of boarding Catawba travelers and stabling their horses. Occasional entries in the Pine Tree Hill store account book refer to payments made to other individuals identified as Native Americans. An April 1775 entry reimbursed Joseph Kershaw for payment made to William Hill, a Catawba, and on other occasions the store paid "Indian John Brown" and "Indian Jamie" for unspecified services.[60]

As a financial institution, the Pine Tree Hill store promoted the expansion of specialized businesses in the backcountry. With the investment credit offered by the central store, the partners and other entrepreneurs established and enlarged commercial ventures in the vicinity of Pine Tree Hill. These included Joseph Kershaw's upper and lower mills, his shipyard, and McGirt's mill. Supplies for the taverns owned by Jasper Sutton and John Cantey were recorded in their respective accounts at the store. Another artisan appearing in the ledger is John Bartlam, a potter who relocated his operation from the lowcountry to Pine Tree Hill in the early 1770s.[61] The store's ledgers included the accounts of others known to have been small storekeepers or traders at some time, but they were not always identified as such. Among the customers were Thomas Wade, who kept a store on Hanging Rock Creek, and Samuel Boykin, in business as a storekeeper when he purchased land on Town Creek in 1772.[62]

Three smaller partnerships stand out as organized mercantile businesses. On the west side of the Wateree, Wilson & Lang relied on the Pine Tree Hill store as a source of goods for sale as well as for the down carriage of produce and up carriage of finished goods. Like Sutton, McGirt, and Cantey, one of the partners also bore ties of kinship to the frontier community's founders. William Lang, who emigrated to South Carolina from Yorkshire in 1770, married Sarah Wyly, the daughter of Samuel Wyly and Dinah Milhous, in 1775 and through this union became a substantial landowner.[63] Archibald Brown & Co., operating out of Charleston, extended business into the backcountry in the late 1760s. Aaron Loocock's marriage to Brown's sister Mary about 1771 further strengthened the latter merchant's ties to Kershaw & Co. Like many lowcountry merchants, Brown invested in interior plantation lands, eventually acquiring twelve tracts totaling 2,656 acres in the Wateree Valley in the vicinity of Pine Tree Hill. He purchased several of these directly from the partners.[64] Charles Ogilvie also began his mercantile career in Charleston following his arrival from England in 1751. He formed a partnership with John Forbes in 1762 and a year later married Mary Michie, an heiress whose estate included 3,880 acres of land in the Wateree Valley formerly owned by her late father, James Michie. Ogilvie operated with varying success as a merchant in Charleston and London before expanding his activities to the interior in the mid-1770s. He acquired additional land in the vicinity of Pine Tree Hill, where he conducted business with the store as well as with several of the partners.[65]

The interaction of Kershaw & Co. with mercantile partnerships in Charleston and the interior was crucial to the economic development in the backcountry. Although established primarily to facilitate business, these ties sometimes became personal through marriage and friendship and reveal the multifaceted nature of relationships among merchants, farmers, millers, wagoners, artisans, and other parties that are characteristic of the network strategy upon which trade depended. The success of this arrangement derived from its continuing value in forging the links necessary to create commercial exchange in the backcountry, ties that allowed individuals to accumulate the capital and credit with which to develop production and to search for opportunities to invest it.

The Rise of Commercial Farming: Plantations on the Wateree

The emergence of plantation farming during the 1760s brought dramatic changes to the economy of the Wateree Valley. Commercial agriculture, based on the employment of enslaved labor, represented an investment of capital and resources in the large-scale production of a narrow range of commodities for an external market. Its incorporation of a capitalist mode of production emphasized the distinct separation of labor from ownership and management, and its intensified levels of production contrasted with the organization of small-scale family farming that supported the regional economy of the frontier.[66] Plantation agriculture altered the structure of colonial society and its use of land in the backcountry, and transactions in the store ledger recorded its growth in the Wateree Valley. Several named plantations or individuals associated with them appear as customers on its pages. The owner of Ely Kershaw's plantation is clear, as is that of Joseph Kershaw's Sowerby. But the proprietorship of Green Hill and Pine Tree Hill plantations is uncertain, although the employment at the latter of a member of the Gaunt family who also managed Joseph

Kershaw's upper mill suggests that this property was Kershaw's as well. Transactions by Parker Quinn and Marlow Pryor, who were overseers for William Ancrum, provide evidence for the operation of his Good Hope and Redbank plantations in the 1770s. Similarly, Joshua English, the overseer of Aaron Loocock's Middleburgh plantation on the Wateree, received goods from the Pine Tree Hill store. The delivery of store supplies to individuals identified simply as "Negroes" or designated only by first names suggests that bondsmen also acted on the part of their owners.[67]

Plantation agriculture changed earlier landholding patterns in the Wateree Valley. The increased scale of farming demanded larger tracts that also possessed characteristics amenable to efficient production. Tracts along the fertile river bottoms now became the most desirable because planters believed they had the potential to yield crops indefinitely. They now saw the high lands covered by oak and other hard woods as being of lower value and the hilly, sandy pine lands, or barrens, as possessing even less agricultural potential.[68] Plantation farming also demanded tracts of sufficient size to produce commercial staples, house the workforce necessary for cultivation, and accommodate crops and livestock necessary for the plantation's subsistence.[69] Because processing and marketing commercial crops depended on access to milling facilities and transportation routes, immigrants sought parcels with access to flowing water to power mills. In an increasingly export-oriented economy, proximity to transportation corridors became much more important, and new planters situated their holdings on navigable water or near principal roads that offered advantages for moving their crops to mills or markets.

The scale of plantation farming encouraged larger landholdings. Many estates grew as entrepreneurial planters such as Samuel Wyly, Joseph Kershaw, William Ancrum, and Aaron Loocock consolidated smaller tracts to form larger parcels. Newer holdings also differed from those of the earlier pioneer period, as owners abandoned the long lots to amass square or rectangular-shaped tracts that permitted them to consolidate lands with environments favorable to large-scale production of commercial crops. Substantial parcels occupied much of the alluvial river bottom lands at and above the Fall Line. These were less prone to flooding than were low, wet, swampy lands downriver. New tracts granted after 1760 also show a distinctive patterning in their distribution of (Fig. 7.4). In addition to occupying the remaining riverine lowlands above the Fall Line, later grantees also favored inland steam valleys. These lands extended into the lower slopes of the Sandhills, where well-drained, sandy to loamy soils were suitable for crops.[70]

Although the transition to commercial agriculture clearly altered patterns of land ownership in the Wateree Valley, it did not result in an immediate increase in production. In the early years, pioneer planters assembled large tracts but lacked the wherewithal to immediately place them in cultivation. Realizing the potential presented by such holdings required the cumulative investment of capital and labor over time and produced a landscape characterized by limited land clearing. This pattern is shown in a contemporary illustration of settlements near the confluence of the Wateree River and Gum Swamp Creek on loamy soils well suited for crops. Here several farms and a few adjacent small cleared fields lie scattered in the forest, surrounded by undeveloped land (Fig. 7.5). All lie on or are connected by roads to the Catawba Path. This pattern of limited land clearing is clearly evident in a 1774 advertisement for a Wateree Valley plantation offering a tract of "200 acres, 10 of it

7.4 Landholdings on the Wateree River in the vicinity of Pine Tree Hill acquired after 1760 (shaded). Their distribution of shows an expansion of holdings away from the river and a preference for large square or rectangular tracts. These parcels, when combined with those along the river, provided alluvial lands for plantation agriculture as well as water power sites in the stream valleys. Author's original map adapted from Kenneth E. Lewis and Frank J. Krist Jr., "Settlement Expansion in Fredericksburg Township, South Carolina, 1740–1770," Report submitted to the Savannah River Archaeological Research Program, South Carolina Institute of Archaeology and Anthropology, University of South Carolina (1997), Part IV, 12–14.

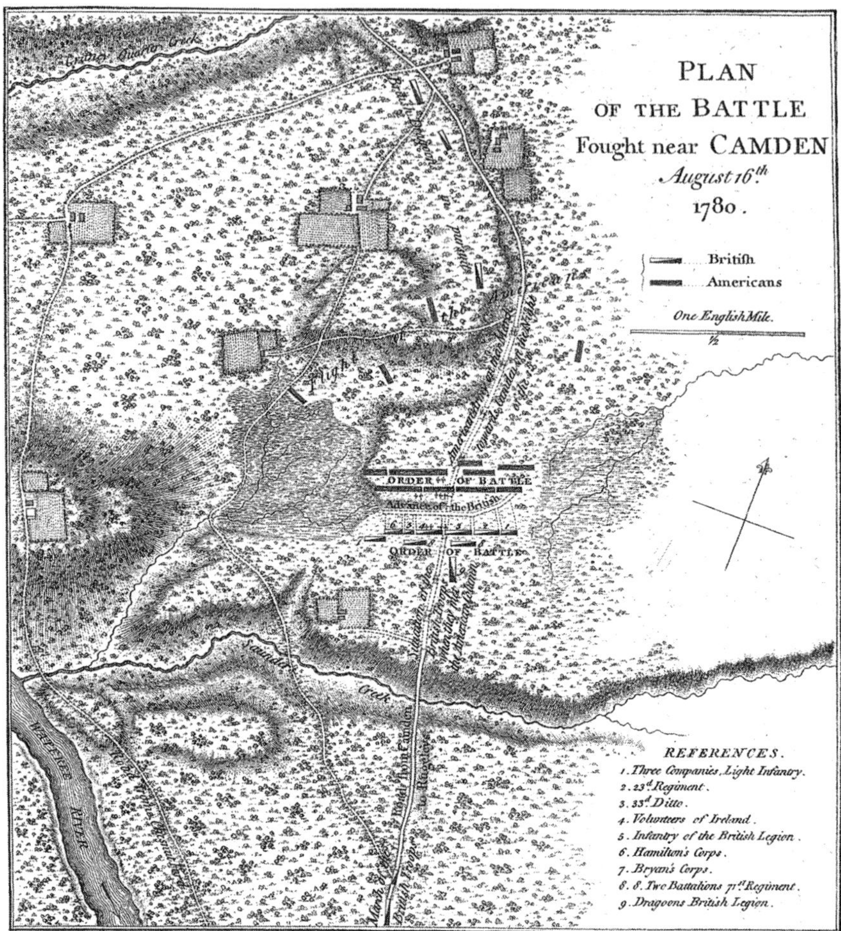

7.5 Rural agricultural settlements in the vicinity of Gum Swamp Creek north of Pine Tree Hill. This detailed map of the battle of Camden in 1780 shows the distribution of settlements on the high terraces above the stream valleys. The limited extent of cleared lands surrounding each homestead reveals a landscape of small, scattered farms linked by a network of trails leading to the Catawba Path running from south to north. Source: Charles Stedman, *History of the American War* (London: J. Murray, 1794), 210.

---

sowed in wheat & rye."[71] Landholding patterns had begun to change in anticipation of the new commercial economy, but altering the organization of agriculture and the scale of land use required other changes as well.

Slavery, Freedom, and the African American Presence

The growth of plantation farming brought the institutionalization of enslaved labor, and the resulting increase in the number of people of African descent began to alter the ethnic composition of the backcountry population. Although slaves were present in early pioneer households, the organization of agricultural production in this newly settled area restricted the use of unfree labor and limited the extent of its influence on the structure of society. The muster roll of 1757, listing the number of militia age men available for duty and their slaves by region, provides an estimate of the proportion of white to black inhabitants in the interior. The eight militia regiments in the Wateree Valley and upper Lynches River listed 206 men and boys, of whom only 19, or 9 percent, were enslaved. If we assume that this figure is representative of the entire population and that every man on the militia roster represents five persons, then, of an estimated total population of 1,030, fewer than 100 African Americans are likely to have inhabited this region. This proportion is comparable to that found in other backcountry regiments.[72]

A growth in the enslaved population accompanied the expanding plantation economy in the Wateree Valley. Of the initial immigrants granted land through 1756, only nine owned five or more bondsmen when they came to the region, and only two had more than ten.[73] But others began to acquire slaves as their landholdings grew and wealth permitted. William Boykin's acquisition of several large tracts between Town and Swift Creeks in 1756 marked his family's entry into plantation farming. By the late 1760s his sons Samuel and John possessed a total of seventy-nine slaves.[74] Other slave owners resident in the Wateree Valley included James Cary, John Marshall, and Charles Woodmason. Kershaw & Co. had begun to import slaves for sale at the store by the 1770s, and their numbers appear to have increased substantially in that decade. By 1777, thirty-six planters owned a sufficient number of bondsmen to provide laborers to construct a magazine at Pine Tree Hill.[75]

The growing number of slaveholding landowners marked the beginning of a shift in the nature of farming in the decade prior to the American Revolution. Although family farms still outnumbered plantations in the Wateree Valley, the inevitable transformation to specialized commercial production was already well under way. There are no comparable figures from which to estimate the growth of the slave population in the Wateree Valley, but the 1790 census for the region lying between the Pee Dee and Broad Rivers reveals an upward trend in the black population of the area during the third quarter of the eighteenth century. By that time blacks already composed more than 23 percent of the total population.[76] These figures indicate that commercial production was still not comparable to that in the lowcountry but was moving in that direction.

Despite the rise of wheat as the backcountry's chief crop, the nature of its production worked to slow the development of plantation agriculture in the region. Unlike rice, tobacco, and indigo, it did not require continuous attention throughout its growing season. Its episodic labor demands, concentrated at planting and harvest, made wheat more conducive to the use of hired help.[77] Nevertheless, backcountry farmers produced smaller crops of tobacco and indigo, whose intensive production demands were more conducive to the use of coerced labor. Tobacco had to be tended constantly prior to harvest, and indigo, which needed less attention during its growing cycle, still required intensive and arduous processing.[78] Although neither came to dominate the region's commercial economy, they introduced the large-scale cultivation of crops that favored enslaved labor.

Despite its slow beginnings, commercial agriculture had already begun to shape the social landscape of the Wateree Valley. Plantation farming, based on the enslavement of people of African descent, introduced efficiencies that enlarged the scale of production and altered its organizational framework by increasingly compartmentalizing agricultural tasks and segregating those associated with them. This shift magnified existing disparities based on race and lay the groundwork for a society whose structure mirrored that of the low-country. But conditions in the backcountry differed from those of the rice coast and produced a transition to specialized commodity production distinct from that of the longer-developed region.

The expansion of plantation farming into South Carolina's interior brought not only Africans who came involuntarily to the new country but also others who saw it as a refuge. As the backcountry economy began its shift toward commercial agriculture, the accompanying shift in the population's composition created an opportunity for black communities to form outside the plantation system. As increasing numbers of people of African descent began to enter the interior in the middle years of the eighteenth century, many found new opportunities for freedom. The sparsely settled frontier possessed bountiful natural resources that remained largely untapped and often uncontested, providing space where those who escaped bondage might find sanctuary.

Despite the dangers posed by vengeful owners and the uncertainties of the wilderness, escape from servitude by flight had always been an option for plantation slaves in South Carolina, and fugitives often found refuge on the periphery of the province. In the early years, the thinly settled countryside of the coastal region and the dispersed nature of plantation settlement allowed relatively unhindered escape from bondage. When officials in Spanish Florida offered sanctuary to Africans held in the nearby British colonies, many fled south. Others instead braved the forests of the interior, where they eluded their owners and formed outlaw communities of maroons, and some sought escape to the sea through Charleston.[79] As slavery entered the backcountry, runaways from the new settlements joined the region's dispersed population. Although many were apprehended and returned to servitude, others appear to have remained free, at least for a time. Traveling in the Wateree Valley in the 1760s, Charles Woodmason encountered "Free Negroes and Mulattoes who greatly abound here" and noted that their number had recently increased markedly. He surmised that some had migrated from the northern colonies, an observation supported by reports of African Americans apprehended in the backcountry. A man named John, for example, passed as a free man after leaving his birthplace in Virginia following the death of his owner, a dancing master in Williamsburg. Jemmy, a native of the Congo/Angola region of central Africa, also escaped from bondage in that province. Like Jemmy, many fugitives were native Africans who had been transplanted to South Carolina from various regions along the western coast of the continent. Bristol, who escaped bondage in Purrysburg, came originally from Guinea, on the coast of West Africa, while Freer, Sancho, Jack, and Isaac were from the Mandingo country in the Gambia River region just to the north, and another Bristol was an Ibo brought from the Niger River delta in present-day Nigeria.[80]

The regular appearance of fugitive slaves implies that survival outside the plantation was possible and took different forms. Some apparently remained in the vicinity of European settlements and worked as wage laborers or supplied commodities such as milk, firewood, oysters, fish, rice, rum, clothes, and corn. Others lived in more distant communities as maroons. Organized by bonds of kinship and the cultural ties associated with plantation work, these communities included people of both sexes and members of varying ages. Some runaways formed groups of armed outlaws who subsisted by robbing and plundering.[81] The perceived threat posed by the last group, together with the slave rebellion at Stono in 1739, led white South Carolinians to fear the increasing number of fugitives and to take more active measures to prevent their escape. The province employed Native peoples, including the Catawbas, to capture runaways, took military action against maroons thought to pose a threat, and strengthened the slave code to require more restrictive patrols by the militia.[82] Despite these measures, enslaved people continued to escape into the interior, where they made up a largely undocumented component of the immigrant population. But those fleeing slavery were not the only people of color in the backcountry.

Many persons of African and mixed descent also came to the interior as free persons. Blacks were not strangers to the frontier, having been involved in livestock keeping as well as the Indian trade during the early days of the colony.[83] Although their presence is poorly documented, numerous skilled African Americans migrated to the South Carolina, North Carolina, and Virginia backcountry during the eighteenth century as farmers or tradesmen. Despite their inferior social position in colonial society, people of color found opportunity in partly settled regions where the regulatory institutions of a slave-based economy had only begun to penetrate.[84] A few are known by name. Burnett, a native of Henrietta County, Virginia, worked with his father as a wagon driver and sawyer in the Long Canes on the upper Savannah, while John Chavis resided in Orangeburg District, and Primes Record apparently lived in the Little River region in the Saluda drainage.[85]

The forks of the Wateree and Congaree Rivers became home to at least one community of African American immigrant families in the decades prior to the American Revolution. Their male members included Edward and Drury Harris, cousins; Gideon and Morgan Griffin, who were brothers; and the Jeffers brothers, Allen, Berry, and Osbourne. The founding members of the Harris and Jeffers families lived originally in Virginia during the 1600s. In the following century their descendants migrated south into eastern North Carolina, where they made up several "free colored" households. Allen Jeffers was born on the Pamlico River, before some of his family emigrated to South Carolina shortly after mid-century. The Griffin family reportedly moved from North Carolina about the same time. All of them earned their living through agriculture, but Berry Jeffers was also a skilled blacksmith. Of moderate means, none of the families are known to have owned land in South Carolina during this time; nevertheless, they established themselves as neighbors in a small rural community that persisted during the transition period and remained intact at least through the early years of the new century.[86]

"The Right of the People When Drove to Desperation": Organized Crime and the Regulator Movement

The growth and survival of the commercial production and trade in the backcountry depended on a secure environment in which to carry out business. Expanding business brought the material wealth of the Atlantic economy to the frontier, but distance and tenuous avenues of communication and exchange placed merchants and residents at risk in a region that lacked political integration. From the time it opened interior lands to settlement, the provincial government failed to provide administrative institutions for the new country and was unable to maintain order over the wide area undergoing settlement. Neither the mechanisms nor the infrastructure existed to enforce laws or to try to punish those who broke them. Justices of the peace possessed limited authority, and the militia dealt only with larger threats. All central judicial institutions lay in the capital of Charleston, which for backcountry residents meant "that the attendance of process and juries were greatly hurtful . . . , by loss of time and expenses that few were able to bear."[87] The absence of an effective means to enforce civil and criminal codes in the backcountry left the region without a governing structure to ameliorate its residents' conflicting interests in the wake of the devastating Cherokee War.[88] By the 1760s, the need for resident courts with jurisdiction over civil actions and authority to try criminal cases became a pressing mater as the backcountry experienced a surge in crime that threatened safety and economic development.[89]

In the chaos that followed the conflict, the emerging commercial economy introduced elements of stability that both shaped the nature of criminal activity and created a basis for its eradication. As networks of trade extended across the interior, linking new settlements to one another and tying them more closely to the entrepôt, the expanding scope of exchange opened new markets for a wider range of goods and services, legitimate or otherwise. The new economy, with its capitalist orientation, encouraged the accumulation of wealth to invest in the land, supplies, equipment, slaves, and other things necessary to enlarge production. The combination of growing portable wealth and increasing access to markets in a region lacking formal institutions of control presented opportunities for criminal activity previously unavailable. The possibility of robbery, theft, and other crimes had always existed in the interior, but changing conditions in the 1760s suddenly made these activities far more lucrative.[90] Operating among the settlements in the principal river drainages of the backcountry, gangs of bandits established their own economic networks, and stolen goods, slaves, and horses passed into neighboring provinces for sale. The bands employed terror to coerce storekeepers and tavern owners to fence stolen goods and to instill fear in those who opposed their activities.[91]

In the 1760s the level and intensity of crime exploded in the Wateree Valley as organized gangs of thieves often resorted to extreme violence to acquire items of high liquidity. The newspapers of the time published lurid accounts of their deeds, which targeted settlers believed to possess portable wealth. A letter from Pine Tree Hill enumerated criminal activities in a region "where robberies have become so frequent lately." The account reported a break-in at John Pain's shop, from which several articles and a stallion were taken. Robbers also stole a horse from Joshua English. Hugh Brennan, who lived on the Lynches Creek road, escaped loss only by removing his goods before the thieves arrived, but his neighbor, a man named Burns, fared far worse. Captured by his assailants, he was tortured with hot irons to force him to reveal the hiding place of his money, after which they burned his house.[92] Several robbers seriously wounded John Huggins at his Waxhaws home. Ancrum, Lance & Loocock reported multiple incidents in which thieves pilfered merchandise on their wagons from Charleston.[93] The vulnerability of settlers to robbery led one to remark, "As matters stand, the lowest state of poverty is to be preferred to riches and affluence, for the person who by his honest labour has earned £50 and lays it up for his future occasions, by this very step endangers his own life, and his whole family, for no man is safe who is reported to have such sums in his possession."[94]

In the Wateree Valley, the growing economic disparity that begun to concentrate wealth and power in fewer hands may have motivated some settlers to turn to banditry as a strategy for coping with change. Some of the gangs were headed by early settlers in the vicinity of Pine Tree Hill who had fallen on hard times. They included Thomas and James Moon and their half brothers George and Govee Black. James Moon had been successfully sued for debt by Joseph Kershaw and sold the latter his land. His brother similarly transferred his property to the planter William Boykin. Kershaw and Samuel Wyly also acquired the Black brothers' tracts, leaving them landless.[95]

During the late summer of 1767 settlers across the interior organized to oppose the bandit gangs. Called the Regulation, the movement's leaders were property owners and slaveholders. As the vanguard of the backcountry's commercial transition, these men believed that their livelihoods and future success depended on restoring stability to the region. Charles Woodmason, a former storekeeper and now a planter and missionary on the Wateree, played a key role by framing the Regulators' demands. His "Remonstrance" specified the need for civil institutions, courts, courthouses, jails, and schools in the backcountry. The Regulators believed that these administrative structures would eliminate the inequities that fueled conflict, protect property, and create a system to enforce conduct.[96] The following spring the Assembly passed an act establishing courts in the interior and appointing law enforcement officials; however, the long process of these changes took another year to complete, and securing the backcountry required immediate action.[97]

The Assembly's more effective response was to authorize two companies of rangers to restore order in the interior. Led by Regulator officers, these mounted units began a three-month long roundup of criminals in the backcountry in late1767. Rendezvousing at Swift Creek on the Wateree, the Regulators moved across the backcountry and ranged as far north as North Carolina and Virginia to pursue stolen property and captives. In the process, a number of outlaws were killed in skirmishes, and sixteen, including Govee Black, were summarily hanged. (His brother George had been executed previously and his brother-in-law Moon incarcerated.) Organized Regular forces captured many more criminals who now faced rapid trial and punishment at the hands of a more sympathetic Court of General Sessions in Charleston. On a broad scale, the Regulators curbed the crime wave in the backcountry and became the de facto authority in the region.[98]

The victory of the Regulators helped to solidify the position of small planters in the fluid social order of the Wateree Valley. The growing commercial economy permitted them to expand their agricultural operations and to establish themselves as an elite group comparable to that of the lowcountry, but this process required a stability achievable only through their combined efforts. It is not surprising that most of the Wateree Regulators and all of the movement's leaders were planters. Among them were Samuel Boykin, a planter, storekeeper, and owner of sixty-four slaves at his Town Creek plantation, and Joseph Kirkland, who possessed 1,141 acres in Fredericksburg Township. Charles Woodmason's experience as a planter, slaveholder, storekeeper, and minor official preceded his current career as a missionary. He and James Cary, one of the region's largest planters, presented his

Remonstrance to the legislature and successfully argued for the support of the movement.[99] At least thirty-eight other residents from Fredericksburg Township and the Waterees participated actively in the movement. Among them were Thomas Charlton, Joshua Dinkins, Joshua English, and John Marshall, who was later politically active in the region (Table 7.6).[100]

Samuel Boykin was among the leaders in the Regulator movement on the Wateree. Accompanied by his younger brother John, he became legendary in his administration of justice to those whose criminal activity or personal behavior violated social standards. A large, powerful, and active individual, he was often called upon to punish those considered to have neglected their responsibilities. In an oft-cited example, he came to the assistance of a Mrs. Dozier, who complained that her husband neglected his family and spent all their resources on drink, leaving them destitute. Arriving at the Dozier house, Boykin and his companions responded to her request to punish the slothful husband and exert a promise to reform his behavior. According to local tradition, the administration of thirty-nine lashes apparently had the desired effect, and Bennet Dozier, who "was not a bad fellow at heart," improved his life and harbored no malice toward Boykin.[101] Samuel Boykin's experience in the Regulator movement marked the beginning of a wider public career.

Although undoubtedly sympathetic to the Regulators' cause, the most influential people in the Wateree Valley did not participate directly in the movement. Joseph Kershaw and his partners, Ely Kershaw, John Chesnut, William Ancrum, and Aaron Loocock, chose not to become involved with Regulator activities, as did the Canteys, the Suttons, the Langs, the Wylys, the McGirts, and others engaged in trade. The powerful Richardson family was also noticeably absent. Their nonparticipation did not indicate their lack of interest in the movement's goals. Certainly it was in their interests to restore order in the face of criminal activity that jeopardized their expanding operations. The central role of the mercantile elite in backcountry society, however, made them far more valuable as politicians than as vigilantes rounding up miscreants. They likely understood that their political influence could be of far greater use in steering the legislative process directed at creating an effective circuit court system to maintain stability in the backcountry.

When opposition to the Regulators surfaced, the Wateree Valley elites took steps to defend them. In 1768, a countermovement, called the Moderators, arose in the backcountry in response to the increasingly strict discipline imposed by the Regulators and the broader political powers its members assumed. Openly and forcefully opposed to the Regulators, the Moderator movement coalesced under the leadership of Joseph Coffel (or Scoffel), a hard-bitten and disreputable former minor official from the Orangeburg area. Although his followers were initially successful in gaining the support of provincial authorities, the prominent backcountry planters Cols. Richard Richardson and William Thomson of Orangeburg soon dealt their cause and its leader a severe blow. Using their influence as militia leaders, justices of the peace, and members of the Assembly from St. Mark's and St. Matthews Parishes, Richardson and Thomson appeared before the governor's Council to denounce Coffel and convinced the Council to withhold support for the movement. Despite this setback, the Moderators continued to gain strength in the backcountry, and a force of several hundred Regulators formed on the Wateree to oppose them in battle. Again Richardson and Thompson acted, this time directly, to prevent major bloodshed. They and

Table 7.6. Regulators from Fredericksburg Township and the Waterees

Andrew Baskin — Little Lynches River
John Boykin — Swift Creek of Wateree River
Samuel Boykin — Town Creek of Wateree River
Richard Burnett — Hanging Rock Creek of Little Lynches River
James Cary — Camden
Thomas Charlton — Camden
Benjamin Cook — Camp Creek of Catawba River
William Deason — Flat Rock Creek of Wateree River
Joshua Dinkins — Old Wateree Loop of Wateree River
Joshua English — Spears Creek of Wateree River
Daniel Gardner — Camden
John Gray — Between Broad and Catawba Rivers
Benjamin Hart — Camden
James Holley — Upper Lynches River
John Holley Sr. — Upper Lynches River
John Holley Jr. — Upper Lynches River
Jonathan Holley — Upper Lynches River
Henry Horn — Fox's Creek of Wateree River
Joshua Horn — Camden District
Henry Hunter — Wateree River, Fredericksburg Township
John Kimbol — Camden District
John Kirkland — White Oak Creek of Wateree River
Joseph Kirkland — Fredericksburg Township
James Marlow — Camden District
John Marshall — Little Lynches River
Thomas Marshall — Little Lynches River
Moses Matthews — Between Broad and Catawba Rivers
John Miles — Camden District
Edward Narramore — Little Lynches River
Averhart Neates — Between Broad and Catawba Rivers
James Nelson — Camden District
William Nettles — Between Broad and Catawba Rivers
John Roden — Wateree Creek of Wateree River
John Scott — Camden
William Simmons — Twenty-five Mile Creek of Wateree River
Matthew Singleton — Melrose Plantation, lower Wateree River
Robert Stark — Camden
Richard Taylor — Between Broad and Catawba Rivers
John Welsh — Little Lynches River
William Welsh — Grannys Quarter Creek of Wateree River
Henry Wimpey — Between Broad and Catawba Rivers
Charles Woodmason — Camden

Source: Richard Maxwell Brown, *The South Carolina Regulators* (Cambridge, Mass.: Belknap Press of the Harvard University Press, 1963), 147–148.

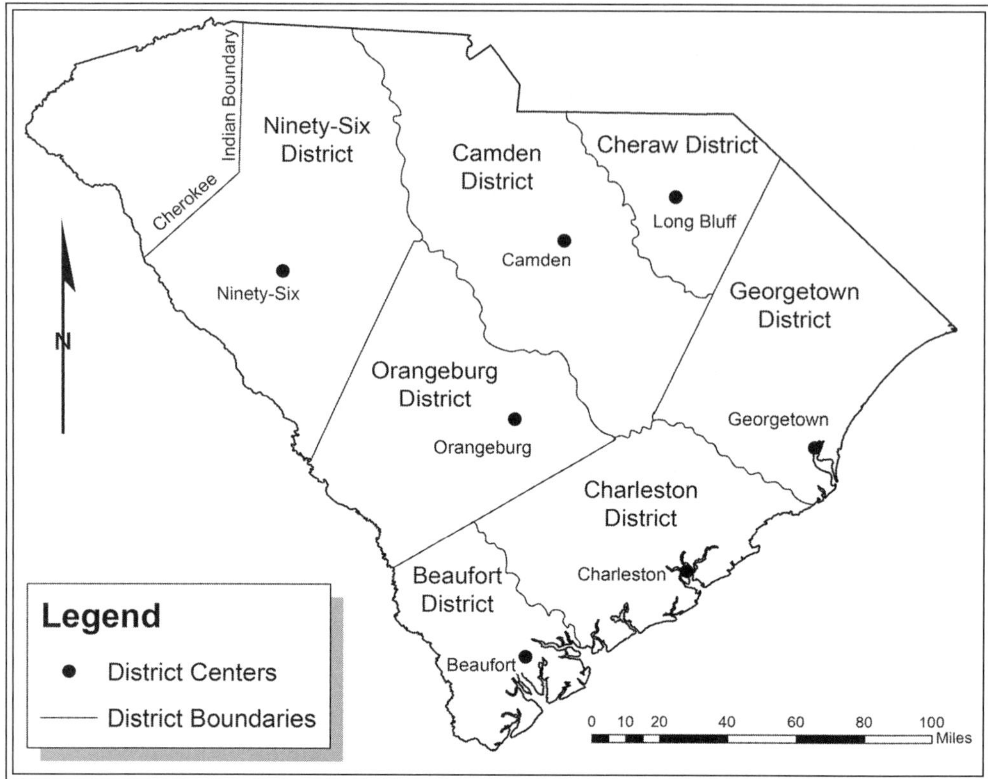

7.6 The judicial districts and seats in South Carolina designated by the Circuit Court Act of 1769. Courtesy of South Carolina Department of Archives and History, Columbia, South Carolina.

Richardson's kinsman Daniel McGirt, son of the prominent Wateree miller James McGirt, arrived as the two sides gathered near the confluence of the Bush and Saluda Rivers. Here they used their personal influence as elites to prevent a pitched battle and negotiate a peace.[102]

Other eminent people with interests in the Wateree Valley acted in support of the Regulators in seeking to influence the lowcountry-dominated legislature. Backcountry voters packed polls in the ancient parish of St. James Goose Creek in 1768 to elect Aaron Loocock and two others sympathetic to their cause as assemblymen. Joseph Kershaw, as a member of the Assembly from St. Mark's Parish, represented Regulator interests the following spring as part of a committee that drafted a bill creating a circuit court system in the interior. When individuals' activities as Regulators left them open to lawsuits by opponents, backcountry inhabitants petitioned the Assembly for a general pardon the following summer. The petition was referred to a committee chaired by Joseph Kershaw, and the legislature quickly supported the request. John Chesnut and the Wateree planter John Cantey led a group of backcountry residents in presenting the Regulators' case to the governor, a request that played a key role in the subsequent pardon.[103]

The Circuit Court Act of 1769 introduced an administrative structure that integrated the vast backcountry with the larger province and established seats of power in the interior. It accomplished this by subdividing South Carolina into seven judicial precincts, three coastal districts centered on the ports of Charleston, Georgetown, and Beaufort and four larger units in the interior. In the backcountry, Cheraws District lay on the upper Pee Dee, Camden District included settlements on both sides of the Wateree, Orangeburg District served those to the west of the Congaree, and Ninety Six District encompassed the northwestern portion of the province (Fig. 7.6). Each judicial district was to be administered by a sheriff, whose authority superceded that of the deputy provost marshal in Charleston. The Circuit Court Act also created commissions to construct district courthouses and jails in each district by 1772 and established a new judiciary whose members rode a circuit of the district courts twice a year. Trials were to be conducted before juries drawn from the inhabitants of each district.[104] Situating these functions in backcountry settlements effectively moved judicial authority from the provincial capital to new centers of authority. But, to serve effectively, the new district seats had to be placed so as to efficiently administer the broader region they served. A court site had to be not only geographically central but also capable of providing convenient access to all parts of the district. As the focus of a trading network that stretched across much of South Carolina's interior, Pine Tree Hill offered an ideal location for the district court in the Wateree Valley, and its selection as such ensured the settlement's continued growth.

Chapter 8

"Camden's Turrets Pierce the Skies"

The Rise of an Urban Center in the Backcountry

On the eve of the American Revolution, George Ogilvie, a Scottish immigrant, found himself in the strange but fascinating world of the rapidly changing South Carolina backcountry. He pondered the nature of the place from "the solitude of the forests" on his infant plantation on Cedar Creek above Pine Tree Hill. In his leisure moments Ogilvie turned to his pen, "to kill the languor of a winter evening, or a sultry noon," and composed a lengthy romantic poem celebrating his new home. The young nephew of the merchant and planter Charles Ogilvie conveyed in verse images of the frontier, a land of primitive beauty and magnificence in the midst of transformation at the hands of European settlers.[1]

> The mountains fertile base, and richer vale,
> Stript of their woods, with harvest promise swell,
> Above extends a length of verdant glade,
> No more a forest, nor depriv'd of shade
>
> Nor through the vale those streams unuseful wind!
> In yonder dell, by potent banks confin'd,
> The' imprison'd waters yield to human law,
> Float the huge raft, impel the lab'ring saw;
>
> Or, thro' the sluice, white foaming o'er the wheel,
> Convert the husky grain to wholesome meal.[2]

But perhaps his most telling lines recognized the individual largely responsible for creating this garden in the wilderness and founding the settlement that became the commercial focus of the South Carolina backcountry: "Thy fame, creative Kershaw! Too shall rise, / As thy own Camden's turrets pierce the skies!"[3]

Joseph Kershaw's prominent role in the region's transition reflected the increasing interconnectedness of economics and politics in the interior. By 1770 the settlement at Pine Tree Hill had emerged as the axis of Kershaw & Co.'s extensive trade network and the managerial center for a large portion of the South Carolina backcountry. Because commercial agriculture and trade dominated the colonial political structure, the settlement's role in business positioned it ideally to play an important part in the region's emerging administrative system. Kershaw's success depended on his close ties with Henry Laurens and other members of the lowcountry mercantile elite and the system of production and trade in which they all participated. These connections undoubtedly worked to align his political interests with theirs at a time when the relationship between the American colonies and the mother country was becoming increasingly strained over economic policy.

In the 1760s political and economic concerns drew closer as colonials found their interests increasingly at odds with those of the Crown, a division expressed by the growing conflict between South Carolina's Assembly and royal officials in the province. Sharp disagreement centered around the legislature's strong opposition to taxation imposed by the Stamp Act of 1765 and the Townshend Acts, passed two years later. These revenue acts, imposed by Parliament, were particularly onerous because their enforcement lay with the Crown-appointed admiralty courts rather than with provincial authorities, depriving South Carolinians of trial by their peers and subjecting them to other abuses of power. Such developments increased fears of a growing imperial prerogative, especially among merchants like Laurens, who were heavily engaged in shipping.[4] Earlier concerns expressed by the Regulators about representation in the colonial legislature increased awareness among lowcountry businessmen of the threat posed by rising imperial power. Support of their interests from Kershaw, Chesnut, and others in the Assembly and from many backcountry leaders fostered a common ideology of resistance to imposed statutes among those engaged in mercantile activity throughout the province.[5] Although backcountry opposition to the Crown was never universal, the common grievances of Laurens and other great lowcountry merchants clearly appealed to entrepreneurs like Joseph Kershaw, whose business depended as much on trade unhindered by onerous regulations as it did upon the maintenance of order. His extensive network built up through trade now took on a political aspect.

Perhaps the most overt manifestation of Joseph Kershaw's alliance with the lowcountry radical elites was the new name he gave the locale of his central store and other facilities. In the winter of 1768 contemporary sources began to refer to Pine Tree Hill as Camden. The name honored Charles Pratt, recently created Baron Camden. A native of Kent, Platt had been a barrister, a member of the Royal Society, a privy councillor, a lord justice of the Court of Common Pleas from 1761to1766, and lord chancellor from 1766 to 1770. As a member of the House of Lords, he opposed Parliament's tax measures for the American colonies, arguing that they were taxation without representation, and he declared the Stamp Act unconstitutional. His position supported the views of American merchants and shippers, including Kershaw and his partners, whose admiration undoubtedly influenced their choice of a name for the hub of backcountry trade and site of administrative authority in the South Carolina interior.[6]

Camden Emerges

At the time authorities chose Camden as the location for the district courthouse and jail, it looked like a center of trade on the frontier. A focus of commercial activity, it had already acquired many of the centralizing functions of market towns in the older settled areas from which many of its residents had come. Nevertheless, the conditions in which Camden developed had influenced its form dramatically, and made it physically distinct from communities on the other side of the Atlantic. European towns of comparable function engaged in interregional trade, carried out specialized production, supported sizable populations involved in a variety of activities, and marketed a wide range of goods. They also incorporated integrative social and political activities that reflected the town's central role in the regions they served. But, unlike settlements on the frontier, such centers had arisen in much more densely populated areas that supported a complex urban hierarchy that included cities, towns, villages, hamlets, and smaller agglomerations, all of which ranked below market towns. Here population density was tied to social complexity and settlement size reflected urban function. Market towns with administrative functions were often large and substantial settlements.[7]

In the South Carolina backcountry, frontier conditions shaped a distinct pattern of settlement. The rapid influx of immigrants dispersed colonists in widely scattered settlements in a region with vast resources and relatively few indigenous inhabitants. Despite continued growth, low population density still characterized the Wateree Valley even as it acquired a commercial economy and an integrated administrative structure. Like other central settlements in the southern interior, Camden remained relatively small during its early development. Its size, however, was unrelated to either the presence of urban functions or a central role in the interior. In the lands from which immigrants came, greater population densities supported a variety of services that were distributed among progressively larger nucleated settlements. Because the dispersed populations of frontier regions in America were not dense enough to reproduce such a hierarchy, the services performed at lower-level settlements shifted upward to those at a higher level. Here these services tended to concentrate at central settlements called "frontier towns." Serving as the focal point for social, economic, political, and religious activities, frontier towns were the principal collecting points for products destined for outside markets and the distribution points for imported goods. As such, they constituted the principal link between the frontier and the entrepôt that connected it with the outside world.[8] A frontier town became the center of multiple activities for the dispersed open-country communities that surrounded it. It was the nucleus of a regional society in which most residents lived outside nucleated settlements.[9] As the hub of the Wateree Valley and regions beyond, Camden emerged as the frontier town for the backcountry.

Frontier conditions influenced the form and configuration of the early town. Because of its role in regional production and trade, numerous activities gravitated to Camden, but some lay outside the nucleated settlement. Some, like Joseph Kershaw's wharf and tobacco warehouses, lay by necessity on the Wateree, and his mills were located at sites along nearby watercourses above and below Camden.[10] Others conducted their businesses at rural locations farther from Camden's center. Daniel Mathis and Jasper Sutton operated taverns to the north along Grannys Quarter and Gum Swamp Creeks, respectively. Robert Milhous's tan yard and bark mill probably lay on his Friend's Neck tract, and John Pain's burglarized blacksmith shop was likely located on his Pine Tree Creek holdings.[11] Nevertheless, the concentration of these services in the vicinity of the Pine Tree store marked its site as the focus of a dispersed community that was beginning to acquire urban functions.

But what of the settlement of Camden itself? As the focus of Kershaw & Co.'s mercantile empire, it began to expand in the 1760s beyond the cluster of earthfast buildings at the intersection of the Catawba Path and the ferry road. Documents and material evidence have revealed the addition of several important new structures that housed activities associated with multiple new functions. The buildings and their distribution set the pattern for Camden's growth ins the years prior to the American Revolution. By agreement, all of the partnership's real properties were held in common prior to its dissolution in 1774, but the appearance of privately owned tracts indicates that the partners had already begun to subdivide the site of Camden. Joseph Kershaw's transfer of land to others implies that he had title to the store site and areas adjacent to it. In 1769 he alienated two parcels, each of which was nearly an acre, to John Chesnut and to his own brother Ely. These lots lay on Kershaw Street, an early thoroughfare in Camden. The properties' north-south boundaries lay 6 degrees east of north, an orientation matching that of the earthfast buildings identically, and implies a systematic survey of the town properties.[12] Unfortunately, the later town survey does not correspond to this configuration, and the location of these tracts and Kershaw Street are uncertain. The subsequent property records for the tract containing the old earthfast store, however, continued to show its northern boundary line deviating several degrees from the axis of the later grid, and this may well be a boundary based on the earlier survey.[13] Although their precise locations are lost, the survey of lots points to a growth of activity in the town in the 1760s. But a more compelling form of evidence is the presence of the new structures.

Several buildings appeared in the vicinity of Camden's original store (Fig. 8.1). Charles Woodmason noted the presence of a meetinghouse belonging to the Society of Friends at Pine Tree Hill in 1766. Although he failed to pinpoint its location, it probably lay near the Quaker cemetery along the ferry road and may be the earlier structure of Samuel Wyly's day. He also mentioned another meetinghouse used by the Presbyterian congregation. It stood at the foot of the present Church Street on the ferry road, not far to the west of its intersection with the Catawba Path. Joseph Kershaw later referred to this location as the "Meeting House ground," consisting of a "lot given to the [Presbyterian] congregation prior to the town of Camden being laid out in lots." Archaeological survey excavations in this area in 1983 revealed building rubble and other artifacts likely to mark the site of this structure.[14]

Joseph Kershaw added the most substantial new addition to the contiguous settlement with the construction of a brewhouse near the southwest corner of the ferry road and the Catawba Path. It was laid out at the same angle as the earthfast structures, implying that it was constructed early in the decade. A comparison of ceramic artifacts recovered in archaeological excavations there suggests that the brewhouse was built by the mid-1760s and was in operation well before Woodmason mentioned it in an admonishing sermon in the summer of 1769. Discovered in 1976 and partially excavated in 1981, the brewhouse rested on a substantial brick foundation typical of those associated with its British counterparts. The massive nature of the structure, its open architecture, and the presence of elements associated with brewing, such as the perforated brick flooring used in grain drying floors, further reflected the building's function. The extremely small proportion of domestic artifacts at the brewhouse and the preponderance of storage and other utilitarian wares recovered

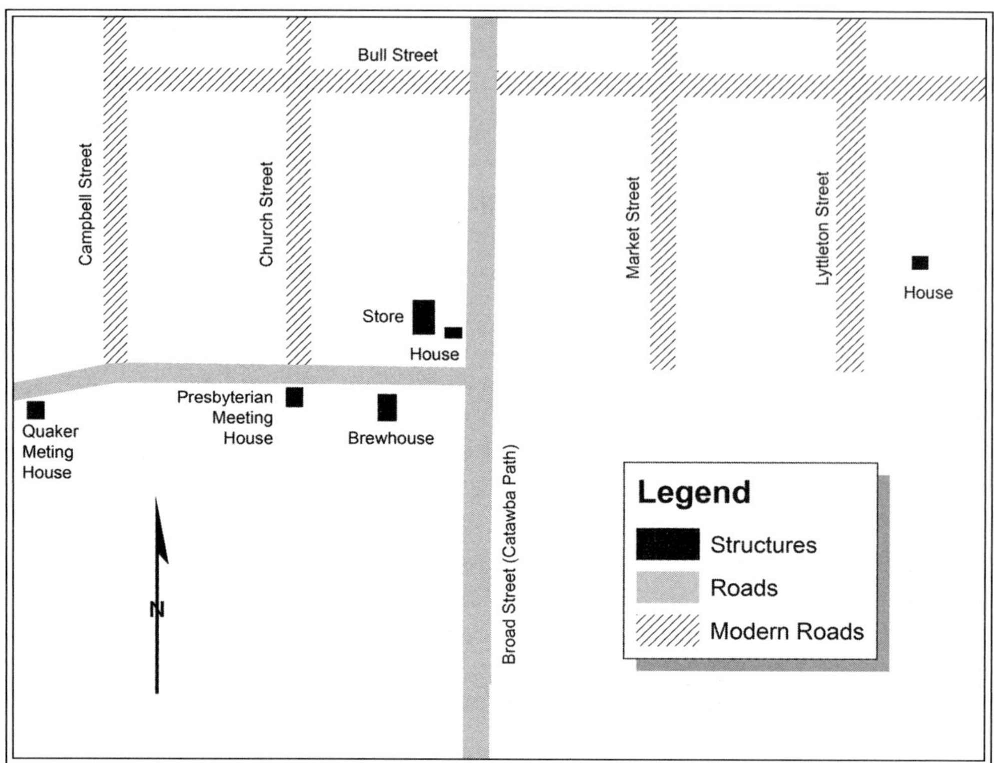

8.1 Locations of known structures at Camden in the 1760s, based on documentary and archaeological sources. Author's original map.

further imply that the structure was not a residence. Like contemporary brewhouses, Kershaw's Camden structure was a specialized industrial building whose workers probably lived elsewhere. Located just a short walk south of the store, the brewhouse was not isolated from other structures in the town.[15]

Directly north of the brewhouse tract, the two earthfast structures described earlier lay on the west side of the Catawba Path. The largest is likely to have been the original store at Pine Tree Hill, dating from at least the time of Joseph Kershaw's arrival. It continued in use as such well past the 1760s, serving as the principal storehouse for Kershaw & Co. at Camden. The assemblages of archaeological materials recovered from the store site reflected its function and longevity. Archaeological excavations also revealed that some of the massive wooden posts on which its frame rested had been replaced, evidence of maintenance efforts to preserve the older structure by keeping it in good repair. An analysis of the ceramic artifacts further testified to the store's use over a long period of time. Here were the slipped earthenwares, delfts, white salt-glazed stonewares that characterized the earlier phases of its occupation and also the hard-paste earthenwares that superseded them in use. The appearance of substantial quantities of creamware was unmistakable at Camden. This industrially produced fine, high-fired earthenware, so effectively marketed by Josiah Wedgwood by the mid-1760s, began to replace the older wares here. The large quantities found on the sites of this and other contemporary structures attest to the shifting economy, and its presence was a harbinger of things to come. Creamware and pearlware, which appeared slightly later, marked the extension of commercial trade into the interior and the continuous use of the building that played a central role in this endeavor.[16]

Artifacts also provide evidence of the store's principal function. The presence of barrel hoops and bale seals, the surviving parts of the containers in which goods were shipped, testify to the store's specialized function as the focus of mercantile activity, as do the variety of finished goods whose fragments found their way into the ground. The excavations yielded a wide array of imported items, including ceramics; glassware; furniture components; tools, hardware, locks, hinges, and other construction materials; clothing items such as shoe buckles, buttons, and cuff links; pins, needles, and thimbles; cooking vessels and implements; eating utensils; vehicle parts; and firearms. The presence of River Burnished wares, produced by Catawba potters at nearby villages in the Waxhaws, indicates a continued reliance on regional products in a transitional economy.[17]

One of the earliest houses at Pine Tree Hill, the smaller earthfast building seems to have been a domestic structure. Its wattle-and-daub chimney in the center of its western wall reflects this function, as do artifacts found there. They include a substantial number of items related to subsistence, the storing, preparation, and consumption of foods, lost or discarded personal items, and the remains of food disposed of as garbage, all of which imply that it was a living area. Artifacts recovered from pits associated with its construction testify to the building's early date, but later ceramics reveal that it continued in use through the 1760s. Built as a pioneer residence, the structure remained home to people associated with the nearby store and brewhouse and perhaps other activities associated with this cluster of businesses in early Camden.[18]

A third earthfast structure lay on a small eminence about a thousand feet to the east of the early settlement cluster along the Catawba Path. It consisted of a single bay, sixteen by sixteen feet square, the frame of which rested on posts set in narrow trenches. Three separate posts supported an overhang, perhaps a porch or platform, on its north side. Situated on lands owned by the partners, this building was probably a domestic structure whose occupants were affiliated with their activities at Camden (Fig. 8.1). Although it sat alone at the time of its construction, the building's location at the future site of Joseph Kershaw's mansion indicates a strong connection with Camden's principal merchant.[19]

Camden's buildings and activities attest to the town's growth and development in the 1760s. The addition of the brewhouse was significant because it introduced an industrial venture that marked the diversification of business activities in the early settlement. With its erection, Joseph Kershaw expanded his endeavors beyond trade to include manufacturing. In colonial America, the appearance of brewhouses accompanied a shift of beer-making beyond the household and was associated with an expansion of production to accommodate larger markets. The number of taverns in the vicinity of Camden, coupled with the partnership's additional stores, provided Kershaw with ample customers for beer and other malt beverages, a market that likely justified the early appearance of this facility.[20] The extensive use of brick in the construction of the brewhouse also points to the manufacture of this building product locally. Brick-making in colonial America generally arose in response to local needs, and its appearance at Camden accompanied the need to supply building materials to complement the products of the sawmills already in operation. Joseph Kershaw is known to have operated a brickyard at Camden before 1770, and the presence of brick in the dated remains of the brewhouse indicates that brick was produced here during the previous decade.[21] The brewhouse and brickyard accompanied the appearance of a diverse manufacturing base and the expansion of retail trade at Camden, trends characteristic of its emergence as a focus of specialized economic activity.

A New Plan for a New Town

Camden's choice as the judicial seat of Camden District brought the addition of a formal government institution that ensured the tiny settlement's role as a political center in the emerging backcountry. But that alone was not responsible for generating the multiple economic and social functions necessary to become a central place. Camden achieved this status because it was home to other regionwide activities, the kind that provided a wide variety of necessary products and services.[22] Camden's paramount role in long-distance trade made it the principal frontier town in South Carolina's interior, and it had already acquired the broad range of manufacturing, repair, and service activities associated with its role as a centralized market. The addition of a judicial function offered those invested in Camden's future an opportunity to consolidate the town's position as an administrative seat in a region in the midst of transition.

Official recognition of a frontier settlement as a corporate entity was an important acknowledgment of its status as a central place. This was particularly difficult to obtain in South Carolina, given the scant provision for local administration that gave no municipality the authority to govern itself.[23] The Assembly, however, granted limited authority to specific communities by allowing them to regulate officially sanctioned fairs. Ashley Ferry, Dorchester, Childsbury, and other centers of periodic trade in the lowcountry acquired charters that facilitated high-volume traffic among merchants in a sparsely populated region. Long accepted as a symbol of market centrality, European fairs served as foci of both wholesale and retail exchange that involved long-distance trade in luxuries rather than for short-term household needs. The exclusive nature of fairs also made them a lucrative source of income and a basis of authority for their managers.[24] Establishing a fair at Pine Tree Hill would provide its leading residents a semblance of corporate authority. As early as 1765 the partners submitted a petition to the Assembly requesting support for a fair to be held on Samuel Wyly's land each spring and fall. Although their initial effort was rebuffed, a subsequent request met with success. In 1774 Joseph Kershaw, Ely Kershaw, John Chesnut, William Ancrum, and Aaron Loocock were granted authority to hold fairs of three days' duration at Camden in April and November. The charter also allowed them to appoint a manager and a clerk with authority to hold a Court of Piepowder, a local tribunal with jurisdiction over disputes between individuals during that time. This provision established, at least for limited periods, a municipal administrative authority apart from that of the district court system.[25] The presence of a fair distinguished Camden as the earliest corporate entity in the interior of South Carolina.

Camden's emergence as a central place brought the promise of physical expansion to the frontier settlement. The charter for the fair entailed laying out grounds for this activity,

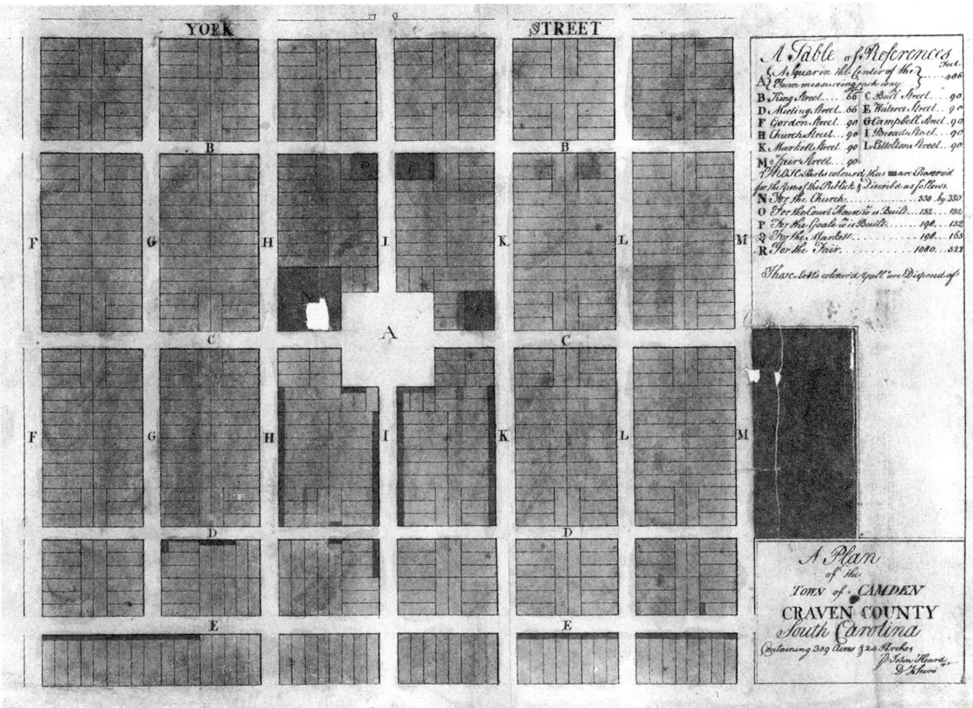

8.2 The plan of Camden surveyed by John Heard in 1771. Broad Street, which followed the Catawba Path, bisects the settlement and intersects its central square. Lots for the courthouse and jail lay one block north of the square, and those reserved for the Church of England and the market were situated to its left and right. The fairgrounds were just east of the town. The shaded lots are those sold in the 1770s. Courtesy of South Carolina Department of Archives and History, Columbia, South Carolina, Series S-213192, Vol.37, 146.

and the pending erection of the new courthouse and jail also demanded specific locations for them to be set aside. Accommodating these additional activities required a systematic plan that enlarged the early settlement situated at the intersection of the Catawba Path and the ferry road. As early as 1771, Deputy Surveyor John Heard prepared a plat for the new town.[26] Laid out on a grid pattern, it featured a central square at the center of a network of streets that met at right angles and formed a number of rectangular blocks (Fig. 8.2). As a focal point for municipal institutions and a gathering place for public activities, the open square was a common centralizing element of urban design in Europe. The central square, when combined with a grid layout, created a compact settlement, facilitated control and movement, and allowed controlled expansion. The design was well adapted to accommodate conditions of rapid settlement by large numbers of people, and English planners successfully applied this arrangement in colonial settlements in Ireland as well as in North America.[27]

The adoption of common urban-planning elements emphasized the close relationship between South Carolina's capital and its central frontier settlement. It undoubtedly reflected the strong ties between backcountry elites and the city's merchants, many of whom also maintained economic and social links to Philadelphia concerns.[28] Camden's square followed a style that appeared in British America at Philadelphia in 1682. This plan, distinguished by major roads diverging from the center of each side, appeared earlier in South Carolina, where planners employed it to situate Charleston's principal public buildings. At Camden the square was located on the Catawba Path, now called Broad Street, at the north end of the block where the early settlement lay. The town's planners not only copied Charleston's square but also employed similar names for its major roads. As in the capital, Broad, Church, Meeting, King, and Church Streets defined the core of the town. Lyttleton, Bull, and possibly Campbell Streets commemorated recent or current governors, Gordon honored the provincial chief justice, York was named for the Kershaws' native Yorkshire, the ferry road on which the Quaker and Presbyterian meetinghouses were situated became Meeting Street, and Wateree commemorated the great river.[29]

Camden's plan also expressed the town's importance through the systematic allocation of space for significant public institutions. Most notably, it provided lots for the courthouse and jail on the block north of the square on the corners of King and Broad Streets. The smallest of the public lots, they enclosed four-tenths of an acre and three-fourths of an acre, respectively. Facing the square on the west was a large tract of two and a half acres reserved for the Church of England at the corner of Bull and Church streets. A market site occupied three-fourths of an acre east of the square at the intersection of Bull and Market Streets. The largest tract bordered Fair Street at the eastern boundary of the town and was set aside for the fairgrounds. This parcel of more than thirteen acres lay at the end of Bull Street. The placement of all of the principal civic institutions either on the central square or along one the streets that intersected it arranged the public functions of the town around a new focal point just north of the initial settlement. The geometry of Camden's new plan governed access to its center and clustered the town's political, social, and economic institutions so as to mark the town as a focus of power for the far-flung rural district it served.[30] As such, it recognized symbolically the elite role of Camden's leaders, who sought to retain their status during the backcountry's commercial transition.

The form of Camden's lots, with their narrow, deep shape, could accommodate a high-density population. Camden's survey subdivided the town site into 630 individual lots, each sixty-six feet wide to maximize the number of parcels with street frontage. Most faced north-south running streets and extended back 264 feet to the center of the block. The shorter 198-foot-deep lots fronted streets at each corner, and twelve lots measuring only 132 feet long faced the square. In order to accommodate the existing Presbyterian churchyard, the southward course of Church Street terminated at Meeting Street. On the sharply descending ground along Wateree Street at Camden's southern edge, the lots all faced northward.[31]

The new town plan clearly sought to reshape the form of settlement at Pine Tree Hill in an urban image, but it had other implications as well. Platting an organized settlement on the corporate property of Kershaw & Co. marked a shift in at the partners' economic strategy. By alienating land and incorporating public institutions on property that lay at the core of their backcountry empire, they abandoned their primary dependence on trade and adopted a new strategy more relevant to the commercial economy, one capable of taking advantage of the new opportunities for growth offered through specialized production and diversified marketing. Increased political stability, an expanding consumer base, and improved transportation opened new avenues for capitalist ventures in the interior, and the partners were not amiss in taking advantage of the changing circumstances. But doing so also prompted changes in their corporate organization.

The Partnership Dissolves

In July 1774 an advertisement appeared in Charleston newspapers announcing the sale of the property belonging to Kershaw & Co., to occur in Camden at the beginning of the next court term on November 7 and to continue until the whole of it was sold. The disposal of goods under such circumstances was common, but this was no unplanned dispersal of a business or an estate. It followed the terms of the agreement that had formed the partnership ten years earlier. The joint stock company had expired at the end of ten years and four months, and all its assets throughout the region were to be liquidated six months after that time, with the proceeds divided among the partners.[32]

A description of the assets involved provides an intriguing look at both the size and scope of the partners' operation at mid-decade. Camden remained the heart of the business, with stores and "houses" on the property and mills and industries situated nearby. In addition to the buildings and "stock of store goods," the partners possessed extensive human property as well, a description of which reveals further the variety of business activities carried out by the company. They included "about one hundred valuable Negroes, being chiefly coopers, millers, bakers, wagoners, jobbing carpenters, boatmen, and field slaves belonging to the late partnership." The sale also advertised the partners' extensive real estate holdings in the Wateree Valley, "amongst which are many settled and well-improved plantations, a great part whereof is rich river low ground, [which] will be set up in convenient tracts of one hundred to one or two thousand acres, so as to accommodate purchasers of all ranks." To facilitate the sale of these assets, the partners offered buyers credit on larger parcels. Clearly the enterprise had expanded beyond trade to include production and, notably, plantation agriculture.[33]

Beyond the Wateree Valley, the sale sought to liquidate the "commodious & well-situated stores [of Chesnut & Co.] at Granby." Apparently still a smaller operation, its assets were not listed separately and were probably included with those of the parent store. In contrast, sales of the more extensive Pee Dee properties were managed separately. Set to be auctioned a week later at the new courthouse at Long Bluff, Ely Kershaw & Co.'s assets included the "valuable plantation called Liberty Hill, and all the adjacent lands at and near Cheraw Hill . . . , together with their stores, houses, mills, and stock of store goods, and about fifty valuable Negroes, employed in everything on their business at Chatham."[34] The Rocky Mount store is conspicuous by its absence, and the partners may well have closed their Waxhaws venture prior to 1774.

The auction met with limited success, and only part of the partnership's assets had passed into the hands of new owners when it concluded on December 8, 1774. A substantial portion of the lands and Camden town lots remained unsold, prompting the announcement of a second public sale in April 1777. In the meantime, the former partners retained control over all of the backcountry stores as well as the outlet in the capital. When the sale concluded, all of the remaining property, including the stores, was divided among them.[35] But even then the firm's estate remained unsettled for some time afterward.[36]

Although largely fragmentary, account records show a continued pattern of interaction among the former partners. Statements of indebtedness and transfer of lands and credits continued to pass between them. William Ancrum dealt with John Chesnut and Ely Kershaw as well as with Kershaw, Boykin & Co., while Chesnut & Kershaw held accounts with Chesnut & Co. and Chesnut & Co. at Granby, and later the firm traded with Ely Kershaw and Samuel Boykin. Despite the formal breakup of the partnership, the ties developed by its former members in succeeding years not only maintained the network forged by Joseph Kershaw but also enlarged it to form a complex system of economic and social linkages that helped them maintain their positions in a changing economy.

The account records attest to a continual shifting of resources following the breakup of the company. In the succeeding years the stores continued to be the cornerstone of their business activity, and each remained in the hands of individual owners who operated them as single businessmen or through new partnerships. At Camden Joseph Kershaw and John Chesnut continued to do business as Kershaw, Chesnut & Co. but also as Chesnut & Kershaw after 1778. Kershaw also maintained accounts as an individual merchant from 1774 to 1776 and as Joseph Kershaw & Co. after 1774. In 1776 he partnered with the Wateree storekeeper Samuel Boykin to form Kershaw, Boykin & Co. In addition, he formed a partnership with Duncan McRa, a young merchant recently arrived from his native Scotland. John Chesnut operated independently but also as Chesnut & Co. of Granby in 1775 and as Chesnut & Co. from Camden after 1775. Ely Kershaw continued the Pee Dee store as Ely Kershaw & Co. at Chatham, and by 1779 he had entered the partnership of Kershaw, Lithgow & Co. William Ancrum engaged in business independently and in partnership with the Charleston merchants Philotheos Chiffelle and Archibald Brown. A third Kershaw sibling, William, emigrated to South Carolina and established himself as an import merchant in Charleston as early as 1778, and by the following year he was supplying his brother's store in Camden with finished goods and slaves in exchange for indigo, tobacco, and other commodities.[37]

Surviving documents reveal the extent of the new firms' business dealings. As Camden's principal merchants, Kershaw, Chesnut & Co. maintained accounts with large overseas suppliers, such as the London mercantile firm Greenwood & Higginson, but also traded with smaller local trading companies such as the Wateree partnership of Kershaw, Boykin & Co. and Robert Stark, a planter and member along with Joseph Kershaw on the commission to clear the Wateree River. They held a standing account with Thomas Sumter as well. An entrepreneur who operated a mercantile business and mills from his wife's plantation in the High Hills of Santee, Sumter became a controversial military and political leader in the turbulent years ahead. He married Mary Cantey, second cousin of both John Cantey of Camden and his sister Mary, who was the wife of the prominent Santee planter and statesman Richard Richardson. Sumter's marriage into the Cantey family provided affinal links to the Richardsons as well as to the merchants Ely Kershaw and John Chesnut.[38]

The arrival of new merchants who established stores or other businesses in the 1770s further complicated the economic picture on the Wateree. Charles Ogilvie came to South

Carolina in 1751 and afterward operated sporadically as a merchant there and in London, most recently as a partner in the Charleston firm of Forbes & Ogilvie. His auspicious marriage to a wealthy heiress, Mary Michie, helped him weather business failures and amass considerable real estate in the backcountry, including several thousand acres in the vicinity of Pine Tree Hill. Ogilvie initially remained in the capital as an absentee owner but later removed to Camden as early as 1773 and resided there at least part-time. He engaged in land and other business transactions with Joseph and Ely Kershaw, John Chesnut, and William Ancrum, as well as with the store at Camden. Charles Ogilvie's nephew George was an attorney who became an indigo planter north of Camden in 1775 and three years later was trading in the town. He also acted as his uncle's agent in business transactions. Through his economic activities as a merchant, planter, and trader, Charles Ogilvie no doubt benefited from his business association with Joseph Kershaw in the years just before the Revolution, a favor he was soon to return in an unexpected way.[39]

Henry Rugeley became an important member of Camden's mercantile community in the 1770s. A native of Huntingdonshire, England, he emigrated to South Carolina in 1769 to join his older brother Rowland, who had accepted a position as register of mesne conveyance for the province three years earlier. Upon Henry's arrival, the brothers entered into a mercantile venture under the name Henry Rugeley & Co., a Charleston partnership that eventually included a third brother, William, who returned to England several years later. Despite an early setback, they succeeded as merchants and began acquiring properties in the interior, particularly in western South Carolina.[40] Henry and Rowland Rugeley shifted the focus of their interest to the Wateree Valley in 1776, however, with the purchase of two tracts totaling 350 acres on Wateree Creek west of the river. In August of the same year Henry acquired three tracts on the east side of the Wateree on Flat Rock and Grannys Quarter Creeks about thirteen miles north of Camden. He combined these parcels to form a five-hundred-acre plantation that he named Clermont. This became his residence and the site of his store and several industrial activities, which employed twenty enslaved laborers. At Clermont he erected a sawmill, a gristmill, two bolting mills, facilities for processing indigo, a tan yard, a substantial log barn, several log houses, a tavern, and his dwelling, described by a contemporary as "elegant."[41] Rowland Rugeley died unexpectedly in 1777, leaving his property and business interests to his brother Henry, who became the owner of substantial assets in addition to his economic venture on the Wateree.[42]

Henry Rugeley operated his Clermont store from January 1776 to at least September 1779, and a surviving ledger reveals the complexity of his activities. From its beginnings, the store appears to have been an operation of considerable size. The enterprise kept separate accounts for the grist- and sawmills, tan yard, the tavern, the plantation, and a second store at Richmond. Its ledger also maintained accounts for the principal commodities traded by its customers—wheat, corn, indigo, tobacco, deerskins, cattle, pork, tallow, and flax seed—as well as for carriage of produce and merchandise to and from Charleston and the rental of slaves. Over the course of its existence, the store held accounts with several hundred customers and did business with other merchants. Joseph Kershaw and John Chesnut, both individually and together, did business with Rugeley, as did Kershaw & Wyly, a new partnership that included John Wyly, son of the late Samuel. The store also hired the services of Zebulon Gaunt, who managed Kershaw's sawmills, and Simon Shy, a Camden blacksmith. The planter and businessman George Ogilvie received the services of the store, and the tavernkeeper Jasper Sutton purchased rum there. Most of Rugeley's customers appear to have been residents of the region, including members of the Adamson and Milhous families, both planters "on the Wateree," and Robert Thompson, who lived "near Clermont," as well as John Marshall, Luke Petty, and George Summerville, who resided farther upriver on Cedar and Beaver Creeks in the Waxhaws.[43] Their individual accounts recorded the flow of produce into the store in exchange for various goods or services it provided.

Other customers came to Rugeley's store from farther afield and their presence reflected the extent of the region's integration into the wider order. Two individuals stand out as representatives of larger political institutions that now extended into the interior. Normally residents of Charleston, they traveled here in an official capacity that reflected the changing times. Thomas Knox Gordon had been appointed Chief Justice of South Carolina by Crown officials eager to install professional British jurists on the bench of its newly created judicial system. Such "placemen" became increasingly unpopular among residents growing restless with the assertion of royal authority in the province. Gordon presided over the first court for Camden District in 1772 and tried cases on the judicial circuit until 1777. He repeated this duty in subsequent years, and his multiple appearances at Rugeley's store were undoubtedly connected with his travels to Camden.[44]

A second visitor, John Rutledge, visited the store only months after his election as president of South Carolina's provincial government of in March 1776. A lawyer by training, Rutledge became politically active as a member of the Assembly. During the 1760s he opposed repressive measures such as the Stamp Act and supported self-government for the American colonies. As relations with the Crown deteriorated, he participated as a delegate to the Continental and Provincial Congresses, and in the spring of 1776 he was chosen to head a new constitutional government in South Carolina. By the time of his visit to Rugeley's store in August, the rift with Great Britain had widened and hostilities already begun.[45] Rutledge's connection with the rising political order made him a central character in the upcoming drama of the American Revolution, and his presence at the store reflected the increasing ties between the backcountry and the larger world, as well as the increasing importance of Camden and its inhabitants in the political structure of South Carolina.

The creation of an official administrative structure in the backcountry began to alter the social structure that had grown around the organization of trade. This judicial institution replaced the less formal arrangements that tied merchants, producers, and customers in a hierarchical system based on kinship, marriage, and reciprocity. With the passage of the Circuit Court Act, the region passed from relative isolation into a much fuller participation in the affairs of the province. No longer did an individual's status rest solely on centrality in a network of relationships that derived from trade. But the links that constituted existing networks did not disappear and in fact proved extremely resilient to the impact of change. Indeed, these ties formed a structure through which individuals retained and built status in the new institutional framework.

In response to the new institutional order, those who had played central roles in the old mercantile networks adapted by shifting away from a reliance on trade and adopted a business strategy linked more closely to market production. Joseph Kershaw, his former partners, and other backcountry elites abandoned their emphasis on maintaining integrated networks of stores and a dependence on retail sales and concentrated instead on increasing the volume of production of export staples and controlling their processing. The partners seem to have foreseen this development when they planned the dissolution of the partnership and the liquidation of its assets. Although this transition did not happen as smoothly as it might have, the strategy provided its membership with capital and flexibility to focus their endeavors in new directions. As a result, they curtailed their larger operation in favor of smaller trading partnerships of more limited scope. Their actions opened the backcountry retail market to new competitors, such as Henry Rugeley, who in turn provided additional outlets for the export staples produced on emerging plantations, which relied on established mills and other facilities developed in the growing town of Camden in the 1770s.

The administrative framework established by the Circuit Court Act helped consolidate a new political order in the backcountry, one that provided residents with an avenue to public positions through which they might achieve and maintain power, wealth, and social status. The Circuit Court Act expanded civil authority farther by moving the administration of justice out of the hands of the provost marshal's office in Charleston and into the separate judicial districts. It authorized the appointment of a sheriff for each district, who oversaw deputies, jailors, and others who administered the courts and jails. The act also empowered the judges of the circuit court to draw grand juries and petit juries from each district to carry out the business of the courts. In addition, it appointed commissioners for each district to superintend the construction of the courthouses and jails, a position that conveyed authority tied directly to urban planning on the frontier.[46] At the same time the Assembly created two new parishes that expanded backcountry representation in the Assembly. In addition to the existing St. Mark's Parish, which encompassed the Wateree drainage, St. Matthew's Parish now included the residents of the Congaree basin, and St. David's Parish provided a political voice for the inhabitants of the Pee Dee. Although parishes were ostensibly ecclesiastical districts intended to support the established church, their broader civil function also established the administrative infrastructure to lay out and maintain roads, conduct elections, and oversee the welfare of orphans and the poor. Although these developments provided services and representation for the backcountry, they failed to establish a structure for local government. They did, however, create a basis for organizing the region politically and provided the means to form an elite comparable to that of the lowcountry.

The Rise of a Political Elite

By the mid-1770s those who had risen to power during the settlement period adopted a new strategy to maintain their status as regional leaders. The shift in emphasis from regional exchange to export market sales presented new opportunities for those who controlled resources to accrue wealth through expanded agricultural production and the growth of processing, transportation, and manufacturing. As the decade began, plantations in the Wateree Valley were beginning to produce substantial quantities of export staples such as wheat, tobacco, and indigo. The yields of the land fed Joseph Kershaw's mills, filled his warehouses at Camden, and passed over his wharf to boats carrying backcountry commodities to lowcountry markets. And his sawmills consumed the pine forests to make lumber for new and larger construction, while his brickyard produced material for substantial buildings to replace the initial log-and-earthfast structures. Kershaw's brewhouse undoubtedly supplied the taverns of John Cantey, Jasper Sutton, and others to quench the thirst of Wateree Valley residents. But the former partners were not the only ones to prosper in the new economy. The McGirt family also operated sawmills, and the growing need to process agricultural products encouraged newcomers like Henry Rugeley to invest in multiple processing ventures at his Clermont plantation.

The backcountry's future lay in commercial agriculture, and those desiring status through wealth needed land for production and investment. By the time of its breakup, members of the partnership had collectively and individually amassed a significant amount of backcountry real estate through grants or purchases of previously owned properties along the Wateree. Joseph Kershaw alone possessed more than seven thousand acres, and the other partners had each accumulated holdings of more than a thousand acres. Both Kershaw brothers, John Chesnut, and William Ancrum had working plantations on their lands in the mid-1770s. But they were not the only rising planters. Samuel Wyly's estate included more than three thousand acres, and the Cantey family collectively owned at least five thousand acres on the Wateree and Santee Rivers, including lands on Town Creek south of Camden. Marriage into the Cantey family also underwrote the success of the rising Santee planter Thomas Sumter, and it provided additional resources for Richard Richardson, who already possessed an estate of eight thousand acres on the Santee. William Boykin, whose son Samuel had been a leader in the Regulator movement, amassed more than 1,400 acres in the vicinity of Swift and Town Creeks. Three other former Regulators, James Cary, Charles Woodmason, and Joshua English, possessed estates of 2,262, 1,600, and 1,200 acres, respectively, and all owned slaves. Cary raised, tobacco, indigo, and livestock in addition to operating a sawmill. Many residents of the Wateree Valley engaged in plantation agriculture, employing enslaved labor on smaller tracts. Among them was the new immigrant George Ogilvie, as well as older colonists like John Adamson, Abraham Belton, Joshua Dinkins, and John Pain.[47] Although large-scale, specialized, commercial agriculture promised a secure and profitable livelihood in the new economy, it did not by itself guarantee its participants membership in the new social elite. To rise to positions of leadership required that planters not only refocus their earlier economic activities but also use their role as large producers to acquire public positions as vehicles through which to advance politically.

Joseph Kershaw stands out as the most successful of those who rose rapidly to political prominence in the Wateree Valley. As the central figure at the Pine Tree Hill store, Kershaw possessed the opportunity to enrich himself financially through trade and to acquire wealth in land and other resources. But the social networks he developed to facilitate the expansion of the store's business also opened doors to public offices that brought access to power and membership in the elite class that controlled South Carolina economically and politically. Soon after his arrival in the backcountry, Kershaw began his public service through his role as supplier and later agent to the Catawbas, positions he continued to hold throughout his life. Gradually he acquired such public offices as were available on the frontier, serving on commissions to open a road from the vicinity of Pine Tree Hill to the Pee Dee in 1762 and another to clear the Wateree two years later. In addition to operating in an official capacity, Kershaw performed other services that benefited the larger community. In the fall of 1766, he provided foodstuffs from the Pine Tree Hill store to settlers in need of provisions during a drought. Later that year he offered critical support for the missionary work of a fellow Anglican, Charles Woodmason, who had recently become rector of St. Mark's Parish. Kershaw was careful to avoid the awkwardness of sponsoring an Anglican church in Camden, but he pledged a large contribution toward erecting a chapel of ease in the High Hills of Santee, a region whose inhabitants were less hostile to the established church. He also maintained an affiliation with the small Anglican body formed in Camden by Woodmason and continued by the Rev. Theodorus Swain Drage following Woodmason's departure in 1772. Membership in this group helped Kershaw cement ties to prominent Anglican planters, such as John Cantey, Richard Richardson, James McGirt, and James Cary.[48]

Joseph Kershaw's central role within the pioneer community on the Wateree facilitated his entry into public service on a provincial level, and he was elected to the Assembly as a representative of St. Mark's Parish in 1769. His office took him to the capital in Charleston, where he mingled with the merchants and planters who formed the colony's elite class of lawmakers as well as with the appointed royal officials who administered South Carolina in the king's name. Membership in the Assembly also renewed his association with fellow legislators Henry Laurens and Aaron Loocock and introduced him to John Rutledge and William Henry Drayton, both of whom would play key roles in Kershaw's political future. South Carolina's legislature was a closely knit group in which established patterns of association, as well as kin ties of blood and marriage, promoted the communication and cooperation that provided access to resources and power. As a member of this body, Kershaw saw his network grow well beyond those associated with trade to include the colony's social and political elite.[49]

Reelected to three additional Assemblies, Joseph Kershaw served in South Carolina's legislature through the remainder of the colonial period. As a representative from St. Mark's Parish, he supported backcountry interests, including demands for increased representation and social services. He chaired a committee that successfully advocated dividing the parish into several smaller administrative units, and he supported building parish churches and providing public schools. Kershaw also served on the committee that brought in the bill to establish the judicial districts in 1769. The Circuit Court Act named him one of the commissioners to build the courthouse and jail at Camden, the construction of which benefited his mercantile businesses directly and promoted the development of his new town. Kershaw's role in creating and implementing the administrative framework of the interior enhanced his political status as well. Following the untimely death in 1772 of the recently appointed Roger-Peter Handasyde Hatley, Joseph Kershaw became the sheriff of Camden District. Upon taking this office, he assumed the paramount position of civil administrative authority in the central South Carolina backcountry.[50]

Residence in the capital afforded Joseph Kershaw frequent opportunities to make contacts that extended his network outside South Carolina to include important merchants and others there on business. His association with Charleston merchants such as Henry Laurens offered access to members of the large and influential Quaker mercantile community in Philadelphia with whom they had regular dealings. His former partners William Ancrum and Aaron Loocock did business directly with John Reynell, and through them

Kershaw developed close ties to this wealthy Philadelphia merchant. He also benefited from his association with the pioneer Wyly family, whose Quaker roots linked them to leading Philadelphia Friends, including Israel Pemberton Jr., a leader of the Quaker party in Pennsylvania and a member of an important merchant family.[51] Through his marriage to Sarah Mathis, who was related to the Pemberton family, Kershaw found a close affinal tie to this mercantile community as well. It is hardly surprising that, when dining with the Kershaws and John Wyly in Charleston during the winter of 1772, the prominent Quaker merchant William Dillwyn remarked not only on the northern ties of the enterprising member of the Assembly from St. Mark's but also on his political and economic status. "He is concerned in a very large Trade," Dillwyn noted, "and besides being one of the most popular Men in the Government, will probably be one of the richest."[52]

Joseph Kershaw realized that, in addition to possessing wealth and forging connections with the political and social elite, he needed to provide a proper education for his family as a key element in maintaining his status in colonial society. Obtaining the necessary schooling to assume a prominent place in society required formal instruction, access to which was uncertain on the frontier and uneven generally in South Carolina. Although both public and private facilities existed in the lowcountry for those who could afford tuition, many settlers enrolled their sons in English public schools. Taking advantage of this opportunity, Joseph Kershaw sent his eldest two sons, James and John, to begin their formal education at Rishworth School, an Anglican institution founded in 1724 in his family's home county of Yorkshire. Following their preparatory classical education there, they attended other schools, probably at Dorchester and Worcester, and in 1778 were enrolled in Dilathorpe's School at Richmond. Both remained in England to complete their education, not returning to South Carolina until the 1780s.[53]

Joseph Kershaw's political star continued to rise as relations between South Carolina's legislature and Crown officials soured. In response to issues involving trade, parliamentary taxation, and imperial policy, conditions deteriorated sufficiently to promote a movement for independence paralleling that occurring in Britain's other North American colonies. In late 1773 influential citizens in Charleston formed a general committee, which called a general meeting of the province to select delegates to a Continental Congress meeting in Philadelphia, the first of two congresses that created a Continental Association to provide a united front to deal with imperial authority. The general meeting formed the basis for a de facto government of South Carolina, and in November it called for the formation of a Provincial Congress as a governing body for the province. Although the lowcountry continued to dominate the new legislature, the fifty-five delegates from thirteen backcountry districts representing the region's interests now comprised nearly 30 percent of the Provincial Congress.[54]

As a member of the Assembly who was well connected with and shared the interests of the province's political and economic elites, Joseph Kershaw played an important role in the First Provincial Congress. In January 1775 he was elected a representative from the District Eastward of Wateree River, a large area that stretched from the Santee to the North Carolina border and east to the Pee Dee River. Here he joined older associates from the region, Richard Richardson and Aaron Loocock, and his brother Ely, as well as the politically ambitious Thomas Sumter. As a member of the Provincial Congress, called into session again in June, Kershaw was elected to the committee formed to carry into execution the Continental Association, a body created to implement a ban on trade with Great Britain. He and other South Carolina's representatives engineered a key compromise that protected the province's precarious agricultural economy by allowing the continued export of rice.[55]

Now an influential public figure in the province, Kershaw represented the Council of Safety, Congress's executive body headed by Henry Laurens, in several important political missions to the backcountry. On its behalf, he journeyed upriver to the Catawba towns in July to deliver a message from the Council, and he negotiated an agreement with the Catawbas to form a regiment of forty to fifty rangers to support the new government under the direction of a white commander.[56] Then in August he joined William Henry Drayton, the Rev. William Tennent, and the Rev. Oliver Hart to assist in a mission sponsored by the Council to convince residents of the interior to support its demands against Great Britain. Rendezvousing with the party at the Congaree store, Kershaw and Richard Richardson accompanied them north into the German-speaking Dutch Fork between the Saluda and Broad Rivers in a generally unsuccessful attempt to gain the backing of its residents.[57] As dissension moved toward open conflict, the Council of Safety began to gather munitions in anticipation of armed confrontation. Kershaw's position as a merchant drew him into their plans in September, when the Council stored powder and lead at his Camden store for use by a militia regiment commanded by Richard Richardson.[58] When Joseph Kershaw formally entered the service of the new government the following month, he did so not only as the backcountry's dominant merchant but also as a member of the region's emerging planter class and South Carolina's political elite.

Although Joseph Kershaw was clearly the central figure in the Wateree Valley in the 1770s, the period also witnessed the rise of John Chesnut to positions of political importance. His significant role in the partnership made him a key member of Kershaw's network, but as a junior partner Chesnut remained in Kershaw's shadow, and his public presence continued relatively modest through the early years of the decade. Chesnut directed his energies toward managing his remaining trading business of Chesnut & Co. at Granby and assembling the land to successfully enlarge his commercial agricultural activities. Nevertheless, his role in public life also began to expand. He occupied the minor positions of tax collector for St. Mark's Parish and Wateree River commissioner, posts he acquired in 1765. Chesnut served on the commission to construct the Camden District courthouse and jail in 1770, and by four years later he had joined the other four partners as a proprietor of the Camden Fair.[59]

Deteriorating relations between Great Britain and its North American colonies provided opportunities that shaped Chesnut's political career. Residents in the District between the Broad and Saluda Rivers elected him to the First Provincial Congress, and with Joseph Kershaw he represented St. Mark's Parish on the committee to implement the Continental Association. The Provincial Congress commissioned Chesnut as an officer in a newly created ranger regiment in May 1775. Following provocative events in neighboring North Carolina that threatened delegates who had issued the radical Mecklenburg Resolves in Charlotte, the Council of Safety directed that the two seditious Salisbury lawyers be arrested and tasked Chesnut with escorting them to Charleston. Later, in August and

September, he placed his store in the Congarees at the disposal of the Drayton-Tennent-Hart mission.[60]

Ely Kershaw's political career grew out of his experience as the partnership's merchant on the upper Pee Dee. In addition to occupying a central position in the region's economy, Kershaw became a leading member of the Anglican community in St. David's Parish and was elected to its vestry in 1770. In this position, he exercised secular responsibilities, such as overseeing the welfare of the poor, and was the collector of a tax to defray the cost of their maintenance. His administrative experience led to his appointment as a commissioner to erect the St. David's Parish church at Cheraw Hill, which was constructed on land he donated in 1774.[61]

As a merchant active in public affairs, Ely Kershaw was selected as a member of the commission to erect the Cheraws District courthouse and jail in 1770. This position placed him in the center of a dispute regarding their location, a controversy that impacted the direction of regional development. Initially the commission proposed that the buildings be erected at Cheraw Hill. As the site of the partners' Chatham store and the parish church, it possessed two integrating functions that made it a likely choice as the court location. Locating an administrative activity there might attract trade to a store that had lost business, because merchants in Cross Creek, North Carolina, had begun to siphon off grain formerly shipped south to Charleston. Cheraw Hill's northerly location far up the Pee Dee, however, placed it away from the geographical center of the district and made it a poor choice for an administrative center serving residents further downriver. In the minds of many, Long Bluff, a site eighteen miles downriver, was a far more convenient location, and their argument convinced the Assembly to override the recommendations of the commission and direct that the facilities be erected there. Despite its role as the district seat, however, Long Bluff remained a small, specialized settlement, and the Chatham store stayed the center of regional trade in the years prior to the Revolution.[62]

The coming crisis with Great Britain also promoted Ely Kershaw's political rise and irrevocably altered his life. With his brother, he was elected to represent the District Eastward of Wateree River at the Provincial Congress in January 1775, and served on its executive committee. Kershaw was also named to the Committee of Observation for St. David's Parish, organized to identify enemies of the provincial government. When Congress created a regiment of rangers under the command of William Thomson of Orangeburg in June, it appointed Kershaw captain of a company to be raised in Camden District. His selection reflected the Council of Safety's realization that holding the backcountry required the loyalty of the region's "most influential gentlemen," whom they designated officers of units assigned there.[63] Ely Kershaw's company encamped with Col. Thompson's regiment at Granby in the Congarees in July, engaged in recruiting and fitting out the militia. By early August his Fourth Company of Rangers reached its full strength. Still without adequate resources, the Council of Safety had to rely on Capt. Kershaw to supply the provincial militia with ammunition. The Council also called on its nascent force to support the Drayton-Tennent-Hart mission, and William Henry Drayton chose Kershaw and Thompson to accompany him as members of the delegation negotiating with Loyalist elements in Ninety Six District.[64]

Others involved in the network of trade in the Wateree Valley also assumed political roles in the changing backcountry. Aaron Loocock expanded his public career in Charleston to include offices with wider breadth. In addition to serving in the Assembly in 1768, he was a member of the General Committee of the Non-Importation Association, which implemented an agreement to boycott British ports. Residents of the District Eastward of Wateree River elected Loocock to the First Provincial Congress in 1775 after he returned from a three-year visit to England to recover his health. He was actively involved with its financial activities, signing certificates of credit issued by the new government and acting as a receiver of pay for William Thompson's regiment.[65] The Boykin brothers, who owned extensive properties on Town and Swift Creeks south of Camden, spread their public service over a wide section of the backcountry. Samuel, the former Regulator, represented Saxe Gotha on the Committee of the Continental Association, created by the First Provincial Congress to prevent seizures of property for debt. When tensions increased in the summer of 1775, the Council of Safety offered him a commission to form and organize a ranger unit composed of Catawba warriors. His younger brothers also occupied public offices. Burwell Boykin served on the vestry of St. David's Parish in 1770, and he represented the parish on the Committee of Continental Association. Francis Boykin was commissioned a lieutenant in Ely Kershaw's company of rangers in 1775.[66] The members of other older families became active politically as well. Samuel Milhous and John Wyly both served on the committee to construct the courthouse and jail, and Wyly, son of the late Quaker leader, assumed the position of Camden District sheriff in 1773.[67]

On the eve of the American Revolution, new formal institutions had begun to replace older social structures based upon kinship and association. The penetration of commercial trade and the creation of the new backcountry parishes and circuit court districts obviated the need for elaborate personal networks that facilitated systematic long-distance exchange and maintained stability in the frontier settlements. These networks arose from the efforts of Joseph Kershaw, the central figure in the partnership that provided the organizational framework for the backcountry economy. Although the firm no longer held the region together, the networks it had created left an indelible imprint on the region's political structure. Individuals capable of managing key administrative positions had emerged from the networks that organized the elements of trade, and the relationships among them endured. By the 1770s, Kershaw had become not only a wealthy merchant and landowner but also one of the most powerful political figures in the interior. Many associated with him employed their ties to rise in a new society that provided a formal structure in which to obtain and exercise power in new arenas. Nowhere in the backcountry was the rise of the new elite more conspicuous than in the principal settlement of Camden.

The Great White House

The 1771 survey of Camden provided a plan for orderly expansion as well as an arrangement of the urban activities associated with its new role. Focused on a main square, Camden's grid accommodated public functions and anticipated the dense occupation of a nucleated settlement. Indeed, the pattern of lots maximized access and provided for orderly growth from the town's center. Elements of the town were already in place by the time of the partnership's sale of the property in 1774. Joseph Kershaw's store, brewhouse, and other buildings, the Presbyterian church, and the Quaker meetinghouse stood on the south side of Meeting Street in the 1760s, and an isolated structure stood on the hill east of Lyttleton Street. Joseph Kershaw also made private transfers of nearby parcels of uncertain provenience to John Chesnut, Ely Kershaw, John Cantey, and James Cary.[68] Commissioners erected the courthouse and jail in1772, and the town's proprietors set aside communal lands for the market and fairgrounds at that time.[69] By the time of the sale, these key structures and activities already formed the core of the settlement.

Apparently the partners' first effort to liquidate real estate at Camden did not go as well as hoped. In late 1774 they sold only two parcels. One consisted of two lots on Broad Street north of the central square, sold to an innkeeper, John Adams, and half of the block southeast of the square was transferred to Thomas Jones, a local landholder. Curiously, he resold it almost immediately to Aaron Loocock.[70] No new land transfers were officially recorded until 1777, but the survey plat of Camden includes the addition of a number of properties as "disposed of" to unknown persons, presumably after the 1774 sale (Fig. 8.2). In addition to the tracts reserved for the courthouse, jail, and other public functions, they included the greater part of the two blocks bordering Broad Street south of the central square, portions of the block south of Meeting Street between Church and Campbell streets, and several blocks of lots situated on the south side of Wateree Street.

The partners attempted to liquidate their jointly held lands again in the spring of 1777, and the results of this sale provide important clues to the emerging pattern of individual land ownership in Camden. Within the span of three days in April they transferred a total of 215 lots into private hands. Thomas Jones, who had earlier acquired land that passed quickly to one of the former partners, was again a key player. He bought 173 of the lots on April 10 and the next day resold them to William Ancrum, Ely Kershaw, and Joseph Kershaw. Jones conveyed twenty lots on the east side of Broad Street to Aaron Loocock. Ancrum's tracts lay along Market, Lyttelton, and Fair Streets, and Ely Kershaw's lay on the west side of Broad. In 1777 Joseph Kershaw possessed much of the remaining property on both sides of Broad Street north and south of the square, as well as half of a block on Lyttelton Street. Kershaw conveyed his lands south of Meeting Street, together with eight lots in his larger tract on the east side of Broad, to John Chesnut later that year, and he sold lots on the southwest corner of the square to John Adamson, a planter and inn holder. [71]

The remaining years of the decade witnessed several other transfers of town lots to smaller owners. Some were nonresident, but all were associates of Camden's leading merchant. Joseph Kershaw's lots southeast of the square passed into the hands of his brother Ely and of Charleston merchant Charles Cook in 1778, and the following year Isaac DaCosta and George Rout, also merchants of the port city, respectively acquired lots on York and Wateree Streets. In 1779 Kershaw and John Chesnut jointly took possession of Aaron Loocock's nine lots on the east side of Broad Street. Robert Carter, a resident of Lynches River and a fellow member of the committee to select delegates to the Continental Association, acquired lots on Lyttelton Street adjacent to Kershaw's and on King Street near the courthouse. Kershaw sold two lots on north Broad Street to his brother-in-law William Nettles, whose lands on Gum Swamp Creek bordered those of Jasper Sutton. The merchant Duncan McRa received sixteen lots on the block northwest of the square, and five lots along Fair Street came into the possession of the potter John Bartlam.[72] By the close of the decade, the lands in the vicinity of the old Pine Tree Hill settlement had been largely redistributed, but most of the lots remained in the hands of four of the former partners.

During the decade preceding the Revolution, Camden was the focus of a rural community whose residents spread along both sides of the Wateree Valley but whose numbers were insufficient to provide a substantial resident urban population comparable to those in contemporary European market centers. Thus, the town remained a small settlement devoted largely to accommodating the integrative functions in areas of a dispersed settlement. The concentration of nonresidential activity there produced a pattern of limited property ownership in the 1770s and would have limited the number of buildings constructed in the town. Some of the new institutions, such as the market and fair, do not seem to have had associated structures, and the land allocated to the Church of England remained vacant. We know that the courthouse and jail occupied the lots set aside for them, and the brewhouse, the old store complex, and the religious structures lay on Broad and Meeting Streets, but what of the rest of the town?

Some of those who did business in Camden are likely to have lived there. Certainly Joseph Kershaw and his family maintained a residence there; however, both William Ancrum and Aaron Loocock were nonresidents, and Ely Kershaw's business interests likely kept him at Cheraw Hill much of the time. John Chesnut and James Cary possessed property here as well, but both also maintained plantations outside Camden. John Adamson, who acquired a large tract on Broad Street in 1777, likely located his residence and inn in Camden. A contemporary resident recalled that in 1777 twenty-six men lived in the town, including innkeeper Adamson, a clerk, two shopkeepers, and two merchants. He also observed that five others lived north of Camden at Logtown, a tract owned by Joseph Kershaw on the Catawba Path about a mile north of the Great Square.[73] Dr. James Clitherall, a Charleston physician who passed through Camden in April 1776, also noted Adamson's establishment, as well as a tavern operated by a Mr. Fagan, and mentioned an unnamed resident blacksmith of "lazy and extravagant" habits. He remarked that Camden was "a well laid out Town [and] has some large Houses in it, among which are the Court House and Gaol." Clitherall also drew attention to a pottery works at Logtown, where he "saw some exceedingly good pans etc. which a man who had set up these found great demand for."[74]

The ceramicist Clitherall mentioned was undoubtedly John Bartlam, a master potter from Stoke-on-Trent who had left England in 1763 to escape debt and improve his lot in America. Emigrating to South Carolina, Bartlam established a pottery factory for the manufacture of a wide variety of fine earthenwares, stonewares, and soft-paste porcelains at Cain Hoy on the Wando River in 1765. In 1770 he moved his operation to Charleston, but within two years he relocated to Camden. Despite the much greater availability of imported creamwares and other fine earthenwares that resulted from the expansion of commercial trade in the late 1760s, Bartlam's wares apparently enjoyed a wide market in the backcountry, and he sold some regularly through Kershaw's store. Although his kilns have not been located, archaeological excavations have yielded a substantial quantity of his earthenwares and stonewares from Camden structures, and the wide use of his wares here attests to the popularity, the competitiveness of his products, and the substantial volume of his business in the 1770s.[75]

Joseph Kershaw's brickyard was one of Camden's earliest industries, and its products provide important clues to the growth and layout of the 1770s settlement and a basis for discerning the nature and distribution of activities there. The location of this industry is still uncertain, but it may have been situated adjacent to Pine Tree Creek on the lowlands occupied by later brickyards. Abundant evidence of its existence is apparent in the town's architecture as early as the 1760s, when the products of its kilns found their way into the foundations of Joseph Kershaw's brewhouse. In the following decade brick became a common element in new buildings erected in Camden, and its archaeological presence has been a key element in ascertaining the form and composition of the pre–Revolutionary War settlement. Although subsequent agricultural activity has obliterated standing structures and aboveground ruins at Camden, the patterning of brick present in the soil can identify the locations of buildings whose form and content provided clues to their functions.[76]

Perhaps the most distinctive brick structure was the Camden jail. Together with the courthouse, the jail housed the institutional elements responsible for the administration of justice in Camden District. In 1770 the contract for constructing the courthouse and jail was let to Joseph Kershaw, John Chesnut, William Ancrum, and Aaron Loocock, who completed the buildings in time for the opening of the court term in November 1772.[77] Written sources provide little information about the Camden jail, but limited archaeological investigations at the jail site uncovered details of its distinctive architecture. These excavations exposed the foundations of a rectangular two-story structure built over a brick cellar, the floor plan of which featured two rooms divided by a central hallway. Its layout shared that of the contemporary jail at Ninety Six, both of which were constructed according to a common plan established by the Circuit Court Act of 1769. The Camden jail must have been an imposing structure in the small settlement, but, despite the utility of its design, it may not have been entirely secure. As early as 1773 a grand jury noted that several prisoners had escaped because the wall surrounding the jail yard was inadequately constructed, and four years later the sheriff, John Wyly, reported that two inmates had "feloniously broke open" the jail to gain their freedom.[78]

Upon its completion in 1772, the Camden jail took on two distinct roles. In response to meeting the need to curb criminal activity in the backcountry, the jail served as a repository for those charged with violating the laws of the province and deemed in need of confinement. As a combined court of common pleas and general sessions, the Camden court tried a variety of cases, and the jail housed those awaiting trial at the sessions held in April and November.[79] In addition to accused criminals, suspected runaway slaves apprehended by patrols established by South Carolina's slave laws were also lodged in the jail. Jailer John R. Hutchins' periodic advertisements describing prisoners "brought to Camden gaol" testify to the growing African American population in the changing economy of the backcountry and offer a glimpse of its diverse composition. Most of the captives were "New Negroes" recently arrived from Africa, and some were not yet fluent in English. The jailer's careful identification of their ethnicity reflected the importance planters attached to contemporary perceptions linking place of origin to temperament and disposition. He noted in particular the ritual scarification or "country marks" on their faces and bodies that identified individuals as Mandingos from the Gambia region and Kearseys, as Kishees from Guinea on the Windward Coast, as Ibos from the Niger Delta and Simboys from the Bight of Benin on the Leeward Coast, and as Bambaras from the Congo, in the interior. Not all were recent arrivals, however, for the captives also included a Jamaican and a native-born cooper from Wray's Ferry near Georgetown.[80]

Archaeology provides the most complete picture of Camden in the 1770s. Investigations I conducted in 1975 employed sampling excavations designed to determine the presence and layout of the town's buildings by plotting the spatial distribution of artifacts linked to architecture. This initial phase of research produced a comprehensive picture of the early town site in its entirety and explored all accessible portions of the early town.[81] Concentrations of brick and brick rubble, nails, window glass, and other structural materials identified a number of potential building sites, the locations of which may be compared to those shown on a 1781 sketch map of Camden.[82] If the recent military features are removed, the drawing provides a map of existing town structures (Fig. 8.3). The distribution of architectural materials in the area sampled corresponds quite closely to that for the buildings shown on the map, and the archaeological remains helped identify their likely locations.

A comparison of the artifacts recovered in the sample excavations indicated that the 1770s settlement was devoted largely to business activities. Clues to the function of the town's structures emerged from a comparison of the contents of the assemblages from each structure's location identified in the sampling. I assumed that assemblages in which domestic artifacts predominated were likely to represent the day-to-day subsistence activities carried out by the occupants of residential structures. Because only three of the ten structures exhibited this pattern, dwellings and their associated buildings appear to have made up only a small portion of the settlement. One was situated on the lots occupied by the tavernkeeper John Adamson west of Broad Street. Another lay on Joseph Kershaw's tract immediately to the south but farther back from Broad Street along what may have been an unnamed east-west cross thoroughfare that divided the block. The third concentration of domestic activities occurred at the edge of Broad Street, also on Kershaw's land, and may be associated with the earthfast house there (Fig. 8.4).

Six of the remaining areas yielded much smaller domestic artifact assemblages, suggesting that they housed businesses in addition to living areas for their proprietor's family or employees. Such an arrangement reflected the mixed use of buildings found in contemporary commercial settlements. Two of the structures were situated on lots owned by John Adamson and are likely associated with his inn and store. Another concentration on Joseph Kershaw's tract marked the location of the Pine Tree Hill store, where subsequent investigations revealed architectural remains of this large earthfast structure that corroborated its commercial function. Two other structural artifact loci lay east of Broad Street on lots owed by Joseph Kershaw and John Chesnut and corresponded to the placement of structures shown on the 1781 map. Although their precise functions remain uncertain, these buildings may also have housed activities and people involved in the mercantile endeavors of their owners or others who conducted business at this focus of backcountry trade. Such undocumented residents might have included renters who occupied the tracts by informal agreement that left no record (Fig. 8.4).

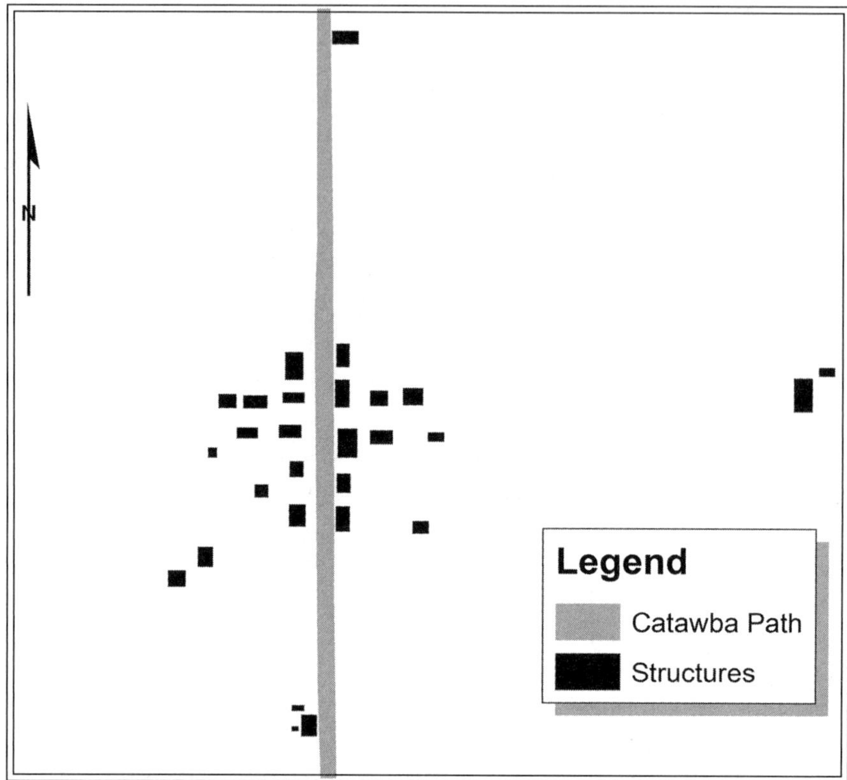

8.3 Buildings in Camden in the 1770s as shown on a 1781 military sketch map of Camden. The layout of the larger buildings defined the course of Broad Street (the Catawba Path) as well as an unnamed east-west street that led toward Joseph Kershaw's mansion, situated east of town. The jail lay to the right of the Catawba Path north of town. Author's original map.

The remaining two artifact concentrations clearly indicated their specialized use and contained little evidence of domestic activity in these structures. Behind the early store, the first marked the location of a brick office or shop, erected adjacent to the store in the 1770s. Completely excavated in the 1990s, this long, narrow, two-storied building enclosed a raised, brick-floored cellar with an open storage area at its west end. An entrance on its south side passed beneath a tower supporting an external stairway to its second floor. The second was a massive concentration of brick rubble south of Meeting Street on the site of the brewhouse. Here archaeological investigations later uncovered the foundations of a substantial brick building divided into large rooms, a plan typical of brewhouses. The perforated paving bricks, designed to permit ventilation and drainage, were commonly used in the floors of malthouses where grain was dried during the brewing process. Their presence here identified the specialized function of the building on the "Brewhouse Square." [83]

In the late 1770s, Camden's appearance changed dramatically with the construction of a new home by the individual whose increasing wealth and political influence paralleled the settlement's growth. Joseph Kershaw marked his achievements by erecting a mansion

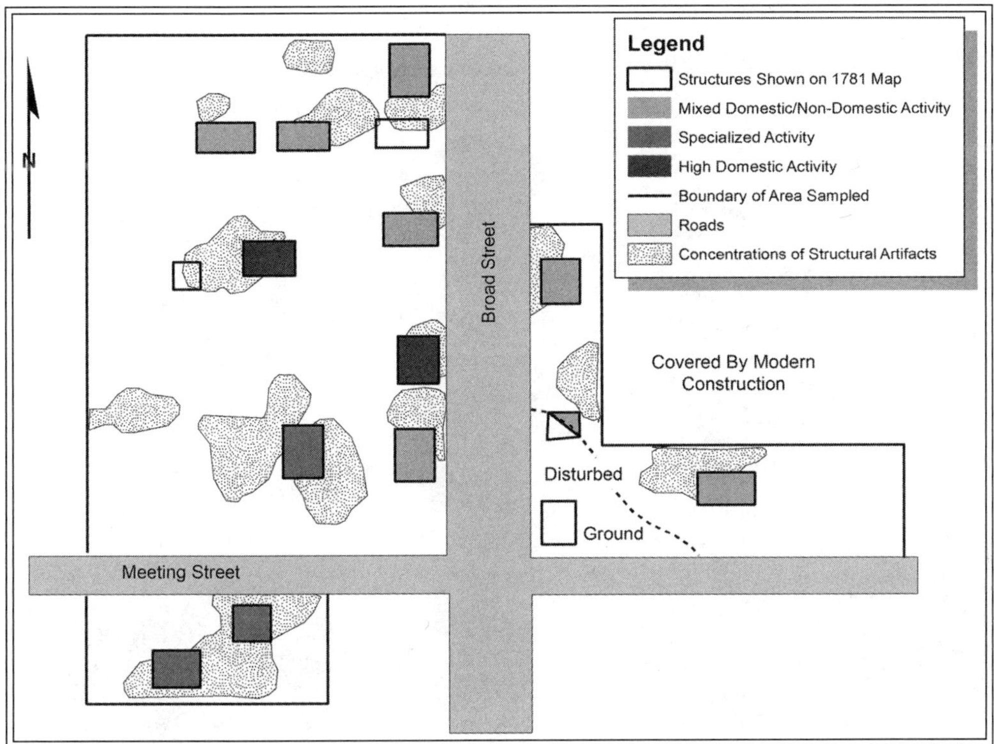

8.4 Concentrations of structural materials revealed by archaeological Investigations compared with the distribution of buildings shown on the 1781 military map of Camden. Author's original map adapted from Kenneth E. Lewis, *Camden: A Frontier Town in Eighteenth Century South Carolina,* Anthropological Studies 2 (Columbia: South Carolina Institute of Archaeology and Anthropology, 1976), 106.

---

the size, style, and location of which proclaimed his position as a leader of society in the central interior. His "Great White House" dwarfed everything in Camden, and it stood alone as perhaps the most impressive example of domestic Georgian architecture in South Carolina's interior. Kershaw situated his new dwelling on rising ground a short distance east of the settled portion of Camden on his tract of fourteen lots on Lyttelton Street. It lay just to the north of the small earthfast building constructed during the previous decade.

Archaeology and contemporary graphic images give us a detailed picture of the house and provide details of its exterior and exterior (Fig. 8.5). Paintings and photographs show a large two-story frame house constructed over a raised brick basement. Excavations revealed a structure measuring forty-eight feet wide by forty-two feet deep. A central hallway divided its interior into two symmetrical blocks of two large rooms, each separated by a wall containing a double fireplace. The facade of the Kershaw mansion was set off by a fifteen-foot-deep two-story pedimented portico, and an eight-foot wide piazza extended along the entire rear of the house. This design was typical of Palladian houses constructed by wealthy individuals in both urban and rural settings in eighteenth-century British North

8.5 Joseph Kershaw's mansion overlooking Camden, the "Great White House." The present building was reconstructed on the foundations of the original structure, excavated in 1968. Author's photo.

America. Known regionally as "double houses," they incorporated Georgian architectural elements that marked them as high-status dwellings. The architecture of the Camden mansion mirrored that of contemporary houses occupied by members of elite society in Charleston, and it was clearly intended to show Kershaw's membership in South Carolina's ruling class.[84]

Diagonally behind the Great White House was a second, more modest structure the architecture of which indicated its role as a service outbuilding (Fig. 8.6, p. 181). Archaeological excavations uncovered the remains of a large frame house that measured thirty-nine by nineteen feet and rested on a brick foundation capable of supporting its story-and-a-half height. It was divided into two rooms separated by a massive central hearth with double fireplaces, the size of which imply its use as a kitchen or laundry. Plantation owners commonly erected structures of this size and layout to accommodate such household activities and the servants who performed them. This structure, which was rebuilt at least once and persisted until the early years of the nineteenth century, was likely to have been the focus of servant households over the course of its existence.[85]

Recognizing the presence of African Americans in the archaeological record requires understanding the differential use of objects by the various groups that made up South

Carolina's creole society. In colonial America, British political and economic policy restricted the range of goods available for use by its residents, both black and white. Consequently, people of African descent found themselves using tools, implements, and other objects that often differed from those of their ancestral homelands. They incorporated these items into their lifeways in a manner that reflected the "deep structures" of culture that had survived the traumatic experiences of their passage into slavery and persisted in colonial America. How they used objects, rather than the nature of the items themselves, can be seen as the link between ethnicity and its material remains. Researchers have discovered that the composition, association, and disposition of goods, rather than the items themselves, are key to recognizing the presence of African Americans in the archaeological record, and their findings are useful in identifying buildings and areas used by people of color at Camden.[86]

An abundance of River Burnished ware provides strong circumstantial material evidence for the presence of the enslaved African American servants upon whom the operation of a mansion's household rested. This unglazed earthenware, produced by the Catawbas for trade, is similar in form and composition to pottery made in the lowcountry and elsewhere. Collectively known as Colonoware, such ceramics were widely employed in food preparation and consumption both on plantations and in urban areas, where cooking was usually done by black hands. Colonoware was manufactured as an trade good by Native Americans and enslaved Africans who were absorbed by the expanding European world economy on the eastern seaboard of North America, as well as in Central America and the Caribbean. Colonoware incorporated physical characteristics of both African and Native American ceramics and exhibited a syncretism resulting from the interaction of potters from both traditions. Although the variation found in Colonoware reflected the social distinctness of the communities that produced it, the economic homogeneity of the broader colonial world the potters inhabited promoted the widespread use of these ceramics. Regardless of its makers, the accessibility and low cost of Colonoware linked its use to the enslaved in colonial South Carolina. The quantity of River Burnished ware in the kitchen at the Kershaw mansion was greater than at any other building excavated at Camden. As refuse that accumulated as servants prepared food for their own and their master's households, these wares testify to a substantial African American presence there.[87]

The recovery of blue beads in the vicinity of the Kershaw mansion further implied the presence of persons of African descent. Although beads were widely used items of personal adornment, the color and form of these objects in combination incorporated important symbolic beliefs, and they played a major role in religious and magical practices. Beads functioned as components of amulets used for protection from harm and illness in animistic religions centered on a spiritual world that required continuous mediation by conjurers who relied on spiritual knowledge and charms to influence all aspects of life. These artifacts played a central role in religious and magical practices in western Africa, and their symbolic characteristics, including color, were key elements of religious beliefs brought to the New World. Such beliefs formed a central institution in African American society in the rural American South, where the color blue was associated with protection, and blue objects, including beads, were used for this purpose. Frequently archaeologists have found blue beads associated with settlements occupied by creolized Africans. Blue beads found in the yard and cellar near the Kershaw mansion provide additional evidence of the presence of enslaved Africans at the home of Camden's leading citizen.[88]

The presence of subfloor pits at the kitchen building further indicates that it was home to an African American household. Despite residing in multiethnic colonial settlements, persons of African descent retained certain cultural traditions that left material manifestations. One such practice was the use of subfloor root cellars beneath the floors of their houses, and such pits are typically associated with the sites of such buildings in Virginia and both Carolinas. These were commonly employed to store root crops and other preserved foods, and some archaeologists believe they may also have served as repositories for ancestor shrines, following West Indian practice. They argue that these cellars represent a subterranean adaptation of the raised shrines commonly employed in West Africa, taken underground to hide them from disapproving masters. Recovered bone fragments, fish scales, and egg shells point to the pits' role in food storage, but the presence of pins, needles, tacks, and two coins indicates a broader role as places to secret household items and valuables. Although the Great White House announced Joseph Kershaw's phenomenal success and Camden's emergence in the changing world of the backcountry, the presence of enslaved African American households bore testimony to the new social order that accompanied the transition to a commercial economy. [89]

The complex of buildings surrounding the Great White House emphasized its role as the focus of a high-status household. Archaeological investigations revealed that when builders completed the mansion in the late 1770s, its yard contained a small complex of outbuildings (Fig. 8.6). In addition to the kitchen and an earlier earthfast structure, it also included a smokehouse and a substantial brick well house and cooling cellar. All of these buildings accommodated activities necessary to support the lifestyle of the owners' household. Their arrangement replicated that found in large town residences of the lowcountry, but the broad range of activities they housed also reflected Camden's still largely rural setting. Part-town mansion and part-farm, the complex served as the visual centerpiece of Joseph Kershaw's backcountry empire.[90]

Despite the rapid changes that accompanied its rise as a central place in the backcountry, Camden in the 1770s retained much of the appearance of a small, unfinished frontier settlement (Fig. 8.7). As a loose arrangement of older earthfast structures and newer frame and brick buildings, the town extended along Broad Street, the old Catawba Path. The great square, a block south of the new courthouse and jail on King Street, still marked the northern limit of the nucleated settlement at the close of the decade. The town's residents had by now largely stripped the immediate area of its original forest cover and begun to plant gardens and fruit trees on the newly cleared ground. Camden's main thoroughfare of Broad Street had been opened to its surveyed width, but as it proceeded north beyond the courthouse and jail toward Logtown it passed through thickly wooded land, with trees and brush along either side of the road. Most of the carefully surveyed town site remained undeveloped, and local thoroughfares in the vicinity of Camden reflected an earlier landscape in which roads and paths connected points along their routes rather than following a surveyed grid. Apart from the small cluster of buildings at Logtown, the only recorded homestead nearby was the home of Thomas Charlton, a physician, planter, and minor official, whose residence lay on the Cheraw road just northeast of town.[91]

8.6 Conjectural bird's-eye view of the Kershaw mansion and its associated outbuildings as they looked in the 1770s. Their locations are based on evidence revealed by archaeological excavations. Courtesy of South Carolina Institute of Archaeology and Anthropology, Columbia, South Carolina.

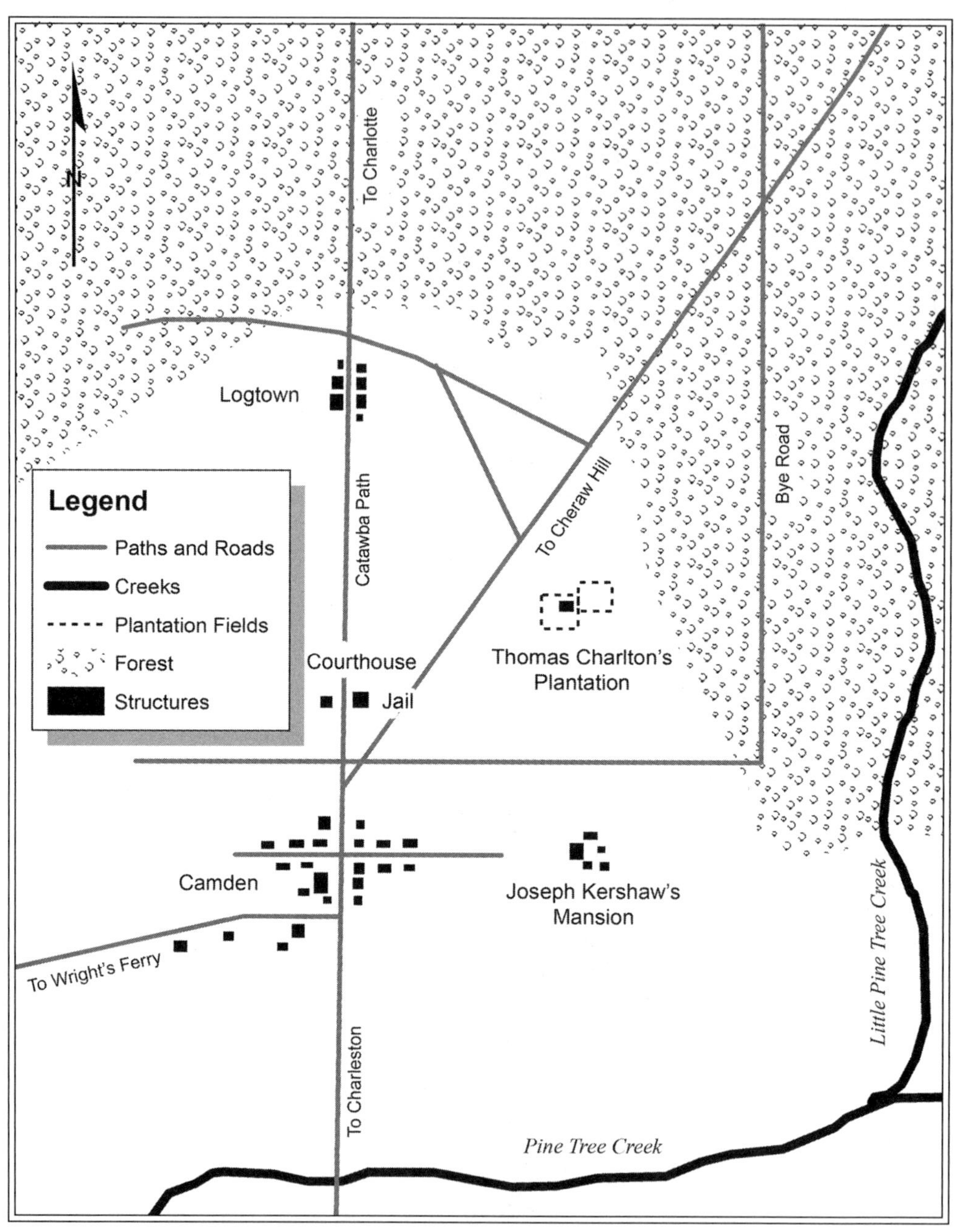

8.7 Camden and vicinity in the late 1770s, based on contemporary sources. Author's original map.

Nevertheless, Camden possessed centralizing urban functions in the rural context of an emerging frontier region, and its institutions served a substantial portion of South Carolina's backcountry. By the mid-1770s Camden possessed the district courthouse and jail; a number of grist- and sawmills; warehouses that stored flour, tobacco, indigo, and other export produce; the stores of several merchants; a pottery that turned out an extensive range of wares; a brickyard; at least two taverns; a brewhouse; a blacksmith; a physician; and the Great White House, home of the region's leading merchant, planter, and politician. Although Camden was still small, its growth and prosperity seemed ensured by its new administrative role and by its central position in the growing commercial economy of the backcountry. But the integrating forces that enmeshed Camden in the larger Atlantic world and helped propel the settlement and its inhabitants to prominence in the new order of the backcountry also contained seeds of discord that soon threatened Camden's success and even its very existence. Dissension between South Carolinians and British authorities had already precipitated a crisis into which the Kershaws and other backcountry leaders were drawn by their position and interests, one that was about to involve them and their associates in a divisive and destructive ordeal. Things were about to change dramatically as the American Revolution spread to the southern colonies.

Chapter 9

"In Consequence of the Above Order"

The Revolution Comes to South Carolina

The closing days of May 1780 found Joseph Kershaw in suddenly reduced circumstances. The statesman whose economic enterprise had dominated the backcountry was now a prisoner of war at Camden, facing exile for his opposition to royal authority in South Carolina during the previous five years. Now the British government had intervened to restore authority over its rebellious colony, and the invasion of 1780 brought to an end the period of independence, replacing it with military rule. Those who had participated in the rebellion were to be punished according to the magnitude of their perceived offenses. As a member of the independent Assembly, a militia leader, and a confidant of the rebel governor, Kershaw was high on the list of traitors. These "notoriously disaffected" individuals were paroled to the coastal islands, where they would no longer influence others inclined to follow their example.[1] His exile brought Kershaw both financial and personal loss and greatly reduced his role as an agent of change in the backcountry.

Kershaw's decline of fortune and the chain of events that led to it mirrored larger changes in colonial South Carolina. Political differences that arose in Britain's North American colonies following the Seven Years' War increasingly divided a diverse frontier population whose members were just beginning to participate in the commercial economy of the larger Atlantic world. Even in the 1770s, the backcountry remained incompletely integrated with the older, longer-settled parts of the province and had only recently come under the authority of a central government. Ethnic, religious, and sectarian loyalties remained strong among people who had more than once been obliged to rely on their own resources to overcome difficulties and threats. As they came increasingly under the sway of broader influences, inhabitants of the interior still depended on ties formed earlier in a society dominated by "men of influence" whose status depended heavily on the networks of linkages that arose in trade. The backcountry remained a political patchwork, the pieces of which were easily prone to fragmentation. The war for American independence only exacerbated this tendency and nearly destroyed all that had been built.

War and Rumors of War

By the mid-1770s, Joseph Kershaw, Richard Richardson, and other prominent business leaders in the interior had allied themselves politically with lowcountry elites whose interests they increasingly shared. Faced with the depressed conditions that resulted from tighter official management of trade, South Carolina's merchants and planters had seen their economic power decline. As a producer of agricultural commodities, South Carolina's economy depended heavily on overseas exchange, and efforts to resist detrimental policies and win back control of trade became more strident as colonials resorted to boycotts and more direct action.[2] In a political move, South Carolina formed a Provincial Congress to replace the Royal Assembly as its elective governing body, and it joined with other colonies to form a Continental Association to deal collectively with grievances against Crown policies. A new governor, Lord William Campbell, arrived in June 1775 but soon found the situation untenable. When he fled five months later, the royal administration authority in the province effectively ended.[3] Led by its executive body, the Council of Safety, the Provincial Congress became South Carolina's de facto government and mapped out an agenda based on its interests.

In 1775, South Carolina's population was hardly unified socially or politically, and for the Revolution to succeed the new rebel government needed the support of backcountry residents. Settlement of the interior was far from complete, and the cultural patchwork of varying religious faiths and ethnicities produced divided loyalties. Dislocation and resettlement occasioned by the Cherokee War ten years earlier complicated the situation further, and farmers just emerging from a regional frontier economy were still only marginally involved in the larger economic issues that influenced the lowcountry. Its inhabitants stood largely apart from the political controversies that had led the colony's leaders to oppose British policies and join the other colonies to resist them.[4]

Uncertain over the support of the backcountry population as the year's events unfolded, the Provincial Congress sought to secure the region. News that hostilities had broken out in Massachusetts in the spring of 1775 brought the threat of military action against the rebellion, and the body took action to safeguard the province. It ordered three regiments of regular troops raised, including a regiment of mounted rangers to secure the backcountry. The new government also drew on the provincial militia system for manpower to support its standing army. Recently reorganized by the General Assembly in response to the Regulator crisis, it consisted of twelve regiments, seven drawn from the interior districts. By recruiting rangers and militia troops from the backcountry, the Provincial Congress hoped to give its residents a stake in the Revolution; however, it could not rely on representation alone to ensure allegiance to the new cause.[5]

Persuasion had drawn communities in the lowcountry to the cause, and the Council of Safety hoped that this strategy would prove effective in the interior as well. But organized resistance arose in the summer of 1775 after the Council ordered the seizure of arms and ammunition at Fort Charlotte (Fig. 9.1). Tory sentiment was concentrated in the western backcountry between the Broad and Saluda Rivers in Ninety Six and western Camden Districts, a region heavily populated by recently arrived colonists recently polarized by the Regulator crisis. Most prominent Regulators sided with the new Whig government, and Tories turned to former anti-Regulators, like the notorious leader Joseph Scoffel whose name soon became a derogatory term that Whigs attached to all Loyalists. Tory opposition centered on the leaders of three loyal militia regiments. Under the leadership of Col. Thomas Fletchall, they gathered stores and supporters, and by the end of July they controlled a substantial area.[6]

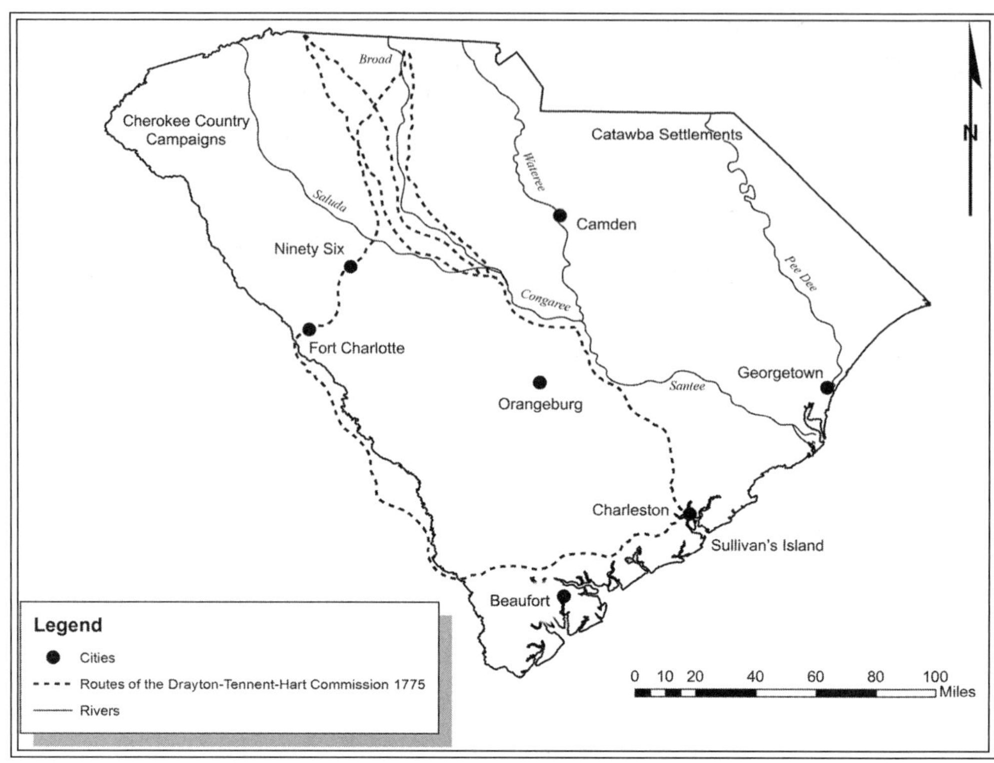

9.1 The American Revolution in South Carolina, 1775–1776. The route of the Drayton-Tennent-Hart mission is shown, as well as the military actions discussed in the text.
Author's original map.

The Council of Safety responded and immediately turned to persuasion to regain support in the western backcountry. Three commissioners, William Drayton, Oliver Hart, and William Tennent, traveled separately up the Santee and Savannah drainages and rendezvoused at the Congarees with two prominent Whig representatives from the eastern interior. Richard Richardson, a prominent planter, militia colonel, and experienced military commander from the High Hills of Santee, and Joseph Kershaw, whose mercantile business stretched from the Granby to the Pee Dee, represented both the military and economic authority of the new government. Their mixed reception at a series of arranged meetings, however, resulted in an increased reliance on intimidation. Threats to deny Loyalists access to the Congaree store at Granby and to cease transporting their goods helped persuade German residents of the Dutch Fork to support the Whig cause. Drayton deployed militia and state troops between the Broad and Savannah Rivers to dissuade opponents of the Provincial Congress and forced Thomas Fletchall to sign the Treaty of Ninety Six, forbidding Tories to take up arms in support of British interests.[7]

But the Treaty of Ninety Six left the political differences that divided backcountry residents unresolved, and armed confrontation soon resumed. When a Saluda River resident, Robert Cunningham, was arrested for openly defying the Provincial Congress, his brother

Patrick raised troops to effect his rescue. Although they failed, the Tory force succeeded in capturing a wagonload of gunpowder the Council of Safety was sending as a gift to the Cherokees. This event triggered military action on the part of the Whigs. Maj. Andrew Williamson and the Long Cane militia marched on Ninety Six to support Whig irregulars there. First blood flowed when Tory forces besieged his command at Ninety Six for three days in November before concluding a temporary truce. Meanwhile, Richard Richardson had raised a large force of several thousand militia and, together with the regiment of rangers, advanced on the Tories the following month. Discouraged by the show of force, many loyalists surrendered, and most of their leaders, including Fletchall, were captured. The remainder under Patrick Cunningham retreated to the edge of the Cherokee boundary, where they were decisively defeated by Richardson in the "Snow Campaign," waged in late December. Richardson's victory blunted loyalist opposition in the backcountry.[8]

Events of the new year sealed the fate of South Carolina's new government. In an attempt at reconciliation, the Provincial Congress enacted a constitution embodying the reforms that its leaders hoped would be acceptable to Crown authorities. British refusal to compromise obliged the governing body to view separation as the only viable alternative to capitulation. Dramatic steps taken by the British government further strengthened the move toward independence. The most direct effort intended to crush the American rebellion by means of military operations, one of which sought to rally loyalist support in the southern colonies. In June 1776 an expedition composed of a naval squadron and landing force arrived off Sullivan's Island at the mouth of Charleston Harbor with the intent of capturing the city. The venture went badly. Crippled by navigational difficulties, the naval bombardment proved ineffective, and land attacks were beaten back by troops at fortifications and elsewhere on the island. This British disaster ended the immediate military threat to South Carolina, giving its government valuable time to deal with other pressing matters.[9]

As the month of the seaborne attack closed, the Cherokee nation, supported by British agents, loyalists, and their Creek allies, joined in a larger uprising against the rebellious colonies. Responding to an attack on refugees on the upper Saluda drainage, the South Carolina Provincial Congress launched an expedition under the command of now Col. Andrew Williamson, who had earlier defended Ninety Six. As part of a general operation mounted by neighboring provinces, his force attacked the Cherokee settlements in an effort to eliminate their subsistence base. Following the destruction of their crops, livestock, and towns on both sides of the mountains, the destitute Indians sued for peace. The Treaty of Dewitt's Corner in 1777 ceded the territory that became the northwestern corner of South Carolina (Fig. 9.1). The Cherokee campaign removed the threat of immediate attack in the west and demonstrated the capability of the militia system as a military force, a role it continued to play in policing internal dissent[10]

The failed British naval attack on Charleston and a successful campaign against the Cherokees in 1776 effectively stabilized the political situation in South Carolina's interior for the next several years. Loyalist opposition was cowed, and new British offensives carried the war into the northern colonies, leaving the newly independent state time to organize the structure of its political and administrative institutions. Crucial to South Carolina's success was the increasing sense of unity of purpose among its residents, particularly those of the backcountry, whose interests had until recently been largely ignored by lowcountry elites. When the Provincial Congress reorganized South Carolina's government in 1776, interior residents gained greater representation in the lower house of the legislature. Two of the region's most prominent members, Joseph Kershaw and Richard Richardson, moved to the upper house, the Legislative Council. The constitution of 1778 increased the region's representation and its political power, and the creation of additional election districts recognized its growing population. The document also officially disestablished the Anglican Church and recognized the equality of other religions. Both efforts helped the new government draw support from the residents of the interior.[11]

Representation of the backcountry districts was based on a political organization that grew out of the frontier experience. In the absence of existing institutions, community leadership still coalesced around prominent "men of influence." Individuals like those who had led the Regulator movement often controlled key resources, such as stores, grist- and sawmills, forges, and other facilities upon which surrounding residents depended. Many had also acquired wealth in land and slaves, and their political power emanated from their economic status. Frequently, militia leaders and those elected to new public offices assumed their positions because of their role in the community. The backcountry elite consisted of those who had forged the region's transition to a commercial economy, and the military organization of the Revolution now drew on this class for its leadership. The militia hierarchy was a mirror of the emerging backcountry's social structure during this crucial period of change.[12]

Accommodation and Allegiance in the Backcountry

The skirmishes of 1775 and 1776 all took place well outside the Wateree Valley, but their impact was nonetheless felt throughout the area as the backcountry settled into an uneasy truce. The zealous and organized Loyalist sentiment found elsewhere seemed to be absent among settlers on the great river, up into the Waxhaws, and in the Pee Dee country. The majority avoided open involvement and instead remained neutral in the absence of provocation. But many men of influence in the region were already active in the revolutionary cause, and their participation influenced the region's political orientation. Joseph and Ely Kershaw and Aaron Loocock served in both the First and Second Provincial Congresses from the District Eastward of Wateree River, while John Chesnut represented the District between the Broad and Saluda Rivers. The Boykin brothers, Burwell and Samuel, participated in the formation of the Continental Association in St. David's Parish and Saxe Gotha District, respectively.[13]

Several of them took an active role in the campaigns against the Loyalists in the west. Ely Kershaw received a captain's commission and led a company in the Regiment of Rangers under Col. William "Old Danger" Thomson in June 1775. Assigned to the Congarees, Kershaw's unit supported the Drayton-Tennent-Hart mission. Kershaw also served as a Whig representative in the negotiations leading to the Treaty of Ninety Six. In the fall of 1775, his unit operated with Thomson's regiment in Amelia Township and the following spring was deployed with it to Charleston to meet the anticipated British attack. Entrenched on Sullivan's Island, Thomson's rangers helped turn back the land assault, an action crucial to the American victory.[14] In addition to his military duties, Ely Kershaw also continued his role as a member of the Provincial Congress, serving on committees charged with identifying Loyalists in St. David's Parish and managing the militia in the backcountry in general. He resigned his commission in the rangers in 1777 and subsequently served as a major in the militia.[15]

Ely Kershaw's ranger company reflected both the composition and the social structure of the community from which its members were drawn.[16] Its commander chose his subordinate officers from among prominent Whigs who resided in the vicinity of Camden. Francis Boykin, of Town Creek, became his first lieutenant. A younger brother of Burwell and Samuel Boykin, he was also a politically active planter. Kershaw's second lieutenant, who also served as a surgeon, was Thomas Charlton, a Maryland physician who had emigrated to the Wateree Valley in the 1760s and settled as a planter near Camden. Both men accompanied the rangers to the Congarees, served in the campaign against the Loyalists in Ninety Six District and later on at Sullivan's Island. Charlton was also involved directly in one of the incidents that led to hostilities following the Treaty of Ninety Six. Dispatched by the Council of Safety to escort the wagons carrying gunpowder to the Cherokees, his small command was captured by Patrick Cunningham's Loyalists and briefly held prisoner. Charlton resigned his commission in July 1776.[17]

Samuel Boykin, the prominent Regulator, also emerged as a military leader. Joseph Kershaw, in his role as liaison to the Catawbas, had secured their support of the Whig faction as well as an offer of military assistance to the new government. Seizing an opportunity to employ their new ally, the Council of Safety called on Boykin to organize and command a Catawba militia unit to support William Thomson's rangers. Formed in the summer of 1775, the unit was called into service the following January and deployed in the parishes north and west of Charleston to scout and capture runaway slaves. Although dismissed in March, the Catawba unit was again called back in the summer and participated in the defense of Sullivan's Island.[18]

Joseph Kershaw's dominant role in the backcountry economy led to his rise as a central figure in the looming drama of the Revolution. Firmly allied with the Whig leaders and a participant in the new government, Kershaw represented its interests in the Wateree Valley. In the summer of 1775 he participated in the Drayton-Tennent-Hart mission, and by the fall his career as a public servant began to take on a military aspect as he participated in activities related directly to the conflict in the backcountry. In September his Camden store stockpiled gunpowder and lead for the upcoming expedition against the Tories, and the following month he officially entered military service as a brigade major under Richard Richardson in the Snow Campaign. Acting as commissary and general treasurer for the expedition, Kershaw played a key role in maintaining this rapidly assembled force. Recognizing his capability as a merchant, the Council of Safety designated him as the supplier of flour and shipbread to the militia. In a day when military logistics were often unreliable, this symbiotic arrangement benefited his business while providing the army with a reliable source of rations. Kershaw continued to furnish both militia and state troops with rations, salt, and other supplies over the next several years, and he even arranged for the burial of a soldier who died en route to Camden.[19]

Joseph Kershaw's role as a military commander increased when the militia organization expanded. He may have advanced from major to lieutenant colonel as early as 1776, when the Provincial Congress subdivided two of the militia regiments in Camden District into four geographically based battalions under the overall command of Col. Richard Richardson.[20] Militiamen served under Joseph Kershaw in the lowcountry campaign in June 1776, participating in Charleston's defense and in subsequent forays to Beaufort and the Savannah River. Willis Whitaker later recalled commanding a company under Kershaw, and Thomas Brown, a resident of the Waxhaws, provided further details of its composition. Drafted into a militia company, he joined Kershaw's unit in Camden and marched with it to Charleston. While serving there, he was attached to companies led by John (presumably James) Kennedy, George Dunlap, and Hugh White, all of whom were company commanders in 1778, when Kershaw commanded a militia regiment. Brown's association with these officers under Kershaw's leadership two years earlier implies that Kershaw was already in charge of a battalion.[21]

Joseph Kershaw's residence at Camden made the settlement a focus for projecting Whig power in the backcountry. His store served as a depot for munitions and captured arms, and his new mansion hosted visiting dignitaries and others whose official business brought them through the Wateree Valley along the inland route from the north to Charleston.[22] Camden's status as a focus of military operations led to its choice by the new government as the site of a magazine to store arms, munitions, and supplies. In 1777 Joseph Kershaw constructed a substantial brick building for this purpose on his land just southeast of the settlement, a project costing £10,000. In the coming year Camden became a hub of activity as South Carolina's leaders responded to increasing uncertainty. As a militia colonel, Joseph Kershaw oversaw military undertakings there, storing and dispensing gunpowder and supplies at the magazine and furnishing provisions and forage for Continental and state troops on the march through Camden or stationed in the town. In its role as a repository for enemies of the state, the new jail also became an important detention facility and fell under Kershaw's purview as well. In 1778 he assumed responsibility for overseeing and repairing the structure and maintaining guards there and at the magazine.[23] As a bastion of Whig strength in the backcountry, Camden discouraged Loyalist activity, but the presence of force did not ensure unity in the doubtful peace that followed the events of 1775–1776.

Although organized hostility had not yet arisen in the eastern backcountry, its residents' loyalties varied considerably. Support for the Crown tended generally to be strongest among Anglicans and weakest among dissenters, but other factors turned individuals to one side or the other. In the Wateree Valley, the initial settlers had become divided in their loyalties, and even the Quakers, whose faith bound them to neutrality, found themselves on both sides. By the 1770s early residents were outnumbered by second- or third-generation Scots-Irish colonists whose strong, interrelated communities, united by kinship and the tenets of evangelical Presbyterianism, shared an inherent hostility to the Crown. Those who arrived later directly from Ireland lacked such community ties, however, and their poverty and adherence to a more traditional Presbyterian religion set them apart and oriented their loyalties quite differently. Residents of the upper Pee Dee River Valley were similarly divided. Welsh Neck Baptists supported the slaveholding Whig Baptists in Charleston with whom they were allied, while Separate Baptists who opposed their authority remained loyal to the Crown. Conflicting interests also divided the Anglicans who attended St. David's Church at Cheraw Hill. Nearby portions of eastern North Carolina that were home to substantial numbers of Highland Scots constituted a bastion of strong Loyalist sentiment.[24] In 1776 the eastern backcountry experienced an uneasy peace.

Existing economic and political institutions continued to operate in the politically ambivalent early years of the American Revolution. Representatives from Camden District and its subdivisions participated in the new government, justices of the peace and magistrates continued to serve, in other district offices were filled, and district commissions for roads and waterways remained intact. Only Whigs served as representatives in the Provincial Congress and its successor, the General Assembly, but some Loyalists continued to occupy local offices in 1776. The planter and lawyer James Cary, who had argued the Regulators' cause before colonial officials, served as a justice of the peace in company with Samuel Boykin, John Cantey, Thomas Charlton, William Lang, and Richard Richardson.[25] As late as 1778 the General Assembly passed ordinances authorizing the district courts at Camden and Ninety Six to remain open and complete current business, and the circuit court at Camden continued to hold sessions, trying criminal and civil cases. By this time, however, the courts had taken on additional political functions, becoming sites for taking oaths of allegiance to the new government and polling places where delegates to the constitutional convention were chosen. Although now under martial authority, the jail still retained its civil functions of housing suspected runaway slaves and those awaiting trial on criminal charges. Activity at the court ceased abruptly in early 1779, when an arsonist, identified as A. Westbury, destroyed the courthouse and set fire to the jail. The General Assembly made provision to restore the court building during the following year, but other events soon suspended all civil activity.[26]

Perhaps the clearest example of cooperation among those with diverging political perspectives was the construction of fortifications at the Camden magazine in 1780 (Fig. 9.2). The magazine had been built three years earlier at the expense of the state. Oriented at the same angle as the town grid, this rectangular buttressed brick structure was fifty feet long by twenty-six feet wide with a raised wooden floor.[27] The magazine was an obvious statement of Whig power, clearly visible along the southern approach to Camden. Under Joseph Kershaw's supervision, enslaved laborers supplied by thirty-six owners erected fortifications around the structure under the direction of James Brown, an engineer and master carpenter, whose carpenters provided the skilled labor. Of the twenty-six contributors whose political affiliation can be determined, seven were Tories, whose desire to maintain harmony must have surpassed their affinity with the Crown. All the Loyalists later took an active role on the side of British in the backcountry. Among them, James Cary became the colonel of a militia regiment he raised and erected a fort on his property across the river from Camden. Robert and Joshua English also served as officers in the Loyalist militia, as did John Adamson and Jonathan Belton, and the merchant Charles Ogilvie collaborated with the military administration at Camden.[28]

The motivations that drove individuals who disagreed so strongly with the rebel cause to participate in this construction project may never be known; however, their cooperation may have grown out of an unwillingness to sever the economic and social relationships they maintained with those who did not share their political views, especially influential people such as Joseph Kershaw and his partners. James Cary had purchased land from Joseph Kershaw and built up his estate around the ferry owned by the millwright Nebo

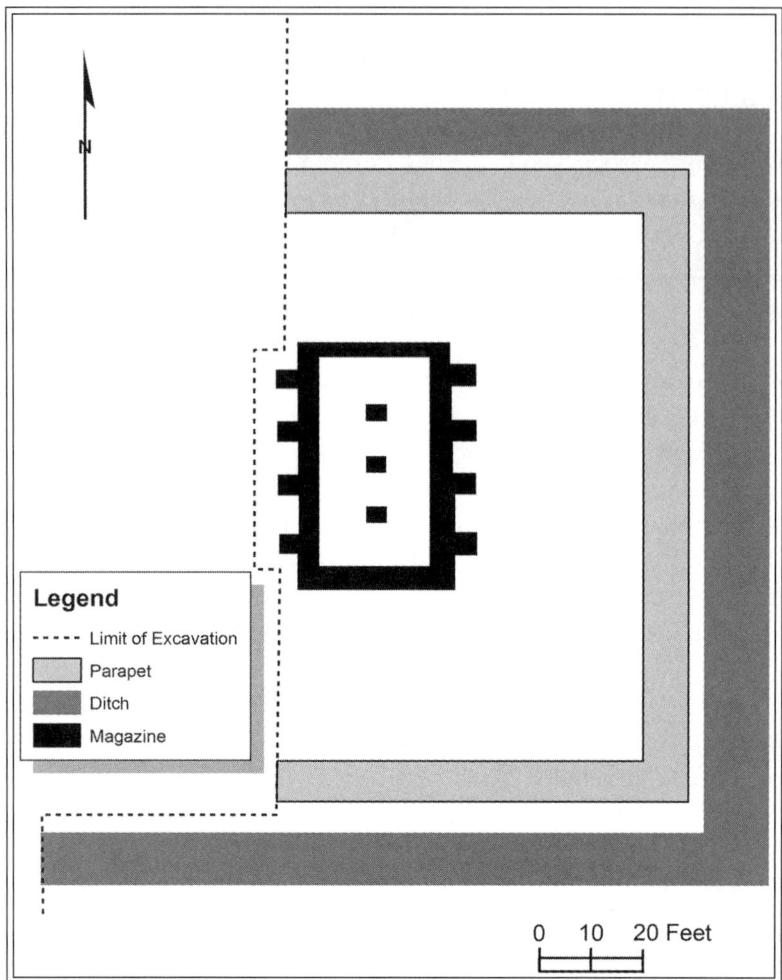

9.2 The Camden magazine erected in 1777 and the fortifications added in 1780. The present foundations and a portion of the surrounding ditch were revealed by archaeological excavations conducted in 1967. Adapted from Alan Calmes, "Report of Excavations at the Revolutionary War Period Fortifications of Camden, South Carolina" (Camden, S.C.: Camden District Heritage Foundation, 1968), Figs. 4,7.

Gaunt, who with his brother Zebulon was an associate of Kershaw. As part of an Anglican minority in the backcountry, James and Mary Cary and Joseph Kershaw shared membership in the small congregation founded at Camden by the Rev. Theopholus Drage in 1773.[29] Members of the English family were among the early Quaker settlers on the Wateree. Its founder, Joshua English, became a substantial landowner south of Camden, a miller, and a prominent member of the community. One of his sons managed Aaron Loocock's Wateree plantation.[30] Preserving the ties that maintained the structure of society in uncertain circumstances encouraged continued cooperation among residents in the activities that constituted daily life, especially public projects, for which compensation provided an added incentive to participate. On the other hand, competition may also have crosscut the fabric of the network by which Joseph Kershaw and his partners had dominated the trade in the backcountry. The English family's involvement in milling and John Adamson's and Henry Rugeley's new stores had the potential to compete with established Whig entrepreneurs. Similar rivalries appear to have motivated the allegiance of many Loyalists in the western backcountry and may well have done so in the Wateree Valley as well. In addition, the Adamsons and the Englishes were also related to each other by blood and to the Belton family through marriage, kin ties that may also have reinforced their political affiliation.[31]

Larger events began to threaten the ambivalent relations between Whigs and Tories in the Wateree Valley. Following the cessation of open hostilities, the new government sought to restore stability by dealing with those who had opposed it. Authorities pardoned and released former enemies and allowed royal officials and those unwilling to take an oath of fidelity to leave, actions that reduced the level of animosity but also pushed Tories farther into the interior.[32] The nearby British provinces of East and West Florida, still loyal to the Crown, became a refuge for those fleeing South Carolina and Georgia and a base from which they could operate against their former neighbors. Violence continued in portions of Ninety Six and Orangeburg Districts, where organized groups of disaffected Loyalists committed depredations against Whig residents. By 1778 this activity began to affect the Wateree Valley. Operations by Col. Andrew Williamson's militia against a large party of Tories attempting to escape to East Florida captured more than one hundred prisoners, half of whom were confined at the Camden jail. Captives taken in other military actions were also housed in district jails, including those at Orangeburg and Long Bluff. But tensions remained high. In nearby Orangeburg District, Loyalists attacked a Whig magistrate and broke open the jail to release prisoners, and on the upper Pee Dee Whig residents feared attacks by Loyalists in nearby North Carolina. Although the Whig militia generally restrained organized Loyalist resistance and stabilized the eastern backcountry for the time being, lingering resentment threatened the return of hostilities if circumstances changed.[33]

The War Turns South

In 1778 the war in America was three years old and not going well for His Majesty's forces in the northern colonies. In the fall of the previous year, they had suffered a humiliating defeat at Saratoga, New York, and by spring the military situation had reached a stalemate. To make matters worse, the rebellious colonies began to strengthen their position by acquiring allies. England's old adversary France declared war against Britain in June 1778, and Spain followed suit the following year. Holland would join the conflict in early 1781. The Crown now perceived its assets in Europe, Africa, and Asia as threatened on several fronts and feared the loss of its valuable sugar islands in the West Indies. To deal with the ominous new circumstances in America, the king and his ministers sought a new strategy to shore up British interests and restore momentum to the war. A campaign in the southern colonies was appealing because it offered a new front against the rebels. The sparsely populated provinces also seemed particularly vulnerable because they were home to a great many Loyalists, whom authorities believed would rally to the Crown. They also believed that the substantial numbers of enslaved Africans in Georgia and South Carolina were unlikely to sympathize with the revolution of their masters. Prompted by the governor of neighboring East Florida, British planners developed a strategy to retake the region by landing in Georgia, from which the army and loyal supporters would then march north to restore royal authority in the errant southern colonies.[34]

The operation began in the closing days of December 1778 with the arrival of a British army under Lt. Col. Archibald Campbell at the mouth of the Savannah River. Early the next month Campbell's troops defeated a small American command defending Savannah and captured the city and port. Reinforced by a larger army marching north from East Florida under Maj. Gen. Augustine Prévost, the British consolidated their forces in the coastal region and set out to extend their control inland, establishing garrisons on the Savannah River as far as Augusta. Military successes in Georgia soon restored British authority there and became an imminent threat to South Carolina's revolutionary government. The presence of an "enemy at the gates" instantly changed the dynamic of the war, as the conflict turned from the suppression of dissent to defense against an invader, and altered the role of its participants.[35]

American military strategy responded immediately to the new threat. Even before the defeat at Savannah, Maj. Gen. Benjamin Lincoln, newly appointed by Congress as the commander of the Southern Department, arrived in Charleston to assemble an army for operations against the British. Seeking a defensive position and a logistics center to support potential offensive operations, Lincoln moved his headquarters to Purrysburg to take advantage of its strategic situation upriver and across from Savannah. Overland routes made Purrysburg accessible from all parts of South Carolina and linked it directly to Charleston. Situated near a river crossing, Purrysburg was also a logical point to enter British-controlled territory. Here Lincoln began assembling an army composed of cavalry, artillery, naval, and infantry units of the Continental line, bolstered by militia from both the Carolinas. The combination of Continental troops who were regulars directly under Lincoln's command and militias that were responsible to state authorities created an awkward and frustrating management situation for the new commander. Underlying these difficulties was the institutional nature of these citizen units, and the manner in which their organization reflected the structure of the society from which their members were drawn.[36]

The Camden Regiment of Militia

As the commander of a militia regiment, Col. Joseph Kershaw occupied a central position in an institution about to assume a wider role in backcountry society. Formed as pioneers settled the region, militia units drew their members from the geographical districts in which they lived and were organized into regiments under appointed commanders. Intended to provide both internal security and defense against external threats, the militia was an integral part of backcountry society. The crisis of 1775 broadened its role by making it an agent of Whig power to crush dissenters and their allies. The need to maintain political control over the militia led the Provincial Congress to install loyal Whigs as regimental commanders and other officers. To increase the readiness of militia regiments, new laws required company commanders to assemble their units regularly, monitor attendance and membership carefully, and have them available to serve at a moment's notice. Despite its expanded role as a military force, the militia remained organizationally separate from the Continental regiments, the regular military units tasked with defending the state in battle against its enemies. Its members were subject to militia law administered by their own officers.[37]

Although the militia had taken on a wider role with the coming of the Revolutionary War, its units still largely reflected the political structure of the communities from which the men came, and Joseph Kershaw's appointment as a regimental commander was as much an extension of his civilian status as it was a recognition of his abilities as a military tactician. The Camden regiment of South Carolina's militia was a microcosm of the regional society from which it was drawn. Its organization drew upon previous relationships among those who inhabited the Wateree Valley. The region's social structure reflected the processes that accompanied the growth and transition of the frontier. Here individual status grew out networks of kinship, affiliation, and trade and the wealth, political prestige, and power they generated during this dynamic period. Clearly Joseph Kershaw's role in the rise of the commercial economy made him the central figure.

At the time of its mobilization at the end of 1778, Joseph Kershaw's regiment was a substantial organization composed of as many as twelve companies of varying size, whose members came from the Waxhaws and the region north and east of Camden. The enlisted ranks were drawn locally in drafts of eligible male inhabitants, and each militia company was commanded by officers whose election implied that they had emerged as community leaders prior to the Revolution. Several of these men had amassed some wealth as farmers, and a few had been active politically.

Several of Kershaw's captains bore ties to their regimental commander. John Marshall (or Marshel) was a former Regulator who possessed 450 acres on Cedar River near the headwater of Little Lynches Creek. The owner of thirty-six slaves, Marshall was active politically and made important contacts with the leaders of the Whig movement prior to the Revolution. In 1775 the Provincial Congress appointed him to the committee to execute the Continental Association, whose members included Joseph Kershaw, Richard Richardson, and Thomas Sumter. He held a senior position among the regiment's officers' and took command in Kershaw's absence.[38] George Wade marketed flour from his plantation on the Catawba River through Kershaw's Camden store in the late 1770s and maintained an active account there. A partner in Kershaw, Wade & Co., he provided supply wagons for the regiment's expedition to Purrysburg in 1779. His relatives Charlotte and Rachael Wade interacted socially with Sarah Mathis Kershaw and her brother Samuel Mathis, implying a close link between the families. Wade also brought military experience, having served in the Snow Campaign during the defense of Charleston.[39] John Chesnut's ties to Joseph Kershaw, his economic success, and his rise as a political figure are well known. He entered military service in 1775 and held the rank of captain in William Thomson's regiment of rangers. Chesnut acted as paymaster of this unit until an attack of rheumatism forced him to resign his commission in 1778. Upon his recovery, he enlisted in the militia at Camden and served as a captain under Joseph Kershaw.[40] John Cook, an early settler in Fredericksburg Township and a former Regulator, became the regiment's quartermaster.[41] Thomas Charlton, a Camden resident, was elected as a representative to the second Provincial Congress from the district east of the Wateree after leaving the ranger regiment in 1776. Although not identified as a company commander, he nevertheless served in some capacity as an officer Kershaw's regiment.[42]

Kershaw's ties to his other company commanders are less certain. Robert Crawford was an ambitious, educated planter and merchant and a member of one of the Irish families from the northern colonies that dominated Waxhaws society. By the 1770s he had accumulated sizable landholding on Waxhaws Creek. Crawford also possessed professional military experience, having held a British commission, which he resigned in 1776 to serve as a militia captain under Richard Richardson.[43] Hugh White, who settled on the Catawba River, and George Dunlap were also members of large kin groups that migrated southward. Robert Montgomery, James Montgomery, and James Kennedy, all lieutenants, were apparently yeoman farmers of lesser means. Crawford and Robert Montgomery had previously served in the Snow Campaign and the defense of Charleston two years earlier.[44] Capt. Middleton McDonald resided on Turkey Quarter Creek, and Capt. George Summerville appears to have lived in the vicinity of Cedar Creek.[45] Luke Petty made his home near Grannys Quarter Creek in the vicinity of the Flat Rock, a well-known granite outcrop on the Catawba Path and a site of early settlement north of Camden.[46] Edward Kennington lived on Flat Creek, a tributary of the Lynches River, and Josiah Evans settled on the Lynches River near relatives who occupied lands on the Pee Dee and the Welsh Neck.[47]

As the commander of the Camden regiment, Joseph Kershaw drew on his existing social prestige and connections to expand his influence through the militia as a social institution. Although his new role as a military leader differed from his previous endeavors, the position nevertheless reflected his status as a backcountry leader. Some of the officers in Kershaw's regiment at the close of 1778 had previous direct personal associations with him, and their subservient positions reflected existing relationships. As residents of the Wateree Valley, the others were to varying degrees clients of the businesses Kershaw and his partners managed through their stores at Camden, Rocky Mount, and Cheraw Hill, where some held accounts. Their positions in the militia grew out of their participation in this extensive economic network, a mutually beneficial arrangement. Kershaw gained political clients upon whom he could rely, and his officers now possessed direct access to a powerful patron. All of Kershaw's officers were community leaders, and several were already men of influence who did not lack ambition and who must have welcomed the opportunity to develop ties to one of the backcountry's central figures. Participation in a revolutionary struggle was not without risk, however, and Kershaw's new role as a military leader was clearly a gamble that offered greater power and prestige if successful but dire consequences if not.

The Kershaws Go to War

The British invasion of Georgia in 1778 drew South Carolina into a conventional war that soon exposed the inadequacy of its defenses. It highlighted the military weaknesses of the militia in particular but nevertheless foreshadowed the role of irregular forces in the conflict that followed. The campaign began even before the fall of Savannah with the appearance of the British invasion fleet off Charleston. The event raised grave concern, and state authorities called for immediate mobilization. On Christmas day 1778 Gov. John Rutledge ordered Joseph Kershaw to assemble his regiment to join a large force of militia gathering under the command of Gen. Richard Richardson in the lowcountry. Upon receiving word from their colonel, the companies under captains John Marshall, Luke Petty, George Summerville, Middleton McDonald, Robert Crawford, George Dunlap, Robert Montgomery, Josiah Evans, and Edward Kennington mobilized and assembled at Camden (Fig. 9.3).[48]

Within days Joseph Kershaw's regiment was on the move. On New Years day 1779 it crossed the Wateree at the Camden ferry, assembled on the Long Causeway on the opposite shore, and began the long march to the Savannah River. Consisting of 190 men and twenty-three wagons, the nine companies of Camden militia spent the next two weeks in transit. They crossed the Congaree at McCord's Ferry on January 4 and reached the Edisto seven days later. As they proceeded beyond the Coosawhatchie along the increasingly impassible lowcountry roads, double teams were required to pull the wagons. At Tulifiny Creek the regiment had to construct its own bridge in order to reach Gen. Richardson's camp near Purrysburg, where they arrived on January 18.[49]

Almost at once the presence of a large militia contingent in a Continental garrison became divisive. Much of the ill feelings grew out of professional soldiers' long-held perception that militia lacked the training and discipline to participate successfully in the traditional style of warfare conducted by European armies and that their short terms of enlistment made them undependable comrades in arms. Images of the militia derived, in part, from the circumstances of their service. Most were farmers, and their call-ups required that they lay aside the continual work of rural production on which the livelihood of their families depended. Militiamen were poorly suited to be away for long periods of training or to be employed in lengthy campaigns far from home, and they perceived their obligation as pursuant to a contract that limited the terms and length of their service.[50] Concerns regarding their performance prevailed at high levels in the new colonial government. A year earlier Maj. Gen. Johann DeKalb, in camp with George Washington's army at Valley Forge, had taken pains to inform Henry Laurens, now president of the Continental Congress, about the difficulties of employing militia in conjunction with regular troops. He warned Laurens of the notoriously unreliable militiaman who "stays in camp but as long as he chooses, and goes home when he pleases, [and for whom] there has not been, to my knowledge any punishment inflicted." Such troops, he lamented, were not only expensive to maintain but also difficult to manage, being "continually on the roads, they eat up, spoil and very often plunder the country." DeKalb, like his commander and many other professional soldiers, preferred a permanent force of regular, disciplined soldiers upon whom he could depend to stand up to the British army.[51] The image of less than useful, undisciplined, and undependable militia troops was not lost on Gen. Lincoln, who observed the careless attitudes toward military service of those at Purrysburg and complained of his inability to control them. Initially assigned fatigue duties, such as road building and other garrison tasks, the men of Kershaw's regiment soon grew restless, provoking a series of events that sealed the fate of the Camden militia in the early campaign.[52]

The controversial role of the militia came to a head as the result of an incident involving members of one of Joseph Kershaw's companies. Placed on guard duty, John Cayle, a private serving under Capt. Luke Petty, deserted his post. When confronted by Petty upon

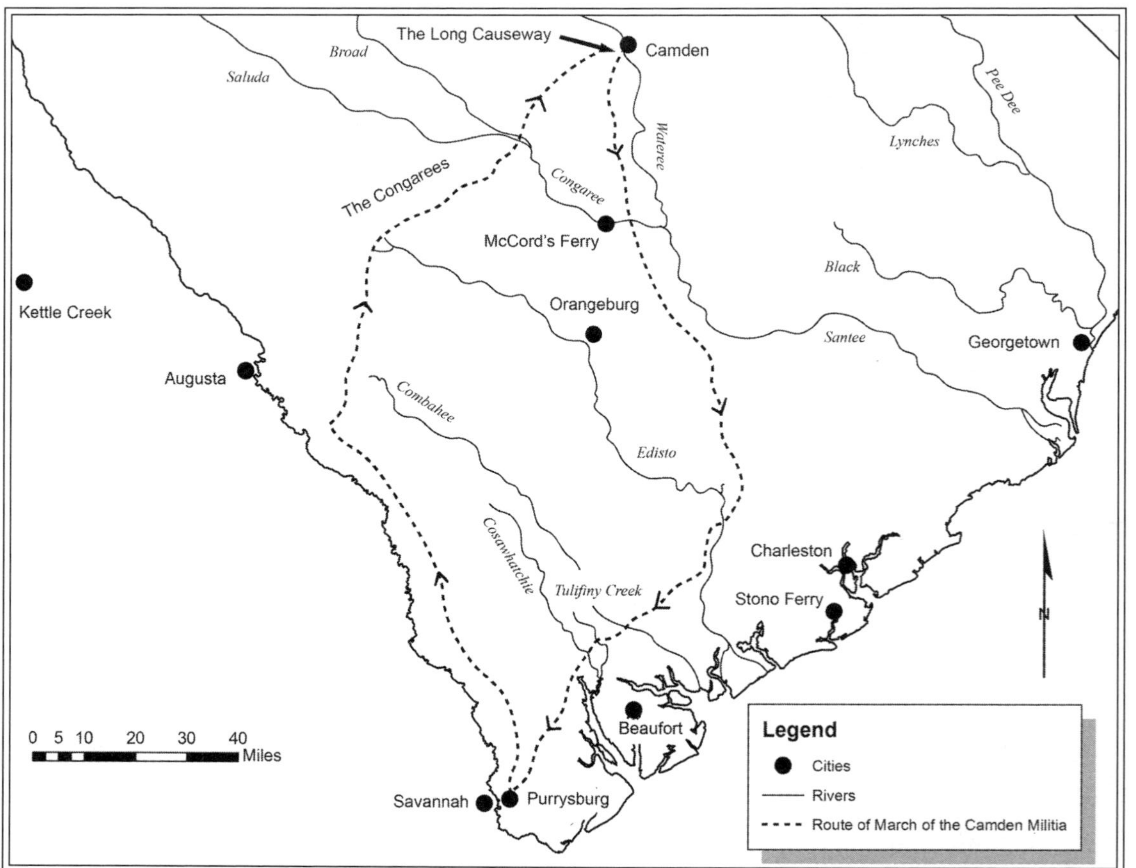

9.3 The seat of war in South Carolina prior to the British invasion of 1780. Major actions of 1778 and 1779 are shown, as well as the route of march of Col. Joseph Kershaw's regiment of Camden militia during the Purrysburg campaign. Author's original map.

his return, Cayle became abusive and threatened Petty's life. Forcibly restrained, the soldier was placed in custody to await punishment. Col. Kershaw attempted to have Cayle tried by a general court martial under the Continental Articles of War and appointed Thomas Charlton judge advocate to prosecute the case. When the court convened, however, its president, Col. Richard Richardson Jr., and seven other militia officers refused to take their oaths as judges. They argued that, because the militia was drafted under state law and did not receive Continental pay or bounties, the prisoner was not subject to the Articles and had to be tried by militia law instead. Their position, supported unanimously by the militia officers, frustrated Gen. Lincoln, who dismissed the South Carolina militia from his command and refused them provisions.[53] This effectively removed the Camden militia regiment from the campaign against Prévost. Decamping from Purrysburg in February, the regiment marched up the Savannah River toward the British post at Augusta. Kershaw's command was joined by Col. Richard Winn's regiment, from the district west of the Wateree, and other militia units, all under orders to place guards at several key ferries. Believing their enlistments were about to expire, however, the militiamen refused to be posted and declined to proceed any farther toward Augusta. Cognizant of the limits of his authority, Kershaw turned his men eastward and discharged them at the Congarees.[54] The initial showing of the Camden regiment of militia had not been auspicious.

The difficulty in defining the militia's role in the larger American military operation reflected the nature of the militia's distinctive social structure. On one hand, the militia represented an institution that had grown out of the conditions of colonization, and it embodied structures that had emerged from the need to organize disparate elements in the absence of an overriding authority. Joseph Kershaw had organized the backcountry economy by employing a strategy that built a network of alliances reliant on ties of kinship, marriage, association, and interdependence. Status in this organization reflected ownership of resources or facilities and the wealth they generated, producing leaders whose influence relied largely on persuasion. This network, linking the inhabitants of a largely rural region through the personal ties of community leaders, created a hierarchy that placed Kershaw in a paramount position to assume the role of a military leader in time of crisis. The militia was composed of small frontier farmers whose livelihood depended on this network and those who controlled it. Drawn from the men of influence in the larger rural community, commanders possessed limited authority based primarily on prestige, a condition that state law recognized and reinforced by separating the militia from the jurisdiction of military courts and offering lenient punishments for crimes such as insubordination. The structure of network relationships provided the authority to organize a military force, but it often worked against those commanding it. Col. Kershaw's demand for a court-martial and the refusal of militia officers to conduct it reflected both the distinctive structure of the militia and its ambiguous role in the larger military organization. The debacle at Purrysburg led the Assembly to pass more stringent laws to regulate the behavior of the militia as a military organization, but throughout the war it remained subject to state control.[55]

Despite its dismissal from Purrysburg, the Camden regiment of militia was soon called upon to again take up arms against the persistent invader. In May, Gen. Prévost's forces bypassed Purrysburg and pressed forward along the coast. To oppose them, Lincoln sent his subordinate William Moultrie with a small force of Continentals and militia. The British advanced on Charleston itself but lacked both the firepower and the transport capacity for a successful siege, and Lincoln's army attacked their rear guard at Stono Ferry just south of the city. Prévost retired to Savannah after the June 20 engagement, leaving a garrison at Beaufort on Port Royal Island.[56]

In response to the British advance, Joseph Kershaw received orders to reassemble his regiment. Less than a month after the Purrysburg expedition, he again faced the task of managing a fragmented military organization. On March 14 he mobilized all the available men, reassigning many to bring the companies to effective strength. Some militiaman, like the recently drafted Richard Clinton, recalled being immediately placed in a new company because his own had so few members.[57] Leaving John Chesnut's company to guard the magazine at Camden, Kershaw dispatched the remainder to reinforce Gen. Andrew Williamson's militia assembling at Orangeburg. Led by the recently promoted Major John Marshall, now officially Kershaw's second in command, the regiment crossed the Wateree on March 28. Their commander joined them en route at Beaver Creek four days later, and they encamped at Orangeburg the next day. Still short of his allotted strength, Kershaw spent much of the next month traveling to militia company musters at Grannys Quarter Creek, Cedar River, Johnson's Old Field in the Waxhaws, and Lynches Creek, encouraging members to turn out at Camden. He also visited the Catawba villages to reaffirm their loyalty and availability to again serve under Samuel Boykin in the coming campaign.[58]

In May the regiment consolidated at Orangeburg and marched to Black Swamp on the Savannah River. From there they participated in William Moultrie's rear-guard action to delay the British advance on Charleston. Private Richard Clinton of John Marshall's company recalled their rapid retreat, "cutting down & destroying every bridge or anything else that would in the least retard the march of the pursuing foe."[59] Under Marshall's command the Camden regiment accompanied Moultrie in his retreat along the coast toward the capital. Kershaw received orders to move three-quarters of his troops to Charleston to await the impending attack. Samuel Boykin's company of Catawbas also arrived in the lowcountry, encamping at Dorchester, northwest of the city. As the threat of an assault faded with the approach of Lincoln's army, the scene of action shifted to Stono Ferry, where some elements of Kershaw's regiment were deployed. Although one of the companies deserted its post, both Marshall's and Luke Petty's companies fought in the ensuing battle on June 20, as did the Catawba company. By this time, however, militia enlistments were again running out, and Gen. Williamson's command began to shrink rapidly. On July 8 all militia troops were discharged.[60] Although the British failed to capture the capital, they established a foothold in the lowcountry and gained valuable information about the surrounding countryside and potential avenues of attack. Their army remained secure in its position in Savannah, where it would defeat an American assault on the city in the fall of 1779. The stage was set for a new campaign the following year.

In the spring of 1779 Ely Kershaw saw action in the western backcountry, the course of which again revealed the nature of the militia as an institution. Activity centered around organized efforts by Loyalists in Georgia to support the British presence on the upper Savannah River. To counter this threat, militia units under Andrew Pickens took to the field in the vicinity of Augusta. Among the units was a detachment of mounted troops formed under Col. Matthew Singleton. A decision by Gen. Williamson, the senior commander, to reassign Singleton elsewhere and replace him with Ely Kershaw, however, brought opposition from Singleton's subordinates, who balked at serving under an unfamiliar leader. Kershaw, who had reentered military service as a lieutenant colonel in the militia, was an outsider in the organization; he had been raised elsewhere and lacked the social prestige necessary for acceptance simply on the basis of an order from higher command. He found himself obliged to rely on the endorsement of both the former commander and Gen. Williamson to persuade the junior officers not only that Singleton had approved of the transfer but also that Kershaw had the credentials to carry out the duties of his new position.[61] He soon found himself in charge of a composite group of militia cavalry, including a company commanded by Lt. Willis Whitaker, who had served with his brother in the Snow Campaign and during the attack on Charleston.[62]

Ely Kershaw distinguished himself in late March while leading an assault against a Loyalist force at Kettle Creek in Georgia. His detachment of horse crossed the Savannah at Beech Island, below Augusta, and attacked a force of about two hundred South Carolina and Georgia Tories. The ensuing battle routed the Loyalists, leaving one of their two commanders dead and the other mortally wounded and a number of prisoners in the hands of the Whigs. Following several weeks spent reconnoitering the area, the unit returned to South Carolina, where some of its members, including Daniel Carter, were discharged at the end of their enlistments. The remainder marched to the lowcountry, took part in the battle at Stono Ferry in June, and later left service at Camden.[63]

Despite his successes, military service took its toll on Ely Kershaw's health and forced him to remain in Charleston following the British retreat. Confined to his house with a debilitating illness that left him barely able to walk, he could no longer continue in his military role and was obliged to conduct even his business activities through others. Ely Kershaw communicated with John Chesnut in Camden and relied on the connections developed earlier through the partnership to coordinate trade in his absence. His confinement in the state's principal port also allowed him to observe directly the war's impact on South Carolina's economy, particularly the restrictions it imposed on the availability of imported goods. But the threat of invasion posed an imminent risk of greater magnitude, and his partner Robert Lithgow, recently returned from Georgia, urged him to settle his business affairs in Charleston with all dispatch, fearing that "the enemy will plague us much this winter." As conditions deteriorated, Ely Kershaw confided his forebodings for the future as he endeavored to return to Camden to plan his next move.[64]

Conquest and Occupation: The Backcountry at War

As 1779 drew to a close, the anticipated apocalypse began to unfold. In late December a British fleet set out from New York and headed south. Under the command of Gen. Sir Henry Clinton and Admiral Marriot Arbuthnot, the combined force aimed to capture Charleston and use South Carolina as a base for a campaign to retake the southern colonies. Their plans avoided the mistakes of the 1776 assault, bypassing the heavily defended harbor to encircle and lay siege to the city. British troops landed on Seabrook Island in February and the following month crossed onto the mainland and headed up the Ashley River. By early April the army had cut off the landward approach to Charleston and begun to construct siege works around the city. At the same time, the fleet advanced from the sea, crossing the bar into Charleston Harbor to complete the noose around Benjamin Lincoln's army and the militia regiments defending the capital.[65]

Even before British troops set foot on South Carolina soil, Gov. Rutledge had prepared the state to meet the coming invasion. In response to his call for a general muster of militia, Joseph Kershaw issued orders in late October to assemble his regiment the following month near Luke Petty's home at Flat Rock for potential deployment to Charleston.[66] As the situation deepened with the new year, Kershaw also made plans to deal with the danger of a renewed war in the interior. The contents of the Camden magazine were a likely military target, and several Tories had already made an unsuccessful attempt to destroy the building. As a result, officials prepared to remove the munitions to a more distant location. By early March 1780 Kershaw had shipped nearly all of the gunpowder and lead to safety in Charlotte, North Carolina. Later that month he began construction of an earthen parapet and ditch surrounding the magazine to protect the remaining munitions there.[67] The Camden jail also took on new significance as tensions rose in the backcountry. As the threat of action by Loyalists increased, many suspected of supporting the Crown found themselves confined there, and a detachment of militia now guarded the jail.[68]

Because of its central location in the transportation network of the backcountry, Camden played an important role in communications as the conflict turned southward. Because Camden was situated on the principal overland route to the north, inland traffic from Philadelphia passed through the town, and it became a stopping place for diplomats and those on official business traveling between the seat of Congress and Charleston. Camden's placement also made it a convenient point of transfer for important correspondence and materials. Just before the fall of Charleston, couriers from Philadelphia met there with Georgia officials to convey $300,000 allocated to that state by Congress.[69] The overland road along the Wateree Valley became a principal military route to the northern interior, and Camden served as a collection point for local militia and state troops in the backcountry as well as for other units moving through the state. During the crisis of 1776, Kershaw's regiment staged at Camden and militia from North Carolina visited the town on their way to Charleston. Following the successful defense of the capital, returning troops passed through Camden, and some were discharged there.[70] In the winter of 1779, Kershaw's regiment bound for Purrysburg assembled at Camden, as did the South Carolina militia headed for Charleston later that year. State troops and militia from Virginia and North Carolina, as well as Gen. Casimir Pulaski's legion, passed through Camden on their way to join the campaigns in coastal South Carolina and Georgia. When the British renewed their offensive against Charleston in the spring of 1780, American forces assembled in the interior to meet the new threat. With the capital surrounded, they attempted to gather relief forces at Orangeburg to break the siege. Camden again became a staging area for local militia and incoming units. On their way south in late April, Col. Abraham Buford, with his Third Virginia Continental Regiment of infantry and artillery, arrived in Camden, where they were joined by Gen. Richard Caswell's regiment and troops from other North Carolina militia units.[71]

Camden's key position in the inland transportation network increased the business of farmers and merchants, but it also created hardships for the residents of the Wateree Valley when the military demand for foodstuffs and forage exceeded the capacity of regional suppliers. These conditions worsened when the failure of the 1779 wheat crop left the region's provisions "much drained." The next spring Joseph Kershaw reported that the price for grain and other supplies had become severely inflated as the state's credit fell. In these circumstances, he drew on his own account to acquire public goods from his established network of suppliers to provide rations, sundries, and transportation for his own regiment during the winter Purrysburg campaign as well as for Col. George Hicks's militia regiment in Orangeburg. In the spring and summer of 1779 he fed and furnished forage for his and Gen. Richard Richardson's regiments en route to the coast, as well as for other Whig forces, including Lt. Col. Archibald Lytle's regiment and Col. Theodorick Bland's Virginia dragoons as they passed through Camden from North Carolina. As the threat to the interior became imminent in 1780, Kershaw attended to matters closer to home, supplying the militia guard at Camden and arranging for the removal and shipment of munitions in the magazine.[72]

To supply the army, Kershaw also relied on the resources of his previous associates. They included his former partners William Ancrum and Kershaw's brother Ely as well as John Cantey, the father-in-law of both Ely Kershaw and John Chesnut. Large landowners and producers such as Benjamin Haile and George White of Lynches River and Robert Crawford of the Waxhaws provided both supplies and transportation, and jailor John Rush Hutchins, who also served as the quartermaster at Camden, supported his establishment. Others, including some in militia service, contributed food, forage, and livestock, as well as tools, wagons, and equipment for use in the campaigns of 1779–1780.[73] As the central figure in the economic development of the Wateree Valley, Joseph Kershaw relied on his ample experience to organize social groups in the absence of higher authority. As a political and military leader, he employed his skills to maintain a government with uncertain influence and now under extreme threat.

In April 1780 Kershaw attempted to assemble his militia regiment for the third time to relieve South Carolina's besieged capital, but he remained behind to tend to affairs in Camden. Although authorities anticipated that his and other militia units would strengthen the defenses at Charleston, the extent to which they did so is uncertain.[74] At least six of his company commanders, John Chesnut, Robert Crawford, George Dunlap, Luke Petty, John Marshall, and Middleton McDonald, served with the Camden regiment at some time during the siege. Several, including Chesnut, were there at the end and, when the city's fall appeared inevitable, urged the American commander to accept Gen. Sir Henry Clinton's terms of surrender. At Camden, Joseph Kershaw continued to collect supplies for the army. Barely a week before Charleston's fall, he ordered Marshall and McDonald to collect cattle and impress horses for the besieged army and later dispatched Crawford to gather any militia he could and proceed to a relief camp at Wright's Bluff on the Santee.[75]

As Kershaw and others struggled to support the doomed Charleston garrison, South Carolina's political leaders began to take steps to relocate the seat of government to a safer location from which they could direct the war. Gov. John Rutledge and key members of his Council escaped from the city via the Cooper River just ahead of British units that were already advancing inland to secure the area north of Charleston. Following the city's surrender on May 12, the army immediately fanned out and defeated American forces at Moncks

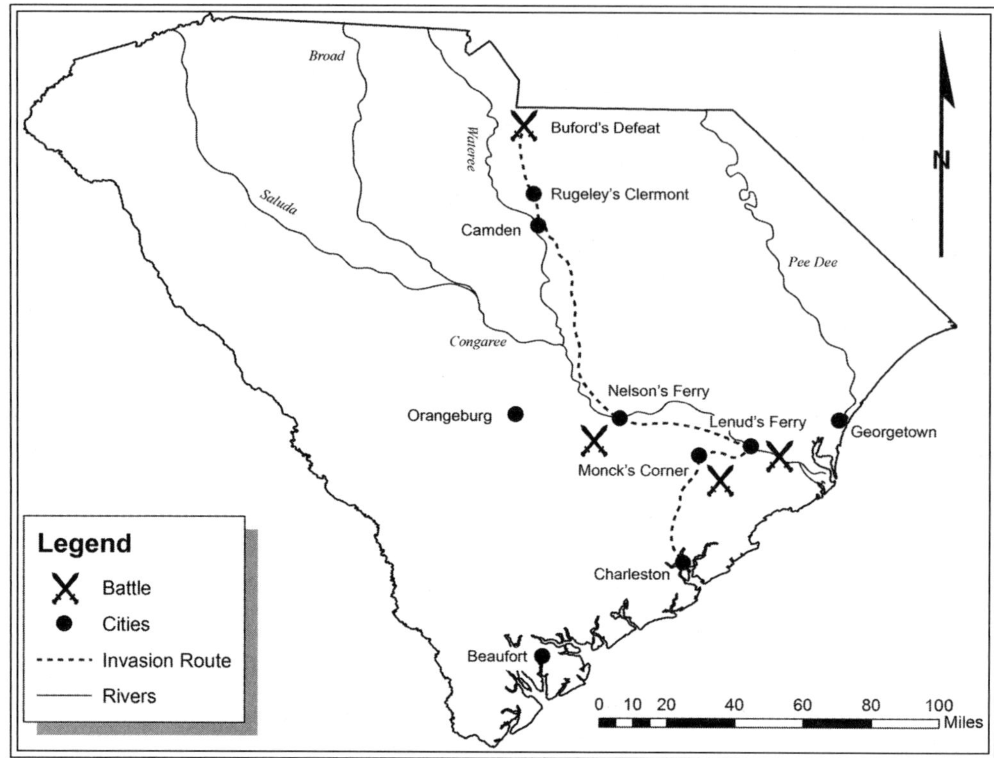

9.4 The British conquest of South Carolina's interior following the fall of Charleston in May 1780. Author's original map.

Corner and Lenud's Ferry, on the lower Santee. When Rutledge encountered Col. Abraham Buford's forces, which were advancing to relieve the capital, he ordered them to immediately fall back to Hillsborough, North Carolina, and his party joined them in their retreat along the road that led to Camden (Fig. 9.4).[76]

Eager to consolidate his victory at Charleston, Clinton immediately turned his attention inland. The enemies of the Crown still ran free in the vast backcountry, and control of South Carolina depended on his occupying and pacifying the interior. Sir Henry believed that suppressing the rebellion hinged on holding key strong points from which the army could crush remaining Whig resistance and support resident Loyalists. To accomplish this, he assigned command of British field forces to his immediate subordinate, Lt. Gen. Charles Earl Cornwallis, a professional soldier whose experience in the American war included the ill-fated attack on Charleston four years earlier. On Clinton's order, Cornwallis struck inland within a week of the surrender, marching up the north side of the Santee toward Camden to cut off the retreat of American units. But the army and its baggage moved slowly, and Buford had several days' head start. To increase the chances of intercepting the Americans, Cornwallis sent a highly mobile force to strike ahead of his advancing army. Led by Lt. Col. Banastre Tarleton, the British Legion was a mixed force of Loyalist and British light cavalry and light infantry that had recently routed Americans forces outside Charleston. Tarleton left the army at Nelson's Ferry on the Santee on May 27 and initiated an aggressive pursuit of a quarry already far inland.[77]

Camden now lay directly in harm's way. Situated on the route of Abraham Buford's retreat into North Carolina, the town once again played host to a passing army. On the same day that Tarleton set out in pursuit, Buford's forces and their baggage train began evacuating Camden up the Catawba Path. Joining them was Luke Petty, Kershaw's militia captain from Grannys Quarter Creek who had recently assisted the colonel in attempting to rally militia troops. Relieved of his mission by circumstances, Petty contributed his services, along with a wagon and team, to assist Buford's army. Gov. Rutledge and his party, who had been staying at Joseph Kershaw's home, preceded the army, leaving the Great White House at eight that morning. Col. Anthony Walton White, survivor of the recent defeat at Lenud's Ferry, remained in Camden throughout the day to destroy any remaining munitions at the magazine and to render the gunpowder there useless. To hinder the British advance, he attempted to burn the bridge over Pine Tree Creek. By the afternoon the army was gone, leaving Kershaw with no means to prevent an aggressive invader from occupying his town.

But he was not alone. Although he lacked military resources, the network of cooperative alliances that Kershaw had built so meticulously earlier was still largely intact. As an arrangement that crosscut political lines, it became a powerful tool through which to negotiate an agreement to salvage what he could. At four in the afternoon Joseph Kershaw notified Camden residents of a meeting to be held two hours later to deal with the imminent threat of a military occupation. Those who attended resolved to deliver a petition under a flag of truce to the British commander, asking for mercy and the protection of their property. The following morning Kershaw, Thomas Charlton, a physician and former ranger, and the Loyalist merchant Charles Ogilvie went out from town to meet with Banastre Tarleton, who agreed to spare the town and requisition only provisions and forage. Tarleton's Legion arrived in Camden in the early afternoon but stayed only long enough for a short rest. By two A.M. on the morning of May 29 they were again on the move.[78]

Meanwhile, Gov. Rutledge's party had proceeded north only as far as Clermont, Henry Rugeley's residence, fourteen miles north of Camden near Grannys Quarter Creek. Here they received the owner's hospitality and settled down to spend the night, only to be awakened later by their host, who had just learned of Tarleton's approach. When he arrived, Tarleton was told the governor had not been there.[79] The failure of Rugeley, a known Loyalist, to divulge the presence of a rebel head of state could imply that he was hedging his bets in a conflict not yet resolved or simply that he did not want to explain Rutledge's presence under his roof. A more plausible explanation is that the strong ties of mutual cooperation and assistance that linked those in the mercantile network of the Wateree Valley imposed social considerations that affected Rugeley's feelings toward and treatment of its members. Closely tied to Kershaw through politics, Rutledge had come to know many of his associates personally and had interacted with Rugeley. The merchant's actions in the wee hours of the 29th preserved social relationships upon which his past success had depended and upon which his future too would rely in these uncertain times. Loyalties that preceded the war continued to strain Henry Rugeley's political allegiance in the months to come as he and other Tories, such as Charles Ogilvie, struggled with the consequences of an occupation that polarized the inhabitants of the backcountry and forced them to engage actively in an increasingly partisan conflict.

During the next few days the British consolidated their hold on the Wateree Valley. On May 29 Tarleton's rapidly moving force caught up with Buford's retreating army in the Waxhaws. When the American commander refused his demand for surrender, Tarleton advanced immediately and completely defeated Buford's troops in a rapacious attack marked by brutality that continued even after the Americans surrendered. Although Buford escaped, his command was destroyed and baggage captured. After the battle, 113 Americans lay dead on the field, and 150 more were badly wounded in the sanguinary affair, among them Luke Petty, whose loss of an arm likely contributed to his death the following year.[80] On his way to Camden with the main body of the army, Earl Cornwallis entertained Charles Ogilvie and Thomas Charleton under a flag of truce the following day and promised the town's residents protection in turn for provisions. In response, Joseph Kershaw exerted his authority as a former militia commander to order three of his captains to round up cattle near Lynches River and used his social prestige to request inhabitants "in and about Camden" to bring corn and provisions to his store to avoid "plundering" by Cornwallis's troops. The army arrived and occupied Camden on June 1. Cornwallis ordered his commissary general, Maj. Charles Stedman, to secure the area and take charge of all facilities and foodstuffs of use to the army.[81]

Kershaw's status now turned against him and immediately affected his treatment. Under the terms of surrender at Charleston, Sir Henry Clinton offered parole to all captured militiamen, allowing them to return home after swearing allegiance to the Crown. But conditions changed when Clinton returned to New York, leaving Cornwallis in charge. The new commander perceived that the need for security demanded that he treat "the most violent Rebels" differently from faithful subjects. He believed field officers of the militia and those who had held civil offices to be disaffected and directed that they lose their protections and be paroled to the coastal islands of South Carolina. Joseph Kershaw and his brother Ely received paroles on June 10 and prepared to leave Camden.[82] Perceiving Kershaw to be "a very violent man [who had] persecuted the loyalists," Cornwallis also confiscated his possessions, ordering Maj. Stedman to seize his property without issuing receipts. The army immediately occupied Kershaw's store, his mills, and his tobacco warehouse on the Wateree and expropriated their contents. Kershaw's losses were compounded by the destruction of the upper mills on Little Pine Tree Creek by fire, an event that severely cut production capacity. In addition, the army requisitioned his horses, cattle, sheep, and hogs as well as his slaves. Cornwallis moved into the Great White House, making it his headquarters, and confined Sarah Kershaw and her five children to a single room.[83]

Now at the mercy of his captors, Joseph Kershaw sought to make arrangements for his brother's health and his family's security during his impending absence. Chief among his concerns was the specter of smallpox, or variola, an epidemic disease that had already ravaged South Carolina twice in the eighteenth century. In the spring of 1779, Casimir Pulaski's legion, which passed through Camden, carried the disease southward on its way to defend Charleston. Smallpox broke out in the capital that summer and raged throughout the siege. Following Charleston's surrender, it followed British troops as they set out to pacify the interior. Variola soon appeared in the vicinity of Camden and contributed to a high rate of sickness among the soldiers of the town garrison. In the yard of Kershaw's house, the large kitchen had already been pressed into service as a hospital. Fearing for the safety of his wife and children, Kershaw received permission to move them to the countryside, where they could receive inoculations against the disease.[84]

He also argued successfully that his brother Ely's condition warranted a delay in meeting the conditions of their paroles and a change in their place of exile. Earl Cornwallis agreed to confine them in Port Royal, Bermuda, and on August 8 the schooner *Savannah* carried them over the Charleston bar en route to Nassau, New Providence. They reached the Bahamas three weeks later and in mid-October sailed for Bermuda on the schooner *Nassau.* Encounters with privateers and rough seas delayed their voyage, and high winds forced them to spend almost a week sheltered in harbor at Eleuthera before continuing on. By this time Ely's condition had worsened considerably and his life slipped away the evening before the ship reached Port Royal harbor. Letters from Charles Ogilvie provided an introduction to Richard and John Jennings, merchants who furnished shelter and made arrangements for Ely's funeral and burial.[85] His arrival in Bermuda ended Joseph Kershaw's journey into exile, and his absence from the Wateree Valley marked a time of dramatic change the course of the region's development.

Confined to the island of Bermuda indefinitely, Joseph Kershaw was alone, removed physically from the region dominated by his presence for the past two decades. Conditions left him isolated and unable to manage his assets in South Carolina. Much of his income-earning property had been confiscated and some of it destroyed outright. With his brother's passing, he had lost both a confidant and a close business partner whose extensive estate was also now in disarray. His home was occupied and his family made refugees in a country that faced an uncertain future. Although the legacy of Kershaw & Co. continued to influence the economy of the backcountry, the absence of the Kershaw brothers created a void that offered opportunities for others to shape the region's economic and political landscape.

Chapter 10

"An Evil Genius about It"

Occupation and War in the Backcountry

The early summer of 1813 found the Earl of Moira traveling on the high seas to assume his new post as governor general of Bengal. A request from a former adversary in the American War for Independence, now thirty years in the past, prompted him to begin a lengthy account of his participation in events that had taken place in South Carolina in 1781. This violent time had witnessed the culmination of the vicious civil war in the backcountry and the collapse of the British military presence established the previous year. As Lt. Col. Francis, Lord Rawdon, he had been stationed at Camden as commander of British forces and their Loyalist allies in the eastern interior (Fig. 10.1). During the year he spent in the backcountry, he saw almost continuous action in a frustrating counterinsurgency campaign against the Americans. More than once he had emerged victorious over Whig forces only to encounter circumstances that made it impossible to exploit his successes and that eventually forced him to abandon the posts under his control and oversee a retreat to Charleston.[1]

There were many reasons for the British failure in South Carolina, but Lord Rawdon's letter emphasized his frustration with an awkward command structure that restricted the geographical scope of his authority and left him subservient to and dependent on the whims of a distant commander at Charleston. Ambiguity surrounding control and responsibility between two competitive officers, coupled with poor communications, hampered Rawdon's ability to carry out his mission effectively and, despite extraordinary efforts, obliged him to witness the collapse of British power in the interior. The American war exacted a toll on the earl's health that forced him to return home from South Carolina on sick leave to recover. Although Lord Rawdon emerged with his reputation untarnished, questions over his role in the conflict continued to demand his attention, even decades later, and brought with them unsettling recollections of a bitter partisan conflict from which few participants emerged unscathed.[2] Camden loomed large in his memory and that of many others who experienced a war that devastated the region and its nascent institutions.

"An Infamous Post"

Earl Cornwallis's choice of Camden as the goal of his initial foray into South Carolina's interior was neither accidental nor capricious. His actions were part of Sir Henry Clinton's

10.1 The Earl of Moira ca. 1800. As Lord Rawdon, he served under Lt. Gen. Earl Cornwallis in the Southern Campaign and commanded the military garrison at Camden in 1780–1781. Author's collection.

larger strategy of pacifying the interior by establishing garrisons at its central settlements. From strongpoints at Camden, Ninety Six, and Augusta, the king's forces could rapidly strike at enemy resistance and secure the region. Such bases also provided foci around which to rally loyal supporters of royal authority. Situated along main routes of overland travel, the fortified settlements served as links between field armies and the principal supply base in Charleston, and they formed the central elements in a defense-in-depth strategy intended to protect the region against external threats and to support a reconquest of the southern colonies.[3]

Soon after the British army occupied Camden, Sir Henry returned to New York, leaving Cornwallis as military commander in the South. Cornwallis's expanded role drew him back to Charleston in June, and command of the Camden garrison shifted to a young subordinate, Lord Rawdon. An experienced and able officer at age twenty-five, he was a logical choice to manage pacification.[4] As the military strongpoint in the Wateree Valley, Camden became a focus for British efforts to control the central and eastern backcountry, serving as a base for regular army units as well as Loyalist elements. To help secure the interior, Rawdon organized four Loyalist militia infantry regiments and one of rangers. All were drawn from inhabitants of the region and placed under influential Loyalists who were commissioned as military officers and given the civil powers of magistrates. He chose James Cary, a well-to-do planter, justice of the peace, and former Regulator who lived across the river from the town, to command the unit west of Camden. Henry Rugeley, merchant, planter, miller, entrepreneur, and recently the savior of the rebel government, commanded the regiment north of Camden from his home on Grannys Quarter Creek. Neither had actively supported the Crown and, with other prominent community members, had recently helped fortify the Camden magazine. Both, however, now pledged their support to the king's forces, gathered supporters, and erected fortifications on their properties to protect the northern and western approaches to Camden.[5]

Just as Camden's success as an economic center had rested upon access, the town's effectiveness as a military strongpoint also depended on the army's ability to keep routes of transportation and communication open to the principal supply depot of Charleston and to other outposts in the interior. Protecting this infrastructure required a broad military presence. To demonstrate their authority in the countryside, British commanders established a number of fortified posts to "awe" the inhabitants and secure points along important routes. Fort Granby at Fridig's Ferry, an important road junction in the Congarees, facilitated communications with the western garrisons at Ninety Six and Augusta. "A chain of small posts" also protected the overland route to Charleston via Moncks Corner, with fortified sites at Mott's house, just south of the Congaree crossing at McCord's Ferry; Fort Watson, on Wright's Bluff north of the Santee; and the important crossing at Nelson's Ferry (Fig. 10.2).[6]

Camden's geographic position made it a key settlement from which to defend South Carolina's interior and launch the planned invasion of the adjacent provinces. Consequently, it became both a garrison town and a supply depot to support offensive operations. Cornwallis recognized Camden's importance by stationing a substantial force of regular troops and militia there.[7] To provision the garrison, British commanders relied on supplies commandeered from the surrounding area. Militiamen ranged as far as the Waxhaws to collect corn and wheat to be ground at Camden's mills and requisitioned cattle, hogs, and sheep from area farms, but the army remained dependent on Charleston for imported supplies such as rum, salt, regimental supplies, and ammunition. To transport materiel, Cornwallis collected wagons from as far away as Ninety Six and the Congarees and employed boats to bring artillery supplies and baggage inland from the capital.[8]

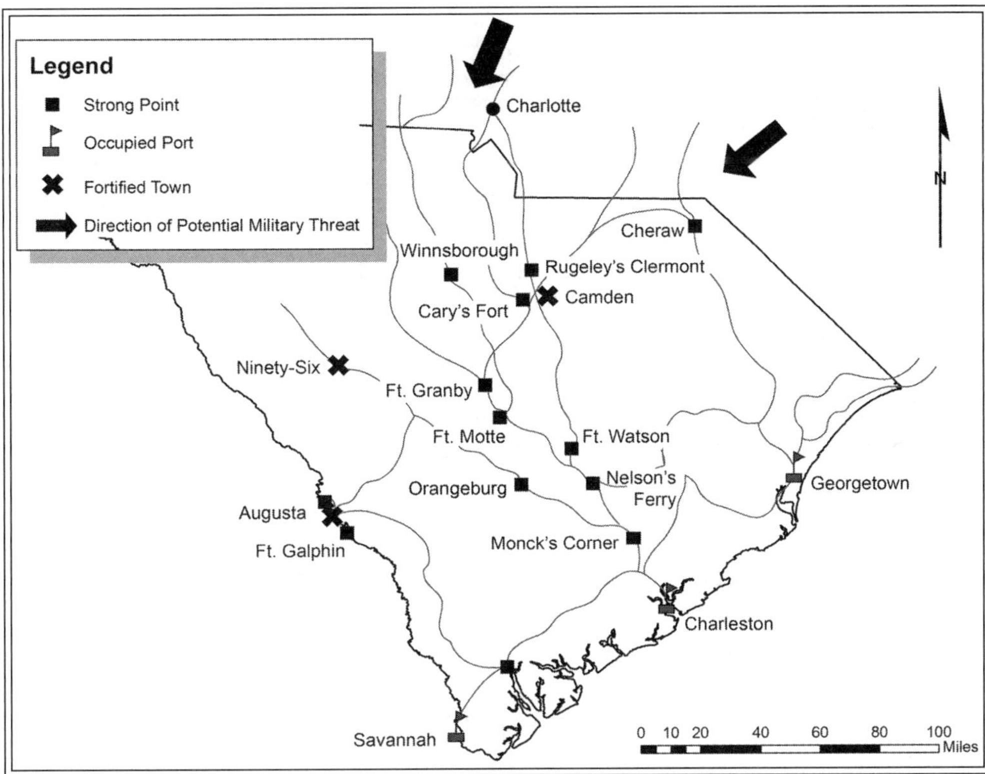

10.2 Garrisons occupied by British and Loyalist forces in South Carolina, 1780–1781. Author's original map.

The military occupation impacted Camden's physical form, as the army made use of existing structures and added others to suit its purposes. Immediately upon their arrival, soldiers seized and appropriated the contents of commercial buildings, including Kershaw's store and brewhouse, his warehouses on the Wateree, and the lower mills on Pine Tree Creek. A substantial permanent garrison required dry space to store its munitions, arms, equipment, and supplies, including a printing press, as well as room for offices and other activities, and Camden's few residences may have been appropriated for military purposes as well. The army also occupied the magazine and employed the jail to house captured Whigs and prisoners of war. Archaeological evidence for the army's extensive use of Camden is reflected in the broad distribution of military artifacts across the entire town site.[9]

Camden's few buildings could not accommodate the army, and Lord Rawdon directed Lt. Henry Haldane of the Royal Engineers to erect rows of barracks near the town to house the troops. Although the barracks were initially intended to occupy the area between the town and the Great White House, no buildings are shown here on the 1781 map, and no archaeological evidence of structures appeared in this area. But the map shows seven similar groups of smaller structures, each consisting of several parallel rows of buildings, arranged

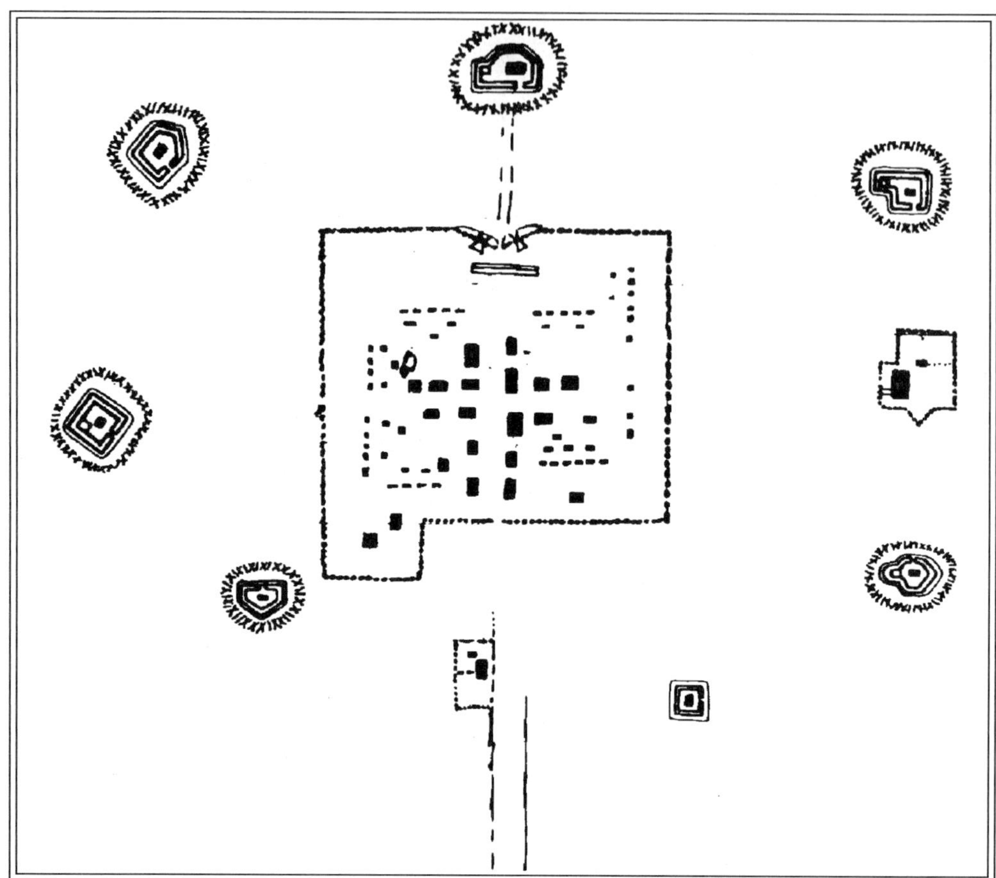

10.3 Plan of the fortified town of Camden in 1781. Palisade walls enclosed the nucleated settlement, Joseph Kershaw's mansion, and a structure to the south. Six redoubts and the fortified magazine surrounded the town to protect it from attack. Each of the heavily fortified redoubts contained a wall, ditch, and abatis. The jail lay within the redoubt north of Camden. Note that the southwest corner of the town palisade was extended to enclose the brewhouse. Adapted from the Nathaniel Greene Papers, Papers of the Continental Congress, National Archives, Washington, D.C.

along the outer edge of the contiguous settlement. The number of clusters corresponds to that of the British and Loyalist units that occupied Camden (Fig. 10.3). Their regular order implies the rigid social hierarchical structure found in military units, with multiple barracks for the common soldiers, fronted by separate structures for noncommissioned officers and officers. Their small size also reflects the desperate conditions under which they were erected. Although Rawdon attempted to acquire sufficient plank and board to construct "some kind of barracks and some huts for officers," a shortage of materials dogged Haldane throughout the summer and fall and delayed construction until late in the year. Fabric for the new quarters sometimes came from existing buildings, such as the Presbyterian meetinghouse, torn down to build a "row, or a street, of huts occupied by the soldiers."[10]

The rapidly deteriorating military situation in the backcountry brought about perhaps the most dramatic additions to Camden. Pacification efforts intended to subdue opposition by pillage or destruction of property only strengthened the resolve of rebels. Executions brought reprisals, and the brutality of Tarleton's tactics created outrage among Whigs, who now sought revenge. Within a month of Cornwallis's victorious advance into the interior, the region erupted in vicious partisan warfare. Organized militia forces resisted the occupation under the leadership of Col. Thomas Sumter and others. Loyalist commanders without military skills failed to cope with a movement that soon threatened the army's mission, and victories by Sumter and other militia commanders at Williamson's Plantation, the Waxhaws, and Hanging Rock emphasized the lack of British control. By early August, Cornwallis concluded that "The whole country between Pedee and Santee has . . . been in an absolute state of rebellion, every friend of the government has been carried off, and his plantation destroyed."[11] But that was not the only problem the earl faced.

Even before the surrender of Lincoln at Charleston, the Continental Congress had created a new army that now moved to regain lost territory in the South. Composed of Maryland and Delaware Continentals, Virginia and North Carolina militia, and units of cavalry and artillery, it descended upon South Carolina under the command of Maj. Gen. Horatio Gates, the architect of the earlier American victory, at Saratoga, New York. The Southern Army approached Camden from the northeast, carefully avoiding British positions on Little Lynches River, then moved westward to Henry Rugeley's plantation to regroup. Meanwhile, Lord Rawdon concentrated his dispersed forces in Camden and called for reinforcements from Ninety Six. With Sumter's forces across the Wateree protecting approaches from the west, Gates advanced at night along the Catawba Path toward a new position from which he hoped to draw Rawdon and the defending forces out of Camden and into an open battle. Earl Cornwallis hurried from Charleston to Camden, assembled the 2,179 troops fit for duty, and immediately marched north on the night of August 15. The two armies encountered each other on Jasper Sutton's farm, just north of Gum Swamp Creek, and skirmished during the early hours of the morning (Fig. 10.4). Before the first light of day on August 16, both armies deployed in line for a traditional battle on the high ground along the main road. The ensuing encounter went badly for the American commander, whose left flank of poorly trained militia units broke and fled when attacked by regular British troops. With their collapse, the Continentals under the command of Maj. Gen. Johann DeKalb came under attack from two sides and suffered heavy losses, and DeKalb fell, mortally wounded. Although Gates escaped, his army was destroyed at the Battle of Camden. Of its original strength of 3,700, about half were killed or wounded, and perhaps as many as 1,000 prisoners of war were rounded up and brought back to Camden.[12]

Despite the rout at Gum Swamp and the subsequent defeat of Thomas Sumter's forces at Fishing Creek, the potential threat of an American advance prompted the British to build significant fortifications at Camden.[13] Cornwallis was aware that the town lay in open country without natural defenses, and he ordered Haldane, the engineer, to construct conventional fortifications to protect its exposed garrison (Fig. 10.3). His plan encircled the nucleated settlement with six strong redoubts. These self-contained forts incorporated earthworks and ditches surrounded by abatis, and each redoubt mounted a light field gun to provide overlapping fields of fire around the town's perimeter. The northernmost redoubt

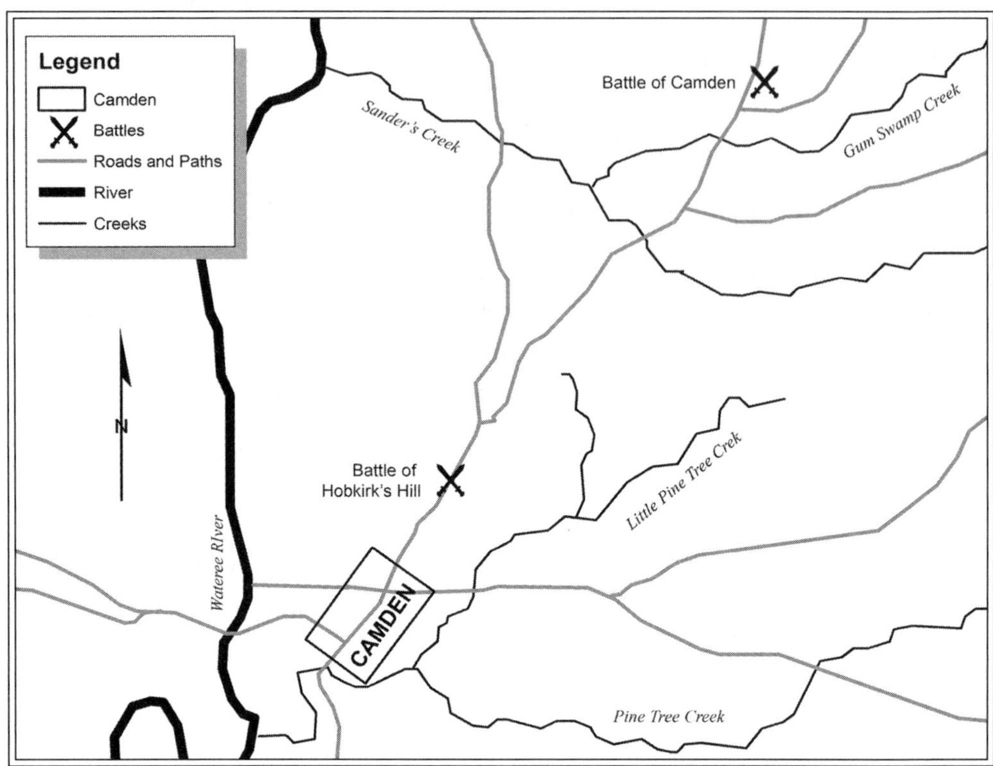

10.4 Two major battles took place in the vicinity of Camden. To the north on Gum Swamp Creek, the Battle of Camden was fought on the morning of August 16, 1780. A second engagement was fought at Hobkirk's Hill on April 25, 1781 and precipitated the British abandonment of Camden two weeks later. Author's original map.

lay on the Catawba Path and enclosed the jail, while the others covered the eastern and western approaches and the road leading to the ferry. Haldane also included Joseph Kershaw's magazine as the southernmost fortification. Construction of the fortifications depended on troops and requisitioned slave laborers, many of whom suffered debilitating illness that slowed construction. Only in late November were the redoubts complete and capable of accommodating the entire garrison.[14]

As a perceptive tactician, Rawdon realized that the isolated redoubts could not protect Camden by themselves. An aggressive assault might pass between them and threaten the undefended town, leaving his stores vulnerable to capture or destruction. Determined to secure a post made increasingly "infamous" by circumstances, he began construction of a stockade wall around the town, as well as smaller stockades to enclose his headquarters and a group of two small structures on the road south of Camden. Archaeological investigations revealed that the town palisade consisted of a single row of posts that enclosed the buildings on either side of Broad Street and extended from Bull to Meeting Street and south to encompass the brewhouse. Its shape varied only slightly from that shown on the 1781 plan, incorporating diagonals to accommodate topography in its northwest corner and

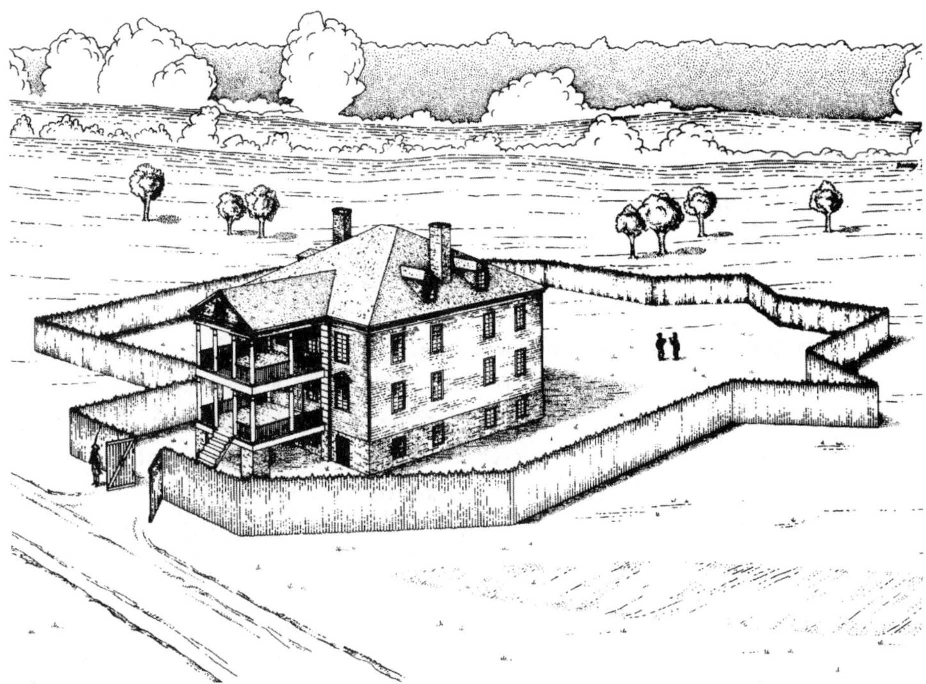

10.5 Conjectural bird's-eye view of the Kershaw mansion surrounded by the palisade fortifications erected during the British occupation. The layout of the palisade was determined by archaeological investigations. Courtesy of South Carolina Institute of Archaeology and Anthropology, Columbia, South Carolina.

at the southern edge of town. Archaeological evidence showed the configuration of the palisade surrounding Kershaw's mansion to be much more complex than indicated. Situated on a hill, its irregular shape followed the sloping terrain and included two bastions, projecting works that permitted defenders to direct flanking fire along adjacent curtain walls (Fig. 10.5). Although not as robust as the earthwork fortifications, the palisade formed a defensible position between the two eastern redoubts. Rawdon also erected detached works to protect two critical resources outside the town, Kershaw's lower mill on Pine Tree Creek and a ferry house on the river.[15]

An increase in hostile activity in the late summer and fall of 1780 led to the fortification of sites beyond Camden as well. The closest was Cary's Fort, situated on the militia colonel's property west of the Wateree. Erected on a small hill, with a creek flanking three sides, it stood about four hundred yards from the ferry and commanded crucial supply and communications routes leading south to McCord's Ferry, north to Winnsboro, Rocky Mount, and Kings Mountain, and west to the Congarees. Although elements under Thomas Sumter surprised the garrison and captured the post during Gates's advance in August, Cary's militia subsequently reoccupied the site as their headquarters.[16]

North of Camden at Grannys Quarter Creek, Henry Rugeley's Clermont occupied a strategic position on the road to the Waxhaws. Briefly abandoned in August 1780, it too was reoccupied by British troops following Gates's defeat. Henry Rugeley strengthened his property in late November as the threat of American attack grew, fortifying his log barn with an earthen wall and abatis. When faced with the prospect of a potentially costly battle to defend his fort against attack in December, Col. Rugeley surrendered Clermont to avoid bloodshed and became a prisoner of war. Although it remained in British hands, the post no longer posed a threat.[17]

The Unhealthiness of the Place

Camden's appearance and composition reflected its occupation by a garrison debilitated by disease while engaged an active war zone. To care for the sick as well as combat casualties, the army established a general hospital for the eastern backcountry at Camden. Intended to accept the overflow of convalescent casualties from regimental and flying hospitals in the field, general hospitals were fixed, stationary facilities situated in relatively safe locations. Under ideal conditions, they provided a haven where patients were cared for until again fit for duty. But because they received all sick and wounded and crowded soldiers recovering from wounds together with those suffering from a variety of infectious illnesses, the conditions in general hospitals often encouraged the spread of disease and actually increased mortality rates.[18]

Such was the case at Camden. Lying just above the river flood plain, the fortified town was subject to seasonal and epidemic disease, prompting more than one perceptive observer to remark on the "unhealthiness of this place." Occupied at the height of the sickly summer season by a population already infected by smallpox, the confined settlement subjected His Majesty's troops to an opponent as threatening as any they would meet on the battlefield. Disease began to take its toll soon after the army arrived in June. In July malaria was already prevalent, and by the following month "fevers and agues" were widespread among the garrison. John Robert Shaw, who arrived in Camden with the Thirty-third Regiment, recalled that he soon fell ill with this "common sickness," and Lord Rawdon himself overcame malaria only with large doses of quinine. When he arrived in Camden to face Gates in battle the following month, Cornwallis found that disease had rendered nearly 800 of his 1,500 regulars ineffective and reported that the garrison was "generally sickly." The "ague" also overcame nearly two-thirds of the troops in the Seventy-first Regiment, encamped at the presumed healthy site of Cheraw, and they were removed to Camden.[19] Conditions failed to improve as the month wore on. "Our sickness is great and truly alarming," wrote Cornwallis, who noted that "every public officer of the Army was incapable of doing his duty" and that Dr. Hays, the British physician general, and all the other surgeons were all "laid up." To add to their woes, dysentery, or the "flux," broke out in Camden. Spread by tainted water and food, it often proved fatal to those already weakened by malaria.[20]

The addition of an estimated 1,000 American prisoners taken at the Battle of Camden on August 16, at least 240 of whom were wounded, compounded the situation at Camden. Newly arrived American casualties and their 245 British counterparts overwhelmed the already strained medical facilities at Camden. Conditions in the crowded settlement, as well as wartime animosities, undoubtedly affected the care of the enemy. British observers, such as Fusilier Shaw, recalled that the captives were "treated with civility," and Commissary

Maj. Stedman stated that "the American wounded were treated with utmost humanity"; however, Virginia militiaman William Allman, who later escaped his imprisonment, painted a grimmer picture of their fate. He reported that "the [American] wounded were very much neglected and when they died were suffered to lay until they stunk horribly in the yard with the other prisoners." High-ranking officers apparently fared better. The mortally wounded Maj. Gen. DeKalb, Gates's second in command, received care at the general hospital, where he died several days after his capture. His aide, the Chevalier DuBuysson, remarked on this civil treatment by British authorities. Following his death, DeKalb was buried with all the honors of war in a funeral attended by all the officers of the British army.[21]

The sudden arrival of American prisoners necessitated a temporary expansion of the medical facilities at Camden, and Cornwallis permitted Dr. Hugh Williamson, an American military surgeon, to cross the lines to administer to the new arrivals. The British commander also took advantage of the services and facilities of Dr. Thomas Charlton, who continued to reside in Camden. The army had confiscated Charlton's medical supplies for the British hospital, effectively curtailing the practice carried out at his plantation just north of town. His skills, however, made him invaluable to the garrison, and he was appointed director of the American hospital. Together he and Williamson supervised the medical treatment of the wounded prisoners they found poorly housed in six small wards, and they later treated British casualties during the occupation. Dr. Isaac Alexander, a North Carolina surgeon, also attended the injured following his capture at the battle of Camden. He dressed the wounds of the mortally wounded Gen. DeKalb and cared for him until he died.[22]

As prisoners captured in actions elsewhere in the interior began to flood into Camden, conditions soon reached crisis proportions. In addition to the wounded, many prisoners became ill with smallpox, typhus, and dysentery, and at least twenty-two eventually died. Aware of the danger posed by their presence, Cornwallis remarked that "The number of prisoners was a great inconvenience to us here in a small village so crowded & so sickly." He recognized that the crowded conditions increased the likelihood of "pestilential fever during the hot weather" and resolved to remove the healthy captives as soon as possible, sending them off in small groups under guard. By October most had been removed to Charleston to languish under appalling conditions in the prison ships. The wounded fared somewhat better, and a small number, some of whom also suffered from smallpox, remained in Camden under the care of surgeon Williamson.[23]

The general hospital dominated Camden throughout the occupation. It was the largest medical facility in the interior and would have occupied a large structure to provide space for a substantial number of casualties from the garrison and units in the field. Guilford Dudley, an American observer, placed the hospital in the southwestern portion of the fortified town, where it lay protected by two of the western redoubts. Local tradition surrounding Gen. DeKalb's death also locates the hospital in this part of town. It relates that he succumbed to his wounds in a structure that lay east of the Presbyterian church and near the corner of Broad and Meeting Streets and that he was buried within yards of that building. A later plat of Camden identified DeKalb's initial burial site, marked by a brick vault topped by a stone slab, on the north side of Meeting Street west of Broad. Although his 1825 reburial obliterated this structure, archaeological excavations in 1975 unearthed brick rubble from the tomb at this location. Joseph Kershaw's store, on the west side of Broad Street just above Meeting Street, was the only substantial building in this portion of the palisaded town. Kershaw himself later indicated that his buildings in Camden had been used as a hospital, and archaeological investigations at the site of the store on Broad Street uncovered uniform buttons and other military objects that confirm its use during the British occupation of the town.[24]

The presence of the general hospital must have altered Camden's landscape further by making the town the final resting place for all those who perished there from wounds and disease. Although most of the ordinary soldiers killed in battle appear to have been buried or left where they fell, hundreds of wounded passed through Camden, and many died there. The area adjacent to the hospital itself was certainly used to inter higher-ranking individuals, including Gen. DeKalb and several British officers, who died of wounds or disease at or near Camden. Those who disposed of the dead at the hospital may also have found it convenient to bury them nearby. But such graves were poorly marked and their locations soon forgotten. Indeed, precise knowledge of DeKalb's resting place became so uncertain in the years following the war that residents had to conduct exploratory excavations to find and mark its location. The undiscovered graves of those who died in Camden are a testament to this dark time.[25]

"A Smooth Tongued Gentleman"

In the summer of 1780, the residents of the Wateree Valley suddenly found themselves subject to a new order that restructured previous social and economic connections. As British authorities strove to establish and maintain political control over the rebellious southern colony, their efforts polarized the backcountry population. Residents found it increasingly difficult to remain neutral in a conflict that now permeated most aspects of everyday life, affecting their livelihoods, their relationships, and often their very existence. Survival meant developing strategies to cope with the perilous new conditions, and those who had supported independence were without institutional support. South Carolina's government, now largely represented by its governor, John Rutledge, was in exile, and opposition to the military regime had taken the form of mobile guerrilla armies operating largely without a territorial base.[26] To persist in the face of the uncertainties of a protracted conflict, residents had again to rely on informal arrangements and turned to networks of relationships developed in previous years.

Four years of intermittent conflict had drawn most men into the militia, an institution whose structure mirrored that of the frontier society from which its members came. Militia leaders included those who were prominent in backcountry trade and politics, men who might be expected to have retained their high status under British military rule. But the terms of the occupation complicated matters. The British victory at Charleston in May resulted in the surrender of the militia forces in the capital as well as those in the interior at Ninety Six and Camden. Although the terms of the surrender attempted to ensure the neutrality of militia members by releasing them as prisoners on parole, a subsequent proclamation requiring them to take an oath of allegiance and actions to imprison and confiscate the estates of prominent militiamen placed the parolees' status in jeopardy.[27]

The war did not destroy the organization of the old networks that underlay backcountry society, although it brought changes in leadership. The most influential rebel militia leaders received harsh punishments that curtailed their power and influence. Former Gen. Richard Richardson had his parole revoked and was imprisoned in Charleston until his health failed. After returning to his plantation, Big Home, on the Santee, he died in September 1780. His son Richard, a major, was paroled to James Island but escaped to take up arms again. Big Home did not long survive its owner. It was burned with other plantations whose owners Banastre Tarleton believed had aided American guerrillas. Joseph Kershaw was exiled from South Carolina and his property in Camden confiscated or destroyed. His brother Ely was similarly banished but did not live to witness the loss of his goods and other property at Cheraw Hill.[28] Such efforts failed to prevent the development of a partisan movement in the backcountry, and new leaders arose. The social and economic structures around which the militia was organized persisted and formed the basis for the guerrilla forces that formed in the wake of the invasion.

A number of prominent Whigs resided in the vicinity of Camden after the fall of Charleston. Some had been associated with the militia previously but were inactive that spring, while others appear to have had no previous military affiliation. Among the former was Francis Boykin, a member of Ely Kershaw's ranger company who had risen to the rank of major at the defense of Ft. Moultrie and commanded a company of Joseph Kershaw's militia at Purrysburg. John Cook occupied the important position of quartermaster on the Purrysburg expedition, and Samuel Boykin organized and led the Catawba Company against the British on at least two occasions.[29] Thomas Charlton, a physician who was active in several campaigns in western South Carolina, had resigned his commission and returned to private practice at Camden; he represented the town's citizens in negotiations with British commanders.[30] Benjamin Haile, a planter on Lynches River, and Duncan McRa, a small merchant, had also served previously as lieutenants in the militia.[31] Other known residents who supported the Whig cause included Joshua Dinkins and John Cantey, by then middle-aged planters, as well as Burwell Boykin, William Wyly, John Milhous, and the merchant William Lang.[32]

The threat to Charleston in the spring of 1780 drew many Camden militia members back into service to oppose the British attack on Charleston, and a number of them were captured when the city surrendered. John Cantey's son James, a veteran officer who had served as a lieutenant in the Snow Campaign of 1775 and later in the ranger regiment of state troops, commanded an outpost on Sullivan's Island at the time of the surrender.[33] Zachariah Cantey and Isaac DuBose also participated in the defense of Ft. Moultrie, and Willis Whitaker and John Chesnut led companies of Kershaw's regiment at Charleston.[34] Other Camden militia members at Charleston included John Whitaker, and Samuel Wyly and his brother John, the sheriff of Camden District, as well as William, youngest of the Kershaw brothers.[35] All became prisoners of war at the surrender and were initially paroled.

Three Whig sympathizers who played a central role in the development of the backcountry economy and who maintained strong connections with Camden resided in Charleston at the time of its capture. The merchants Archibald Brown, Aaron Loocock, and William Ancrum all possessed stocks of goods, stores, and warehouses there, as well as substantial economic holdings in the interior, and the invasion jeopardized the security of their assets. Loocock and Brown were partners in business in the capital and were further tied by Loocock's marriage to Brown's sister Mary. Ancrum's mercantile activities were also centered largely in Charleston, and he maintained an active trade with his former partners at Camden. All three merchants owned backcountry plantations, whose location in an active war zone put their operation at risk. The necessity of maintaining their livelihood under the arbitrary conditions of military rule placed them in the awkward position of now being obliged to do business with their recent enemies. Although noncombatants, they were subject to the conditions of parole under the terms of surrender. Fearful of having their property seized by military authorities, the merchants were obliged to demonstrate their acceptance of the new regime by signing a congratulatory address to the victorious British commanders, Sir Henry Clinton and Adm. Mariot Arbuthnot. This act, later seen by their countrymen as treasonous, provided an avenue to integrate former enemies into the new order. Perhaps because of their previous public roles, all three received civil appointments. Ancrum and Loocock became commissioners of the streets, and Ancrum was made firemaster of Charleston and was commissioned to investigate the depreciation of paper currency. Brown briefly commanded a loyalist militia company charged with keeping the peace. In return, the merchants retained the freedom to conduct business in the metropolis and the backcountry, an arrangement that served British interests as well as their own.[36]

Merchants played a crucial role in supplying the king's military garrisons and interior settlements during the occupation. Maintaining their businesses required that they actively manage the enterprises firsthand, traveling to plantations, stores, and mills to oversee trade and production. Because of their essential economic importance and their acquiescence to British authority, their business faced minimal scrutiny and few restrictions. Nevertheless, operating in a war zone exposed them to continuous risk. Conducting business in the backcountry in 1780 not only exposed civilian activities to disruptive field operations that destroyed crops and property, interrupted trade, and endangered lives but also subjected valuable commodities to seizure by military authorities. Loocock and Brown lost twenty-two casks of indigo stored on a lowcountry plantation, taken by the army shortly after the surrender of Charleston. At Camden, William Ancrum recovered only a small portion of his indigo captured and held by the military commissary there.[37] The ebb and flow of military action also curtailed the movement of goods to lowcountry markets, at times cutting off trade altogether. Uncertain markets also affected the availability and price of goods, once leaving Archibald Brown watching helplessly in Charleston while the price of his tobacco, stored in Camden, fell. Wartime conditions also threatened the production of agricultural commodities in the backcountry, leaving planters like William Ancrum to face additional risks to their livelihood.[38]

The changing conditions of commerce prompted different responses among the three merchants. Aaron Loocock fled the capital, retiring to his Middleburgh plantation below Camden near the Great Raft on the Wateree. Circumstances threatening his business interests in Charleston soon forced his return, but the unstable political situation and his own ambivalent status led him to liquidate both his assets in the former Kershaw & Co. and a current partnership with Archibald Brown and, in October 1780, to leave the province. Removing to London, he remained in exile for the next three years. Brown, however, remained

10.6 William Ancrum was one of the original partners in the Pine Tree Hill venture. A wealthy Charleston merchant, he was also a backcountry planter who maintained close ties with his former associates at Camden. His involvement in commercial activities there continued during the British occupation, and he remained a presence in Camden throughout his life. Courtesy of the Ancrum Family Trust, Monroe, North Carolina.

in South Carolina as a merchant, maintaining a low profile while managing his business affairs and those of his former partner.[39]

In contrast, William Ancrum remained active as a planter and merchant (Fig. 10.6). Although residing in Charleston, he continued to monitor the management of his four backcountry plantations. Despite the disruption of war, at least one of them, Redbank, near Camden, remained in operation and was a continuing source of revenue throughout the occupation. In partnership with a Mr. Lord, Ancrum supplied corn, grain, cattle, and forage from Redbank and perhaps from other plantations to the British forces at Camden and in the field. Ancrum's business activities at Camden, however, may have been motivated by more than an interest in profit. Earl Cornwallis quickly became distrustful of the former Whig, suspecting that Ancrum was using his access to the garrison as a means of collecting intelligence. In correspondence to Lt. Col. Nesbit Balfour, commander at Ninety Six, Earl Cornwallis expressed his doubts, acknowledging that "Mr. Ancrum is a smooth-tongued gentleman, but I very much suspect his loyalty. His overseers were constantly going backward & forward to [Gen. Thomas] Sumter, & everyone he recommends is inclined to rebellion. . . . I do not trust Mr. Ancrum." Although the political inclinations of

10.7 John Chesnut joined Kershaw & Co. as a clerk and quickly rose to become a member of the partnership. Active in the militia during the Revolutionary War, he returned to Camden on parole and assumed a central role in its merchant community. In the postwar years Chesnut expanded his landholdings and achieved great wealth as one of South Carolina's most successful cotton planters. Portrait of John Chesnut by Gilbert Stuart reproduced by permission of Mulberry Plantation, Camden, South Carolina.

Marlow Pryor, Redbank's early overseer, are unknown, his replacement by former militia captain Samuel Boykin must have caused concern. Ancrum continued to ship goods and produce overland to Charleston as well, a crucial channel of information between the capital and the backcountry.[40]

Ancrum's trading activities facilitated the rise of John Chesnut as the central figure in the wartime economy of the Wateree Valley (Fig. 10.7). With the breakdown of civil institutions, commerce again relied on a network of social ties, the organization of which mirrored those that had arisen earlier. In the absence of Joseph Kershaw and his brother Ely, the network coalesced around the individual who possessed the economic wherewithal and the connections around which to organize exchange. When William Ancrum conducted business in occupied Camden, he addressed his correspondence to his old partner John Chesnut, now paroled to his plantation at Knight's Hill, north of the town. His choice of Chesnut reflected more than mere sentiment. In addition to having already established himself as a planter and merchant, Chesnut had also demonstrated his ability as an efficient manager, a public office holder, and a militia officer. Furthermore, he possessed important ties through kinship with leading families in the area. His wife, Sarah, was a member of the large Cantey family of prominent planters, and through her sister Mary, Chesnut was Ely Kershaw's brother-in-law. Sarah Cantey Chesnut's mother was Mary McGirt, the daughter of James McGirt, who as a lieutenant colonel in Col. Richard Richardson's militia regiment had played an active role in resolving the Regulator-Moderator conflict in 1769. Indeed,

Mary Cantey, Sarah's aunt, was Richardson's wife. Sarah Cantey Chesnut's brother, Zachariah Cantey, had married Sarah Boykin, daughter of Samuel Boykin, erstwhile Regulator and militia captain and now overseer at Redbank. A more distant cousin, Mary Cantey, was married to Gen. Thomas Sumter, the American guerrilla leader destined to play a major role in the backcountry war.[41]

John Chesnut had maintained a strong commercial presence in the Wateree Valley. Following the breakup of Kershaw & Co., he had continued in business with Joseph Kershaw at Camden and operated the store at Granby in the Congarees. Now, under the occupation, he altered his strategy to cope with changing circumstances. With Duncan McRa and the Camden merchant John Adamson, he formed the partnership Adamson & Co. The inclusion of a Loyalist like Adamson in the firm made it possible for the two paroled Whig militiamen to operate freely within the garrison.[42] Chesnut's experience allowed him to play a key role in marketing the produce of local farmers and planters. He helped arrange for the sale of grain and corn from Ancrum's Redbank plantation and from others in the area and conducted business with the storehouse managed by members of the British garrison. Michael Egan, a Loyalist major from Charleston, formed a partnership with two Tory militia officers, Capt. Joshua English and his brother Col. Robert English, who commanded the First Regiment of Camden Loyalist militia. Their firm, established to supply the troops with imported sugar, rum, and dry goods, also took in crops and livestock in trade from Samuel Mathis, Sarah Kershaw, James Bettie, and others and may have been a significant buyer of local livestock and produce.[43]

As the sole member of the original mercantile firm resident at Camden, John Chesnut was obligated by custom and law to look after the interests of his former partners and soon found himself in the role of assisting the larger community of merchants at Camden. In the wake of the occupation, the exiled Kershaw brothers' assets lay in disarray. Ely Kershaw's active involvement in the Revolution had drained his resources and left his business enterprises neglected. As the only one of his executors in residence in the backcountry, Chesnut had the task of looking after Kershaw's properties. He made arrangements with a local planter, Thomas Wade, and his son Holden to care for the goods and stores at Cheraw Hill and oversee the management of properties in the Pee Dee Valley. The estate took years to settle and involved Chesnut in his brother-in-law's affairs long after war's close.[44] His proximity to Camden drew Chesnut into Joseph Kershaw's concerns as well. Following the town's occupation, Sarah Kershaw and her family had been evicted from their Camden home, and they resided with her brother, Samuel Mathis, at their Burndale plantation, west of the Wateree. The Great White House, Kershaw's mills, and stores had been confiscated, and most of his other enterprises had fallen into neglect. The overseer of his plantation near Camden quit his position when it was "entirely broke up," leaving Chesnut with the responsibility of maintaining Kershaw's slaves and property. Although Mathis assumed the primary role of managing Kershaw's estate in his absence, Chesnut maintained contact with him and others throughout this critical period.[45]

Perhaps nowhere is John Chesnut's emerging central social role in the wartime network of merchants better illustrated than in his relationship with Henry Rugeley, the entrepreneur and ill-fated Loyalist militia colonel whose infamous surrender disgraced him in the eyes of his British superiors. In the previous decade Rugeley had operated a store and other rural industries near the fork of Flat Rock and Grannys Quarter Creeks north of Camden. During the early years of the Revolution in South Carolina, he maintained an ambivalent political position and took no active role in the struggle. When the events of 1780 brought the conflict to the Wateree Valley, Rugeley engaged in several apparently contradictory actions, first aiding rebel Gov. John Rutledge in his escape and then, almost immediately, volunteering to lead one of the new Loyalist militia units organized to pacify the backcountry. Some interpreted his conduct to a desire to maintain stability in the region and curtail the bloodshed that had accompanied the recent invasion. His precipitous capitulation has been attributed to this motive, although British commanders suspected collusion between Rugeley and the enemy.[46]

But Rugeley's behavior may also have reflected more than altruism. As a regional merchant, he participated in the network of traders that included the Kershaw brothers, John Chesnut, William Ancrum, and their associates. He not only supplied produce and sold goods through the Camden business but also participated in the complicated transfers of funds upon which the business of long-distance trade depended.[47] Like Charles Ogilvie, who provided Joseph Kershaw with a crucial introduction to Bermuda merchants, Rugeley remained loyal to his fellow businessmen, despite their political differences, and avoided doing them harm. Rugeley attempted to protect the property of his friends in their absence, and he even tried unsuccessfully to prevent the kidnapping of Ely Kershaw's slaves. When Rugeley entered exile, Chesnut looked after his financial obligations and arranged to accommodate his niece Betsey on family land near Camden.[48] Henry Rugeley's close ties to John Chesnut reflected the persistence of the network of merchants as well as Chesnut's ascendency within it.

Despite John Chesnut's success in commerce, he operated in a dangerous political environment where his status as a rebel on parole often made his actions suspect. Chesnut and others suffered for their affiliation with the Whig cause, particularly during the violent summer of 1780. Samuel Wyly II, son of the early storekeeper, was murdered by Tory militiamen who purportedly sought revenge on his older brother John, the former sheriff. Another Wyly brother, William, was imprisoned, as were more than 160 other Camden residents who refused to take up arms in support of the Crown.[49] Among them was John Chesnut, accused of hoarding goods and slaves belonging to the army with the intent of selling them in the country. Captured by a party of dragoons at his plantation at Knight's Hill, Chesnut was briefly imprisoned and kept in irons; however, a lack of evidence that his property was stolen or that he had communicated with the enemy brought about his release. John Chesnut's role as the rising figure in regional trade made him a leading suspect in the matter of illegal exchange with the rebels. Circumstances limited Chesnut's ability to assist the Whigs directly, and he likely focused the bulk of his mercantile activities on overseeing exchange between civilian producers and merchants or, through his new partnership, with the Camden garrison. Nevertheless, a subsequent receipt of £181.8.4 in compensation for provisions, livestock, and sundries supplied by Chesnut to the Continental army during this period implies that Rawdon's suspicions were perhaps not entirely without foundation.[50] Now a central figure in the regional network that maintained relationships between merchants and producers across political boundaries, John Chesnut found that his support for the American cause was not without risk in a time of great uncertainty.

In the Territory of an Enemy Awed Solely by Apprehension of Our Force

In the fall of 1780 the conflict in the backcountry evolved rapidly. Following the American defeat at the Battle of Camden in August, the emphasis shifted from formal engagements between regular armies toward guerrilla warfare. The war itself moved away from Camden temporarily as Earl Cornwallis began his northern offensive. Hoping to defeat rebel opposition and galvanize Loyalist support to win back the backcountry, he departed with most of the units originally assigned there, leaving Lord Rawdon in command of a smaller garrison and convalescents unable to march. The success of his campaign was predicated on support by backcountry Tories, but the defeat of a large Loyalist militia force at Kings Mountain in November ended such hopes. The loss there of Maj. Patrick Ferguson, commander of loyal militia in the province, crippled British efforts to organize support in the interior and encouraged Whigs to join the growing partisan movement. The absence of a general Loyalist uprising, Ferguson's defeat at Kings Mountain, and his own failure to advance beyond Charlotte convinced Cornwallis to curtail his campaign. In late October he returned to South Carolina and took up winter quarters at Winnsboro, a small settlement on the headwaters of Jackson's Creek about midway between the Wateree and the Broad. The late fall and winter brought a marked rise in guerrilla warfare directed by Col. Francis Marion in the Pee Dee drainage and the lower Santee and by Gen. Thomas Sumter in the Waxhaws. Brig. Gen. Daniel Morgan's decisive victory over Banastre Tarleton at Cowpens in January brought a second major British defeat, boosting the rebel cause and reigniting the partisan war in the backcountry.[51]

The new year saw a renewal of British efforts in the South, pinned on hopes of defeating the Americans in a decisive battle. Earl Cornwallis again advanced into North Carolina in pursuit of Morgan and a new American army under the command of Maj. Gen. Nathanael Greene. Recognizing that his relatively weak army could not prevail if he employed a conventional military strategy, Greene chose to fight a mobile war that drew Cornwallis deep into North Carolina, where his supplies and reinforcements were cut off and losses could not be made up. The two armies finally clashed at Guilford Courthouse, where Cornwallis won an expensive tactical victory. Afterward, Greene's army escaped intact, but heavy British losses forced Cornwallis to retire to the coast to resupply his exhausted troops. Greene was now free to turn his attention to retaking South Carolina. As part of his unconventional strategy, he integrated the irregular forces operating in the area with his Continentals in a combined effort aimed at capturing the British garrisons in the interior.[52] As the principal base in the eastern interior, Camden again faced a direct threat.

Defending British interests in South Carolina and expanding them in the southern colonies depended on a protected food supply. Control of the interior required a regular supply of men and materiel from Charleston and a regular provision of food from the surrounding countryside, and British planners had carefully laid out their interior posts with subsistence in mind. As the key points for projecting power in the backcountry, Camden and Ninety Six were fortified and became the principal garrisons that collected foodstuffs to support themselves and forces in the field. Smaller posts protected the roads connecting them with each other and with the capital and secured areas from which produce and livestock might be gathered. But the increasing level of hostilities and strategic setbacks in the fall of 1780 intensified the vulnerability of Camden and the other garrisons.[53]

Subsistence was always a problem for the commander at Camden. Years later, Lord Rawdon recalled the difficulties created by the town's location, which separated him from resources west of the Wateree River. Hostilities had left much of the surrounding area "so wasted as to afford nothing beyond precarious and incidental supplies." The uncertainty of local provisions obliged him to seek supplies from Orangeburg and the Congarees, strategic assets that were controlled by Nesbit Balfour at Ninety Six.[54] The rising level of guerrilla activity further aggravated the situation. "In the territory of an enemy awed solely by apprehension of our force," wrote Rawdon, the British army found itself "betrayed on every side by the inhabitants," who constantly threatened its food supply. As early as the fall of 1780, Americans openly impeded the acquisition and movement of provisions bound for Camden. They attacked threshing parties and foragers to the north, captured wagons in the Waxhaws, and prevented the transport of corn and wheat from Santee. "Unless we can make these Rebels retreat," wrote a subordinate to Rawdon, "we shall not be able to get it in."[55] Recognizing the importance of maintaining Camden as a center for regional defense, Cornwallis ordered that efforts be made to retain two weeks' provisions there in addition to the stockpile of supplies for his 1781 campaign.[56]

In the new year, the Americans tightened the noose around Camden. The town's fortifications made a direct attack unfeasible, but its location made it vulnerable to isolation if routes of supply and communications could be cut. As Cornwallis pursued Greene in North Carolina, the American general directed his mobile war farther south. Operating in concert with militia units in South Carolina, he moved to attack the subsistence base that supported strategic inland garrisons. In December, he ordered Col. John Marshall, formerly Kershaw's brigade major, to work with Col. Thomas Wade's North Carolina militia forces to round up all the hogs in the vicinity of Camden and Lynches River. To further isolate the garrison, Greene requested Thomas Sumter's forces to restrict the sources of Camden's subsistence. In February they captured provisions, including a "great quantity of meal," destined for Camden at the Congarees and later moved to cut off livestock being driven from Orangeburg.[57] To gather intelligence, Greene directed Marshall to watch the roads along the Catawba River for troop movements and to send "trustworthy women to take provisions into Camden daily" in order to gather information regarding the garrison itself.[58]

Despite American exertions to curtail the movement of supplies into Camden, Rawdon managed to retain access to local subsistence resources and control of facilities sufficient to sustain the garrison into the spring of 1781. In an effort to attack the supply of local provisions, Greene instructed Sumter to destroy the gristmill that supplied the garrison with flour. Presumably this was Kershaw's surviving mill below the town on Pine Tree Creek. Because of its strategic significance, a detachment of British soldiers defended this facility, and, although attacked at least once by Whig militia, the mill continued to operate throughout the occupation.[59] But food was becoming increasingly scarce, and other circumstances soon made Rawdon's situation even more perilous.[60]

In April, Greene's army entered South Carolina and moved on Camden. Advancing south from the Waxhaws, he paused at Logtown to reconnoiter Camden's defenses. There he discovered not only that Rawdon had strengthened the redoubts protecting the town but also that his troops had destroyed all buildings obstructing their fields of fire. Thomas Charlton's plantation northeast of Camden and all of the structures at Logtown had been burned to the ground.[61] Recognizing that his force was too small to invest or storm the town, Greene regrouped his army to consolidate his position. To isolate Camden, he sent a combined force under Gen. Francis Marion of the South Carolina militia and the Continental officer Lt. Col. Henry (Light Horse Harry) Lee to cut off communications with Charleston by eliminating posts on the principal land routes. Fort Watson, the key to movement along the Santee, fell to an innovative assault, and Fort Motte, guarding the western approach along the river, soon came under siege.[62] But Rawdon did not remain complacent, and, as Greene waited for reinforcements north of Camden, he seized the initiative and moved against his camp at Hobkirk's Hill (Fig. 10.4). The hard-fought battle left Rawdon with a tactical victory but a severe loss of irreplaceable troops. Greene avoided the decisive encounter Rawdon desired and again kept his army intact.[63]

The costly British victory at Hobkirk's Hill marked the beginning of the collapse of British control in the backcountry. Believing that command of the region now required a powerful field army, Rawdon consolidated the units currently scattered among the interior posts. He precipitated this process by abandoning Camden on May 10 and moving his command south along the Santee toward Moncks Corner and Charleston.[64] As Rawdon reconstituted his forces, many smaller posts came under attack. Sumter forced the surrender of the Orangeburg garrison on May 11, Fort Motte fell to Lee and Marion the next day, and Fort Granby in the Congarees capitulated on May 15. On the Savannah River, Lee's forces accepted the surrender of Fort Galphin, and Augusta's two forts fell in early June. By the late spring of 1781, only the fortified settlement of Ninety Six remained in British hands. Unaware that Rawdon had ordered its abandonment, the Loyalist garrison remained and came under a lengthy siege by Greene's forces. Rawdon's field force broke the siege at Ninety Six and forced Greene to retreat. The debilitating summer heat curtailed further action by both armies, and Rawdon abandoned Ninety Six and retreated to Orangeburg to regroup. Meanwhile, the loss of Georgetown to Marion restricted the area of British control to the capital and a portion of the lowcountry. With Greene now encamped in the High Hills of Santee, the seat of war at last moved away from the Wateree Valley. Although isolated hostilities continued in the backcountry into the coming year, the occupation was over, and recovery from the darkness could begin at last.[65]

"Camden seems to have an evil genius about it," wrote Nathanael Greene. "Whatever is attempted near that place is unfortunate."[66] Throughout the occupation, the situation at Camden had frustrated the British as well as their opponents, and Greene's harsh words seem especially appropriate to describe the conditions that prevailed at his enemy's departure. On May 9, Lord Rawdon informed the garrison of his intent to evacuate Camden immediately and to have the process completed by the following day. His decision to abandon the post once again brought dramatic changes to the town. As the principal British garrison in the backcountry, Camden represented a major component of the physical infrastructure necessary to support the army. In addition to the fortifications and other military structures, the town held carefully husbanded provisions as well as stores of supplies and equipment. As evening fell on May 9, Rawdon dispatched its baggage under a strong escort, but his wagons could carry only a portion of the materiel stockpiled at Camden. "We brought off all the stores of any kind of value," he reported, "destroying the rest." Contemporary sources reported that Rawdon burned the remaining stores but disposed of some in other ways as well.[67]

The destruction that accompanied the evacuation that night impacted the fabric of the town as well. Although a Loyalist observer claimed that the army "left all the town burning" and Gen. Greene himself characterized what remained as "little better than a heap of rubbish," the destruction was well planned, and avoided substantial parts of the town.[68] The British deliberately burned buildings of strategic importance, including the jail, the barracks, and Joseph Kershaw's mill on Pine Tree Creek, and began to tear down the town's defensive works. Because some of the immovable stores were housed in existing structures, the army destroyed some private property as well. Although the evacuation left Camden a shadow of the prewar village, much of the town seems to have survived. An observer passing through the town early the following year noted that residents occupied a half-dozen houses, and many other standing buildings remained vacant due to their damaged condition.[69] In fact, a number of prominent buildings greeted Greene on his arrival.[70] One of the most conspicuous was the hospital, now filled with casualties from the recent encounter on Hobkirk's Hill. Here lay thirty-one American and fifty-eight British soldiers, who were too badly wounded to move.[71] Joseph Kershaw's brewery, a massive brick structure situated south of Meeting Street, also survived the evacuation intact.[72] Rawdon also abandoned his headquarter at the Great White House, and within two weeks Samuel Mathis moved his sister's family back into their home.[73]

Archaeological investigations revealed the actual extent of destruction in Camden. Few of the numerous buildings identified in the excavations exhibited evidence of burning. On the west side of Broad Street, the hospital and the two nearby buildings, the brewhouse, and other structures remained intact in 1781, although all were used for military purposes during the occupation. Several concentrations of brick rubble and charcoal identified the sites of burned structures, but these generally lay behind the row of principal buildings along Broad Street. Their locations correspond to those of the barracks complexes situated near the palisade wall. One burned area, however, lay on John Adamson's property and may represent remains of the store he operated during the occupation. Supplies held here would probably have been destroyed during the evacuation, perhaps along with the structure itself. The general absence of burning west of Broad Street contrasts with evidence for the destruction of several buildings east of that thoroughfare. These included at least two early structures near the center of town, as well as the barracks situated in its southeastern corner.[74] Archaeological excavations near the palisade in that part of the town uncovered a large rectangular pit containing a number of British "Brown Bess" infantry muskets, balls, gunflints, and gun parts that had been deliberately buried there to prevent their falling into American hands. To the north of town, excavations at the site of the jail contained the burned debris produced by the fire that destroyed it.[75]

Camden's extensive fortifications also seem to have been generally undamaged. Rawdon hoped to deny the Americans use of the redoubts and palisades that had successfully prevented the town's capture by force, but the rear guard he left behind to destroy them only partially completed its task. Nathanael Greene's troops found them largely intact when they occupied the town. But fortified bases had no role in his mobile campaign, and the

American commander immediately ordered his subordinates to "collect all the militia & negroes you can about the country & march into Camden in order to destroy the works there. Let the parapets be leveled," he declared, "the palisades cut down, & the abatis burnt, those at the ferry as well as those in town." Greene placed militia Col. John Marshall in charge of the task and threatened planters who failed to supply labor. By the first of June the works were "chiefly demolished."[76]

Camden's central role in the occupation affected the social fabric of its community. As a fortified settlement in a country increasingly beset by partisan violence, it became not only a base for Loyalist units but also a haven for their families and other resident Tories who gravitated to the safety of its defenses.[77] When Lord Rawdon evacuated the town, he offered "every assistance we could afford" to those who chose to accompany his troops to the lowcountry. Fearing retribution, many Loyalists cast their fate with Rawdon, whose caravan "brought off the militia who had been with us at Camden, but also all of the well-affected neighbors on our route, together with the wives, children, negroes, and baggage of almost all of them."[78] Among the Loyalists who fled Camden were several merchants, including the Charleston militiamen Thomas Hopper, the partner of Thomas Charlton, and Michael Egan, who operated a store with Robert English, a local planter. The Camden merchant John Adamson, who facilitated the mercantile activities of his Whig neighbors Duncan McRa and Samuel Mathis, also left Camden. So did the merchant Jonathan Belton and the planter James Cary. The widow of the late potter John Bartlam, who cast his lot with the Crown as a member of the Loyalist militia, left with the army, as did Jane Gibbes, whose former husband, William Downs, had been killed by the Whig militia. Abandoning their lands and all property that could not be transported quickly, all faced an uncertain future as refugees in the British enclave around Charleston.[79]

Through the remainder of the year and into the next, hostilities continued in South Carolina as the sphere of British influence continually shrank. Although Camden was no longer a fortified town, its position placed it directly on routes traversed by troops and supplies moving into the coastal theater of war. Situated on the main interior road from the North, the town played host to units from Virginia, Pennsylvania, and North Carolina, as well as those operating within its own state. The American army continued to keep a presence at this hub of logistical activity. Greene maintained his headquarters at Camden while operating immediately south in the High Hills of Santee, and it served as a supply base for operations closer to the coast. Camden became a storehouse for the army's tents, clothing, provisions, and other military supplies and even supported its official printing office.[80] The Quartermaster General's Department for the Southern Army oversaw the acquisition of corn, wheat, potatoes, cattle, sheep, and other foodstuffs that flowed into the town to supply the troops, and Nathanael Greene appointed the experienced merchant Samuel Mathis as quartermaster at Camden in the fall of 1781.[81]

The general hospital always played an important role in wartime Camden. In addition to the wounded brought there during the occupation, smallpox and seasonal epidemic diseases remained a constant problem in the crowded settlement, and their victims filled its wards. In a heroic effort to combat smallpox, Dr. Thomas Charlton inoculated British troops as well as others in the village. But disease persisted as spring approached, and operations in the surrounding countryside brought a continual influx of prisoners. Among them was the future president Andrew Jackson, who contracted the disease while interned in the Camden jail with about 250 Whig inmates.[82] The Battle of Hobkirk's Hill in late April flooded the hospital with the wounded from both sides. Rawdon left his casualties at the hospital when he evacuated Camden, together with an equal number of Continental prisoners to exchange for them so that they might be paroled after their recovery.[83] Afterward Greene maintained the medical facility at Camden as a Continental line hospital, and Thomas Charlton continued to direct its operations during the transitional period.[84] When the army returned to the field, the Camden hospital again received the sick and wounded who were capable of being moved by wagon, including prisoners. The large number of casualties from the Battle of Eutaw Springs, fought in early September, severely strained its resources, and, despite the waning of malaria and other "seasonal fevers" in the colder weather of late fall, conditions remained deplorable into the new year. Presumably the Camden hospital continued operations until the general hospital removed to Charleston following the British evacuation in December 1782.[85]

A divisive civil war brought devastation to much of South Carolina's interior, and the occupation weighed particularly heavily on Camden, whose residents had seen their town occupied as a military garrison. Its new role transformed the town into a fortress inhabited by strangers whose interests were far different from those of the people who had built the settlement. With its economy largely shut down, its political institutions eliminated, its most prominent business leader exiled, and its residents split by divergent loyalties, the old networks of relationships that had facilitated Camden's emergence now took on a new role as inhabitants adapted to changed conditions. By the summer of 1782, the war moved largely to the lowcountry, and, despite sporadic violence, the region generally lay quiet and exhausted. It was time for rebuilding the damaged town and the institutions that had fallen into disrepair during the war years. But the dramatic events that destroyed property and lives also affected Camden's society and economy, and nowhere were these changes more evident than in the merchant community.

"We D_mn'd Scooffs"

The British occupation of South Carolina's interior in 1780 brought an abrupt end to the toleration that had prevailed in the Wateree Valley over the previous five years. By polarizing the civilian population, it directly crosscut networks of mutual dependence that linked backcountry merchants of different political affiliations, the personal ties upon which the regional economy depended.[86] Among the principal merchants, the Kershaw brothers were exiled and their property confiscated. John Chesnut fared somewhat better. Paroled to his Camden estate, he engaged in local trade and looked after the interests of his fellow merchants. In Charleston, Aaron Loocock gave up his business and returned to England, leaving his affairs in the hands of his partner, Archibald Brown, while William Ancrum continued in trade and planting on a restricted scale. Henry Rugeley, a Camden Loyalist, chose to participate actively in the conflict and saw his property at Clermont destroyed and his liberty curtailed as a prisoner of war. A fellow Tory, Charles Ogilvie, initially remained in occupied Camden as a merchant but soon returned to London. All these men marked time during the occupation, and none gained substantially from a war that tore the old order asunder.

The political situation in the backcountry changed abruptly when the British army left Camden, dramatically shifting the fortunes of many who had participated in the wartime economy. The removal of royal military authority from most of the state's territory opened the door for the restoration of civil government in South Carolina. Under the protection of Greene's army, the Fourth General Assembly convened at the small town of Jacksonborough, about thirty miles inland from occupied Charleston. For the first two months of 1782, its delegates enacted legislation intended to punish those who had been part of the British regime.[87] The Assembly passed laws that defined classes of Loyalists perceived to have committed particularly egregious crimes, banishing them and confiscating their estates. These individuals fell into three categories. The first included those who had signed or who were alleged to have signed a congratulatory address to Sir Henry Clinton and Admiral Arbuthnot following the surrender of Charleston. William Ancrum, Aaron Loocock, and Archibald Brown were judged to have committed this offense. John Adamson, Jonathan Belton, James Cary, Robert English, Charles Ogilvie, and Henry Rugeley fell into a second category, those who bore civil or military commissions under the British government. Finally, Charles Ogilvie's brother William and his nephew George, as well as the heirs of Rowland Rugeley, found themselves listed among those British subjects who owned land in South Carolina but had never submitted to the American government.[88] The 1782 acts punished Loyalists deemed guilty of other less serious offenses with amercements based on the value of their property and fined former combatants who had met the terms of a general pardon offered the previous fall. Some, however, escaped the vengeful hands of the victors entirely. Joshua English, who served as a captain in his brother Robert's regiment of Camden militia, was not included. Neither was Daniel McGirt, who served in the Loyalist rangers and later became a bandit leader in Georgia and East Florida.[89]

The severity of the new punitive acts threatened many whose interests and livelihoods were vested in the Wateree Valley and whose futures depended on their ability to avoid the imposed consequences. Their fates varied considerably, and the extent of their suffering seems to have depended as much on their connections as on their alleged crimes. The success of efforts by the Charleston merchants to have their estates and rights restored depended heavily on personal ties. The key to obtaining relief from the penalties of the Confiscation Acts was convincing the General Assembly that ameliorating circumstances warranted exoneration. William Ancrum, Aaron Loocock, and Archibald Brown all presented cases for clemency, but having a strong advocate in the new legislature was also important in obtaining a favorable outcome.[90]

Events in the late summer of 1781 led to Joseph Kershaw's sudden reappearance as a prominent civic figure in South Carolina. On August 23, two weeks after his release in a general exchange of prisoners, Kershaw arrived in Philadelphia from Bermuda and was soon reunited with "many hundreds of our Carolina friends." There, as befitting a member of the political elite, he met and dined with the celebrities of the Revolution, including "the Minister of France in company with Gen. [George] Washington & and [Henry] Knox, [Comte de] Rochambeau, [Marquis de] Chastellux, [William] Moultrie and many other officers of the army, together with the President and many members of Congress."[91] Kershaw remained in Philadelphia until late September and arrived back in Camden on October 3. Soon he began to travel, renewing his social and political ties within the region. He ventured into the Waxhaws to visit the Catawbas on the reservation to which they had retired at the close of hostilities. He congratulated them for their active support of the American cause in "this long and Bloody war" but reminded them to be conscious of their land rights guaranteed by treaty, warning them to be vigilant against future encroachments on their estate. Observing the Indians' poverty, he assured them that a grateful state would soon provide aid.[92] In November he was in Salem, North Carolina, where the governor and members of the state assembly were staying. While there, he also met with Moravian merchants, from whom he purchased provisions and cooking supplies for the new South Carolina Assembly preparing to meet in Jacksonburgh.[93] In December, Kershaw attained public office as the new representative from the District Eastward of Wateree River in a special election, and he was reelected the following year. His appointment as a justice of the peace for Camden District two months later further reaffirmed his civil status within the region.[94] Despite his absence of nearly a year and a half, Kershaw remained a powerful figure in backcountry politics.

Joseph Kershaw's presence in the state legislature when the acts affecting the fate of the South Carolina Loyalists were promulgated proved fortunate for many of those with whom he had long-term ties. Perhaps the most conspicuous of those condemned by the Confiscation Act were his old associates William Ancrum, Aaron Loocock, and Archibald Brown. Ancrum remained in Charleston as a merchant, holding civil offices in St. Philips Parish, until forced to leave when the British evacuated the city. In January he was in London with two other Charleston merchants applying for compensation for property taken by the army, and by the end of the month he had filed a petition to be relieved of the penalties of the Confiscation Act.[95] Since October 1780, Aaron Loocock had been a merchant in London. Under the advice of Henry Laurens, then recovering his health following his imprisonment in the Tower of London, Loocock filed a petition for relief and returned to South Carolina in January 1783 to await news of its outcome. The initial response to his request was hostile, and Loocock was confined to the Provost.[96] Archibald Brown also remained in Charleston through the waning months of the war. Aware of the unfortunate change in his legal status, he removed to St. Augustine in British East Florida in October 1782, leaving his wife, Mary, to file a petition for his relief the following February.[97]

The fate of the Charleston merchants changed dramatically in the winter of 1784 when the Fifth General Assembly passed an act to remove a number of individuals from the banishment and confiscation list.[98] Ancrum and Brown were amerced 12 percent of the value of their property, and Brown was disqualified from public office. Aaron Loocock was taken off the lists with no further punishment. Undoubtedly the merchants' connections with politically powerful individuals, such as Henry Laurens and Brown's father-in-law, John Deas, helped strengthen their case for relief. However, their close ties to Joseph Kershaw, who had not only suffered at the hands of the British but also now walked among the leading figures of the Revolution, would almost certainly have influenced those determining the fate of South Carolinians charged with aiding and abetting the British cause.[99]

All three merchants remained in the state after the war and prospered. Ancrum remained in business, independently and in partnership with his brother George and Philotheos Chiffelle, operating in Charleston, Camden, and elsewhere in the backcountry. Throughout the following decade he successfully pursued relief from amercement and received compensation for the loss of slaves, produce, and other property during the war or through subsequent confiscation.[100] Although Archibald Brown's properties in Camden District were confiscated and sold at auction in 1783, he recovered financially and continued to live as a planter in the lowcountry. There he acquired five plantation properties totaling 1,332 acres on the Ashley and Cooper Rivers, including two inherited from his brother-in-law John Deas Jr.[101] In spite of the unpleasant reception he received upon his return, Aaron Loocock resumed his career as a successful businessman in Charleston, where he and his partners, Nathaniel Russell and Andrew Lord, operated the Rumney Distillery. In addition to his house on Tradd Street, he also owned a rental house in Camden and maintained plantations in St. Johns Goose Creek and Middleburgh on the Wateree.[102] Loocock also continued his active public life. He supported internal improvements as a director of the Inland Navigation Company and was an advocate for the construction of the Santee Canal. Loocock took an active role in the Society for the Relief of the Widows and Orphans of the Clergy of the Protestant Episcopal Church in South Carolina, and he was a director of the South Carolina State Bank. His political and civic offices included service as a vestryman of St. Michael's Parish, road commissioner for St James Goose Creek Parish, and delegate to the state's Constitutional Convention. In 1791 he was elected to the Ninth General Assembly from St. James Goose Creek Parish.[103]

In addition to the three Charleston merchants, two Camden businessmen who espoused the Loyalist cause also gained relief from the Confiscation Act through the help of their friends. Henry Rugeley figured prominently on the list of those who held British commissions. As a colonel, he commanded one of the four regiments of Camden District Loyalist militia. After his surrender in December 1780, Rugeley was held prisoner for four months in Virginia, after which he was exchanged and returned to Charleston, where he lived on his Retreat plantation. Devastated financially by the fortunes of war, he endeavored to keep his creditors at bay and remain solvent. For his immediate support, he relied on his salary as the register of mesne conveyance, an office previously held by his late brother, Rowland, while he sought other sources of income. In the spring of 1781, when the army proposed raising a British regiment in Charleston for service in the West Indies under Lord Charles Montagu, Rugeley had accepted a lieutenant's commission. He sailed with the unit when the British abandoned the city and arrived in Jamaica in late February1783. Rugeley then resigned his commission and spent the next year and a half on the island operating a small leased plantation, Mount Prospect, while he attempted to sort out his business affairs.[104]

Initially banished and faced with the loss of his property by the Confiscation Act, Henry Rugeley relied on a network of kin and former associates to help look after his interests. During his exile in Jamaica, his brothers William and Matthew managed his financial accounts in England and facilitated his use of bills of credit to cover debts and expenses. His sister Frances Rugeley offered him assistance in seeking redress for his losses in London.[105]

In South Carolina, the fate of Rugeley's business affairs depended on developments in the legislature, where his powerful allies Joseph Kershaw and John Rutledge now sat, but also on the efforts of his former mercantile associates elsewhere in the state.[106] Rugeley had already relied on John Chesnut for numerous favors. Chesnut oversaw the care of his young niece Betsey until his new wife, Elizabeth, was settled on his property near Camden. Rugeley had recently married the daughter of John Cook, the old Regulator and wagoner who had served with Kershaw's regiment at Purrysburg. Chesnut also assisted in recovering a stolen still and looked after horses left with him for safekeeping. Rugeley's correspondence reveals ties with other influential Camden residents who had supported the Whig cause, including the merchants Joseph Kershaw and Duncan McRa and the sheriff and justice of the peace John Wyly.[107]

Such support for a former Loyalist colonel contrasted sharply with the raw hatred felt toward other Tories and reflected a general perception that, "although on the British side, [Rugeley] was thought to be an American." Finding it impossible to remain neutral in a bitter civil war, he attempted to use his influence to "procure mercy for and from both parties." The argument presented in his petition for relief was that he accepted the commission at the request of his Whig neighbors "to prevent it from falling into the hands of a person who would have distressed them." His subsequent behavior at "Rugeley's Defeat" seems to confirm this intent. Decades later, his son perhaps did not exaggerate when he recalled that "his good opinion and favorable representation, were life and salvation to hundreds on both sides."[108] Rugeley himself seemed comfortable enough with the goodwill that existed between him and his backcountry associates to engage in a bit of self-deprecation prior to his departure for Jamaica. In a letter he chided his friend John Chesnut with the facetious comment "I fancy I hear you cry, a happy riddance to you all, and now we have got the d_mned Tories (I mean Scoofs) all away; we shall do very well again." Rugeley intended to return to South Carolina, and his faith was rewarded when the Amercement Act of 1784 removed him from the Confiscation and Banishment list. By October he and his family again resided at Clermont.[109]

John Adamson was another merchant whose ties within the larger Camden community helped him avoid punishment under the Confiscation Act. Immigrating to South Carolina with his family from his birthplace in Ireland in the 1760s, he acquired a number of parcels on the Wateree during the following decade. He settled on a large tract north of Camden in 1775 and operated a store in Camden on eleven town lots that he acquired on Broad Street two years later. Like many in the Wateree Valley, Adamson remained neutral during the early years of the Revolution and did not participate in political or military activities prior to 1780, although, he did contribute labor to construct the fortifications at the Camden magazine that spring.[110]

Things changed abruptly with the British invasion in June, an event that prompted Adamson to enlist as a lieutenant in Col. Henry Rugeley's militia regiment. The following month found him attached to a force under the command of the notorious Capt. Christian Huck, a Tory officer in Tarleton's Legion. Huck was known for his brutal treatment of rebels in the upper Wateree Valley, and his men had purportedly murdered Samuel Wyly II, brother of the sheriff. Huck's force moved north into present York County to capture Col. William Bratton, one of Thomas Sumter's militia leaders. There they occupied Bratton's plantation, where one of his men threatened the life of Martha Bratton when she refused to reveal her husband's whereabouts. In an action that soon became legendary, an officer named Adamson intervened to save her life. The following day's Battle of Williamson's Plantation, or "Huck's Defeat," left Huck and many of his men dead and marked the first British setback in the interior. In its aftermath, Martha Bratton returned the favor and nursed the severely wounded Adamson. Two Loyalist officers with this surname received injuries at Huck's Defeat, and the identity of Mrs. Bratton's defender is uncertain; however, later accounts attributed the noble act to Lt. John Adamson.[111]

Exchanged at Cornwallis's request, Adamson returned to Camden, where he resumed his role in the merchant community. There he became the catalyst that allowed two of its Whig members to remain in business during the British occupation. His partnership with John Chesnut and Duncan McRa permitted them to trade directly with the enemy garrison, and his ability to accept bonds for merchandise from the British regiments kept funds flowing into local hands, capital that supported merchants and suppliers and helped maintain important links with old and influential friends. Obliged to leave when the British evacuated Camden, Adamson followed the army to Charleston and remained there until the end of the war. Finding himself included in the Confiscation Act, he left when the city was evacuated to await his fate in East Florida.[112]

Support for Adamson's relief came almost as soon as he began his exile. In January 1783 he filed a petition claiming that, like Rugeley, he had accepted the commission at the request of his neighbors to prevent its being given to someone likely "to oppress them." A petition signed by twenty-three citizens testified to Adamson's reputation as a defender of his "friends and connections" in the Camden community from the villainy of the Tories. The petitioners stressed his efforts to protect distressed Americans, particularly widows, orphans, and the families of exiles, from British injustices and begged that he be relieved of punishment. The signers included a number of prominent individuals, including the planters William Boykin, William Lang, and Joshua Dinkins and others, including John Boykin, William Wyly, and John Dinkins, who had actively opposed the British and suffered in the war. Joseph Kershaw, John Chesnut, and Samuel Boykin offered Adamson protection to return to South Carolina while the Assembly considered his petition. His efforts were successful, and John Adamson became a leading member of Camden's postwar community.[113]

Jonathan Belton, who held a commission in James Cary's Loyalist militia regiment, also found himself on the Confiscation list. He traveled to St. Augustine with his brother-in-law John Adamson and from there filed a petition for relief. The Assembly revoked his punishments and amerced his property in the spring of 1784, after which he returned to Camden, where he died six years later.[114]

Others were not so fortunate. Several prominent Wateree Valley Loyalists named in the Confiscation Act were unable to maintain their residence or save their estates. James Cary, a planter, lawyer, prominent Regulator, and, later, justice of the peace, commanded a regiment of Loyalist militia in 1780. Although his loyalty remained unquestioned by his superiors, his military and management skills apparently left much to be desired, and plundering by his troops earned him the enmity of local residents.[115] He and his wife, Mary, retreated to Charleston with the British army. Cary apparently did not envision returning to his estates in South Carolina. He failed to petition for redress when his name appeared on the Confiscation Act list, and within the next few years the state sold his lands. Attempting to start anew, the Carys removed to Jamaica, where he went into partnership in a planting venture. To compensate for his confiscated property, Cary took with him captured slaves, many of whom belonged to Whig residents in the Camden area. This act further discredited his reputation and embroiled him in lawsuits for years to come.[116] James and Mary Cary spent the rest of their lives in exile. After much difficulty, he eventually obtained a pension from the Royal Commission charged with examining Loyalist claims and retired to London in ill health. Following his death in 1794, Mary returned to America to live with her sister in Virginia.[117]

The Confiscation Act also banished Charles Ogilvie and his nephew George, who also lost their extensive estates in South Carolina. Although they chose not to petition for relief from the act, Charles and George attempted to recover their losses by applying to the Royal Commission for compensation and by aggressively prosecuting claims against American debtors, including Ely Kershaw and John Chesnut. Under the terms of the Treaty of Paris, which officially ended the war in 1783, British creditors were allowed to call in debts in the United States, but American courts limited such suits to Loyalist merchants, and, despite numerous attempts, the Ogilvies failed to recoup their losses. Charles did, however, succeed in having the property his children had inherited from their mother excluded from his confiscated lands.[118] The terms of the 1783 peace treaty also allowed Loyalists a year to settle affairs in the state, and George returned briefly to South Carolina. But "finding his stay in the country unpleasant," he returned to Scotland, where he eventually became comptroller of customs in Aberdeen. Charles continued as a merchant in London until his death in 1788, never realizing compensation for his American losses. More than three decades later, in the last years of his life, George finally received an award from the Crown.[119]

Robert English and Joshua English were sons of one of the early Quaker settlers on Swift Creek south of Camden. Both apparently remained neutral in the early years of the Revolution and contributed to construction of the Camden magazine fortifications. In 1774 Joshua managed Aaron Loocock's Wateree plantation. But the invasion of 1780 changed everything, and the brothers joined the Loyalist militia. As a captain, Joshua served as a company commander under James Cary in 1780. The following year, Robert was appointed a lieutenant colonel to command a regiment formed of the remnants of Cary's and Rugeley's. Both were partners in a mercantile enterprise at Camden in 1781 but lost all their assets in the evacuation.[120]

Although both English brothers participated actively in the militia, only Robert was subject to banishment and confiscation. When the army evacuated Charleston, he left South Carolina forever, although his son, John, and his daughter, Amelia, apparently remained in the state. With his brothers-in-law, Jonathan Belton and John Adamson, he took refuge first in St. Augustine, but, rather than seeking relief from his punishment, he began anew elsewhere. Following the return of East Florida to Spain, English settled in British Honduras, where he died in 1788. Despite the state's attempt to dispose of his confiscated lands in the summer of 1783, not all were sold, and later his son, John, successfully petitioned the Assembly to acquire the remainder of the estate. His brother, Joshua English, returned to Camden at the close of hostilities and apparently rejoined the community without incident.[121]

The aftermath of the Revolution, however, was generally much less kind to Loyalists. Some, like Michael Egan, a Charleston Loyalist who had been Robert English's brigade major and a mercantile partner in Camden, and Thomas Hopper, another Charleston resident who operated a store in occupied Camden, became refugees who could only hope for redress from the British government.[122] Other Tories in South Carolina fared much worse when Whigs who had suffered during the occupation sought revenge for acts perpetrated against them or their friends. On Fishing Creek in upper Camden District, residents routed former Loyalists from their homes, which they then burned. In the region between the Broad and Saluda Rivers, where Loyalist sentiment had been strong, militia patrols captured, tried, and executed several of their former enemies.[123] One incident involved the grisly murder of Francis Tidwell, a former captain of the Jackson's Creek Loyalist militia regiment. Dragged from his home, he was allegedly shot and wounded, carried off, and summarily hanged by a party of ten vengeful residents of the Camden area, whose lives had been deeply touched by the Revolution. Among them was John Dinkins, son of the Wateree planter, whose response to his family's suffering at the hands of James Cary's militia had earlier led him to threaten the life of the Loyalist leader at the capture of Cary's Fort. His brother Samuel and his companion Kit Gales had been captured by Rawdon during an attempted ambush, an incident that brought Gales's immediate execution and Dinkins's imprisonment at Camden. Willis Whitaker, who had served as a company commander with Joseph Kershaw's regiment at Purrysburg and was captured after the surrender of Charleston, was also involved. Their activity contrasts with the absence of subsequent criminal behavior in the lives of these men, several of whom had distinguished public careers. But, like others, they apparently had scores to settle at the close of this "worst of times."[124]

On the other hand, sometimes even the most notorious Loyalists escaped punishment for their actions and continued to reside unmolested in South Carolina. Perhaps the most infamous was Daniel McGirt. Initially a member of the Whig militia, he changed sides abruptly when an officer, who coveted his beloved horse, had McGirt tried and punished on trumped-up charges. Making his escape, McGirt fled to East Florida and became a leader of the Loyalist rangers. By 1779 his unit had become a bandit gang of diverse refugees who stole horses, slaves, and other property in South Carolina, including the Wateree Valley. That year he joined Gen. Augustine Prévost's ill-fated foray into coastal South Carolina and took part in the destruction and theft of property that accompanied this invasion. McGirt and his followers remained active in Georgia and, following the end of hostilities, retreated to East Florida, where they turned to plundering Loyalist plantations. Despite his capture and imprisonment multiple times, McGirt continued his activities in the now Spanish province for at least another decade before retiring to South Carolina, where he passed the remainder of his life in seclusion.[125]

The closing chapter of Daniel McGirt's unlikely odyssey speaks less to his role as a partisan combatant than it does to the ties that preceded his participation in the conflict. He was the son of an early settler, James McGirt, a commissioner for establishing St. Mark's Parish and an officer under Col. Richard Richardson in the Cherokee campaign. Daniel became active in public life and played an important role in resolving the Regulator crisis, and his rise was undoubtedly helped by his kin relations. His sister Mary married a prominent planter, Capt. John Cantey, and, through their daughters, Mary and Sarah, he was tied to their husbands, Ely Kershaw and John Chesnut, respectively. His sister's sons, James and Zachariah Cantey, married Martha Whitaker, the sister of Willis Whitaker, and Sarah Boykin, the daughter of Samuel Boykin, respectively. The Boykins and the Whitakers were further connected by the sequential marriage of Catherine and Mary Whitaker, the daughters of Willis's uncle William Whitaker, to Burwell Boykin. Another of William's daughters married Alexander Irvin, whose mother was the sister of John Chesnut.[126]

These kin links enmeshed McGirt in the social and economic network of the Wateree Valley prior to the war, and the strength of its ties is reflected in several incidents that may account for his favorable treatment later. The first involved his interaction with Lt. James Cantey, whose party was escorting a small convoy carrying funds from Augusta to Charleston. Shadowing the convoy, McGirt called out for Cantey, to leave as he intended to annihilate the escort to gain the money they protected. Cantey's refusal to do so called McGirt's bluff, and the bandit withdrew, calling out to him, "You had better thank your stars that you happen to be my nephew." On another occasion McGirt risked discovery to communicate with a party of Whig cavalry commanded by John Boykin, a group to which members of the Whitaker and Irvin families belonged. His warning allowed them time to escape an imminent attack by Banastre Tarleton's Legion. McGirt also freed his childhood friend Anthony Hampton from British custody by cutting the ropes that bound him while in transit to Charleston. These instances of altruism reflect the continuing strength of earlier ties that persisted despite the political division that rent the backcountry during the Revolution. Although McGirt was an enemy combatant and bandit, his kin repaid his loyalty after the hostilities ended. His eventual return from East Florida brought him to South Carolina in ill health, and he spent his remaining years living first with his wife's brother John James and later on the estates of his nephews Zachariah and James Cantey at Camden.[127]

McGirt's fate, like that of other Camden Loyalists, appears to have depended less on his role in British service than on his behavior toward those with whom he was connected by bonds that grew out of the social and economic networks of the frontier. Their altruistic motives for entering the king's service and their compassionate behavior in office helped John Adamson and Henry Rugeley escape the harsh retribution suffered by James Cary, Robert English, Jonathan Belton, Charles Ogilvie, and others who held commissions. Contending that they had used their positions to protect rather than persecute the community, they drew on a network of influential associates to support their case as useful and integral members of the backcountry community. Although condemned for acknowledging the British victory, William Ancrum, Aaron Loocock, and Archibald Brown could call upon powerful associates to support their assertion that they did so under duress and sought not only to protect their assets but also to preserve the commerce and trade upon which backcountry residents depended. Their economic role was integral to the region's survival during the recent troubles, and all of them would continue to play an important role in the region's postwar recovery.

In the fall of 1781 Joseph Kershaw returned to a community that had only begun to recover from an experience that had badly shaken both its physical structure and its social fabric. During his brief absence, the inhabitants of the central backcountry had persisted in the face of extreme adversity and adapted to radically changed circumstances. Now they faced the difficult task of rebuilding their lives as well as the shattered infrastructure of production, trade, and administration. Although the Revolution failed to halt the Wateree Valley's development, it affected the course of its transition from a frontier to a commercial economy. The war altered the community and changed the lives of those in it. In the coming years, things in Camden would not be the same.

Chapter 11

"To Promote and Enjoy the Blessings of Peace"

Rebirth and Change in the Early National Period

Samuel Boykin was a product of the frontier. The eldest son of a pioneer family from Virginia, he settled with his kin on lands near Town Creek south of Pine Tree Hill in the mid-1750s and became a planter and small merchant. Ambitious and vigorous, he was soon a forceful personality in the Wateree Valley. His nephew Edward Boykin recalled that "he was an able and energetic man, admirably suited to the rough times in which he lived, of great personal strength, six feet high, and although he weighed 225 pounds, muscular and active withal, with a brain as active and powerful as his body."[1] After his father's death in 1760, Samuel rose to become the head of a family whose interests looked to the region's commercial growth. When criminal elements arose to threaten the stability that underlay the area's development, he took a leading role in the Regulator movement that arose to suppress them. Never one to suffer the indignity of what he considered inappropriate behavior, he did not hesitate to act, even in the absence of formal authority, to impose order when and where he deemed it necessary. Boykin's growing wealth in land and slaves, as well as the strength of his assertive personality, helped him rise to become a member of the small group of merchants and planters who formed the backcountry elite. An active supporter of the Whig cause, Boykin assumed both military and civil roles in the revolutionary government, while continuing to manage his own plantations and those of others. In the decade following the war he continued to enlarge his land holdings and held political office in the newly formed county where his properties lay. Samuel Boykin epitomized the pioneer planter who overcame great odds through his own initiative to reap the rewards of the struggle to build a commercial economy and a stable society in a region still in the process of transition.[2]

One morning in late 1791, Samuel Boykin's past collided with the reality of the present when he once again faced the challenge of restoring order in a changing world. His plantation on the east side of the Wateree lay near the heavily traveled highway that had been the Catawba Path, now the principal wagon road to the Waxhaws and points north. Informed that a group of wagoners from North Carolina had camped on his land, Boykin reacted immediately and in a familiar manner. In the past, the absence of institutionalized authority had left residents with no alternative but to take matters of this sort into their own hands, and Samuel Boykin had not hesitated to do so when the situation arose. Now in middle age, he again took direct action against those who dared trespass on his property. Alone, he went out to effect their removal. During the face-off that followed, the wagoners became belligerent, and a fight ensued. In the uneven struggle he received a beating that left four of his ribs broken, but the resourceful planter persevered and escaped on his horse, riding off to gather supporters to help him complete his mission. When they returned to the camp, Boykin's party "punished" the trespassers severely, evicting them and burning their wagons. His victory was short-lived, however, for the wounds he received in the fight had taken their toll on Boykin's aging body. He returned home to his plantation to recuperate, but inflamation set in, and on December 28 Samuel Boykin passed from the world he had helped create.[3] The death of the legendary Regulator marked not only the loss of a prominent pioneer but also the waning of the old order in the Wateree Valley. It foreshadowed the profound changes beginning to take place in a region recovering from the destruction of the Revolution and now on the verge of being fully incorporated within the larger sphere of South Carolina's economy and society. No longer living on the frontier, its residents found it imperative to adapt to the conditions imposed by a new world.

"Destroyed beyond Description or Belief": The Impact of the War

In the 1780s Camden began to emerge from the shadow of the Revolution. The conflict touched all parts of South Carolina, but its effects were particularly ruinous in the backcountry, where economic growth was jeopardized by the wanton destruction of life and property. The intensity of the conflict had so wasted the countryside that the American commander Nathanael Greene characterized it as "in the utmost danger of becoming a desert."[4] The devastation went beyond the immediate actions of combat. The accompanying violence had forced residents to abandon their lands, livestock, and crops. It had claimed their houses and outbuildings, as well as the mills, warehouses, ironworks, courthouses, jails, and other institutional elements upon which the growth of this emerging region depended. So thorough was the destruction that even three years after the British retreat, the chimneys of burned farmsteads still marked the road from Camden to Charleston.[5] In addition to causing the loss of physical infrastructure, the war had also removed enslaved laborers upon whom plantation agriculture depended. The loss of slaves, taken away by Loyalist owners or kidnapped by the British upon their departure, immediately impacted production and made their replacement essential to restoring the state's agricultural economy. Taking stock of his backcountry ventures that had suffered so badly in the war, Joseph Kershaw perhaps did not exaggerate when he lamented that "this part of the country is destroyed beyond description or belief."[6]

In addition to the physical losses, a combination of increasing debt and shrinking markets hampered the restoration of agricultural commodity production. South Carolinians had always depended heavily on British imports, and the early years of the war dramatically reduced the volume of trade. The capture of Charleston restored commerce in 1780, flooding the city with British merchants. The newcomers soon developed extensive commercial arrangements and had become such crucial suppliers to South Carolina's coastal planters that they could negotiate an agreement with the new government to continue in business after the evacuation. Distressed planters, needing to replace lost slaves and rebuild their operations, eagerly accepted lenient terms offered by the merchants and quickly added new debts that postwar economic conditions made it difficult to repay. The distribution of goods in South Carolina involved merchants and their customers in a complex network of links that created a web of indebtedness so complex that small farmers as well as large planters suffered when outstanding obligations were called in. The difficulty of paying off the costs of restoring production was compounded further by shrinking produce markets that stifled the generation of new wealth. The lucrative rice market in the British West Indies was now gone, and external competition reduced British and French markets for tobacco and decreased the demand for rice in Portugal. The British bounty on indigo also disappeared, and the cultivation of this crop in the French colonies hurt both coastal and interior growers. The road to recovery would be neither easy nor rapid.[7]

The Debt Crisis and Administrative Change

The widespread debt crisis that gripped South Carolina's farmers and planters focused attention on the administrative structure in the backcountry. Responding to demands, the General Assembly attempted to defuse the situation by deferring or restricting the collection of debts. In 1784 legislators allowed creditors to file suits to recover interest for prewar debts but postponed further the collection of the principal. Although this law provided some assistance, it did nothing to aid debtors while the economic situation in the state continued to deteriorate.[8] As a legal issue, however, the collection of debts involved South Carolina's courts and emphasized their role as a central institution in the postwar backcountry.[9] Suits stemming from debt cases generally came to trial at the district courts established by the Act of 1769, and these now became the focus of social resistance.

As the seat of Camden District, the old frontier town took center stage in a crisis that helped shape the postwar backcountry. In the spring of 1785 Judge John F. Grimke arrived from Charleston to conduct a session of the Court of Common Pleas, at which cases against debtors were presented. There he encountered a large, unruly crowd that had formed to prevent the court from hearing these cases.[10] The number of protesters not only held up the proceedings but also intimidated authorities. As a result, the sheriff was unable to arrest their leader, and the jurors, fearing for their safety, fled town that evening. Although Grimke conducted criminal trials the following day, civil resistance forced him to abandon his attempt to preside over those involving civil suits. Grimke noted with apparent surprise the failure of the "gentlemen of the district" to come to his support, a stance that reflected both their solidarity with the debtors and their desire for effective legislation to bring them relief. The Camden riot was the first of several similar disturbances in South Carolina that year. So great was the opposition that by August sheriffs dared to serve civil writs only within the city of Charleston, and courts had ceased to operate outside the capital. Camden's role in this movement illustrates the seriousness of the debt crisis, particularly in the backcountry, but also emphasizes the town's continued role as a focus of political activity in postwar South Carolina.[11]

The General Assembly now attempted to deal with the debt crisis by instituting radical measures that precipitated new allegiances between the rising backcountry planters and those of the lowcountry. During the turbulent summer of 1785, a special session of the legislature passed the Sheriff's Sale, or Pine Barren, Act. This legislation, broadly supported by representatives of Camden District and leading backcountry residents, allowed debtors to substitute title to marginal lands for cash payments owed creditors. The Sheriff's Sale Act was followed by a Currency Act that issued paper currency, backed by mortgages of land, gold, or silver, that served as scrip that could be used to pay off creditors. Because both acts allowed differential land values to be employed as the basis for liquid assets, the laws benefited large landowners more than smaller ones Two years later an Installment Act allowed debts to be paid over time, a compromise measure that also appeased merchants because it also banned slave imports, which they saw as a chief source of spiraling planter debt. As the decade advanced, rice production began to recover as exports increased, and planters generally became less supportive of the earlier radical assistance measures that now benefited them less. Consequently, the legislature did not renew the first two acts, and efforts to ensure the value of lands transferred to creditors failed to gain support. On the other hand, an Installment Act that forestalled payments owed found backing among the planters of the lowcountry as well as the emerging planter class of the interior. The increasing alignment of backcountry interests with those of the coastal elites reflected the revival of commercial development in both regions. The changing economy produced a more visible social stratification in the interior and fostered political ties among those engaged in large-scale agriculture throughout the state.[12]

Administrative Reform and Institutional Growth

The social disruption and economic desolation that followed the war demanded the extension of state authority to stabilize the region. In addition to displacing large numbers of people and destroying property, the civil war in the backcountry left deep divisions among South Carolinians that persisted into the postwar years. A destitute vagrant population familiar with the use of violence to achieve its ends created conditions similar to those two decades earlier, when an increase in crime followed in the wake of the Cherokee War and precipitated the Regulator Movement. The absence of authority in the backcountry during the 1780s encouraged the spread of criminal activity; bands of thieves and robbers victimized settlers, traders, and travelers, and their presence again brought demands for a return to vigilante justice.[13]

Reconstructing the district court system became paramount to restoring order in the interior. Even before hostilities closed, Gov. Rutledge recognized the need for the new government to project its authority, and he appointed ordinaries to conduct proceedings in the backcountry. Wood Furman, a member of the newly elected legislative delegation from Camden District, became the first ordinary for his region. In its winter session of 1782, the General Assembly at Jacksonburgh passed acts to hold circuit courts of oyer and terminer to try criminal cases in each of South Carolina's judicial districts and authorized the governor to appoint judges to preside over them.[14]

As the seat of the district court, Camden retained the institutions critical to maintaining its administrative role in the Wateree Valley. Because the war had destroyed its courthouse and jail, the district lacked physical public facilities for conducting judicial business in the interior. Ordinary Furman was obliged to hold court at his home in the High Hills of Santee, and his successor, Col. Henry Hampton, worked out of his plantation near Winnsboro.[15] Such arrangements were inadequate to conduct legal proceedings or confine criminals, and the legislature soon passed an ordinance to rebuild or repair the district courthouses and jails. In the spring of 1783 Joseph Kershaw submitted a proposal and plans for these facilities at Camden to his fellow legislators, who approved them and appropriated funds for construction. A year later, with the project nearly completed, Kershaw received reimbursement for the last of his expenses. Kershaw's contractors finished the buildings in time for the ill-fated session of 1785.[16]

Reestablishing the district courts helped reassert the authority of the central government in the state's war-torn interior, but the small number of facilities and the distances between them made access to their services difficult for many of the region's residents and led to demands for more efficient arrangements. In response, the legislature passed the Court Act of 1785, dividing the state's seven judicial districts into thirty-four counties. Each county court was to hold quarterly sessions administered by three justices who had limited jurisdiction over civil and criminal cases.[17] The restructuring of the court system apportioned the Wateree Valley into six counties and placed Camden near the juncture of four of them (Fig. 11.1). Situated at the southern edge of Lancaster County, the town lay across the Wateree from Richland and Fairfield Counties and just above Claremont County. To ensure access to the new courts, the Act specified that each be held at "the most convenient part of each county" with regard to its form and the distribution of its inhabitants. Because Camden's location left it on the periphery of the new counties, its courts were relocated elsewhere, sometimes away from nucleated settlements. The Lancaster County court, for example, met at the residence of James and Margaret Ingram on Hanging Rock Creek. Although the new county courts diminished Camden's public function, the town remained the seat of the Camden District Court. State judges heard district-level cases there, and the Court of Ordinary continued in operation for two more years.[18]

The awkward situation created by dispersing administrative functions away from the most significant urban center in South Carolina's backcountry brought efforts to restore Camden's former status. In March 1787 a "large body of people" from the four Wateree counties petitioned the legislature to remedy the situation by creating a new county, named DeCalb after the ill-fated general Johann DeKalb, with Camden as its seat. In addition to pointing out the financial and logistical advantages of using public facilities already available there, the petitioners lamented that the current political boundaries divided the productive agricultural estates concentrated in the region among multiple administrative units, complicating their management and deterring trade. With an eye to supporting Camden's commercial community, they also maintained that its location in the more densely populated Wateree Valley was far more likely to generate business for the courts than would placing public facilities in the poor "barren regions" that lay at the centers of the present counties.[19] Despite the endorsement of Joseph Kershaw and John Chesnut, efforts to create the new county proceeded slowly, perhaps because of the difficulty of establishing boundary lines with the surrounding counties. But in the winter of 1791 the legislature finally ratified acts to establish the county, now named after Kershaw, and placed its courts in Camden. Two years later the Assembly finally fixed the boundaries of Kershaw County (Fig. 11.2).[20]

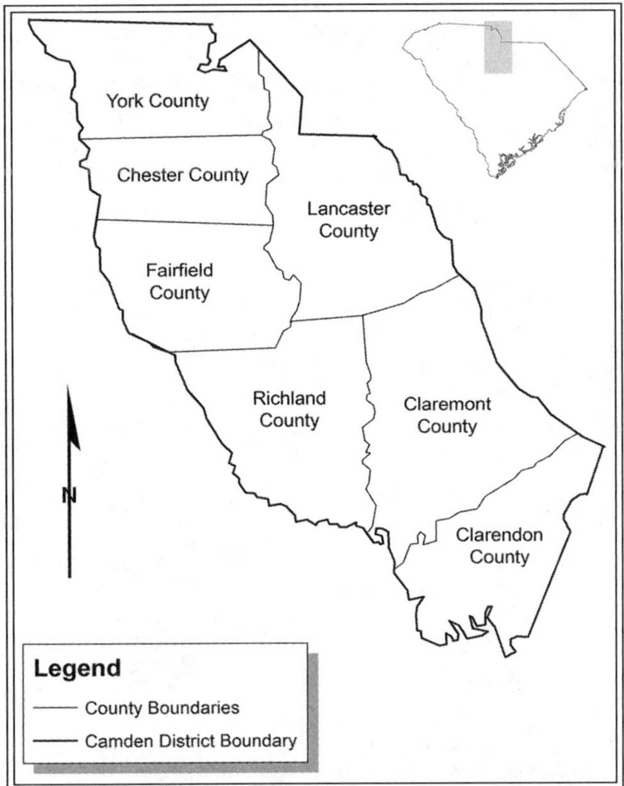

11.1 Camden District in 1785. The Court Act of that year subdivided South Carolina's seven judicial districts into thirty-four counties. As the seat of Camden District, Camden lay at the juncture of four counties, which gained many of its court functions. Courtesy of South Carolina Department of Archives and History, Columbia, South Carolina.

A county court system with locally appointed officials relied on the existing social and political structure that provided a framework for administrative governance. In staffing the courts, the system took advantage of those already possessing social prestige and reinforced their power through the civil authority of their office. Many justices, such as Wade Hampton of Richland County, Richard Richardson Jr. of Clarendon County, and Richard Winn of Fairfield County, were prominent planters and militia leaders in the recent war, and residents' acceptance of their social status undoubtedly contributed to the success of the county courts in the communities they served. Their achievement was significant in light of their courts' role in enforcing civil law during hard economic times, during which opposition arose from those who resented their authority. Nevertheless, the dispersed county courts allowed backcountry settlers with limited means access to legal redress for small claims and suits, and their authority to deal with petty crime addressed a growing need in the backcountry. By reinforcing the existing social order, the county court system became the basis for emergence of new political structures in the region.[21]

The return of administrative functions to Camden brought not only the new courthouse and jail but also an influx of state funds to refurbish and improve them. Barely four

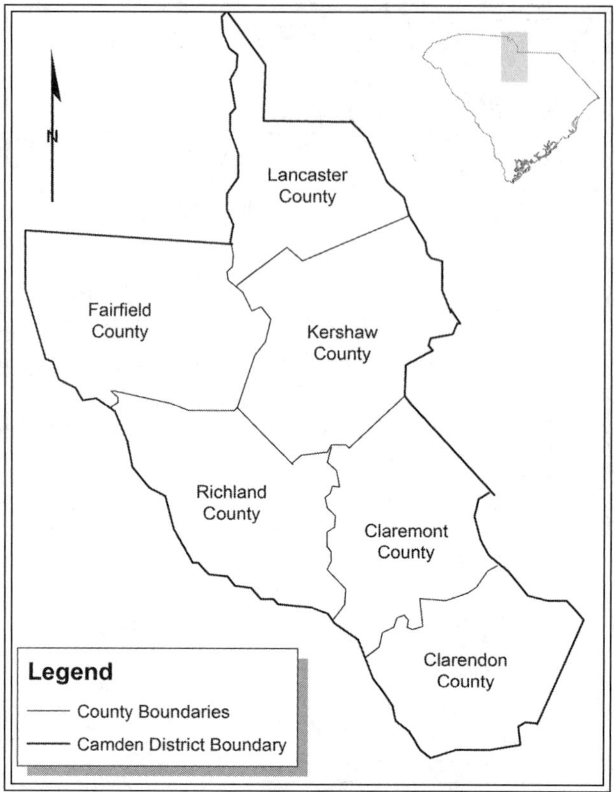

11.2 In 1791 Camden regained its court functions with the creation of Kershaw County. The judicial district lines were also redrawn that year, reducing the size of Camden District. Courtesy of South Carolina Department of Archives and History, Columbia, South Carolina.

years after its completion, a legislative committee found the Camden jail already in want of repairs and in 1788 appropriated £850 to cover the cost. Two years later, the courthouse too had fallen into disrepair, prompting the Camden District Grand Jury to request that it be rebuilt. In the following year £1,000 was provided for this project.[22] Efforts to maintain and upgrade these structures reflected the significance of their role in the developing interior as well as Camden's continued importance as a regional center.

Organized religion had always been an important element of colonial society in the Wateree Valley, and churches continued to serve as one of the region's principal integrating institutions. Prior to the Revolution, the Quaker community held its meetings at Pine Tree Hill, and a Presbyterian congregation later erected its meetinghouse nearby on the ferry road not far from Joseph Kerhsaw's store and brewhouse. By 1782 so many of the Quakers had migrated from the area that those remaining discontinued the Camden meeting.[23] In contrast, the Presbyterians remained active and rebuilt their meetinghouse on the old site in the 1780s.[24] Baptists also flourished on the Wateree and by the 1770s focused their activities around a church at the High Hills of Santee. Aware of Camden's emerging importance in the postwar era, its leaders acquired two lots there in 1784 and 1785 to found a daughter church and organized a formal congregation in 1810.[25] Methodist itinerant preachers operated in the Wateree Valley as early as the 1760s. Following the Church's formal organization in 1784, Methodists established a circuit organization to extend its influence in South Carolina's interior. Circuit preachers began holding regular services in Camden in 1787, and the Church erected a formal structure around the turn of the century.[26]

Institutions of faith flourished in the countryside of the Wateree Valley in the postwar years as well and served as a basis for reintegrating a rural population recovering from the war's devastation. Preachers from several denominations held religious meetings at private homes as well as outdoors, and by 1786 at least five meetinghouses stood on both sides of the river in the vicinity of Camden. The decade also witnessed the appearance north of town of a number of formal congregations identified only by the names of creeks and other natural landscape features found at the locations where they met.[27] The rapid growth of rural congregations continued to play an important role in the social integration of a still largely dispersed population.

The established Church of England was always poorly represented in a backcountry heavily populated by evangelicals. Early efforts by the Rev. Woodmason to proselytize his countrymen in the 1760s met generally with failure, and Anglican Church membership was confined largely to elite families such as the Kershaws, the Carys, the Richardsons, and the Canteys. Camden's small Anglican congregation organized by the Rev. Drage dissolved at his death in 1775. Although Camden's developers anticipated its presence in the new town and took pains to allot space for the established Church on the town square, a structure was never built there, and the lot became a cemetery. After the war, the Church of England in America reorganized as the Episcopal Church, but many in South Carolina's interior recalled with disfavor its Anglican roots. Despite missionary efforts, a half-century passed before an Episcopalian congregation formed and erected a church in Camden.[28]

Institutional growth in the backcountry received its most visible support when the legislature agreed in 1786 to remove the seat of government to the Congarees. Demands for an inland state capital grew out of postwar economic hardships as well as the political resurgence of the backcountry. Many local residents saw such a move as a means to curb the power of resident British merchants in Charleston and their coastal supporters, while backcountry residents argued that the move would eliminate inconveniences they presently endured in conducting public and private business with offices in a distant capital. Residents from both sides of the Wateree River strongly advocated relocation and authored petitions enumerating its advantages.[29] Although several possible locations, including Camden, were proposed as sites of the new capital, after much political wrangling the legislature situated it on the east bank of the Congaree River near Fridig's Ferry in the vicinity of Granby. Subsequent legislation authorized the purchase of lands, the erection of public buildings, and the removal of all public offices to the new settlement, called Columbia, by the close of 1789.[30]

Removing the capital to Columbia greatly increased the accessability of government to those living in the South Carolina's interior. It shifted important public administrative functions away from the coastal region and placed the state's decision-making body closer to the homes of backcountry legislators. Important civil offices now resided in Columbia, as did the Courts of Chancery and Sessions and Pleas. Their presence not only facilitated the transaction of business and the settlement of disputes in the interior but also fostered the growth of a system of formal regulatory institutions that replaced earlier, looser, informal arrangements. Coastal interests continued to dominate a legislature still largely apportioned on the basis of wealth, but the new capital's convenience helped increase the influence of backcountry representatives who formed interregional alliances that favored their interests. The historian Rachel Klein has argued that this process unified planter elites in both regions and encouraged backcountry planters to become mediators between interior interests and lowcountry political leadership.[31]

Restoring the Economic Infrastructure

Agriculture remained the basis of the Wateree Valley's economy as it emerged from the devastation of the Revolutionary War. The two decades after the end of the fighting witnessed the region's slow revival and reorientation around a new cash crop. Postwar conditions created uncertain markets that encouraged farmers to maintain diverse production of older commodities while raising livestock for export.[32] Wheat continued to be the major export crop raised in the Wateree Valley, and the demand for grain provided sufficient impetus to rebuild the mills and other processing facilities destroyed in the war. Raising the capital necessary for these construction projects depended heavily on prewar networks of association, and several individuals who had previously been successful in trade became actively involved in mill construction and operation. Duncan McRa, a Scotsman who had moved to Camden from St. David's Parish on the Pee Dee, became a partner with John Chesnut and John Adamson in Camden during the occupation. By the late 1780s he joined Chesnut and Samuel Boykin to form Chesnut & Co., later Chesnut, Boykin & Co. A widower, McRa married Chesnut's eldest daughter, Mary, in 1789 and he, Samuel Boykin, and Zachariah Cantey became managers of his new father-in-law's property. Cantey, formerly Nathanael Greene's quartermaster and now a merchant, was also linked to Samuel Boykin through marriage to his daughter Sally. In 1794 McRa and Cantey joined with Thomas Broom, a Maryland merchant, to form the partnership of McRa & Cantey. Broom's recent marriage to Samuel Boykin's widow, Elizabeth, further solidified the relationship with his new partners. As a soldier during the recent war, Broom had visited Camden and noted the potential of Kershaw's old mill sites on Pine Tree Creek below the town. With the wherewithal provided by his new business associates, he rebuilt and operated large mills there. The success of their ventures permitted the partners to expand their operations, and several years later McRa & Cantey erected large grist- and sawmills on a substantial acreage on Pine Tree Creek and a sawmill on Sanders Creek north of Camden. Described as a "great establishment," McRa's Flouring Mills received wheat from much of the Wateree Valley, as well as the Pee Dee River country and the southern counties of North Carolina. Duncan McRa also built a mill on Little Pine Tree Creek and another northeast of Camden.[33]

Entrepreneurs in the Wateree Valley were eager to invest in the export market for grain and built mills farther from Camden along swift-flowing streams that provided suitable sites. Burwell Boykin dammed Swift Creek on family lands south of Camden and built a gristmill there. Joshua English operated a mill on his thousand-acre tract on Spears Creek and another on Town Creek, just above the site of John Chesnut's newly constructed mill. Chambers's and Moore's Mills also lay downstream from Camden. The former militia leader John Marshall erected a mill to the east near Lynches River, and Peoples's mill also lay between that watercourse and Camden. North of town, Archer's Mill was situated between Hanging Rock Creek and the Wateree.[34]

Although wheat was the chief commodity produced, area farmers and planters grew other crops for sale as well. Primarily a subsistence crop for home consumption and fodder, corn became an important item of trade. The fertile river lands of planters such as John Chesnut were well suited to corn and yielded large crops. His accounts record the regular sales of substantial amounts of it to numerous customers through the mid-1790s. Although most of his crop seems to have remained in the backcountry, some was delivered as far away as Charleston.[35] With the decline of indigo exports in the 1780s, tobacco enjoyed a resurgence, and production increased markedly in the Wateree Valley. Sufficient quantities of this crop regularly passed through the hands of Chesnut, Boykin, Cantey, and other Camden merchants for the state to make Camden one of three interior tobacco inspection points, with inspectors assigned to the town. The Wyly family maintained and operated one of two or more tobacco warehouses on the Wateree.[36] Despite the loss of the British subsidy, indigo remained a profitable but less important crop throughout the late eighteenth century in the backcountry. Wateree and Pee Dee planters continued to raise indigo on dry lands along the drainages, but the postwar boom in indigo production was short lived. John Chesnut sold two casks at its peak in 1792, but its market declined rapidly when England's wars with France cut off the European markets. Henry Rugeley remained hopeful of selling indigo grown on his reclaimed estate but abandoned the crop by mid-decade.[37] In addition to produce, beef and pork raised to the east of the Wateree became export staples. Processed in Camden or by individual planters, meat products joined other commodities shipped to market in Charleston.[38]

Shipping increasing quantities of wheat and other heavy bulk agricultural commodities to Charleston strained the system of overland transport, which relied on largely unimproved roads. To alleviate this problem, producers increasingly turned to the great river as an avenue of commerce. By the 1780s the Wateree raft obstructing navigation below Camden had been removed, allowing free passage as far as the mouth of the Santee. However, the absence of a protected passage to Charleston still required goods to be transferred from shallow-bottomed river craft to seaworthy vessels.[39] This meant that Camden merchants trading with the state's chief port had to coordinate their movements with other shippers. Samuel Mathis ran two boats a month from Camden to a store operated by James Mouzon near the mouth of the Santee, from which point Mouzon's schooner carried their cargoes to the entrepôt.[40] Camden became a collection point for corn, indigo, tobacco, barreled beef and pork, and other heavy bulk goods produced in the Wateree Valley. The payment of storage and wharfage fees for produce passing through the town reflected its role as a collection hub for agricultural commodities moving to destinations downriver. Export trade now consumed a greater share of production, but not all cargoes went to Charleston markets. The opening of river commerce also allowed planters to market subsistence goods like corn to other locations in the interior, and several Camden residents employed their own boats in this trade. John Chesnut shipped his corn by water to customers along the

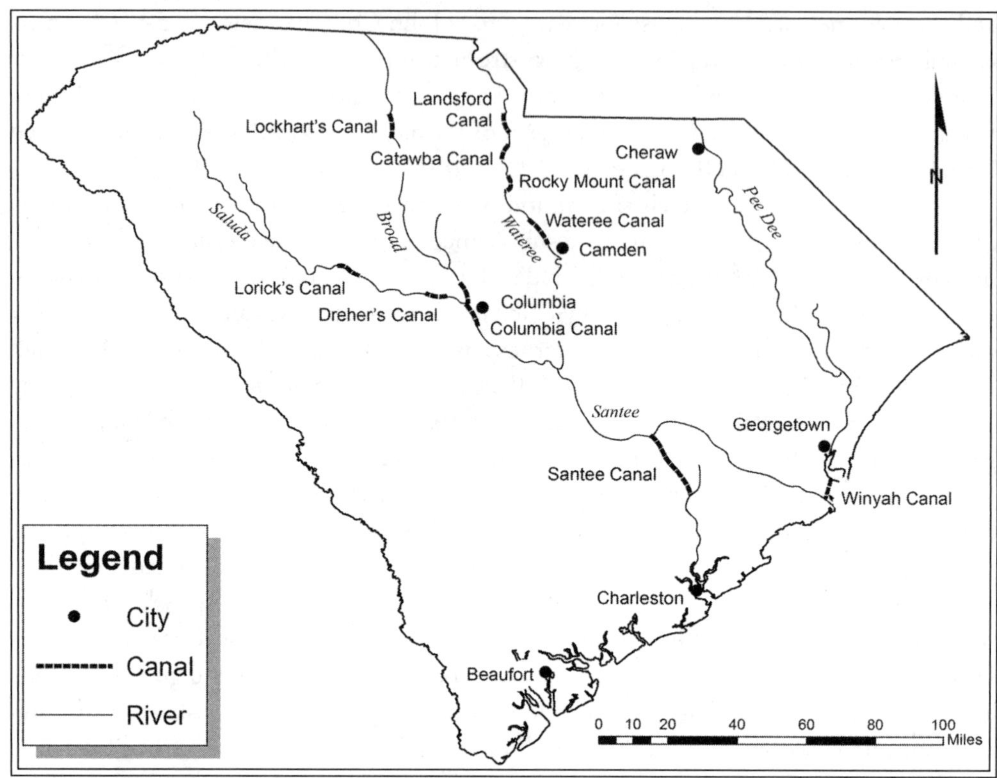

11.3 Canals constructed in South Carolina between 1792 and 1825. South Carolina carried out these river improvements to support the development of plantation agriculture in the state's central interior. Author's original map adapted from Kovacik and Winberry, *A Geography*, 21.

---

inland rivers, and boats owned by McRa & Cantey and James Kershaw carried their own and others' produce.[41]

Inland navigation received a boost with the opening of the Santee Canal in 1800. This project, conceived by Charleston interests eager to capture the trade of the immense Santee drainage, promoted the canal's construction to allow Charleston merchants direct access to settlements on the Wateree and Congaree Rivers. Its completion in 1792 connected the interior directly with Charleston and encouraged entrepreneurs who incorporated companies to open the Wateree Valley to navigation as far as the North Carolina line.[42] The Wateree projects became part of a massive campaign to canalize the state's inland rivers (Fig. 11.3). By the first quarter of the new century, canals offered the entrepôt access to the produce of a large portion of South Carolina's interior, and John Chesnut's boats now passed directly to the city via the new waterways. Rivers now dominated the flow of commerce in the state, and the growing reliance on water transport promoted the growth of inland towns like Camden, Granby, and Augusta at the expense of Orangeburg, Williamsburg, and others that had occupied central locations in the state's road network.[43]

In the last two decades of the eighteenth century, the rapid expansion of river shipping gave rise to a boat-building industry at Camden. Local craftsmen constructed cargo boats capable of carrying up to 120 barrels of rice or fifteen to twenty cords of wood. Perhaps the best-known boatbuilder was Kirkpatrick. His yard employed many enslaved skilled workers, including Cato, a carpenter hired from the Kershaw family. The total number of boats constructed is unknown, but ten were built from 1795 to 1799 and seven in 1800 alone. James Kershaw mentioned eleven specific vessels, eight of which were named, that operated during this time. Owned by local planters or merchants, these vessels expedited the movement of their produce to South Carolina's chief port.[44]

The expansion of mail service into the interior in the 1790s facilitated the exchange of information crucial to integrating the backcountry within the larger economy. Business depended on the transmission of written documents to order merchandise, maintain accounts, keep track of credit, and arrange marketing agreements between parties over long distances. Official mails to South Carolina from the outside arrived regularly at Charleston and Georgetown by sea or flowed along land routes that paralleled the Atlantic Coast, but no official interior postal routes existed, and mail to the central and eastern backcountry moved by private hands.[45] The situation changed abruptly in 1792, when an Act of the United States Congress established regular official mail service by shifting the principal north-south post road inland to pass from North Carolina through the central part of South Carolina and into Georgia. This move connected Camden, Columbia, Cheraws Court House (Long Bluff), and Cambridge (Ninety Six) with Fayetteville, North Carolina, and Augusta, Georgia, and provided a direct route from Charleston to the Wateree Valley. Subsequent federal legislation expanded the network of post routes to much of South Carolina's interior, facilitating postwar business and further integrating the backcountry with the outside world.[46]

Despite the deleterious impact of the recent war, the final decades of the eighteenth century brought developments that lay the groundwork for economic recovery in the backcountry. These changes had important implications for a society that had so recently settled this region and whose structure was still shaped by its frontier experience. The transition of the regional economy depended on the availability of both resources and capital, as well as a strategy capable of implementing production for a high-demand market. The new infrastructure that made this goal feasible created the economic and social environment that shaped the antebellum landscape of the backcountry.

Consolidating the Postwar Economy

The proliferation of mills and the growth of production in the 1780s and 1790s reflected the recovery of Wateree Valley processors as well as their further integration within the larger market economy, a process that increasingly concentrated wealth in the hands of a small number of people and stimulated the emergence of an economic elite. The milling consortium formed by Chesnut, McRa, Boykin, and Cantey effectively cornered business in Camden during the postwar years, and its members prospered as the economy revived. Export demand for flour remained strong at the close of the eighteenth century, and Camden millers found profitable markets in New York, Philadelphia, and Jamaica. But processing was only part of their strategy for success.[47]

Wealth in South Carolina had always been linked to large-scale agricultural production of commercial crops. Rice growing dominated the lowcountry, and its high return on invested capital helped make the region home to some of the richest individuals in North America.[48] Prior to the Revolution, many backcountry merchants anticipated the rise of commercial agriculture in the region and began to invest profits in land and slaves. They hoped to employ the profitable strategy of Henry Laurens and other lowcountry merchants who enhanced their income from trade with profits derived from planting. Success in planting promised not only greater wealth but also a closer association with the powerful coastal elites. Changing conditions in the postwar world facilitated the economic transformation of the backcountry and consolidated the social and political position of the region's planter class.[49]

Plantation agriculture could not exist without substantial amounts of real estate under single management, land that could be devoted to both staple production and subsistence crops, pasture, forage, workers' quarters, and maintenance activities, as well as the owner's house and associated buildings. Although some planters, such as the partners and associates of Kershaw & Co., had managed to amass large estates in the years preceding the war, the closure of the provincial land office in 1773 ended the free distribution of the public domain and limited the acquisition of land to purchases from previous owners. All this changed in 1784 when the state legislature once again authorized the distribution of land for modest fees. Acquiring new land appealed to residents as a means of enlarging their estates as well as obtaining collateral for debts, but the new laws also opened the door to speculation on the anticipated rise in land values. In the following decade, South Carolinians accumulated an estimated eight million acres in speculative tracts, nearly 90 percent of which were in the backcountry. The sudden availability of cheap land gave ambitious planters and those with political influence an opportunity to obtain vast holdings in the developing interior and to profit from the expanding agricultural economy. Among them were Richard Winn and Thomas Sumter, who owned the town sites of Winnsboro and Stateburg, respectively, while the site of the new capital of Columbia lay on lands in the Congarees granted to Thomas and James Taylor and to Wade Hampton.[50]

The ability to obtain new lands benefited many residents with established business interests in the backcountry's development. By the late eighteenth century, the merchants Samuel Boykin, John Chesnut, Duncan McRa, and Zachariah Cantey emerged as Camden's wealthiest citizens, and two of them were among the largest landowners in the Wateree Valley as well. These men acquired the greater part of their real property, and in one case all of it, after 1784. Chesnut's holdings were among the largest in the region. Built on an estate of nearly six thousand acres, he added an estimated eleven thousand more in the postwar era. Cantey's estate was also extensive, comprising more than fourteen thousand acres, most of which were obtained after 1786. At the time of his death, Samuel Boykin's estate included a portion of his father's 1,100-acre estate, as well as 3,832 acres in state grants and at least 800 additional acres purchased. Duncan McRa obtained all of his holdings after the war. Although somewhat smaller than those of the others, they were not insubstantia; not including the mill properties in Camden, they totaled 1,255 acres.[51] The investment value of their substantial holdings nevertheless allowed each of them to generate the capital necessary for commercial agricultural expansion.

The success of commercial enterprises also required the development of institutions that facilitated production and trade. In the past, the extension of credit had always depended on the resources available to individual merchants or producers. Commerce in the internally focused regional economy of the frontier involved exchange based largely on equivalencies, and early commercial trade was financed by the personal wealth of individuals such as Charles Ogilvie or by the capital of lowcountry merchants such as Ancrum, Lance & Loocock. By the end of the eighteenth century, however, the volume of production and trade in the United States had so substantially increased the demand for credit that the leaders of the new federal government recognized the need for a formal financial institution, a bank whose services would increase the medium of trade, regulate contracts, expedite the payment of taxes, and provide a depository for funds. To these ends, in 1791 they established the Bank of the United States, a branch of which opened in Charleston the following year. By1801 eleven states and the District of Columbia also chartered thirty-one additional commercial banks to accommodate the growing capital market. The Bank of South Carolina, organized in 1792, was both a depository and a bank of issue. It not only provided credit for working capital to finance mercantile activities but also issued notes that became a stable and convertible currency that could circulate widely. Although the value of notes still varied with the issuing bank's reputation, notes permitted regional exchange in the absence of a national currency. The rise of early American banking brought fiscal changes that facilitated the growth of export trade in the South, but the success of this commerce was contingent upon the adoption of a staple whose returns were capable of sustaining the cost of large-scale production.[52]

In the 1790s the introduction of cotton accelerated the growth of commercial agriculture in South Carolina's interior. During that decade, the increased demand for cotton generated by Great Britain's expanding textile industry opened a vast market for a crop well adapted to South Carolina's climate. This development coincided with the fortuitous appearance in 1793 of Eli Whitney's gin, a machine that overcame the difficult process of separating seeds from short staple cotton and made its production cost-effective. Short staple cotton was an ideal crop for backcountry farmers because it not only grew well but also could be produced with low capital investment. A prospective cotton grower required little more than a plow, hand tools, and access to a gin and bailer. The promise of cotton led to its rapid spread in the interior at the expense of wheat, tobacco, indigo, and other crops. So great was its growth in Camden District that residents anticipated the need for a cotton inspector as early as 1796.[53]

The wealth cotton brought to the backcountry increased the capital available for the purchase of durable goods as well as for investment, but the economy's expansion also depended on institutional regulation of trade. The stability provided by the new court system made it possible for storekeepers and those in trades to control the credit on which an expansion of retail business depended. By 1790 the tenuous conditions that existed immediately after the war had improved sufficiently for Henry Rugeley to conclude that South Carolina's interior was now "a fine place for a country store." Having returned from exile, the former Camden Loyalist described the region as "a thick settled part of the country, with able planters," but he also emphasized the lower the risks of doing business. "I am almost certain I could carry on business," he wrote, "now [that] the . . . courts are fix'd, [and customers] are obliged . . . to pay their debts."[54]

The lower production costs for cotton and the high returns presented opportunities for wealth to small landowners, but they offered even greater prospects to large planters who already possessed the wherewithal to expand their production. Seven years into the new century, a traveler to the vicinity of Camden from Maryland visited one of the largest cotton plantations. "Col. C[hesnut] is one of the richest cotton planters in Carolina," he remarked, adding that his plantation was a largely self-contained operation where cotton was not only grown but also ginned and packed "for the Charleston market, where it is sent in large boats by the river." Cotton also allowed Chesnut to "bring into use land which from its barrenness was not worth a farthing," increasing the value of the upland tracts he and other entrepreneurs had recently amassed. The capital Chesnut, Cantey, and McRa had acquired in trade and invested in land now generated a rate of return sufficient to place them among the region's wealthiest residents and largest slaveholders. Cotton made the fortunes for those who shaped the postwar economy and who would take their place among the antebellum landed elite.[55]

The Fate of the Kershaws

Ironically, Joseph Kershaw was not among the planters who flourished in the postwar years. Previously Kershaw had been the central figure in the region's development, and his efforts had been the driving force behind its transition to a commercial economy. Kershaw's efforts underwrote the rise of Camden as South Carolina's principal inland settlement, and he supported the Revolution with his wealth as well as his person. But, following the British occupation of South Carolina, his fortunes declined sharply. As a notorious rebel leader, he saw his property confiscated and damaged by outright destruction as well as neglect. His confinement in Bermuda removed him from affairs in the backcountry, and the loss of his brother Ely deprived him of a valuable associate. War and exile changed things forever.

During Kershaw's year in Bermuda, his activities there and the disastrous events in South Carolina brought about economic reversals that irreparably damaged the business empire that he had carefully built over the previous two decades. Through Charles Ogilvie's letter of introduction Kershaw became acquainted with the prominent Bermuda merchants Richard and John Jennings, partners of Henry Tucker and others in the firm of Jennings, Tucker & Co. Despite being a loyal British possession, Bermuda had an economy that was heavily dependent on trade with the American colonies mounting a revolution, and the continued success of its leading merchants and shipowners rested on maintaining illicit but profitable economic relations with them. Henry Tucker had relatives and business connections in Virginia as well as in South Carolina, and these connections undoubtedly affected his sympathy for American interests. He and the Jennings brothers had been involved in the contraband trade with the rebellious colonies from the beginning of hostilities.[56]

Eager to share in the profits of a new business venture, Jennings, Tucker & Co. joined with Joseph Kershaw in a venture that placed both their resources at risk. At Kershaw's instigation, they provided £9,000 worth of clothing and military stores to be conveyed to the mainland. Lacking direct access to capital for the speculative venture, Kershaw acquired the goods on credit by posting a bond that mortgaged seventy lots he owned in Camden, including the tract upon which the Great White House stood. Unfortunately the enterprise failed with the capture of the ship and the seizure of its contents by the British authorities. Unable to repay his creditors or receive official redress from the state or Congress for his losses, Kershaw was at the mercy of the Bermudan partners, whose demands now placed his entire estate in jeopardy. The occupation of South Carolina had been costly and left him with few resources to draw upon. Kershaw estimated that his losses from the destruction and theft of property at Camden and elsewhere amounted to nearly £20,000, for which he eventually received only about £4,000 in compensation. Additional prewar business obligations of more than £12,000 left him further indebted.[57]

To settle his liabilities, Kershaw was forced to liquidate his estate. He conveyed the seventy mortgaged Camden properties to Jennings, Tucker & Co. in 1786 and sold off a large number of other town lots and rural properties.[58] But all did not actually pass out of his hands. He conveyed the tract containing the original store at the intersection of Broad and Meeting Streets to William Ancrum and the sixteen lots immediately to the south of it "where the brewhouse now stands" to Aaron Loocock, both former partners. Because Ancrum and Loocock did not reside in Camden, neither used these properties, making their purchases not so much transfers of property as movements of funds to assist a distressed associate. Kershaw's subsequent offer of the store as rental property in 1786 and his son James Kershaw's ongoing involvement with the brewhouse implies that the family continued to manage these buildings. Archaeological investigations at the sites of both structures recovered ceramics whose dates testify that they remained in use through the first decade of the new century.[59]

Despite his declining fortunes, Joseph Kershaw remained active in civil and political affairs in the last years of his life. Voters in the District Eastward of Wateree River elected him to the Fourth and Fifth General Assemblies, where he served from 1782 to 1784. During this time he received appointments as commissioner to rebuild the courthouse and jail at Camden and to clear the Wateree river. As a member of the house committee charged with recommending compensation for the Catawbas' wartime service, he continued his advocacy for a people whose sufferings were compounded by the threat of encroachment by white settlement. For his efforts and sacrifice on behalf of the state, the new administrative unit around Camden was named Kershaw County in his honor. When Camden was formally incorporated in 1791, he was elected the first intendant. As its chief officer, he exercised the prestigious duty of presiding over the reception committee that welcomed President George Washington to Camden during his tour of the southern states that year. Kershaw's star still burned bright, but it could not erase the economic disaster that had befallen him and crippled his enterprises.[60]

In the end, Joseph Kershaw could not escape the financial difficulties that now forced him to liquidate his estate. In 1790 he sought to expedite the payment of his debts by placing the remainder of his property in the hands of five trustees, among whom were William Ancrum and Kershaw's eldest son, James. He also authorized his second son, John, to act as their attorney in disposing of the lands. This lengthy process was complicated by conflicting claims of creditors as well as by family members' continued occupation and management of the properties as specified in the terms of Joseph Kershaw's 1788 will. John Kershaw assumed control of the estate upon his father's death in the closing days of 1791 and continued its liquidation, offering plantations and other rural properties in Camden, Pinckney, and Ninety Six Districts in the spring of 1794. Working with William Ancrum and others, John Kershaw began selling off lands, slaves, and other property, much of which was apparently not alienated for several decades. They sold two large tracts that encompassed 170 lots in Camden and eight hundred acres at the mouth of Pine Tree Creek and settled a number of major debts before1803. The property containing the Great White House soon passed from the hands of the Kershaw family into the ownership of the Camden Orphan Society, a private school, well before the surviving partners of Jennings, Tucker & Co. sued to acquire it for debts owed them by the Kershaw estate. Although the family still possessed nearly 250 surveyed lots in Camden and more than seventeen thousand acres of rural property as late as 1819, the magnificent town mansion, the mill tracts, the site of the magazine, and the nearby Hermitage plantation, where the Kershaw family had taken refuge during the late war, were all now gone.[61]

Despite the loss of wealth and property, the Kershaws persisted and retained influential in the county named after the family's founder. Joseph Kershaw's central role in the network of partnerships and alliances ensured that his descendants remained in the region's social elite, and several went on to play significant roles as military, political, and religious leaders in South Carolina during the turbulent times to come. Although the family continued to be actively involved in the agricultural economy of the antebellum backcountry, the integrative role of its pioneer merchant, spokesman, and administrator had now been assumed by the institutions his actions helped create. And the individuals who had risen in Joseph Kershaw's footsteps now stood ready to shape the destiny of the region that had emerged as a result of his efforts.[62]

The Revolutionary War also brought the financial collapse of Ely Kershaw's enterprises, but the network that promoted his success in business now rescued his family from ruin at the hands of enemies and creditors. During his absence, the Chatham store had been burned and other property destroyed or stolen, leaving his affairs as in "great confusion." Despite the devastation, his plantations remained intact, and Holden Wade, his conscientious overseer, had preserved their records, providing a basis for the estate's administration. William and Joseph Kershaw, John Chesnut, and Joseph Kershaw's former partner William Ancrum saw to the liquidation of Ely Kershaw's estate to provide for his three minor children, a complicated task that took his executors decades to complete. Indeed, it occupied several of them for the rest of their lives.[63] To raise funds, Joseph Kershaw and John Chesnut rented the Pee Dee plantations and other lands, as well as his buildings at Cheraw Hill and lands in Lancaster County.[64] But paying off the extensive debts necessitated the sale of the estate's assets. The disposal of Ely Kershaw's plantations, rural properties, and lots in Camden began with sheriff's sales in 1788. As a creditor as well as an executor, William Ancrum worked to maximize the value of the properties, managing advertising and sales and even offering to purchase property himself until it could be sold at higher prices to benefit the estate.[65] In the end, John Chesnut supervised the bulk of the estate's administration. He not only handled the rental and sale of the estate's property but also oversaw the receipt of accounts for Ely Kershaw's Revolutionary War claims, handled suits with Ely's creditors and debtors, and maintained accounts of the transactions over the years. As the new century dawned, William Ancrum's increasing infirmity left the task of settling the estate to John Chesnut, a task he finally completed by the close of the first decade.[66]

Despite the economic distress into which his estate had fallen, Ely Kershaw's legacy survived his demise and that of Mary Cantey Kershaw, to be carried forward by their descendants. Although now orphaned, their three children benefited from an extensive kin network that included the wealthiest individuals in the region. All reached their maturity in the 1790s, but only their daughter Rebecca's children carried the family into the next generation. Her marriage to Joseph Brevard, a rising planter as well as a prominent lawyer, judge, and, later, congressman, ensured the family's membership in the antebellum elite. Their four offspring, produced before her early death in 1802, continued the family's legacy in the changing world of antebellum South Carolina.[67]

The destiny of the Kershaws now diverged from that of the town their efforts had helped create, but Camden's future progress was a direct result of the process Joseph Kershaw had set in motion. His mercantile network, that knit together a large portion of the backcountry, laid the groundwork for the formation of economic, social, and political institutions that transformed the region and made it part of the larger Atlantic world. The emergence of a commercial economy in the backcountry nevertheless marked a watershed in the region's development, one that had implications for the lives of its inhabitants and those yet to reside there.

The Changing Composition of Society in the Backcountry

By the close of the eighteenth century, a shift toward large-scale export production of agricultural commodities had already begun to change the composition of the region's population and alter the nature of its landscape. The decades following the American Revolution witnessed the resurgence of the flour trade, now made more lucrative by transportation improvement, as well as a search for new agricultural export staples. Because profitability was linked to scale of production, success in commercial agriculture encouraged investment in land and the growth of plantation farming. The adoption of cotton as a cash crop in the 1790s accelerated this process, increasing the number of large holdings and expanding the role of slave labor.

The growth of agriculture in the backcountry did not come immediately. As long as the region depended on earlier cash crops with a limited market, planters felt little pressure to expand their operations after the war. In contrast to their counterparts in the lowcountry, who were eager to replace slaves lost in the war, planters in the interior did not face an acute shortage of laborers. Indeed, when rice planters began acquiring substantial numbers of slaves from abroad, Wateree Valley representatives supported legislation passed in 1787 to prohibit the importation of foreign slaves and backed an extension of the restriction into the 1790s.[68] But the introduction of cotton agriculture in the century's closing years presented backcountry planters with an enormous opportunity for growth and brought an abrupt change in their position. Just as the adoption of tidal swamp agriculture had increased coastal planters' demand for labor to realize the potential of a larger scale of production, the expansion of cotton intensified the need for new workers in the backcountry and led the state to lift the ban on imported slaves in 1803. In the five years before a constitutional prohibition finally ended the slave trade in 1808, thousands of captive Africans came into the interior.[69]

The growth of cotton agriculture transformed the demography of the backcountry. Although involuntary servitude accompanied the first wave of European immigration to the backcountry, slaves accounted for a relatively small portion of the new inhabitants. The earliest estimate of the interior population, derived from the 1757 Muster Roll of the militia, indicates that slaves then made up less than 10 percent of the region's males and were probably a smaller segment of the total immigrant population. In the years following the American Revolution, this proportion changed dramatically. The first United States census, taken a year before Kershaw County's creation in1790, shows that slavery had already made serious inroads in the Wateree Valley (Table 11.1). Enslaved people already made up nearly 40 percent of the population in the counties of Claremont and Richland below Camden but constituted fewer than a quarter of the residents in Fairfield and Lancaster counties above the town. The demography of Camden District, which included the Wateree Valley as well as portions of the Congaree, Broad, Lynches, and upper Santee drainages, reveals how this patterned changed. Slaves accounted for less than a quarter of its residents in 1790, but their numbers rose rapidly afterward (Table 11.2), more than doubling by 1800. In the next thirty years slaves became the majority of its inhabitants. The enslaved population in Kershaw County, which became Kershaw District in 1800, increased even faster. Slaves already accounted for a third of the population at the beginning of the new century, and within a decade the number of enslaved people nearly equaled the number of free whites (Table 11.3).[70]

The growth of plantation agriculture not only brought substantial overall growth in the number of enslaved persons in the Wateree Valley but also increased their concentration

Table 11.1. Composition of the Population in Claremont, Fairfield, Lancaster, and Richland Counties in 1790

Population Totals

County	*Free White*	*Slave*	*Totals*
Claremont	4,428	2,712	7,140
Fairfield	6,138	1,485	7,623
Lancaster	4,864	1,438	6,302
Richland	2,479	1,451	3,930
Totals	17,909	7,086	24,995
Population Percentages			
Claremont	62.0%	38.0%	100.0%
Fairfield	80.5%	19.5%	100.0%
Lancaster	77.2%	22.8%	100.0%
Richland	63.1%	36.9%	100.0%
Totals	71.7%	28.3%	100.0%

Table 11.2. Composition of the Population in Camden District, 1790–1830

Date of Census	Free White	Slave	Totals
Population Totals			
1790	29,242	9,023	38,265
1800	42,306	18,768	61,074
1810	43,174	34,460	77,634
1820	54,059	51,078	105,137
1830	56,308	67,165	123,573
Population Percentages			
1790	76.4%	23.6%	100.0%
1800	69.3%	30.7%	100.0%
1810	55.6%	44.4&	100.0%
1820	51.4%	48.2%	100.0%
1830	45.6%	53.4%	100.0%

in larger agricultural operations. As plantation production expanded over time, more people owned slaves and the number of large slave owners rose. Table 11.4 shows that there was a steady growth of substantial slaveholdings in Kershaw District during the first three decades of the nineteenth century. Of particular interest is an increase in the number of owners possessing one hundred or more slaves. In 1800 only John Chesnut and Isaac DuBose owned this many of their fellow human beings, but a decade later the number had increased to eight. Between 1820 and 1830 the largest slaveholders nearly doubled the number of their bondsmen. For the remainder of his life John Chesnut remained the county's leading planter, owning 234 slaves in 1810 and 205 at his death three years later. By the close of the century's second decade, his son James had assumed his father's position, with a substantial estate that included 320 slaves. The revolutionary generation, many of whom had prospered

Table 11.3. Composition of the Population in Kershaw District, 1800–1830

Date of Census	Free White	Slave	Free Colored	Totals
Population Totals				
1800	4,706	2,530	104	7,340
1810	4,911	4,832	78	9,821
1820	5,625	6,692	112	12,429
1830	5,016	8,333	196	13, 545
Population Percentages				
1800	64.1%	34.5%	1.4%	100.0%
1810	50.0%	49.2%	0.8%	100.0%
1820	45.3%	53.8%	0.9%	100.0%
1830	37.0%	61.5%	1.4%	99.9%

Table 11.4. Concentration of Slave Ownership in Kershaw District, 1800–1830

	1800	*1810*	*1820*	*1830*
Owners of 100 or More Slaves	2	8	11	20
Owners of 70 or More Slaves	5	11	17	30
Owners of 50 or More Slaves	5	16	23	35

in the postwar economy, dominated the planter elite in 1810. It included not only John Chesnut, Burwell Boykin, Isaac DuBose, and Zachariah Cantey but also relative newcomers such as Joseph Brevard and William Ancrum II, the nephew and namesake of the pioneer merchant. John Adamson, the former Loyalist now restored to grace, also ranked among the region's wealthiest planters.[71]

The acquisition of substantial numbers of slaves by Wateree planters in the closing years of the eighteenth century was somewhat remarkable in light of the war's impact on agriculture. Conventional and guerrilla activity by both sides had destroyed the physical infrastructure of plantations and frequently dispersed their enslaved populations. Many plantation workers escaped, some to form maroon communities. Others absconded in response to British offers of freedom to those slaves who joined them. Although some found freedom in British service, others were returned to Loyalist owners by authorities eager to avoid losing their support. Many became captives of one or the other side, pressed into service or treated as war booty. During the dark days in the spring of 1781, Thomas Sumter encouraged his militiamen to extend their enlistments with the promise of receiving slaves captured from Loyalist owners as payment for their service. Slaves belonging to rebels were often likewise appropriated to be sold outside the province or carried away by their British and Loyalist captors. Between 1775 and 1783 South Carolina lost perhaps as many as twenty-five thousand slaves.[72]

Fearful of losing slaves to escape or predation, many owners attempted to shift their most valuable property away from the seat of war, moving them frequently and over great distances. As the British threat loomed in Georgia, large slave owners, such as the Indian trader and planter George Galphin, removed their slaves from the Savannah River to the interior. The lowcountry planter Adam Fowler Brisbane, who subsequently settled in Camden, also moved his slaves to avoid their capture by the invading enemy. In 1780 he gathered bondsmen from his family's estates and took them first to James Island, and subsequently into the interior; he finally sought refuge in North Carolina and Virginia. His efforts took their toll, however, and he retained only half of the original number when he returned to South Carolina.[73] Although planters and their agents actively worked to keep their laborers together, most lost slaves in the war. Several belonging to the Loyalist James Cary were stolen or escaped, and Sumter's troops appropriated thirty-one of the fifty-four removed from William Ancrum's Wateree and Pee Dee estates. Slaves who escaped from the Kershaw brothers and John Chesnut to join the British were taken by departing Loyalists or otherwise disappeared during the course of the occupation. Occasionally planters relied on former ties to help compensate for wartime losses of slaves. Previously affiliated in happier times, James Cary and Joseph Kershaw found themselves on opposite sides in the Revolution. Nevertheless, their families apparently remained on amiable terms during the occupation, and the Carys permitted Samuel Mathis to recover escaped Kershaw slaves who had sought refuge on his plantation. When the Carys fled South Carolina with their human assets in 1781, they left two skilled bondsmen, Cato and Quash, as reimbursement for several Kershaw slaves with whom they absconded. Both later became the legal property of John Kershaw.[74]

Although African Americans made up an increasingly larger proportion of the postwar population in the Wateree Valley, information about them is far from complete. Most were presumably agricultural laborers, but some possessed practical and managerial skills that were recorded. John Chesnut counted several specialists among his bondsmen, including the blacksmiths Frank, Cesar Campbell, and Harry Gaston, as well as Ben, a bricklayer, Pompey, a tanner, and Moses, a cobbler. These men undoubtedly worked at the family's forge, which produced iron and steel, or at their tannery, which made leather used to manufacture shoes. Chesnut and other large planters, such as Burwell Boykin, Zachariah Cantey, and Duncan McRa, all had skilled workers engaged in small industries. Their modest output implies that much of their work was consumed by the plantation, but Ben's building skills, as well as those of Duncan McRa's cooper, Tom, and the large output of shoes and boots produced by Zachariah Cantey's leatherworkers may also have generated outside income.[75]

Renting the services of slaves in response to changing labor needs permitted planters and craftsmen to acquire skilled labor for specific tasks. James Kershaw rented Cato, an experienced boatman and boat carpenter, to several individuals. Cato worked for the Camden boatbuilder Kirkpatrick on several occasions and was employed on a boat owned by Daniel Brown, a town lawyer. Kershaw also rented Cato to Benjamin Carter, a tanner, and contributed his expertise as a boatman to a joint plantation venture with Joseph English, uncle of his wife, Sarah English Kershaw. Another of Kershaw's bondsmen, Sam, was also a boatman and worked with Cato for Kirkpatrick, Brown, and English. When he needed specialized labor, James Kershaw also engaged the services of craftsmen owned by others, as when he rented the masons Geoff and Tom to build a chimney on his plantation.[76]

Although the closing years of the eighteenth century witnessed the rapid expansion of slavery, they also saw a rise in the number of free African Americans in the backcountry. There had always been small numbers of free people of color in the interior, but the postwar period saw their numbers grow through manumission and self-purchase by slaves. An influx of fugitive free blacks came during the 1793 exodus precipitated by the slave revolt in Saint Domingue.[77] As many as 1,800 free blacks lived in South Carolina by 1790, and their number increased by three-quarters during the following decade. One hundred and four free persons of color appear in the census of 1800 for Kershaw District, all but seventeen of whom were attached to the households of white families that also owned slaves.[78] Free people of color who possessed skills practiced in slavery continued to work in these trades after becoming free and often accumulated substantial propertied estates. Bonds Conway, for example, was a skilled carpenter who emigrated with his owner, Edwin Conway, from Virginia. With the proceeds acquired by hiring himself out, he purchased his freedom with the assistance of Zachariah Cantey in 1793 and subsequently acquired property, including several houses in Camden. Another free black who lived and worked in Camden was Levi, described as a "French Negro," who purportedly came with Lafayette as a soldier during the Revolution. Wounded at the Battle of Camden, he remained after the war as a servant. At least nine other free men of color traded in Camden in the 1790s, but the names of these men are now lost.[79]

An affiliation with a member of the slaveholding class could bring more than the economic security provided by a patron whose word might recommend the services of a manumitted slave or bring business to the shop of a black craftsperson. Certainly Bonds Conway's ties to a planter as prominent as Zachariah Cantey would have been advantageous to his business as a carpenter, but an alliance with a member of the elite also brought ties to one who held political power. Such a patron's influence was certainly helpful in civil matters and provided protection from the threat of vigilantes who might seek to take advantage of the vulnerability of nonwhites in a society in which status and race were increasingly synonymous. Because the planters and their allies who dominated South Carolina were always mindful of the potential for a slave insurrection, free people of color occupied an awkward position as persons who were free but did not share equal rights with white citizens. Consequently, most free blacks found it in their best practical interest to work within the structure of a society divided by race and avoid the conflict inherent in making the overt demands for equality heard in states where abolition had occurred. Instead, they created a parallel society defined by color, within whose bounds individuals could rise in status on the basis of achievement and that conducted political affairs with the larger world in private through the protection provided by clientage.[80]

Although vastly outnumbered by their enslaved brethren, free small farmers of African descent lived in the Wateree Valley in the postwar era. Charles Woodmason and other observers noted the presence of free people of color in the region as early as the 1760s. Some, like the members of the Harris, Griffin, and Jeffers families, had emigrated to South Carolina from nearby Virginia and North Carolina and accounted for part of a rural community west of the Wateree by the 1770s. Several of their members enlisted in the Third South Carolina Continental Regiment during the Revolutionary War, and at least four received bounty land grants in recognition of their service.[81] The names of other free persons of color appearing in legislative documents attest to the presence of rural black farmers and artisans in the Wateree Valley. Among them was Miller Sam. Taken from his Loyalist owner and freed at the close of the war, he became a prosperous miller in Chester County. In 1793, twenty-three men, describing themselves as "a poor needy people" with "large families to support," petitioned for exemption from a recent ordinance taxing "all free Negroes, Mustizoes, and Mulattoes." Their endorsements by Richard Winn of Fairfield County and by John Cook and other prominent white citizens of Kershaw County imply a widespread free black population in the region. Tied by bonds of kinship, as well as by their common racial status, these free blacks were not large landholders but nonetheless remained a viable part of the agricultural landscape in the Wateree Valley.[82]

Archaeologists have observed the continuing presence of African Americans through the artifacts present at the sites of early structures that persisted into the new century. Blue beads and River Burnished ceramics were uncovered at Joseph Kershaw's Great White House as well as at the Broad Street store and an adjacent shop building. The first two structures were occupied during and after the war, even as the properties on which they stood began to pass into the hands of others, and the presence of these artifacts reflects their continued use by blacks during that time. The nearby shop, however, found a new use in the 1790s. As the workshop of the tinworker Gayeton Aiguier, it was remodeled, and the archaeological deposits associated with his later use contained blue beads as well. Aiguier owned four slaves, among them Ipolite, a skilled shop assistant. Aiguier's slaves, like the human chattel of the Kershaws and others in postwar Camden, continued to leave material evidence of their presence there.[83]

The Catawbas' New World

In 1781 the Catawba Nation emerged from the disruption of war to face new challenges in the rapidly changing backcountry, where new conditions taxed the viability of old arrangements. The Catawbas participated early in the conflict as allies of the rebels and suffered during the British occupation. Catawba warriors were active throughout the Southern campaign, and the Catawba Nation provided supplies for the Americans. It became a refuge for Whig militia leaders and a rallying point for forces under Thomas Sumter following the capture of Charleston. But residence in the seat of war and an affiliation with the rebel cause put the Catawba people at risk and forced them to seek refuge in North Carolina in 1780. When the Indians returned to the Waxhaws the following spring, they found their towns sacked and their livestock driven away, severely impacting their livelihood. The Catawbas had to begin anew and abandoned their old settlements to build a new town farther upriver.[84]

Throughout this time the Catawbas' welfare remained an important concern of Camden's leading merchant. Joseph Kershaw understood the Indians' precarious position as the British advanced into the backcountry and implored Earl Cornwallis to respect the Catawba land claims and to protect their neutrality during the occupation. Despite his attempts to protect their interests, the ensuing civil conflict left the Catawbas uprooted and destitute. Following his return from exile, Kershaw immediately sought aid for the state's Indian allies. As an elected official, he arranged for the provision of food and goods. Beginning in the winter of 1782, the General Assembly empowered the governor to contract with Samuel Mathis & Co. to furnish corn, blankets, cloth, and other supplies to the Catawbas in compensation for their service. The state also authorized renting reservation lands to whites as a source of tribal income and established schools on their lands.[85] Throughout the following decade, Kershaw played a central role in relations with the Catawbas, delivering supplies, advising them on relations with their white neighbors, and defending their treaty rights. He encouraged them to be wary of squatters on their lands and to employ the services of an agent to handle their financial affairs. When white renters failed to make payments, he brought the Catawbas' case before the legislature and continued to represent their interests for the remainder of his life.[86]

Changes in the emerging backcountry economy further affected the Catawbas, now dependent on the Americans as protectors, suppliers of cash and goods, and consumers of Native products. The Indians adapted to the new order by solidifying their image as friendly, acculturated, and productive Indians. They adopted republican elements, such as substituting elected for hereditary leadership, expressed openness to Christian missionaries, and expanded their manufacture of ceramics for trade. But their reduced numbers and proximity to settlers had left them poverty-stricken and denigrated. "In common with every other Indian tribe in proximity to the whites," wrote a contemporary traveler, "they exhibited a melancholy picture of the singular and fatal ravages of the vices, with which they have become contaminated from an association with their civilized neighbors." South Carolina lumped the Catawbas legally with other free persons of color, a designation that left them socially marginal in the new state. Although their status continued to alienate the Catawbas from the larger society, by keeping them apart it helped them retain their cultural identity in an altered world.[87]

Deprived of their traditional livelihood, the Catawbas relied on two strategies to meet their economic needs: renting their reservation lands and expanding their production of ceramics. Despite the passage of federal legislation in 1790 that forbade the lease or alienation of Indian lands, the State of South Carolina allowed the regulated leasing of Catawba lands. Renting lands to white farmers was a lucrative source of income for the Catawba people, and it became increasingly central to their subsistence, but it threatened to deprive them of their domain if it continued unabated. When defaulting tenants and trespassers placed their traditional estate in jeopardy, the Catawbas petitioned the state for assistance. This provided some relief but failed to halt the onslaught and only delayed the ultimate loss of most of their lands.[88]

Long the makers of ceramics for a wider market, the Catawbas adapted to meet the needs of customers following the Revolution. In a new economy characterized by the increasing availability of inexpensive imported tablewares, Catawba potters expanded their production to include food storage and preparation vessels. Archaeological investigations at the postwar Catawba towns have revealed evidence of this growth in ceramic manufacturing. Excavations uncovered tools and clay-curing facilities associated with large scale pottery-making, as well as waster dumps with the discarded sherds of the vast array of jars, bowls, plates, bottles, cups, handled pots, and other forms made for sale to outsiders. By the early nineteenth century these wares were in great demand on plantations, and itinerant Catawba potters regularly traveled as far as the lowcountry to supply the region's needs. The pottery trade served a wider political purpose beyond just generating cash income. As an indigenous industry with deep roots in the country's unsettled past, the manufacturing of such distinctive wares helped maintain a public awareness of the Catawbas' existence and came to symbolize the survival of a resilient Native people continually faced with absorption by the wider society.[89]

Camden Rebounds

The political consolidation of the backcountry and its slow but steady economic resurgence in decades following the Revolution fostered the rebirth of the region's chief settlement. Fortified as a military strongpoint, abused by an occupying army, and hastily abandoned as the British retreated, Camden had been devastated by the war. Although much of the town apparently survived the war intact, its mills and industrial structures had been damaged or destroyed, and many of its buildings had suffered injury at the hands of the resident garrison and the legions of American troops that had passed through Camden before and after the occupation. The war had been less kind to structures on the margins of the nucleated settlement. Soldiers had torn down the Presbyterian meetinghouse for building material, and, as Green's army approached in April 1781, Camden's defenders had destroyed all the buildings outside the ring of redoubts to provide open fields of fire around the town. They also had burned Thomas Charlton's plantation northeast of town and set fire to the buildings in Logtown along the Catawba Path. Camden survived the war, but it was only a shadow of the earlier town.[90]

Camden's central role in commerce and its position in the state's administrative structure fueled its slow recovery, and visitors described the town's emergence in the postwar years. An American officer described conditions shortly after the British retreat, remarking that "there is not more than a dozen houses [that] can be occupied, the remainder either being totally demolished, or so much [w]recked by the British that the[y] are abandoned by their owners."[91] Two years later a visitor, J. F. D. Smyth, found that Camden was again "a place of considerable commerce," but the jurist and planter William Drayton noted that the town still bore "marks of the British having been here."[92] David Humphreys found Camden still a small village in the late 1780s, containing fewer buildings than Augusta, Georgia's inland center of trade on the Savannah River. He believed, however, that Camden's houses were "larger and better built," a sentiment shared by the Lutheran missionary Arnold Roschen, who also remarked on their "handsome" architecture. Both estimated that the town contained from thirty to fifty dwellings, indicating a slow but steady growth in the first decade of peace.[93] The next ten years saw Camden expand rapidly from the approximately 70 buildings described by the traveler William Loughton Smith in 1791 to the 120 recorded by the geographer Jedidiah Morse at mid-decade. Morse also revealed that Camden was South Carolina's third largest settlement, behind only Charleston and Georgetown. Gov. John Drayton's account estimated that Camden contained two hundred dwellings in 1802. Camden was recognized as by far the most substantial town in the interior, and its size reflected its importance as an economic and administrative center.[94]

Camden grew along the plan laid out in 1771, a design that accommodated the rapid expansion of the postwar town. Both Morse and John Drayton commented on Camden's regular layout, "with streets intersecting others at right angles [and] having a large square in the center."[95] The established grid determined the placement of the new jail, courthouse, and market as well as the arrangement of commercial and residential structures, but the distribution of new buildings in the closing years of the century also reveals that the town was expanding beyond its former limits. Following the British evacuation, residents reoccupied much of the old town, reclaiming and repairing many of the surviving structures. Situated on the blocks immediately south of the town square, Adamson's and Kershaw's stores, the brewery, and associated structures as well as other buildings along Broad Street formed the nucleus of the new town. As Camden grew, however, settlement did not spread outward in all directions but rather pushed north along the Catawba Path toward Logtown, where several stores were erected. The areas to either side of the old town remained undeveloped. Joseph Kershaw's mansion stood alone east of town looking down on a vacant field that served as a muster ground (Fig. 11.4). The remains of the British redoubts that once surrounded the fortified town were still in evidence in the spring of 1791, when President

11.4 The Kershaw mansion and vicinity in antebellum times. Camden now lay to the north of the old town site on Magazine Hill, and the broad expanse in front of the mansion served as a muster ground for militia units that assembled there on parade. The old house became a grandstand where spectators gathered to watch the festivities on the Fourth of July and other patriotic occasions. Courtesy of Historic Camden Foundation, Camden, South Carolina.

George Washington visited Camden and noted their presence. Indeed, they were still discernible a half-century later.[96]

By the early nineteenth century, most new settlement in Camden lay north of the old square, although several residences and businesses still occupied the original town site. Sarah Thompson Alexander, a contemporary resident, provided perhaps the most complete picture of Camden in 1800 in a reminiscence penned at mid-century. She recalled that the "Blue House," the office and residence of her husband, Dr. Isaac Alexander, lay on the west side of Broad Street facing John Dinkins's tavern. Farther north, John Adamson's house and store lay west of the square, while to the east the store and residence of Joseph Mickle and the houses of J. Brown, Samuel Mathis, and Abram Blanding, a lawyer, all faced the old square. "From Blanding's corner up to the court house, on each side of the street, [were] stores and private buildings closely connected," and the town was "closely built up" as far as York Street. Residents placed a public pump on the square, and as early as 1791 a market building stood at the public market. Far to the east of the town's built-up area, the "old Kershaw house" was the sole structure on the distant hill. Elizabeth Thornton also lived in postwar Camden. Late in life, the widow of the merchant and postmaster Phinehas Thornton recalled the Presbyterian church at the foot of Church Street, built in the 1780s on the site of the earlier meetinghouse. James Kershaw's sketch map of Camden in 1811 showed the blocks south of the great square largely vacant. It situated Samuel Mathis's store and house

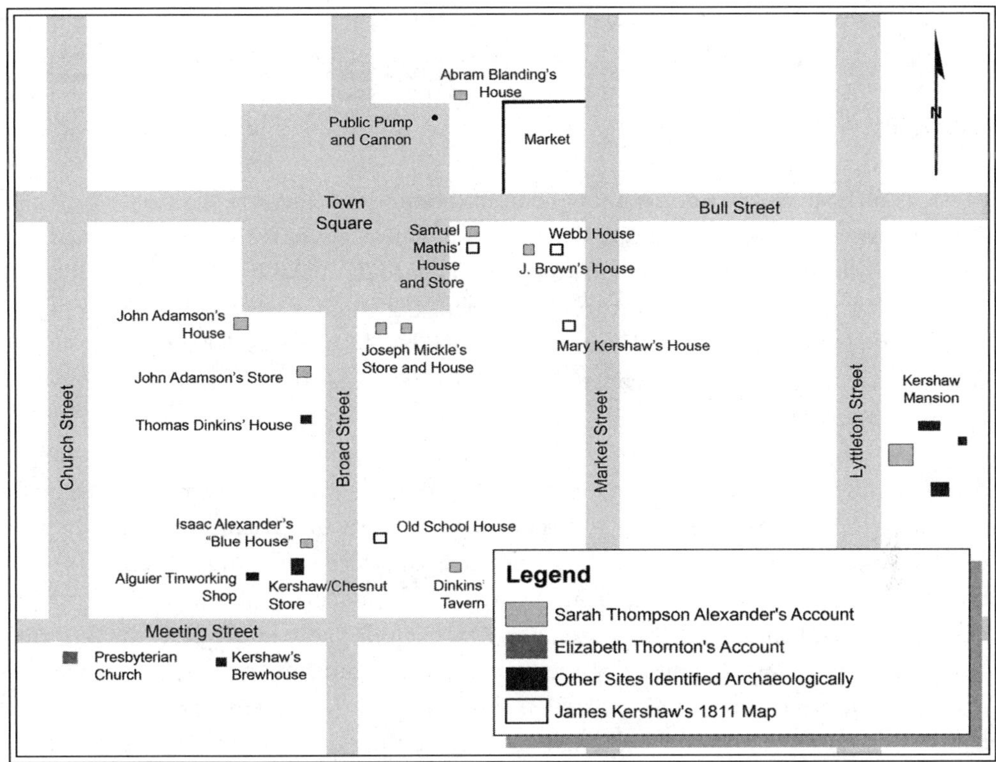

11.5 Structures on the site of the original settlement of Camden ca. 1800, based on contemporary accounts, public records, reminiscences, and archaeological evidence. Author's original map.

and the Webb house on the south side of Bull Street as well as Mary Kershaw's house on the west side of Market Street. Farther south, on the east side of Broad Street stood the "old school house." This structure is likely associated with the "old school lot" behind it facing Market Street and may be the "Red House," a dwelling that had served as a "boarding house for young ladies" prior to 1786 (Fig. 11.5). Other documents reveal that the brewhouse, though perhaps no longer in use, still stood as late as 1803.[97] Archaeological investigations have discovered architectural evidence of several structures that persisted to the end of the century as well. They include both Adamson's buildings and Dinkins's tavern, the Kershaw store and the brewhouse, as well as the Blue House. The discovery of Gayeton Aiguier's tin-working shop near the store testifies to the property's continued use following its sale by the Kershaw family. Architectural remains north of the Blue House may be those of Thomas Dinkins's residence.[98]

Camden's postwar appearance reflected its place in the commercial economy of a region that had completed the transition from its frontier roots. The geographer Judith Schulz's analysis of deed records and other sources shows that by the mid-1790s the town's business section had grown north past the courthouse and jail to fill the block south of King Street. The intersection of Broad and King Streets became the center of the town's business district, surrounded by fashionable residences. John Chesnut's new town house lay nearby at the corner of King and Fair Streets. As one of the finest dwellings of the postwar period, it reflected the economic success and the social ascendency of the planter and civic leader who hosted President George Washington during his 1791 visit to Camden. Other residences lined Broad Street north as far as the causeway that crossed a low marsh north of York Street, the northern town boundary shown on the 1771 plat. Settlement also began to spread east and west along York Street. In 1798 a legislative act, accompanied by a new survey, formally extended the town's boundaries to double the size of the original settlement (Fig. 11.6). In 1801 the construction of the "Big Ditch" drained the marsh and permitted settlement to extend farther north. Camden had become a substantial town by the early nineteenth century, one whose composition reflected its function as an important trading center and court town.[99]

The rising agricultural economy of the new century supported an increasing number of businesses whose diversity stood in marked contrast to the limited array of enterprises that characterized Camden's settlement period. The variety of offerings went far beyond a narrow range of basic services to include the offices of both lawyers and physicians, several taverns, and specialized retailers, including boot- and shoemakers, a silversmith, a watchmaker, a printer, a tailor, and a hatmaker. Retailing exploded after 1810. Nearly thirty dealers advertised general merchandise, dry goods, or groceries. Gunsmiths, saddlers, confectioners, bakers, jewelers, bookbinders, glaziers, milliners, druggists, dancing school masters, hairdressers, and purveyors of "fancy goods" offered their wares and services in Camden. Makers of cotton gins, cabinets, and furniture found business in the town, which now boasted two hotels.[100] The postwar jail underwent repairs and improvements in the 1790s to address its deteriorated state, and it was relocated in the 1810s to make room for a new town market.[101]

Camden maintained its wide political presence in the new state. The town served as an election site for representatives of the District Eastward of Wateree, and in 1788 it was considered briefly as a temporary state capital, pending the completion of the public buildings at Columbia. Although Camden never rose above the level of a county seat, its influence as an urban center was much broader, and the Assembly recognized its role in the winter of 1791 by passing an act of incorporation. This legislation was significant in that it made Camden the first inland town in South Carolina to achieve this designation, and it was only the second municipality after Charleston. Its new status officially established a town government, vesting Camden's administration in an elected intendant and wardens for each of four wards.[102]

Camden's shift to a commercial economy and the expansion of its service sector were closely intertwined with an influx of immigrants following the Revolution. Many newcomers were small farmers, driven out of Virginia, Maryland, and Pennsylvania by declining prices for tobacco and grain and by shortages of land, but business prospects also attracted planters, who perceived opportunities for success in the developing South Carolina backcountry.[103] Camden's increasing urban role also attracted those engaged in trade, specialized production, and professional services. Some, like the merchants Paul Francis Villepigue and Pierre Laurent Jumelle and the tinworker Gayeton Aiguier, found refuge in Camden after fleeing the slave revolt in Saint Domingue, but others migrated here to open new

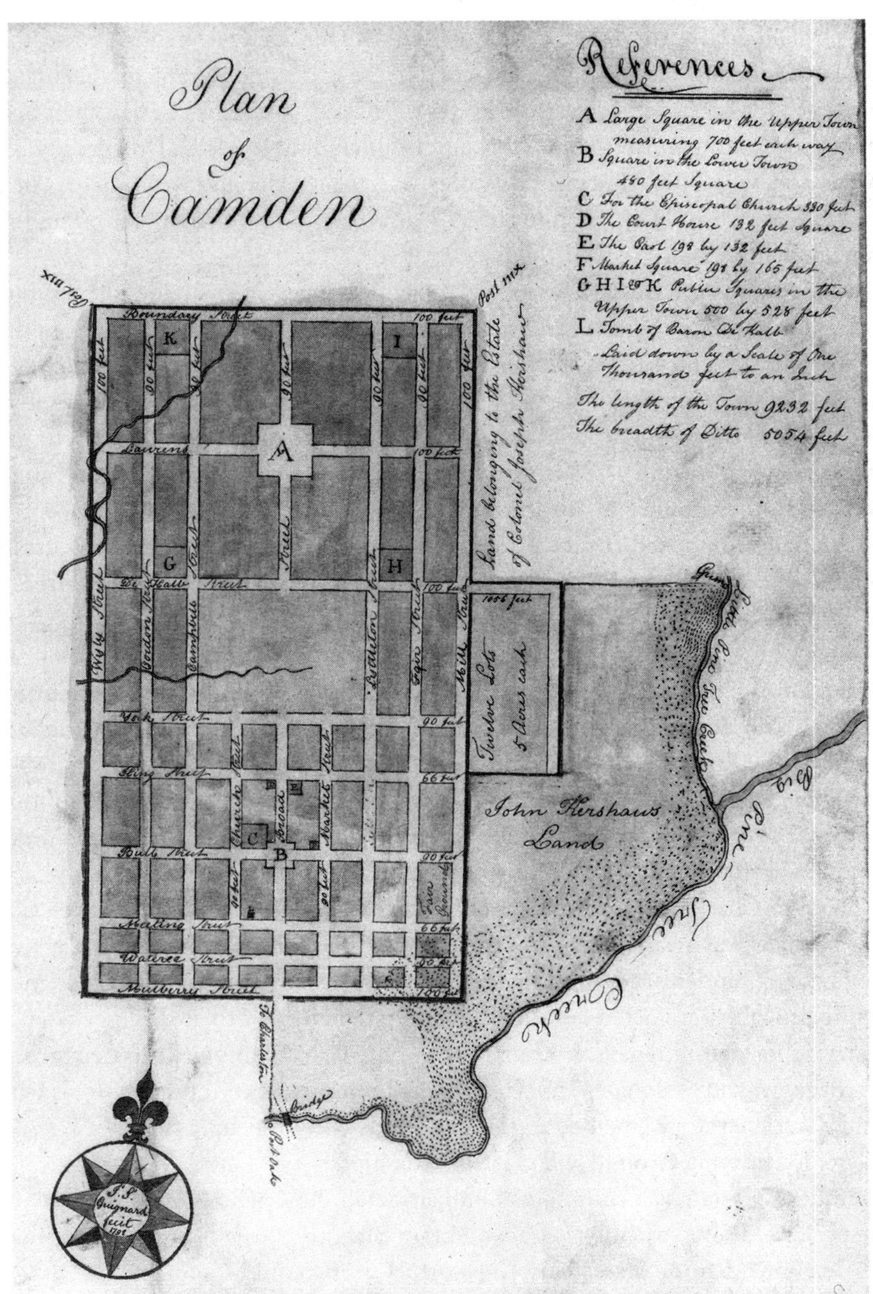

11.6 The 1798 plan of Camden extended the boundaries of the town northward, more than doubling its area. The plan retained the grid pattern of the earlier survey as well as the lots set aside for public facilities. It also created five new public squares in the upper town. The "big ditch" had yet to drain the marsh between York and DeKalb Streets, and the course of Broad Street remained unsurveyed. In the lower town, DeKalb's gravesite lay on the north side of Meeting Street just west of Broad. Some of the extensive landholdings of the Kershaw family east of Camden are also noted. Courtesy of South Carolina Department of Archives and History, Columbia, South Carolina, Series S-213192, Vol. 37, p. 146.

markets.[104] Gilbert Thornton moved to Camden with his family from New Jersey, followed by his son Phinehas. His daughters married three other immigrant merchants, Daniel Carpenter of Massachusetts, Jonathan Eccles of Ireland, and James L. Clarke of Scotland. Several other Scots merchants came to Camden, including James K. Douglas and Alexander Matheson, who opened dry goods stores, and the jeweler and watchmaker Alexander Young. Others, such as Daniel White and William Hutchinson, also carried on trade briefly in Camden before 1800.[105]

The late eighteenth century witnessed the appearance of a small Jewish community in Camden. Jews were among the earliest settlers in South Carolina, first arriving in the closing years of the seventeenth century. As merchants and shopkeepers, they thrived in the relatively tolerant political climate of the province and gravitated to its urban center. Most resided in Charleston, where their numbers grew sufficiently to permit them to organize a formal congregation and establish synagogues, cemeteries, social service organizations, schools, and other important institutions by the middle of the eighteenth century. Although initially composed largely of Sephardic Jews of Iberian ancestry, the Charleston community increasingly attracted Ashkenazic elements from other parts of Europe around the time of the Revolution.[106]

Among the Ashkenazim were Samuel Levy and Mordecai Lyon, who came from Germany and Poland, respectively. Both arrived in Charleston as sutlers during the British occupation but subsequently shifted their sympathies to the American cause. In the turbulent aftermath of the Revolution, when state authorities investigated the loyalty of many who remained in business in the occupied capital, both were exonerated of collaboration with the British. Following the war, Levy and Lyon extended their mercantile activities to the backcountry. Both became permanent residents of Camden. Moses Sarzedas, a pharmacist, immigrated to Charleston from Savannah, Georgia, in 1790 and later moved to Camden. Joseph Kershaw was aware of a nascent Jewish community in Camden in the 1780s. Most of the Jews in Camden were likely fellow merchants, shopkeepers, or businessmen with whom he probably interacted, although the precise nature of their dealings is unknown. Kershaw also recognized that the permanence of a Jewish community was tied to establishing a synagogue and a cemetery, its two principal central institutions, and in his will, written in the summer of 1788, he bequeathed to "God's antient People the Jews . . . Lot 315 in Camden for a burying Ground and place of Worship."[107]

Camden's growth as a commercial hub attracted those who offered professional and other specialized services. The attorneys Abram Blanding, Joseph Brevard, and Benjamin Perkins emigrated from Massachusetts, North Carolina, and Connecticut, respectively. The town acquired three physicians, John A. Trent from New Jersey, William Blanding, who followed his brother from Massachusetts, and Isaac Alexander, who returned to the settlement where he had treated the mortally wounded Gen. DeKalb in 1780.[108] The Rev. Thomas Adams, a graduate of Harvard College, came to Camden as pastor of the Presbyterian congregation in 1789. Richard Champion was an English merchant and potter from Bristol who had pioneered the development of English porcelain. But his unpopular political views and financial reverses led him to America, and he resettled his family north of Camden in 1784.[109] The development of trade also attracted planters with wealth to invest in agricultural production. Among them was Adam Fowler Brisbane, son of Dr. William

Brisbane of Charleston, a wealthy merchant, pharmaceutical dealer, and planter. Having inherited his father's estate, Brisbane purchased substantial property in the Wateree Valley and Camden, where he settled after the war. William Ancrum II, nephew and namesake of the founding merchant, inherited his uncle's extensive backcountry estate and settled in Camden, where he married Brisbane's daughter Elizabeth.[110]

The influx of newcomers enhanced the variety and tempo of activities in Camden, reflecting its role as a rising urban center. But the fabric of society in the new town still looked to its prewar roots, and recent immigrants sought to blend into the social structure that had emerged from the earlier frontier experience. Many elite families were allied by blood, and newer arrivals often joined the establishment through marriage. Benjamin Perkins married Joseph Kershaw's daughter Sarah, and Joseph Brevard wed Rebecca Kershaw, the child of the founder's brother Ely. Dr. Isaac Alexander took Amelia Adamson, daughter of the forgiven Loyalist John Adamson, as his second wife, and Mary DuBose, whose father, Isaac, was a substantial planter, married first Dr. John Trent and subsequently R. L. Champion, son of the noted ceramicist.[111] Establishing affinal ties helped bind those who composed Camden's new class of planters, artisans, shopkeepers, and professionals to the network of merchants and agriculturists who had preceded them in the Wateree Valley.

But Camden's residents old and new entered a world different from that of the recent frontier. The official political and economic institutions that accompanied the region's development had begun to transform life in the backcountry, increasingly replacing the networks of kinship and association around which pioneer settlers had organized society, production, and trade. Formal courts oversaw disputes and promoted security; goods and produce traveled on roads and waterways maintained by the state; regulated fairs and markets facilitated regional commerce; a municipal government now oversaw Camden's administration and development; constitutional reforms restructured the political divisions of the interior and brought increased representation of backcountry interests in the state legislature; state inspectors oversaw the quality of tobacco; and South Carolina's new capital shifted central government to the backcountry. Religious organizations had always played a central role in community organization and now expanded their influence as denominations became more systematic and structured. Formal education came to Camden with the appearance of private schools, the most notable of which opened under the auspices of the Camden Orphan Society in 1791.[112] Although their influence had begun to pervade all aspects of society, the new institutions failed to diminish the role played by bonds of blood and affinity. Family ties continued to matter in a world dominated by plantation agriculture. On a still largely rural landscape, large and small farmers constituted an integrated agrarian community, one that was characterized by an unequal distribution of wealth but linked through the interdependency between the elites and those upon whose labor and services they depended. Thus the ties that had served to connect individuals in the diverse and eclectic society of the frontier remained, but the strategies that forged these bonds were dramatically reshaped by the region's new commercial orientation.[113] As South Carolina entered the new century, the expansion of plantation agriculture enmeshed the backcountry firmly within the capitalist economy of antebellum America, an entity whose structure had already altered a world that was still within living memory.

Chapter 12

"A New Generation and a New Town"

In his lifetime Phinehas Thornton witnessed Camden's rise from the ashes of the Revolutionary War and its emergence as a county seat in a stable world far removed from the frontier of the previous century. Now Camden was a central place on a landscape dominated by plantation agriculture. Cotton replaced wheat as the staple crop. As an urban center in a still largely rural region, Camden continued to be a focus of processing and transportation, but one linked more closely to the larger world by increasingly efficient transportation and more complex marketing arrangements that enmeshed it in a wealthy and dynamic national economy. By the second decade of the nineteenth century, the rise of a planter elite in the backcountry brought the interests of the region's leaders closer to those of their counterparts in the lowcountry, a trend that united the regions and facilitated the state's political integration. Although the inequities inherent in the increasingly hierarchical nature of society in antebellum South Carolina produced contradictions that reflected larger political and economic tensions, these stresses were ameliorated by a republican ideology that united small farmers and plantation owners. The political landscape it created emphasized their mutual interests, diminished the inherent conflicts between them, and sanctioned the use of unfree labor in production. The common purpose it espoused brought a stability that was underlain by the economic success of an efficient and profitable, if distinctive, system of capitalist agriculture.[1] Camden became part of the new order so completely during Thornton's fifty-seven years residence that he felt he had witnessed "a new generation and a new town, sprung up in that time."[2]

The evolving world of antebellum South Carolina brought changes that many contemporary observers believed physically separated Camden from its past and its residents from their traditions. Writing at mid-century, Sarah Thompson Alexander observed, "Change is the irrecov[er]able decree of all beneath the Sun, but in no small place perhaps do you see so great a change in a small community as here." She recalled with sadness how the old town site was abandoned. "About the year 1817, a spirit of migration began to agitate the houses," she wrote. "Sickness had driven the inhabitants to seek out summer resorts and the buildings took a notion they would not be left behind. So one moon light night they started up to Logtown." Soon the old site was empty, abandoned "for the benefit of the planters. Should anyone curious in the matters of antiquity set out to find the Camden of Revolutionary memory," she continued, "they would be badly disappointed, for not a vestige now remains of that once memorable city." A new and much larger Camden, whose business center lay nearly a mile to the north, had replaced the colonial settlement. Situated on higher, healthier ground and connected to the outside world by roads and water routes and later by railroads and the telegraph, Camden became part of a new world in which rapid communications and the increasing availability of investment capital quickened the pace of marketing activity and promoted growth. Mid-century Camden flourished in the expanding cotton economy, and to many older residents the town seemed to have abandoned its past.[3]

Mrs. Alexander went on to remind her readers of the loss of traditional values. She emphasized how recent changes had altered not only the physical world but also perceptions of it. "Steam cars or telegraph were never dreamt of, cows grazed quietly in their pastures without disturbance from the whistle or fear of being crushed beneath the wheels, and people were content to travel in the stage to Charleston at a rate of three miles an hour, . . . happy if they got there in a week with life and whole bones." Earlier residents, she believed, had sacrificed for the common good, were practical in dress and frugal in their wants, polite in their discourse, honest, trusting, and with limited disagreement in politics. "So recently escaped from a common danger [and] all perfectly satisfied with a government of their own creation, they felt secure in the present and [had] no fears for the future." While nostalgia may have softened her recollections of a bygone era that was certainly not without discord, the world of Sarah Alexander's past must have seemed much less divisive than the current one racked by economic uncertainties and political dissension that threatened the union. Market fluctuations affecting cotton and external competition for rice, coupled with the depression that followed the Panic of 1837, created uncertainties in South Carolina's specialized agricultural economy, and the state's growing and increasingly contentious involvement in the national debate over tariffs, abolition, and other issues presented a disquieting picture of internal disunity.[4]

A Rage for Emigration

Sarah Alexander and Phinehas Thornton lived through a time in which the agricultural economy of South Carolina's backcountry became a victim of its own success. The "utilitarian age" that accompanied the rise of cotton favored specialized production centered on this staple, a strategy that brought prosperity to both large and small cotton growers who were all tied to the larger market economy. As a result, productivity became paramount to farmers and planters, who continuously cropped lands to maximize profits.[5] Such a non-sustainable practice rapidly depleted soil fertility, and, as the size of crops declined, many planters abandoned older lands and moved their operations to newly opened territories to the West. A contemporary observer wrote, "the whole country about the Wateree and Congaree, including Columbia, is literally breaking up and moving en masse to the west." Kershaw County was taken with the "restless, moving spirit" and suffered substantial population loss as residents left for the new country. In the winter of 1834 an article in the *Camden Journal* proclaimed that "The rage for emigration southwesterly has . . . increased in the past year beyond all calculation." Its editor reported witnessing caravans of as many as two hundred persons leaving the county in a single day. In one week the following year as many as eight hundred people, both blacks and whites, passed through Camden. To older residents these losses were "so great as to make one melancholy," but emigrants' motivations made it clear that optimism rather than despair drove them to abandon their farms to seek improved circumstances as commercial farmers in the West. Far from the restive "poorer class," of destitute people envisioned by Mrs. Alexander, most who left were established residents whose resources would have enabled them "to live comfortably anywhere," people who clearly saw the decision to migrate as an entrepreneurial enterprise, an opportunity to expand production and increase their wealth by acquiring part of the extensive public domain and the substantial resources it offered.[6]

Slowed only by the Panic of 1837 and the subsequent slump in the cotton market, the out-migration from South Carolina continued throughout the antebellum period. Although many emigrants were of moderate means, the movement also included representatives of successful families who sought to increase their wealth by extending their operations to new lands. John Chesnut's daughter Margaret accompanied her husband, John Deas, to Alabama in 1835, the state that also became home to Mary Camber Brisbane, daughter of the planter Adam Fowler Brisbane, and her husband, Samuel Nettles, son of the Revolutionary War veteran and pioneer settler Capt. William Nettles. Two of Francis Boykin's children, Eliza and Samuel, moved to Milledgeville, Georgia, as did James Cantey, the wartime opponent and later protector of his uncle Daniel McGirt. Benjamin Haile, whose Lynches River property had recently yielded deposits of gold ore sufficient to ensure his family's financial future, nevertheless lost three sons who emigrated south with their families to acquire lands in the vicinity of Gainesville, Florida.[7]

The rapid out-migration of residents impacted the growth and composition of South Carolina's population in several ways. The loss of white residents occurred throughout the antebellum period. White emigrants totaled twenty times the number of white settlers who came into the state in 1850 alone. Two decades earlier the movement of farm families and the children of planters seeking opportunities to the West had already reversed the previously steady growth in Kershaw County's white population, and at mid-century whites constituted only a third of the county's residents. In contrast, the African American population continued to rise after 1830, despite the loss of an unknown number of slaves who moved with their owners. The need for labor to sustain the growth of plantation production increased the proportion of blacks in Kershaw County, and they were almost 68 percent of the population in 1850 (Table 12.1). The demographic shift in Kershaw County's population completed the process of settlement begun a century earlier.[8]

Are You Going to Winnsboro Fair? A Narrower Role in the New Economy

Camden's emergence as an economic and administrative center was tied to access. Just as its trade and communications networks opened the backcountry, they maintained the antebellum commerce of the interior. Trade drew the backcountry into the wider economy, and the town's paramount position attracted additional services and activities that made it the logical choice to become the seat of the Camden District Court in 1769. Five years later the town's proprietors gained permission to hold a biannual fair at Camden, officially sanctioning their management of exchange. As a key settlement in the interior, Camden attracted

Table 12.1. Composition of the Population of Kershaw District, 1820–1850

Date of Census	Free White	Free and Enslaved Colored	Totals
Population Totals			
1820	5,628	6,804	12,432
1830	5,016	8,529	13,545
1840	3,988	8,293	12,281
1850	4,681	9,792	14,773
Population Percentages			
1820	45.3%	54.7%	100%
1830	37.0%	63%	100%
1840	32.5%	67.5%	100%
1850	32.3%	67.7%	100%

Source: Julian J. Petty, *The Growth and Distribution of Population in South Carolina* (Columbia: South Carolina State Planning Board, 1943; reprint ed., Spartanburg, S.C.: The Reprint Co., 1975), 226–229

emerging public institutions and became the state's second incorporated municipality. But the process that led to Camden's rise as a key frontier settlement also set in motion changes that diminished the scope of its role. As the backcountry matured, access improved, and services once only available at Camden came to other settlements as well.

Camden remained a regional center but no longer occupied the paramount position of earlier years. Its role as the region's major trading center had already begun to fade when Kershaw & Co. dissolved in the 1770s. Aware of the opportunities offered by commercial agriculture in the backcountry, the partners deliberately shifted their resources from trade to planting and processing. As new firms arose to carry out trade across the region, the institutions that oversaw its organization became more formalized. Camden's fair was the only officially regulated market in the backcountry before the Revolution, but by 1785 three other interior communities successfully petitioned to hold fairs. Markets opened at Belleville, near McCord's Ferry on the Congaree; at Greenville on the Long Bluff of the Pee Dee; and at Winnsborough, west of the Wateree. Virtually surrounding Camden, these locales provided alternate venues for exchange that effectively limited the range of the older town's retail trade. The new regional markets offered a potentially wide variety of goods for sale, as witnessed by the petition of the merchants John and Richard Winn. Seeking a market at their namesake town, the brothers anticipated that a fair would "expose for sale horses, cattle, grain, hemp, flax, tobacco, indigo, and all sorts of produce and merchandize."[9]

The expansion of internal improvements in the 1820s promoted Columbia's rise as the marketing center of the interior (Fig. 12.1). Improvements in river navigation and the construction of canals expedited bulk commodity shipping to Charleston via the Santee River system and extended commerce well beyond the head-of-navigation of its major tributaries. The new canals extended trade on the upper Wateree above Camden and opened the extensive western country drained by the Broad and Saluda Rivers. Situated at the center of

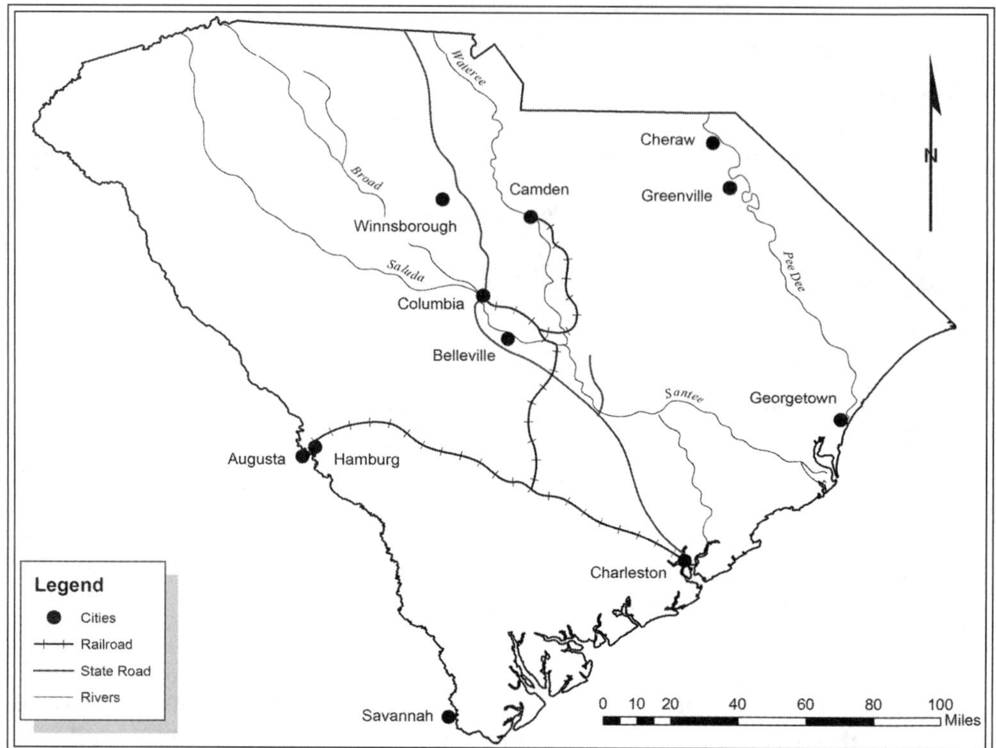

12.1 Improvements in overland transportation ensured the dominance of Columbia in commerce. The State Road passed directly through the capital, as did the trunk line of the railroad, leaving Camden at the end of a branch. Author's original map.

the vast interior drainage, Columbia and its trade benefited greatly from such public works. A new State Road, or turnpike, connecting the settlements of the upper Piedmont with Charleston also passed through the capital but left Camden on the sideline. In the 1830s lowcountry interests constructed a railroad line as far inland as Hamburg, across from Augusta, bypassing Savannah and extending Charleston's economic hinterland well up the Savannah River drainage. In the following decade, the tracks of the South Carolina Railroad entered the central interior. Camden's business interests attempted to draw the line toward the Wateree Valley, but despite their efforts they were unable to prevail over those in the capital, and the line was completed to Columbia in 1842. Only six years later did a branch of the railroad reach Camden.[10] By mid-century the capital had become South Carolina's largest inland town.[11]

The transportation system connected Camden and other inland towns ever more closely in the postwar era, but the expanding network of overland routes brought increased competition for trade territory and reduced the role of each settlement in the larger economy. Nowhere is this phenomenon better illustrated than in the development of the United States postal system. American postal officials saw the mail service as crucial to binding society and integrating the new nation's economy and planned a system capable of linking

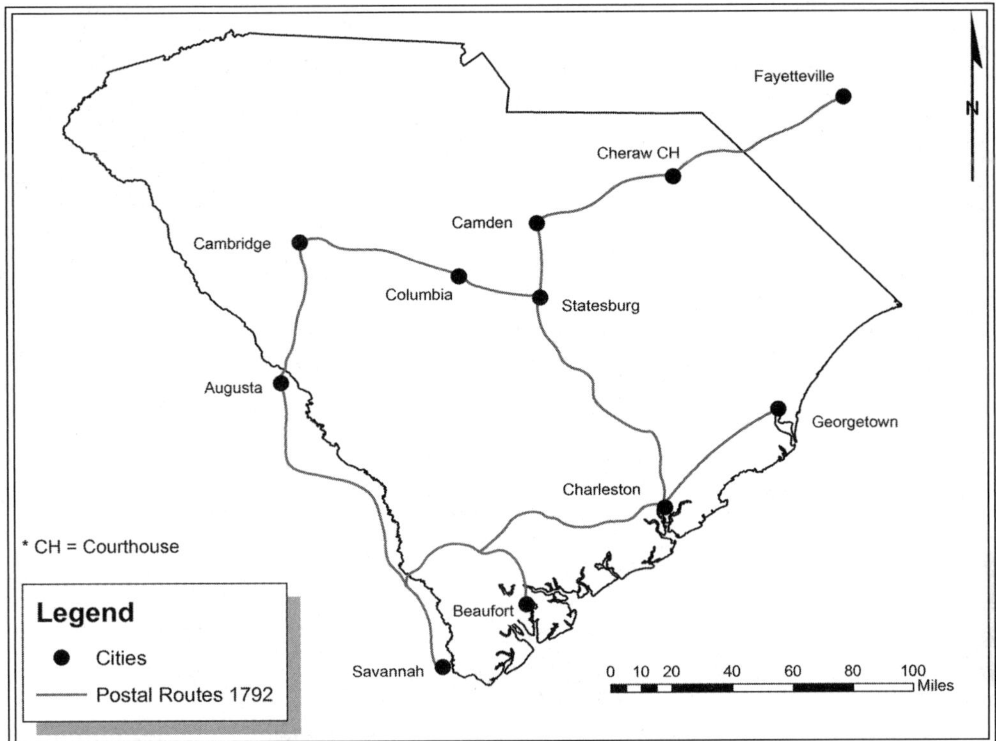

12.2 The expansion of federal postal routes into South Carolina's interior in 1792 recognized Camden's central position in the overland road network and linked the town directly to the interior postal route from the north. Author's original map adapted from Harvey S. Teal and Robert J. Stets, *South Carolina Postal History and Illustrated Catalog of Postmarks, 1760–1860* (Lake Oswego, Ore.: Raven Press, 1989), 17.

its settlements.[12] Initially the state's residents could send and receive official mail only at the coastal ports of Charleston and Georgetown, but in 1792 the postal service employed the earlier dendritic transportation pattern of routes to enter the interior. Proceeding up the Santee drainage from Charleston, the principal route divided just above the confluence of the Congaree and Wateree Rivers, with its two branches passing through Camden and Columbia (Fig. 12.2). But within five years, this route centered on the new capital. By 1810 the pattern of postal routes radiated outward in all directions from Columbia to link most of the interior settlements with one another (Fig. 12.3). Fewer links to smaller centers such as Camden reflected the towns' reduced hinterlands.[13]

Camden's role as a regional center was manifested by the courthouse and jail, state institutions that now provided services at county level. In 1826 a fine new courthouse replaced the deteriorating structure built after the war. The noted architect Robert Mills, South Carolina's superintendent of public buildings, designed the imposing Greek Revival structure, one of twenty-one county courthouses and jails built or rehabilitated by the state.[14] Public funds also enhanced Camden's role as a commercial center. The state erected

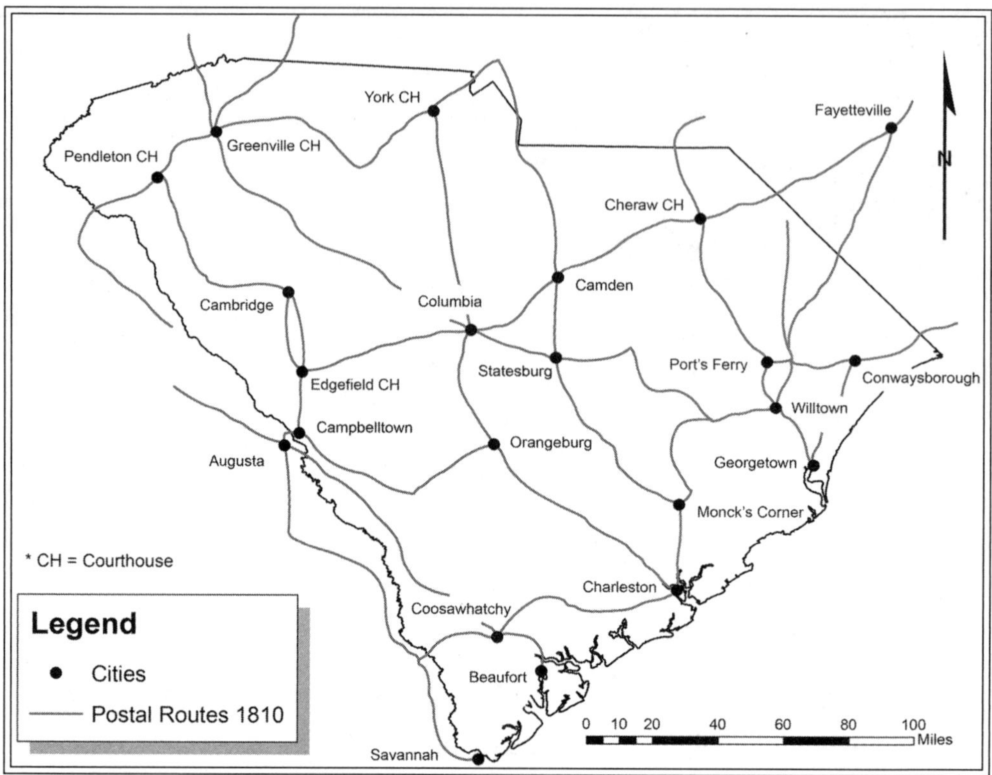

12.3 By 1810 the network of postal routes had expanded to connect all parts of South Carolina. Although Camden possessed direct connections with points in all directions, including the capital, Columbia had become the focus of the state's mail system. Author's original map adapted from Harvey S. Teal and Robert J. Stets, *South Carolina Postal History and Illustrated Catalog of Postmarks, 1760–1860* (Lake Oswego, Ore.: Raven Press, 1989), 30.

a structure to house Camden's market as early as 1791, and when a fire destroyed the building in 1812, the legislature responded by authorizing the construction of a replacement. Opened in 1816, an "elegant brick market and library room" rested on the site of the old jail, which was relocated elsewhere in the town.[15]

Camden was home to other public institutions as well. In 1822 it became one of four county seats to house branches of the Bank of South Carolina. A quasi-official fiscal agency of the state, the bank supported commercial interests, and its interior branches financed the activities of merchants and planters.[16] Camden was also among the few interior towns to acquire educational institutions. Despite backcountry residents' early interest in providing public schools, South Carolina began to fund them only in 1811, leaving nearly all education still in private hands. Local organizations arose to sponsor schools in the interior, and as early as the 1770s the legislature gave official sanction to the first of several academies.[17] Among the most successful of these was the Camden Orphan Society, which began operation in 1791. Supported by tuition as well as by county funding, this academy operated at various locations throughout the antebellum period, augmented by several private schools that opened for shorter periods.[18]

Churches remained one of the most important institutions and grew as formal organizations in antebellum Camden. The appearance of church buildings emphasized religion's role as a key element in the town's social structure. Immediately after the war, the Presbyterians replaced the destroyed building at the foot of Church Street and formally organized as the Bethesda congregation in 1805. The church's rapid expansion brought the need for a larger sanctuary, which was constructed seven years later on DeKalb Street just east of Camden's emerging business district. Camden's Methodists erected a house of worship on King Street before 1804, but their growing congregation also moved north to a larger structure on DeKalb Street in 1828. The Baptists built a church at the corner of York and Market Streets in 1809 and organized a congregation the following year. Like the other denominations, it outgrew its early building, and the congregation moved to a new location on Broad Street north of DeKalb in 1836. Although the Episcopalian denomination was tainted by its affiliation with the Church of England, its adherents eventually organized in Camden. They formed Grace Church congregation in 1830 and erected a church on Broad Street below DeKalb two years later.[19] As local expressions of larger denominational organizations, Camden's churches grew out of the community, whose members supported them and oversaw their administration. Like other formal institutions in the changing backcountry, they now served areas circumscribed by the town's decreased sphere of influence.

"My Own Dear Town"

Despite its diminished status, Camden remained distinctive. Now an antebellum county seat, the town settled into the role of a regional center whose once extensive influence had waned and whose focus had turned inward. But it was more than another central settlement on a landscape dominated by the commercial economy of cotton. Although now submerged in a web of multiple ties to the larger world, Camden enjoyed a heritage that distinguished it from its contemporaries. In a state always conscious of its history and the events that had shaped its past, residents still recalled Camden as the hub of frontier trade in South Carolina's interior and as the settlement at the eye of the revolutionary storm in the eastern backcountry. Throughout the nineteenth century published accounts repeated a narrative centered on the dual themes of frontier economic development and wartime adversity and heroism.

As the central figure in the expansion of backcountry trade and the embodiment of Whig dissent on the Wateree, Joseph Kershaw encompassed both themes. Recognized by his contemporaries for his central role in peace and war, he remained a popular figure and, despite his financial setbacks, maintained considerable influence and held offices of public trust throughout his lifetime. Upon Camden's incorporation in 1791, Kershaw became its first intendant, and the newly created county was named for him the same year. Already the legend had emerged that linked his stores and mills to the trade and prosperity that ushered in a successful commercial plantation economy. Kershaw's role forever elevated him to head the pantheon of Camden's founders, and his exploits appeared in early published accounts of the region's history. Both Robert Mills's and William Gilmore Simms's geographies

12.4 Surrounded by a high wooden fence, the vacant Kershaw mansion stood in disrepair at mid-nineteenth century. Caretakers living in the nearby outbuilding oversaw curious visitors to the historic old house that many then believed to be haunted. Courtesy of Davie Beard Collection, Camden, South Carolina.

attributed the region's successful growth to Kershaw's presence, and historical narratives of the town always included biographical sketches of his life. The Great White House, now lying abandoned, became a widely known landmark in antebellum Camden (Fig. 12.4). Linked to its founder's economic success as well as to the town's Revolutionary War occupation, the Kershaw mansion attracted comment before and even after its destruction in 1865, in the closing months of a subsequent conflict.[20]

Kershaw's role as a Whig leader in the Revolution tied him to the second theme in Camden's past. As the site of major engagements in the Revolutionary War, Camden assumed a prominent place in participant histories of the conflict. Chroniclers of the war noted Kershaw's significant public role in the revolutionary government and as a military commander prior to his capture and exile in 1780. Although he participated in none of the major actions that earned Camden a prominent place in the conflict, the strength of his presence linked Kershaw with the town and its fate. The presence of important enemy military figures such as Earl Cornwallis and Lord Rawdon in Camden and their use of his mansion as a headquarters spread the prestige of the town and Kershaw even farther.[21] Camden's reputation attracted visits by George Washington in 1791 and the Marquis de Lafayette in 1825, and both recalled the town's seminal role in the War for Independence and recognized its historical distinctness among settlements of the South Carolina backcountry.[22] So significant was the revolutionary tie that when two Camden residents, Thomas J. Kirkland and Robert M. Kennedy, set out to compile a definitive history of their birthplace at the beginning of the twentieth century, they found these two seminal themes dominating their work. When completed, the first volume of *Historic Camden* devoted nearly three-quarters of its four hundred pages to the Revolutionary War and its aftermath and interwove the career of its leading citizen with these events. Appearing at the close of an eventful and traumatic century, long after the founders and their initial settlement were gone, the book drew Camden's identity from a much earlier time. Camden was indeed a special place that was unique even as its mythology connected it to events and personalities whose significance extended beyond its limits and well outside the State of South Carolina.[23]

But the history of Camden and the Wateree Valley and the form of its settlement could not be divorced from the processes that created it. Writing a descriptive account of the town and its vicinity in 1853, Margaret Maxwell Martin recognized the importance of landscape and the emotional connection to place when she addressed her local audience. "Camdenian," she implored, "do you desire to love your country, or what is the same, your town? Then get by heart her features."[24] In verse, she stressed further the importance of history to her sense of place. Of Camden she continued,

And more thy churches and thy graves
All, all the past in memory down,
O, may these let no adverse waves
Drift me, from my own dear Town.[25]

Her understanding of the influence of the past upon the present and the important relationship between earlier events and the locations where they occurred reflected not only a keen observation of the world around her but also a prescient explanation of how it came to be.

Mrs. Martin's acknowledgment of the relationship between the patterning of the geographical features she observed and the forces that affected the region's past emphasized the importance of historical processes in shaping the form and content of the landscape it generated. As elsewhere, the process of settlement in the Wateree Valley was affected by broad conditions associated with agricultural colonization on the periphery of the expanding European world economy, and the region shared much in common with other frontiers in British North America. But more than the economic and political factors that shaped other places influenced colonization in South Carolina's interior. European settlers encountered conditions distinctive to the region. Perceiving the province as vulnerable to external and internal threats, its officials sought to settle the interior with free farmers whose presence would offset demographic disparities in the lowcountry and defend against outside attack. British settlement of the Wateree Valley brought a rapid influx of immigrants who quickly outdistanced existing mechanisms of exchange and administration. In the absence of formal structures, individuals developed strategies to overcome the isolation of the frontier and generated new institutions that organized the region's economy and society and integrated the backcountry and its inhabitants into the larger milieu of British North America. These institutions persisted through the trial of war and the challenges of political change that followed to become the foundations of society in the state.

Central to the success of these institutions were the strategies that created them. Without a formal institutional framework in which to operate, personal social networks assumed both economic and political significance. Joseph Kershaw's networks combined the capital, resources, and expertise necessary to erect and manage the infrastructure required to establish staple production and carry out export trade. Relying on relationships formed by common interest, association, and kinship, his networks organized exchange and helped integrate the diverse social entities on the frontier. The growth of central mercantile concerns and the success of their business became the catalyst for the ascension of commercial agriculture and the rise of an elite class of merchants, processors, and planters. The drive to protect the interests of this new elite led to administrative changes that made the backcountry an integral part of South Carolina, and the shared economic concerns of elites of the interior and coastal regions became a crucial factor in the political unification of the state following the Revolution.

Network-building in the backcountry bound the region's diverse religious and ethnic elements, uniting them for the purpose of organizing a functioning commercial economy on the frontier, and was instrumental in the rise of a regional elite. The partners in trade Joseph and Ely Kershaw and John Chesnut all became successful business and community leaders, and their Charleston associates William Ancrum, Aaron Loocock, and Archibald Brown also profited from the enterprise. The extensive network of backcountry exchange also supported smaller regional traders such as Charles Ogilvie and Henry Rugeley and contributed to the success of John Adamson, the Boykins, the Canteys, James Cary, John Cook, the Englishes, the Mathises, the McGirts, the Wylys, and members of other early planting families with whom the firm interacted.

As the principal agent of regional development, Joseph Kershaw assumed a central position in trade that brought him not only wealth but also important civil responsibilities in the emerging political order of the region. Elected to represent his region multiple times in the Royal Assembly, he subsequently served in the Provincial Congresses that challenged British rule and in the General Assembly of the independent state. Kershaw's many ties to members of the lowcountry elite enhanced his role as an advocate for the backcountry, and he became one of its most powerful and influential political figures. When war came to the Wateree Valley, Joseph Kershaw again took on a central role as commander of the Camden militia. For its leadership he drew on his network for officers, who included his partner John Chesnut, his business associate George Wade, the physician Thomas Charlton, and successful regional planters such as John Marshall, Robert Crawford, and Francis Boykin.

The organization of networks formed to facilitate trade not only underlay the rise of the backcountry economy but also helped create its administrative institutions. Economic success depended on civil order, and the crisis of the 1760s involved prominent community members such as John and Samuel Boykin, James Cary, Joshua Dinkins, Thomas Charlton Joshua English, and John Marshall in the Regulation. Direct and often violent in nature, the movement reflected the needs of a rising backcountry elite whose livelihood depended on stability, and the success of their efforts helped lay the foundation for the administrative organization that precipitated the political incorporation of the backcountry. Not simply a mechanism to facilitate Joseph Kerrshaw's economic success, his networks became the cornerstone for the consolidation of the region and a crucial element in its transition.

Participation in trade did not guarantee future material wealth, but individual prestige often reflected the structure of earlier networks of interaction. For many businessmen, the economic opportunities accrued through mercantile activities became the basis for accumulating capital for investment in new commercial ventures. Frequently those who had thrived in trade became successful millers or planters as the century drew to a close, but prosperity did not always follow mercantile achievement. Some merchants, such as John Chesnut, fared well. Already established in agriculture by the time of the Revolution, he became a leading figure in a region enveloped by war, and his efforts helped protect and maintain the estates of many of his fellow planters. When peace returned, he invested wisely and became the region's most successful and wealthiest planter. But Chesnut and others nevertheless remained in the shadow of the region's pioneer merchant. Joseph Kershaw's seminal role in developing the Wateree Valley allowed him to amass immense prestige and influence and considerable property. Despite the wartime misfortunes that impoverished him and limited the opportunities of his heirs, he endured as the region's most revered individual and the namesake of the county. Celebrated in life and afterward, he remained the figure associated with Camden and colonial settlement in the Wateree Valley. The die cast in early days determined the course of historical memory.

Looking back over the six decades he had lived in Camden, Phinehas Thornton correctly perceived that a "new town" and a "new generation" had "sprung up" during his residence. Observing that only five or six people and but two buildings remained from the time of his arrival, he and other old residents were only too aware of the distance between the present and the time that set the region on its present course. Now almost beyond living memory, the Wateree Valley frontier had become the history of other days. But despite the gap wrought by time, antebellum observers recognized that their community was tied to its roots in the previous century and that the landscape they inhabited still betrayed the forces that had created it. In a world lacking established institutions, colonization in the Wateree Valley was shaped by economic processes influenced by the agency of individuals whose strategies molded society and guided change. These circumstances at once directed the backcountry's development and determined its legacy.

Notes

Chapter 1. "So Great a Change in a Small Place"

1. Phinehas Thornton to Clarissa Martin, Dec. 20, 1850, letter in author's possession.

2. Northern immigration to South Carolina, and particularly Camden, during the closing decades of the eighteenth century is discussed in John Drayton, *A View of South Carolina, as Respects Her Natural and Civil Concerns,* Vol. 1 (Charleston, S.C.: W. P. Young, 1802; reprint ed., Spartanburg, S.C.: The Reprint Co., 1972), 103; Thomas J. Kirkland and Robert M. Kennedy, *Historic Camden, Vol. 2: Nineteenth Century* (Columbia, S.C.: State Printing Co., 1926), 100; Julian J. Petty, *The Growth and Distribution of Population in South Carolina* (Columbia: South Carolina State Planning Board, 1943; reprint ed., Spartanburg, S.C.: The Reprint Co., 1975), 141.

3. Phinehas Thornton's biography is detailed in "Introduction," in P. Thornton, *The Southern Gardener and Receipt Book* (Newark, N.J.: A. L. Dennis, 1845; reprint ed., Birmingham, Ala.: Oxmoor House, 1984).

4. Phinehas Thornton to Clarissa Martin, Dec. 20, 1850; "Items from the Reminiscences of Mrs. Phineas [*sic*] Thornton, Dec. 11, 1856," Elizabeth Thornton Papers (ETP), South Caroliniana Library, University of South Carolina, Columbia. For Thornton's role in the Methodist Episcopal Church, see Joan A. Inabinet, *Lyttleton Street United Methodist Church of Camden, S.C.* (Camden, S.C.: Pine Tree Publishing Co., 2003), 64, 67, 69. An entry in the diary of James Kershaw revealed that the Thorntons interacted socially with at least one of Camden's most prestigious families. James Kershaw Diary with Meteorological Observations, May 11, 1810, James Kershaw Papers, 1786–1825 (hereafter JKP), South Caroliniana Library, University of South Carolina, Columbia.

5. Phinehas Thornton to Clarissa Martin, Dec. 20, 1850.

6. Camden's history in the eighteenth century has been examined extensively in two regional histories written a century apart, by Thomas J. Kirkland and Robert M. Kennedy, *Historic Camden, Vol. 1: Colonial and Revolutionary* (Columbia, S.C.: State Printing Co., 1905), and, more recently, by Joan A. Inabinet and L. Glen Inabinet, *A History of Kershaw County, South Carolina* (Columbia: University of South Carolina Press, 2011). Its economic development is the subject of an extensive study by Judith J. Schulz: "The Rise and Decline of Camden as South Carolina's Major Trading Center, 1751–1829: A Historical Geographic Study" (M.A. thesis, University of South Carolina, 1972), and is summarized by Kenneth E. Lewis, "Economic Development in the South Carolina Backcountry: A View from Camden," in *The Southern Colonial Backcountry: Interdisciplinary Perspectives on Frontier Communities,* ed. David Colin Crass, Steven D. Smith, Martha A. Zierden, and Richard D. Brooks (Knoxville: University of Tennessee Press, 1998), 87–107.

7. The economic expansion of Europe following the fifteenth century has long been recognized as the key factor in shaping the form of colonization of North America. Several authors have specifically linked the geography of global colonization with the organization of the emerging European economy and particularly its capitalist mode of production. Immanuel Wallerstein, in *The Modern World-System, Vol. 1: Capitalist Agriculture and the Origins of the European World-Economy in the Sixteenth Century* (New York: Academic Press, 1974); Wallerstein, "The Rise and Future Demise of the World Capitalist System: Concepts for Comparative Analysis," *Comparative Studies in Society and*

History 16 (1974), 387–415; and Fernand Braudel, *Civilization and Capitalism: 15th–18th Century, Vol. 3: The Perspective of the World,* trans. Siân Reynolds (New York: Harper & Row, 1984).

8. The term "institution" is used here in a general anthropological sense to refer to a complex of behavior patterns organized around the common interest of the group involved. Institutions concerned with the production and distribution of goods, for example, are considered economic institutions, while those associated with administration and government may be characterized as political institutions.

9. Comparative studies of frontier colonization have stressed the organizational aspects of settlement systems. Classic approaches include Joseph B. Casagrande, Stephen I. Thompson, and Philip D. Young, "Colonization as a Research Frontier," in *Process and Pattern in Culture: Essays in Honor of Julian H. Steward,* ed. Robert A. Manners (Chicago: Aldine, 1964), 281–325; Jerome O. Steffen, *Comparative Frontiers: A Proposal for Studying the American West* (Norman: University of Oklahoma Press, 1980).

10. Scholars have found the term "community" a useful concept to link people with locale, defining it on the basis of social relations rather than geography alone. As a basic unit of integration and transmission, the organization of a community rather than its form is the key to recognizing its boundaries. See Conrad M. Arensberg, "The Community as Object and Sample," *American Anthropologist* 63 (1961): 248. An understanding of the complex nature of rural communities arose from the work of rural sociologists, anthropologists, and historians who investigated the nature of social and economic integration in dispersed agricultural societies and its role in their formation. Examples include John Mack Faragher, "Open-Country Community: Sugar Creek, Illinois, 1820–1850," in *The Countryside in the Age of Capitalist Transformation: Essays in the Social History of Rural America,* ed. Steven Hahn and Jonathan Prude (Chapel Hill: University of North Carolina Press, 1985), 236–237, 245–247; Stephen I. Thompson, *Pioneer Colonization: A Cross-Cultural View,* Addison-Wesley Modules in Anthropology 33 (Reading, Mass.: Addison-Wesley, 1973), 8–9; C. J. Galpin, *The Social Anatomy of an Agricultural Community,* AES Research Bulletin no. 34, University of Wisconsin, Madison, 1915; Lowry Nelson, *Rural Sociology* (New York: American Book Co., 1952), 72–77; and G. J. Lewis, "Rural Communities," in *Progress in Rural Geography,* ed. Michael Pacione (London: Croom Helm, 1983), 149. Pertinent historical community studies in South Carolina include George D. Terry, "'Champaign Country': A Social History of an Eighteenth Century Lowcountry Parish in South Carolina, St. Johns, Berkeley" (Ph.D. diss., University of South Carolina, 1981); Peter N. Moore, *World of Toil and Strife: Community Transformation in Backcountry South Carolina, 1750–1805* (Columbia: University of South Carolina Press, 2007); and Arlin C. Migliazzo, *To Make This Land Our Own: Community, Identity, and Cultural Adaptation in Purrysburg Township, South Carolina, 1732–1865* (Columbia: University of South Carolina Press, 2007).

11. See, for example, the works of Robert Mills, *Statistics of South Carolina* (Charleston, S.C.: Hurlbut and Lloyd, 1856; reprint ed., Spartanburg, S.C.: The Reprint Co., 1972), 590–591, and William Gilmore Simms, *The Geography of South Carolina* (Charleston, S.C.: Babcock, 1843), 89–90. Elizabeth Thompson Alexander, an insightful contemporary observer, commented on the impact of wider factors in the town's development in "Camden Fifty Years Ago," [1850], Thomas J. Kirkland Papers (hereafter KP), Box 2–23, South Caroliniana Library, University of South Carolina, Columbia.

12. KP. See also Inabinet, *Lyttleton Street United Methodist Church,* 8–10.

13. As a term encompassing a group of people, often related by real or fictive kinship, who share space and frequently have common interests and engage in related activities, "household" has been a useful unit of analysis in social science. One of its foremost advocates has been Peter Laslett, "The Comparative Study of the Household and Family," *Journal of Social History* 4 (1970), 75–87; Laslett, "Introduction: The History of the Family," in *Household and Family in Past Time,* ed. Peter Laslett (Cambridge: Cambridge University Press, 1972), 1–89. The phrase "household mode of production," referring to an economic arrangement directed toward producing and distributing goods on the basis of need rather than price, derives from the notion of households as both producing and consuming units in societies for which markets play a limited role. For its use by historians of early America, see James A. Henretta, "Families and Farms: *Mentalité* in Pre-Industrial America," *William and Mary*

Quarterly, 3rd ser., 35 (178): 15–16; Christopher Clark, *The Roots of Rural Capitalism: Western Massachusetts, 178–1860* (Ithaca, N.Y.: Cornell University Press, 1990); Michael Merrill, "Cash Is Good to Eat: Self-Sufficiency and Exchange in the Rural Economy of the United States," *Radical History Review* 3 (1977): 52–57.

14. The literature of social science has long recognized the role the individual in social change. Early authors on this topic include Emile Durkheim, *The Elementary Forms of Religious Life*, Joseph Ward Swain, trans. (New York: Free Press, 1995); Karl Marx, *Capital: A Critique of Political Economy*, ed. Paul Eden, trans. Paul Cedar (reprint ed., New York: E. P. Dutton, 1930); and Max Weber, *Economy and Society*, ed. Guenther Roth and Claus Wittich, trans. Ephraim Fischoff (Berkeley: University of California Press, 1978). Later anthropologists such as Bronislaw Malinowski, "The Group and Individual in Functional Analysis," *American Journal of Sociology* 44 (1939): 938–964; Morris Opler, *An Apache Life-Way: The Economic, Social, and Religious Institutions of the Chiricahua Indians* (Chicago: University of Chicago Press, 1941); and John J. Honigman, *Personality and Culture* (New York: Harper & Bros., 1954), followed this theme. More recently, studies of the relationship of the individual to society have encompassed in the examination of "agency," a broad term that has been used to address a variety of issues ranging from cognitive structure and social practices to resistance to power inequities and free will. The most notable recent works are those by Pierre Bourdieu, *Outline of Theory and Practice* (New York: Cambridge University Press, 1977), and Anthony Giddens, *Central Problems in Social Theory: Action, Structure, and Contradiction in Social Analysis* (Berkeley: University of California Press, 1979); see also Sherry B. Ortner, "Theory in Anthropology since the Sixties," *Society for Comparative Study of Society and History* 26, no. 1 (1984):126–166, and Elizabeth M. Brumfiel, "Distinguished Lecture in Archaeology: Breaking and Entering the Ecosystem—Gender, Class, and Faction Steal the Show," *American Anthropologist* 94 (1992): 559.

15. Numerous scholars have analyzed South Carolina's colonial history and the events that shaped the backcountry during the eighteenth century. Of the many volumes compiled during the past two centuries, the lengthiest perhaps is Yates Snowden, *History of South Carolina*, 5 vols. (New York: Lewis Publishing Co., 1920). The most recent comprehensive works are Robert M. Weir's *Colonial South Carolina: A History* (New York: KTO Press, 1983; reprint ed., Columbia: University of South Carolina Press, 1997), and Walter Edgar's *South Carolina: A History* (Columbia: University of South Carolina Press, 1998).

Chapter 2. "More Valuable to the Mother Country Than Any Other Province"

1. Philip M. Hamer et al., eds., *The Papers of Henry Laurens* (hereafter *HLP*), 12 vols. (Columbia: University of South Carolina Press, 1968–1990), Vol. I, xv; Vol. III, xvii–xviii.

2. Ibid., 56n; Daniel Thorp, *The Moravian Community in Colonial North Carolina: Pluralism on the Southern Frontier* (Knoxville: University of Tennessee Press, 1989), 136–137.

3. Henry Laurens to David Webb, 20 July 1764, Hamer et al., eds., *HLP*, 4: 346; Henry Laurens to Richard Oswald, Apr. 27 1768, Hamer et al., eds., *HLP*, 5: 665.

4. Henry Laurens to Richard Oswald & Co., Feb. 15, 1763, Hamer et al., eds., *HLP*, 3: 260.

5. For recent discussions of the founding and early development of the South Carolina colony, see Robert M. Weir, *Colonial South Carolina: A History* (New York: KTO Press, 1983; reprint ed., Columbia: University of South Carolina Press, 1997), Chs. 2–3; Walter Edgar, *South Carolina: A History* (Columbia: University of South Carolina Press, 1998), Ch. 6.

6. Richard S. Dunn, "The English Sugar Islands and the Founding of South Carolina," *South Carolina Historical Magazine* 72 (1971): 83–85; Jack P. Greene, "Colonial South Carolina and the Caribbean Connection," *South Carolina Historical Magazine* 88 (1987): 192–197; Edgar, *South Carolina*, 47–49.

7. The concept of a capitalist world system as I employ it here was introduced by Immanuel Wallerstein in his *The Modern-World System, Vol. 1: Capitalist Agriculture and the Origins of the European World-Economy in the Sixteenth Century* (New York: Academic Press, 1974), 347–351.

8. Central to a capitalist economy were the mechanisms associated with production. Here, the process of *commodification*, by which all activities involving production, exchange, saving, or borrowing

were monitized, allowed all of them to be appropriated for purposes of capital accumulation. In such an economy, cost-effectiveness encouraged *multiple modes of labor control.* In addition to wage labor, producers employed coerced labor, including slavery, to restrain the demands of workers and keep costs low. In order to integrate production in a capitalist economy, it was also necessary to create efficient *commodity chains,* connected paths by which a resource is gathered, transformed into a commodity, and then distributed. These chains link all productive activities throughout the entire division of labor. Commodity chains gave capitalists the ability to integrate often geographically separated elements that employed vastly different types of production and labor control into vertical chains, whose parts could be manipulated for the benefit of those who controlled them. In addition to the core and periphery, *semiperipheral areas,* smaller states lying outside the political arena of the core, facilitated this system of global exchange. Unable to compete with the core states, they became collection points for vital skills and services needed to operate the world economy, such as providing transportation or finance and credit, and also served to deflect political pressures aimed at core states by peripheral areas. Like the core states and peripheral areas, semiperipheral areas were vital components of the world economy. For a more complete discussion of the institutions of the world economy, see Immanuel Wallerstein, "The Modern World System and Evolution," *Journal of World Systems Research* 1, no. 19 (1995): 3–9; Wallerstein, "The Rise and Future Demise of the World Capitalist System: Concepts for Comparative Analysis," *Comparative Studies in Society and History* 16 (1974): 400; Barry K. Gills and Andre G. Frank, "5000 Years of World Systems History: The Cumulation of Accumulation," in *Core/Periphery Relations in Pre-Capitalist Worlds,* ed. Christopher K. Chase-Dunn and Thomas D. Hall (Boulder, Colo.: Westview, 1991), 84–85, 90–93; H. Peter Gray, *A Generalized Theory of International Trade* (New York: Holmes and Meier, 1976), 235–236.

Despite its ability to operate in a market extending beyond the bounds of individual states, the world economy depended heavily on the security provided by political units at its core. A strong state offered a structure that encouraged the interests of the emerging group of capitalists by legitimizing them and protecting them from both internal and external threats. To these capitalists, the state represented a customer for their services and a mode of social legitimation. It also constituted a shield against local unrest and international brigandage, provided protection from the actions of other states, and helped thwart the formation of strong states that might jeopardize their interests in the periphery. The taxation required to support the state's administrative machinery was a reasonable cost for these services. Wallerstein, *Modern World System,* Vol. 1, 355; Wallerstein, "Modern World System and Evolution," 9–10.

9. Challenged by crises of unemployment and the outflow of specie in foreign trade during the seventeenth century, advocates of mercantilism responded to the slowdown in economic growth in the core states of Europe by arguing for the adoption of mercantilist state policies. K. G. Davies, *The North Atlantic World in the Seventeenth Century* (Minneapolis: University of Minnesota Press, 1974), 315–317; Paul M. Sweezy and Harry Magdoff, "Capitalism and the Distribution of Income and Wealth," *Monthly Review* 39, no. 5 (1987): 3; Peter Coclanis, *The Shadow of a Dream: Economic Life and Death in the South Carolina Low Country, 1670–1920* (New York: Oxford University Press, 1989), 16–19.

10. Scholars have long recognized that colonies devoted to the production of specialized staples for export possessed distinctive characteristics. Jack P. Greene and J. R. Pole, "Reconsidering British-American Colonial History: An Introduction," in *Colonial British America: Essays on the History of the Early Modern Era,* ed. Jack P. Greene and J. R. Pole (Baltimore: Johns Hopkins University Press, 1984), 11–12. Earlier, sociologist James G. Leyburn, *Frontier Folkways* (London: Yale University Press, 1935), 231–233, explored at length the influence of a colony's economic base on its organization and institutions and identified a number of colonial types based on variations he observed. He introduced the term "exploitative plantation" (Ch. 8) to describe those based on the large-scale, labor-intensive, commercial production of crops. More recently, Gray emphasized the role of noncompetitive goods as a crucial factor in determining the organizational nature of colonization: *Theory of International Trade,* 125–126. See also Ida C. Greaves, "Plantations in the World Economy," in *Plantation Systems of the New*

World, Social Science Monographs 7 (Washington, D.C.: Pan American Union, 1959), 13–23; Elena Padilla, "Colonization and Development of Plantations," in *Plantation Systems of the New World,* Social Science Monographs 7 (Washington, D.C.: Pan American Union, 1959), 26–37.

11. See Kenneth E. Lewis, *The American Frontier: An Archaeological Study of Settlement Pattern and Process* (Orlando, Fla.: Academic Press, 1984), 264–267, 277–286, for a discussion of types of frontier settlement associated with noncompetitive colonization. Jerome O. Steffen, whose lengthy essay called attention to the significance of the relationship between the nature of settlement and the intensity of the economic and social ties between the colony and homeland, introduced the term "cosmopolitan" to describe these colonies. *Comparative Frontiers: A Proposal for Studying the American West* (Norman: University of Oklahoma Press, 1980), xii–xvii.

12. The nature of colonies devoted to the production of competitive staples is discussed by Gray, *Theory of International Trade,* 130, and Robert E. Baldwin, "Patterns of Development in Newly Settled Regions," *Manchester School of Social and Economic Studies* 24 (1956): 130–131.

13. Although part of the world system, insular colonies were often economically "marginal areas" because of their participation in commercial market exchange between core and periphery. Carol A. Smith, "Beyond Dependency Theory: National and Regional Patterns of Underdevelopment in Guatemala," *American Ethnologist* 5 (1978): 581. The role of a colony's insularity in shaping its structure and institutions and its relationship with the homeland is examined in Gray, *Theory of International Trade,* 130; Steffen, *Comparative Frontiers,* xi–xii; and Robert M. Weir, "Who Shall Rule at Home: The American Revolution as a Crisis of Legitimacy for the Colonial Elite," *Journal of Interdisciplinary History* 6 (1976): 685–686.

14. The physiographic zones are based on those described in Charles F. Kovacik and John J. Winberry, *South Carolina: A Geography* (Boulder, Colo.: Westview Press, 1987), 18–26.

15. William Hilton, "A Relation of a Discovery Lately Made on the Coast of Florida, 1664," in *Narratives of Early Carolina, 1650–1708,* ed. Alexander S. Salley Jr. (New York: Charles Scribner's Sons, 1911), 43–44; Robert Sandford, "A Relation of a Voyage on the Coast of the Province of Carolina, 1666," in *Narratives of Early Carolina, 1650–1708,* ed. Alexander S. Salley Jr. (New York: Charles Scribner's Sons, 1911), 107.

16. See Peter A. Coclanis, "Bitter Harvest: The South Carolina Low Country in Historical Perspective," *Journal of Economic History* 45 (1985): 252; Coclanis, *Shadow of a Dream,* 14–26.

17. The Fundamental Constitutions of 1669, which outlined the provincial government under the Proprietary rule, gave the Lords Proprietors authority to establish a feudalistic society dominated by landed aristocracy and characterized by the systematic distribution of land to colonists. They intended to control the colony's development through a series of rigid administrative institutions that relied on a complex subdivision of colony's territory into regular units of progressively smaller size, whose ownership was shared among the Proprietors, a hereditary nobility, and freeholders. Because the possession of land brought with it fealty to the Proprietary government, its ownership was also meant to ensure political stability and maintain proprietary authority. By manipulating land, the Proprietors hoped to create a compact pattern of settlement centered on nucleated towns. Robert K. Ackerman, *South Carolina Colonial Land Policies* (Columbia: University of South Carolina Press, 1977), 15–16; Meaghan N. Duff, "Creating a Plantation Province: Proprietary Land Policies and Early Settlement Patterns," in *Money, Trade, and Power: The Evolution of Colonial South Carolina's Plantation Society,* ed. Jack P. Greene, Rosemary Brana-Shute, and Randy J. Sparks (Columbia: University of South Carolina Press, 2001)1–2; Weir, *Colonial South Carolina,* 56–57. The Fundamental Constitutions of Carolina are found in Langdon Cheves, ed., *The Shaftesbury Papers and Other Records Relating to Carolina . . . prior to 1676* (Charleston, S.C.: South Carolina Historical Society, 1897); reprint ed., *The Shaftesbury Papers* (Charleston, S.C.: Tempus, 2000), 93–117.

18. Samuel Wilson, "An Account of the Province of Carolina, in America, 1682," in *Historical Collections of South Carolina, . . . to 1776,* Vol. 1, ed. B. R. Carroll (New York: Harper & Bros., 1836), 27; Thomas Ashe, "Carolina; or a Description of the Present State of that Country, 1682," in Salley,

Narratives of Early Carolina, 141–142; Thomas Newe, "Letters of Thomas Newe, 1682," in Salley, *Narratives of Early Carolina*, 182–184; Maurice Mathews to Lord Ashley, Aug. 30, 1671, in Cheves, ed., *Shaftesbury Papers*, 332–333; Henry Woodward, "A Faithful Relation of My Westoe Voyage, 1674," in Salley, *Narratives of Early Carolina*, 130; Mark Catesby, "Mark Catesby's *Natural History*, 1731–47," in *The Colonial South Carolina Scene: Contemporary Views, 1697–1774*, ed. H. Roy Merrens (Columbia: University of South Carolina Press, 1977), 94.

19. Greene, "South Carolina and the Caribbean Connection," 198; Converse D. Clowse, *Economic Beginnings in South Carolina, 1670–1730* (Columbia: University of South Carolina Press, 1971), 53–54. For comparisons with Barbadian plantations, see Jerome S. Handler and Frederick W. Lange, *Plantation Slavery in Barbados: An Archaeological and Historical Investigation* (Cambridge, Mass.: Harvard University Press, 1978), 46; Frederick W. Lange and Jerome S. Handler, "The Ethnohistorical Approach to Slavery," in *The Archaeology of Slavery and Plantation Life*, ed. Theresa A. Singleton (Orlando, Fla.: Academic Press, 1985), 17–18.

20. Kovacik and Winberry, *South Carolina: A Geography*, 69; Weir, *Colonial South Carolina*, 61. Archaeological surveys confirmed that seventeenth-century settlement sites in the Edisto and Stono River drainages, situated southwest of Charleston, were associated with locations where high ground met the deep-water channel of the rivers and streams. Stanley South and Michael Hartley, "Deep Water and High Ground: Seventeenth Century Settlement Patterns on the Carolina Coast," in *Structure and Process in Southeastern Archaeology*, ed. Roy S. Dickens Jr. and H. Trawick Ward (Tuscaloosa: University of Alabama Press, 1985), 263–286.

21. Settled temporarily in 1684, Port Royal was permanently occupied only when Beaufort was established in 1711. Weir, *Colonial South Carolina*, 62, 83; Georgetown was founded in 1729 as a center for growing settlement on the lower Santee and Pee Dee Rivers. Clowse, *Economic Beginnings*, 249. The definition of Outer Coastal Plain is based on Kovacik and Winberry, *South Carolina: A Geography*, 18–23. The extent of colonial settlement is illustrated graphically in Lewis, *American Frontier*, 162–165.

22. Originating in Africa and brought to the New World with the spread of slavery, the disease accompanied colonization in the Caribbean and North America. In South Carolina, settlers came to associate agues and fevers with the summer and the debilitating physical effects of that season's excessive heat. Prevalent from August through November, malaria was often fatal in its own right and lowered its victims' resistance to other maladies. It soon became a significant scourge in the lowcountry, producing a disproportionately higher death rate generally and increasing infant and child mortality dramatically. In addition to malaria, there were epidemics of smallpox, yellow fever, filariasis, influenza, dysentery, typhus, and typhoid fever. Joseph Ioor Waring, *A History of Medicine in South Carolina, 1670–1825* (Columbia: South Carolina Medical Association, 1964), 18–47; Coclanis, *Shadow of a Dream*, 41–443; Jim Potter, "Demographic Development and Family Structure," in *Essays in the New History of the Early Modern Era*, ed. Jack P. Greene and J. R. Pole (Baltimore: Johns Hopkins University Press, 1984), 148. Despite the high mortality endured by residents of the lowcountry, eighteenth-century observers were slow to recognize the association between malaria and environmental variables. Colonists persisted in their belief that in summer inland locations along the rivers and swamps were healthier than the coast and the area around Charleston. Only gradually, as lowcountry residents became aware of the regional variation in the occurrence of malaria in South Carolina, did they begin to understand its connection to swamps and low, wet lands and revise their perceptions of disease. Situated away from stagnant water, the coastal settlements of Charleston, Beaufort, and Georgetown became refuges, and inland locales, exhibiting higher elevations and covered by pinelands, attracted planters and others who could afford to move seasonally. H. Roy Merrens and George D. Terry, "Dying in Paradise: Malaria, Mortality and the Perceptual Environment in Colonial South Carolina," *Journal of Southern History* 50 (1984): 540–549.

23. Fundamental Constitutions of Carolina, in Cheves, ed., *Shaftesbury Papers*, 115–116; Weir, *Colonial South Carolina*, 54. Coclanis, *Shadow of a Dream*, 50–51; Robert D. Mitchell, *Commercialism and Frontier: Perspectives on the Early Shenandoah Valley* (Charlottesville: University of Virginia Press, 1977), 4; Lewis, *American Frontier*, 271–275.

24. Clowse, *Economic Beginnings,* 57–60. Archaeological excavations have revealed physical evidence of these early experiments at the original Albemarle Point settlement. In 1968 traces of the vineyard ditches appeared: Stanley South, "Excavating the Fortified Area of the 1670 Site of Charles Towne, South Carolina," *Conference on Historic Site Archaeology, Papers, 1969* 4 (1971): 41; South, *Archaeological Pathways to Historical Site Development* (New York: Kluwer, 2002), 76–79, 81. Barbadian redware ceramics recovered there in 1999 represented types associated with sugar production on the island. Michael J. Stoner and Stanley A. South, *Exploring 1670 Charles Towne: 38CH1 A/B, Final Archaeology Report,* Research Manuscript Series 230 (Columbia: University of South Carolina Institute of Archaeology and Anthropology, 2001), 58–59.

25. Imported into the colony from Virginia and the West Indies, livestock thrived on the Coastal Plain, and herds grew rapidly. As early as the 1680s, cattle already numbered several thousand head, and some planters possessed herds of seven hundred to eight hundred. Maurice Mathews, "A Contemporary View of Carolina in 1680," *South Carolina Historical Magazine* 55 (1954): 157; Wilson, "Account of the Province of Carolina," 29. The number of both cattle and hogs continued to increase in the early years of the eighteenth century and seemed to be limited only by the amount of land available for grazing and the length of time the owner devoted to stock raising. [John Norris], "A Description, or True Relation, of South Carolina (1712)," in *Settling a New World: Two Colonial South Carolina Promotional Pamphlets,* ed. Jack P. Greene (Columbia: University of South Carolina Press, 1989), 101. By this time South Carolina was an important exporter of hides and salted barreled beef and pork for the West Indies, and its meat products industry had become a major commercial enterprise in the young colony. John Solomon Otto, "Livestock-Raising in Early South Carolina, 1670–1700: Prelude to the Rice Plantation Economy," *Agricultural History* 61, no. 4 (1987): 23–24. For other discussions of the significance of the livestock industry in early South Carolina, see Lewis Cecil Gray, *History of Agriculture in the Southern United States to 1860,* Vol. 1 (Gloucester, Mass.: Peter Smith, 1933), 55–57, and Terry G. Jordan, *North American Cattle-Ranching Frontiers: Origins, Diffusion, and Differentiation* (Albuquerque: University of New Mexico Press, 1993), 109–120. The economic viability of livestock raising as an economic strategy is discussed in Arnold Strickon, "The Euro-American Ranching Complex," in *Man, Culture, and Animals,* ed. Anthony Leeds and Andrew P. Vayda (Washington, D.C.: American Association for the Advancement of Science, 1965), 229–258. The definition of Highland Britain follows that of L. Dudley Stamp, *Britain's Structure and Scenery* (London: Collins, 1946), 5, and falls within the "hardscrabble" zone of Europe, where unstable environmental conditions have traditionally favored diversified agricultural adaptations, including herding. Terry Jordan and Matti Kaups, *The American Backwoods Frontier: An Ethnic and Ecological Interpretation* (Baltimore: Johns Hopkins University Press, 1989), 33–34; John Solomon Otto, "The Origins of Cattle-Ranching in Colonial South Carolina, 1670–1715," *South Carolina Historical Magazine* 87 (1986): 120–122.

26. Clowse, *Economic Beginnings,* 61–63; Weir, *Colonial South Carolina,* 143–145; Kovacik and Winberry, *South Carolina: A Geography,* 70–71; John J. Murray, "Baltic Commerce and Power Politics in the Early Eighteenth Century," *The Huntington Library Quarterly* 6 (1943): 300–302; Clarence L. Ver Steeg, *Origins of a Southern Mosaic* (Athens: University of Georgia Press, 1975), 120–121; [Thomas Nairne], "A Letter from South Carolina (1710)," in *Settling a New World: Two Colonial South Carolina Promotional Pamphlets,* ed. Jack P. Greene (Columbia: University of South Carolina Press), 40–41; [Norris], "A Description," 95–96, 105.

27. Eric R. Wolf, *Europe and the People without History* (Berkeley: University of California Press, 1982), 79. Numerous studies have examined the Native societies of South Carolina and neighboring areas. For overviews of these groups, see Gene Waddell, *Indians of the South Carolina Lowcountry, 1562–1751* (Spartanburg, S.C.: The Reprint Co., 1980); Charles M. Hudson, *The Southeastern Indians* (Knoxville: University of Tennessee Press, 1976); James H. Merrell, *The Indians' New World: Catawbas and Their Neighbors from European Contact through Removal* (Chapel Hill: University of North Carolina Press, 1989); Chapman Milling, *Red Carolinians* (Chapel Hill: University of North Carolina Press, 1940); Paul Quattlebaum, *The Land Called Chicora* (Gainesville: University of Florida Press, 1956); John R. Swanton, *Early History of the Creek Indians and their Neighbors,* Smithsonian Institution, Bureau

of American Ethnology, Bulletin 73 (Washington, D.C.: Government Printing Office, 1922); and James Mooney, *The Siouan Tribes of the East,* Smithsonian Institution, Bureau of American Ethnology, Bulletin 22 (Washington, D.C.: Government Printing Office, 1894).

Slavery had come to the Carolina colony with its first European settlers. Emigrating from the British Caribbean, where a colonial economy based on the use of slave labor of Africans had already proved successful, its founders emulated a system that was common to the periphery of the European world system. England placed the jurisdiction over enslavement in the hands of colonial authorities, a practice that permitted Europeans seeking salable commodities to expand the commerce in African slaves to captives acquired in North America. The prospect of exchanging enemy prisoners for weapons, metal tools, and other European goods introduced a new dimension to Native warfare just as it created source of supply for a growing export market in Indian slaves. First exploited by English traders in Virginia, the practice spread into South Carolina as rivalry for land and resources made it practical for aboriginal peoples seeking European products to accommodate the English presence and seek alliances that could help them face an uncertain future in a state of increasing dependency. Alan Gallay, *The Indian Slave Trade: The Rise of the English Empire in the American South, 1670–1717* (New Haven, Conn.: Yale University Press, 2002), 42–48; William L. Ramsey, "'All & Singular the Slaves': A Demographic Profile of Indian Slavery in Colonial South Carolina," in *Money, Trade, and Power: The Evolution of Colonial South Carolina's Plantation Society,* ed. Jack P. Greene, Rosemary Brana-Shute, and Randy J. Sparks (Columbia: University of South Carolina Press, 2001), 166–186; Edgar, *South Carolina: A History,* 21–24, 28–33, 46–48; David Brian Davis, *The Problem of Slavery in Western Culture* (Ithaca, N.Y.: Cornell University Press, 1966), 180. Dependency is a product of the expansion of the capitalist world system. It involves the economic collapse of aboriginal subsistence systems and their integration into world markets controlled by the states at the system's core. Dependency is accompanied by a loss of economic control, which brings about profound political and social changes. Richard White, *The Roots of Dependency: Subsistence, Environment, and Social Change among the Choctaws, Pawnees, and Navajos* (Lincoln: University of Nebraska Press, 1983), xv–xix.

28. For a discussion of the role of war in the acquisition of Native estates, see Francis Paul Prucha, *The Great Father: The United States Government and the American Indians* (Lincoln: University of Nebraska Press, 1984), 5–7. Edgar, *South Carolina: A History,* 86–87, 100–102; Verner W. Crane, *The Southern Frontier, 1670–1732* (Ann Arbor: University of Michigan Press, 1956), 162–186; Gallay, *Indian Slave Trade,* 329–335; Ramsey, "All & Singular the Slaves," 178–179; Weir, *Colonial South Carolina,* 142–143; Charles M. Hudson, *Elements of Southeastern Indian Religion,* Iconography of Religions 10 (Leiden: E. J. Brill, 1984), 22.

29. Deerskins found a ready market for clothing in England, and the large numbers of deer in the eastern woodlands of North America provided an almost inexhaustible source of hides to those able to obtain them by hunting. The trade in deerskins grew rapidly, reaching an average of 54,000 annually by the beginning of the eighteenth century. In order to maintain this volume, traders extended their activities farther into the interior, involving Native peoples increasingly distant from Charleston. The exchange also became more specialized, with its control gravitating to traders attracted by its lucrative nature. Motivated by profit, the Carolina traders ignored attempts by the Proprietors to control their activities and established arrangements with groups and shifted them to others when convenient, taking advantage of an increasingly unstable political situation in the interior. Ver Steeg, *Origins of a Southern Mosaic,* 109–114; Edgar, *South Carolina: A History,* 136; Crane, *Southern Frontier,* 108–136.

30. *SC&AGG,* Feb. 19, 1768.

31. Jan de Vries, *The Economy of Europe in an Age of Crisis, 1600–1750* (Cambridge: University Press, 1976); Wallerstein, *Modern World System, II: Mercantilism and the Consolidation of the European World Economy, 1600–1750* (New York: Academic Press, 1980); R. C. Nash, "South Carolina and the Atlantic Economy in the Late Seventeenth and Eighteenth Centuries," *Economic History Review* 45 (1992): 697; Weir, *Colonial South Carolina,* 165–166.

32. The Proprietors recognized the potential of rice as a commercial crop in Carolina even before English colonization began. Duke of Albemarle to Lord Willoby, Aug. 31, 1663, in Cheves, ed., *Shaftesbury*

Papers, 15. They may have sent rice seed there as early as 1672, but certainly by 1677. Rice purportedly was planted in South Carolina as early as 1685, and by 1691 it was considered a promising crop, Cheves, ed., *Shaftesbury Papers,* 377n.; Drayton, *View of South Carolina,* 115; Gray, *History of Agriculture,* 1: 277–278; Ver Steeg, *Origins of a Southern Mosaic,* 118–119. Recent genetic research has revealed that the rice imported to South Carolina was most likely Ghanaian in origin. African rice, *Oryza glaberrima,* was domesticated on the upper Niger River as early as 1500 B.C. and was grown extensively along the West African coast when Europeans arrived there in the fifteenth century. This region supplied the bulk of the enslaved Africans imported into South Carolina, and it is not unreasonable to assume that their familiarity with the crop in whose success they later played so large a role had a similar origin. Judith Ann Carney, *Black Rice: The Origins of Rice Cultivation in the Americas* (Cambridge, Mass.: Harvard University Press, 2001), Ch. 2.

33. Rice production rose in the first decade of the eighteenth century, and the province exported 12,677 barrels in 1713. Exports of rice climbed to 32,384 barrels by 1729 and kept rising. They were double this volume in the 1750s and sometimes nearly triple. The volume of rice passing through the port of Charleston peaked at 130,500 barrels in 1771, and on the eve of the American Revolution South Carolina's entrepôt shipped 118,279 barrels of rice. David Ramsey, *History of South Carolina, From Its First Settlement in 1670, to the Year 1808,* Vol. 2 (Charleston, S.C.: David Longworth, 1809), 115; Clowse, *Economic Beginnings,* 233, 256–257; Gray, *History of Agriculture,* 2: 1021–1023; Petty, *The Growth and Distribution of Population,* 214.

34. Peter A. Coclanis, "Rice Prices in the 1820s and the Evolution of the South Carolina Economy," *Journal of Southern History* 48 (1982): 540–541; Stephen G. Hardy, "Colonial South Carolina's Rice Industry and the Atlantic Economy," in *Money, Trade, and Power: The Evolution of Colonial South Carolina's Plantation Society,* ed. Jack P. Greene, Rosemary Brana-Shute, and Randy J. Sparks (Columbia: University of South Carolina Press, 2001), 115–117.

35. Nash, "South Carolina and the Atlantic Economy," 694–696.

36. Discussions of the technology of tidal rice cultivation illustrating the components of the irrigation system and the spatial extent of tidal rice agriculture in South Carolina and Georgia appear in Sam B. Hilliard, "The Tidewater Rice Plantation: An Ingenious Adaptation to Nature," *Geoscience and Man* 12 (1975): 58–65, and Hilliard, "Antebellum Tidewater Rice Culture in South Carolina and Georgia," in *European Settlement and Development in North America: Essays on Geographic Change in Honor of Andrew Hill Clark,* ed. James R. Gibson (Toronto: University of Toronto Press, 1978), 97–115; Kovacik and Winberry, *South Carolina,* 73. Peter H. Wood, *Black Majority: Negroes in Colonial South Carolina from 1670 through the Stono Rebellion* (New York: Alfred A. Knopf, 1974), first emphasized the role of African knowledge in the cultivation of rice in South Carolina, a topic further explored by Daniel C. Littlefield, *Rice and Slaves: Ethnicity and the Slave Trade in Colonial South Carolina* (Urbana: University of Illinois Press, 1981), Ch. 4, and explicitly by Judith A. Carney, "From Hands to Tutors: African Expertise in the South Carolina Rice Economy," *Agricultural History* 67, no. 3 (1993): 1–30, and Carney, "Landscapes of Technology Transfer: Rice Cultivation and African Continuities," *Technology and Culture* 37 (1996): 5–35.

37. In South Carolina, Eliza Lucas successfully grew indigo with the assistance of knowledgeable French Huguenot immigrants as early as 1744, but its production languished until midcentury conflicts curtailed traditional sources in France and Spain and encouraged domestic production. The sudden rise in demand brought a Parliamentary bounty on indigo grown in British colonies, and its cultivation steadily increased in South Carolina until exports reached more than a million pounds annually on the eve of the American Revolution, after which it declined as the political factors that provided its market disappeared King George's War (1739–1748) provided the initial impetus for indigo production, but afterward demand declined rapidly as older sources again became available. Demand rose again with the outbreak of the Seven Years' War (1754–1763). New tariffs on foreign indigo followed this conflict and, together with colonial bounties, provided the impetus for its growth as a cash crop in South Carolina. G. Terry Sharrer, "Indigo in Carolina, 1671–1796," *South Carolina Historical Magazine* 72 (1971): 94–103; Gray, *History of Agriculture,* 1: 1024; Ramsey, *History of South Carolina,* Vol. 1 118–119;

David L. Coon, "Eliza Lucas Pinckney and the Reintroduction of Indigo Culture in South Carolina," *Journal of Southern History* 42 (1976): 68–76. For the significance of indigo in the textile industry, see Susan Fairlie, "Dyestuffs in the Eighteenth Century," *Economic History Review,* 2nd ser., 17 (1965): 498. Gray, *History of Agriculture,* Vol. 1 292–293; Weir, *Colonial South Carolina,* 150.

38. John J. McCusker and Russell R. Menard, *The Economy of British America, 1607–1789* (Chapel Hill: University of North Carolina Press for the Institute of Early American History and Culture, 1985), 182–183; Clowse, *Economic Beginnings,* 234–235. This trade involved a complex web that reached far beyond a bilateral exchange between Europe and America. An observer noted in 1761 that the deerskins, forest products, rice, and indigo sent directly from South Carolina to Great Britain only partially covered the cost of the imported finished goods and enslaved Africans. To make up the deficit, colonists engaged in extensive trading relationships with New England and the northern British colonies, the West Indies, and the Portuguese islands. "A Description of South Carolina," in *Historical Collections of South Carolina,* Vol. 2, ed. B. R. Carroll (New York: Harper & Bros., 1836), 254–256.

39. The correlation between settlement and crop-processing requirements was postulated by Carville Earle and Ronald Hoffman, "Staple Crops and Urban Development in the Eighteenth Century South," *Perspectives in American History* 10 (1976): 66. Coclanis, *Shadow of a Dream,* 146–147, stressed the degree to which the self-sufficient tendencies of lowcountry plantations inhibited town growth in the region; however, surplus goods produced by slaves were marketed outside the plantation. Although slaves exchanged some of their produce in town markets, much of it appears to have been sold through itinerant watermen who traversed the rivers between plantation and port. Ira Berlin, *Many Thousands Gone: The First Two Centuries of Slavery in North America* (Cambridge, Mass.: Belknap Press of Harvard University Press, 1998), 164–166.

40. George C. Rogers Jr., *Charleston in the Age of the Pinckneys* (Norman: University of Oklahoma Press, 1969), 12; Coclanis, *Shadow of a Dream,* 146; Henry A. M. Smith, "Some Forgotten Towns in Lower South Carolina," *South Carolina Historical Magazine* 13 (1914): 198–203; William B. Barr, "Childsbury Towne and Ashley Ferry Town: Elements of Control in the Economic Landscape of Colonial South Carolina," *Underwater Archaeology Proceedings from the Society for Historical Archaeology Conference 1994,* ed. Paul Forsythe Johnson (1995), 88–93. In an attempt to induce settlement growth, the provincial legislature attempted to encourage "handycraft tradesmen, shopkeepers, and others to settle in towns and villages along the rivers." *Journal of the Commons House of Assembly* (hereafter *JCHA*), South Carolina Department of Archives and History, Mar. 13, 1746.

41. Petty, *Growth and Distribution of Population,* 49–50; H. Roy Merrens, *Colonial North Carolina in the Eighteenth Century: A Study in Historical Geography* (Chapel Hill: University of North Carolina Press, 1964), 13; Rogers, *Charleston,* 7–9; Jacob M. Price, "Economic Function and the Growth of American Port Towns in the Eighteenth Century," *Perspectives in American History* 8 (1974): 161–163; McCusker and Menard, *Economy of British North America,* 184–185; Weir, *Colonial South Carolina,* 123; Kovacik and Winberry, *South Carolina,* 82. For a discussion of the concept of "second nature" and its role in the development of central places in regions undergoing settlement, see William Cronen, *Nature's Metropolis: Chicago and the Great West* (New York: W. W. Norton, 1991), 55–57.

42. Rogers, *Charleston,* 14–21; Edgar, *South Carolina,* Chs. 6 and 7.

43. George C. Rogers Jr., *The History of Georgetown County, South Carolina* (Columbia: University of South Carolina Press, 1970); Leila Sellers, *Charleston Business on the Eve of the American Revolution* (Chapel Hill: University of North Carolina Press, 1934), 6–7; Close, *Economic Beginnings,* 249; Drayton, *A View of South Carolina,* 207–208; Robert Mills to Sarah Mills, 1804, in "Letters from Robert Mills," *South Carolina Historical Magazine* 39 (1938): 114; "A Short Description of the Province of South Carolina," in *Historical Collections of South Carolina,* ed. B. R. Carroll, Vol. 2 (New York: Harper & Bros., 1836), 490–491.

44. Drayton, *View of South Carolina,* 208–209; "A Short Description of South Carolina," 490; A Young Gentleman, "A Gentleman's Account of His Travels, 1733–34," in *The Colonial South Carolina Scene: Contemporary Views, 1697–1774,* ed. H. Roy Merrens (Columbia: University of South Carolina Press, 1977), 121.

45. Richard Waterhouse, *A New World Gentry: The Making of a Merchant and Planter Class in South Carolina, 1670–1770* (Charleston, S.C.: The History Press, 2005), 108.

46. Ver Steeg, *Origins of a Southern Mosaic,* 65–68; Weir, *Colonial South Carolina,* 64.

47. The transition from Proprietary government to a royal administration was a lengthy process that grew out of growing dissatisfaction with the old regime in the first decades of the eighteenth century. A bloodless coup, the Revolution of 1719, reconstituted South Carolina's colonial government, declared Proprietary rule incompetent, and requested that the Crown appoint a royal governor. The following year the British government recognized that colony was under its control and appointed a governor, who took office in 1721. Despite these events, legal title to South Carolina remained with the Proprietors until 1729, when seven of the eight agreed to sell their shares in the colony to the king. With this transfer the transition to Royal government was complete. Edgar, *South Carolina,* 103–111.

48. Jack P. Greene, "The Role of the Lower House of Assembly in Eighteenth Century Politics," *Journal of Southern History* 27 (1961): 455. Robert M. Weir, "'The Harmony We Were Famous For': An Interpretation of Pre-Revolutionary South Carolina Politics," *William and Mary Quarterly,* 3rd ser., 26 (1969): 479–482, and Weir, *Colonial South Carolina,* 134–136, has linked the political philosophy that underlay unification in eighteenth-century South Carolina to the rise of "country ideology," a body of ideas and assumptions currently fashionable throughout the British Empire. These derived from the notion that maintaining individual freedom was paramount; however, because human nature was unreliable, social order could be maintained by limiting the exercise of that freedom. Maintaining order fell to government, but if it failed in its responsibility people had the duty to resist it. This could be achieved by instituting checks on the power of government, one of which was an elected representative legislature that protected the people from abuses of executive power. Members of the legislature bore an obligation to employ political expertise in the service of their constituents, a capability that required education and economic independence. These qualifications limited membership in the legislature to the elite, whose wealth attested to their success in these endeavors. Although self-interest might tempt representatives toward factional actions, it subverted the power of the legislature and diminished its ability to thwart executive power. Consequently, a unified legislature was perceived as the key strategy for achieving success in its role as the people's representative.

49. Edgar, *South Carolina,* 125–129; Weir, *Colonial South Carolina,* 107; Waterhouse, *New World Gentry,* 103–105; M. Eugene Sirmans, *Colonial South Carolina, A Political History, 1663–1763* (Williamsburg, Va.: For the Institute of Early American History by the University of North Carolina Press, 1966), 250–251.

50. Waterhouse, *New World Gentry,* 91–92; Edgar, *South Carolina,* 128; Weir, *Colonial South Carolina,* 107; Sirmans, *Colonial South Carolina,* 166.

51. In 1716 the Assembly passed legislation changing the units of representation from counties to parishes and designating parish churches polling places for elections. Weir, *Colonial South Carolina,* 98; Waterhouse, *New World Gentry,* 93; Edgar, *South Carolina,* 125.

52. Edgar, *Colonial South Carolina,* 112–113.

Chapter 3. "That Remote Part of the Country"

1. James de St. Julien was the son of Peter de St. Julien, who, with his brother Louis, had come to South Carolina from Vitré in the province of Brittany in 1686 as part of the wave of Huguenot immigrants who fled France after the revocation of the Edict of Nantes. The St. Juliens had been members of the lower gentry, and Peter became one of the largest landholders on the upper Cooper River in St. Johns Parish, Berkeley County. His sons, James, Henry, and Peter Jr., all acquired substantial estates there. N. Louise Bailey, Mary L. Morgan, and Carolyn R. Taylor, *Biographical Directory of the South Carolina Senate, 1776–1985,* Vol. 2 (Columbia: University of South Carolina Press, 1986), 583–585; Bertrand Van Ruymbeke, "The Huguenots of Proprietary South Carolina: Patterns of Migration and Integration," in *Money, Trade, and Power: The Evolution of Colonial South Carolina's Plantation Society,* ed. Jack P. Greene, Rosemary Branna-Shute, and Randy J. Sparks (Columbia: University of South Carolina Press, 2001), 37–38; George D. Terry, "'Champaign Country': A Social History of an Eighteenth

Century Lowcountry Parish in South Carolina, St. Johns Berkeley County" (Ph.D. diss., University of South Carolina, 1981), 53–55.

2. For the participation of James and Peter de St. Julien in the Indian trade and James's role in the settlement of the Georgia colony, see Verner W. Crane, *The Southern Frontier, 1670–1732* (Ann Arbor: University of Michigan Press, 1956), 120; Phinizy Spandling, "South Carolina and Georgia: The Early Days," *South Carolina Historical Magazine,* 69 (1968), 85–86; Arthur Henry Hirsch, *The Huguenots of South Carolina* (Columbia: University of South Carolina Press, 1999), 45.

3. Although the Wateree River constitutes a single watercourse from its confluence with the Congaree to the North Carolina line, it possesses two names. Its southern portion, comprising about half its length, is called the Wateree, while the remainder is known as the Catawba. Unfortunately, the events and processes of the region's history overlap both parts of this single though arbitrarily divided entity, introducing an additional layer of complexity to their discussion. To avoid confusion, I have employed the term "Wateree Valley" to refer to the entire length of this river in South Carolina.

4. The antiquity of the human presence in the southeastern United States, and South Carolina in particular, has been a topic of controversy among archaeologists in recent years. Traditionally, they assigned dates for the earliest human occupation on the basis of the presence of lanceolate stone tool types associated with peoples known as Paleoindian. Situated in many portions of the state, they implied a Paleoindian presence between 9,500 and 8,000 B.C. Albert C. Goodyear III, James L. Michie, and Tommy Charles, "The Earliest Carolinians," in *Studies in South Carolina Archaeology: Essays in Honor of Robert L. Stephenson,* ed. Albert C. Goodyear III and Glen T. Hanson, Anthropological Studies 9 (Columbia: South Carolina Institute of Archaeology and Anthropology, University of South Carolina, 1989), 42–43. More recently, discoveries of earlier Paleoindian sites in the Southeast and elsewhere in the Americas indicate a human presence at least 15,000 years ago and possibly before 20,000 B.P. The oldest claim of human occupation in North America is at the Topper site, on the lower Savannah River in South Carolina, but the 50,000 B.P. dates for tools found here remain controversial. Albert C. Goodyear, "The 2010 Activities of the Southeastern Paleoindian Survey," *South Carolina Institute of Archaeology and Anthropology, Legacy* 15, no. 1 (2011): 8–15; Ted Goebel, Michael R. Waters, and Dennis H. O'Rourke, "The Late Pleistocene Dispersal of Humans in the Americas," *Science* 319 (2008): 1500. The environmental changes that occurred in South Carolina during and after the close of the Pleistocene are based on a palynological sequence taken from White Pond, located in the Wateree Valley on the inner Coastal Plain near Camden. W. A. Watts, "The Late Quaternary Vegetation History of the Southeastern United States," *Annual Review of Ecological Systematics,* 11 (1980): 398, 403; Watts, "Late Quaternary Vegetation History at White Pond, South Carolina," *Quaternary Research* 13 (1980): 192–194.

5. The Archaic Period in South Carolina is discussed in David G. Anderson and Glen T. Hanson, "Early Archaic Settlement in the Southeastern United States: A Case Study from the Savannah River Valley," *American Antiquity* 53 (1988): 262–286, and Kenneth E. Sassaman and David G. Anderson, *Middle and Late Archaeological Records of South Carolina: A Synthesis for Research and Resource Management* (Columbia: Council of South Carolina Professional Archaeologists, 1994). The Woodland Period in the Carolinas was defined by Joffre L. Coe, "The Formative Cultures of the Carolina Piedmont," *Transactions of the American Philosophical Society,* n.s., 54 (1964), and discussed in Michael B. Trinkley, "An Archaeological Overview of the South Carolina Woodland Period: It's the Same Old Riddle," in *Studies in South Carolina Archaeology: Essays in Honor of Robert L. Stephenson,* ed. Albert C. Goodyear III and Glen T. Hanson, Anthropological Studies 9 (Columbia: South Carolina Institute of Archaeology and Anthropology, University of South Carolina, 1989), 73–89. A synthetic summary of the precontact history of South Carolina is not currently available in published form; however, a useful discussion may be found in John S. Cable, "Cultural Background," in "Archaeological Data Recovery at Sites 38SU45, 38SU133, and 38SU145, with Results of Test Excavations Conducted at Sites 38SU136, 38SU137, and 38SU141, Poinsett Electronic Combat Range, Sumter County, South Carolina," U.S. Air Force Air Combat Command Series, Report of Investigations 7, Geo-Marine, Inc. (Plano, Tex., 1998), 21–34.

6. Classic definitions of the Mississippian follow James B. Griffin, "Eastern North American Archaeology: A Summary," *Science* 156, no. 3772 (1967): 189; Bruce D. Smith, "Variation in Mississippian Settlement Patterns," in *Mississippian Settlement Patterns,* ed. Bruce D. Smith (New York: Academic Press, 1978), 486, 488.

7. The term "chiefdom" has been used in the anthropological literature to describe complex societies organized on the basis of ranked hierarchical leadership. Morton H. Fried, *The Evolution of Political Society: An Essay in Political Anthropology* (New York: Random House, 1967) and Elman R. Service, *Primitive Social Organization: An Evolutionary Perspective* (New York: Random House, 1962). Traditional studies postulated that the redistribution of surpluses was central to the rise of this form of political organization; however, more recent works have found less evidence for the economic role of leaders and instead emphasized the organizational advantages associated with their political, religious, and military functions. See for example Christopher S. Peebles and Susan M. Kus, "Some Archaeological Correlates of Ranked Societies," *American Antiquity* 42 (1977): 427–431, and Timothy Earle, *Chiefdoms, Power, Economy, and Ideology* (Cambridge: Cambridge University Press, 1991).

Changes associated with the Mississippian involved managing greater numbers of people and coordinating the production and distribution of foodstuffs, as well as other goods. Success depended on the ability of leaders to control activities within the polities they oversaw. As in other emerging complex societies, leadership was based on a ranked form of social organization in which the individual occupying the highest status exercised power based on prestige. In Mississippian society, status was ascriptive, that is, it was conferred by birth and determined by one's position in a system of ranked kin groups, usually lineages. The individual who occupied the highest-ranked position in a highest-ranked lineage was a hereditary chief, whose position conferred political, religious, and military authority, through which all aspects of society could be regulated. Centralized leadership was advantageous for large, sedentary societies in which efficient decision making and expeditious information processing facilitated the mobilization of resources to ward off famine or protect the community from outside aggression. Possessing advantages of effective control and flexibility, complex societies, called "chiefdoms," came to dominate much of eastern North America, including the Southeast.

The organization of chiefdoms fostered the growth of large but inherently unstable polities in the Southeast. Because authority grew out of an individual's position in a kin network, leaders lacked coercive political power and the permanent institutions of the highly centralized government found in early states. Expansion and incorporation of new lands and disparate peoples could make extending control into new regions tenuous and threaten the stability of the system. The succession of chiefs might also create uncertainty. Although ascribed, positions of leadership also required charisma, and rivalry among potential successors introduced inherently dangerous factionalism. The success of Mississippian leaders in developing social networks that allowed them to accumulate political capital by manipulating information, prestige goods, and surplus labor allowed them to enlarge their polities and often control substantial areas, but the absence of formal political institutions made the system essentially unstable. Over time, the size of Mississippian polities grew and the power wielded by leaders increased, but the exclusionary strategies upon which their authority was based encouraged competition and intensified factionalism among chiefdoms, magnifying their instability and resulting in periodic collapse and reorganization. Indeed, most southeastern chiefdoms had declined by 1400. David G. Anderson, *The Savannah River Chiefdoms: Political Change in the Late Prehistoric Southeast* (Tuscaloosa: University of Alabama Press, 1994), and Adam King, "Leadership Strategies and the Nature of Mississippian Chiefdoms in Northern Georgia," in *Leadership and Polity in Mississippian Society,* ed. Brian M. Butler and Paul D. Welch, Occasional Paper 33 (Carbondale: Center for Archaeological Investigations, Southern Illinois University, 2006), 73–90. The distinction between chiefdoms and early states follows that of Kent V. Flannery, "The Cultural Evolution of Civilizations," *Annual Review of Ecology and Systematics* 3 (1972): 403–404.

8. Anderson, *Savannah River Chiefdoms,* 326–329; Chester DePratter, "The Kingdom of Cofitachequi," in *The Forgotten Centuries: Indians and Europeans in the American South, 1521–1704,* ed. Charles Hudson and Carmen Chaves Tesser (Athens: University of Georgia Press, 1994), 198–199.

9. The Mulberry mounds and the Adamson mound, as well as others in the vicinity of Camden, have been the subject of scholarly inquiry since the middle of the nineteenth century. Ephraim G. Squire and E. H. Davis, *Ancient Monuments of the Mississippi Valley* (Washington, D.C.: Smithsonian Institution, 1848), 105–108. The results of archaeological work at Mulberry have been compiled in Leland G. Ferguson, ed., "Archaeological Investigations at the Mulberry Site," *South Carolina Institute of Archaeology and Anthropology, Notebook* 6, nos. 3–4 (1974), and the results of more recent research are listed in DePratter, "Kingdom of Cofitacheque," 224, n. 72.

10. Estimates of the size and extent of Cofitacheque vary considerably. Those based on Spanish accounts of the de Soto and Pardo expeditions have traditionally included a wider territory; see Steven G. Baker, "Cofitacheque: Fair Province of Carolina" (M.A thesis, University of South Carolina, 1975); however, a more recent examination of these materials together with archaeological evidence has led one author to conclude that the chiefdom encompassed a more restricted zone; see DePratter, "Kingdom of Cofitacheque," 213–214, 219–221.

11. Baker, "Cofitacheque," 123–182.

12. Charles Hudson et al., "On Interpreting Cofitachequi," *Ethnohistory* 55 (2008): 469–471; Anderson, *Savannah River Chiefdoms,* 242–244; DePratter, "Kingdom of Cofitacheque," 197, 221; John Lawson, *A New Voyage to Carolina,* ed. Hugh Talmage Lefler (Chapel Hill: University of North Carolina Press, 1967), 233; Steven G. Baker, "The Working Draft of: The Historic Catawba Peoples: Exploratory Perspectives in Ethnohistory and Archaeology" (Columbia: Office of Research, University of South Carolina, 1975), 27–36; Charles M. Hudson, *The Juan Pardo Expedition: Exploration of the Carolinas and Tennessee, 1556–1568* (Washington, D.C.: Smithsonian Institution Press, 1990), 181; Hudson, *The Catawba Nation* (Athens: University of Georgia Press, 1970), 28–30; Crane, *Southern Frontier,* 13.

13. Baker, "Historic Catawba Peoples," 45–48, 55–56; Lawson, *New Voyage,* 46, 49.

14. For a discussion of the multiple causes and outcomes of the Yamassee War, see Alan Gallay, *The Indian Slave Trade: The Rise of the English Empire in the American South, 1670–1717* (New Haven, Conn.: Yale University Press, 2002), 329–335, 338–341. The role of drought and its impact on aboriginal societies in the Southeast may be found in David G. Anderson, David W. Stahle, and Malcolm K. Cleaveland, "Paleoclimate and the Potential Food Reserves of Mississippian Societies: A Case Study from the Savannah River Valley," *American Antiquity* 60 (1995): 258–286.

15. Baker, "Historic Catawba Peoples," 56–58, 80–83; James E. Merrell, "The Indians' New World: The Catawba Experience," *William and Mary Quarterly,* 3rd ser., 41 (1984): 544; Merrell, *The Indians' New World: Catawbas and Their Neighbors from European Contact through the Era of Removal* (Chapel Hill, University of North Carolina Press for the Omohundro Institute of Early American History and Culture, 1989), 133; Samuel Cole Williams, ed., *Adair's History of the American Indians* (Johnson City, Tenn.: Watauga Press, 1930), 235–236; Frank G. Speck, "Siouan Tribes of the Carolinas as Known from Catawba, Tutelo, and Documentary Sources," *American Anthropologist* 37 (1935): 216–221. As late as 1721, Native cartographers identified eleven separate groups situated north of Charleston. "The Catawba Map" (London: British Museum, Additional MS 4723, c. 1721), in Mark Warhus, *Another America: Native American Maps and the History of Our Land* (New York: St. Martin's Press, 1997), 77–80. Seven years later, the Catawbas were clearly identified as a single entity. The location of the "Katawba" towns and routes of access to them were illustrated in George Hunter's early map of the interior "The Charecke Nation by Col. Herbert's Map & My Own Observations with the Path to Charles Town . . ." (Washington, D.C.: Geography and Map Division, Library of Congress, 1730).

16. The factory erected was erected near the location where the trading paths to the trading routes to the Cherokees and the Catawbas crossed just below the point where the Broad and Saluda Rivers join to form the Congaree. Constructed in 1718, this fortified settlement remained in use until 1722. It was situated on a bend in Congaree Creek, which lies on the west side of the Congaree River southwest of present-day Columbia. Archaeologists discovered the remains of the Congaree factory on the north side of Congaree Creek in Lexington Couty and investigated the site in 1989. James L. Michie, *The Discovery of Old Fort Congaree,* Research Manuscript Series 208 (Columbia: South Carolina Institute

of Archaeology and Anthropology, 1989); Crane, *Southern Frontier,* 194; Baker, "Historic Catawba Peoples," 65–69.

17. Anticipating a visit from the "Catawba and Charrow Indians" in the spring of 1739, the provincial governor requested funds for the "usual reception and entertainment" from the Assembly. "Message from Gov. William Bull," *JCHA,* June 5, 1739. In subsequent years the legislature regularly appropriated funds for clothing, supplies, liquor, corn, beef, medicines, arms and ammunition, and other items. See, for example, "Accounts of Expenses" and "Presents," *JCHA,* Mar. 29, 31, 1740; Jan. 19, 1742; June 8, 1748; May 14, 1750; Jan. 28, 1751: 268, 280, 283, 315, 294–295, 462, 207. For examples of lists of goods supplied the Catawbas at the Congarees, see William L. McDowell, ed., *Documents Relating to Indian Affairs, May 21, 1750–August 7, 1754* (Columbia: South Carolina Department of Archives and History, 1958), 217–218, and McDowell, *Documents Relating to Indian Affairs, 1754–1765* (Columbia: South Carolina Department of Archives and History, 1970), 34–35. On April 1746 Gov. James Glen met with the Catawbas on the Santee River to reaffirm the Natives' support of the colony in the face of French threats from the west. Emphasizing past loyalty between their peoples and the common danger from external enemies, Glen stressed the necessity of maintaining their alliance and pledged South Carolina's continued material backing of the Catawbas: *South Carolina Gazette* (hereafter *SCG*), June 2, 1746.

18. Robert L. Meriwether, *The Expansion of South Carolina, 1729–1765* (Kingsport, Tenn.: Southern Publishers, 1940), 17–19; Arlin C. Migliazzo, *To Make This Land Our Own: Community, Identity, and Cultural Adaptation in Purrysburg Township, South Carolina, 1732–1865* (Columbia, University of South Carolina Press, 2007), 31.

19. Meriwether, *Expansion of South Carolina,* 20–21.

20. Migliazzo, *To Make This Land Our Own,* 31; John W. Shy, "A New Look at Colonial Militia," *William and Mary Quarterly,* 3rd ser., 20 (1963): 179–181; [Robert Johnson], "A Governor Answers a Questionnaire, 1719/20," in *The Colonial South Carolina Scene: Contemporary Views, 1697–1774,* ed. H. Roy Merrens (Columbia: University of South Carolina Press, 1977), 57–58; [William Bull], "Governor William Bull's Representation of the Colony, 1770," in ibid., 261; Clyde R. Ferguson, "Functions of the Partisan Militia in the South during the American Revolution: An Interpretation," in *The Revolutionary War in the South: Power, Conflict, and Leadership: Essays in Honor of John Richard Alden,* ed. W. Robert Higgins (Durham, N.C.: Duke University Press, 1979), 242. Statistics of militia membership prior to 1790 have been summarized in Appendix E in Julian J. Petty, *The Growth and Distribution of Population in South Carolina* (Columbia: South Carolina State Planning Board, 1943; reprint ed., Spartanburg, S.C.: The Reprint Co., 1975), 220–225.

21. Meriwether, *Expansion of South Carolina,* 34–35; Petty, *Growth and Distribution of Population,* 35–37. Purry envisioned his colony as a private enterprise to establish a closely knit village in the wilderness, but the Purrysburg project faced the tasks of accommodating people of different ethnicity and religious persuasion, establishing and maintaining civil authority, and developing a functioning economy in a region lacking a substantial population, adequate capital for investment, and an infrastructure for production and transportation. For a discussion of Purry's ideas and theories about colonization, the background to his South Carolina enterprise, and its development, see Migliazzo, *To Make This Land Our Own,* Ch. 2.

22. Meriwether, *Expansion of South Carolina,* 46, 50, 62, 66–70; Petty, *Growth and Distribution of Population,* 40, 41–42.

23. Alexander Gregg, *History of the Old Cheraws* (Columbia, S.C.: The State Co., 1867; reprint ed., Greenville, SC: Southern Historical Press, 1991), 45–54; Meriwether, *Expansion of South Carolina,* 82–83, 94; Petty, *Growth and Distribution of Population,* 39–40; Hunter, "The Charecke Nation."

24. Meriwether, *Expansion of South Carolina,* 99–100; Petty, *Growth and Distribution of Population,* 40–41. The route of the principal Indian trade routes of the eighteenth century are based on William E. Myer, "The Trail System of the Southeastern United States in the Early Colonial Period," in "Indian Trails of the Southeast," in *Annual Report of the Bureau of American Ethnology* 42 (1928): 727–857.

25. The process of integrating the interior of South Carolina was both economic and political in nature. The latter aspect of unification has been explored extensively by Rachel N. Klein, *Unification of a Slave State: The Rise of the Planter Class in the South Carolina Backcountry, 1760–1808* (Chapel Hill: University of North Carolina Press for the Institute of Early American History and Culture, 1990).

26. For an example of this approach to frontier expansion in South Carolina, see Kenneth E. Lewis, *The American Frontier: An Archaeological Study of Settlement Pattern and Process* (Orlando, Fla.: Academic Press, 1984), Chs. 5–8.

27. "Plat of the Town of Fredericksburg on Wateree River, Surveyed by James de St. Julian," Feb. 2, 1734, Copies of Plats and Plans, 1728–1800, S213187 (CCP), Vol. 1, 47, South Carolina Department of Archives and History, Columbia. For the role of frontier maps as devices to impose authorities notions of social order, see Gregory H. Nobles, "Straight Lines and Stability: Mapping the Political Order of the Anglo-American Frontier," *Journal of American History* 80 (1993): 9–35.

28. Carolina Bays are a distinctive geological feature consisting of large oval or elliptically shaped depressions that contain embayments of water. They are unique to South Carolina's Outer Coastal Plain. Charles F. Kovacik and John J. Winberry, *South Carolina: A Geography* (Boulder, Colo.: Westview Press, 1987), 18–21; Charles B. Hunt, *Physiography of the United States* (San Francisco: W. H. Freeman, 1967), 145; William C. Overstreet and Henry Bell III, *The Crystalline Rocks of South Carolina,* U.S. Department of the Interior, Geological Survey, Bulletin 1183 (1965), 81; Santee-Wateree Planning Council, *Land Use Sketch Plan, Santee-Wateree Planning District, June 1972* (Columbia, S.C.: n. p., 1972), 8–11.

29. Kovacik and Winberry, *South Carolina: A Geography,* 40–41; Cleveland J. Mitchell Jr., *Soil Survey of Kershaw County Area, South Carolina* (Washington, D.C.: U.S. Department of Agriculture, Soil Conservation Service, in cooperation with the South Carolina Agricultural Experiment Station and the South Carolina Land Resources Conservation Commission, 1989), 5–11,101; Ronald Morton, *Soil Survey of Kershaw County Area, South Carolina,* U.S. Department of Agriculture, Soil Conservation Service, in cooperation with the South Carolina Agricultural Experiment Station and the South Carolina Department of Natural Resources (Washington, DC: 1989), 5–17, 129–130; George H. Wittkowsky and J. L. Moseley Jr., *Kershaw County: Economic and Social* (Columbia: Department of Rural Social Science, University of South Carolina, 1923), 16.

30. Although historic land use activities have removed nearly all of South Carolina's interior forest cover, ecologists and other researchers have reconstructed its composition on the basis of undisturbed secondary growth, surviving stands, and an understanding of trends in forest succession. E. Lucy Braun, *Deciduous Forests of Eastern North America* (Philadelphia: Blakiston Co., 1950), 259–260, 284–285, 290–300; E. H. Frothingham and R. M. Nelson, *South Carolina Forest Resources and Industries,* U.S. Department of Agriculture Miscellaneous Publication No. 552 (Washington, D.C.: Government Printing Office, 1944), 20–22; A. W. Kuchler, *Potential Natural Vegetation of the Coterminous United States,* Special Publication 36 (New York: American Geographical Society, 1964); John M. Barry, *Natural Vegetation of South Carolina* (Columbia: University of South Carolina Press, 1980; U.S Army Corps of Engineers, *Provisional Reconnaissance Inventory of the Charleston District* (Washington, D.C.: Office of the Chief of Engineers, Engineer Agency for Resources Inventories, 1972), 10–11; Pete Laurie and David Chamberlain, *The South Carolina Aquarium Guide to Aquatic Habitats of South Carolina* (Columbia: University of South Carolina Press, 2003), 94–95, 109–113.

31. Mark Catesby, "Mark Catesby's *Natural History,* 1731–47," in *The Colonial South Carolina Scene: Contemporary Views, 1697–1774,* ed. H. Roy Merrens (Columbia: University of South Carolina Press, 1977), 93–94.

32. Immigrants' assessment of the value of a new environment has always been influenced heavily by their needs and experience, and the images they formed reflect a comparison of the environments with those with which they were familiar. The importance of establishing mixed farming led most frontier settlers to evaluate an environment on the basis of its utility rather than on notions of its romantic, picturesque, or ecological qualities. John A. Jakle, *Images of the Ohio Valley: A Historical Geography of Travel, 1740–1860* (New York: Oxford University Press, 1977), 9–13; Klaus G. Loewald, Beverly Starika, and Paul S. Taylor, eds., "Johann Martin Bolzius Answers a Questionnaire on Carolina and

Georgia, Part II [1751]," *William and Mary Quarterly,* 3rd ser. (1958): 15, 249–250; "A Short Description of the Province of South Carolina (1763)," in *Historical Collections of South Carolina,* ed. B. R. Carroll (New York: Harper & Bros., 1836), 468; Louis De Vorsey Jr., ed., *De Braham's Report of the General Survey in the Southern District of North America* (Columbia: University of South Carolina Press, 1971), 72–76; George Fenwick Jones, ed. and trans., "Commissary [Georg Philipp] von Reck's Report on Georgia, [1734]," *Georgia Historical Quarterly* 47 (1963): 98–99. These quotes are from the following sources, respectively: De Vorsey, ed., *De Brahm's Report,* 75–76; Lionel Chalmers, "A Sketch of the Climate, Weather, and Soil in South Carolina, . . . Written in 1776," *The American Museum and Universal Magazine* 3 (1788): 319; Thomas Griffiths, "A Journal of the Voyage to South Carolina in the Year 1767," in *The Colonial South Carolina Scene: Contemporary Views, 1697–1774,* ed. H. Roy Merrens (Columbia: University of South Carolina Press, 1977), 242; Walter L. Robbins, ed., "John Tobler's Description of South Carolina (1753)," *South Carolina Historical Magazine* 71 (1970): 150.

33. De Vorsey, ed., *De Brahm's Report,* 76; "Short Description," 467. For discussions of the perception of disease and its impact on settlement in South Carolina, see Charles F. Kovacik, "Health Conditions and Town Growth in Colonial and Antebellum South Carolina," *Social Science and Medicine* 12 (1978): 131–133; and H. Roy Merrens and George D. Terry, "Dying in Paradise: Malaria, Mortality, and the Perceptual Environment in Colonia South Carolina," *Journal of Southern History* 50 (1984): 547–550.

34. "Report of the Committee . . . to Prepare a Statement of the Pretensions of this Province," *JCHA,* Apr. 28, 1757.

35. "Petition of the Inhabitants of the Upper Part of the Parish of Prince Frederick," *JCHA,* Feb. 25, 1741.

36. "Report of the Committee Appointed to Enquire Where Any Vacant Mainorable Lands may be Ascertained and Set Apart for the Accommodation of Foreign Protestants Who Shall Arrive Here from Europe," *JCHA,* Dec. 1, 1752.

37. Greene to Continental Congress, Apr. 22, 1781, Nathaniel Greene Papers/Papers of the Continental Congress (hereafter NGP/PCC), M247, R 175, I 155, Vol. 2, 43, microfilm (Washington, D.C.: Library of Congress, 1966); Rawdon to Col. McMahon, Jan. 19, 1801, in A. Aspinall, ed., *The Correspondence of George, Prince of Wales, 1770–1812,* Vol. 4 (London: Cassell, 1963–1971), 192.

38. "Plat of the Town of Fredericksburg."

39. Accounts of the systematic burning of forests to clear land appear in De Vorsey, ed., *De Brahm's Report,* 80–81. European settlers continued to employ burning as a method of clearing and maintaining agricultural land in the backcountry, as exemplified in the entries of Evan Pugh, a settler in the Welsh Neck. Horace Fraser Rudisill, ed., *The Diaries of Evan Pugh (1762–1801)* (Florence, S.C.: St. David's Society, 1993), 346, 368, 377, 378, 397, 398.

40. Both Maj. Montcrief to Cornwallis, Cornwallis Papers, Great Britain, Public Records Office (hereafter CP), 30/11/64: 122–123, and Guilford Dudley, "Sketch of the Military Services Performed by Guilford Dudley, Then of the Town of Halifax, North Carolina, During the Revolutionary War," *Southern Literary Messenger* 3 (1845), 146, mention the open nature of the pine forests that correspond to the longleaf pine fire subclimax forests discussed by Braun, *Deciduous Forests,* 284–286. No less than George Washington noted the "miserable" nature of the pine barrens in the sand hills. Archibald Henderson, ed., *Washington's Southern Tour, 1791* (Boston: Houghton Mifflin, 1923), 260.

Chapter 4. "Those Townships Being the Frontier Places"

1. "Petition of the Inhabitants on the Wateree River," *JCHA,* May 9, 1752, 328–329; "Petition of the Inhabitants of the Upper Part of the Parish of Prince Frederick," *JCHA,* Feb. 25, 1741, 504; "Statement from James Glen, Governor of South Carolina, to the Queries from the Commissioners of Trade and Plantations," *JCHA,* May 6, 1749; "Report of the Committee Appointed to Take under Consideration the Governor's Letters to the Lords of Commissioners of Trade and Plantations," *JCHA,* May 16, 1749.

2. Legislation supporting the immigration fund frequently appeared throughout the second quarter of the eighteenth century, see for example *JCHA,* Dec. 10, 1737; Oct. 28, 1741; Nov. 25, 1750;

Nov. 24, 1752; *SCG*, July 16, 1741. *JCHA*, Feb. 3, 1738; Nov. 28, 1739; Mar. 30, 1743; Nov. 23, 1749; Jan. 14, 1746, 34; *South Carolina Gazette and Country Journal* (hereafter *SCG&CJ*), June 30, 1767.

3. Walter Edgar, *South Carolina: A History* (Columbia: University of South Carolina Press, 1998), 55–62.

4. Anthropologists have traditionally defined an institution as a complex of behavior patterns that are organized around a dominant interest of a group and that constitute the established forms or set methods of procedure governing the group's actions. Institutions are basic to all societies and underlie the structure of communal life. For a classic general discussion of social institutions see Robert H. Lowie, *Social Organization* (New York: Holt, Rinehart, 1948), Chs. 4–9. For discussions of social and economic institutions in contemporary England, see Peter Laslett, *The World We Have Lost: England before the Industrial Age*, 2nd ed. (New York: Charles Scribner's Sons, 1971), Ch. 3; J. H. Plumb, *England in the Eighteenth Century* (Baltimore: Penguin, 1972), 14–27; and Carl Bridenbaugh, *Vexed and Troubled Englishmen, 1590–1642* (New York: Oxford University Press, 1968), 83, 119–121. Fernand Braudel examined the structure of French social institutions in *The Identity of France, Vol. 1: History and Environment*, trans. Siân Reynolds (New York: Harper & Row, 1986), 66–77, 150–160, 180–190, and more generally in *Civilization and Capitalism, Vol. 2: The Wheels of Commerce*, trans. Siân Reynolds (New York: Harper & Row, 1979), 29–30, 81–85. For Germany, see Jurgen Schlumbohm, "From Peasant Society to Class Society: Some Aspects of Family and Class in a Northwest German Protoindustrial Parish, Seventeenth–Nineteenth Centuries," *Journal of Family History* 17 (1992): 183–199.

Household here refers to a residence unit composed of the members of one or more families or related people and may include inmates, lodgers, and servants, who act cooperatively on a day-to-day basis. Peter Laslett, "Introduction" to *The World We Have Lost*, 28–36; R. M. Netting, R. R. Wilk, and E. J. Arnould, eds., *Households, Historical and Comparative Studies of the Domestic Group* (Berkeley: University of California Press, 1984).

5. Richard Waterhouse, *A New World Gentry: The Making of a Merchant and Planter Class in South Carolina, 1670–1770* (Charleston, S.C.: The History Press, 2005), 117–119; Richard Maxwell Brown, *The South Carolina Regulators* (Cambridge, M: Belknap Press of Harvard University Press, 1963), 13–15; Rachel N. Klein, *Unification of a Slave State: The Rise of the Planter Class in the South Carolina Backcountry, 1760–1808* (Chapel Hill: University of North Carolina Press for the Institute of Early American History and Culture, 1990), 39–42.

6. Studies of regional settlement on the eastern seaboard of British colonial America have revealed that the initial motivation of colonists was almost always an intent to enter commercial production as soon as conditions permitted. Robert D. Mitchell, "The Commercial Nature of Frontier Settlement in the Shenandoah Valley," *Proceedings of the Association of American Geographers* 1 (1969), 109–113; Mitchell, "The Shenandoah Valley Frontier," *Annals of Association of American Geographers* 62 (1972), 475–476; Mitchell, *Commercialism and Frontier*, 4–6; Winifred B. Rothenberg, "The Market and Massachusetts Farmers, 1750–1855," *Journal of Economic History* 42 (1981): 283–314; Allan Kulikoff, *The Agrarian Origins of American Capitalism* (Charlottesville: University Press of Virginia, 1992), 16–17; Kulikoff, "Households and Markets: Toward a New Synthesis of American Agrarian History," *William and Mary Quarterly*, 3rd ser., 50 (1993): 343–344; Kulikoff, *From British Peasants to Colonial American Farmers* (Chapel Hill: University of North Carolina Press, 2000), 205–207.

7. Of the major inland rivers in South Carolina, only the Savannah appears to have been free of natural obstructions. Mark Catesby, "Mark Catesby's *Natural History*, 1731–47," in *The Colonial South Carolina Scene: Contemporary Views, 1697–1774*, ed. H. Roy Merrens (Columbia: University of South Carolina Press, 1977) 96, reported that this watercourse was "open, devoid of rocks below the falls." This was not the case elsewhere. Rafts were reported on the Black and Pee Dee Rivers, *SCG*, Mar. 20, 1738; "Presentment of the Grand Jury of Cheraws District," *SCG*, Nov. 16, 1772; Nov. 15, 1773. The Edisto was similarly blocked and not cleared for navigation until 1774, *SCG*, July 4, 1774; and navigation on the Wateree River was impeded by a massive raft as late as 1773, "Petition from the Inhabitants of the Wateree River," *JCHA*, May 9, 1752, 329; "Presentment of the Grand Jury of Camden District," *SCG&CJ*, Dec. 15, 1772; *SCG*, Dec. 27, 1773.

8. Caroline E. MacGill, *History of Transportation in the United States before 1860* (Washington, D.C.: Carnegie Institution of Washington, 1917; reprint ed., Gloucester, Mass.: Peter Smith, 1948), 276–277.

9. The course of major roads leading to Fredericksburg Township and the upper Wateree are illustrated in the earliest comprehensive maps of South Carolina's interior. These include James Cook, *A Map of the Province of South Caro*lina (London, 1773); Henry Mouzon, *An Accurate Map of North and South Caro*lina, with Their Indian Frontiers (London: Robert Sayer and J. Bennett, 1775); and William Faden, *A Map of South Caro*lina and a Part of Georgia (London, 1780). For the position of these routes in lager geographical context, see William E. Myer, "Indian Trails of the Southeastern United States in the Early Colonial Period,"in "Indian Trails of the Southeast," Annual Report of the Bureau of American Ethnology 42 (1928): 727–857.

10. The initial pattern of transport development in South Carolina followed the first phases of an ideal typical sequence identified in other colonial areas by Edward J. Taaffe, Richard L. Morrill, and Peter R. Gould, "Transport Expansion in Underdeveloped Countries: A Comparative Analysis," *Geographical Review* 53 (1963): 503–511.

11. "Petition of the Inhabitants of the Townships of New Windsor, Orange Burgh, Saxe Gotha and Fredericks Burgh," *JCHA,* Jan. 19, 1738, 393; "Petition from the Inhabitants of the Upper Part of the Parish of Prince Frederick," *JCHA,* Feb. 25, 1741; "Petition from the Inhabitants of the Wateree Valley," *JCHA,* May 9, 1752; "Petition of the Inhabitants of Fredericksburg Township," *JCHA,* May 10, 1754; Petition of the Inhabitants of Orangeburgh Township, the Forks of the Edisto, and West Side of Steads Creek," *JCHA,* May 9, 1752; "Petition from the Inhabitants of Winyaw," *JCHA,* Jan. 27, 1744; "Petition of John Jacob Reminsperger and Inhabitants of Saxe Gotha Township," *JCHA,* Nov. 27, 1746.

12. Gregory H. Nobles, "Breaking into the Backcountry: New Approaches to the Early American Frontier, 1750–1800," *William and Mary Quarterly,* 3rd ser., 46 (1989): 652–653; Andrew Hill Clark, "Suggestions for the Geographical Study of Agricultural Change in the United States, 1790–1840," *Agricultural History* 46 (1972): 165–166; Kulikoff, "Households and Markets," 353–354; Daniel H. Usner Jr., "The Frontier Exchange Economy of the Lower Mississippi Valley," *William and Mary Quarterly,* 3rd ser. (1987): 166–167; Peter N. Moore, *World of Toil and Strife: Community Transformation in Backcountry South Carolina, 1750–1805* (Columbia: University of South Carolina Press, 2007), 45.

13. Terry Jordan and Matti Kaups, *The American Backwoods Frontier: An Ethnic and Ecological Interpretation* (Baltimore: John Hopkins University Press, 1989), 211–213.

14. As elsewhere in North America, the abundance of wild animals in South Carolina impressed European observers. See Thomas Ashe, "Carolina; or a Description of the Present State of that Country, 1682," in Salley, *Narratives,* 72–73 and Peter Purry, "A Description of the Province of South Carolina, 1731," in Salley, *Narratives,* 134; cf. William Cronon, *Changes in the Land: Indians, Colonists, and the Ecology of New England* (New York: Hill and Wang, 1982), 22–24. John M. Logan, *A History of the Upper Country of South Caroina,* Vol. 1 (Charleston, S.C.: Courtenay, 1859), 22–23, 35–36, 39–40; *JCHA,* Apr. 16, 1746, 195; Richard J. Hooker, ed., *The Carolina Backcountry on the Eve of the Revolution: The Journal and Other Writings of Charles Woodmason, Anglican Itinerant* (Chapel Hill: University of North Carolina Press, 1953), 39.

15. Walter L. Robbins, ed. and trans., "John Tobler's Description of South Carolina (1753)," *South Carolina Historical Magazine* 71 (1970): 159–160; Robert L. Meriwether, *The Expansion of South Carolina, 1729–1765* (Kingsport, Tenn.: Southern Publishers, 1940), 162; "Presentment of the Cheraws Grand Jury, Nov. 156, 1773," *SCG,* Dec. 27, 1773; Klein, *Unification of a Slave State,* 53.

16. Terry G. Jordan, *North American Cattle Ranching Frontiers: Origin, Diffusion, and Differentiation* (Albuquerque: University of New Mexico Press, 1993), 14–17; Arnold Strickon, "The Euro-American Ranching Complex," in *Man, Culture, and Animals,* ed. Anthony Leeds and Andrew P. Vayda (Washington, D.C.: American Association for the Advancement of Science, 1965), 230. A contemporary observer, Lionel Chalmers, outlined the advantages of livestock raising, remarking that "Any person who inclines . . . to raise black cattle, hogs, or horses, marks out a few hundred acres of land in some unsettled part of the country, where he finds a good range; and drives thither as many cows, bulls, hogs,

stallions and mares as he pleases, where they increase without any more trouble. . . . As to the black cattle and horses, they are drove up once every year, in order to mark and brand the increase. After which they are again suffered to feed at large, . . . unless it be required to get some of them for sale, when they are wanted. In this manner, some persons have stocked such farms with 50 or more black cattle &c., have in 15 or 20 years marked 3,000 or 4,000 calves yearly, and hogs without number." Lionel Chalmers, "A Sketch of the Climate, Water, and Soil in South Carolina, . . . Written in 1776," *The American Museum or Universal Magazine* 3 (1788): 29.

17. Gary S. Dunbar, "Colonial South Carolina Cowpens," *Agricultural History* 35 (1961): 125–126, 128; John Solomon Otto, "Livestock-Raising in Early South Carolina, 1670–1700: Prelude to the Rice Plantation Economy," *Agricultural History* 61, no. 4 (1987): 23; Otto, "The Origins of Cattle Ranching in Colonial South Carolina, 1670–1715," *South Carolina Historical Magazine* 87 (1986): 123–124; Logan, *History of the Upper Country,* 151–152; Jordan, *North American Cattle-Ranching Frontiers,* 171–177, 189–191; Mart A. Stewart, "'Whether Wast, Deodand, or Stray': Cattle, Culture, and the Environment in Early Georgia," *Agricultural History* 65 (1991): 14. The sites of two mid-eighteenth-century cowpens on the Inner Coastal Plain have been comprehensively studied by archaeologists. The Catherine Brown cowpen and the Thomas Howell Site on the Savannah River in present Barnwell County have yielded remains of structures, pens, and activity areas associated with these settlements. Richard David Brooks, "Cattle Ranching in Colonial South Carolina: A Case Study in History and Archaeology of the Lazarus/Catherina Brown Cowpen" (M.A. thesis, University of South Carolina, 1988); R. D. Brooks, M. D. Groover, and S. C. Smith, *Living on the Edge: The Archaeology of Cattle Raisers in the South Carolina Backcountry,* Savannah River Archaeological Research Papers 10 (Columbia: University of South Carolina Institute of Archaeology and Anthropology, 2000); and Mark D. Groover and Richard D. Brooks, "The Catherine Brown Cowpen and Thomas Howell Site: Material Characteristics of Cattle Raisers in the South Carolina Backcountry," *Southeastern Archaeology* 22 (2003): 92–111.

18. Cronon, *Changes in the Land,* 140–141.

19. Otto, "Livestock-Raising in Early South Carolina," 20–21; John T. Schlebecker, "Stockmen and Drovers during the Revolution," *Proceedings of the Pioneer America Society* 2 (1973): 4–5. Logan, *History of the Upper Country,* 152. Some idea of the extent of the Charleston livestock market may be gained by regular newspaper advertisements, see, for example, *SCG,* June 23, 1757; Mar. 8, 1773; Sept. 6, 1773; Apr. 4, 1774.

20. Strickon, "Euro-American Ranching Complex," 232; Otto, "Livestock-Raising in Early South Carolina," 24; Meriwether, *Expansion of South Carolina,* 162; Dunbar, "Colonial Carolina Cowpens," 128–129; Jordan, *North American Cattle-Ranching Frontiers,* 189–191; Louis Cecil Gray, *A History of Agriculture in the Southern United States to 1860,* 2 vols. (Washington, D.C.: Carnegie Institution of Washington, 1933; reprint ed., Gloucester, Mass.: Peter Smith, 1958), Vol. 1, 210; Cornelius Oliver Cathey, *Agricultural Developments in North Carolina, 1783–1860,* James Sprunt Studies in History and Political Science, Vol. 38 (Chapel Hill: University of North Carolina Press, 1956), 199. A midcentury observer near Augusta on the Savannah River described the conflict between agricultural settlers and livestock raisers, "who have large stocks of cattle and very wide ranges, which they consider as their property, without any legal title to them; hence whenever a new settler comes near them; they look upon it as an encroachment, & don't fail to set the Indians upon destroying their cattle & giving them all manner of disturbance." Henry F. Ellis to William Henry Lyttelton, May 1, 1757, William Henry Lyttelton Papers (hereafter WHLP), William L. Clements Library, University of Michigan, Ann Arbor.

21. The communal organization of simple commodity production accounts for its distinctiveness from capitalist economic production, in which the link between labor and the means of production is severed and production is controlled by those with the wealth to possess it. In simple commodity production the household is the unit of production in which both owners and laborers are a part and the quantity of labor available remains fixed. Surpluses accrued remain the property of the household, and its redistribution among household members takes precedence over maximization of profit. As long as members are part of the household, the surpluses can be invested in farm expansion and improvements. When it becomes necessary or desirable to divide the household, a portion of the surplus

is transferred through wage labor to household members seeking to set up farms of their own. The redistribution of surpluses to create new units of production is central in the reproduction of simple commodity production. Harriet Friedmann, "World Market, State, and family Farm: Social Bases of Household Production in the Era of Wage Labor," *Comparative Studies in Society and History* 20 (1978): 559–562; Friedmann, "Simple Commodity Production and Wage Labour in the American Plains," *Journal of Peasant Studies* 6 (1979): 96.

22. The salient characteristics of the household mode of production parallel economic arrangements found in societies lacking central government institutions. The anthropologist Marshall Sahlins noted the association of exchange based on the use value of goods with societies that lack commoditized markets. Here economic goals center around maintaining a way of living rather than generating abstract wealth. Such a "domestic mode of production" results in little incentive to create a surplus greater than that needed to exchange for necessities and limits the total volume of production. Marshall Sahlins, *Tribesmen* (Englewood Cliffs, N.J.: Prentice Hall, 1968),75–81; Sahlins, *Stone Age Economics* (New York: Aldine, 1972), 83–84. Several historians have emphasized the association of the household mode of production with a precommercial market phase of agriculture on the Atlantic seaboard, especially in the Northeast. For discussions, see Michael Merrill, "Cash Is Good to Eat: Self-Sufficiency and Exchange in the Rural Economy of the United States," *Radical History Review* 3 (1977): 52–54; James A. Henretta, "The Transition to Capitalism in America," in *The Origins of American Capitalism: Collected Essays,* ed. James A. Henretta (Boston: Northeastern University Press, 1991), 263–264; Henretta, "Families and Farms: *Mentalité* in Pre-Industrial America," *William and Mary Quarterly,* 3rd ser., 35 (1978): 15–16; Edwin J. Perkins, *The Economy of Colonial America* (New York: Columbia University Press, 1980), 50; and Charles Sellers, *The Market Revolution in Jacksonian America, 1815–1846* (New York: Oxford University Press, 1991), 5. Kulikoff, "Households and Markets," 353, applied the term "communal self-sufficiency" to economic systems characterized by regional exchange on the Eastern seaboard and later frontier areas. For discussions of regional exchange, see Warren R. Hofstra and Robert D. Mitchell, "Town and Country in Backcountry Virginia: Winchester and the Shenandoah Valley, 1730–1800," *Journal of Southern History* 59 (1993): 627–628; Christopher Clark, *The Roots of Rural Capitalism: Western Massachusetts, 178–1860* (Ithaca, NY: Cornell University Press, 1990), 28–30, 64–65; Daniel P. Jones, *The Economic and Social Transformation of Rural Rhode Island, 1780–1850* (Boston: Northeastern University Press, 1992), 6–10; James T. Lemon, "Household Consumption in Eighteenth-Century America and Its Relationship to Production and Trade: The Situation among Farmers in Southeastern Pennsylvania," *Agricultural History* 41 (1967): 68–69; John J. McCusker and Russell R. Menard, *The Economy of British America, 1607–1789* (Chapel Hill: University of North Carolina Press for the Institute of Early American History and Culture, 1985), 301–302. For specific reference to the South Carolina backcountry, see Moore, *Toil and Strife,* 2, 5.

23. Although it rarely involved cash, this form of exchange avoided the pitfalls associated with simple *barter,* which involves the direct exchange of goods for goods, the value of which must be agreed upon and is not necessarily constant. The use of a good on constant value provides a common denominator of value. Although it lacks the homogeneity, portability, divisibility, and durability of money, the presence of such goods brings order into calculations of value and makes *money barter* an effective system for conducting business. Providing a medium of exchange, money barter allows the development of markets and the rise of mechanisms of credit. Melville J. Herskovits, *Man and His Works* (New York: Alfred A. Knopf, 1948), 276–279. Formal bookkeeping provided the means to accurately record and prove the details of lengthy exchanges, and its use by traders and storekeepers on the frontier permitted them to keep track of the accounts of numerous customers and suppliers involving mostly goods. W. T. Baxter, "Accounting in Colonial America," in *Studies in the History of Accounting,* ed. A. C. Littleton and B. S. Yamey (London: Sweet & Maxwell, 1956), 273–278. This form of exchange is also known as *truck* and is common in isolated economies in economically peripheral areas of the world economy, where the supply of cash is limited and direct exchanges of goods and services predominate. Gerald M. Sider, *Culture and Class in Anthropology and History: A Newfoundland Illustration* (Paris: Cambridge University Press, 1991), 22–23, 56; Carole Shammas, "How Self-Sufficient Was Early

America?," *Journal of Interdisciplinary History* 13 (1982): 263. [William Bull], "Governor William Bull's Representation of the Colony, 1770," in *The Colonial South Carolina Scene: Contemporary Views, 1697–1774*, ed. H. Roy Merrens (Columbia: University of South Carolina Press, 1977), 268.

24. The term "composite farming" was introduced by Richard Lyman Bushman, "Markets and Composite Farms in Early America," *William and Mary Quarterly*, 3rd ser., 55 (1998): 364–365.

25. Catesby, "Catesby's Natural History," 98–99; Purry, "A Short Description," 134; E. Alfred Jones, ed., "Von Reck's Second Report from Georgia," *William and Mary Quarterly*, 3rd ser., 22 (1965): 324–325; Alexander Garden, "A Letter from a Scientist (1757)," in *The Colonial South Carolina Scene: Contemporary Views, 1697–1774*, ed. H. Roy Merrens (Columbia: University of South Carolina Press, 1977), 214; Klaus G. Loewald, Beverly Starika, and Paul S. Taylor, ed., "Johann Martin Bolzius Answers a Questionnaire on Carolina and Georgia, Part II [1751]," *William and Mary Quarterly*, 3rd ser. (1958): 236; *North Carolina Magazine* (hereafter *NCM*), Jul. 20, 1764, 55; *SCG*, July 4, 1768; Nicholas P. Hardeman, *Shucks, Shocks, and Hominy Blocks: Corn as a Way of Life in Pioneer America* (Baton Rouge: Louisiana State University Press, 1981), 54–55; Meriwether, *Expansion of South Carolina*, 165–166. Traveling east of the Wateree River in the winter of 1767, Charles Woodmason lamented that the diet of local residents consisted of "Indian Corn, Pork in Winter and Bacon in Summer." Hooker, ed., *Carolina Backcountry*, 13, 196.

26. *SCG*, Apr. 1, 1745; *JCHA*, May 22, 1749; Apr. 28, 1750; Catesby, "Catesby's Natural History," 100; Samuel Wylie to Gov. William Lyttelton, Oct. 27, 1758, WHLP.

27. Loewald, ed., "Bolzius Answers a Questionnaire," 239. Charles Woodmason noted the abundance of fruit trees among the farms on the upper Wateree and remarked that "the poor people . . . are reduced to the sad necessity of of gathering apples, peaches, &c. green from the trees and boiling them for food." Hooker, ed., *Carolina Backcountry*, 23, 48.

28. "Message from Gov. James Glen," *JCHA*,Mar. 5, 1748. For a discussion of historic American alcohol consumption, see W. J. Rorabaugh, *The Alcoholic Republic: An American Tradition* (New York: Oxford University Press, 1979), Ch. 1, app. 5. Typical references to brandy made from peaches appear in *SCG*, Aug. 3, 1747; Hooker, ed., *Carolina Backcountry*, 53; Horace Fraser Rudisill, ed., *The Diaries of Evan Pugh (1762–1801)* (Florence, S.C.: St. David's Society, 1993), 372; to rum in ibid., 121, 166, 176; and to whiskey in Hooker, ed., *Carolina Backcountry*, 30, 53.

29. For example, Nath. Scott, a Charleston brewer, advertised "Carolina" beer in barrels and kegs at his brewhouse on Queen Street. *SCG*, Feb. 22, Nov. 20, 1752. An enterprising German immigrant to Saxe Gotha Township, Christopher Bendeker, tried unsuccessfully to have the Assembly appropriate funds to equip his brewery in 1750. *JCHA*, Feb. 9, 1750. The initially promising attempt by the Huguenot immigrant Jean Louis de Mesnil du St. Pierre to establish a wine industry on land granted to him at the French settlement of New Bordeaux on the Savannah also culminated in failure when funds did not materialize. Arthur Henry Hirsch, *The Huguenots of Colonial South Carolina* (Durham, N.C.: Duke University Press, 1928; reprint ed., Columbia: University of South Carolina Press, 1999), 205–210; Philip M. Hamer et al., eds., *The Papers of Henry Laurens* (hereafter *HLP*), Vol. 8 (Columbia: University of South Carolina Press, 1968–1990), 140n.

30. Susan Fairlie, "Dyestuffs in the Eighteenth Century," *Economic History Review*, 2nd ser., 17 (1965): 498; "A Description of South Carolina," in *Historical Collections of South Carolina*, ed. B. R. Carroll (New York: Harper & Bros., 1836), 203–204. Indigo growing and processing in South Carolina was discussed in detail by "Agricultor" in *SCG*, Jan. 19, 26, 1747. For its encouragement in the backcountry, see *SCG*, Aug. 27, 1748; *JCHA*, Jan. 20, 21, 1752; Jan. 30, Apr. 27, 1754. Meriwether, *Expansion of South Carolina*, 167.

31. Purry, "Short Description," 133; Lionel Chalmers, *An Account of the Weather and Diseases of South Carolina*, Vol. 1 (London: Edward and Charles Dilly, 1776), 28. The success of hemp as a backcountry crop did not come until the mid-1760s, following the passage of bounties by Parliament and the South Carolina Assembly. Hamer et al., eds., *HLP*,5: 132–133n; *SCG&CJ*, July 15, 1766; *SCG*, Nov. 10, 1766. Even as late as 1770, Gov. William Bull noted the role of flax in the regional economy of the backcountry. "The Irish from Belfast," he wrote, "have now raised flax for their own wear, and barter

the superfluous linen to supply . . . their neighbours." Bull, "Governor Bull's Representation of the Colony," 265.

32. Laslett, *The World We Have Lost,* 8, 11–14; Laslett, "Introduction," 34–36; Clark, *Roots of Rural Capitalism,* 21.

33. Laslett, *The World We Have Lost,* 9–11.

34. M. M. Postan, *The Medieval Economy and Society: An Economic History of Britain, 1100–1500* (Berkeley: University of California Press, 1972), 111–112; Laslett, *The World We Have Lost,* 64–65; Kulikoff, *From British Peasants to American Farmers,* 14.

35. C. M. L. Bouch and G. P. Jones, *A Short Economic and Social History of the Lake Counties, 1500–1830* (Manchester: Manchester University Press, 1961), 161; Elinor Trotter, *Seventeenth Century Life in the County Parish* (London: Frank Cass, 1968), 2–3.

36. [Robert Johnson], "A Governor Answers a Questionnaire, 1719/20," in *Colonial South Carolina Scene: Contemporary Views, 1697–1774,* ed. H. Roy Merrens (Columbia: University of South Carolina Press, 1977), 57–58; Alan D. Watson, "The Quitrent System in Royal South Carolina," *William and Mary Quarterly,* 3rd ser., 33 (1976), 184; Kulikoff, *From British Peasants to American Farmers,* 206.

37. The study of peasant societies has been a major focus of anthropological study. The definitions used here are drawn primarily from the work of Alfred Kroeber, *Anthropology* (New York: Harcourt Brace, 1948, 184; Robert Redfield, *Peasant Society and Culture* (Chicago: University of Chicago Press, 1956), Ch. 2; Eric R. Wolf, "Types of Latin American Peasantry: A Preliminary Discussion," *American Anthropologist* 57 (1955): 453–454; Wolf, *Peasants* (Englewood Cliffs, N.J.: Prentice Hall, 1966), 2; Michael Kearney, "Peasants," in *International Encyclopedia of the Social Sciences,* Vol. 6, ed. William A. Darity Jr. (Detroit: Macmillan Reference USA, 2008), 195–196.

38. Eric R. Wolf, *Europe and the People without History* (Berkeley: University of California Press, 1982), 317–318.

39. The recognition that peasants represent economically marginal societies arose from the realization that peasant villages and other small communities are related to a larger integral whole and that their relationships to the outside help determine both the community's character and its continuity. For definitions of peasants, see Wolf, "Types of Latin American Peasantry," 454–455, and Wolf, *Peasant Wars of the Twentieth Century* (New York: Harper & Row, 1969), xiv–xv.

40. Wolf, *Peasants,* 4–10.

41. John M. Wantanabe, "Ritual Economy and the Negotiation of Autarky and Interdependence in a Ritual Mode of Production," in *Mesoamerican Ritual Economy: Archaeological and Ethnological Perspectives,* ed. E. Christian Wells and Karla L. Davis-Salazar (Boulder: University of Colorado Press, 2007), 311–312; Eric R. Wolf, "Distinguished Lecture: Facing Power-Old Insights, New Questions," *American Anthropologist* 92 (1990): 586; Wolf, *Peasants,* 7.

42. Wantenabe, "Ritual Economy," 302–304.

43. Ibid., 313–314. Although generally associated with religion, anthropologists have also recognized the role of ritual as a routinized, formal, prescribed, highly stereotyped, stylized, and repetitive pattern of behavior that symbolizes the basic tenets of an ordered universe and that serves to maintain equilibrium or restore it following a crisis. These characteristics have composed the definition of ritual in anthropological texts; see Eliot D. Chapple and Carleton S. Coon, *Principles of Anthropology* (New York: Henry Holt, 1942), 706; Robbie Davis-Floyd, "Rituals," in *International Encyclopedia of the Social Sciences,* Vol. 7, ed. William A. Darity Jr. (Detroit: Macmillan Reference U.S.A., 2008), 259–264.

44. Redfield, *Peasant Society and Culture,* 42–58.

45. The bulk of agricultural immigration to South Carolina originated in Great Britain and the German states, and most immigrants came to America to escape economic conditions that had deteriorated over the previous century. Farmers, laborers, and craftspersons had grown up in the context of European peasant villages and were familiar with the institutions that governed this way of life, and they brought this knowledge with them to the New World. Bridenbaugh, *Vexed and Troubled Englishmen,* 48–53; Kulikoff, *From British Peasants to American Farmers,* 167–184; Jean-Louis Flandrin, *Families in Former Times: Kinship, Household, and Sexuality* (New York: Cambridge University Press, 1979),

74–78, 85–88; Kenneth W. Keller, "The Outlook of Rhinelanders on the Virginia Frontier," in *Diversity and Accommodation: Essays on the Cultural Composition of the Virginia Frontier,* ed. Michael J. Puglisi (Knoxville: University of Tennessee Press, 1992), 100–103.

Chapter 5. "The Great Inconveniences of People in Those Remote Places"

1. "Petition of Inhabitants of Saxe Gotha," *JCHA,* Apr. 16, 1746, 195.

2. The concept of "community" links populations of people and a locale, emphasizing their social relations. As a basic unit of integration and cultural transmission, its organization rather than its form is the key to recognizing its structure and boundaries. Conrad M. Arensberg, "The Community as Object and Sample," *American Anthropologist* 63 (1961): 248–250. An understanding of the complex nature of rural communities has arisen from the work of social scientists and historians who investigated the nature of social and economic integration in dispersed agricultural societies and its role in their formation. See, for example, Arensberg, "American Communities," *American Anthropologist* 57 (1955), 155–156; John Mack Faragher, "Open-Country Community: Sugar Creek, Illinois, 1820–1850," in *The Countryside in the Age of Capitalist Transformation: Essays in the Social History of Rural America,* ed. Steven Hahn and Jonathan Prude (Chapel Hill: University of North Carolina Press, 1985), 236–237, 245–247. For discussions of communities of accretion, see Kenneth E. Lewis, *West to Far Michigan: Settling the Lower Peninsula, 1815–1860* (East Lansing: Michigan State University Press, 2002), 133–141. Communities of accretion dominated the South Carolina backcountry and stood in marked contrast to *covenanted communities,* organized around a set of common principles and shared purposes expressed in a "covenant" that guided their lives and activities around a common set of rules and expectations. The solidarity inherent in such planned frontier communities as Purrysburg on the Savannah River and Wachovia in North Carolina provided security and an organizational structure that helped them weather the challenges of pioneering. Common religious beliefs often sanctioned such groups and justified an organization that provided a unified social and economic structure to oversee relations among individual households and ensure their mutual support. Page Smith, *As a City upon a Hill: The Town in American History* (New York: Alfred A. Knopf, 1966),17–21. For example, the Wachovia settlement founded in 1753 by the Moravian Church in North Carolina relied on a theocratic government to manage relations among the colony's residents, regulating its members' internal affairs as well as their relations with the outside world. Its organization permitted leaders to look after the needs of its residents in the context of the larger community, an arrangement that ensured the survival of both and also ensured that the goods and services they produced became an important component of the wider backcountry economy. Daniel Thorp, *The Moravian Community in Colonial North Carolina: Pluralism on the Southern Frontier* (Knoxville: University of Tennessee Press, 1989), Chs. 4 and 5. Studies of Wachovia and Purrysburg may be found, respectively, in Thorp, *The Moravian Community in Colonial North Carolina,* and in Arlin C. Migliazzo, *To Make This Land Our Own: Community, Identity, and Cultural Adaptation in Purrysburg Township, South Carolina, 1732–1865* (Columbia: University of South Carolina Press, 2007).

3. Karl Polanyi, *The Great Transformation: The Political and Economic Origins of Our Time* (Boston: Beacon Press, 1957), 61–62.

4. Oscar Handlin, "Peasant Origins," in *Tribal and Peasant Economies: Readings in Economic Anthropology,* ed. George Dalton (Garden City, N.Y.: Natural History Press, 1967), 462–463. Warren R. Hofstra and Robert D. Mitchell, "Town and Country in Backcountry Virginia: Winchester and the Shenandoah Valley, 1730–1800," *Journal of Southern History* 59 (1993): 628, emphasized the role for cooperation in the frontier economy of the Shenandoah Valley of Virginia.

5. Henri Pirenne, "Aspects of Medieval European Economy," in *Tribal and Peasant Economies: Readings in Economic Anthropology,* ed. George Dalton (Garden City, N.Y.: Natural History Press, 1967), 432–434; Georges Duby, *Rural Economy and Country Life in the Medieval West,* trans. Cynthia Postan (London: Edward Arnold, 1968), 347–348.

6. The fair at Childsbury, at Strawberry Ferry on the Cooper River, was established by statute in 1723 as well as at Ashley Ferry and Dorchester, on the Ashley. Thomas J. Cooper and David J. McCord,

ed., *Statutes at Large of South Carolina,* Vol. 4 (Columbia, S.C.: A. S. Johnson, 1838), 204; Walter Edgar, *South Carolina: A History* (Columbia: University of South Carolina Press, 1998), 171; *SCG,* Oct. 1, 1750; Sept. 16, 1751; William J. Barr, "Strawberry Ferry and Childsbury Towne: Elements of Control in the Economic Landscape of Colonial South Carolina," in Underwater Archaeology Proceedings from the Society for Historical Archaeology Conference, ed. Paul Forsythe Johnson (Pleasant Hill, Calif.: Society for Historical Archaeology, 1994), 88- 93.

7. Michael Woods, "The Culture of Credit in Colonial Charleston," *South Carolina Historical Magazine* 99 (1998): 358; Michael V. Kennedy, "'Cash for Turnips': Agricultural Production for Local Markets in Colonial Pennsylvania," *Agricultural History* 74 (2000): 588–592.

8. Daniel B. Thorp, "Doing Business in the Backcountry: Retail Trade in Colonial Rowan County, North Carolina," *William and Mary Quarterly,* 3rd ser., 48 (1991): 387–408; Thorp, "Taverns and Communities: The Case of Rowan County, North Carolina," in *The Southern Colonial Backcountry: Interdisciplinary Perspectives on Frontier Communities,* ed. David Colin Crass, Steven D. Smith, Martha A. Zierden, and Richard D. Brooks (Knoxville: University of Tennessee Press, 1998), 76–86.

9. Conveyance Books, Public Register S372001 (hereafter CBPR), Vol. I-I, June 2, 1750, 26; Vol. I-I, Aug. 31, 1751, 235; Vol. O-3, Apr. 27, 1769, 422; Vol. O-O, July 3, 1752, 200; Vol. K-3, Dec. 19, 1767, 360; Vol. K-3, Aug. 4, 1767, 153, South Carolina Department of Archives and History, Columbia; Migliazzo, *To Make This Land Our Own.,* 189–190.

10. *JCHA,* May 25, 1738; Nov. 28, 1739.

11. Petitions to build mills in Saxe Gotha and Orangeburg Townships appeared within four years after settlement began in 1735. *JCHA,* Oct. 6, 1738, 336; Mar. 1, 1739. In the Welsh Tract, millers requested funds within two years of the area's 1737 opening: George Lloyd Johnson Jr., *The Frontier in the Colonial South, South Carolina Backcountry, 1736–1800* (Westport, Conn.: Greenwood Press, 1997), 23.

12. Robert L. Meriwether, *The Expansion of South Carolina, 1729–1765* (Kingsport, Tenn.: Southern Publishers, 1940), 100–101, 104–105; Colonial Plat Books, S213184 (hereafter CPB), Vol. 4, Feb. 7, 1743, 223, South Carolina Department of Archives and History, Columbia; CPB, Vol. 12, Apr. 25, 1745, 141; CPB, Vol. 6, Nov. 20, 1751, 56; CBPR, Vol. W-W, Nov. 10, 1758, 156; CPB, Vol. 6, June 13, 1752, 56; CPB, Vol. 7, Apr. 22, 1761, 156; Memorial Books (hereafter MB), S111001, Vol. 7, Dec. 19, 1761, 391, South Carolina Department of Archives and History, Columbia; Richard J. Hooker, ed., *The Carolina Backcountry on the Eve of the Revolution: The Journal and Other Writings of Charles Woodmason, Anglican Itinerant* (Chapel Hill: University of North Carolina Press, 1953), 49.

13. Meriwether, *Expansion of South Carolina,* 100–105; Julian J. Petty, *The Growth and Distribution of Population in South Carolina* (Columbia: South Carolina State Planning Board, 1943; reprint ed., Spartanburg, S.C.: The Reprint Co., 1975), 40–41. Population estimates are those derived by Kaylene Hughes, "Populating the Backcountry: The Demographic and Social Characteristics of the South Carolina Frontier, 1730–1760" (Ph.D. diss., Florida State University, 1985), 42–50. For the form of population spread, see Herman R. Friis, "A Series of Population Maps of the Colonies and the United States, 1625–1790," Mimeographed Publication Series, No. 3 (New York: American Geographical Society, 1940); Kenneth E. Lewis, *The American Frontier: An Archaeological Study of Settlement Pattern and Process* (Orlando, Fla.: Academic Press, 1984), 62–69.

14. Allan Kulikoff, *From British Peasants to Colonial American Farmers* (Chapel Hill: University of North Carolina Press, 2000), 220–221; Hofstra and Mitchell, "Town and Country in Backcountry Virginia," 627; Rachel N. Klein, *Unification of a Slave State: The Rise of the Planter Class in the South Carolina Backcountry, 1760–1808* (Chapel Hill: University of North Carolina Press for the Institute of Early American History and Culture, 1990), 26–27.

15. Peter Laslett, "Introduction: The History of the Family," in *Household and Family in Past Time,* ed. Peter Laslett (Cambridge: Cambridge University Press, 1972), 23–28; Robert V. Wells, "Household Size and Composition in the British Colonies in America, 1675–1775," *Journal of Interdisciplinary History* 4 (1974): 545–546; James A. Henretta, *The Evolution of American Society, 1700–1815: An Interdisciplinary Analysis* (Lexington, Mass.: D. C. Heath, 1973), 24–25; Jean-Louis Flandrin, *Families in Former Times Families in Former Times: Kinship, Household, and Sexuality* (New York: Cambridge University

Press, 1979), 4–10; David Warren Sabean, *Property, Production, and Family in Neckarhausen, 1700–1870* (Cambridge: Cambridge University Press, 1990), 107–123.

16. For this study, the upper boundary of the area examined is situated at the northern limit of Fredericksburg Township, at the approximate point where Grannys Quarter Creek joins the Wateree on the east and Sawneys Creek intersects the western bank of the river. The study area's southern boundary is extended below the likely boundary of the township to include the tracts clustered at the confluence of Swift Creek and the Wateree River.

17. Hughes, "Populating the Backcountry," 35–40; Petty, *Growth and Distribution of Population,* 34; Robert M. Weir, *Colonial South Carolina: A History* (New York: KTO Press, 1983; reprint ed., Columbia: University of South Carolina Press, 1997), 48.

18. These figures are derived from information contained in the following record groups: CPB; Township Grants, S213016 (hereafter TSG); and Colonial Land Grants (hereafter CLG/CS), S213019, all in the South Carolina Department of Archives and History, Columbia. Johnson, *Frontier in the Colonial South,* 29, Table 3.

19. James Michie was a prominent lawyer who served as a member of the Assembly and the Council and as Chief Justice of South Carolina and who also held many other public offices. Michie was also a planter who owned 12,362 acres and 118 slaves, including the 50 slaves for whom he claimed the right to 2,500 acres on the Wateree. Walter B. Edgar and N. Louise Bailey, *Biographical Directory of the South Carolina House of Representatives, Vol. 2: The Commons House of Assembly, 1692–1775* (Columbia: University of South Carolina Press, 1977), 452–453; Brent H. Holcomb, ed., *Petitions for Land from the South Carolina Council Journals* (hereafter *PL*), Vol. II (Columbia, S.C.: SCMAR, 1996–2009), 19.

20. Holcomb, ed., *PL,* I: 173; I: 201.

21. Holcomb, ed., *PL,* I: 173, 307, 317; II: 28.

22. Holcomb, ed., *PL,* II: 14; 10–11, 64.

23. Holcomb, ed., *PL,* II: 239, 28; I: 258.

24. Holcomb, ed., *PL,* II: 219, 220; Kenneth L. Carroll, "The Irish Quaker Community at Camden," *South Carolina Historical Quarterly* 77 (1976): 70–72.

25. See, for example, *SCG,* Nov. 20, 1749; Dec. 3, 1750; Nov. 13, 1752; Feb. 5, 1753; Oct. 8, 1753; Dec. 12, 1754. Occasionally individuals with special skills, such as the "servant lad who spoke Dutch [Deutsch], English, and French" or the English woman skilled in sewing and other domestic tasks, were advertised separately: *SCG,* Jan. 15, 1756; June 18, 1753. See also Warren R. Smith, *White Servitude in Colonial South Carolina* (Columbia: University of South Carolina Press, 1961).

26. Holcomb, ed., *PL,* IV: 196–197.

27. The act to benefit "poor foreign Protestants" was funded through a tax on new purchasers of slaves: *JCHA,* Oct. 6, 1752. The immigrant households that benefited from this act were those of George Jones, Archibald Watson, and John Jessops. Holcomb, ed., *PL,* IV: 102–103.

28. For discussion of the link between slave and land ownership and household size, see Wells, "Household Size and Composition," 554, 568. Meriwether, *Expansion of South Carolina,* 100, 102; *JCHA,* May 13, 1751; May 9, 1752.

29. Holcomb, ed., *PL,* II: 27; CBPR, Vol. B-B, Mar. 22, 1744, 56; CLG/CS, Vol. 5, Oct. 6, 1752, 25.

30. Holcomb, ed., *PL,* I: 305; II, 21; CPB, Vol. 5, Dec. 27, 1747, 101; CLG/CS, Vol. 4, Feb. 25, 1747, 148; Miscellaneous Records, S213003 (hereafter MR), Vol. 2H, 218, South Carolina Department of Archives and History, Columbia; Mar. 1, 1749; *JCHA,* May 13, 1751; Thomas J. Kirkland and Robert M. Kennedy, *Historic Camden, Vol. 2: Nineteenth Century* (Columbia, S.C.: State Printing Co., 1926), 71–73; CPB, Vol. 4, Feb. 25, 1747, 400; Will Transcripts, S108093 (hereafter WT), Pkt.: Apt. 60, Pkg. 2137, South Carolina Department of Archives and History, Columbia.

31. MR, Vol. 25, Aug. 10, 1741, 228; Petitions to the General Assembly, S165015 (PGA), Item 3735, n.d., South Carolina Department of Archives and History, Columbia; Holcomb, ed., *PL,* II: 243; MR, Vol. 5, Mar. 14, 1753, 357; Vol. 2G, Aug. 10, 1748, 361.

32. The smaller size of families among initial settlers was noted by Philip J. Greven Jr., "The Average Size of Families and Households in the Province of Massachusetts in 1762 and in the United States

in 1790: An Overview," in *Household and Family in Past Time,* ed. Peter Laslett and Richard Wall (Cambridge: Cambridge University Press, 1972), 552. See also Terry Jordan and Matti Kaups, *The American Backwoods Frontier: An Ethnic and Ecological Interpretation* (Baltimore: John Hopkins University Press, 1989), 66. The subsequent rapid growth of families in newly settled regions became a significant factor in the rapid growth of the colonial population of British North America. See Robert Wells, "The Population of England's Colonies in America: Old English of New American?," *Population Studies* 46 (1992): 85–89; Russell R. Menard, "What Ever Happened to Early American Population History," *William and Mary Quarterly,*3rd ser., 50 (1993): 363; David Hackett Fischer, *Albion's Seed: Four British Folkways in America* (New York: Oxford University Press, 1989), 666–667. For the growing size of immigrant families on the southern frontier in particular, see Johnson, *Frontier in the Colonial South,* 29–30; Alan D. Watson, "Household Size and Composition in Pre-Revolutionary North Carolina," *Mississippi Quarterly* 31 (1978): 551–569. Observing pioneer families in the Wateree Valley in the 1760s, the Rev. Woodmason attributed large household size and high rate of increase to early marriage: Hooker, ed., *Carolina Backcountry,* 39, a conclusion supported by demographic historians. Rudy Ray Seward, *The American Family: A Demographic History* (Beverly Hills, Calif.: Sage Publications, 1978), 57–60.

33. Although earlier scholars of the frontier experience emphasized the role of individualism and its importance in overcoming previous social arrangements (for example, Frederick Jackson Turner, "The Significance of the Frontier in American History," *Annual Report of the American Historical Association for the Year 1893* [Washington, D.C.: Government Printing Office, 1893], 107, 165), more recent studies of American communities have stressed the role of kinship and its importance in maintaining the social and economic fabric. See, for example, John Demos, *A Little Community: Family Life in Plymouth Colony* (New York: Oxford, 1970). For the role of kin groups in migration, see Robert E. Bieder, "Kinship as a Factor in Migration," *Journal of Marriage and the Family* 35 (1973): 434; John Mack Faragher, *Sugar Creek: Life on the Illinois Prairie* (New Haven, Conn.: Yale University Press, 1986, 57–58; Fischer, *Albion's Seed,* 25–26, 229, 434, 610. Kin-based clusters in frontier settlement have been noted by Roger D. Mason, *Euro-American Settlement Systems in the Central Salt River Valley of Northeast Missouri,* Publications in Archaeology, No. 2 (Columbia: American Archaeology Division, University of Missouri–Columbia, 1984), and Dale Ray Borders, "The Effect of Kinship on the Settlement Patterns on the Southwest Michigan Frontier" (Ph.D. diss., Michigan State University, 2003).

34. Kirkland and Kennedy, *Historic Camden,* 2: 399–400; CPB, Vol. 5, July 28, 1753, 417; CBPR, Vol. P-P, Apr. 2, 1753, 152, South Carolina Department of Archives and History, Columbia; MB, Vol. 7, June 4, 1759, 249; CPB, S, Vol. 5, July 27, 1753, 353.

35. CPB, Vol. 5, Apr. 17, 1749, 34; Vol. 4, May 17, 1749, 482; Vol. 4, Dec. 23, 1749, 71; Vol. 4, Dec. 26, 1749, 411.

36. CPB, Vol. 4, Feb. 25, 1747, 400; Vol. 5, Sept. 21, 1749, 286.

37. CPB, Vol. 12, Apr. 19, 1749, 112; Vol. 12, Apr. 20, 1749, 112; Vol. 4, June 6, 1749, 496; Meriwether, *Expansion of South Carolina,* 102.

38. CPB, Vol. 6, Nov. 20, 1751, 56; Vol. 6, Aug. 29, 1757, 335; MB, Vol. 9, Apr. 11, 1768, 468.

39. CBPR, Vol. O-O, Jan. 9, 1753, 120; CPB, Vol. 6, Nov. 3, 1753, 434; Vol. 6, May 10, 1754, 435; Vol. 5, Oct. 21, 1752, 394; Vol. 5, Sept. 17, 1754, 456; Vol. 5, Oct. 21, 1752, 370; Vol. 7, Apr. 8, 1756, 185; Thomas J. Kirkland and Robert M. Kennedy, *Historic Camden, Vol. 1: Colonial and Revolutionary* (Columbia, S.C.: State Printing Co., 1905), 74.

40. Edgar and Bailey, *Biographical Directory,* 2: 739; Charlotte Boykin Salmond Brunson, *Kershaw County Cousins* (Columbia, S.C.: R. L. Bryan, 1978), 210; Kirkland and Kennedy, *Historic Camden,* 1: 74, 84, 86–87.

41. Robert W. Lowie, "Religion in Human Life," *American Anthropologist* 65 (1963): 539; Thomas J. Little, "'Adding to the Church Such as Shall Be Saved': The Growth and Influence of Evangelicalism in Colonial South Carolina, 1740–1775," in *Money, Trade and Power: The Evolution of Colonial South Carolina's Plantation Society,* ed. Jack P. Greene, Rosemary Brana-Shute, and Randy J. Sparks (Columbia: University of South Carolina Press, 2001), 368–374, 377–378). For discussions of the role of religion

as an integrative mechanism as well as a cause of friction in frontier communities, see Stephen I. Thompson, "Religious Conversion and Religious Zeal in an Overseas Enclave: The Case of the Japanese in Bolivia," *Anthropological Quarterly* 41 (1968): 201–208, and Thompson, *Pioneer Colonization: A Cross-Cultural View,* Addison-Wesley Modules in Anthropology 33 (Reading, Mass.: Addison-Wesley, 1973), 16.

42. Immigrants to Purrysburg, Saxe Gotha, Orangeburg, New Windsor, and Amelia Townships were largely German and German-speaking Swiss; Scots-Irish colonists flocked to Williamsburg; Queensborough and the Welsh Tract were settled predominantly by those of Welsh origin; and Scots-Irish from the northern colonies occupied the Waxhaws region above Fredericksburg. Petty, *Growth and Distribution of Population,* 38–42. Migliazzo, *To Make This Land Our Own,* 299.

43. Little, "Growth in Influence of Evangelicalism," 377. John Wesley Brinsfield, *Religion and Politics in Colonia South Carolina* (Easley, S.C.: Southern Historical Press, 1983), 48–49; Christine Leigh Heyrman, *Southern Cross: The Beginnings of the Bible Belt* (New York: Alfred A. Knopf, 1997), 10–11; Hooker, ed., *Carolina Backcountry,* xxiv; R. J. Dickson, *Ulster Emigration to Colonial America, 1718–1775* (Belfast: Ulster Historical Foundation, 1966), 49–52.

44. Edgar, *South Carolina,* 62; Meriwether, *Expansion of South Carolina,* 105–106.

45. Hooker, *Carolina Backcountry,* 241.

46. Meriwether, *Expansion of South Carolina,* 107; *JCHA,* Jan. 21, 1756, 38; *SCG,* May 26, 1757; Hooker, ed., *Carolina Backcountry,* 22, 42; Lacy K. Ford, *Origins of Southern Radicalism: The South Carolina Upcountry, 1800–1860* (New York: Oxford, 1988), 20.

47. Carroll, "Irish Quaker Community at Camden," 69–70; Williston Walker, *A History of the Christian Church,* rev. ed. (New York: Charles Scribner's Sons, 1959), 420.

48. Carroll, "The Irish Quaker Community at Camden," 70–71; Fischer, *Albion's Seed,* 423–424, 430.

49. Heyrman, *Southern Cross,* 141–142.

50. Carroll, "Irish Quaker Community at Camden," 76–83. Robert Milhous's large family, for example, dispersed within a generation. Kirkland and Kennedy, *Historic Camden,* 1: 77, 83–84; Evelyn Perry Milhous, *History of the Milhous Family in South Carolina* (Miami, Fla.: By the Author, 1944), 10.

51. Carroll, "Irish Quaker Community at Camden," 70–72, 75; Kirkland and Kennedy, *Historic Camden,* 1: 78–81.

52. TSG, Vol. 2F, Mar. 7, 1754, 108; Vol. 2G, Mar. 14, 1754, 3; Vol. 8, Dec. 9, 1754, 605; CPB, Vol. 8, Dec. 9, 1754; Vol. 6, Jan. 21, 1756, 177; Vol. 6, Feb. 11, 1757, 187; Vol. 7, Apr. 22, 1761, 156; MB, Vol. 7, June 8, 1757, 151; CBPR, Vol. M-M, Aug. 23, 1752, 177; Vol. O-O, Jan. 9, 1753, 120; Vol. P-P, Nov. 18, 1754, 135; Vol. Y-Y, Jan 28, 1762, 342.

53. By the late 1750s, Wyly's "Pinetree store" had become a central place for the distribution of goods on the Wateree. Catawbas Headmen to William Lyttelton, Aug. 23, 1759, WHLP; Estate of Samuel Wyly, July 20, 1768, Inventories of Estates (hereafter IE), Book X, 373, South Carolina Department of Archives and History, Columbia; Kirkland and Kennedy, *Historic Camden,* 1: 75, 78–79; Meriwether, *Expansion of South Carolina,* 104–105.

54. Kulikoff, *From British Peasants to Colonial American Farmers,* 220–223; Gregory Nobles, "The Rise of Merchants in Rural Market Towns: A Case Study of Eighteenth-Century Northampton, Massachusetts." *Journal of Interdisciplinary History* 24 (1990): 9.

55. Richard Waterhouse, *A New World Gentry: The Making of a Merchant and Planter Class in South Carolina, 1670–1770* (Charleston, S.C.: The History Press, 2005), 91. For Samuel Wyly's appointment s as justice of the peace, see *SCG,* Nov. 4, 1756, Oct. 19, 1765; for his appointments as deputy surveyor, see Edgar and Bailey, *Biographical Directory,* 739; MR, Vol. KK, 403–405.

56. Hooker, ed., *Carolina Backcountry,* 126–127; Klein, *Unification of a Slave State,* 40–41.

57. Richard Maxwell Brown, *The South Carolina Regulators* (Cambridge, Mass.: Belknap Press of Harvard University Press, 1963), 16; Jo Anne McCormick, "The Quakers of Colonial South Carolina, 1670–1807" (Ph.D. diss., University of South Carolina, 1985), 111–112.

58. James H. Merrell, *The Indians' New World: Catawbas and Their Neighbors from European Contact through Removal* (Chapel Hill: University of North Carolina Press, 1989), 555; John Evans to Gov.

James Glen, Dec. 16, 1755, and Gov. James Glen to King Haigler, Feb. 12, 1756, William L. McDowell, ed., *Documents Relating to Indian Affairs, May 21, 1750-August 7, 1754* (Columbia: South Carolina Department of Archives and History, 1958), 89, 95–96.

59. *SCG,* Mar. 8, 1760; *JCHA,* May 6, 1751; Edgar and Bailey, *Biographical Directory,* 739.

60. *SCG&CJ,* Dec. 17, 1765; Edgar and Bailey, *Biographical Directory,* 2: 739. St. Mark's Parish was created in 1757 to include the region above the upper Santee River to include lands between the Saluda and Lynches Rivers. Edgar, *South Carolina,* 215; Brown, *South Carolina Regulators,* 19.

61. Merrell, "Indians' New World," 547–548.

62. Committee on Indian Affairs Report, *JCHA,* Oct. 8, 1737; Gov. James Glen's Message to the Catawbas, Apr. 24, 1746, *SCG,* June 2, 1746.

63. Steven G. Baker, "The Working Draft of: The Historic Catawba Peoples: Exploratory Perspectives in Ethnohistory and Archaeology" (Columbia: Office of Research, University of South Carolina, 1975), 98–100; Merrell, "Indians' New World," 554–555.

64. The social processes of identity formation as a consequence of their incorporation within expanding capitalist societies is discussed in Eric R. Wolf, "Incorporation and Identity in the Making of the Modern World," in *Pathways of Power: Building and Anthropology of the Modern World,* ed. Eric R. Wolf with Sydel Silverman (Berkeley: University of California Press, 2001), 353–369.

65. Examples of accounts for items in these categories appear in *JCHA,* Jan. 28, 1739; Mar. 29, 1740; Mar. 31, 1740; May 25, 1741; Jan. 19, 1742; Mar. 23, 1743; May 8, 1744; Apr. 25–26, 1745; Mar. 31, 1746; June 8, 1748, 294–295; Feb. 9, 1750; Mar. 14, 1750; May 7, 1752; McDowell, ed., *Documents, 1754–1765,* Jan. 21, 1755. For a discussion of the value of presents as an indicator of Indians' economic worth, see Peter C. Mancall, Joshua L. Rosenbloom, and Thomas Weiss, "Indians in the Economy of Eighteenth Century South Carolina," in *The Atlantic Economy during the Seventeenth and Eighteenth Centuries: Organization, Operation Practice, and Personnel,* ed. Peter A. Coclanis (Columbia: University of South Carolina Press, 2005), 304–311.

66. *JCHA,* May 25, 1741, 35; Plat Collection of John McCrady (hereafter PCJM), L10005, Reel 1, Plat 88; Mabel L. Webber, "Death Notices from the South Carolina and American General Gazette, and Its Continuation the Royal Gazette: May 1766–June 1782," *South Carolina Historical Magazine* 17 (1916): 46; Kenneth Scott, "Sufferers in the Charleston Fire of 1740," South *Carolina Historical Magazine* 64 (1963): 211; *JCHA,* Jan. 19, 1742; CPB, Vol. 1, Jan. 2, 1733, 516; *JCHA,* Jan. 27, 1750; CPB, Vol. 4, Sept. 11, 1749, 497; Vol. 13, Mar. 19, 1757, 501.

67. Samuel Wyly supplied corn to the Catawbas as early as 1755: John Evan to Gov. James Glen, McDowell, ed., *Documents, 1754–1765,* Dec. 16, 1755. Conscious of transportation costs, Gov. Glen pointed out the advantage of purchasing corn from frontier farmers, Message, Nov. 25, 1755, *JCHA,* 7–8. His purchases from Milner and Narney are mentioned in Message from Gov. Henry Lyttelton, *JCHA,* Mar. 31 1757. MB, Vol. 7, May 29, 1756.

68. *JCHA,* Apr. 1, 1757; Samuel Wyly to William Lyttelton, Apr. 20, 1759, WHLP.

69. Meriwether, *Expansion of South Carolina,* 104.

70. Committee Report on Governor's Message to the Catawbas, *JCHA,* Oct. 8, 1737; *JCHA,* Mar. 1, 1737; Edmund Atkin to William Lyttelton, Oct. 24, 1757, Nov. 23, 1757, WHLP. James H. Merrell, "Minding the Business of the Nation: Hagler as Catawba Leader," *Ethnohistory* 33 (1986): 60–61.

71. For opposition to surveying lands of Indians in general, see Message of Gov. William Bull, *JCHA,* Jan. 27, 1738, and for legislative opposition to the transfer of lands by the Catawbas in particular, see "Report of the Committee to Examine Thomas Brown's Petition", *JCHA,* Apr. 20, 1744. Merrell, "Indians' New World," 556–557. Encroachment on Catawba lands was exacerbated by confusion over their boundary as well as over the boundary between North and South Carolina, sometimes resulting in erroneous surveys by officials from both colonies. One such survey involving Samuel Wyly resulted in the removal of a grantee and a resurvey of his land at a new location. Holcomb, ed., *PL,* IV: 39–40. Old Indian agricultural fields appear on settlers' plats on both sides of the Wateree as the river begins its great meanders just below the Fall Line. Extensive old fields, often rising above the surrounding swamplands, were noted on William Newitt Edwards's tract near Friends Neck, CPB, Vol. 4, Dec. 28,

1749, 508, and they constituted a major portion of the five hundred acres Roger Gibson claimed nearby along a bend in the river: CPB, Vol. 4, Feb. 25, 1747, 400. James Ousley's tract noted "Indian old fields" along the west side of the Wateree: CPB, Vol. 5, Dec. 23, 1748, 108; and a plat of a neighboring property granted to Luke Gibson revealed two "Indian Ditches" extending from the river: CPB, Vol. 5, Feb. 15, 1749, 27. Much farther to the south, James Michie's 2,500-acre tract included "Ragland's Old Fields" adjacent to the river, CPB, Vol. 5, June 13, 1749, 168.

72. Perhaps the most notorious of these incidents were the murders of a family near Pine Tree Creek in 1736, a crime for which Catawbas leaders purportedly put the ringleaders to death. *JCHA,* Dec. 7, 1726; Feb. 25, 1737; Feb. 24, 1737; *SCG,* July 7, 1739. A group of Catawbas was also accused of stealing horses and attempting to rob houses in the Waxhaws, as well as severely beating a woman there. Robert Davies to Samuel Wyly, Apr. 16, 1759, WHLP; Spangenberg Diary, Nov. 11, 1752, Adelaide L. Fries, Kenneth G. Hamilton, Douglas L. Rights, and Minnie J. Smith, eds., *Records of the Moravians in North Carolina* (hereafter *RMNC*), Vol. 1 (Raleigh: North Carolina Historical Commission, 1922–1969), 48; Baker, "Historic Catawba Peoples," 100–101; Merrell, "Indians New World," 555–556.

73. Baker, "Historic Catawba Peoples," 101–102. In an attempt to reduce the hostilities between the Catawbas and the Six Nations, the provincial governments of South Carolina brokered a peace settlement in 1752. Message from Gov. James Glen, *JCHA,* May 17, 1752. Nevertheless, persistent warfare with other groups continued, *SCG,* June 18, 1753, and deteriorating relations between the colony and the Cherokees brought the Catawbas into conflict with this group by the close of the decade: *SCG,* June 9, 1759. Hagler and Other Head Men and Warriors of the Catawba Nation to William Lyttelton, WHLP, June 16, 1757; Fred Anderson, *Crucible of War: The Seven Years' War and the Fate of Empire in British North America, 1754–1766* (New York: Vintage Books, 2000), 15–16.

74. For the impact of the 1738 epidemic and a "pestilential fever" that struck the following year, see *SCG,* June 1, 1738, and Petition to His Majesty, *JCHA,* July 23, 1740. In an attempt to prevent an epidemic among the European population on the Wateree, Samuel Wyly "set up several advertisements among ye next inhabitants to ye Indians, forbidding trade with them on any terms." Wyly to William Lyttelton, Nov. 5, 1759, WHLP.

75. Catawba Headmen to William Lyttelton, Oct., 1759, WHLP; *SCG,* Dec. 8–15, 1759. Baker, "Historic Catawba Peoples," 106–107.

76. Catawba Headmen to William Lyttelton, June 11, 1759, WHLP; James Adamson to William Lyttelton, June 12, 1759, WHLP.

77. The significance of economic interactions among colonizers and Native peoples has been investigated at length by Daniel H. Usner Jr., "The Frontier Exchange Economy in the Eighteenth Century," *William and Mary Quarterly,* 3rd ser. (1987): 166–192, and Usner, *Indians, Settlers, and Slaves in a Frontier Exchange Economy: The Lower Mississippi Valley Before 1783* (Chapel Hill: University of North Carolina Press for the Institute of Early American History and Culture, 1992). This phenomenon occurred elsewhere in South Carolina and neighboring regions;, see Verner W. Crane, *The Southern Frontier, 1670–1732* (Ann Arbor, University of Michigan Press, 1956), 118; Martha Zierden, "Frontier Society in South Carolina: An Example from Willtown (1690–1800)," in *Another's Country: Archaeological and Historical Perspectives on Cultural Interactions in the Southern Colonies,* ed. J. W. Joseph and Martha Zierden (Tuscaloosa: University of Alabama Press, 2002), 183–185; Joshua Piker, "Colonists and Creeks: Rethinking the Pre-Revolutionary Southern Backcountry," *Journal of Southern History* 70 (2004): 503–540.

78. Douglas Summers Brown, *The Catawba Indians: The People of the River* (Columbia: University of South Carolina Press, 1968), 232–233, 254–255; Charles M. Hudson, *The Catawba Nation* (Athens: University of Georgia Press, 1970), 28–30; 50–51, 74; Baker, "Historic Catawba Peoples," 185–187; Merrell, "Minding the Business of the Nation," 59.

79. Contemporary observers reported that Catawba women produced pottery during historic times, and this tradition has persisted until the present. See M. R. Harrington, "Catawba Potters and Their Work," *American Anthropologist* 10 (1908): 399–407; Vladimir J. Fewkes, "Catawba Pottery-Making, with Notes on Pamunkey Pottery-Making, Cherokee Pottery-Making, and Coiling," *Proceedings of the*

American Philosophical Society 88 (1944): 69, 71–72; Lorene B. Harris, Thomas J. Blumer, and Brett H. Riggs, "Glimpses of a Nearby Nation: The Making of Catawba Pottery with Georgia Harris and Edith Brown," *Southern Cultures* (Winter 2008): 102–111. The Catawbas considered it vital to maintain a record of their past through oral accounts kept by a designated individual. This role seems to have fallen to a woman who was by custom the authorized historian of her people. Merrell, *Indians' New World,* xxi–xxii, 262.

80. For the original type descriptions for Lamar ceramics, see Jesse D. Jennings and Charles H. Fairbanks, "Pottery Type Descriptions," *Southeastern Archaeological Conference Newsletter* 1, no. 2 (1939): 2, 4. Discussions of Lamar in the context of the Catawba-Wateree region appear in Chester B. DePratter and Chris Judge, "Wateree River," in *Lamar Archaeology: Mississippian Chiefdoms in the Deep South,* ed. Mark Williams and Gary Shapiro (Tuscaloosa: University of Alabama Press, 1990), 56–58, and David Moore, *Catawba Valley Mississippian: Ceramics, Chronology, and Catawba Indians* (Tuscaloosa: University of Alabama Press, 2002). The results of recent archaeological work on Catawba settlement sites of the early historic period appear in Brett H. Riggs, "Temporal Trends in Native Ceramic Traditions of the Lower Catawba River Valley," *Southeastern Archaeology* 29 (2010): 31–43.

81. Merrell, *Indians' New World,* 210–211.

82. The regiments for Grenville, Colleton, and Berkeley Counties were assigned to the western half of the province. The Craven County regiment served all the territory north and east of the Santee, which included the townships of Williamsburg, Kingston, and Queensborough and the Welsh Tract, as well as Fredericksburg on the Wateree. William A. Schaper, "Sectionalism and Representation in South Carolina, a Sociological Study," *Annual Report of the American Historical Association for the Year 1900,* Vol. 1 (Washington, D.C.: Government Printing Office, 1901), 333–334; Sally E. Hadden, *Slave Patrols: Law and Violence in Virginia and the Carolinas* (Cambridge, Mass.: Harvard University Press, 2001), 43; Edgar, *South Carolina,* 73–75; Jean Martin Flynn, *The Militia in Antebellum South Carolina Society* (Spartanburg, S.C.: The Reprint Co., 1991), 31–34, 216–217.

83. For the exemption of backcountry townships from the establishment of patrol districts, see *SCG,* May 17, 1740; *JCHA,* Apr. 28, 1757. Flynn, *Militia,* 36–37.

84. For the locations of militia companies on the Wateree and the number of their members, see Petty, *Growth and Distribution of Population,* 46, Fig. 6, 217.

85. Patterns of settlement expansion by decade are illustrated in Lewis, *American Frontier,* 162–169. For the character of militias, see Hadden, *Slave Patrols,* 44–46; Klein, *Unification of a Slave State,* 40–41; Hooker, ed., *Carolina Backcountry,* 96–97.

86. Geographers have long recognized the role of human societies in creating landscapes and influencing their form over time. Carl Ortwin Sauer, "The Morphology of Landscape (1925)," in *Land and Life, a Selection from the Writings of Carl Ortwin Sauer,* ed. John Leighly (Berkeley: University of California Press, 1963), 343. Consequently, landscapes are seen as an outcome of human activities and a reflection of the societies that created them. Peirce F. Lewis, "Axioms for Reading the Landscape: Some Guides to the American Scene," in *The Interpretation of Ordinary Landscapes,* ed. Donald W. Meinig (New York: Oxford University Press, 1979); John R. Stilgoe, *Common Landscapes of America,1580 to 1845* (New Haven, Conn.: Yale University Press, 1982); James Duncan and Nancy Duncan, "(Re)Reading the Landscape," *Environment and Planning D: Society and Space 6* (1988). Landscapes may also be perceived in differing contexts based on the particular experiences of the individuals or groups involved. David Lowenthal, "Geography, Experience, and Imagination: Towards a Geographical Epistemology," *Annals of the Association of American Geographers* 51 (1961): 260; D. W. Meinig, "The Beholding Eye, Ten Versions of the Same Scene," in *The Interpretation of Ordinary Landscapes,* ed. D. W. Meinig (New York: Oxford University Press, 1979), 43–45. Settlement patterning is a significant aspect of landscape, and archaeologists have emphasized its role in investigating the relationship of its form and composition to the adjustments of societies of varying levels of complexity to their social and natural environments. See, for example, Bruce Trigger, "The Determination of Settlement Patterns," in *Settlement Archaeology,* ed. K. C. Chang (Palo Alto, Calif.: National Press, 1968), 53–78.

87. Mitchell, *Soil Survey of Kershaw County,* 5–10.

88. *JCHA,* Dec. 12, 1752; H. Roy Merrens and George D. Terry, "Dying in Paradise: Malaria, Mortality and the Perceptual Environment in Colonial South Carolina," *Journal of Southern History* 50 (1984): 547–550.

89. Holcomb, ed., *PL,* II: 224.

90. Holcomb, ed., *PL,* II: 10, 41.

91. Similar land patterns of long lots appeared elsewhere in colonial British North America, along the Connecticut, Mohawk, Delaware, and Savannah Rivers, as well as among the French settlements along the Mississippi River in Louisiana and Illinois and the St. Lawrence in Canada. D. W. Meinig, *The Shaping of America: A Geographical Perspective on 500 Years of History, Vol. 1: Atlantic America, 1492–1800* (New Haven, Conn.: Yale University Press, 1986), 242–243. For discussions of long lots and their adaptability to frontier situations, see John Fraser Hart, *The Look of the Land* (Englewood Cliffs, N.J.: Prentice Hall, 1975), 48–49, and T. Lynn Smith, *The Sociology of Rural Life,* 2nd ed. (New York: Harper & Bros., 1947), 256–260. Bishop Spangenberg to Graf Zinzendorf, June 11, 1760, Fries et al., eds., *RMNC,* 2: 540–541. A preliminary study of early landholding patterns along the Wateree River revealed the extensive use of long lots during the initial settlement period. Kenneth E. Lewis and Frank J. Krist Jr., "Settlement Expansion in Fredericksburg Township, South Carolina, 1740–1770," Vol. V, Report submitted to the Savannah River Archaeological Research Program, South Carolina Institute of Archaeology and Anthropology, University of South Carolina (1997), 15–16.

92. CPB, Vol. 4, Apr. 23, 1745, 436; Vol. 5, Oct. 19, 1749, 103; Vol. 5, Nov. 13, 1749, 439; Vol. 5, Nov. 14, 1749, 412; Vol. 5, Aug. 16, 1749, 49.

93. European ceramics, particularly those produced in Great Britain, underwent extensive change during the eighteenth century. Innovations in the technology of their manufacture during this time produced a wide variety of types, the morphological characteristics of which are readily discernible even on broken specimens. Because of the rapid rate of change in the industry, individual ceramic types had relatively short use ranges and are useful time indicators. Aggressively marketed to an increasingly style-conscious consumer society, new ceramics spread rapidly throughout the British colonial world, making their manufacturing and use dates virtually identical. Documentation relating to the production and marketing of these ceramics is sufficiently complete to allow historical archaeologists to accurately calculate the use ranges for each type. They have found the identity and relative quantity of the types to be extremely useful in establishing chronologies for the sites on which they are found. Ivor Noël Hume, *A Guide to Artifacts of Colonial America* (New York: Alfred A. Knopf, 1970). Statistical methods have compared the median date for the range for each ceramic type and the type's frequency of occurrence to calculate a mean date for the ceramic assemblage. Because the intensity of artifact deposition during the period over which a site's occupation occurred forms a unimodal curve, this mean usually falls near the midpoint of a site's occupation and is helpful in determining this date. A comparison of the documented date ranges for each type is helpful in bracketing the time in which an assemblage of types used together accumulated. The bracketing technique and mean ceramic dating formula are presented in Stanley South, "Evolution and Horizon as Revealed in Ceramic Analysis in Historical Archaeology," *Conference on Historic Site Archaeology, Papers* 6 (1972), 71–116, and South, *Method and Theory in Historical Archaeology* (New York: Academic Press, 1977), 207–218.

94. Site Survey Record, South Carolina Institute of Archaeology and Anthropology, University of South Carolina, Columbia; Michael Trinkley and Natalie Adams, *Archaeological Survey of the Santee-Cooper Lugoff-Allied Signal Transmission Line, Kershaw County, South Carolina,* Chicora Foundation, Research Contribution 65 (Columbia, S.C., 1991), 12–13; CPB, Vol. 5, May 27, 1749, 156; Vol. 5, May 29, 1749, 187; Vol. 5, Dec. 23, 1748, 108.

95. Hooker, ed., *Carolina Backcountry,* 19.

96. CPB, Vol. 5, Feb. 23, 1749, 103; Vol. 5, Feb. 24, 1749, 91.

97. CPB, Vol. 5, Feb. 15, 1749, 27.

98. CPB, Vol. 5, Feb. 27, 1749, 205; Vol. 4, June 14, 1749, 500.

99. CPB, Vol. 5, Oct. 18, 1749, 125; Vol. 5, Feb. 16, 1754, 415; Vol. 8, Oct., 1752, 225; Vol. 6, June 14, 1757, 317.

100. CPB, Vol. 5, Feb. 15, 1749, 27; *JCHA*, Jan. 19, 1737/38, 393; Feb. 9, 1749/50, 198.

101. CPB, Vol. 5, Oct. 16, 1749, 49; Vol. 5, Nov. 13, 1749, 439; Vol. 5, Nov. 14, 1749, 412; *JCHA*, Mar. 10, 1752, 137; May 10, 1754, 522. The course of this road is described in John Tobler, *The South Carolina Almanack, for 1755* (Germantown, Pa.: Christopher Sower for Jacob Viart, 1754).

102. *JCHA*, Mar. 29, 1753.

103. The notion of centrality is drawn from central place theory, which is based on the assumption that settlements in a region may be organized hierarchically on the basis of their role as market centers, with higher-order settlements supplying the goods and services for lower-order settlements as well as producing a higher order of goods and services that set them apart from central places of a lower order. These settlements are distributed spatially so that those of a higher order are more widely spaced and those of a lower order are contained within, or "nest" within, their trade areas. The relative proportion of the two types of settlements, as well as their spatial arrangement, varies according to the principles underlying the economic organization of the region. J. Garner, "Models of Urban Geography and Settlement Location," in *Models in Geography*, ed. Richard J. Chorley and Peter Haggett (London: Methuen, 1967), 306–308; Brian J. L. Berry, *Geography of Market Centers and Retail Distribution* (Englewood Cliffs, N.J.: Prentice Hall, 1967), 2–3.

104. CPB, Vol. 5, Nov. 13, 1749, 439; Vol. 5, Oct. 16, 1749, 49; Vol. 5, Oct. 18, 1749, 125; Vol. 6, Jan. 30, 1756, 129.

105. *JCHA*, Mar. 10, 1752, 137; May 10, 1754, 522–523; Edward M. Boykin, *History of the Boykin Family, from Their First Settlement in Virginia 1685, and in South Carolina, Georgia, and Alabama, to the Present Time* (Camden, S.C.: Colin MacRae, 1876), 5. Map of Camden, n.d., Chesnut-Miller-Manning Papers (hereafter CMMP), 12/34/20, South Carolina Historical Society, Charleston.

106. Meriwether, *Expansion of South Carolina*, 108–109, 136–146; Peter N. Moore, *World of Toil and Strife: Community Transformation in Backcountry South Carolina, 1750–1805* (Columbia: University of South Carolina Press, 2007), 19–29; Merrell, "Indians' New World," 555–558.

107. Alexander Gregg, *History of the Old Cheraws* (Columbia, S.C.: The State Co., 1867; reprint ed., Greenville, S.C.: Southern Historical Press, 1991), 47–51; Meriwether, *Expansion of South Carolina*, 91–93; Johnson, *Frontier in the Colonial South*, 19–25, 31.

108. G. D. Bernheim, *History of the German Settlements and the Lutheran Church in North and South Carolina* (Philadelphia: The Lutheran Book Store, 1872; reprint ed., Spartanburg, S.C.: The Reprint Co., 1972), 126–137; Edgar, *South Carolina*, 55–56.

109. Meriwether, *Expansion of South Carolina*, 133–135.

Chapter 6. The Pine Tree Store

1. Joseph Kershaw was born on Mar. 26, 1728, the son of Joseph Kershaw and Mary Ryly, who operated a small tenant farm in Baitings Gate, near the main packhorse road from Halifax in Yorkshire, to Rochdale, in neighboring Lancashire. The Kershaws rented their land from the Royd family of Beestonhirst Hall in Soyland, a family of large landowners resident in the area since the thirteenth century. Deriving their wealth from the woolen industry that had come to dominate the economy of the West Riding of Yorkshire in the early eighteenth century, the Royds employed rural tenant weavers and presumably became acquainted with Joseph Kershaw through their association with his family. John Royd and his brother Jeremia inherited a large amount of capital from their father and situated their mercantile business in Bucklersbury, London. John later established a mortgage, banking, and insurance firm in Halifax. John Royd died on May 23, 1781. Information regarding the Royd family is derived from Hugh P. Kendall, "Beeston Hirst and Thrum Hall in Soyland: The Royde Family," (Halifax, UK: Halifax Antiquarian Society, 1915); Giles Brocklebank, "Royds Family Pedigree, from the Work of Sir Clement Royds (1910)," (1952), http://www.fitzwalter.com/afh/Royds/roydspl.html; "Revealed at Last—Halifax's Hidden Gem," [Halifax] *Evening Courier*, June 8, 2007, http:www.halifaxcourier.co.uk/somersethouse/Revealed-at-last-Halifax39s.2941363.jp; West Yorkshire England, Baptisms, Marriages and Burials, 1512–1812, Yorkshire Parish Records, WDP138/1/1/2, West Yorkshire Archive Service: Wakefield, Yorkshire, England; Unpublished genealogical research by Hazel M. Whiteley and her

paper, "Joseph Kershaw of Baitingsgate: Transcribed from Original Sources," Ripponden, UK, 2001 (photocopied). The quote is from Joseph Kershaw to Joseph Kershaw in Sowerby, June 13, 1748, in Peter G. D. Kershaw, "A Kershaw Family, 1670–1970," p. 67, Port Charlotte, Fla., 1974 (photocopied).

At the time of his association with Joseph Kershaw, John Ainslie was an import merchant whose business in Charleston involved "all sorts of goods." Amassing substantial wealth and property as a result of two subsequent marriages, Ainslie removed to St. George Dorchester as a planter, eventually owning three working estates. He was elected to the Assembly several times, participated in the Cherokee Campaign of 1760–1761, and held other public offices, including service on the Council of East Florida. Ainslie retired to his plantation, Windsor Hill, where he died on Jan. 11, 1774. Walter B. Edgar and N. Louise Bailey, *Biographical Directory of the South Carolina House of Representatives, Vol. 2: The Commons House of Assembly, 1692–1775* (Columbia: University of South Carolina Press, 1977), 25–26.

2. Jacob Motte was born in 1700 in Dublin and emigrated with his family to South Carolina. He entered a business partnership but operated independently after 1725 and eventually became one of the three largest merchant bankers in Charleston. The firm of Laurens & Motte existed from 1751 to 1755. Elected to the Assembly in 1739, he resigned to become public treasurer four years later. Despite Motte's apparent incompetence in this office, he was not removed and, after repaying the missing £90,000 to the trustees of his estate in 1759, he continued in the position until his death in 1770. The owner of a town house in Charleston, he owned in addition a plantation in Christ Church Parish and twenty slaves. Edgar and Bailey, *Biographical Directory,* 2: 478–479. Joseph Kershaw, with Jacob Motte, confirmed the sale of a portion of Archer's Island. He also witnessed the transfer of a town lot in Charleston and the assignment of Motte's estate. CBPR, Book L-L, Nov. 26, 1751, 117; Book L-L, Feb. 11–12, 1752, 85; Book N-N, Dec. 29–30, 1752, 70.

James Laurens (1728–1784) pursued a successful career as a merchant in Charleston. His partnership with Jacob Motte lasted from 1751 to 1755, during which time they imported ironware, ship chandlery, and sundries including supplies for the provincial government. *JCHA,* Jan. 16, Apr. 21, May 7, 1752; Jan. 15, 1755; *SCG,* Dec. 12, 1754; July 5, 13, 17, Nov. 6, 20, 1755; Jan. 8, 1756. He continued in business as James Laurens & Co. until 1775, when he retired to England to recover his health. Philip M. Hamer et al., eds., *The Papers of Henry Laurens* (hereafter *HLP*), Vol. 1 (Columbia: University of South Carolina Press, 1968–1990), 193n; *SCG,* Feb. 12, 1756; Mar. 10, 1757. Kershaw advertised with James Laurens & Co. in *JCHA,* Feb. 8, 1756–Mar. 30, May 31, 1757; *SCG,* Aug. 1, 1754, and Apr. 8, 22, May 1, 22, and June 5, 10, 1756. For the significance of Henry Laurens's purchase of Wambaw plantation, see Hamer et al., eds., *HLP,* 2: 180.

In addition to the profits he acquired as a merchant, Kershaw also inherited the estate of William Hope Meall. South Carolina, Records of the Secretary of State, Wills (RSS/W), Book 1752–1756, 62, Apr. 3, 1754, 62, Caroline T. Moore, ed., *Abstracts of the Wills of the State of South Carolina, 1760–1784,* (Columbia, S.C.: R. L. Bryan, 1969), 173.

3. William Ancrum was born in Northumberland County, England, in 1722 and sometime before 1750 immigrated to Charleston, where he became a successful merchant. Ancrum paid customs duties as an independent importer of general merchandise from 1754 to 1756 and as a partner with Nowell & Davies from 1761 to 1765. Thomas J. Kirkland and Robert M. Kennedy, *Historic Camden, Vol. 1: Colonial and Revolutionary* (Columbia, S.C.: The State Co., 1905), 344; Stuart O. Stumpf, "South Carolina Importers of General Merchandise, 1735–1765," *South Carolina Historical Magazine* 84 (1983): 5, 6. Lambert Lance was a merchant in Charleston by 1747, selling agricultural products. He also possessed five hundred acres of land in Colleton County. *SCG,* June 8, 1747, Nov. 20, 1755; *JCHA,* Mar. 24, 1756. Born in England in 1733, Aaron Loocock arrived in Charleston in 1755. "Inscriptions from the 'Chapel of Ease' of St. James Goose Creek, Situated Near Mt. Holly, S.C.," *South Carolina Historical Magazine* 13 (1912): 68; Hamer et al., eds., *HLP,* 5: 424–425. Lance and Loocock formed a partnership in 1756 and a year later constituted the firm of Ancrum, Lance & Loocock, engaged in the trade of deerskins and slaves. *SCG,* May 13, 1756, Jan. 20, 1757; Stumpf, "South Carolina Importers," 4; Walter B. Edgar and N. Louise Bailey, *Biographical Directory of the South Carolina House of Representatives, Vol. 2: The Commons House of Assembly, 1692–1775* (Columbia: University of South Carolina Press, 1977), 411–412.

A native of England, Charles Woodmason was born about 1720 and seems to have lived in London. He left his wife and son there when he emigrated to South Carolina sometime in the summer of 1752. MR, Vol. 21, May 11, 1752, 221. In August of that year he had opened a store on the corner of Tradd and Church streets in Charleston, selling books, clocks, looking glasses, and a variety of other imported goods. The following year he moved to a situation on the bay where he offered an expanded inventory to include mercery, haberdashery, millinery wares, printed matter, and flour. *SCG,* Aug. 17, 1752, Jan. 22, 1753. By 1754 he was apparently doing business in Craven County, where he acquired land and described himself as a planter and merchant. MR, Vol. 2K, 247; CPB, Vol. 6, 98. He opened the Black Mingo Creek store in 1757. A staunch Anglican, he was a church warden and later a vestryman in Prince Fredericks Winyaw Parish. He occupied several public offices in Craven County and Charleston, serving as a lieutenant in the Black River Church company of militia and also as justice of the peace, constable, tax collector, and coroner. In 1762, with his affairs in South Carolina in a tangled state, he returned briefly to England. Richard J. Hooker, ed., *The Carolina Backcountry on the Eve of the Revolution: The Journal and Other Writings of Charles Woodmason, Anglican Itinerant* (Chapel Hill: University of North Carolina Press, 1953), xii–xvi.

4. Woodmason's account of his role in the opening of the Wateree store and in assisting Joseph Kershaw in obtaining his position is contained in "A Letter to John Chesnut," in Hocker, ed., *Carolina Backcountry,* 140–141. Joseph Kershaw was described as a "merchant in Fredericksburgh Township," when he witnessed a land transaction there the following year: CBPR, Vol. V-V, Feb. 2, 1759, 466.

5. Jacob M. Price, *Capital and Credit in British Overseas Trade: The View from the Chesapeake* (Cambridge, Mass.: Harvard University Press, 1980), 19; John J. McCusker and Russell R. Menard, *The Economy of British America, 1607–1789* (Chapel Hill: University of North Carolina Press for the Institute of Early American History and Culture, 1985), 335. The structure of partnerships, which limited ownership to the partners, ensured their control over the enterprise and access to the profits it generated. But it also restricted the firm's resources to those available to the partners, a condition that could make raising capital problematic. Thomas Carson, ed., *Gale Encyclopedia of U.S. Economic History,* Vol. 2 (Detroit: Gale Group, 1999), 775.

6. Russell R. Menard, "Financing the Lowcountry Export Boom: Capital and Growth in Early South Carolina," *William and Mary Quarterly,* 3rd ser., 51 (1994): 670–676.

7. Henry Laurens to John Ettwein, Jan. 19, 1761, Hamer et al., eds., *HLP,* 3: 56; John Ettwein to Henry Laurens, Mar. 20, 1762, Bethabara Diary, Oct. 23, 1764, Adelaide L. Fries, Kenneth G. Hamilton, Douglas L. Rights, and Minnie J. Smith, eds., *Records of the Moravians in North Carolina* (hereafter *RMNC*), Vol. 1 (Raleigh: North Carolina Historical Commission, 1922–1969), 91, 290.

8. Michael Woods, "The Culture of Credit in Colonial Charleston," *South Carolina Historical Magazine* 99 (1998): 365–367; Michael Chatfield, *A History of Accounting Thought* (New York: Robert E. Krieger, 1977), 56–60, 66–67; W. T. Baxter, "Accounting in Colonial America," in *Studies in the History of Accounting,* ed. A. C. Littleton and B. S. Yamey (London: Sweet & Maxwell, 1956), 275–280; John J. McCusker, *Money and Exchange in Europe and America, 1600–1775: A Handbook* (Chapel Hill: University of North Carolina Press, 1978), 6.

9. Kershaw & Co. Charleston Store Account Book (hereafter KCCSAB), Historic Camden Foundation, Camden, S.C.

10. Henry Laurens to Joseph Kershaw, Apr. 30, 1765, Hamer et al., *HLP,* 4: 618.

11. CPB, Vol. 6, June 4, 1758, 353.

12. CPB, Vol. 6, June 5, 1758, 353; Kirkland and Kennedy, *Historic Camden,* 1: 77–80; Kenneth E. Lewis, *Camden: Historical Archaeology in the South Carolina Backcountry* (Belmont, Calif.: Thomson Wadsworth, 2006), 90, 97–100.

13. Cary Carson, Norman F. Barka, William M. Kelso, Gary Wheeler Stone, and Dell Upton, "Impermanent Architecture in the Southern American Colonies," in *Material Life in America, 1600–1860,* ed. Robert Blair St. George (Boston: Northeastern University Press, 1988), 113–158. For archaeological examples of earthfast architecture in the South Carolina backcountry, see Stephanie Holschlag and Michael J. Rodeffer, *Ninety Six: Exploratory Excavations in the Village* (Ninety Six, S.C.: Star Fort

Historical Commission, 1977), 90–92; David Colin Crass and Bruce Penner, "The Struggle for the South Carolina Frontier: History and Archaeology at New Windsor Township," *South Carolina Antiquities* 24 (1992): 37–56; Mark D. Groover, "Evidence for Folkways and Cultural Exchange in the Eighteenth Century South Carolina Backcountry," *Historical Archaeology* 28, no. 1 (1994): 46–48.

14. The occupation dates for these buildings were determined on the basis of the ceramic artifacts recovered in the excavations of their sites. For a discussion of the derivation of dates for these structures, see Lewis, *Camden: Historical Archaeology,* 113–114.

15. The formal layout of the later settlement of Camden is presented in Ch. 9.

16. Lewis, *Camden: Historical Archaeology,* 104–106, 119–120.

17. CPB, Vol. 6, Nov. 16, 1758, 415; Vol. 6, Nov. 16, 1758, 416.

18. "Petition of the Inhabitants of the Townships of New Windsor, Orangeburgh, Saxe Gotha, and Fredericksburgh," *JCHA,* Jan. 19, 1738; "Petition from Settlers on the Northeast Side of Congaree River," *JCHA,* May 14, 1752.

19. Geographers have identified the appearance of such routes as the initial phase in the development of transport systems in colonial regions. See Edward J. Taaffe, Richard L. Morrill, and Peter R. Gould, "Transport Expansion in Underdeveloped Countries: A Comparative Analysis," *Geographical Review* 53 (1963): 506.

20. Leila Sellers, *Charleston Business on the Eve of the American Revolution* (Chapel Hill: University of North Carolina Press, 1934), 34–35; "Petition from Commissioners of the Highways in the Parish of St. James Goose Creek", *JCHA,* Mar. 10, 1757.

21. John Tobler, *The South Carolina Almanack for 1755* (Germantown, Pa.: Christopher Sower for Jacob Viart, 1754).

22. Several developments during the course of the eighteenth century regularized the delivery of transatlantic mail. Contract delivery of mail between England and the American colonies began with the establishment of a packet service in 1702, and when the British Post Office assumed authority over all colonial post offices in 1710, it fixed mail routes and rates. Transatlantic mail service by private carriers operated sporadically until 1755, when it came under the control of the General Post Office. In 1765 a packet service directly to Charleston and other southern ports began, and it continued in operation until the outbreak of the American Revolution, after which transatlantic packet service resumed. *SCG,* Jan. 5, 1769; *SC&AGG,* Oct. 7, 1780; Alex L. Ter Braake, "Trans-Atlantic Mail in Colonial and Revolutionary Days," in *The Posted Letter in Colonial and Revolutionary America,* ed. Alex L. Ter Braake (State College, Pa.: American Philatelic Research Library, 1975), F-22–30, 44; Kenneth A. Wood, *Post Dates: A Chronology of Intriguing Events in the Mails and Philately* (Albany, Ore.: Van Dahl, 1985). Mail packets were indispensable for transoceanic commerce, and merchants such a Henry Laurens relied on the regularity with which correspondence passed between him and his correspondents overseas. Henry Laurens to Richard Oswald & Co., Aug. 6, 1756, Hamer et al., eds., *HLP,* 2: 275. Despite the establishment of official mail service between coastal ports, the private carriage of overland mail continued throughout the colonial period. Frank H. Norton, ed., *Journal Kept by Hugh Finley, Surveyor of the Post Roads on the Continent of North America, during His Survey of the Post Office between Falmouth and Casco Bay in the Province of Massachusetts, and Savannah in Georgia* (Brooklyn, N.Y.: Frank H. Norton, 1867), 55.

Throughout the colonial period Charleston remained the principal port through which mail passed from South Carolina to Europe, the Caribbean, and the provinces of British North America. Consequently, correspondence from secondary ports such as Georegtown as well as that from the interior entered the mailstream via South Carolina's entrepôt. Alex L. Ter Braake and Nicholas J. Johnson, "The Early Letter Post of Charlestown, S.C.," in *The Posted Letter in Colonial and Revolutionary America, 1628–1690,* ed. Alex L. Ter Braake (State College, Pa.: American Philatelic Research Library, 1975), N-8–11.

23. Wesley Everett Rich, *The History of the United Sates Post Office to the Year 1829* (Cambridge, Mass.: Harvard University Press, 1924), 25–31; *SCG,* May 3, 1739; *JCHA,* Apr. 27, 1743; *SCG,* Aug. 19, 1756; Harvey S. Teal and Robert J. Stets, *South Carolina Postal History and Illustrated Catalog of Postmarks,*

1760–1860 (Lake Oswego, Ore.: Raven Press, 1989), 8, 16–17. Rates for mail on overland routes between post offices in the American colonies were based on distance and generally exceeded rates for mail carried by water between ports. "Mail Rates of British Post Offices," *SCG*, Aug. 26, 1765.

24. Dependent on maintaining close ties between the parent church and its far-flung congregations, Moravian leaders paid close attention to communication by mail in the absence of an official postal system. Bethabara Diary, 1758, Fries et al., eds.,1: 192. "You will be able to send and receive many letters by the hands of friends and neighbors as they travel to an fro," wrote Bishop Spangenberg, "if you give them a stipulated *douceur* for the service, if it is generally known that you will give such reward, many will mention their intention of going and offer this service. . . . For instance, if a man delivers your letters in Bethlehem, and receives a piece-of-eight as 'trinkgeld,' and if the man who brings your letters from Bethlehem also receives a certain sum, men will be found who will serve you." He also stressed the flexibility of such a network, reminding his correspondents that"as you have acquaintances in Charlestown, and vessels frequently sail from there to Philadelphia, you will often be able to send letters by water to Pennsylvania. And if you can learn from what point in Virginia the post rider goes direct to Philadelphia, that will be a way you can send letters, if necessary, at less expense than by express messenger." Spangenberg to the Conference at Bethabara, July 28, 1763, Fries et al., eds., *RMNC*, 2: 552. The routing of a parcel from Germany illustrates the movement through private channels. "The package was started by Br. Broderson on Sept. 9th of this year; was forwarded four weeks later from London on the *Hope* to Mr. Nicholson in Charlestown; he sent it to Mr. Kirshaw [*sic*] at Pine Tree; he to Mr. Mitchell at Salisbury; and he sent it on by our neighbor Mr. Phelps." Bethabara Diary, Dec. 8, 1763, Fries et al., eds, *RMNC*, 2: 277. Joseph Kershaw also forwarded mail from Charleston to Bethabara. Henry Laurens to John Ettwein, Mar. 13, 1764, Hamer et al., eds., *HLP*, 4: 208.

25. The Rev. Evan Pugh, who resided at Cashaway Neck on the Pee Dee River, regularly received and sent letters from various places overland via Charleston by the early 1760s. Horace Fraser Rudisill, ed., *The Diaries of Evan Pugh (1762–1801)* (Florence, S.C.: St. David's Society, 1993), 4, 6, 10, 17, 18, 19. *SC&AGG*, Sept. 4, 1777; George Lloyd Johnson Jr., *The Frontier in the Colonial South, South Carolina Backcountry, 1736–1800* (Westport, Conn.: Greenwood Press, 1997), 105–106.

26. Lewis Cecil Gray, *History of Agriculture in the Southern United States to 1860* (Gloucester, Mass.: Peter Smith, 1933), Vol. 1, 161, 171–172; Nicholas P. Hardeman, *Shucks, Shocks, and Hominy Blocks: Corn as a Way of Life in Pioneer America* (Baton Rouge: Louisiana State University Press, 1981), Chs. 12 and 13; Samuel R. Aldrich and Earl R. Leng, *Modern Corn Production* (Cincinnati: The Farm Quarterly, 1965) 17–18; W. J. Rorabaugh, *The Alcoholic Republic: An American Tradition* (New York: Oxford University Press, 1979), Ch. 1, app. 5.

27. Gray, *History of Agriculture*, Vol. 1, 161. For a discussion of the suitability of wheat for cultivation as a commercial crop in the colonial Eastern Seaboard colonies, see Harold B. Gill Jr., "Wheat Culture in Colonial Virginia," *Agricultural History* 52 (1978): 380–393.

28. Gov. James Glen commented that New York and Philadelphia were "draining us of all the little money and bills that we could gather from other places for the bread, flour, beer, . . . and other produce." *JCHA*, May 6, 1749. For the wheat bounty, see *SCG*, Apr. 1, 1745; *JCHA*, May 16, 22, 27, 1749; Apr. 28, May 31, 1750; May 14, 17, 1751; Joseph A. Ernst and H. Roy Merrens, "The South Carolina Economy of the Middle Eighteenth Century: A View from Philadelphia," *West Georgia College Studies in the Social Sciences* 12 (1973): 19.

29. "Petition of Inhabitants of the Wateree River," *JCHA*, May 9, 1752; "Petition from Settlers on the North Side of Congaree River," *JCHA*, May 14, 1752.

30. *SCG*, Aug. 18, 1759.

31. G. G. Powell to William H. Lyttelton, Oct. 20, 1759, WHLP.

32. Carville Earle and Ronald Hoffman, "Staple Crops and Urban Development in the Eighteenth Century South," *Perspectives in American History* 10 (1976): 8–11, 22–25, 31–38.

33. Douglass C. North, "Agriculture and Regional Economic Growth," *Journal of Farm Economics* 41 (1959): 948; Charles M. Tiebout, "Exports and Regional Economic Growth," *Journal of Political Economy* 64 (1956): 164. Morton Rothstein, "Antebellum Wheat and Cotton Exports: A Contrast in

Marketing Organization and Economic Development,"*Agricultural History* 40 (1966): 94; Earle and Hoffman, "Staple Crops," 66–67.

34. R. J. Forbes, "Power to 1850," in *A History of Technology, Vol. IV: The Industrial Revolution, c. 1750 to c. 1850*, ed. Charles Singer, E. J. Holmyard, A. R. Hall, and Trevor I. Williams (New York: Oxford University Press, 1958), 151–152, 156. Richard Bennett and John Elton, *History of Corn Milling, Vol. II: Watermills and Windmills* (New York: Burt Franklin, 1898), 294–295. The relative efficiency of waterwheels is discussed in A. Stowers, "Watermills, c. 1500–c. 1850," in *A History of Technology, Vol. IV: The Industrial Revolution, c. 1750 to c. 1850*, ed. Charles Singer, E. J. Holmyard, A. R. Hall, and Trevor I. Williams (New York: Oxford University Press, 1958), 202–205; Martha Zimiles and Murray Zimiles, *Early American Mills* (New York: Bramhall House, 1973), 11–15. John Storck and Walter Dorwin Teague, *Flour for Man's Bread* (London: Oxford University Press, 1952), 113–114; J. Allen, "Hydraulic Engineering," in *A History of Technology, Vol. V: The Late Nineteenth Century, c. 1850 to c. 1900*, ed. Charles Singer, E. J. Holmyard, A. R. Hall, and Trevor I. Williams (New York: Oxford University Press, 1958), 528–530.

35. CPB, Vol. 7, Nov. 23, 1761, 152; Vol. 7, Aug. 6, 1762, 264; Vol. 7, Oct. 13, 1762, 282.

36. CBPR, Vol. Y-Y, Apr. 29, 1761, 389; Vol. Y-Y, Jan. 28, 1762, 342; Vol. Y-Y, Jan. 28, 1762, 404.

37. Kershaw acquired the Milhous tract from William Ferrall, who had purchased it four years earlier from Robert Milhous's heirs. CBPR, Vol. Y-Y, Jan. 25, 1762, 420; Y-Y, May 3, 1762, 382; CPB, Vol. 7, 136.

38. CBPR, Vol. M-3, Dec. 23, 1762, 442; Vol. M-3, Aug. 1, 1763, 452.

39. Various advertisements in *SCG*, July 26; Aug. 23, 30; Oct. 11; Nov. 22,1760.

40. Moore, comp. and ed., *Abstracts of Wills*, 1: 198–199; CBPR, Vol. Y-Y, Jan. 25, 1762, 420. Further information on the Milhous descendants may be found in Evelyn Perry Milhous, *History of the Milhous Family in South Carolina* (Miami, Fla: By the Author, 1944). Harvey S. Teal, ed., *Old Times in Camden: Pen Pictures of the Past, by William M. Shannon* (Camden, S.C.: Kershaw County Historical Society, 1996), 3.

41. *SCG*, Mar. 8, 1760. For the context of the conflict between Cherokee and South Carolina's authorities, see Fred Anderson, *Crucible of War: The Seven Years' War and the Fate of Empire in British North America, 1754–1766* (New York: Vintage Books, 2000), 457–461.

42. Kershaw supplied corn for the Catawbas: Samuel Wyly to Gov. William Lyttelton, Apr. 23, 1759, WHLP. He also carried official correspondence for Wyly and helped convince the Catawbas to deliver correspondence to isolated provincial garrisons in the Cherokee country: *Pennsylvania Gazette* (hereafter *PG*), Apr. 17, May 22, 1760; Kirkland and Kennedy, *Historic Camden*,1: 53. His continuing role as agent is indicated in Gov. William Bull to Joseph Kershaw, Mar. 1, 1766, Joseph Brevard Kershaw Papers (hereafter JBKP), South Caroliniana Library, University of South Carolina, Columbia.

43. Douglass C. North, "Institutions," *Journal of Economic Perspectives* 5 (1991): 97–98.

44. The concept of political economy has been employed to describe production, distribution, and exchange in the context of politically enforced economic relationships. Discussions of political economy in the context of the colonial world owes much to the work of anthropologists who studied the formation of communities in Puerto Rico and elsewhere in the Caribbean and in Latin America. See for example, Eric R. Wolf, "Specific Aspects of Plantation Systems in the New World," in *Plantations Systems of the New World* (Washington, D.C.: Pan American Union, 1959), 136–147; Eric R. Wolf and Sidney W. Mintz, "Haciendas and Plantations in Middle America and the Antilles," *Social and Economic Studies* 6 (1957): 380–412.

45. William Roseberry, "Political Economy," *Annual Review of Anthropology* 17 (1988): 167–169.

46. Ibid., 171–172. Studies involving the role of agency have been integral to the examination of variation on forms of production, See, for example, Harriet Friedmann, "Household Production and the National Economy: Concepts for the Analysis of Agrarian Formations," *Journal of Peasant Studies* 7 (1980): 158–184. Carol A. Smith, "Forms of Production in Practice: Fresh Approaches to Simple Commodity Production," *Journal of Peasant Studies* 11 (1984): 201–221.

47. Recently archaeologists have begun to focus on the role of the individual in social change and its impact on the form and composition of the material record. Robin A. Beck Jr., James A. Brown,

Douglas J. Bolender, and Timothy K. Earle, "Eventful Archaeology: The Place of Space in Structural Transformation," *Current Anthropology* 48 (2007): 833–860, have examined the explanatory role of agency in archaeological interpretation. They assume that archaeological patterning reflects the articulation between the resources and schemas that characterize social structures and that alteration in such patterning occurs when their articulation is disrupted. Because dramatic events resulting from human agency are seen as the likely cause of such disruptions, examining the nature of such events holds the key to explaining structural change and its manifestations in the archaeological record.

48. This view of the role of human agency assumes that cultural systems are contingent and negotiated and that change is the result of intentional decisions and actions by rational individuals whose motives can be recognized through the context of their participation in larger social systems and the process of affecting them. Elizabeth Brumfiel, "Distinguished Lecture in Archaeology: Breaking and Entering the Ecosystem—Gender, Class, and Faction Steal the Show," *American Anthropologist* 94 (1992): 559. See also Jennifer L. Dornan, "Agency and Archaeology: Past, Present, and Future Directions," *Journal of Archaeological Method and Theory* 9, no. 4 (2002): 311–312, 320.

49. Motivated by personal interests, individual actions on one hand serve the purpose of implementing the course of larger social processes, but they can also produce unintended consequences. Such effects may be "emergent" in the sense that they are more than the sum of the parts. Although the patterning of the resulting system is recognizable, its relationship to the individual elements that produced it cannot necessarily be explained by what is known of them. George W. Salt, "A Comment on the Term Emergent Properties," *American Naturalist* 113, no. 1 (1979): 145; B. J. Cole, "A Reply to D. Gordon," *American Naturalist* 137, no. 2 (1991): 262; J. Stephen Lansing, "Complex Adaptive Systems," *Annual Review of Anthropology* 32 (2003): 185.

50. Richard E. Blanton, Gary M. Feinman, Stephen A. Kowalewski, and Peter N. Pergrine, "A Dual Processual Theory for the Evolution of Mesoamerican Civilization," *Current Anthropology* 37, 1 (1996): 2; Lansing, "Complex Adaptive Systems," 196–198.

51. Carole L. Crumley, "Heterarchy and the Analysis of Complex Societies," *Archaeological Papers of the American Anthropological Association* 7, 1 (1995): 3. Blanton et al., "Dual Processual Theory," 4–5; Timothy Earle, *Bronze Age Economics: The Beginnings of Political Economies* (Boulder, Colo.: Westview, 2002)17, 69, 348–349.

52. Henry Gallman to William Lyttelton, Feb. 12, 1760, WHLP; *PG*, Mar. 20, 1760.

53. Anderson, *Crucible of War*, 459–468.

54. *PG*, Apr. 17, 1760.

55. Catawba Headmen to William Lyttelton, Aug. 23, 1759, WHLP; Samuel Wyly to William Lyttelton, Aug. 23, 1759, WHLP; *PG*, May 22, 1760.

56. *PG*, July 24, Aug. 28, 1760; Steven G. Baker, "The Working Draft of: The Historic Catawba Peoples: Exploratory Perspectives in Ethnohistory and Archaeology" (Columbia: Office of Research, University of South Carolina, 1975), 129–131; James H. Merrell, *The Indians' New World: Catawbas and Their Neighbors from European Contact through Removal* (Chapel Hill: University of North Carolina Press, 1989), 558–559; Kirkland and Kennedy, *Historic Camden*, 1: 55.

57. Merrill, *Indians' New World*, 195. A map published a dozen years later indicates that this village was situated on the north side of Pine Tree Creek to the east of the European settlement. Henry Mouzon, *An Accurate Map of North and South Carolina, with Their Indian Frontiers* (London: Robert Sayer and J. Bennett, 1775).

58. Lamar ceramics in the Catawba River Valley exhibit surfaces decorated with paddle stamping, cord marking, incising, punctations, and corn cob marking. Forms include open bowls, cazuela bowls, collared jars, and pots with slightly constricted orifaces. Brett H. Riggs, "Temporal Trends in Native Ceramic Traditions of the Lower Catawba River Valley," *Southeastern Archaeology* 29 (2010): 31–37; Leland G. Ferguson, "Lowland Plantations, the Catawba Nation, and River Burnished Pottery," in *Studies in South Carolina Archaeology: Essays in Honor of Robert L. Stephenson*, ed. Albert C. Goodyear III and Glen T. Hanson, Anthropological Studies 9 (Columbia: South Carolina Institute of Archaeology and Anthropology, 1989), 187–190.

59. Native groups' participation in colonial economies as pottery producers has been documented for the Pamunkeys in Virginia. Frank G. Speck, "Chapters on the Ethnology of the Powhattan Tribes of Virginia," *Museum of the American Indian, Indian Notes and Monographs,* 1, no. 5 (1928): 402–409, and Ivor Noël Hume, "An Indian Ware of the Colonial Period," *Quarterly Bulletin of the Archaeological Society of Virginia,* 17, no. 1 (1962): 2–14. There is also documentation from coastal North Carolina and from Spanish colonial sites in Georgia and Florida. Steven G. Baker, "Colono-Indian Pottery from Cambridge, South Carolina, with Comments on the Historic Catawba Pottery Trade," *South Carolina Institute of Archaeology and Anthropology, Notebook* 4, no. 1 (1972): 9–10. For a discussion of the role of ceramics in Pamunkey adaptation, see Nancy Oestreich Lurie, "Indian Cultural Adjustment to European Civilization," in *Seventeenth Century America,* ed. James Morton Smith (Chapel Hill: University of North Carolina Press, 1959), 33–60.

60. Kenneth E. Lewis, "Archaeological Investigations in Southwestern Camden: Report of the 1996–1998 Project," Report to Historic Camden Foundation, Camden, S.C., 1999, 166–167; Baker, "Colono-Indian Pottery," 13–15; Vladimir J. Fewkes, "Catawba Pottery-Making, with Notes on Pawmunkey Pottery-Making, Cherokee Pottery-Making, and Coiling," *Proceedings of the American Philosophical Society* 88 (1944): 69–72; R. P. Stephen Davis and Brett H. Riggs, "An Introduction to the Catawba Project," *North Carolina Archaeology* 53 (2004): 53, 4–5, 37–38; Lewis, *Camden: Historical Archaeology,* 136–137.

61. Samuel Wyly to William Lyttelton, May 6, 1759; John Evans to William Lyttelton, Sept. 7, 1759, WHLP; *SCG,* Sept. 12, 1760; *PG,* June 7, July 27, 1760; Peter N. Moore, *World of Toil and Strife: Community Transformation in Backcountry South Carolina, 1750–1805* (Columbia: University of South Carolina Press, 2007), 29; Kirkland and Kennedy, *Historic Camden,*1: 56, 64.

62. Both Alexander Chesnut and Mary Ross were born in Ulster in Ireland. The Ross family emigrated to Frederick County, Virginia, in 1719, and Alexander arrived in Philadelphia with his brother Benjamin early in the century. Following their marriage in 1740, Alexander Chesnut settled among his wife's relatives on the Virginia frontier, where he worked as a surveyor. Jasper Sutton, Mary's second husband, had roots in New England and New Jersey. In 1771 he and John Chesnut arranged for the sale of the abandoned Virginia lands. Martha Daniels, "Mulberry Plantation's Family," paper presented to the South Carolina Genealogical Society, Columbia, S.C., July 11, 2014; William B. White Jr., *The Ross-Chesnut-Sutton Family of South Carolina* (Franklin, N.C.: Genealogy Publishing Services, 2002); Mulberry Plantation Archives, Camden, S.C.; Charlotte Boykin Salmond Brunson, *Kershaw County Cousins* (Columbia, S.C.: R. L. Bryan, 1978), 149; Richard W. Lloyd, "Inscriptions from Cemeteries in and Near Camden," *South Carolina Historical Magazine* 25 (1924): 48; Hooker, ed., *Carolina Backcountry,* 136n; Brent H. Holcomb, ed., *Petitions for Land from the South Carolina Council Journals* (hereafter *PL*), Vol. V (Columbia, S.C.: SCMAR, 1996–2009), 113. Chesnut's presence at Pine Tree Hill is indicated by his appearance as a witness to the transfer of land between Govee Black and Samuel Wyly, CBPR, Vol. Y-Y, Jan. 29, 1762, 342.

63. CLG/CS, Vol. 10, Oct. 7, 1762, 347; CLG/CS, Vol. 12, July 17, 1765, 535; CLG/CS, Vol. 14, June 1, 1767, 404. Reference to Sutton as an "inn holder" appeared in a deed, CBPR Vol. M-3, Mar. 15, 1769, 466; CLG/CS, Vol. 25, Oct. 5, 1771, 302; State Plat Books, Charleston Series (hereafter SPB/ChS), Vol. 5, Oct. 19, 1784, 385; and SPB/ChS, Vol. 15, May 20, 1785, 347. Sutton's Tavern occupied this location in 1780. William Seymour, "A Journal of the Southern Expedition, 1780–1783, by William Seymour, Sergeant-Major of the Delaware Regiment," *Pennsylvania Magazine of History and Biography* 7 (1883): 289. The cleared portion of Sutton's Farm apparently lay just north of the ford of the Charleston Road at Gum Swamp Creek. H. L. Landers, *The Battle of Camden, South Carolina, August 16, 1780,* H.R. 37, 71st Cong., 1st sess., 1929, 41. Although much of the Sutton property remained wooded in the eighteenth century, it later became known as "Parker Old Field" after a subsequent owner. Benjamin J. Lossing, *Pictorial Field Book of the Revolution,* Vol. 1 (New York: Harper & Bros., 1860), 460; Kirkland and Kennedy, *Historic Camden,* 1: 169.

64. Meriwether, *Expansion of South Carolina,* 136–146.

65. Thomas J. Little, "'Adding to the Church Such as Shall Be Saved': The Growth and Influence of Evangelicalism in Colonial South Carolina, 1740–1775," in *Money, Trade and Power: The Evolution of Colonial South Carolina's Plantation Society,* ed. Jack P. Greene, Rosemary Brana-Shute, and Randy J. Sparks (Columbia: University of South Carolina Press, 2001), 367–368; Moore, *World of Toil and Strife,* 1–3.

66. Christine Leigh Heyrman, *Southern Cross: The Beginnings of the Bible Belt* (New York: Alfred A. Knopf, 1997), 10–11.

67. Hooker, ed., *Carolina Backcountry,* 141, 144.

68. Ibid., 144. James Chesnut was born in 1745, the youngest child of Alexander and Mary Ross Chesnut. Daniels, "Mulberry Plantation Family"; White, *Ross-Chesnut-Sutton Family.*

69. Holcomb, ed., *PL,* V: 80; CBPR, Vol. Y-Y, Feb. 17, 1762, 416; Vol. H-3, Mar. 18, 1763, 266; MB, Vol. 11, Aug. 22, 1772, 366; Kirkland and Kennedy, *Historic Camden,*1: 67, 77; Joseph B. Kershaw, Notes in Equity (hereafter JBKNE), June 14, 1780.

70. Holcomb, ed., *PL,* V: 91, 92, 126; CPB, Vol. 9, Oct. 10, 1763, 110; Vol. 10, Feb. 20, 1768, 210. For the date of Kershaw's marriage, see Kirkland and Kennedy, *Historic Camden,*1: 380, and also Hooker, ed., *Carolina Backcountry,*145.

71. Kirkland and Kennedy, *Historic Camden,* 1: 75, 86.

72. Daniel Thorp, *The Moravian Community in Colonial North Carolina: Pluralism on the Southern Frontier* (Knoxville: University of Tennessee Press, 1989), 35–40.

73. Ibid., 113–115. The extent of trade and the diversity of customers are illustrated by the arrival of three wagons of grain at the Bethabara mill from a Quaker settlement in present Guilford County and two from an Irish settlement in present Davidson County. Bethabara Diary, Dec. 14, 1756, Fries et al., eds., *RMNC,* 1: 173.

74. Stanley South, "The Ceramic Forms of the Potter Gottfried Aust at Bethabara, North Carolina, 1755 to 1771," *Conference on Historic Site Archaeology, Papers, 1965–1966,* 1 (1967): 33–38; South, *Historical Archaeology in Wachovia: Excavating Eighteenth Century Bethabara and Moravian Pottery* (New York: Kluwer/Plenum, 1999).

75. Bethabara Diary, Feb. 14, Aug. 25, 1763; May 28, 1764; Diary of Bethabara and Bethania, Nov. 12, 1762, Fries et al., eds., *RMNC,* 1: 261, 275, 288, 251; John F. Bivins Jr., *The Moravian Potters in North Carolina* (Chapel Hill: University of North Carolina Press, 1973).

76. Thorp, *Moravian Community,* 135–141; Hamer et al., eds., *HLP,* 3: 95n; Memorabilia of Wachovia, 1762, Bethabara Diary, Oct. 14, 1762, Bethabara Diary, 1763, Fries et al., eds., *RMNC,* 1: 241, 250, 269.

77. Bethabara Diary, Dec. 2, 1765; Wachovia Diary, Nov., 1768, Fries et al., eds, *RMNC,* 1: 307, 373. In addition to the shipments to the Pine Tree Hill store, at least one other trader, John Moore, acquired pottery for his store on the Catawba River. Diary of Bethabara and Bethania, Nov. 12, 1762, Fries et al., eds., *RMNC,* 1: 251. Moravian ceramics have appeared in the archaeological record at Pine Tree Hill, farther west at Ninety Six, as well as in Charleston. Kenneth E. Lewis, *Camden: A Frontier Town in Eighteenth Century South Carolina,* Anthropological Studies 2 (Columbia: South Carolina Institute of Archaeology and Anthropology, 1976), 171; Lewis, *The American Frontier: An Archaeological Study of Pattern and Process* (Orlando, Fla.: Academic Press, 1984), 130–132.

78. Lewis, *Camden: Historical Archaeology,* 123; Lewis, "Archaeological Investigations in Southwestern Camden," 164–165, 183–184.

79. Lorna Weatherill, *The Growth of the Pottery Industry in England, 1670–1815* (New York: Garland, 1986), 170–183; N. Kendrick, "Josiah Wedgwood: An Eighteenth-Century Entrepreneur in Salesmanship and Marketing Techniques," *Economic History Review,* new ser., 12 (1960): 408–433; George L. Miller, "Marketing Ceramics in North America: An Introduction," *Winterthur Portfolio* 19 (1984): 1–5; Ivor Noël Hume, *A Guide to Artifacts of Colonial America* (New York: Alfred A. Knopf, 1970), 106–129.

80. Lewis, "Archaeological Investigations in Southwestern Camden," 180–182.

81. *SCG,* Nov. 5, 1763.

Chapter 7. "Kershaw & Co's Store"

1. *SCG&CJ*, Feb. 19, 1770. This act, known as the Circuit Court Act of 1769, is contained in *Acts of the General Assembly of South Carolina, Passed in the Year 1769* (Charleston, S.C.: Peter Timothy, printer, 1769), and is reproduced in Maxwell Brown, *The South Carolina Regulators* (Cambridge, M: Belknap Press of Harvard University Press, 1963), 98–102, 148–158.

2. The appearance of courts here reflects a traditional role they have played historically in expanding trade by providing an institution capable of protecting merchants as well as enforcing contracts, both of which offer the incentive of lowering business costs. Douglass C. North, "Institutions," *Journal of Economic Perspectives* 5 (1991): 107, 109.

3. John J. McCusker and Russell R. Menard, *The Economy of British America, 1607–1789* (Chapel Hill: University of North Carolina Press for the Institute of Early American History and Culture, 1985), 79–80, 194; William S. Sachs and Ari Hoogenboom, *The Enterprising Colonials: Society on the Eve of the Revolution* (Chicago: Argonaut, 1965), 41; Allan Kulikoff, *Tobacco and Slaves: The Development of Southern Cultures in the Chesapeake, 1680–1800* (Chapel Hill: University of North Carolina Press, 1986), 120; Jon Butler, *Becoming America: The Revolution before 1776* (Cambridge, Mass.: Harvard University Press, 2000), 60–61; William H. Siener, "Charles Yates, The Grain Trade, and Economic Development in Fredericksburg, Virginia, 1750–1810," *Virginia Magazine of History and Biography* 93 (1985): 412–413.

4. For a discussion of these settlements, see H. Roy Merrens, *Colonial North Carolina in the Eighteenth Century: A Study in Historical Geography* (Chapel Hill: University of North Carolina Press, 1964), 116–118, 155–1160.

5. M. G. Smith, *Corporations and Society: The Social Anthropology of Collective Action* (Chicago: Aldine, 1974), 94–98.

6. Jacob M. Price, *Capital and Credit in British Overseas Trade: The View from the Chesapeake* (Cambridge, Mass.: Harvard University Press, 1980), 24, 59–60.

7. "Memorandum of Agreement between Joseph Kershaw, John Chesnut, Ely Kershaw, William Ancrum, and Aaron Loocock, Jan 4, 1764," CMMP, 12/33/5. Although the new partnership divided its assets formally among its members, it was not a joint stock company in that its legal identity remained tied to its owners and only they possessed shares in the concern. As a partnership, the organization existed only as long as the original owners participated and had to reorganize itself in response to the changes in the partnership's composition. Thomas Carson, ed., *Gale Encyclopedia of U.S. Economic History*, 2 vols. (Detroit: Gale Group, 1999), 1: 514; 2: 775.

8. Economists have observed that the phenomenon in which the most skilled or productive people tend to gravitate together to form the largest business groups occurs widely, suggesting that inefficiency limits group size and that partnership size is correlated with the ability of members. Joseph Farrell and Suzanne Scotchmer, "Partnerships," *Quarterly Journal of Economics* 103 (1988): 279–297.

9. John Chesnut was identified as a "merchant" when he witnessed the transfer of two hundred acres on Jumping Gully from Hardyrice and Needham Jernigan to Joseph Kershaw & Co. CBPR, Vol. E-3, May 15, 1764, 244.

10. Memorandum of Agreement, Jan. 4, 1764.

11. Ely Kershaw was baptized Sept. 24, 1743, West Yorkshire, England, Baptisms, Marriages and Burials, 1512–1812, WDP138/1/1/2; Peter G. D. Kershaw, "A Kershaw Family, 1670–1970," p. 67, Port Charlotte, Fla., 1974 (photocopied), 8. Ely Kershaw was resident at Pine Tree Hill when he witnessed a deed conveying 350 acres on the Wateree River from James and Priscilla McGirt to his brother. CBPR, Vol. Y-2, Apr. 29, 1761, 169. Ely Kershaw was appointed a tax inquirer and collector in 1764 and 1766 for St. Mark's Parish and held this office until 1767. Created in 1757 as an ecclesiastical unit to accommodate rapid population growth in the backcountry, St. Mark's Parish served as a provincial administrative entity as well. *SCG*, Sept. 22, 1766; *SCG&CJ*, Jan. 20, 1767; Brown, *South Carolina Regulators*, 26; John Wesley Brinsfield, *Religion and Politics in Colonia South Carolina* (Easley, S.C.: Southern Historical Press, 1983), 53–54.

12. Memorandum of Agreement, Jan. 4, 1764.

13. CBPR, Vol. F-3, Aug. 22, 1766, 748; Vol. H-3, May 26, 1767, 22.

14. This ferry was located on three hundred acres granted to Joseph Joyner at the fork of the Congaree and Wateree Rivers in 1752. Its location made it a major overland outlet for inhabitants in that region seeking a market for their produce. CPB, Vol. 4, Jan. 9, 1752, 564; *JCHA,* Mar. 10, 1752; John Hammond Moore, *Columbia and Richland County: A South Carolina Community, 1740–1990* (Columbia: University of South Carolina Press, 1993), 11. Joseph Kershaw later acquired the ferry site by purchase. CBPR, Vol. Y-Y, May 1, 1761, 410.

15. These figures have been compiled from grants (CLG/CS), plats (CPB), and conveyance books (CBPR).

16. The Waxhaws region has no certain boundaries. Traditionally it has been delineated as the area encompassed within a ten-mile radius centered on the confluence of Waxhaw Creek and the Catawba River. The Waxhaw Settlement extended into North Carolina and included residents of the valleys of neighboring Twelve Mile Creek to the north and Cane Creek to the south. "Waxhaws," *Southern Home,* Oct. 6, 1873; Peter N. Moore, *World of Toil and Strife: Community Transformation in Backcountry South Carolina, 1750–1805* (Columbia: University of South Carolina Press, 2007); Walter Edgar, *South Carolina: A History* (Columbia: University of South Carolina Press, 1998), 56–57. Because of the region's indefinite nature, the term "Waxhaws" is used loosely here to refer to all areas of European settlement in the upper Wateree/Catawba River Valley.

17. Moore, *World of Toil and Strife,* 52–54.

18. Richard J. Hooker, ed., *The Carolina Backcountry on the Eve of the Revolution: The Journal and Other Writings of Charles Woodmason, Anglican Itinerant* (Chapel Hill: University of North Carolina Press, 1953), 14. In the spring of 1772, William Moultrie characterized the Waxhaws settlements as having "pretty good lands [and] a great many wheat fields." Charles Davis, ed., "The Journal of William Moultrie While a Commissioner on the North and South Carolina Boundary Survey, 1772," *Journal of Southern History* 8 (1942): 552.

19. Patrick Bready to John Chesnut and Ely Kershaw, CBPR, Vol. E-3, Oct. 9, 1765, 280; CPB, Vol. 10, Apr. 27, 1768, 217; Vol. 17, Dec. 13, 1771, 445; CLG/CS, Vol. 11, Oct. 20, 1763, 333.

20. Wyly completed his survey of the Catawba Reservation the following year; however, the Assembly, noting that the work was not authorized by its body, requested that he receive reimbursement from the office of the Superintendent of Indian Affairs for the Southern District *JCHA,* Mar. 5, 13, 14, 1765. For a discussion of the factors that complicated the survey of the Catawba lands, see Steven G. Baker, "The Working Draft of: The Historic Catawba Peoples: Exploratory Perspectives in Ethnohistory and Archaeology" (Columbia: Office of Research, University of South Carolina, 1975), 134–140.

21. James E. Merrell, "The Indians' New World: The Catawba Experience," *William and Mary Quarterly,* 3rd ser., 41 (1984): 559–560; Adelaide L. Fries, Kenneth G. Hamilton, Douglas L. Rights, and Minnie J. Smith, eds., *Records of the Moravians in North Carolina* (hereafter *RMNC*), Vol. 1 (Raleigh: North Carolina Historical Commission, 1922–1969), 331; Hooker, ed., *Carolina Backcountry,* 20.

22. For Joseph Kershaw's role in supplying goods to the Catawbas, see William Bull to Joseph Kershaw, Mar. 1, 1766, JBKP. Kershaw was officially asked by the Catawbas to represent them in grievances against settlers on their lands. "At a Meeting Held with the Catawbas," March 26, 1771, JBKP.

23. For Moore, see CPB, Vol. 7, Jan. 11, 1757, 186; Diary of Bethabara and Bethania, Nov. 12, 1762, Fries et al., eds. *RMNC,* 1: 251. For Patten, see Moore, *World of Toil and Strife,* 49–50, and Judgement Rolls, Court of Common Pleas (hereafter JRCCP), South Carolina Department of Archives and History, Columbia, Box 88A, Item 130A, Oct. 19, 1770. For Wade, see CPB, Vol. 7, 184; CBPR, Vol. E-3, 785. For Crawford, see Moore, *World of Toil and Strife,* 24, 56; CPB, Vol. 9, Apr. 17, 1768, 234; Vol. 13, Nov. 2, 1772, 239; CBPR, Vol. K-4, 132; Hendrik Booraem, *Young Hickory: The Making of Andrew Jackson* (Dallas, Tex.: Taylor Trade Publishing, 2001), 30–31, 553–55.

24. For the distinction between wholesale merchants and general retailers or shopkeepers, see Stephanie Grauman Wolf, *As Various as Their Land: The Everyday Lives of Eighteenth-Century Americans* (New York: HarperCollins, 1993), 190–191.

25. Alexander Gregg, *History of the Old Cheraws* (Columbia, S.C.: The State Co., 1867; reprint ed., Greenville, S.C.: Southern Historical Press, 1991), 45–49; Julian J. Petty, *The Growth and Distribution of Population in South Carolina* (Columbia: South Carolina State Planning Board, 1943; reprint ed., Spartanburg, S.C.: The Reprint Co., 1975), 39–40; Robert L. Meriwether, *The Expansion of South Carolina, 1729–1765* (Kingsport, Tenn.: Southern Publishers, 1940), 92–93; George Lloyd Johnson Jr., *The Frontier in the Colonial South, South Carolina Backcountry, 1736–1800* (Westport, Conn.: Greenwood Press, 1997), 25, 30–31; Johnson, "The Welsh in the Carolinas in the Eighteenth Century," *North American Journal of Welsh Studies* 4 (2004): 17–18.

26. John J. Winberry, "Reputation of Carolina Indigo," *South Carolina Historical Magazine* 80 (1979): 243–244; Johnson, *Frontier in the Colonial South,* 40–41.

27. Johnson, *Frontier in the Colonial South,* 50.

28. Discussions of the early traders in the Welsh Tract appear in Meriwether, *Expansion of South Carolina,* 49–50, and Johnson, *Frontier in the Colonial South,* 50–54. Christopher Gadsden was a merchant and planter who operated stores in Charleston and Georgetown. Although he registered three of his five ships in Georgetown and developed a working plantation on the Pee Dee, he maintained his main store in the capital, where he built his wharf and warehouses. Walter B. Edgar and N. Louise Bailey, *Biographical Directory of the South Carolina House of Representatives, Vol. 2: The Commons House of Assembly, 1692–1775* (Columbia: University of South Carolina Press, 1977), 259–260. For the location of lands surveyed for Nicholas Rogers and Christopher Gadsden, see CPB, Vol. 4, Jan. 6, 1742, 45, and Vol. 6, Apr. 15, 1757, 213.

29. Nearby road locations in this vicinity are shown in the plats of lands belonging to Thomas Wade, CPB, Vol. 11, Dec. 12, 1766, 64, and Vol. 21, May 26, 1772, 250.

30. These tracts included a total of 650 acres owned by Ely Kershaw, CBPR, Vol. Z-4, Jan. 4, 1770, 467; CPB, Vol. 11, May 12, 1770, 551; Vol. 17, June 30, 1775, 439; 250 acres acquired by Aaron Loocock, CLG/CS, Vol. 19, Oct. 31, 1769, 19; and 400 acres to all the partners collectively, CPB, Vol. 16, May 22, 1772, 406. The overland route west of Cheraw led northwest and intersected another road that passed out of North Carolina in a southwesterly direction. This road passed through the Lynches River drainage above the fork of Lynches and Little Lynches Rivers and intersected the Catawba Path at Pine Tree Hill. Its route in 1773 is illustrated in James Cook, *A Map of the Province of South Carolina* (London, 1773), and in 1775 in Henry Mouzon, *An Accurate Map of North and South Carolina, with Their Indian Frontiers* (London: Robert Sayer and J. Bennett, 1775).

31. "Memorandum of Agreement"; Records of activities of the store appear in Ely Kershaw, Account Book, 1769–1774 (hereafter EKAB), South Carolina Historical Society, Charleston. This date corresponds to the traditional opening date of the Kershaw store at Cheraw Hill. Gregg, *History of the Old Cheraws,* 118–119.

32. EKAB; Account Books of Joseph Kershaw, 1774–1775 (JKAB). Microfilm 478, Wisconsin Historical Society, Madison.

33. These stores are discussed in Johnson, *Frontier in the Colonial South,* 51–54. For the location of Thomas Elerbee's tracts, see CPB, Vol. 4, Jan. 1, 1742, 195; Vol. 4, Jan. 23, 1747, 398; MR, Vol. 21, 330.

34. For Woodmason's role in promoting the Church of England in the upper Pee Dee drainage, see Hooker, ed., *Carolina Backcountry,* 13, 19. Johnson, *Frontier in the Colonial South,* 148–150.

35. *SC&AGG,* Apr. 15, 1768; Brent Holcomb, ed., *Saint David's Parish, South Carolina, Minutes of the Vestry,1768–1832, Parish Register, 1819–1924* (Easley, S.C.: Southern Historical Press, 1979), 9–11, 13–15; Gregg, *History of the Old Cheraws,* 174–175, 177, 179, 185.

36. Johnson, *Frontier in the Colonial South,* 151; Klein, *Unification of a Slave State,* 277.

37. Capt. John Cantey was the son of William Cantey of Craven, settled in Prince Fredericks Parish, presumably, where he was the owner of extensive plantation lands and served as Tax Commissioner for English Santee in 1715. William Cantey's father was George Cantey of Berkeley, a Goose Creek planter who owned one thousand acres on the Ashley River and the son of Teige Cantey, one of the original 1670 settlers from Barbados. John Cantey moved to the Wateree some time before 1752

and became a large landowner there, amassing at least 3,510 acres by 1771. He lived on his plantation, Live Easy, south of Town Creek. Appointed a commission for St. Mark's Parish on its creation in 1757, Capt. John Cantey also served as a justice of the peace and magistrate for Craven County. His title derived from his service in Gov. Henry Lyttelton's Cherokee campaign of 1759–1760. Joseph S. Ames, "Cantey Family," *South Carolina Historical Magazine* 11 (1910): 204–205, 207–208, 212–213, 224–225; Henry A. M. Smith, "The Upper Ashley: And the Mutations of Families," *South Carolina Historical Magazine* 20 (1919), 192; Thomas J. Kirkland and Robert M. Kennedy, *Historic Camden, Vol. 1: Colonial and Revolutionary* (Columbia, S.C.: State Printing Co., 1926), 356; *SCG*, Oct. 19, 1765, Oct. 26, 1767; Martha Daniels, "Mulberry Plantation's Family," paper presented to the South Carolina Genealogical Society, Columbia, S.C., July 11, 2014.

38. Ames, "Cantey Family," 242. For the McGirts' initial landholding, see TSG, Vol. 2F, May 14, 1752, 67. John Cantey witnessed the sale of the McGirts' land to Robert Milhous the following year: CBPR, Vol. P-P, May 12, 1753, 119. He purchased fifty acres of this tract the same day: CBPR, Vol. E-3, 160. Cantey received by gift four acres at Pine Tree Hill from Samuel Wyly (CBPR, Vol. E-3, Jan. 25, 1764, 184) and acquired six acres from Joseph Kershaw adjacent to the road to the Waxhaws: CBPR, Vol. R-3, Apr. 22, 1765, 393. Charles Woodmason referred to Cantey's tavern disparagingly in 1767 and also alluded to Cantey's social ties to Samuel Wyly and the Kershaws: Hooker, ed., *Carolina Backcountry,* 12, 138. Curiously, the marriage notice of Nov. 19, 1769, lists Ely Kershaw's residence as Rockingham, perhaps in reference to the settlement just across the North Carolina northeast of Cheraw: *SCG,* Nov. 30, 1769; *SC&AGG,* Dec. 4, 1769. Sarah Cantey was born Feb. 15, 1753. Richard W. Lloyd, "Inscriptions from Cemeteries in and Near Camden," *South Carolina Historical Magazine* 25 (1924): 48. Her marriage to John Chesnut occurred on June 19, 1770. *SCG&CJ,* June 14, 1770; "Records Kept by Col. Isaac Hayne," *South Carolina Historical Magazine* 11 (1910): 93.

39. Edgar and Bailey, eds., *Biographical Directory,* 2: 557–558; Ames, "Cantey Family," 213.

40. For these routes, see William DeBrahm, *A Map of South Carolina and a Part of Georgia,* (London: T. Jefferys, 1757); Cook, *Map of the Province of South Carolina;* and Mouzon, *Accurate Map of North and South Carolina.*

41. Meriwether, *Expansion of South Carolina,* 58–61; Edwin L. Green, *A History of Richland County,* Vol. 1 (Greenville, S.C.: Southern Historical Press, 1996), 26–32; 63, 138–139; Petty, *Growth and Distribution of Population.,* 41, 47; Moore, *Columbia and Richland County,* 64–65; G. D. Bernheim, *History of the German Settlements and the Lutheran Church in North and South Carolina* (Philadelphia: The Lutheran Book Store, 1872; reprint ed., Spartanburg, S.C.: The Reprint Co., 1972), 232–233.

42. CBPR, Vol. M-3, Jan. 15, 1768, 419; Vol. Y-4, Dec. 22, 1769, 186.

43. CPB, Vol. 9, Aug. 8, 1768, 322; Brown, *South Carolina Regulators,* 116–117.

44. The tract was granted to John Matthews in 1738. A decade later Martin Fridig acquired the land and established the namesake ferry. CPB, Vol. 9, Feb. 7, 1736, 384; *JCHA,* May 11, 1754. Fridig's heirs subsequently conveyed 2 3/4 acres of this land to Chesnut. CBPR, Vol. V-5, Dec. 29, 1772, 317; Green, *Richland County,* 18; Moore, *Columbia and Richland County,* 16. For the tract granted to Martin Fridig, see CPB, Vol. 9, 443; CLG/CS, Vol. 41, 672; CBPR, Vol. W-5, 672. The roads are shown on, DeBrahm, *Map of South Carolina.* For settlement in Saxe Gotha Township, see Katherine H. Richardson, "The Impact of the Township System on the Backcountry of South Carolina: From Garrison Towns to 'Traditional' Towns," paper presented at Southern Colonial Backcountry Conference, Columbia, S.C., Oct. 15, 1993. The location the Congaree Fort is based on archaeological investigations: James L. Michie, *The Discovery of Old Fort Congaree,* Research Manuscript Series 208 (Columbia: South Carolina Institute of Archaeology and Anthropology, 1989).

45. "Memorandum of Agreement, Jan. 4, 1764"; Moore, *Columbia and Richland County,* 29.

46. H. T. Cook, *The Hard Labor Section* (Greenville, S.C.: By the Author, 1923), 6; Bernheim, *History of the German Settlements,* 161–166; Arthur Henry Hirsch, *The Huguenots of South Carolina* (Columbia: University of South Carolina Press, 1999), 40–43; J. W. Joseph and Martha Zierden, "Cultural Diversity in the South Colonies," in *Another's Country: Archaeological and Historical Perspectives on*

Cultural Interactions in the Southern Colonies, ed. David Colin Crass, Steven D. Smith, Martha A. Zierden, and Richard D. Brooks (Tuscaloosa: University of Alabama Press, 2002), 6–7; Petty, *Growth and Distribution of Settlement,* 38.

47. Samuel Francis to William Henry Lyttelton, Aug. 29, 1759, WHLP; Edmund Atkin to William Henry Lyttelton, Feb. 5, 1760; John Pearson to William Henry Lyttelton, Feb. 8, 1760, WHLP; Patrick Calhoun to William Henry Lyttelton, Feb. 25, 1760, WHLP; Brown, *South Carolina Regulators,* 5–7.

48. Meriwether, *Expansion of South Carolina,* 131–135, 169–170; Petty, *Growth and Distribution of Population,* 41.

49. Kenneth Coleman, *Colonial Georgia: A History* (New York: Charles Scribner's Sons, 1976), 215.

50. Francis Harper, ed., *The Travels of William Bartram,* Naturalist's Edition (New Haven, Conn.: Yale University Press, 1958), 201.

51. An informative estimate of the extent of trade emanating from the Pine Tree Hill store appears in Judith J. Schulz, "The Hinterland of Revolutionary Camden, South Carolina," *Southeastern Geographer* 16 (1976): 91–97. The author based this work on an analysis of the customers identified in Joseph Kershaw Account Books 1774–1775 (JKAB) (see below) and persons appearing in the 1790 manuscript census. Kershaw County Historical Society, *First Federal Census, Population, 1798, South Carolina, Camden District.* Camden, S.C., Kershaw County Historical Society, 1969.

52. Michael Woods, "The Culture of Credit in Colonial Charleston," *South Carolina Historical Magazine* 99 (1998): 366–367.

53. The Kershaw & Co. Ledgers (hereafter JKAB) are the source of all further references to transactions associated with the store at Pine Tree Hill. They include accounts with stores operated by Kershaw, Chesnut & Company at Pine Tree Hill; Kershaw, Chesnut & Kershaw at Rocky Mount; the Chatham store of Ely Kershaw & Company at Cheraw Hill; and that of John Chesnut & Company at Granby in the Congarees.

54. Sowerby Plantation was situated near Pine Tree Hill. Samuel Mathis, Joseph Kershaw's brother-in-law, stayed there briefly following his return from military service in July 1781. Samuel Mathis Diary, in Kirkland and Kennedy, *Historic Camden,* 1: 403. James McGirt was the grandfather of Mary and Sarah Cantey, the wives of Ely Kershaw and John Chesnut, respectively.

55. Kenneth E. Lewis, *Camden: Historical Archaeology in the South Carolina Backcountry* (Belmont, Calif.: Thomson Wadsworth, 2006), 123; Ivor Noël Hume, "An Indian Ware of the Colonial Period," *Quarterly Bulletin of the Archaeological Society of Virginia,* 17, no. 1 (1962): 269–271.

56. For the marketing of wheat, see *SCG,* Jan. 17, 27, Feb. 2, 1765; Jan. 4, 11, 1772. By 1769 the amount of flour produced had increased to the extent that its value exceeded that of any other backcountry export crop indigo. Klein, *Unification of a Slave State,* 16–18.

57. For tobacco production in the Backcountry, see *JCHA,* Apr. 10, 1753; *SCG,* Nov. 10, 1766. References to indigo production on the Pee Dee appear in EKAB, 1769–1770; Johnson, *Frontier in the Colonial South,* 41–42. Evan Pugh mentioned indigo raising at his Cashaway plantation as early as 1770. Horace Fraser Rudisill, ed., *The Diaries of Evan Pugh (1762–1801)* (Florence, S.C.: St. David's Society, 1993), 102; Henry Laurens to Joseph Kershaw, July 23, 1766, Philip M. Hamer et al., eds., *The Papers of Henry Laurens* (hereafter *HLP*), Vol. 5 (Columbia: University of South Carolina Press, 1968–1990), 139. Joseph Kershaw is reported to have erected an indigo works and a tobacco warehouse at Pine Tree Hill before 1770. Thomas J. Kirkland and Robert M. Kennedy, *Historic Camden, Vol. 2: Nineteenth Century* (Columbia, S.C.: State Printing Co., 1926), 14–15. References to the acquisition, use, and repair of boats for the transport of tobacco appear in JKAB, Apr. 11, 12, 13, 25, 29, 1775. Demand for tobacco inspectors appeared in the *SCG,* Nov. 14, 1768, but inspectors were not actually appointed until 1784. Gregg, *History of the Old Cheraws,* 430. The Wateree River raft was situated below Camden near the river's confluence with the Congaree. Robert Mills, *Atlas of the State of South Carolina, 1825,* with an Introduction by Gene Wadell (Greenville, S.C.: Southern Historical Press, 1980), Map of Sumter District. Early settlers realized the importance of clearing the river of obstructions, and during the 1750s

provincial funds were used to open the Wateree and maintain its navigability. Meriwether, *Expansion of South Carolina,* 106–107.

58. Pine Tree Hill's role in communications was recognized by the Moravian community at Bethabara, North Carolina, as early as 1763 when it determined that its access to Charleston offered the most rapid connection with London. Bethabara Diary, Dec. 8, 1763, Fries et al.,eds., *RMNC,* 1: 277. Letters and packages were delivered to Pine Tree Hill to be picked up or forwarded. Henry Laurens to John Ettwein, Mar. 13, 1764, Hamer et al., eds., *HLP,* 4: 207–208; Charles Woodmason Journal, Aug. 16, 1768, Hooker, ed., *Carolina Backcountry,* 57. For the link to Augusta, see Friedrich Marshall and Elizabeth Marshall to Bishop John M. Groff, Mar. 21–31, 1775, Fries et al., eds., *RMNC,* 2: 918. The fortnightly private post from Charleston was mentioned in William Ancrum's correspondence to Christian Girving, Aug. 15, 1777, and John Chesnut, Aug. 29, 1777, William Ancrum Account and Letter Book, 1757–1782 (hereater WAALB), South Caroliniana Library, University of South Carolina, Columbia.

59. William Bull to Joseph Kershaw, Mar. 1, 1766; Joseph Kershaw to William Bull, July 9, 1771; "Copy of Proclamation of William Bull to King Frow and the Principal Chiefs of the Catawba Nation," Feb. 18, 1773, "Account of a talk between Mr. Drayton and the Catawba Indians, John Wyly to Joseph Kershaw," June 28, 1773; "Copy of a talk from Superintendent of Indian Affairs delivered to the Catawbas Apr. 15, 1773," and "Warning to sundry persons to remove off the Catawbas' lands, certified by Joseph Kershaw," Oct. 1, 1785, JBKP.

60. Joseph Kershaw Account Record with Kershaw & Co, 1772–1774, JBKP. JKAB, Feb. 27, Mar. 24, 1775.

61. Bradford L. Rauschenberg, "John Bartlam, Who Established 'New Pottworks in South Carolina' and Became the First Successful Creamware Potter in America," *Journal of Early Southern Decorative Arts* 17, no. 2 (1991): 17, 19–20.

62. CPB, Vol. 7, May 19, 1761, 184. Wade is identified as a storekeeper in CBPR, Vol. E-3, Apr. 5, 1762, 785. For Boykin, see Conveyance Books, Register of Mesne Conveyance (hereafter CBMC), S363001, Vol. C-4, Aug. 12, 1772, 67, South Carolina Department of Archives and History, Columbia.

63. William Lang was born in Wakefield, Yorkshire, Feb. 16, 1746, the son of Obadiah Lang and Elizabeth Wilson. He emigrated to South Carolina in 1770, settled in the vicinity of Pine Tree Hill the following year, and married Sarah Wyly in 1775. CPB, Vol. 16, Nov. 11, 1771, 282; Vol. 33, Sept. 9, 1774, 282; Kirkland and Kennedy, *Historic Camden,* 1: 385.

64. Archibald Brown was born in 1752, the son of the Goose Creek physician and surgeon Robert Brown, M.D., and Elizabeth Hubbard. Lothrop Withington, "South Carolina Gleanings from England," *South Carolina Historical Magazine* 8 (1907): 215; "Inscriptions from the 'Chapel of Ease' of St. James Goose Creek, Situated Near Mt. Holly, S.C.," *South Carolina Historical Magazine* 13 (1912): 67; Edgar and Bailey, eds., *Biographical Directory,* 2: 106–107; Caroline T. Moore, comp. and ed., *Abstracts of the Wills of Charleston District, South Carolina, and Other Wills Recorded in the District, 1783–1800* (Columbia, S.C.: R. L. Bryan, 1974), 307. Brown's land holdings are summarized in CBPR, D-5, Oct. 6, 1776, 300–303, and CBMC, N-5, Oct. 27, 1784, 208–213.

65. Charles Ogilvie was born in 1731 in Auchiries, Aberdeenshire, Scotland, the son of James Ogilvy, the sixth Earl of Findlater and Earl of Seafield. Because his elder brother James had served with the Jacobite army in the unsuccessful rebellion of 1745, he found it expedient to immigrate to South Carolina. Alan Valentine, *The British Establishment, 1760–1784: An Eighteenth Century Biographical Dictionary,* Vol. 2 (Norman: University of Oklahoma Press, 1970), 656–657. Although Mary Michie had become the sole heir to her father's substantial fortune, a settlement executed at the time of her marriage passed only a portion of the estate to her husband. By this settlement she also retained ownership of her estate during her lifetime and passed it directly to her children. CBPR, Vol. C-3, Oct. 19, 1763, 1; CBMC, S363001, 1776–1785, Vol. Z- 5, Mar. 15, 1786, 1; *Journal of the House of Representatives* (hereafter *JHR*), Jan. 20, 1783. Charles Ogilvie retained his share of the interior land upon Mary Michie Ogilvie's death in 1769 and acquired additional lands in the Wateree Valley by grants and purchases. He eventually owned several thousand acres: *SCG,* Aug. 4, 1766; CPB, Vol. 16, Jan. 30, 1771, 544; CBPR,

Vol. L-4, Nov. 11, 1773, 219; CLG/CS, Vol. 34, Nov. 25, 1774, 167. Ogilvie sold 557 acres to John Chesnut and Ely Kershaw: CBPR, Vol. M-4, Mar. 7, 1774, 63. In addition to his business interactions with the Pine Tree Hill store, he had additional dealings with William Ancrum and Joseph Kershaw: WAALB, May 13, June 12, 1777.

66. The distinctive nature of the plantation economy, the influences that shaped it, and their social implications have long interested social scientists. See discussions in Lewis Cecil Gray, *History of Agriculture in the Southern United States to 1860,* Vol. 1 (Gloucester, Mass.: Peter Smith, 1933), 302–203; Pan American Union, *Plantation Systems of the New World,* Social Science Monographs VII (Washington, D.C.: Research Institute for the Study of Man and the Pan American Union, 1959); and, more recently, Ira Berlin, *Many Thousands Gone: The First Two Centuries of Slavery in North America* (Cambridge, Mass.: Belknap Press of Harvard University Press, 1998), 97–100.

67. Ancrum's Wateree Valley plantations and their overseers are mentioned in his correspondence in WAALB, passim. Joseph Kershaw's ties to the Gaunt family are mentioned in JBKNE, June 14, 1780.

68. The relative agricultural value of these three land categories is based on an assessment made by a committee of the South Carolina House of Representatives in shortly after independence. Concerned with establishing an ad valorem tax on real estate, the committee evaluated land by region and assigned monetary values based on perceived production potential. *JHR,* Mar. 3, 1784.

69. Merle Prunty Jr., "The Renaissance of the Southern Plantation," *Geographical Review* 45 (1955): 460–461.

70. Cleveland J. Mitchell Jr., *Soil Survey of Kershaw County Area, South Carolina* (Washington, D.C.: U.S. Department of Agriculture, Soil Conservation Service, in cooperation with the South Carolina Agricultural Experiment Station and the South Carolina Land Resources Conservation Commission, 1989), 76–78, 88; Kenneth E. Lewis and Frank J. Krist Jr., "Settlement Expansion in Fredericksburg Township, South Carolina, 1740–1770," Vol. IV, Report submitted to the Savannah River Archaeological Research Program, South Carolina Institute of Archaeology and Anthropology, University of South Carolina (1997), 12–14.

71. The drawing is from the "Plan of the Battle Fought Near Camden, August 16th, 1780," map, in Banastre Tarleton, *History of the Campaigns of 1780 and 1781* (London: T. Cadell, 1787; reprint ed., Spartanburg, S.C.: The Reprint Co., 1967); the advertisement appeared in *SCG&CJ,* Apr. 5, 1774. The soil descriptions and capabilities are based on Mitchell, *Soil Survey of Kershaw County,* 37, 51.

72. The ratio of five persons to each man in the militia follows Petty's estimate, based on a comparison of the militia totals and a contemporary estimate of the white population. The ratio of whites to slaves in the Wateree Valley and along the upper Lynches River compares well with that found for the twenty-three other backcountry militia regiments, where the 334 African Americans constituted only 12percent of the total 2,487 militia members. The total population of the backcountry was determined by employing Petty's estimate that militia member constituted one-fifth of the total population: Petty, Growth and Distribution of Population, 45, 217.

73. Slaves owned by immigrant households and the total number of slaves by household are shown in various tables in the text.

74. Holcomb, ed., *PL,* IV: 277; CBPR, Vol. R-R, 369, 375; Edward M. Boykin, *History of the Boykin Family, from Their First Settlement in Virginia 1685, and in South Carolina, Georgia, and Alabama, to the Present Time* (Camden, S.C.: Colin MacRae, 1876), 5–6.

75. Brown, *South Carolina Regulators,* 145. The individuals who contributed the labor of their slaves included James Brown, who served as engineer and master carpenter, as well as John Adamson, William Ancrum, Abraham Belton, James Bettie, Burwell Boykin, Samuel Boykin, Archibald Brown, James Cary, Nathaniel Cary, John Chesnut, Joseph Clay, Joshua Dinkins, Samuel Elbert, Joshua English, Robert English, Joseph Habbersham, John Hope, John Hutchins, Ely Kershaw, Joseph Kershaw, William Lang, William LeConte, George McIntosh, John May, Malachi Murphy, David Nelson, Charles Ogilvie, John Pain, John Platt, Isabella Reid, James Seesom, James Whitaker, Richard Whitaker, William Whitaker Sr., William Whitaker Jr.,and John Wyly. Kirkland and Kennedy, *Historic Camden,* 1:

129–130. The number of slaves sold by the store was relatively small, but their high value nonetheless made their sale a lucrative part of its business. Unidentified Camden Account Book, 1779–1780 (UCAB), Historic Camden Foundation, Camden, S.C.

76. Ibid., 70–71.

77. Carville V. Earle, "A Staple Interpretation of Slavery and Free Labor," *Geographical Review* 68 (1978): 54–56.

78. Gray, *History of Agriculture,* 1: 218–219, 294–297; 2: 430. G. Terry Sharrer, "The Indigo Bonanza in South Carolina, 1740–90," *Technology and Culture,* 12 (1971): 449–454; *Pennsylvania Gazette,* Mar. 5, 1754; John Drayton, *A View of South Carolina, as Respects Her Natural and Civil Concerns* (Charleston, S.C.: W. P. Young, 1802; reprint ed., Spartanburg, S.C.: The Reprint Co., 1972), 127.

79. Berlin, *Many Thousands Gone,*67, 70, 72–73; Herbert Aptheker, "Maroons within the Present Limits of the United States," in *Maroon Societies: Rebel Slave Communities in the Americas,* ed. Richard Price (Garden City, N.Y.: Anchor Books, 1973), 152–153; John Hope Franklin and Loren Schweninger, *Runaway Slaves: Rebels on the Plantation* (Oxford: Oxford University Press, 1999), 86–87; Daniel E. Meaders, "South Carolina Fugitives as Viewed through Local Colonial Newspapers, with Emphasis on Runaway Notices, 1732–1801," *Journal of Negro History* 60 (1975): 303–305.

80. Henry Gallman advertised for the return of a runaway slave from Saxe Gotha as early as 1750: *SCG,* July 16, 1750. Meaders, "South Carolina Fugitives," 305; Hooker, ed., *Carolina Backcountry,* 12, 25, 297; *SCG,* Oct. 24, 1774, Feb. 20, Nov. 21, 1775. Europeans attributed behavioral characteristics to the ethnicity of Africans and selected them on the basis of their perceived qualities. Joseph Kershaw, for example, carefully noted the presence of purchased Ibos because they were considered less desirable as slaves; planters believed them to be inclined to be melancholy and suicidal, sickly, unattractive, and superstitious. Account with Robert Stack, Dec. 25, 1772, CMMP, 12/33/10. For a discussion of contemporary European images of African peoples, their origins, and their characteristics, see Daniel C. Littlefield, *Rice and Slaves: Ethnicity and the Slave Trade in Colonial South Carolina* (Urbana: University of Illinois Press, 1981), 8–31.

81. Meaders, "South Carolina Fugitives," 307; Michael P. Johnson, "Runaway Slaves and Slave Communities in South Carolina, 1799 to 1830," *William and Mary Quarterly,* 3rd ser., 38 (1981): 430–436; Aptheker, "Maroons," 152–153.

82. Sally E. Hadden, *Slave Patrols: Law and Violence in Virginia and the Carolinas* (Cambridge, Mass.: Harvard University Press, 2001), 23–24; Weir, *South Carolina,* 192–194; Aptheker, "Maroons," 153.

83. John Solomon Otto, "Livestock-Raising in Early South Carolina, 1670–1700: Prelude to the Rice Plantation Economy," *Agricultural History* 61, no. 4 (1987): 121–122; Terry G. Jordan, *North American Cattle-Ranching Frontiers: Origins, Diffusion, and Differentiation* (Albuquerque: University of New Mexico Press, 1993), 117; Alan Gallay, *The Indian Slave Trade: The Rise of the English Empire in the American South, 1670–1717* (New Haven, Conn.: Yale University Press, 2002), 348–349.

84. J. Susanne Schramm Simmons, "Augusta County's Other Pioneers: The African American Presence in Frontier Augusta County," in *Diversity and Accommodation: Essays on the Cultural Composition of the Virginia Frontier,* ed. Michael J. Puglisi (Knoxville: University of Tennessee Press, 1997), 160–163.

85. *SCG&CJ,* Dec. 29, 1767; Bobby G. Moss and Michael C. Scoggins, *African-American Patriots in the Southern Campaign of the American Revolution* (Blacksburg, S.C.: Scotia-Hibernia Press, 2004), 56, 194.

86. Information regarding the Harris, Griffin, and Jeffers families is contained in their petitions for pensions for service in the Revolutionary War. Michael C. Scoggins, "'Voluntarily Enlisted as a Soldier in the Revolution': A Case Study of Free African-Americans in the South Carolina Continental and State Troops During the Revolutionary War," Research paper, Cultural & Heritage Museums (York, S.C., 2008), 1, 4, 5, 11; Moss and Scoggins, *African-American Patriots,* 109–110; Roland Harris, for Edward Harris, Pension Application, R4649; Revolutionary War Pension and Bounty Land Warrant Application File, Microfilm Series M804 (hereafter RWPBLWAF), National Archives and Records

Administration, Washington, D.C.; Gideon Griffin, Audited Account, Accounts Audited of Claims Growing out of the Revolution (hereafter AA), S108092, Reel 61, Frame 17, F 3110A, South Carolina Department of Archives and History, Columbia. Additional information about the families is found in Paul Heinegg, *Free African Americans of North Carolina and Virginia* (Baltimore, Md.: Genealogical Pub. Co., 1994), 321–326, 360–362.

87. Petition by the Inhabitants of Winyah, *JCHA,* Feb. 16, 1743.

88. The rise in criminal activity in South Carolina's interior arose from many causes. The influx of new agricultural settlers exacerbated old tensions with hunters and herders, who viewed the newcomers as encroaching on their traditional domain. Pioneer households faced with establishing themselves with limited means often turned to hunting and foraging, introducing further competition for wild resources. Both these conflicts were enhanced by the violence of the Cherokee War, which had killed immigrants, destroyed their property, and caused the temporary abandonment of settlements in the western and central interior. Large numbers of settlers had become refugees from the violence, only to languish in backcountry forts, where they suffered under corrupt officials. Many emerged with few prospects at the close of hostilities and appropriated livestock and property abandoned by others as a strategy for survival in a world that had left them destitute. Brown, *South Carolina Regulators,* 9–12; Klein, *Unification of a Slave State,* 54–56.

89. "Petition on Inhabitants of Winyaw," *JCHA,* Feb. 16, 1743; "Petition of Several Inhabitants in Craven County," *JCHA,* Mar. 3, 1750; "Petition from Residents of Granville County", *JCHA,* Mar. 8, 1750.

90. In his discussion of violence on the frontier, H. C. Allen, *Bush and Backwoods: A Comparison of the Frontier in Australia and the United States* (East Lansing: Michigan State University Press, 1959), 101–103, linked this phenomenon closely with the degree to which government established firm control during the initial stages of settlement.

91. Brown, *South Carolina Regulators,* 33–34.

92. *SC&AGG,* Aug. 4, 1767.

93. *SCG,* Apr. 30, 1763; *SC&AGG,* Dec. 12, 16, 1766.

94. *SC&AGG,* Aug. 7, 1767.

95. Brown, *South Carolina Regulators,* 29–30; Klein, *Unification of a Slave* State, 58–59; *SCG&CJ,* Oct. 20, 1767. For the original landholdings of these individuals, see Table 5.1. CBPR, Vol. Y-Y, Dec. 22, 1755, 367; Vol. Y-Y, Jan. 22, 1755, 367; Vol. B-3, Mar. 7, 1763, 485.

96. Hooker, ed., *Carolina Backcountry,* 230–233.

97. *SC&AGG,* Oct. 30, 1767, Apr. 15, 1768; *SC&AGG,* July 31, 1769; *SC&AGG,* Feb. 1770: *SCG&CJ,* Aug. 4, 11, 1767.

98. Brown, *South Carolina Regulators,* 44–45, 51–52.

99. Hooker, ed., *Carolina Backcountry,* 172–173, 283; Kirkland and Kennedy, *Historic Camden,* 1: 348; Brown, *South Carolina Regulators,* 350.

100. All of these men would play prominent roles during the coming Revolutionary War in the backcountry, Charlton, Dinkins, and Marshall as rebels, English as a Tory.

101. Boykin, *History of the Boykin Family,* 7; Brown, *South Carolina Regulators,* 50–51.

102. Edgar and Bailey, eds., *Biographical Directory,* 2: 558, 669–671; Klein, *Unification of a Slave State,* 72–74; Brown, *South Carolina Regulators,* 90–95.

103. Edgar and Bailey, eds., *Biographical Directory,* 2: 412; *SCG,* July 7, 1769; Brown, *South Carolina Regulators,* 62, 96–97, 103–105.

104. W. Hardy Wickwar, *300 Years of Development Administration in South Carolina* (Columbia: Bureau of Government Research and Service, University of South Carolina), 50.

Chapter 8. "Camden's Turrets Pierce the Skies"

1. George Ogilvie was born at the Auchires estate of Hatton, in Aberdeenshire in northeastern Scotland about 1750. His father, Alexander Ogilvie, was the brother of Charles Ogilvie, who emigrated to South Carolina as a merchant in 1751. George Ogilvie was taken into his uncle's mercantile house in

London at the age of fourteen in 1764 and emigrated to Charleston a decade later to take charge of a property on the Wateree River. He later acquired 1,100 acres there in his own name, including the 400-acre tract on Cedar Creek. In addition to owning plantation properties, George Ogilvie acted as his uncle's attorney and in 1778 operated a business in Camden. George Ogilvie Diary (hereafter GOD), South Caroliniana Library, University of South Carolina, Columbia; Gerald Stranraer-Mull, *A Parish History of the Churches in Ellon and Cruden Bay,* http://freespace.virgin.net/gerald.stranraer-mull/parish/history.htm, 12; Peter Wilson Coldham, ed., *American Loyalist Claims, Vol. 1, Abstracted from the Public Record Office, Audit Office Series 13, Bundles 1–35 & 37* (Washington, D.C.: National Genaeological Society, 1980), 202, 371; CLG/CS, Vol. 35, Feb. 3, 1775, 51; Vol. 35, Feb. 3, 1775, 52; Vol. 35, Feb. 10, 1775, 244; *SC&AGG,* June 18, 1778.

2. [George Ogilvie], *Carolina; or, ThePlanter, Written in 1776* (London, 1790), 78.

3. Ibid., 80.

4. Robert M. Weir, *Colonial South Carolina: A History* (New York: KTO Press, 1983; reprint ed., Columbia: University of South Carolina Press, 1997), 294–301.

5. Richard J. Hooker, ed., *The Carolina Backcountry on the Eve of the Revolution: The Journal and Other Writings of Charles Woodmason, Anglican Itinerant* (Chapel Hill: University of North Carolina Press, 1953), 260–261; Rachel N. Klein, *Unification of a Slave State: The Rise of the Planter Class in the South Carolina Backcountry, 1760–1808* (Chapel Hill: University of North Carolina Press for the Institute of Early American History and Culture, 1990), 80–81.

6. A newspaper notice of Samuel Wyly's death on February 13, published as late as early March, referred to him as a resident of Pine Tree Hill; however, the Act of Assembly of April 12 used the name Camden, "lately called Pine Tree Hill." Subsequent mention of the settlement later that year also noted the change in name. *SCG&CJ,* Mar. 8, 1768; Thomas J. Kirkland and Robert M. Kennedy, *Historic Camden, Vol. 1: Nineteenth Century* (Columbia, S.C.: State Printing Co., 1926), 90–95; *SCG,* Oct. 24, 1768; Alan Valentine, *British Establishment, 1760–1784: An Eighteenth Century Biographical Dictionary,* Vol. 2 (Norman: University of Oklahoma Press, 1970), 719–720.

7. Brian W. Blouet, "Factors Influencing the Evolution of Settlement Patterns," in *Man, Settlement and Urbanism,* ed. Peter J. Ucko, Ruth Tringham, and G. W. Dimbleby (London: Gerald Duckworth, 1972), 3–15; David Grove, "The Function and Future of Urban Centres," in *Man, Settlement and Urbanism,* ed. Peter J. Ucko, Ruth Tringham, and G. W. Dimbleby (London: Gerald Duckworth, 1972), 559–565; H. S. A. Fox, "Going to Town in Thirteenth-Century England," in *Man Made the Land: Essays in English Historical Geography,* ed. Alan H. R. Baker and J. B. Harley (Newton Abbot, Devon: David & Charles, 1973), 73; P. Flatres, "Hamlet and Village," in *Man and His Habitat: Essays Presented to Emyr Estyn Evans,* ed. R. H. Buchanan, Emrys Jones, and Desmond McCourt (New York: Barnes and Noble, 1971), 70.

8. Brian J. L. Berry, *Geography of Market Centers and Retail Distribution* (Englewood Cliffs, N.J.: Prentice Hall, 1967), 33–34. Edward K. Muller, "Regional Urbanization and Selective Growth of Towns in North American Regions," *Journal of Historical Geography* 3 (1977): 21–40; C. F. J. Whebell, "Corridors: A Theory of Urban Systems," *Annals of the Association of American Geographers* 59 (1969): 3–4, 10–11. Although the term "frontier town" has been widely used, the specific meaning employed here is that introduced by Joseph B. Casagrande, Stephen I. Thompson, and Philip D. Young, "Colonization as a Research Frontier," in *Process and Pattern in Culture: Essays in Honor of Julian H. Steward,* ed. Robert A. Manners (Chicago: Aldine, 1964), 312–313, in their cross-cultural study of processes of agricultural colonization. Their work stressed the function of these settlements as supply centers linking the area of colonization with the entrepôt and the outside world. Frontier towns also served as the jumping-off point for new colonists entering the area and as the terminus of its transportation network. The authors emphasized the towns' central role as the focal point of social, economic, political, and religious activity and their associated institutions.

9. This definition of community follows that of Conrad M. Arensberg, "The Community as Object and Sample," *American Anthropologist* 63 (1961): 248. For examples of similar open country communities in the colonial South, see Warren R. Hofstra and Robert D. Mitchell, "Town and Country in

Backcountry Virginia: Winchester and the Shenandoah Valley, 1730–1800," *Journal of Southern History* 59 (1993): 619–646; Robert D. Mitchell, "The Settlement Fabric of the Shenandoah Valley, 1790–1860: Pattern, Process, and Structure," in *After the Backcountry: Rural Life in the Great Valley of Virginia, 1800–1900,* ed. Kenneth E. Koons and Warren R. Hofstra (Knoxville: University of Tennessee Press, 2000), 34–36; G. Rebecca Dobbs, "Frontier Settlement Development and 'Initial Conditions': The Case of the North Carolina Piedmont and the Indian Trading Path," *Historical Geography* 37 (2009): 114–137.

10. Thomas J. Cooper and David J. McCord, eds., *Statutes at Large of South Carolina, Vol. 5,* Act. No. 1006, 1771 (Columbia, S.C.: A. S. Johnson, 1839).

11. Thomas J. Kirkland and Robert M. Kennedy, *Historic Camden, Vol. 2: Nineteenth Century* (Columbia, S.C.: State Printing Co., 1926), 15; Richard Maxwell Brown, *The South Carolina Regulators* (Cambridge, Mass.: Belknap Press of Harvard University Press, 1963), 36; MB, Vol. 7, Aug. 3, 1761, 373; Vol. 7, Dec. 24, 1761, 290.

12. Both tracts were measured from a cornerstone on Kershaw Street, with the same angles for each of their four sides. One lot was 3 rood, 30 perches, or 0.937 acre, and the other was 3 rood, 37 perches, or 0.98 acre. CBPR, Vol. Q-3, Nov. 16, 1769, 250, 252.

13. The east-west boundary line deviates at an oblique angle of 3 degrees south of east from the earliest plan of Camden, drawn by John Heard in 1771. "Accurate Survey of the Town of Camden, Craven County, South Carolina," Copies of Plats and Plans, Vol. 1, p. 7 (hereafter CPP), ca. 1798, South Carolina Department of Archives and History, Columbia. This survey established the present layout of streets and lots in Camden. Joseph Kershaw to William Ancrum, May 5, 1786, Lancaster County, Records of the Clerk of Court, Conveyances (hereafter LCRCC/C), Vol. B, 11. For a discussion of the property boundaries, see Kenneth E. Lewis, *Camden: Historical Archaeology in the South Carolina Backcountry* (Belmont, Calif.: Thomson Wadsworth, 2006), 104–105.

14. Hooker, ed., *Carolina Backcountry,* 6; Joseph Kershaw, Will, Kershaw County, Records of the Probate Judge, Estates (hereafter KCRPJ/E), Apt. 37, Pkg. 1354, Sept. 21, 1815; Kenneth E. Lewis, "Report of Archaeological Work at the Southwest Redoubt and the Presbyterian Cemetery, Nov. 1–2, 1983," report submitted to the Camden Historical Commission, Camden, S.C., 1983, 2.

15. Mean ceramic dating indicates that the brewhouse was built as early as 1762. Lewis, *Camden: Historical Archaeology,* 94–95. Hooker, ed., *Carolina Backcountry,* 137–138. For descriptions of eighteenth-century brewhouses in England, Scotland, and colonial North America, see D. Gillian Hurst, "Post-Medieval Britain in 1966," *Post-Medieval Archaeology* 2 (1967): 118; Geoff Egan, "Post-Medieval Britain and Ireland in 1988," *Post-Medieval Archaeology* 23 (1989): 46–47; Michael Ponsford, "Post-Medieval Britain and Ireland in 2002," *Post-Medieval Archaeology* 37, pt. 2 (2003): 295–296; Leonie Driver, Malcolm Hislop, Stephen Litherland, and Eleanor Ramsey, "The North Service Range, Ashton Hall, Birmingham: Excavation and Recording, *Post-Medieval Archaeology* 41, no. 1 (2008): 121–122; and Daniel Simoneau, "The Intedant's Palace Site: New Insight into Its Physical Evolution and Initial Occupation," *Post-Medieval Archaeology* 43, no. 1 (2009): 172–176.

16. Lewis, *Camden: Historical Archaeology,* 98–99.

17. Lewis, "Archaeological Investigations in Southwestern Camden,"162–164; Lewis, *Camden: Historical Archaeology,* 118–123, 135–138.

18. Lewis, *Camden: Hist. Arch.,* 94–95, 98–99.

19. Kenneth E. Lewis, *Archaeological Investigations at the Kershaw House, Camden (38KE1), Kershaw County, South Carolina,* Research Manuscript Series 78 (Columbia: South Carolina Institute of Archaeology and Anthropology, 1975), 26–29; Lewis, *A Functional Study of the Kershaw House Site in Camden, South Carolina,* Research Manuscript Series 110 (Columbia: South Carolina Institute of Archaeology and Anthropology, 1977), 46, 70–72: Lewis, *Camden: Historical Archaeology,* 90. The hill in question is a topographic feature that lies at about the same elevation as the early town of Camden. It is an extension of the high terrace above Pine Tree Creek and is separated from the settlement by a shallow, sloping depression that drains the lands to the north, a feature that accentuates its height.

20. South Carolinians brewed beer widely in the eighteenth century, and the Rev. Woodmason made reference to its availability and consumption in the backcountry. Walter L. Robbins, ed., "John

Tobler's Description of South Carolina (1753)," *South Carolina Historical Magazine* 71 (1970): 156–157; Mark Catesby, "Mark Catesby's *Natural History,* 1731–47," in *The Colonial South Carolina Scene: Contemporary Views, 1697–1774,* ed. H. Roy Merrens (Columbia: University of South Carolina Press, 1977), 100; Hooker, ed., *Carolina Backcountry,* 137–138. A similar evolutionary shift in the scale of beer production occurred in colonial New England when the industry centralized to accommodate specialization and the development of larger markets. James E. McWilliams, "Brewing Beer in Massachusetts Bay, 1640–1690," *New England Quarterly* 71 (1998): 561–566.

21. Gary M. Walton and James F. Shepherd, *The Economic Rise of Early America* (London: Cambridge University Press, 1979), 49. The traditional date for the opening of a brickyard is associated with the construction of the jail and other brick buildings around 1771. Judith J. Schulz, "The Rise and Decline of Camden as South Carolina's Major Trading Center, 1751–1829: A Historical Geographic Study" (M.A. thesis, University of South Carolina, 1972), 105. For the use of brick at Camden, see Lewis, *Camden: Historical Archaeology,* 107–109.

22. For a discussion of central places in marketing networks, see Berry, *Geography of Market Centers,* 2–3.

23. The Assembly refused to allow the development of local governments that might challenge its authority and instead relied on appointed commissions to oversee and administer municipal offices. No municipalities were incorporated, and even the city of Charleston's myriad offices were administered by commissions, although here citizens elected these officials. Weir, *Colonial South Carolina,* 138–139; Walter Edgar, *South Carolina: A History* (Columbia: University of South Carolina Press, 1998), 125–129.

24. Margaret T. Hodgen, "Fairs in Elizabethan England," *Economic Geography* 18 (1942): 389–390; R. Epstein, "Regional Fairs, Institutional Innovation, and Economic Growth in Late Medieval Europe," *Economic History Review* 47 (1994): 468.

25. Under English law, courts of piepowder were organized on the occasion of a market and had jurisdiction over disputes between merchants as well as over acts of thefts and violence. *JCHA,* Mar. 20, 1765; "An Act to Establish Biennial Fairs in Camden," *MR,* Oct. 28, 1774; Kirkland and Kennedy, *Historic Camden,* 1: 12–14; Leila Sellers, *Charleston Business on the Eve of the American Revolution* (Chapel Hill: University of North Carolina Press, 1934), 90–91; Jo Anne McCormick, "The Camden Backcountry Judicial Precinct, 1769–1790" (M.A. thesis, University of South Carolina, 1975), 52–54.

26. Although the plat itself bears no date, the time of its creation is implied by the notations for the locations of the courthouse and jail. In both cases the phrase "which is built" is used to describe the lots set aside for these buildings. "Plan of the Town of Camden," CPP. The need to situate the courthouse and jail properly required that the survey on which the plan was based be made before these two buildings were completed in 1771, although the actual plan may have been drawn later.

27. John W. Reps, *The Making of Urban America: A History of City Planning in the United States* (Princeton, N.J.: Princeton University Press, 1965), 177; Reps, *Tidewater Towns: City Planning in Colonial Virginia and Maryland* (Williamsburg, Va.: Colonial Williamsburg Foundation, 1972), 22; Carl Feiss, "Early American Public Squares," in *Town and Square: From the Agora to the Village Green,* ed. Paul Zucker (Cambridge, Mass.: MIT Press, 1970), 237–239.

28. Joseph A. Ernst and H. Roy Merrens, "The South Carolina Economy of the Middle Eighteenth Century: A View from Philadelphia," *West Georgia College Studies in the Social Sciences* 12 (1973): 16–29.

29. Edward T. Price, "The Central Courthouse Square in the American County Seat," *Geographical Review* 58 (1968): 39–44. For the origin of street names, see Kirkland and Kennedy, *Historic Camden,* 1: 31–32. Attributing the name of Campbell Street to the last royal governor, Lord William Campbell, is tenuous given his short rule and his association with the end of British civil authority in South Carolina in 1775. Weir, *Colonial South Carolina,* 325.

30. Several scholars have noted the relationship between the spatial geometry of the courthouse square and regional power. See Price, "The Central Courthouse Square," 58–60; Arensberg, "American Communities," 1151–1152.

31. Kirkland and Kennedy, *Historic Camden,* 1: 31. In his will Joseph Kershaw bequeathed two lots, Nos. 287 and 288, to the Presbyterian Church, extending its property as far south as Wateree Street. Kershaw County, KCRPJ/E, Apt. 37, Pkg. 1354, June 1, 1788.

32. Memorandum, Jan. 4, 1764, CMMP, 12/33/5; *SC&AGG,* July 22, 1774.

33. *SC&AGG,* July 22, 1774. The partners offered twelve months' credit on all sales of more than £100 to those paying interest from the day of sale and providing approved security. *SCG,* July 25, 1774.

34. *SC&AGG,* July 22, 1774.

35. *SC&AGG,* Jan. 16, 1777; Response by John Chesnut, 1786, CMMP, 33/33.

36. Miscellaneous accounts may be found in CMMP, 12/33/19, 12/33/33, and 12/33/36.

37. Information regarding the post-1774 partnerships has been abstracted from accounts contained in John Chesnut's papers, in CMMP and *SC&AGG,* Aug. 16, 1780.

Ely Kershaw & Co. at Chatham, 12/33/9
John Chesnut, 12/33/13
Chesnut & Co., 12/33/15
Kershaw & Co., 12/33/16
Kershaw, Chesnut & Co., 12/33/17
Chesnut & Kershaw, 12/33/23
William Ancrum, 12/34/6
Ancrum & Chiffelle, 12/34/13
Chesnut & Co. at Granby, 12/34/15

Additional partnerships were recorded in the accounts of a Camden store for 1779, Unidentified Camden Account Book, 1779–1780, Historic Camden Foundation, Camden, S.C. The parnterships include:

Kershaw, McRa & Co.
Kershaw, Boykin & Co.
William Kershaw & Co.
Kershaw, Lithgow & Co.

Duncan McRa was born in Rosshire, Scotland, Apr. 26, 1754. Kirkland and Kennedy, *Historic Camden,* 1: 387; Kershaw County Cemetery Survey Project, *Kershaw County, South Carolina, Cemetery Survey Project* (hereafter *KCCSP*), Vol. 3 (Camden, S.C.: Kershaw County Historical Society, 1991), 44.

William Kershaw was born at Baiting's Gate, Yorkshire, the youngest son of Joseph Kershaw and Mary Ryley, and baptized Feb. 15, 1746. He advertised the sale of cloth, paper, hardware, wine, boots, shoes, and other imported goods as well as Carolina flour, indigo, and other "country produce" at his store on the corner of Church and Broad Streets in Charleston as early as the summer of 1778. West Yorkshire, England, Baptisms, Marriages and Burials, 1512–1812 (hereafter WYEBMB), WDP138/1/1/3; Peter G. D. Kershaw, "A Kershaw Family, 1670–1970," p. 67, Port Charlotte, Fla., 1974 (photocopied), 5–7; *SC&AGG,* July 2, 30, Aug. 27, 1778.

38. CMMP, 12/33/11/; 12/33/16; 12/33/17; 12/33/22; Kirkland and Kennedy, *Historic Camden,* 2: 35; Klein, *Unification of a Slave State,* 32–33; Joseph S. Ames, "Cantey Family," *South Carolina Historical Magazine* 11 (1910): 213, 224–35; John Buchanan, *The Road to Guilford Courthouse: The American Revolution in the South* (New York: John Wiley, 1997), 390–393. William Greenwood and his nephew William Higginson were the surviving partners in a London firm that was founded by John Beswicke in 1744. By the mid-1770s the firm of Greenwood & Higginson was the largest Carolina trader in London. George C. Rogers Jr., *Charleston in the Age of the Pinckneys* (Norman: University of Oklahoma Press, 1969), 13–14.

39. Evidence of Ogilvie & Forbes appears in suits, for example, Charles Ogilvie and John Forbes vs. Meyer Moses, Judgement Rolls, Court of Common Pleas, South Carolina Department of Archives and History, Columbia (hereafter JRCCP), Box 97A, Item 154A, 1773. Charles Ogilvie acquired large quantities of land on the Wateree through his marriage. *SCG,* Aug. 4, 1764. In addition, he purchased

one hundred acres, CBPR, Vol. L-4, Nov. 11, 1773, 219. He sold three tracts to John Chesnut and Ely Kershaw the following year: CBPR, Vol. M-4, Mar. 8, 1774, 63–70; CMMP, 12/33/15. His dealing with William Ancrum appeared in WAALB, May 13, 1777. George Ogilvie's business involved trade in indigo: CLG/CS, Vol. 35, 244; *SC&AGG*, June 18, 1778; Coldham, Peter Wilson, ed. *American Loyalist Claims*, Vol. 1, abstracted from the Public Record Office Series 13, Bundles 1–35 and 37. Washington, D.C. National Genealogical Society, 1980, Vol. 1, 202, 373.

40. Henry Rugeley was born the third son of Rowland and Elizabeth Rugeley on March 8, 1742/43 at St. Ives, Huntingdonshire, England. His father was a well-to-do draper and a neighbor of Lord Charles Greville Montagu, who became South Carolina's royal governor in 1766, and several of the Rugeley brothers are said to have served under Lord Charles in the Huntingdonshire militia. As a result of this connection, Henry's older brother Rowland received an offer to came to South Carolina to assume the office of register of mesne conveyance, a position for which the officeholder supported himself on a portion of the fees collected. The two brothers apparently shared the duties of the office. Helen Hoskins Rugeley (compiler), *Rugeleys in America, Vol. II: English and American Ancestors* (Austin, Tex.: Rugeley Family Association, 1997), 40–41. Rowland Rugeley recorded his first deed in 1769, and Henry, as deputy register, did so the following year. CBPR, Vol. M-3, Feb. 13, 1769, 163; Vol. O-3, Jan. 20, 1770, 432. The company name appeared in a 1772 suit: JR, Box 94A, Item 285A. The Rugeleys purchased ten interior tracts between 1772 and1776: two tracts of unknown size on Fair Forest Creek and Little River; three tracts on Saluda River totaling 650 acres; 250 acres in Purrysburgh Township; and 250 acres the Enoree River, as well as two 300-acre parcels on Long Cane Creek and 500 acres in Berkeley County: CBPR, Vol. P-4, June 8, 1775, 310; Vol. P-4, Feb. 26, 1773, 315; Vol. P-4, Aug. 25, 1772, 321; Vol. X-4, Sept. 20, 1776, 190; Vol. X-4, Nov. 11, 1776, 193; Vol. W-4, Mar. 6, 1778, 552; Vol. X-4, Sept. 12, 1775, 180; Vol. W-4, May 19, 1775, 21. William Rugeley apparently left the partnership and returned home before 1777. William Rugeley to Father, [1777], Helen Hoskins Rugeley (compiler), *Rugeley Papers: Blue-Blooded Brits in Reduced Circumstances* (Austin, Tex.: By the Author, 1997), X311.92, 25.

41. For the Wateree Creek purchases, see CBPR, Vol. X-4, July 29, 1776, 184; Vol. X-4, Apr. 18, 177[6], 195. William Ancrum's purchase of Rugeley's indigo is recorded in WAAB, Dec. 9, 1777. Descriptions of Clermont appear in Rugeley (compiler), *Rugeleys in America, Vol. II*, 42, and Robert Stansbury Lambert, *South Carolina Loyalists in the American Revolution* (Columbia: University of South Carolina Press, 1987), 117. The extensive barn is described in Rawdon to Cornwallis, Dec. 2, 1780, CP 30/11/4, 271.

42. Rowland Rugeley died on Dec. 23, 1776, leaving half his estate and half the profits from his office of register of mesne conveyance to his brother Henry and half to his brother William and his three sisters: *PG*, Feb. 12, 1777; Henry Rugeley to Mathew Rugeley, Mar. 18, 1777; Copy of Will of Rowland Rugeley, Dec. 22, 1776, Rugeley (compiler), *Blue-Blooded Brits*, X311.90, 23, 24.

43. Henry Rugeley, Ledger, 1776–1790 (HRL). Thomas J. Kirkland Papers, South Caroliniana Library, University of South Carolina, Columbia. James Adamson received a grant on the south side of the Wateree in 1754, and his nephew John Adamson settled on the Wateree River in 1765 on land above Pine Tree Hill. CLG/CS, Vol. 5, Mar. 7, 1754, 365; Kirkland and Kennedy, *Historic Camden*, 1: 130. For the locations of Marshall's, Petty's, and Summerville's lands, see CLG/CS, Vol. 21, Oct. 12, 1770, 174; Vol. 32, Aug. 19, 1774, 342; Vol. 18, June 2, 1769, 338; SPB/Ch, Vol. 17, Feb. 14, 1787, 14.

44. Brown, *South Carolina Regulators*, 107–108; Geraldine M. Meroney, "William Bull's First Exile from South Carolina, 1777–1781," *South Carolina Historical Magazine* 80 (1979): 92–93. Information regarding the presiding judges for the Camden Circuit Court prior to 1783 is unavailable because court records no longer exist. Kirkland and Kennedy, *Historic Camden*, 2: 252.

45. Walter B. Edgar and N. Louise Bailey, *Biographical Directory of the South Carolina House of Representatives, Vol. 2: The Commons House of Assembly, 1692–1775* (Columbia: University of South Carolina Press, 1977), 578–579; Weir, *Colonial South Carolina*,350–352.

46. Alexander Gregg, *History of the Old Cheraws* (Columbia, S.C.: The State Co., 1867; reprint ed., Greenville, S.C.: Southern Historical Press, 1991), 162–166; W. Hardy Wickwar, *300 Years of Development*

Administration in South Carolina (Columbia: Bureau of Government Research and Service, University of South Carolina), 49–50; Edgar, *South Carolina,* 215; "The Circuit Court Act of 1769," in Brown, *South Carolina Regulators,* 148–158.

47. These figures are based on data contained in plat books (CBP), grant records (CLG/CS), and conveyances (CBMC, CBPR). Edgar and Bailey, *Biographical Directory,* 2: 375, 558; Brown, *South Carolina Regulators,* 145–147; Kirkland and Kennedy, *Historic Camden,* 1: 47, 77n; Robert S. Lambert, "A Loyalist Odyssey: James and Mary Cary in Exile, 1783–1804," *South Carolina Historical Magazine* 79 (1978): 169.

48. Kirkland and Kennedy, *Historic Camden,* 1: 53; 2: 281; Edgar and Bailey, *Biographical Directory,* 2: 376; Hooker, ed., *Carolina Backcountry,* xxxi, 7, 10; Philip M. Hamer et al., eds., *The Papers of Henry Laurens* (hereafter *HLP*), Vol. 15 (Columbia: University of South Carolina Press, 1968–1990), 222n; Frederick Dalcho, *An Historical Account of the Protestant Episcopal Church in South Carolina, from the First Settlement to the War of the Revolution* (Charleston, S.C.: E. Thayer, 1820), 323.

49. Edgar and Bailey, *Biographical Directory,* 2: 208–209, 391, 394, 412–413, 578, 581; Edgar, *South Carolina,* 123.

50. For a summary of Joseph Kershaw's political career, see Edgar and Bailey, *Biographical Directory,* 2: 375–377. His election to the Twenty-ninth Royal Assembly is recorded in *SCG,* Dec. 7, 1769; the Thirtieth Assembly in *SC&AGG,* Mar. 30, 1772; the Thirty-first Assembly in *SCG,* Oct. 8, 1772; and the Thirty-third Assembly in *SCG,* Mar. 29, 1773. He was named a commissioner to oversee the district courthouse and jail in the Circuit Court Act of 1769: Brown, *South Carolina Regulators,* 154.

Born in England, Roger-Peter Handasyde Hatley emigrated to South Carolina in 1766 in the entourage of the newly appointed governor Lord Charles Grenville Montague. He served as deputy collector of customs for the port of Charleston from 1767 to 1769 and again in 1772. In the wake of a controversy arising from his last appointment, he left this office to assume the position of sheriff of Camden District in June 1772. Caroline T. Moore, comp. and ed., *Abstract of the Wills of the State of South Carolina, 1760–1784* (Columbia: R. L. Bryan, 1969), 186; Hamer et al., eds, *HLP,* 5: 303n; *HLP,* 6: 9; *PG,* Oct. 17, 1769; July 16, 1772; June 18, 1772; *SCG&CJ.* His appointment as sheriff was reported in *SCG&CJ,* June 30, 1772, and his death four months later in *SCG,* Nov. 5, 1772, purportedly at Joseph Kershaw's house in Camden. Kirkland and Kennedy, *Historic Camden,* 1: 377.

51. Hamer et al., eds, *HLP,* 1: 58n, 247n; Kenneth L. Carroll, "The Irish Quaker Community at Camden," *South Carolina Historical Quarterly* 77 (1976): 73; Theodore Thauer, "The Quaker Party in Pennsylvania, 1755–175," *Pennsylvania Magazine of History and Biography* 71 (1947): 20; Marc Egnal, "The Economic Development of the Thirteen Continental Colonies, 1720–1775," *William and Mary Quarterly,* 3rd ser., 32 (1975): 215. The relationship between Charleston merchants, and particularly Joseph Kershaw, and the powerful Quaker mercantile community in Philadelphia has been explored by Joseph A. Ernst and H. Roy Merrens, "The South Carolina Economy of the Middle Eighteenth Century: A View from Philadelphia," *West Georgia College Studies in the Social Sciences* 12 (1973): 24–25; Ernst and Merrens, "'Camden's Turrets Pierce the Skies!': The Urban Process in the Southern Colonies during the Eighteenth Century," *William and Mary Quarterly,* 3rd ser., 30 (1973): 563–564, 566.

52. A. S. Salley, ed., "Diary of William Dillwyn during a Visit to Charles Town in 1772," *South Carolina Historical Magazine* 36 (1935): 33, 34.

53. Weir, *Colonial South Carolina,* 248–251. John Kershaw studied law and returned to South Carolina in 1783. Seeking additional training, James Kershaw may also have worked with a mercantile house prior to returning in 1784. Hazel M. Whiteley, "Joseph Kershaw of Baitingsgate: Transcribed from Original Sources," Ripponden, UK, 2001 (photocopied)4; Kirkland and Kennedy, *Historic Camden,* 1: 276; Joseph Kershaw to Henry Laurens, Jan. 5, 1780, Hamer et al., eds., *HLP,* 15: 221.

54. Edgar, *South Carolina,* 219–223.

55. Kershaw represented St. Mark's Parish on the committee to implement the Continental Association. William E. Hemphill and Wylma A. Waites, eds., *Extracts from the Journals of the Provincial Congresses of South Carolina, 1775–1776 (JPC)* (Columbia: South Carolina Department of Archives

and History, 1960), Jan. 11, 1775; Kirkland and Kennedy, *Historic Camden,* 1: 110; Weir, *Colonial South Carolina,* 315–316.

56. John Rutledge to Joseph Kershaw, July 25, 1775, quoted in Kirkland and Kennedy, *Historic Camden,* 1: 111, 118.

57. Weir, *Colonial South Carolina,* 321; John Drayton, *Memoirs of the American Revolution, from the Commencement to the Year 1776,* Vol. 1 (Charleston, S.C.: A. E. Miller, 1821), 324, 363–376; William Henry Drayton to Council of Safety, Aug. 9, Aug. 21, 1775, Hamer et al., *HLP,* 10: 286, 349–350.

58. Council of Safety to William Henry Drayton, Sept. 5, 1775, Hamer et al., *HLP,* 10: 365; Joseph Kershaw to John Rutledge, Feb. 24, 1784, quoted in Kirkland and Kennedy, *Historic Camden,* 1: 379.

59. Brown, *South Carolina Regulators,* 154; Kirkland and Kennedy, *Historic Camden,* 1: 13; Kirkland and Kennedy, *Historic Camden,* 2: 35; *SCG&CJ,* Dec. 15, 1772; *SCG,* May 31, 1773.

60. Kirkland and Kennedy, *Historic Camden,* 1: 109–110; "Papers of the First Council of Safety of the Revolutionary Party in South Carolina, June–November 1775" (hereafter PFCS), *South Carolina Historical Magazine* 2 (1901): 191–193; "Mecklenburg Declaration of Independence, reprinted in "*Southern Home,* May 10, 1875; William T. Graves, ed., "Reverend Oliver Hart's Diary of the Journey to the Backcountry," *Southern Campaigns of the American Revolution,* 2, no. 4 (2005): 27–29.

61. Brent Holcomb, ed., *Saint David's Parish, South Carolina, Minutes of the Vestry, 1768–1832, Parish Register, 1819–1924* (Easley, S.C.: Southern Historical Press, 1979), 10, 13, 15, 18; Gregg, *History of the Old Cheraws,* 174–175, 179.

62. Gregg, *History of the Old Cheraws,* 185–193. For the rise of Cross Creek, see H. Roy Merrens, *Colonial North Carolina in the Eighteenth Century: A Study in Historical Geography* (Chapel Hill: University of North Carolina Press, 1964), 165; Ernst and Merrens, "Camden's Turrets," 567. Despite the impact of Cross Creek and other new outlets along the Cape Fear drainage on the trade in eastern North Carolina, Charleston remained the chief link to the Atlantic economy for the more westerly Moravian settlements. Daniel Thorp, *The Moravian Community in Colonial North Carolina: Pluralism on the Southern Frontier* (Knoxville: University of Tennessee Press, 1989), 138. The settlement at Long Bluff consisted of a cluster of buildings scattered between the courthouse, situated on the road to Georgetown, and the river landing. Kenneth E. Lewis, *An Archaeological Survey of Long Bluff State Park, Darlington County, South Carolina,* Research Manuscript Series 129 (Columbia: South Carolina Institute of Archaeology and Anthropology, 1978), 24–29, 52–67.

63. Hemphill, ed., *JPC,* June 11, 12, 1775, 46–48, 66; Ames, "Cantey Family," 242; Kirkland and Kennedy, *Historic Camden,* 1: 49, 109; Gregg, *History of the Old Cheraws,* 236–237; Wilmot G. DeSaussure, *The Names . . . of the Officers Who Served in the South Carolina Regiments of the Continental Establishment; [and] . . . in the Militia* (Columbia: Presbyterian Printing House for the State Society of the Cincinnati of South Carolina, 1886), 9, 14–15.

64. William Henry Drayton to Council of Safety, Aug. 7, 1775, William Thompson to Henry Laurens, Aug. 25, 1775, Hamer et al., *HLP,* 10: 281–282, 350; James H. O'Donnell, ed., "A Loyalist View of the Drayton-Tennent-Hart Mission to the Upcountry," *South Carolina Historical Magazine* 67 (1966): 22n. The quote is from William Moultrie, *Memoirs of the American Revolution, as Far as It Relates to the States of North Carolina, South Carolina, and Georgia,* Vol. 1 (New York: David Longworth, 1802), 64. Ely Kershaw's company of rangers included two lieutenants, two sergeants, a drummer, and 30 privates. PFCS, 199–121.

65. Aaron Loocock's Charleston offices included inspector under the Flax Act (1770), commissioner of the workhouse and markets (1770–1771), and churchwarden of St. Michael's Parish (1771–1772). Edgar and Bailey, eds., *Biographical Directory,* 2: 412; *SCG&CJ,* Apr. 2, 1771. He was also a proprietor of the Camden Fair. Kirkland and Kennedy, *Historic Camden,* 1: 13. For Loocock's visit to England, see *SCG&CJ,* June 22, 1772, and *SCG,* Mar. 14, 1774. For his election and activities associated with the First Provincial Congress, see Hemphill, ed., *JPC,* Jan. 11, 1775; PFCS, 192; Kirkland and Kennedy, *Historic Camden,* 1: 109; Louis Jordan, "South Carolina Currency, June 1, 1775," *Colonial Currency, a Project of the Robert H. Gore, Jr. Numismatic Endowment, University of Notre Dame, Department of Special Collections* (1998), http://www.coins.nd.edu/ColCurrency/CurrencyText/SC-06-01-75b.html.

66. Kirkland and Kennedy, *Historic Camden,* 1: 110, 118; *SCG,* Jan. 30, 1775; Holcomb, ed., *Saint David's Parish, South Carolina,* 17; Gregg, *History of the Old Cheraws,* 227; DeSaussure, *Names of Officers,* 6.

67. Brown, *South Carolina Regulators,* 154; *SCG&CJ,* Oct. 26, 1773.

68. CBPR, Vol. R-3, Apr. 22, 1765, 393; Vol. Q-3, Nov. 16, 1769, 250; Vol. Q-3, Nov. 16, 1769, 252; Vol. R-3, Oct. 12, 1770, 369.

69. *SC&AGG,* Feb. 19, 1770; *SCG,* Feb. 21, 1770; *SCG,* Apr. 30, May 14, May 28, Nov. 5, 1772.

70. CBPR, P-4, 490; CBMC, D-6; Kershaw-Chesnut Papers, Preston Davie Collection, Southern Historical, University of North Carolina, Chapel Hill (hereafter KCP/PDC).

71. CBMC, Vol. W-4, Apr. 11, 1777, 350; Vol. G-5, Apr. 10, 1777, 26; Kershaw County, Records of the Clerk of Court, Conveyances (KCRCC/C), Vol. H, Apr. 10, 11, 1777, 198, 301; Lancaster County, Records of the Clerk of Court, Conveyances (hereafter LCRCC/C), Vol. B, 11; KCRCC/C, Vol. H, 301; CBMC, Vol. C-5, Apr. 9, 1777, 65; LCRCC/C, Vol. D, 1779, 8; Vol. BB, May 5, 1786, 220; CBMC, Vol. T-5, May 5, 1786, 120; Vol. T-5, May 9, 1786, 113, 117; Vol. Y-5, 408; KCRPJ/E, Book C, 59; Plat, Preston Davie Collection, Southern Historical Collections, University of North Carolina, Chapel Hill (PDC), Nov. 8, 1786.

72. CBMC, Vol. Z-4, Apr. 11, 1778, 133; Plat, 1778, PDC; CBMC, Vol. B-5, July 12, 1779, 212; Vol. Y-5, Apr. 2, 1781, 198; Vol. E-5, Dec. 14, 1779, 90; Plat, Apr. 11, 1777, PDC; LCRCC/C, Vol. D, 8; Plat, Apr. 8, 1777, PDC; KCRCC/C, Vol. B, 1788, 132. William Nettles's second wife was Mary Mathis, sister of Sarah Mathis. Kirkland and Kennedy, *Historic Camden,* 1: 86, 392. For Cook, DaCosta, and Carter, see ibid., 109, 359, 387.

73. Cantey Family Papers 10 MSS, 14 Sept. 1771–15 Oct. 1823, South Caroliniana Library, University of South Carolina, Columbia, quoted in Judith J. Schulz: "The Rise and Decline of Camden as South Carolina's Major Trading Center, 1751–1829: A Historical Geographic Study" (M.A. thesis, University of South Carolina, 1972), 27. Situated on a tract of higher ground, Logtown was a distinct location named for the log houses occupied by its early residents. Kirkland and Kennedy, *Historic Camden,* 1: 18.

74. James Clitherall Diary, 1776, Southern Historical Collection, University of North Carolina, Chapel Hill, quoted in Ernst and Merrens, "Camden's Turrets," 564–565.

75. John Bartlam's life and works have been traced extensively in Bradford L. Rauschenberg, "John Bartlam, Who Established 'New Pottworks in South Carolina' and Became the First Successful Creamware Potter in America," *Journal of Early Southern Decorative Arts* 17, no. 2 (1991): 1–66. For discussions of Bartlam's ceramics, see Stanley South, *The Search for John Bartlam at Cain Hoy: America's First Creamware Potter,* Research Manuscript Series 219 (Columbia: South Carolina Institute of Archaeology and Anthropology, 1993); and South, "John Bartlam's Porcelain at Cain Hoy, 1765–1770," in *Ceramics in America, 2007,* ed. Robert Hunter (Milwaukee: The Chipstone Foundation, 2007), 196–202. For the occurrence of Bartlam's wares in the archaeological remains at Camden, see Kenneth E. Lewis, *Camden: A Frontier Town in Eighteenth Century South Carolina,* Anthropological Studies 2 (Columbia: South Carolina Institute of Archaeology and Anthropology, 1976), 169–173; "Archaeological Investigations in Southwestern Camden: Report of the 1996–1998 Project," Report to Historic Camden Foundation, Camden, S.C., 1999, 147–150; Lewis, *Camden: Historical Archaeology in the South Carolina Backcountry* (Belmont, Calif.: Thomson Wadsworth, 2006), 58–59, 88, 139–140. Records of Bartlam's dealings with the store are contained in Unidentified Camden Account Book.

76. Lewis, *Camden: A Frontier Town,* 96–98.

77. Brown, *South Carolina Regulators,* 105.

78. Stephanie L. Holschlag, Michael J. Rodeffer, and Marvin L. Cann, *Ninety Six: The Jail* (Ninety Six., S.C.: Star Fort Historical Commission, 1978), 50–76; Kenneth E. Lewis, "The Camden Jail and Market Site: A Report on Preliminary Investigations," *South Carolina Institute of Archaeology and Anthropology, Notebook* 16 (1984): 15–32; Lewis, *Camden: Historical Archaeology,* 129. For the jail breaks, see *SCG,* May 31, 1773; *SC&AGG,* Aug. 7, 1777.

79. Courts were scheduled in April and November at Camden: *SCG,* May 28; the governor appointed district sheriffs and clerks of the common pleas: *SCG,* June 4, 25, July 16, 1772. The first grand jury for Camden District met in November 1772: *SCG,* Dec. 10, 1772. For a discussion of the operations of the early district court, see Jo Anne McCormick, "The Camden Backcountry Judicial Precinct, 1769–1790" (M.A. thesis, University of South Carolina, 1975), 45–50.

80. *SCG,* Nov. 8, 1773; *SC&AGG,* May 8, 1776; May 22, 1776; Mar. 20, 1777. For a discussion of South Carolinians' identification of ethnic groups based on geographical origin and planters' perceptions of their behavioral characteristics and understanding of "country marks," see Daniel C. Littlefield, *Rice and Slaves: Ethnicity and the Slave Trade in Colonial South Carolina* (Urbana: University of Illinois Press, 1981), 9–21, 117–126.

81. The sampling excavations covered about three-fourths of the town site south of Bull Street on both sides of Broad Street. Because modern sports facilities and an auditorium covered the remaining portions of the site, it could not be examined archaeologically. Lewis, *Camden: A Frontier Town,* 35.

82. Plan of Camden, May 12, 1781, Letters, 1774–1789, NGP/PCC, 175/2/161.

83. For contemporary brewhouses, see Driver et al., "The North Service Range," 121–122; Simoneau, "The Intendant's Palace," 172–174; Egan, "Post-Medieval Britain and Ireland in 1988," 46–47; Hurst, "Post-Medieval Britain in 1966," 117. Lewis, *Camden: A Frontier Town,* 118–126; Lewis, *Camden: Historical Archaeology,* 63–66, 122, 127.

84. Lewis, *Functional Study of the Kershaw House Site,* 9–12, 16, 37–42; Lewis, *Camden: Historical Archaeology,* 124–125. The closest parallel example to the Kershaw mansion in Charleston is the William Washington house on South Battery and Church Streets, built by Thomas Savage about 1768. Miles Brewton, a wealthy merchant, constructed a house of similar design in brick on King Street in 1765. Alice R. Huger Smith and D. E. Huger Smith, *The Dwelling Houses of Charleston, South Carolina* (Philadelphia: J. B. Lippincott, 1917), 93, 190. Kershaw described his mansion as the "Great White House" in CBMC, Vol. T-5, May 5, 1786, 120.

85. Lewis, *Camden: Historical Archaeology,* 146–148. For a discussion of plantation kitchen structures, see John Michael Vlach, *Back of the Big House: The Architecture of Plantation Slavery* (Chapel Hill: University of North Carolina Press, 1993), 43–62. Double pen houses with a single central chimney opening into both rooms constitute a classic style of architecture in the upland South and are sometimes referred to as "saddlebag" houses. Milton B. Newton Jr., *Louisiana House Types: A Field Guide,* Mélanges, No. 2 (Baton Rouge: Louisiana State University, Museum of Geoscience, 1971), 7–8.

86. The term "creole" is used to refer to colonial societies that are recognized as having elements distinct from those of the places from which their inhabitants came. The nature of a creole society reflects the larger context in which it developed. The system of New World plantation agriculture that depended extensively on enslaved labor and the incorporated people whose geographical origin and racial status set them apart from Europeans encouraged the retention of a disparate identity and fostered resistance to incorporation. The inflexible multiethnic organization of plantation production created a creole society formed by the nature of its specialized economy and its need to accommodate heterogeneous social elements. Richard N. Adams, "On the Relation between Plantation and 'Creole Cultures," in *Plantation Systems of the New World: Social Science Monographs VII* (Washington, D.C.: Pan American Union, 1959), 73–74. Creolization resulted in the use of objects commonly understood to have one meaning in new ways. To use a linguistic analogy, the deep structures of African culture brought to the New World, like a grammar employing new words from a broader lexicon, incorporated European and African elements into a new colonial culture. Charles Joyner, *Down by the Riverside: A South Carolina Slave Community* (Chicago: University of Illinois Press, 1984), xxi–xxii. By analogy, artifacts, regardless of their origin, may also have new meanings and must also be interpreted according to the structural context of their users. Leland G. Ferguson, *Uncommon Ground: Archaeology and Early African America, 1650–1800* (Washington, D.C.: Smithsonian Institution Press, 1992), xli–xliv.

87. Although archaeologists are still exploring its role in the social and economic milieu of colonial America, recent studies of Colonoware have examined its variety and its meaning within this

larger context. See Ronald B. Anthony, "Colono Wares," in *Home Upriver: Rural Life on Daniel's Island, Berkeley County, South Carolina,* Vol. 1, ed. Martha Zierden, Lesley Drucker, and Jeanne Calhoun (Columbia: South Carolina Department of Highways and Public Transportation, 1986), 7-22–7-51; Anthony, "Tangible Interaction: from Stobo Plantation," in *Another's Country: Archaeological and Historical Perspectives on Cultural Interactions in the Southern Colonies,* ed. J. W. Joseph and Martha Zierden (Tuscaloosa: University of Alabama Press, 2002), 45–64; Theresa A. Singleton and Mark Bograd, "Looking for the Colono in Colonoware," in *Lines That Divide: Historical Archaeologies of Race, Class, and Gender,* ed. James Delle, Stephen A. Mrozowski, and Robert Paynter (Knoxville: University of Tennessee Press, 2000), 3–21; Laurie Wilkie and Paul Farnsworth, *Sampling Many Pots: An Archaeology of Memory and Tradition at a Bahamian Plantation* (Gainesville: University Press of Florida, 2005), 152–254, 269; Rainer Schreg, "Panamanian Coarse Handmade Earthernware—A Melting Pot of African, American, and European Traditions?," *Post-Medieval Archaeology* 44, no. 1 (2010): 135–164; Charles R. Cobb and Chester B. DePratter, "Multisited Research on Colonowares and the Paradox of Globalization," *American Anthropologist* 114 (2012): 446–461. For the role of Colonoware in food preparation in African American households, see Ferguson, *Uncommon Ground,* 90–96.

Recent research has affirmed the Catawbas' geographically widespread itinerant ceramic trade in South Carolina during the first half of the nineteenth century as not only an economic phenomenon but also a politically useful tool that kept the residents of the Catawba Nation visible in an era when their identity as well as their resources came under increasing threat. Brett H. Riggs, "Temporal Trends in Native Ceramic Traditions of the Lower Catawba River Valley," *Southeastern Archaeology* 29 (2010): 38–41. The association of River Burnished wares with the African American populations on coastal plantations has long been recognized: Steven G. Baker, "Colono-Indian Pottery from Cambridge, South Carolina, with Comments on the Historic Catawba Pottery Trade," *South Carolina Institute of Archaeology and Anthropology, Notebook* 4, no. 1 (1972): 13–16; Ferguson, "Lowcountry Plantations, the Catawba Nation and River Burnished Pottery," 186, 188; Ronald W. Anthony, "Tangible Interaction: Evidence from Stobo Plantation," in *Another's Country: Archaeological and Historical Perspectives on Cultural Interactions in the Southern Colonies,* ed. J. W. Joseph and Martha Zierden (Tuscaloosa: University of Alabama Press, 2002), 63.

88. For an extensive discussion of the symbolism of blue beads, their use by African Americans, and their relevance to the archaeological sites of African American settlements, see Linda France Stine, Melanie A. Cabak, and Mark D. Groover, "Blue Beads as African American Cultural Symbols," *Historical Archaeology* 30, no. 3 (1996): 49–75.

89. William M. Kelso, *Kingsmill Plantations, 1619–1800* (Orlando, Fla.: Academic Press, 1984), 104–105, discusses the association of root cellars with slave quarters. The ritual significance of these pits was explored by Patricia M. Samford, "The Archaeology of African-American Slavery and Material Culture," *William and Mary Quarterly,* 3rd ser., 53 (1966): 89–91, 100; Samford, *Subfloor Pits and the Archaeology of Slavery in Colonial America* (Tuscaloosa: University of Alabama Press, 2007), 184–187. The structure near the Kershaw mansion and its contents are described in Lewis, *Camden: Historical Archaeology,* 125, 145–149.

90. For discussions of smokehouses and springhouses, see Vlach, *Back of the Big House,* 63–80. Discussions of the Kershaw house complex may be found in Lewis, *Functional Study of the Kershaw House Site,* 51–91; Lewis, *Camden: Historical Archaeology,* 126–127, 130.

91. Broad Street was not cleared to its surveyed ninety-foot width until 1780, and its course remained "woody on each side of the road & in some places (near the Town) very thick." Samuel Mathis to William Richardson Davie, June 26, 1819, Samuel Mathis Papers (hereafter SMP), South Caroliniana Library, University of South Carolina, Columbia. The American General Nathanael Greene also described the hills along the main road north of Camden as being "covered with timber": *PG,* May 30, 1781. The location of Thomas Charleton's property is shown on a "Sketch of the Battle of Hobkirk's Hill According to Plan by Capt. C. Vallancey of the Volunteers of Ireland," reproduced in Kirkland and Kennedy, *Historic Camden,* 1: 235.

Chapter 9. "In Consequence of the Above Order"

1. The policy for the treatment of rebel leaders was outlined in Cornwallis to Clinton, June 30, 1780, in Charles Ross, ed., *Correspondence of Charles, First Marquis Cornwallis,* Vol. 1 (London: John Murray, 1859), 485–486. As a notorious rebel, Joseph Kershaw saw his real and personal property, including livestock, slaves, goods, and produce, confiscated and his family forced to move from his house in Camden. JBKNE, June 14, 1820, 1780.

2. Marc Egnal and Joseph A. Ernst, "An Economic Interpretation of the American Revolution," *William and Mary Quarterly,* ser. 2, 29 (1972): 18–24.

3. Walter Edgar, *South Carolina: A History* (Columbia: University of South Carolina Press, 1998), 224–225.

4. Gary D. Olson, "Loyalists and the American Revolution: Thomas Brown and the South Carolina Backcountry, 1775–1776," *South Carolina Historical Magazine* 68 (1967): 202; Egnal and Ernst, "Economic Interpretation," 31.

5. Robert Stansbury Lambert, *South Carolina Loyalists in the American Revolution* (Columbia: University of South Carolina Press, 1987), 34; Clyde R. Ferguson, "Functions of the Partisan Militia in the South during the American Revolution: An Interpretation," in *The Revolutionary War in the South: Power, Conflict, and Leadership,* ed. W. Robert Higgins (Durham, N.C.: Duke University Press, 1979), 241–243.

6. Although members of the older German-speaking communities of Orangeburg and Saxe Gotha remained loyal but largely passive and the Quakers were neutral, many newer English and Scots-Irish immigrants actively resisted the new government. Richard Maxwell Brown, *The South Carolina Regulators* (Cambridge, Mass.: Belknap Press of Harvard University Press, 1963), 123–126; Robert M. Weir, *Colonial South Carolina: A History* (New York: KTO Press, 1983; reprint ed., Columbia: University of South Carolina Press, 1997), 322–323; Rachel N. Klein, "Frontier Planters and the American Revolution: The South Carolina Backcountry, 1775–1782," in *An Uncivil War: The Southern Backcountry during the American Revolution,* ed. Ronald Hoffman, Thad W. Tate, and Peter J. Albert (Charlottesville: University Press of Virginia for the United States Capitol Historical Society, 1985), 41–43, 55; Lambert, *South Carolina Loyalists,* 35–38.

7. Lambert, *South Carolina Loyalists,* 38–42; John Wesley Brinsfield, *Religion and Politics in Colonia South Carolina* (Easley, S.C.: Southern Historical Press, 1983), 92–97; Olson, "Loyalists and the American Revolution," 208–214; *SCG&CJ,* Oct. 6, 1775.

8. Lambert, *South Carolina Loyalists,* 29–32; Olson, "Loyalists and the American Revolution," 216–218; Weir, *Colonial South Carolina,* 324–325.

9. Weir, *Colonial South Carolina,* 327–328; John W. Gordon, *South Carolina and the American Revolution: A Battlefield History* (Columbia: University of South Carolina Press, 2003), 35–46.

10. Ibid., 46–54.

11. Richard R. Beeman, "The Political Response to Social Conflict in the Southern Backcountry: A Comparative View of Virginia and the Carolinas during the Revolution," in *An Uncivil War: The Southern Backcountry during the American Revolution,* ed. Ronald Hoffman, Thad W. Tate, and Peter J. Albert (Charlottesville: University Press of Virginia for the United States Capitol Historical Society, 1985), 131–132; William Moultrie, *Memoirs of the American Revolution, as Far as It Relates to the States of North Carolina, South Carolina, and Georgia,* Vol. 1 (New York: David Longworth, 1802), 25, 129; Edgar, *South Carolina,* 226–227; Brinsfield, *Religion and Politics,* 122–124.

12. Rachel N. Klein, *Unification of a Slave State: The Rise of the Planter Class in the South Carolina Backcountry, 1760–1808* (Chapel Hill: University of North Carolina Press for the Institute of Early American History and Culture, 1990), 84–88.

13. William E. Hemphill and Wylma A. Waites, eds., *Extracts from the Journals of the Provincial Congresses of South Carolina, 1775–1776* (hereafter *JPC*) (Columbia: South Carolina Department of Archives and History, 1960), Jan. 11, 1775; *SCG&CJ,* Jan. 13, 30, 1775; *SCG,* Sept. 7, 1775; *Gazette of the*

State of South Carolina (hereafter *GSSC*), Dec. 8, 1779; Thomas J. Kirkland and Robert M. Kennedy, *Historic Camden, Vol. 1: Colonial and Revolutionary* (Columbia, S.C.: State Printing Co., 1905), 109, 110; Walter B. Edgar and N. Louise Bailey, *Biographical Directory of the South Carolina House of Representatives, Vol. 2: The Commons House of Assembly, 1692–1775* (Columbia: University of South Carolina Press, 1977), 376–377, 412- 413; Alexander Gregg, *History of the Old Cheraws* (Columbia, S.C.: The State Co., 1867; reprint ed., Greenville, S.C.: Southern Historical Press, 1991), 227.

14. Hemphill and Wates, ed., *JPC,* June 12, 1775, 47; Wilmot G. DeSaussure, *The Names . . . of the Officers Who Served in the South Carolina Regiments of the Continental Establishment; [and] . . . in the Militia* (Columbia: Presbyterian Printing House for the State Society of the Cincinnati of South Carolina, 1886),14; William Thomson to Council of Safety, July 22, 1775, in Philip M. Hamer et al., eds., *The Papers of Henry Laurens* (hereafter *HLP*), Vol. 10 (Columbia: University of South Carolina Press, 1968–1990), 239–240; William Henry Drayton and William Tennant to Council of Safety, July 29, 1775, in Hamer et al., eds., *HLP,* 10: 281–282; James H. O'Donnell, ed., "A Loyalist View of the Drayton-Tennent-Hart Mission to the Upcountry," *South Carolina Historical Magazine* 67 (1966): 22n. John Buchanan, *The Road to Guilford Courthouse: The American Revolution in the South* (New York: John Wiley, 1997), 8, 13. Draftee Thomas Brown recalled that his company marched from Camden to Charleston, crossing the Santee at Nelson's Ferry. Upon arrival, the rangers were attached to the larger army under Maj. Gen. Charles Lee. Acting first as a sentinel, Brown later joined his unit on Sullivan's Island. Application of Thomas Brown, RWPBLWAF, R-132, Application S3059.

15. Hemphill, and Wates, eds., *JPC,* June 22, 1775, 66, Feb. 18, 1776, 195–196; Gregg, *History of the Old Cheraws,* 237.

16. Although disagreement exists as to the military effectiveness of the colonial militia in frontier regions, its integrative social role in binding members of the rural community and reinforcing its hierarchical structure has been widely observed. John Shy, "The American Revolution: The Military Conflict Considered as a Revolutionary War," in *Essays on the American Revolution,* ed. Stephen G. Kurtz and James H. Hutson (Chapel Hill: University of North Carolina Press, 1973), 148–149; Shy, "A New Look at Colonial Militia," 182; Harry S. Lavier, "Rethinking the Social Role of Militia: Community-Building in Antebellum Kentucky," *Journal of Southern History* 68 (2002): 780, 815–816.

17. Kirkland and Kennedy, *Historic Camden,* 1: 112–115; Moultrie, *Memoirs of the American Revolution,* 1, 97; Olson, "Loyalists and the American Revolution," 216.

18. Henry Laurens to Joseph Kershaw, July 25, 1775, Hamer et al., eds. *HLP,* 10: 246–247; Samuel Boykin to Council of Safety, Oct. 16, 1775, Hamer et al., eds., 10: 471; Henry Laurens to Samuel Boykin, Jan. 14, 1776, Hamer et al., eds., *HLP,* 11: 28; Kirkland and Kennedy, *Historic Camden,* 1: 119–120.

19. Council of Safety to William Henry Drayton, Sept. 5, 1775, Hamer et al., *HLP,* 10: 365; Richard Richardson to Henry Laurens, Jan. 2, 1776, Hamer et al., *HLP,* 10: 612; Joseph Kershaw to John Rutledge, Feb. 24, 1784, quoted in Kirkland and Kennedy, *Historic Camden,* 1: 379; Hemphill and Wates, eds., *JPC,* Feb. 24, 1776; Kirkland and Kennedy, *Historic Camden,* 1: 131–132; John Lewis Gervais to Henry Laurens, Aug. 2, 1777, in Raymond Starr, ed., "Letters from John Lewis Gervais to Henry Laurens, 1777–1778," *South Carolina Historical Magazine* 66 (1965): 21; AA, Reel 83, Frame 152, File 4259; July 5, July 15, Aug. 25, Oct. 30, Dec. 25, 1778; Mar. 18, Mar. 27, Apr. 2, 1779.

20. Joseph Kersaw is likely to have been given command of the new regiment that corresponded to the election district known as District Eastward of the Wateree, an area that included the Waxhaws and stretched east to Lynches River. Hemphill and Wates, eds., *JPC,* Mar. 23, 1776, 251

21. Peter G. D. Kershaw, "A Kershaw Family, 1670–1970," p. 67, Port Charlotte, Fla., 1974 (photocopied), 11; Thomas Brown Application, RWPBLWAF, R-132, Application S3059. Willis Whitaker, who had served as a lieutenant in the Snow Campaign, also recalled that immediately afterward he was ordered to Charleston, where he served as a company commander under Joseph Kershaw. AA, Reel 156, Frame 303, File 8410; Kirkland and Kennedy, *Historic Camden,* 1: 396.

22. Camden's situation on the principal overland route leads to Charlotte, Salisbury, and Salem in neighboring North Carolina, as well as to the complex system of roads linking Halifax, the port of Edenton and settlements in Virginia, and points farther north. H. Roy Merrens, *Colonial North Carolina in*

the Eighteenth Century: A Study in Historical Geography (Chapel Hill: University of North Carolina Press, 1964), 144–157. Henry Laurens advised correspondents that the route through Halifax and Camden was the best road from Philadelphia to Charleston. Henry Laurens to Lachlan McIntosh, Aug. 11, 1777, Hamer et al., *HLP,* 11: 441–442. On Feb. 16, 1778, for example, Joseph Kershaw hosted a party of officers that accompanied the Marquis de Lafayette as he traveled from Charleston to Philadelphia and became involved with the ill-fated shipment of some of their luggage. Two months later the military engineer John Christian Senf, who accompanied Baron de Holtzendorf, stayed at his house while en route to Charleston. Baron DeKalb to Henry Laurens, Apr. 16, 1778, Hamer et al., *HLP,* 13: 124–125; Apr. 16, 1778, 124–125; Hamer et al., *HLP,* 12: 452n; Baron de Holtzendorf to Henry Laurens, Apr. 16, 1778, Hamer et al., *HLP,* 1: 13, 120.

23. AA, S108092, Reel 83, Frame 152, File 4259; Kirkland and Kennedy, *Historic Camden,* 1: 131–132.

24. William H. Nelson, *The American Tory* (Boston: Basic Books, 1961), 89; Kevin Phillips, *The Cousins' Wars: Religion, Politics, and the Triumph of Anglo-America* (New York: Basic Books, 1999), 56–57, 179–183, 200–204; Klein, "Frontier Planters and the American Revolution," 41; Jo Anne McCormick, "The Quakers of Colonial South Carolina, 1670–1807" (Ph.D. diss., University of South Carolina, 1985), 159–160; Peter N. Moore, "Local Origins of Allegiance in Revolutionary South Carolina: The Waxhaws as a Case Study," *South Carolina Historical Magazine* 107 (2006): 29–30; George Lloyd Johnson Jr., *The Frontier in the Colonial South, South Carolina Backcountry, 1736–1800* (Westport, Conn.: Greenwood Press, 1997), 129–130; Merrens, *Colonial North Carolina,* 56–57.

25. Richard J. Hooker, ed., *The Carolina Backcountry on the Eve of the Revolution: The Journal and Other Writings of Charles Woodmason, Anglican Itinerant* (Chapel Hill: University of North Carolina Press, 1953), 197, 210; *SCAGG,* May 8, 1776; *Journal of the General Assembly of South Carolina, Mar. 26, 1776–April 11, 1776, September 17–October 20, 1776* (hereafter *JGA*) (Columbia: South Carolina State Historical Commission, 1906, 1909), Mar. 30, 1776, 19 R-3.

26. Jo Anne McCormick, "The Camden Backcountry Judicial Precinct, 1769–1790" (M.A. thesis, University of South Carolina, 1975), 63–68; *GSSC,* Oct. 13, Oct. 28, 1778; *SC&AGG,* Mar. 20, 1777; Aug. 7, 1777; *GSSC,* Sept. 15, 1777; Thomas J. Kirkland and Robert M. Kennedy, *Historic Camden, Vol. 2: Nineteenth Century* (Columbia, S.C.: State Printing Co., 1926), 252; William W. Hemphill, Wylma A. Wates, and R. Nicholas Olsberg, eds., *Journals of the General Assembly and the House of Representatives, 1776–1780 (JGA&HR)* (Columbia: University of South Carolina Press, 1970), 281.

27. Archaeological investigations conducted in 1967 exposed the Camden magazine and examined its architecture and contents. Despite being extensively damaged by its demolition and the subsequent use of the site as a plant nursery, the form of the building was intact, as were features associated with it. Alan Calmes, "Report of Excavations at the Revolutionary War Period Fortifications of Camden, South Carolina" (Camden, S.C.: Camden District Heritage Foundation, 1968), 3, 6–9, Figs. 3 and 4.

28. The list of contributors of slaves for the construction of the magazine appears in Kirkland and Kennedy, *Historic Camden,* 1: 129–130. Lambert, *South Carolina Loyalists,* 118–119; Alfred E. Jones, ed., "The Journal of Alexander Chesney, a South Carolina Loyalist in the Revolution and After," *Ohio State University Bulletin* 26, no. 4 (1921): 114; Murtie June Clark, *Loyalists in the Southern Campaign of the Revolutionary War,* 3 vols. (Baltimore: Genealogical Publishing Co., 1981), 113–118; 1: 147, 149; Earl Cornwallis to James Cary, Oct. 3, 1780, CP/30/11/81:13. For a more recent presentation of Cornwallis's correspondence, see Ian Saberton, ed., *The Cornwallis Papers: The Campaigns of 1780 and 1781 in the Southern Theatre of the American Revolutionary War* (East Sussex: Naval & Military Press, 2010).

29. James Cary was born in Nansemond County, Viginia, in the 1730s and moved to North Carolina about 1750. There he served as an attorney in Johnston and Edgecombe Counties. In 1759 he married Mary Bennett, a widow, and five years later they relocated to South Carolina, residing in St. James Parish, Goose Creek. In 1768 he was listed as Regulator. In 1770 Cary moved to the vicinity of Camden, where he managed a plantation for John Milhouse but subsequently acquired landholdings of 1,600 acres and owned forty-two slaves. Lambert, "A Loyalist Odyssey," 167–169; CBPR, Vol. R-3, Oct. 12, 1770, 394; Kirkland and Kennedy, *Historic Camden,* 1: 77; 2: 281.

30. Joshua English I was born in King's County, Ireland, emigrated to South Carolina in 1753, and subsequently acquired four hundred acres on Spears Creek south of Camden. He was a Regulator in 1768 and was a member of several district grand juries. He married Sarah Adamson, daughter of James Adamson, who was killed at Fort Loudon during the Cherokee War in 1760. They had three sons, Joshua II, Robert, and John, and one daughter, Elizabeth. Kirkland and Kennedy, *Historic Camden,* 1: 74, 77, 87, 96, 106–108; Charlotte Boykin Salmond Brunson, *Kershaw County Cousins* (Columbia, S.C.: R. L. Bryan, 1978), 210; Brown, *South Carolina Regulators,* 145.

31. Klein, *Unification of a Slave State,* 87–88; McCormick, "Quakers of Colonial South Carolina, 159–160. John Adamson, born in Antrim County, Ireland, in 1744, was a nephew of James Adamson of Cherokee War fame. He settled on the Wateree River as a planter north of Camden in 1765 and married his cousin Elizabeth Adamson about 1770. Kirkland and Kennedy, *Historic Camden,* 1: 65, 76, 290; Draper Manuscript Collection, Sumter Papers (hereafter DMC/SP), microfilm, State Historical Society of Wisconsin, Madison, Wis., 4vv, 229–231. Abraham and Jonathan Belton settled on the Wateree in 1767 and acquired land adjacent to that of John Adamson. Jonathan married Mary English, a sister of Joshua and Robert English, in the 1770s. Kirkland and Kennedy, *Historic Camden,* 1: 74, 76, 285.

32. Lambert, *South Carolina Loyalists,* 51, 59–61, 67–70; Olson, "Loyalists and the American Revolution," 218; John Lewis Gervais to Henry Laurens, June 22, 1778, Hamer et al., *HLP,* 13: 520.

33. [Robert Gray], "Colonel Robert Gray's Observations on the War in Carolina," *South Carolina Historical Magazine* 11 (1910): 153; Rawlins Lowndes to Henry Laurens, Sept. 22, 1778, Hamer et al., *HLP,* 14: 343; *JGA,* Oct. 1, 1776, 71; *SCG&CJ,* May 11, 1778; Gregg, *History of the Old Cheraws,* 274–278.

34. Henry Lumpkin, *From Savannah to Yorktown: The American Revolution in the South* (Columbia: University of South Carolina Press, 1981), 27–29; Buchanan, *Road to Guilford Courthouse,* 25–26; Christopher Hibbert, *Redcoats and Rebels: The American Revolution through British Eyes* (New York: Avon Books, 1990), 226–235.

35. Hibbert, *Redcoats and Rebels,* 242.

36. Arlin C. Migliazzo, *To Make This Land Our Own: Community, Identity, and Cultural Adaptation in Purrysburg Township, South Carolina, 1732–1865* (Columbia: University of South Carolina Press, 2007), 256–257.

37. Ferguson, "Functions of the Partisan Militia," 242–244; Hemphill and Wates, eds., *JPC,* 44, 54, 133–134, 142, 143, 146–147, 151.

38. Brown, *South Carolina Regulators,* 125, 159–160; JBKNE, Dec. 28, 1778; Mar. 28, 1779; CLG/CS, Vol. 21, Oct. 12, 1770, 174; Vol. 32, Aug. 19, 1774, 346; CBPR, Vol. D-4, Mar. 28, 1773, 300; CBP, Vol. 18, May 22, 1773, 20; Kirkland and Kennedy, *Historic Camden,* 1: 109.

39. CBPR, Vol. P-3, Jan. 5, 1768, 285; CBP, Vol. 11, Mar. 4, 1770, 361; CLG/CS, Vol. 21, 52; "Memorial of Militia Now Doing Duty in Charles Town, Feb. 24, 1776," Robert W. Gibbes Collection of Revolutionary War Manuscripts (RWGCRWM), S 213089, Box 2, Folder 57, South Carolina Department of Archives and History, Columbia; KCCSAB; CMMP, 12/33/36; Stub Entries to Accounts of Revolutionary Claims (SEIRC), William L. Clements Library, University of Michigan, Book Z, No. 450, 293; Samuel Mathis Plantation Journal (SMPJ), South Caroliniana Library, University of South Carolina, Columbia, Mar. 30, 1781.

40. "PFCS," *South Carolina Historical Magazine* 2 (1901), 191; DeSaussure, *Names of Officers,* 6; Kirkland and Kennedy, *Historic Camden,* 1: 367; Provision Return for Capt. John Chesnut's Company, Oct. 9, 1779, RWGCRWM, Box 3, Folder 31; Hamer et al., eds., *HLP,* 10: 182n.

41. Kirkland and Kennedy, *Historic Camden,* 1: 75, 77, 89; Brown, *South Carolina Regulators,* 145, 159; JBKNE, Jan. 4, 1779.

42. Hemphill, et al., *JGA&HR 1779, 321;* JBKNE, Jan. 24, 1779.

43. Peter N. Moore, *World of Toil and Strife: Community Transformation in Backcountry South Carolina, 1750–1805* (Columbia: University of South Carolina Press, 2007), 48, 56–58, 62; Hendrik Booraem, *Young Hickory: The Making of Andrew Jackson* (Dallas, Tex.: Taylor Trade Publishing, 2001), 7–8, 30–31.

44. MB, Vol. 8, Oct. 20, 1768, 290; CPB, Vol. 14, Apr. 18, 1772, 496; CLG/CS, Vol. 33, Sept. 30, 1774, 448; CPB, Vol. 18, Nov. 23, 1772, 495; Vol. 28, 1; CLG/CS, Vol. 5, Feb. 13, 1768, 284; CLG/CS, Vol. 16, 232;,

CLG/CS, Feb. 23, 1768; JBKNE, Dec. 25, 1778; Booraem, *Young Hickory,* 21; Moore, *World of Toil and Strife,* 22, 48, 74; "Memorial of Militia Now Doing Duty in Charles Town, Feb. 24, 1776," RWGCRWM, Box 2, Folder 57.

45. CLG/CS, Vol. 16, Feb. 23, 1768, 232; JBKNE, Apr. 14, 1779.

46. Kirkland and Kennedy, *Historic Camden,* 2: 13; Kershaw County Historical Society, *A Guide to Historic Sites in Camden, South Carolina* (Camden, S.C.: 1992), 55.

47. MB, Vol. 12, July 7, 1773, 286; SPB/ChS, Vol. 3, 223; JBKNE, Dec. 28, 1778, Gregg, *History of the Old Cheraws,* 52n, 100.

48. JBKNE, Dec. 25, 1778; *PG,* Jan. 27, 1779. Daniel Carter, a draftee who resided in the lower Wateree Valley, recalled that his company was among the units integrated with those of Kershaw's regiment as it proceeded to Purrysburg. RWPBLWAF, R 155, Application S 3126. Thomas Gill also mentioned that his company, commanded by Captain Philip Walker, was attached to the Camden regiment when it deployed. Application, DMC/SP, 15vv, 131. Following the regiment's arrival at Purrysburg, it grew further with the addition of light troops from Col. Summers's brigade. "Order Book of John Faucherand Grimke, August 1778 to May 1780," *South Carolina Historical Magazine,* 14 (1913): 163. Col. Richard Richardson had been promoted to general in the South Carolina militia in March 1778. Edgar and Bailey, eds., *Biographical Directory,* 2: 559.

49. JBKNE, Jan. 4, 17, 18, 1779.

50. William T. Graves, "The South Carolina Backcountry Whig Militia: 1775–1781, An Overview,"- *Southern Campaigns of the American Revolution* 2, no. 5 (2005): 8; Fred Anderson, *A People's Army: Massachusetts Soldiers and Society in the Seven Year's War* (Chapel Hill: University of North Carolina Press, 1984), 167–195.

51. Baron DeKalb to Henry Laurens, Jan. 7, 1778, Hamer et al., eds., *HLP,* 12: 265–266; Robert C. Pugh, "The Revolutionary Militia in the Southern Campaign," *William and Mary Quarterly,* 3rd ser., 14 (1957): 156–158.

52. Migliazzo, *To Make This Land Our Own,* 257; JBKNE, Jan. 21, 1779.

53. JBKNE, Jan. 24, 1779; Moultrie, *Memoirs of the American Revolution,* 1: 273; Joseph Johnson, *Traditions and Reminiscences Chiefly of the American Revolution in the South* (Charleston, S.C.: Walker & James, 1851), 465; Kirkland and Kennedy, *Historic Camden,* 1: 121–122.

54. JBKNE, Feb. 14, 16, 17, 18, 25; Joseph Kershaw to Benjamin Lincoln, Feb. 18, 1779, Benjamin Lincoln Papers (hereafter BLP), microfilm, Massachusetts Historical Society, Cambridge.

55. Kirkland and Kennedy, *Historic Camden,* 1: 123.

56. Gordon, *South Carolina and the American Revolution,* 64–70.

57. Charles B. Baxley, ed., "Annotated Pension of Richard Clinton," *Southern Campaigns of the American Revolution,* 2, no. 3 (2005): 14.

58. JBKNE, Mar. 13, 20, 27, 28; Apr. 1, 2, 9, 13–17, 20.

59. Baxley, "Annotated Pension of Richard Clinton," 14.

60. The Indians' participation was mentioned in Gov. Rutledge's orders to Kershaw for dispatching militia from Camden: JBKNE, May 8, 1779; Kirkland and Kennedy, *Historic Camden,* 1: 124–125; Moultrie, *Memoirs of the American Revolution,* 1: 474. Both Moses Beard of Capt. Luke Petty's company and Richard Clinton, who served under John Marshall, mentioned participating in the Battle of Stono Ferry. RWPBLWAF, R 67, Application S 5818; Baxley, ed., "Annotated Pension of Richard Clinton," 14.

61. Deposition by Two Members of Lt. Col. Kershaw's Horse Brigade and Col. Singleton's Summary of Assignment of His Proposed Command to Lt. Col. Kershaw, n.d., Matthew Singleton Papers (hereafter MSP), South Caroliniana Library, University of South Carolina, Columbia.

62. AA, Reel 156, Frame 303, File 8410; Kirkland and Kennedy, *Historic Camden,* 1: 396.

63. *SC&AGG,* Apr. 9, 1779; *PG,* May 12, 1799; George White, RWPBLWAF, R 859, Application S32057; Daniel Carter, RWPBLWAF, R 166, Application S 3126; William Barret, RWPBLWAF, R 53, Application S 30846; Gordon, *South Carolina and the American Revolution,* 63.

64. Ely Kershaw to John Chesnut, Oct. 29, 1779, Nathaniel Greene Papers, William L. Clements Library, University of Michigan, Ann Arbor (NGP/CL).

65. Gordon, *South Carolina and the American Revolution,* 71–82; Buchanan, *Road to Guilford Courthouse,* 42–48.

66. JBKNE, Oct. 23, 1779.

67. Kershaw shipped 262 barrels (26,200 pounds) of gunpowder and almost one thousand pounds of lead to Charlotte, leaving about 3,400 pounds and thirty boxes of cartridges in Camden. Joseph Kershaw to Benjamin Lincoln, Mar. 8, 1779, BLP; Joseph Kershaw to John Rutledge, Apr. 25, 1780, quoted in Kirkland and Kennedy, *Historic Camden,* 1: 127–129, 132. Archaeological excavation conducted by Alan Calmes in 1967 uncovered evidence of this fortification ditch and wall, together with the gunpowder and munitions once stored in the magazine, including solid shot of various sizes, split shot, hollow shot (or bombs), grape shot cannonballs, grapeshot, and musket balls. Calmes, "Excavations at the Revolutionary War Period Fortifications," 9–13, Fig. 7. For identification of these, see Harold L. Peterson, *Round Shot and Rammers: An Introduction to Muzzle-Loading Land Artillery in the United States* (New York: Bonanza Books, 1969), 27–30.

68. For example, on New Years Day 1779 Joseph Kershaw had Ephram Ponder of the militia confined for trying to raise mutiny and sedition: JBKNE, Jan. 1, 1779. Ten months later, members of Capt. Luke Petty's company escorted a group of Tory prisoners accused of attempting to destroy the Camden magazine to the Camden jail. John Rush Hutchins, AA, Reel 76, Frame 379, File 3899. Militiaman William Barret recalled that he had served as a jail guard under the command of Lt. James Canada for two months, from March through May 1780. William Barret, RWPBLWAF, R 53, Application S 30846.

69. Henry Laurens to Lachlan Mcintosh, Aug. 11, 1777, Hamer et al., eds., *HLP,* 11: 441–442; Extract from Minutes of the Treasury Office, Oct. 17, 1780, *Papers of the Continental Congress, 1774–1789* (hereafter *PCC*) (Washington, D.C.: National Archives and Record Service, General Services Administration, 1971), M 227, R 147, I 136, Vol. 4, 625–627.

70. Richard Richardson to Henry Laurens, Jan. 1776, Hamer et al., eds., *HLP,* 11: 56; Joseph Chapman, RWPBLWAF, R 177, Application S 21691; James Harris, Pension Account Application W 11223, in Bobby G. Moss and Michael C. Scoggins, *African-American Patriots in the Southern Campaign of the American Revolution* (Blacksburg, S.C.: Scotia-Hibernia Press, 2004), 112–113.

71. Jethro Sumner Letter, Dec. 8, 1778, Jethro Sumner Papers (hereafter JSP), William L. Clements Library, University of Michigan, Ann Arbor; Joseph Kershaw to Benjamin Lincoln, July 31, 1779, BLP; Kirkland and Kennedy, *Historic Camden,* 1: 125–126, 134–135; John Lewis Gervais to Henry Laurens, Apr. 28, 1780, Hamer et al., eds., *HLP,* 15: 285; Joseph Kershaw, AA, Reel 83, Frame 152, File 4259.

72. Joseph Kershaw, AA, Reel 83, Frame 152, File 4259; Joseph Kershaw to Benjamin Lincoln, July 31, 1779, BLP; Joseph Kershaw to John Rutledge, Apr. 25, 1780, Kirkland and Kennedy, *Historic Camden,* 1: 127.

73. William Ancrum, SEIRC, N, No. 67, 200; Ely Kershaw, AA, Reel 83, Frame 141, File 4258; John Chesnut, AA, Reel 22, Frame 218, File 1230; SEIRC, Q, No. 434, 10; John Cantey, AA, Reel,19, Frame 98, File 1047; Benjamin Haile, AA, Reel 63, Frame 107, File 3215; SEIRC, W, No. 495, 269; George White, AA, Reel 156, Frame 407, File 8424; Robert Crawford, AA, Reel 106, Frame 371, File 5314; John Rush Hutchins, AA, Reel 76, Frame 379, File 3899. Other known contractors included provisioners William Baird, SEIRC, Y-Z, 62; George Ross, AA, Reel 82, Frame 357, File 4234; Stephen Smith, SEIRC, X, 108; Y-Z, 32; and Amos Way, SEIRC Y-Z, 36; wagoners Thomas Durin, George Ganter, Daniel Horton, AA, Reel 83, Frame 152, File 4259; Nicholas Robinson, SEIRC Y-Z, 141; and George Wade, SEIRC, Y-Z, 293.

74. *PG,* Mar. 22, 1780; Henry Laurens to Henry Young, Apr. 1, 1780, Hamer et al., eds., *HLP,* 15: 267.

75. Robert Crawford served at least part of this time as sergeant-major in the regiment commanded by Col. Richard Richardson, II, AA, Reel 106, Frame 371, File 5314; Luke Petty, AA, Reel 117, Frame 450, File 5906; JBKNE, Apr. 30, May 9, 1780. Camden residents signing the petition included Ely Kershaw's and John Chesnut's brothers-in-law James and Zachariah Cantey; Joseph Kershaw's brother-in-law Samuel Mathis; Isaac DuBose; John W. Whitaker; Willis Whitaker; and Samuel Wyly II. Kirkland and Kennedy, *Historic Camden,* 1: 126; 133; Joseph S. Ames, "Cantey Family," *South Carolina Historical Magazine* 11 (1910): 127, 243, 246.

76. Gordon, *South Carolina and the American Revolution,* 82–84; Buchanan, *Road to Guilford Courthouse,* 80.

77. William B. Willcox, ed., *The American Rebellion: Sir Henry Clinton's Narrative of His Campaigns, 1775–1782, sith an Appendix of Original Documents* (New Haven, Conn.: Yale University Press, 1954), 175; Buchanan, *Road to Guilford Courthouse,* 81.

78. Alan Calmes found evidence of Col. White's efforts to destroy the munitions in his excavations of the Camden powder magazine fortification ditch. A deposit of gunpowder at the bottom of the ditch had accumulated where it had been dumped to render it ineffective, and cannonballs, grapeshot, and musket balls scattered in the ditch and elsewhere indicate further efforts to deny their use to the British. Calmes, "Report of Excavations," 10. JBKNE, May 27, 28, 1780; Buchanan, *Road to Guilford Courthouse,* 82.

79. Banastre Tarleton, *History of the Campaigns of 1780 and 1781* (London: T. Cadell, 1787; reprint ed., Spartanburg, S.C.: The Reprint Co., 1967), 27; Kirkland and Kennedy, *Historic Camden,* 1: 135; Buchanan, *Road to Guilford Courthouse,* 82.

80. Charles Stedman, *History of the American War* (London: J. Murray, 1794), 193; Buchanan, *Road to Guilford Courthouse,* 82–85. Capt. Luke Petty had recently commanded a detachment of the regiment at Camden, and he was not in Charleston during the siege. Evidence for his presence at Buford's defeat is his residence in Camden uninjured at the time of Buford's retreat, his furnishing a wagon and team "destroyed by the British Legion at the defeat of Abraham Buford," and the testimony of Joseph Kershaw, who certified that he lost his arm while in militia service. John Rush Hutchins, AA, Reel 76, Frame 379, File 3899; Luke Petty, AA, Reel 117, Frame 450, File 5906; KCRPJ/E, Estate Book A-1, Apt. 130, Pkg. 5113.

81. Stedman, *American War,* 193–194n; JBKNE, May 30, 31, June 1, 1780.

82. Moultrie, *Memoirs of the American Revolution,* 2: 100; "A Plan for Regulating the Province and Forming a Militia," June 4, 1780, CP 11/30/2, 58–59; Cornwallis to Patterson, June 10, 1780, CP 30/11/77, 3; Cornwallis to Clinton, June 30, 1780, in Ross, ed., *Correspondence of Cornwallis,* 486; Paroles of Joseph Kershaw and Ely Kershaw, June 10, 1780, CP 30/11/2, 120, 121.

83. Joseph Kershaw to Alexander Ross, June 2, 1780; Joseph Kershaw to Earl Cornwallis, June 18, 1780, JBKNE.

84. Elizabeth A. Fenn, *Pox Americana: The Great Smallpox Epidemic of 1775–82* (New York: Hill and Wang, 2001), 110–112, 116–118. By summer, residents reported smallpox on local plantations, and at least eight hundred of the troops at Camden were sick with this or other diseases. Cornwallis to Clinton, Aug. 10, 1780; Stedman, *American War,* 205–206; JBKNE, June 18, June 20, 1780.

85. JBKNE, June 18, Aug. 24, Aug. 29, Oct. 5, Oct. 13, 1780; Ely Kershaw to John Chesnut, Aug. 1, 1780, NGP/CL.

Chapter 10. "An Evil Genius about It"

1. Earl of Moira to Henry Lee, June 24, 1813, in Henry Lee, *Memoirs of the War in the Southern Department of the United States* (New York: University Publishing Co., 1869; reprint ed., New York: Arno Press, 1969), 613–620; Alan Valentine, *The British Establishment, 1760–1784: An Eighteenth Century Biographical Dictionary,* Vol. 2 (Norman: University of Oklahoma Press, 1970), 732.

2. John Buchanan, *The Road to Guilford Courthouse: The American Revolution in the South* (New York: John Wiley, 1997), 130–131; John W. Gordon, *South Carolina and the American Revolution: A Battlefield History* (Columbia: University of South Carolina Press, 2003), 158.

3. William B. Willcox, ed., *The American Rebellion: Sir Henry Clinton's Narrative of His Campaigns, 1775–1782, sith an Appendix of Original Documents* (New Haven, Conn.: Yale University Press, 1954), 175; Gordon, *South Carolina and the American Revolution,* 87–88.

4. Of Anglo-Irish background, Rawdon was educated at Harrow and Oxford before entering the army. As a young officer, he served under the Duke of York at Flanders and, posted to America at the outbreak of hostilities, was wounded at Bunker Hill in 1775. An enthusiastic member of Sir Henry Clinton's staff at Boston and New York, Rawdon fought under him at Monmouth three years later.

When Clinton organized a Provincial regiment in Philadelphia in 1778, Rawdon became its commander. Valentine, *British Establishment,* 732; Christopher Hibbert, *Redcoats and Rebels: The American Revolution through British Eyes* (New York: Avon Books, 1990), 60, 122, 126, 252; Buchanan, *Road to Guilford Courthouse,* 130–131.

5. Cornwallis to Balfour, June 13, 1780, CP 30/11/77, 8; Robert Stansbury Lambert, *South Carolina Loyalists in the American Revolution* (Columbia: University of South Carolina Press, 1987), 118–119. Farther from Camden, two provincial infantry regiments guarded approaches from the west and the Waxhaws. One of these formed a garrison under John Phillips at Winnsboro on Jackson's Creek, and Mathew Floyd commanded an advanced post at Rocky Mount on the Catawba River. Like Cary and Rugeley, both were local "men of influence" who could draw on the support of their neighbors, but, unlike the former, neither had previously expressed ambivalence regarding his political position. Phillips and Floyd had been staunch Loyalists from the beginning and had been imprisoned for their actions. To secure the territory to the east between the Wateree and Pee Dee Rivers, Cornwallis found a commander for the ranger regiment in John Harrison, a Loyalist resident of Sparrow Swamp on Lynches River. A somewhat less than reliable subordinate whose unit's actions were often less than honorable, Harrison and his rangers nonetheless remained active in the British cause throughout the conflict, as did Phillips's regiment. Cornwallis hoped that the provincial units he raised would be sufficient to secure the extensive territory between the Broad River and the Cheraws, but he realized that its inhabitants lacked the Loyalist sentiment of those in the western country and that Britain's control would always be tenuous. Cornwallis to Clinton, June 30, 1780, Charles Ross, ed., *Correspondence of Charles, First Marquis Cornwallis,* Vol. 1 (London: John Murray, 1859), 485, 485; Lambert, *South Carolina Loyalists,* 115–166, 118.

6. "Colonel Robert Gray's Observations on the War in Carolina," *South Carolina Historical Magazine* 11 (1910): 147; Cornwallis to Germain, Aug. 20, 1780, Ross, ed., *Correspondence of Cornwallis,* 489; Charles Stedman, *History of the American War* (London: J. Murray, 1794), 195; Roger Lamb, *An Original and Authentic Journal of Occurrences during the Late American War from Its Commencement to the Year 1783* (Dublin: Wilkinson & Courtney, 1809), 301; A. S. Salley, ed., *Colonel William Hill's Memoirs of the Revolution* (Columbia: Historical Commission of South Carolina, 1921), 6.

7. The garrison at Camden included two veteran elite regular infantry regiments, the Twenty-third, the Royal Welsh Fusiliers, and the Thirty-third Infantry, Cornwallis's own regiment. The remainder consisted of Loyalist units, the Volunteers of Ireland, the dragoons of the British Legion, and Brown's and Hamilton's corps of North Carolina provincials. Nearby at Cheraw were two battalions of the Seventy-first Infantry Regiment. Mark Urban, *Fusiliers: The Saga of a British Redcoat Regiment in the American Revolution* (New York: Walker, 2007), 73, 205; Stedman, *American War,* 195;

8. William Davidson to Jethro Sumner, Sept. 15, 1780, JSP; Richard Lee to Henry Laurens, July 27, 1780, Philip M. Hamer et al., eds., *The Papers of Henry Laurens* (hereafter *HLP*), Vol. 15 (Columbia: University of South Carolina Press, 1968–1990), 318; Cornwallis to Clinton, June 2, 1780, CP 30/11/73, 14; Cornwallis to Clinton, July 14, 1780, Ross, ed., *Correspondence of Cornwallis,* 51–52; Cornwallis to Clinton, CP 30/11/78, 34–35, 44; Rawdon to Cornwallis, Dec. 29, 1780, CP 30/11/4, 419; Stedman, *American War,* 319n.

9. Joseph Kershaw, AA, 83, Frame 152, File 4259; Stedman, *American War,* 194–195n. For the printing press, see England to Cornwallis, Sept. 19, 1780, 30/11/64, 79. The army also needed space for captured equipment, such as the 150 French muskets shipped from Winnsborough for repair at Charleston: Cornwallis to Rawdon, Nov. 14, 1780, CP 30/`11/82, 67. For the use of the jail, see Samuel C. Williams, ed., "General Richard Winn's Notes—1780," *South Carolina Historical Magazine* 43 (1942): 202; Tarleton to Cornwallis, Aug. 5, 1780, CP 30/11/63, 20. For the distribution of military artifacts, see Kenneth E. Lewis, *Camden: A Frontier Town in Eighteenth Century South Carolina,* Anthropological Studies 2 (Columbia: South Carolina Institute of Archaeology and Anthropology, 1976), 140–143; Lewis, "Archaeological Investigations in Southwestern Camden: Report of the 1996–1998 Project," Report to Historic Camden Foundation, Camden, S.C., 1999," 169–177.

10. Joseph Kershaw mentioned Haldane's orders to a Mr. Brown to collect and transport building materials to erect "on pile of barracks . . . in the interval between Mr. Kershaw's house and Mr. Brown's, equidistant from each. The other pile of barracks to be erected on the other side of Mr. Kershaw's house at the same distance, fronting the village in a line with the proposed street." JBKNE, June 20, 1780. Later building methods were mentioned in Rawdon to Cornwallis, Nov. 19, 1780, CP 30/11/4, 146; Cornwallis to Rawdon, Nov. 18, 1780, CP 30/11/82, 61; and Rawdon to Cornwallis, Nov. 19, 1780, CP 30/11/4, 161. Many years later, Mary Kershaw recalled that soldiers tore down the Presbyterian meetinghouse for material to erect the southwest row of barracks along Meeting Street. The information is contained in a testimony recorded by the Rev. Francis B. Lee, rector of the Grace Episcopal Church in Camden, on Jan. 5, 1843. It was provided by an unnamed niece of Mary Kershaw, who witnessed these events as a child of ten. Thomas J. Kirkland and Robert M. Kennedy, *Historic Camden, Vol. 2: Nineteenth Century* (Columbia, S.C.: State Printing Co., 1926), 281.

11. Gordon, *South Carolina and the American Revolution,* 88, 90–92.

12. H. L. Landers, *The Battle of Camden, South Carolina, August 16, 1780,* H.R. 37, 71st Cong., 1st sess., 1929, 22–23, 39–50, 61–62; Gordon, *South Carolina and the American Revolution,* 91–94; Return of Killed, Wounded and Missing of the Troops under the Command of Lt. Gen'l. Earl Cornwallis in the Action Near Camden, 16 Aug't., 1780, Mackenzie Papers (hereafter MP), William L. Clements Library, University of Michigan, Ann Arbor; Cornwallis to Cruger, Aug. 18, 178, Ross, ed., *Correspondence of Cornwallis,* 56. Archaeologists have recently traced the course of the battle spatially through analyses of munitions and other material remains. James B. Legg, Steven D. Smith, and Tamara S. Wilson, *Understanding Camden: The Revolutionary War Battle of Camden as Revealed through Historical, Archaeological, and Private Collections Analysis* Columbia: South Carolina Institute of Archaeology and Anthropology, 2005), 63–74.

13. For a contemporary account of these events, see *SC&AGG,* Sept. 6, 1780; Gordon, *South Carolina and the American Revolution,* 94–95.

14. The necessity of defending Camden as a key post was recognized early. Rawdon to Cornwallis to Germain, Aug. 20, 1780, Great Britain, Public Records Office, British Headquarters (Sir Guy Carleton) Papers, 1747 (1777)–1783 (hereafter GCP) (Washington, D.C.: Microfilming Service, Recordak Corp., 1957), 2971, 26a-b; Rawdon to Clinton, Oct. 20, 1780, CP 30/11/3, 298–299; Turnbull to Rawdon, Oct. 31, 1780, CP 30/11/3, 328. The redoubts and other fortifications are described in British documents as well as those gathered by American intelligence: Cornwallis to Rawdon, Nov. 19, 1780, CP 30/11/82, 67; Rawdon to Cornwallis, Nov. 24, 1780, CP 30/11/4, 188; Rawdon to Cornwallis, Nov. 27, 1780, CP 30/11/4, 209; Plan of Camden, May 12, 1781, Letters, 1774–1789/ NGP/PCC, M 247, R175, I 155, Vol. 2, 161; Harrington to Gates, Nov. 5, 1780, PCC, R174, I 54, Vol. 2, 319–320; Greene to Huntington, Dec. 7, 1780, PCC, M 243, R 175, I 155, Vol. 1, 476; Edward Boykin to Lyman Draper, Mar. 13, 1874, DMC/SM, 17vv, 239. As detached works enclosed on all sides, redoubts were placed around a fortified site to extend the depth of its defense into the open country surrounding it. Christopher Duffy, *Fire & Stone: The Science of Fortress Warfare, 1660–1860* (Newton Abbot, Devon: David & Charles, 1975), 63, 185. Archaeological excavations were carried out at the northeast redoubt by Alan Calmes in1968 and the following year by Robert Strickland. Lewis, *Camden: Historical Archaeology,* 31–34. Their work revealed evidence of the structure's parapet and the raised firing steps behind it as well as the filled-in ditch. Alan Calmes, "Report of Excavations at the Revolutionary War Period Fortifications of Camden, South Carolina" (Camden, S.C.: Camden District Heritage Foundation, 1968),17–19, Figs. 11–13; Robert N. Strickland, "Camden Revolutionary War Fortifications (38KE1): 1969–70 Excavations," *South Carolina Institute of Archaeology and Anthropology, Notebook* 3, no. 3 (1971): 57–59.

15. Rawdon expressed the need for palisade defenses in Rawdon to Cornwallis, Nov. 27,1780, CP 30/11/4, 215–216. Duffy, *Fire & Stone,* 45–46. Archaeological investigations conducted by Calmes and Strickland also revealed the locations of the palisade walls around the town and at Kershaw's mansion house. Calmes, "Report of Excavations,"13–17, 21–22, Figs. 9, 10, 14; Robert N. Strickland, "Archaeological Excavations at Camden, 1971–1973," report to the Camden Historical Commission, Camden, S.C.,

1976; Strickland, "Camden Revolutionary War Fortifications," 59–68, Figs. 5–7. Rawdon referred to the town as an "infamous" post in Rawdon to Cornwallis, Nov. 24, 1780, CP 30/11/4, 202–203. The impact of smallpox and other diseases on the rate of construction appears in Trumbull to Cornwallis, Nov. 3, 1780, CP 30/11/4, 15.

16. Cary's Fort is mentioned in Edward M. Boykin to Lyman Draper, Mar. 13, 1874, DMC/SP, 17vv, 239–240; Thomas J. Kirkland and Robert M. Kennedy, *Historic Camden, Vol. 1: Colonial and Revolutionary* (Columbia, S.C.: State Printing Co., 1905), 153; H. W. Harrington to Horatio Gates, Nov. 5, 1780, PCC/R 174, I 154, Vol. 2, 329. For Cary's area of operation, see, Cornwallis to Balfour, Sept. 3, 1780, CP 30/11/80, 2; Cornwallis to Rawdon, Nov. 17, 1780, CP 30/11/82, 58. Apparently not entirely safe in his home, Cary was the subject of a kidnap attempt by rebels in December: Rawdon to Cornwallis, Dec. 6, 1780, CP 30/11/4, 209.

17. The garrisons posted at Clermont, Hanging Rock, and Rocky Mount were all withdrawn upon the advance of Gates's army. Stedman, *History of the American War,* 205; Kirkland and Kennedy, *Historic Camden,* 1: 152–153; Horatio Gates to Continental Congress, Aug. 28, 1780, Horatio Gates Letters/ Papers of the Continental Congress (hereafter HGL/PCC), National Archives and Records Service, General Services Administration, Washington, D.C., 1957. Following the American defeat, Rugeley again occupied Clermont and began to fortify the barn there. Lt. Col. William Washington surrounded the barn and demanded Rugeley's surrender, threatening to destroy the fort with a "field piece" made out of a pine log. Apparently impressed, Rugeley surrendered himself and his command. Kirkland and Kennedy, *Historic Camden,* 1: 213; Johnson, *Life and Correspondence of Nathanael Greene,* 2: 509; Rawdon to Cornwallis, Dec. 2, 1780, CP 30/11/4, 271.

18. Oscar Reiss, *Medicine and the American Revolution: How Diseases and Their Treatments Affected the Colonial Army* (Jefferson, N.C.: McFarland, 1998), 39–40.

19. John Robert Shaw, *A Narrative of the Life and Travels of John Robert Shaw, the Well-Digger, Now Resident of Lexington, Kentucky* (Lexington, Ky.: Daniel Bradford, 1807), 49; Rawdon to Cornwallis, July 17, 1780, CP 31/11/2, 330; Cornwallis to Clinton, Aug. 10, 1780, Ross, ed., *Correspondence of Cornwallis,* 55; Stedman, *American War,* 205–206; Cornwallis to George Germain, Aug. 20, 1780, Ross, ed., *Correspondence of Cornwallis,* 490, 491, 492.

20. Cornwallis to Clinton, Aug. 23, 1780, GCP, 11; England to Cornwallis, Sept. 18, 1780, CP 30/11/64, 71. Malaria and dysentery are described in Reiss, *Medicine,* 14, and in C. Keith Wilbur, *Revolutionary Medicine* (Old Saybrook, Conn.: Globe Pequot Press, 1980, 14, 16. The quote is from a badly wounded and paroled American officer. Thomas Pinckney to Money, Sept. 22, 1780, CP 30/11/3, 84.

21. Cornwallis to George Germain, Aug 21, 1780, Willcox, ed., *American Rebellion,* 454; "Return of Killed, Wounded and Missing of the Troops under the Command of Lt. Gen'l Earl Cornwallis in the Action Near Camden 16th Aug't 1780," MP; Shaw, *Narrative,* 53; Stedman, *American War,* 211; "Examination of William Allman of Col. Stubblefield's Regiment of Virginia Militia, Who was Wounded in the Action of the 16th and Escaped from the Enemy," PCC 247, R 174, I 154, Vol. 2, 57; Joseph Ioor Waring, *History of Medicine in South Carolina, 1670–1825* (Columbia: South Carolina Medical Association, 1963), 102, 198–199, 377. Accounts of DeKalb's burial include Chevalier DuBuysson to unknown recipient, quoted in Kirkland and Kennedy, *Historic Camden,* 1: 190–191; Lamb, *Journal of Occurrences,* 304; A. S. Salley, "Journal of General Peter Horry," *South Carolina Historical Magazine* 39 (1938): 128. Louis C. Duncan, *Medical Men in the American Revolution, 1775–1783* (Carlisle Barracks, Pa.: Medical Field Service School, 1931), 315.

22. Thomas Charlton resigned from American military service in 1776 and returned to Camden. He was elected as a representative to the Second and Third Provincial Congresses in 1778 and 1779, respectively, and appointed a justice of the peace for Camden District in 1779. Charlton accompanied Joseph Kershaw's military expedition to Purrysburg that year. Residing in Camden at the time of the British arrival, he negotiated terms of treatment of the American wounded with Earl Cornwallis. William W. Hemphill, Wylma A. Wates, and R. Nicholas Olsberg, eds., *Journals of the General Assembly and the House of Representatives, 1776–1780 (JGA&HR)* (Columbia: University of South Carolina Press, 1970), 321;; Waring, *History of Medicine,* 198; Jan. 24, 1779, May 27, May 30, 1780, Dennis M. Conrad,

The Papers of Nathanael Greene (hereafter *PNG*): *Vol. 9: 11 July 1781–2 December 1781* (Chapel Hill: University of North Carolina Press for the Rhode Island Historical Society, 1997), 213.

Isaac Franklin Alexander was born in Charlotte, N.C., the son of Abram Alexander, a leading magistrate in Mecklenburg County. He graduated from Princeton College in September 1772, after which he presided over an academy in Charlotte, N.C., for five years. During this time he studied medicine and qualified himself for practice by attending military hospitals. Dr. Alexander later served for ten months as a surgeon with the rank of sergeant in Col. William Polk's regiment in Gen. Thomas Sumter's brigade of militia. Later he entered the practice of medicine. *Southern Home,* May 24, 1875; Waring, *History of Medicine,* 341; Isaac Alexander, AA, Reel 2, Frame 151, File 66A; *PG,* Oct. 14, 1772; Elizabeth H. Jervey, "Marriage and Death Notices in the *City Gazette* and *Daily Advertiser,*" *South Carolina Historical Magazine* 37 (1936): 85–86; E. Haviland Hillman, "The Brisbanes," *South Carolina Historical Magazine* 14 (1913): 129; Kirkland and Kennedy, *Historic Camden,* 1: 342–343.

23. Hugh Williamson to Thomas Bentley, Dec. 1, 1780, quoted in Duncan, *Medical Men in the American Revolution,* 315–316; Cornwallis to Clinton, Aug. 29, 1780, CP 30/11/72, 47; Cornwallis to Jaynes, Aug. 25, 1780, PCC/M 243, R 85, 71, Vol. 1, 543. The notorious conditions in the Charleston prison ships have been discussed elsewhere: see Waring, *History of Medicine,* 102–103; Elizabeth A. Fenn, *Pox Americana: The Great Smallpox Epidemic of 1775–82* (New York: Hill and Wang, 2001), 121–122. Hugh Williamson to Cornwallis, Oct. 2, 1780, CP 30/11/93, 3–4.

24. Hill to Cornwallis, Sept. 21, 1780, CP 30/11/64, 93. The description of Camden in 1781 is by Guilford Dudley, RWPBLAF, R 254, Application W-8681. "Plan of Camden," CPP, ca. 1798. The traditions regarding DeKalb's death appeared in the *Camden Journal,* July 31, 1830, as quoted in Kirkland and Kennedy, *Historic Camden,* 1: 188–189. Joseph Kershaw, AA, Reel 83, Frame 152, File 4259. The 1798 Plan of Camden is filed with "Plan of the Town of Camden," CCP, ca. 1798. For the archaeological evidence, see Lewis, *Camden: A Frontier Town,* 104, Fig. 43. Excavations at the site of the Kershaw store uncovered a substantial number of military artifacts, including buttons identifying the Twenty-third Regiment and Hamilton's North Carolina provincials, as well as weapons parts and munitions. Specialized medical instruments were valuable items that usually remained the property of individual military surgeons, and their absence in the archaeological record is not surprising. Neither is the absence of medical supplies. Composed of lint, cloth, wood, and other perishable materials, these would not have been preserved. Lewis, "Archaeological Investigations in Southwestern Camden," 19, 174–175.

25. Elkanah Watson reported in 1786 that "unburied bones of men and horses" marked the Battle of Camden site. He also observed DeKalb's grave, together with those of several British officers, enclosed by palings site. Winslow C. Watson, ed., *Men and Times of the Revolution; or, Memoirs of Elkanah Watson* (New York: Dana, 1856), 297. George Washington visited the grave during his Southern Tour of 1791. Terry W. Lipscomb, *South Carolina in 1791: George Washington's Southern Tour* (Columbia: South Carolina Department of Department of Archives and History and History, 1993), 73. The account of the rediscovery of DeKalb's grave is found in Kirkland and Kennedy, *Historic Camden,* 2: 76–77. Its location is shown on the "Plan of Camden by J. P. Guignard," Thomas J. Cooper and David J. McCord, ed., *Statutes at Large of South Carolina, Vol. 5* (hereafter *SLSC*) (Columbia, S.C.: A. S. Johnson, 1838),Act No. 1702, 1798. Edwin J. Scott, who lived in Camden as a child, described the brick tomb, lying "in the middle of a lonely old field at the Southwest part of Camden," in 1815. Edwin J. Scott, *Random Recollections of a Long Life, 1806–1876* (Columbia, S.C.: C. A. Calvo, 1884), 18.

No other burials associated with the Revolutionary War have been identified in Camden. A tradition, attributed to the childhood memories of Joseph's daughter, Mary Kershaw, indicated that American dead were buried in "long trenches" in the yard and vicinity of the Kershaw mansion. Kirkland and Kennedy, *Historic Camden,* 1: 275. Extensive archaeological investigations conducted in this area revealed no evidence of burials. Strickland, "Archaeological Excavations," 2. A number of graves of those killed in action at the Battle of Camden, north of the town, are situated on the site of this action. Legg et al. *Understanding Camden,* 59, and contemporary sources also reported soldiers' graves at Hobkirk's Hill. Kirkland and Kennedy, *Historic Camden,* 2: 26.

26. Walter Edgar, *Partisans and Redcoats: The Southern Conflict That Turned the Tide of the American Revolution* (New York: William Morrow, 2001), 50.

27. Stedman, *American War,* 186, 191–192; Walter Edgar, *South Carolina: A History* (Columbia: University of South Carolina Press, 1998), 233.

28. N. Louise Bailey, Mary L. Morgan, and Carolyn R. Taylor, *Biographical Directory of the South Carolina Senate, 1776–1985,* Vol. 2 (Columbia: University of South Carolina Press, 1986), 559; Joseph S. Ames, "Cantey Family," *South Carolina Historical Magazine* 11 (1910): 247; Buchanan, *Road to Guilford Courthouse,* 247–248; Stedman, *American War,* 194n; Joseph Kershaw to Henry William Harington, Sept. 25, 1781, Henry William Harrington Papers, 1748–1809 (hereafter HWHP) #314, Southern Historical Collections, University of North Carolina, Chapel Hill.

29. Francis Boykin served as first lieutenant in Capt. John Chesnut's company. JBKNE, Jan. 4, 24, 1779; Francis Boykin, AA, Reel 12, Frame 325, File 680; Edward M. Boykin, *History of the Boykin Family, from Their First Settlement in Virginia 1685, and in South Carolina, Georgia, and Alabama, to the Present Time* (Camden, S.C.: Colin MacRae, 1876), 11–12; Kirkland and Kennedy, *Historic Camden,* 1: 117, 349; John Cook, AA, Reel 12, Frame 325, File 680; Kirkland and Kennedy, *Historic Camden,* 1: 58, 124.

30. JBKNE, May, 27, 30, 1780; Waring, *History of Medicine,* 198.

31. Benjamin Haile, AA, Reel 63, Frame 107, File 3215; Alexander Gregg, *History of the Old Cheraws* (Columbia, S.C.: The State Co., 1867; reprint ed., Greenville, S.C.: Southern Historical Press, 1991), 290; Kirkland and Kennedy, *Historic Camden,* 1: 289.

32. Joshua Dinkins was a former Regulator who sympathized with the Whig cause and furnished the military with supplies. Richard Maxwell Brown, *The South Carolina Regulators* (Cambridge, Mass.: Belknap Press of Harvard University Press, 1963), 160. A justice of the peace, John Cantey was a member of the Camden District Grand Jury that sent presentations opposing Parliamentary taxation. Cantey, Dinkins, and Wyly provided labor to erect fortifications at the Camden magazine in 1780. Kirkland and Kennedy, *Historic Camden,* 1: 107–108, 129–130.

33. Ames, "Cantey Family," 245; Kirkland and Kennedy, *Historic Camden,* 1: 301, 357.

34. Ames, "Cantey Family," 245; Kirkland and Kennedy, *Historic Camden,* 1: 357, 371, 396.

35. Ames, "Cantey Family," 246; Kirkland and Kennedy, *Historic Camden,* 1: 133; John Wyly, Parole, CP 30/11/2, 122; John Lewis Gervais to Henry Laurens, May 13, 1780, Hamer et al., eds., *HLP,* 15: 290; *JHR,* Jan. 22, 1783.

36. All three merchants had supported the Whig cause. Brown and Ancrum had supplied labor to fortify the Camden magazine, and Brown had served as an officer in the militia and acted as courier of correspondence between South Carolina's rebel government and its representatives in Congress at Philadelphia. Ancrum and Loocock both served in the Third Provincial Congress, representing the District Eastward of the Wateree and St. James Goose Creek, respectively. Kirkland and Kennedy, *Historic Camden,* 1: 129; Robert Bentham Simons, "Regimental Book of Captain James Bentham, 1778–1800," *South Carolina Historical Magazine* 54 (1953): 39; Hamer et al., eds., *HLP,* 14: 28, 35; *Gazette of the State of South Carolina,* Dec. 8 1779; Edgar and Bailey, *Biographical Directory,* 2: 412. A bill to confiscate the estates of and to banish persons who committed acts believed to demonstrate their disloyalty included the names of all three merchants. They later argued that they were persuaded by the argument that acquiescing to the demands that they sign would maintain the peace, and Loocock claimed that his name was added without his knowledge or consent while he was absent at Camden. "William Ancrum Petition," *JHR,* Jan. 30, 1783; "Petition from Mary Brown," *JHR,* Feb. 15, 1783; "Memorial from William Clarkson on Behalf of Aaron Loocock," *JHR,* Jan. 24, 1783. *SCAAG,* Aug. 23, Oct. 14, 1780; Wilmot G. DeSaussure, *The Names . . . of the Officers Who Served in the South Carolina Regiments of the Continental Establishment; [and] . . . in the Militia* (Columbia: Presbyterian Printing House for the State Society of the Cincinnati of South Carolina, 1886).

37. "Petition of Aaron Loocock and Archibald Brown to Sir Henry Clinton," May 30, 1780, Henry Clinton Papers (hereafter HCP) 102, 11, William L. Clenents Library, University of Michigan, Ann Arbor; William Ancrum to John Chesnut, Dec. 11, 1780, NGP/CL, 11: 67.

38. John Chesnut to Archibald Brown, Aug. 20, 1782, NGP/CL, 66: 80; William Ancrum to Duncan McRa, Nov. 14, 1780, NGP/CL, 11: 11.

39. Edgar and Bailey, *Biographical Directory,* 2: 412–413; *SC&AGG,* Sept. 6, Oct. 7, 1780; CBMC, Vol. K-5, Nov. 13, 1781, 13.

40. Cormwallis's opinion of Ancrum is expressed in Cornwallis to Nesbit Balfour, Sept. 3, 1780, CP 30/11/80, 2. Francis Rawdon to Charles Stedman, Sept. 3, 1780, CP 30/11/80, 2; Henry Haldane to William Ancrum, Dec. 29, 1780, CP 30/11/83, 93; William Ancrum to Duncan McRa, Nov. 14, 1780, NGP/CL, 11: 11; William Ancrum to John Chesnut, Nov. 27, 1780, NGP/CL, 11: 25.

41. Ames, "Cantey Family," 224–225, 234–235, 243–244, 246; Edgar and Bailey, *Biographical Directory,* 2: 558; Kirkland and Kennedy, *Historic Camden,* 1: 298.

42. The Rocky Mount store was apparently no longer in operation and was not listed in the properties owned by Kershaw & Co. at the time of its breakup in 1774. *SC&AGG,* July 22, 1774. Because McRa and Chesnut were "looked upon by the garrison as Enemies," British units at Camden refused to post bonds for payment with them. As a Loyalist merchant through whom the regiments could carry on business, John Adamson provided the mechanism by which regiments could do business with the partnership. Kirkland and Kennedy, *Historic Camden,* 1: 289.

43. William Ancrum to John Chesnut, Nov. 27, 1780, NGP/CL, 11: 25; Michael Egan, Memorial, South Carolina Loyalist Claims (hereafter SCLC), Vol. 54, 449, microfilm, South Carolina Department of Archives and History, Columbia. Kirkland and Kennedy, *Historic Camden,* 1: 100–101; SMD, Apr. 8, 9, 1781, in ibid, 1: 401. This regiment was formed in 1781 and was consisted of about 150 men who had previously served with James Cary, Henry Rugeley, or other Loyalist leaders whose units had dissolved. Lambert, *South Carolina Loyalists,* 220.

44. Ely Kershaw's other executors were Joseph Kershaw, William Kershaw, and William Ancrum. Ely Kershaw, Will, Book A, Aug. 1, 1780, 47, Caroline T. Moore, comp. and ed., *Abstracts of the Wills of Charleston District, South Carolina, 1783–1800, and other Wills Recorded in the District,* (Columbia, S.C.: R. L. Bryan, 1974), 7–8. Joseph Kershaw characterized his brother's affairs as being in "great confusion." Joseph Kershaw to Henry William Harrington, Sept. 25, 1781, HWHP. Thomas Wade acquired land on Lynches River as early as 1758, owned a mill on Broad River, and amassed sizable holdings there and on the Pee Dee River. Some of these lands lay adjacent to the property acquired by partners at Cheraw Hill in 1769. Wade was a vestryman for St. David's Parish and a magistrate for Cheraws District. He served as a colonel in the South Carolina militia during the Revolution and was appointed Commissary for the South State in December 1780. In this capacity Gov. John Rutledge directed him to oversee Ely Kershaw's Pee Dee plantation as a "publick concern." Gregg, *History of the Old Cheraws,* 348; Wade Holden to John Chesnut, Jan. 2, 1782, NGP/CL, 51: 50; Brent H. Holcomb, ed., *Petitions for Land from the South Carolina Council Journals* (hereafter *PL*), Vol. V (Columbia, S.C.: SCMAR, 1996–2009), 37, 68, 182, 185, 253; CLG/CS, Vol. 17, Oct. 4, 1768, 5; CBPR, Vol. H-5, 318; CPB, Vol. 11, Sept. 23, 1769, 64. Holden Wade was one of two sons of Thomas Wade: Nicholas Eveleigh vs. Hoden Wade and Thomas Wade, JRCCP, Box 141A, Item 471A.

45. William Ancrum to John Chesnut, Nov. 27, 1780, NGP/CL, 11: 25. The location of Burndale is identified in Harvey S. Teal, "Samuel Mathis—Another Look," paper presented to the Kershaw County Historical Society, Camden, S.C., October 23, 1988. SMD, Mar. 27, 28, 1781, in Kirkland and Kennedy, *Historic Camden,* 1: 401.

46. In an 1819 interview with W. Faux, Henry Rugeley's son Rowland commented that "Although [his father was] on the British side, he was thought to be an American at heart; and his extensive influence . . . was generally exerted in doing good, and procuring mercy for and from both parties." W. Faux, *Memorable Days in America: Being a Journal of a Tour to the United States* (London: W. Simkin and R. Marshall, 1823), 62; reprinted in Harvey S. Teal, ed., *Five Visitors to Kershaw District, 1806–1832,* Preserve Pamphlet 7, Kershaw County Historical Society [Camden, S.C., 1997]). Rawdon was concerned about Rugeley's behavior when he failed to retire in the face the American advance and suspected him of collusion with the enemy. Rawdon to Cornwallis, Dec. 3, Dec. 6, 1780, CP 30/11/66, 8. Considering

him a traitor, Cornwallis went so far as to imply that Rugeley had been "bought off for table money." Cornwallis to Rawdon, Dec. 3, 1780, CP 30/11/66, 7; Cornwallis to Tarleton, Dec. 4, 1780, CP 30/11/83, 13.

47. In one instance he carried $4,000 from John Chesnut in Camden to Robert Lithgow in Charleston to pay the sum due on bonds held in accounts held by several individuals and partnerships. Robert Lithgow to John Chesnut, May 9, 1778, NGP/CL, 2: 18. Following Rugeley's capture, John Chesnut covered Rugeley's debts to Mary Marshall. Mary Marshall to John Chesnut, Jan. 20, 1781, CMMP, 12/33/39.

48. Henry Rugeley to John Chesnut, Dec. 9, 1782, NGP/CL, 72: 53. Although staunch Whig, John Cook made son-in-law Henry Rugeley as one of his two executors. John Cook, Will, KCRPJ/E, Book A I, p. 256, Apt. 130/S110.

49. Kirkland and Kennedy, *Historic Camden,* 1: 439–140, 143–144; Ames, "Cantey Family," 244.

50. Rawdon to Cornwallis, July 27, 1780, CP/30/11/2, 371–372; AA, John Chesnut, Reel 22, Frame 218, File 1230; John Chesnut, SEIRC, Book Q, No. 434, 276; SEIRC, Book R, No. 45, 10; Book W, No. 387, 252.

51. Stedman, *American War,* 222–227; Buchanan, *Road to Guilford Courthouse,* 241–251; Willcox, ed., *Sir Henry Clinton's Narrative of His Campaigns,* 230–231.

52. Gordon, *South Carolina and the American Revolution,* 144–148. For discussions of Greene's strategy, see Russell F. Weigley, *The Partisan War: The South Carolina Campaign of 1780–1782* (Columbia: University of South Carolina Press, 1970), 46–47; John Morgan Dederer, "Making Bricks without Straw: Nathanael Greene's Southern Campaigns and Mao Tse-Tung's Mobile War," *Military Affairs* 47 (1983): 118–120. See also Dederer, *War in America to 1775: Before Yankee Doodle* (New York: New York University Press, 1990).

53. Johnson, *Life and Correspondence of Nathanael Greene,* 1: 314; Rawdon to Clinton, Oct. 20, 1780, CP 30/11/3, 298–299.

54. Earl of Moira to Henry Lee, June 24, 1813, in Lee, *Memoirs of the War,* 615.

55. The estimate of the situation is from Rawdon to Cornwallis, Dec. 5 1780, Ross, ed., *Correspondence of Cornwallis,* 501. Arthur McArthur to Cornwallis, Oct. 7, 1780, CP 30/11/3, 199; William Lee Davidson to Jethro Sumner, Oct. 12, 1780, JSP; George Turnbull to Rawdon, Oct. 30, 1780, CP 30/11/3, 322.

56. Rawdon to Clinton, Oct. 20, 1780, CP 30/11/3, 298–299; Rawdon to Stedman, Oct. 31, 1780, CP 30/11/7, 8; Rawdon to Clinton, Oct. 29, 1780, Ross, ed., *Correspondence of Cornwallis,* 63; Cornwallis to Balfour, Nov. 16, 1780, CP 30/11/ 82, 47; Rawdon to Cornwallis, Dec. 29, 1780, CP 30/11/4, 419; Stedman, *American War,* 319n.

57. Marquis de Malmedy to Nathanael Greene, Jan. 10, 1781, Conrad, ed., *PNG,* 7: 92; "Henry Felder, Petition for Relief for Family losses in the Revolution," *JHR,* Feb. 18, 1785. The meal stored at the Congarees was mentioned in Cornwallis to Rawdon, Jan. 9, 1781, CP 30/11/84, 44. For the importance of these provisions and their capture by Sumter's forces the following month, see Thomas Wade to Nathanael Greene, Feb. 25, 1781, Conrad, ed., *PNG,* 7: 349.

58. Nathanael Greene to John Marshall, Dec. 30, 1780, Conrad, ed., *PNG,* 7: 26.

59. The Americans planned to attack the Camden mill in an effort to starve the garrison into submission: Greene to Thomas Sumter, Feb. 21, 1781, Conrad, ed., *PNG,* 7: 28. The Rev. James Jenkins, an early Methodist circuit preacher in Camden, reported the attempt to burn the mill. J. Jenkins, *Experience, Labours, and Sufferings of Rev. James Jenkins of the South Carolina Conference* (Columbia, S.C.: By the Author, 1842), quoted in Kirkland and Kennedy, *Historic Camden,* 1: 252–253.

60. William R. Davie to Nathanael Greene, Apr. 11, 1781, Conrad, ed., *PNG,* 8: 84; Rawdon to Cornwallis, May 2, 1781, CP 30/11/6, 21.

61. Nathanael Greene to Continental Congress, Apr. 22, 1781, NGP/PCC, M 247, R 175, I 155, Vol. 2, 41–42. Guilford Dudley, a lieutenant colonel in a North Carolina militia regiment, recalled that upon their arrival, "Logtown [was] then in flames, and the houses crumbling down, the enemy having, upon our approach, . . . applied the torch to that small appendage to the village of Camden." Guilford Dudley, RWPBLWAF, R 254, Application W-8682.

62. Gordon, *South Carolina and the American Revolution,* 148–151. Archaeological investigations have revealed not only the sites of the fortifications at Fort Watson and Fort Motte but also detailed evidence of the battles fought at each of these locations. Leland G. Ferguson, "An Archaeological-Historical Analysis of Fort Watson: December 1780–April 1781," in *Research Strategies in Historical Archaeology,* ed. Stanley South (New York: Academic Press, 1977), 41–71; Steven D. Smith, James B. Legg, Tamara S. Wilson, and Jonathan Leader, *"Obstinate and Strong": The History and Archaeology of the Siege of Fort Motte* (Columbia: South Carolina Institute of Archaeology and Anthropology, 2007).

63. Weigley, *Partisan War,* 49–52.

64. Rawdon to Cornwallis, May 24, 1781, CP 30/11/6, 108; *PG,* June 20, 1781.

65. Gordon, *South Carolina and the American Revolution,* 151–158; Stedman, *American War,* 372–376. Discussions of the battles at Ninety Six have accompanied the extensive archaeological research conducted to investigate the fortifications. These have uncovered detailed evidence of the fortifications as well as the siegeworks associated with Greene's attack. For the results of these efforts, see Stanley South, "Exploratory Archaeology at Holmes' Fort, the Blockhouse, and Jail Redoubt at Ninety Six," *Conference on Historic Site Archaeology Papers 1970* 5 (1971): 35–50; South, *Ninety Six Fortification Search: Ninety Six National Historic Site,* Research Manuscript Series 232 (Columbia: University of South Carolina Institute of Archaeology and Anthropology, 2006); Stephanie L. Holschlag and Michael J. Rodeffer, *Ninety Six: Siegeworks Opposite Star Redoubt* (Ninety Six, S.C.: Ninety Six Historic Site, 1976).

66. Nathanael Greene to Joseph Reed, May 4, 1781, Conrad, ed., *PNG,* 8: 201.

67. Rawdon to Cornwallis, May 24, 1781, in R. W. Gibbes, ed., *Documentary History of the American Revolution,* Vol. 3 (Columbia, S.C.: Banner Steam Power Press, 1852), 79.

68. Benjamin Ingraham, Excerpt from the Diary of Benjamin Ingraham, Sergeant in the King's American Regiment, Historic Camden Foundation, Camden, S.C.; Nathanael Greene to Samuel Huntington, May 14, 1781, NGL/PCC, R 175, I 155, Vol. 2, 59.

69. Joseph Lee Boyle, ed., "The Revolutionary War Diaries of Captain Walter Finney," *South Carolina Historical Magazine* 98 (1997): 134.

70. Stedman, *American War,* 362; Nathaniel Pendleton to Francis Marion, May 10, 1781, in Gibbes, *Documentary History,* 3: 69.

71. These were largely casualties from the recent engagement at Hobkirk's Hill. Rawdon left British wounded who could not be moved, together with Continental prisoners to be used for exchange. Rawdon to Cornwallis, May 14, 1781, in Gibbes, *Documentary History,* 79; Nathanael Greene to Samuel Huntington, May 14, 1781, NGP/PCC, R 175, I 155, Vol. 2, 59.

72. James Kershaw, Diary, Feb. 12, 1793, JKP. Deeds transferring the property as late as 1801 referred to the property as that "where the Brewhouse now stands." Lancaster County, Records of the Clerk of Court, Conveyances (LCRCC/C), Book B, May 6, 1786, 10.

73. Samuel Mathis Plantation Journal, May 23, 1781, SMP.

74. Kenneth E. Lewis, "'Little Better Than a Heap of Rubbish': History. Legend, and the Archaeological Record at Camden," *South Carolina Historical Magazine* 114 (2013): 242–246; Lewis, *Camden: A Frontier Town,* 140–143; Lewis, "Archaeological Investigations in Southwestern Camden," 169–177; Lewis, *Camden: Historical Archaeology,* 72–74, 118–130.

75. Strickland, "Camden Revolutionary War Fortifications," 55–71; Kenneth E. Lewis, "The Camden Jail and Market Site: A Report on Preliminary Investigations," *South Carolina Institute of Archaeology and Anthropology, Notebook* 16 (1984): 31.

76. Nathanael Greene to Samuel Huntington, May 14, 1781, NGL/PCC, R 175, I 155, Vol. 2, 59; Johnson, *Correspondence of Nathanael Greene,* 2, 118; Nathanael Greene to John Marshall, and Nathanael Greene to Arthur Brown Ross, May 11, 1781, in Conrad, ed., *PNG,* 8: 238–239; William Seymour, "A Journal of the Southern Expedition, 1780–1783, by William Seymour, Sergeant-Major of the Delaware Regiment," *Pennsylvania Magazine of History and Biography* 7 (1883): 304. Arthur Brown Ross was a planter who settled on the west side of the Wateree River in 1771. MB, Vol. 10, Apr. 3, 1771, 368; CPB, Vol. 20, Aug. 13, 1775, 199.

77. Stedman, *American War*, 195–196; Henry William Harrington to Horatio Gates, Sept. 16, 1780, NGP/PCC, M247, R 85, I 71, Vol. 1, 429.

78. Rawdon to Cornwallis, May 24, 1781, in Gibbes, *Documentary History*, 3: 69, 79.

79. Thomas Hopper, Memorial, SCLC, Vol. 36, 303; Michael Egan, Memorial, SCLC, Vol. 54, 449; Kirkland and Kennedy, *Historic Camden*, 1: 286, 289; DMC/SP, 17vv, 229–230; Lambert, "A Loyalist Odyssey," 171; Bradford L. Rauschenberg, "John Bartlam, Who Established 'New Pottworks in South Carolina' and Became the First Successful Creamware Potter in America," *Journal of Early Southern Decorative Arts* 17, no. 2 (1991): 23; Jane Gibbes, Memorial, SCLC, Vol. 52, 365; Christopher Moore, *The Loyalists: Revolution, Exile, Settlement* (Toronto: McClelland & Stuart, 1994), 135.

80. Greene to President of Continental Congress, PCC, M 247, R 175, I 155, Vol. 2, 241; *PG*, Sept. 26, 1781; Edward Carrington to Nathanael Greene, July 15, 1781, John Hamilton to Nathanael Greene, Aug. 31, Sept. 10, 1781; Peter Horry to Nathanael Greene, Sept. 28, 1781, Nathaniel Pendleton to Nathanael Greene, Nov. 24, 1782, Conrad, ed., *PNG*, 9: 12, 273, 312, 406, 682.

81. Quartermaster General's Department for the Southern Army, Pay for Services, 1783, PCC, M 247, R 175, I 155, Vol. 2, 615–616. Among the local residents supplying livestock for the use of Continental troops at Camden were Isaac Ross, SEIRC, Book Y, No. 495, 32; Abraham Belton, AA, Reel 8, Frame 110, File 432A; Christian Kinesler, SEIRC, Book Y, No. 375, 68; Burwell Boykin, AA, Reel 12, Frame 319, File 679; Samuel Mathis, SEIRC, Book Y, No. 495, 83; and Jesse Perry, AA, Reel 117, Frame 226, File 5869. Samuel Mathis served as Green's quartermaster at Camden from 1781 to 1783. Nathaniel Pendleton to Nathanael Greene, Nov. 22, 1781, Conrad, ed., *PNG*, 9: 611–612. For reference to troop movements through Camden, see Nathanael Greene to Thomas Sumter, July 3, 1781, Nathanael Greene to John Armstrong, July 4 and July 8, 1781; Nathanael Greene to Henry Lee, Aug. 22, 1781; Nathaniel Pendleton to Nathanael Greene, Nov. 24, 1781; Nathanael Greene to William Henderson, Aug. 24, 1781; all in Conrad, ed., *PNG*, 8: 89, 506; 9: 23, 222–223, 484, 622; *PG*, Aug. 15, 1781; William Henry Egle, ed., "Journal of Lieut. William McDowell, of the First Penna. Regiment, in the Southern Campaign, 1781–1782," *Pennsylvania Archives*, 2nd ser., 15 (1893): 309–310; Boyle, ed., "Diaries of Captain Walter Finney," 133; James Chitwood, RWPBLWAF, R 183, Application S-1751.

82. Thomas Charleton to Nathanael Greene, Aug. 20, 1781; Conrad, ed., *PNG*, 9: 213; Sam B. Smith and Harriett Chapell Owsley, eds., *The Papers of Andrew Jackson, Vol. 1: 1770–1803* (hereafter *AJP*) (Knoxville: University of Tennessee Press, 1980), 7.

83. Rawdon to Greene, Apr. 26 1781, PDC, #3406; Rawdon to Cornwallis, May 24, 1781, CP 30/11/6, 108; Otho H. Williams to Nathanael Greene, June 1, 1781, Conrad, ed. *PNG*, 8: 439.

84. Otho Williams to Francis Smith, June 22, 1781, Conrad, ed., *PNG*, 8: 439; John Armstrong to Nathanael Greene, July 10, 1781, *PNG*, 8: 504; Richard Bearden, RWPBLWAF, R 68, Application. Nathaniel Greene to President of the Continental Congress, July 17, 1781, NGL/PCC, M 247, R 175, I 155, Vol. 2, 195; Dr. David Oliphant, who had become deputy director of the Medical Department of the Southern Army in May, appointed Charlton, but his assistant director, Robert Johnson, questioned Charlton's loyalty, and these charges led to Charlton's dismissal. Although apparently threatened with court-martial, Charlton successfully refuted the accusations in letters to Oliphant and Greene, and action against him proceeded no farther. Samuel Huntington to President of Continental Congress, May 24, 1781; Waring, *History of Medicine*, 198–199, Hamer et al., eds., *HLP*, 10: 285n.

85. Greene established a flying hospital to accompany the army in August and directed the deputy quartermaster at Camden to arrange wagon transportation. He also ordered that those "sick and unable to march" remain at Camden. To assist the limited medical staff, he requested that "a sufficient number of women," who presumably accompanied the army, and "particularly those with children be left as nurses." General Greene's Orders, Aug. 24, 1781, Conrad, ed., *PNG*, 9: 233. Following the battle of Eutaw Springs, a flying hospital caring for a large number of wounded existed near McCord's Ferry on the road between the battlefield and Camden. Nathaniel Pendleton to Nathanael Greene, Sept. 19, 1781, Conrad, ed., *PNG*, 9: 377. Conditions at the Camden hospital, which included shortages of medicines, food, clothing, and other supplies, were exacerbated by sickness among the staff, which limited their ability to treat patients. Nathanael Greene to Thomas McKain, Oct, 25, 1781, PCC, M 247, R 175,

I 155, Vol. 2, 36363–36364; Samuel Vickers to Nathanael Greene, Nov. 20, 1781, Conrad, ed., *PNG,* 9: 595. Waring, *History of Medicine,* 97, 104–107. The Camden hospital continued to rely on local suppliers for meat as indicated by indents for beef and supplied in 1781. Samuel Mathis, SEIRC, Book D, No. 35, 139; John Bradley, SEIRC, Book D, No. 176,164; James Bettie, AA, Reel 8, Frame 588, File 473; Abraham Galloway, SEIRC, Book N, No. 212, 283.

86. Weigley, *Partisan War,* 12–13.

87. The Assembly's motivation for enacting this legislation undoubtedly grew from the desire to punish those who had recently sided with the enemy, a feeling shared with their counterparts in other states. Historians have pointed out, however, that their action in passing the Confiscation Act also had the effect of averting potential violence against Loyalists by vengeful Whigs, particularly those in the backcountry, where the civil conflict had often become vicious and personal. By choosing to make an example of prominent individuals easily identified by their presence on documents such as congratulatory proclamations, the Assembly avoided the perception of leniency but still left open the door to relief through individual acts of clemency. Robert M. Weir, "'The Violent Spirit,' the Reestablishment of Order, and the Continuity of Leadership in Post-Revolutionary South Carolina," in *An Uncivil War: The Southern Backcountry during the American Revolution,* ed. Ronald Hoffman et al. (Charlottesville: University Press of Virginia for the United States Capital Historical Society, 1985), 71–74, 83–84, 95–97; Rachel N. Klein, *Unification of a Slave State: The Rise of the Planter Class in the South Carolina Backcountry, 1760–1808* (Chapel Hill: University of North Carolina Press for the Institute of Early American History and Culture, 1990), 120–122.

88. Lambert, *South Carolina Loyalists,* 237–240. The "Act for Disposing of Certain Estates, and Banishing Certain Persons, Therein Mentioned" became law on Feb. 26, 1782. Cooper and McCord, eds., *Statutes,* Vol. 4, Pt. 2, No. 1153, 1782. The names of those affected were published a month later in the *Royal Gazette* (hereafter *RG*), [Charleston, S.C.], Mar. 20, 1782.

89. Lambert, *South Carolina Loyalists,* 240; Moultrie, *Memoirs of the American Revolution,* 2, 411–412; Alfred E. Jones, ed., "The Journal of Alexander Chesney, a South Carolina Loyalist in the Revolution and After," *Ohio State University Bulletin* 26, no. 4 (1921): 114; Clark, ed., *Loyalists of the Southern Campaign,* 1: 113; Kirkland and Kennedy, *Historic Camden,* 1: 300–301; Klein, *Unification of a Slave State,* 98–99.

90. Lambert, *South Carolina Loyalists,* 286–287.

91. JBKNE, Aug. 23, 31, 1781.

92. Address to "To the Brave Genl New King & the Rest of the Headmen, Warriors of the Catawba Nation," [1781], JBKP.

93. Diary of the Congregation in Salem, Nov. 29, Dec. 6, 1781, Adelaide L. Fries, Kenneth G. Hamilton, Douglas L. Rights, and Minnie J. Smith, eds., *Records of the Moravians in North Carolina* (hereafter *RMNC*), Vol. 4 (Raleigh: North Carolina Historical Commission, 1922–1969), 1705, 1737. The supplies included flour, butter, iron pots, and a Dutch oven, all of which were shipped to Jacksonborough via Camden. Joseph Kershaw, AA, Reel 83, Frame 152, File 4259.

94. Edgar and Bailey, eds., *Biographical Directory,* 2: 376; Kirkland and Kennedy, *Historic Camden,* 1: 285–286; A. S. Salley, ed., *Journal of the Senate of South Carolina* (hereafter *JS*), *January 8, 1782–February 26, 1782* (Columbia: The State Co. for the South Carolina Historical Commission, 1941), Feb. 16, 1782.

95. John Tobler, *The Charlestown Directory for 1782* (Charleston, S.C.: R. Wells & Son, 1782; reprint ed., Charleston, S.C.: Historical Commission of Charleston, 1951); *RG,* Apr. 21, 1781; Apr. 3, 1782; William Ancrum, William Greenwood, and John Hopton to James Simpson, Jan. 4, 1783, HCP, 197, 43; Jones, ed., "Journal of Alexander Chesney," 119–120; "Petition to the House of Representatives from William Ancrum," *JHR,* Jan. 30, 1783.

96. *SC&AGG,* Oct. 7, 1780; "Memorial from William Clarkson in Behalf of William Ancrum," *JHR,* Jan. 24, Feb. 17, 1783; "Memorial on Behalf of Aaron Loocock," *JHR,* Jan. 24, 1783; "Petition from Aaron Loocock Praying to be Liberated from His Confinement in the Provost," May 25, 1783, Adele Stanton Edwards, ed., *Journals of the Privy Council, 1783–1789* (hereafter *JPrC*) (Columbia: University of South Carolina Press, 1971), 62; Lambert, *South Carolina Loyalists,* 289–290.

97. Archibald Brown to John Chesnut, Oct. 29, 1782, NGP/CL, 40: 49; "Petition from Mary Brown on Behalf of Her Husband Archibald Brown," *JHR,* Feb. 15, 1783.

98. Bill to Relieve from the Pains and Penalties of an Act Entitled, "An Act for Disposing of Certain Estates and Banishing Certain Persons Therein Mentioned, but to be Amerced of Each of them Twelve Per Cent," *JHR,* Mar. 14, 1784.

99. The list of those included in the Amercement Act appeared in *JHR,* Mar. 14, 1784, and SCG, Mar. 27, 1784. John Deas was a wealthy and powerful merchant who served as an attorney for several petitioners who had been forced to leave South Carolina. A prominent resident of Charleston during the war, Deas was included on the Amercement Act, but favorable testimony led to his relief. Lothrop Withingham, ed., "South Carolina Gleanings in England," *South Carolina Historical Magazine* 8 (1907): 211–216; Stuart O. Strumpf, "South Carolina Importers of General Merchandise, 1735–1765," *South Carolina Historical Magazine* 84 (1983): 7; Lambert, *South Carolina Loyalists,* 287, 288, 295. Possessing alliances seems to have been an important factor in winning the remission of penalties under the Confiscation and Amercement Acts, and those who could find support generally escaped confiscation. Edward Rutledge and other legislators worked hard to keep their friends and relatives off the list. Weir, "The Violent Spirit," 83–84.

100. Bailey et al., *Biographical Directory,* 2: 305; William Ancrum Petitions for exemption from amercement, *JHR,* Mar. 1, 1785; Feb. 18, 1786; William Ancrum, Indents and awards, SEIRC Book Y, No. 518, 86; Book Z, No. 35, 236; Jan. 25, 1788; Feb. 28, 1788; Mar. 13, 1789; SEIRC, Book Z, 311; SEIRC. Book Z, Nos. 593, 594, 595, 311–312; William Ancrum, Discount of Amercement, *JHR,* Jan. 19, 1790; James Kershaw Diary, Jan. 6, 1794, James Kershaw Papers (hereafter JKP), South Caroliniana Library, University of South Carolina; Kirkland and Kennedy, *Historic Camden,* 1: 344.

101. Henry A. M. Smith, "The Baronies of South Carolina, XVI, Quenby and the Eastern Branch of Cooper River," *South Carolina Historical Magazine* 18 (1917): 24–26; Smith, "The Ashley River: Its Seats and Settlements," *South Carolina Historical Magazine* 19 (1919): 36. His status is reflected by his membership in the prestigious St. Thomas Hunting Club. J. H. Easterby, "The St. Thomas Hunting Club,"*South Carolina Historical Magazine* 46 (1945): 125, 210.

102. Edgar and Bailey, eds., *Biographical Directory,* 2: 412; Kirkland and Kennedy, *Historic Camden,* 2: 262; Moore, comp. and ed., *Abstracts of the Wills of Charleston District,* 307.

103. Ellen Heyward Jervey, "Items from a South Carolina Almanac [1793]," *South Carolina Historical Magazine* 32 (1931): 75; *JHR,* Feb. 7, 1786; Edgar and Bailey, eds., *Biographical Directory,* 2: 412–413; Edwards, ed., *JPrC,* Apr. 19, 1787, 193.

104. Henry Rugeley to Father and Mother, Mar. 18, 1781, X311.108; William Rugeley to Mother, Mar. 31, 1782, X311.112; Henry Rugeley to William Rugeley to Matthew Rugeley, Dec. 10, 1782, X311.116; Henry Rugeley to Matthew Rugeley, Oct. 10, 1783, X311.120; Frances Rugeley to William Rugeley, June 9, 1785, X311.129, all in Helen Hoskins Rugeley (compiler), *Rugeley Papers: Blue-Blooded Brits in Reduced Circumstances* (Austin, Tex.: By the Author, 1997), 34, 36, 38, 41, 47; Henry Rugeley to John Chesnut, Apr. 21, 1782, NGP/CL, 58: 53. Lord Montagu, the former royal governor, was sent to Charleston with a warrant to raise a unit composed of Continental prisoners of war confined in the prison ships there. In exchange for their freedom, the Americans agreed to join the Duke of Cumberland's Regiment in the West Indies with the stipulation that they would never have to serve against their own countrymen. Lambert, *South Carolina Loyalists,* 203–204; Carl P. Borick, *Relieve Us of This Burthen: American Prisoners of War in the Revolutionary South, 1780–1782* (Columbia: University of South Carolina Press, 2012). Henry Rugeley was commissioned Feb. 19, 1781, Dates of Commissions by General Dalling, Register of Officers in the Right Honorable Lord Montagu's Corps, Feb. 25, 1781, Clark, *Loyalists in the Southern Campaign,* 1: 478–479. Rugeley joined more than 1,200 Loyalists and their 2,600 slaves who sailed on a fleet of twenty vessels for Jamaica. They were part of a larger armada concentrated in Charleston to remove British, German, and provincial military personnel as well as South Carolina residents to St. Lucia, Jamaica, St. Augustine, New York, and Nova Scotia in the fall of 1782. Lambert, *South Carolina Loyalists,* 254–256.

105. Henry Rugeley to Matthew Rugeley, July 6, 1784, X311.124, in Rugeley, ed., *Rugeley Papers,* 43.

106. Although no longer possessing the extraordinary powers he had been accorded as governor during the occupation, Rutledge remained active politically. He continued to serve in the legislature as the representative from St. Andrews Parish in the Fourth and Fifth General Assemblies (1782–1784) and was a delegate to the Constitutional Convention (1782–1783). Edgar and Bailey, eds., *Biographical Directory,* 2: 579

107. Henry Rugeley married Elizabeth Cook on Nov. 28, 1782, Henry Rugeley to Matthew Rugeley, Dec. 10, 1782, X311.116, Rugeley, ed., *Rugeley Papers,* 38. Henry Rugeley to John Chesnut, Apr. 21, 1782, NGP/CL, 58: 53; Henry Rugeley to John Chesnut, Sept. 1782, NGP/CL, 68: 73; Henry Rugeley to John Chesnut, Oct. 9, 1782, NGP/CL, 69: 44; Henry Rugeley to John Chesnut, Dec. 9, 1782, NGP/CL, 72: 53; Kirkland and Kennedy, *Historic Camden,* 1: 77, 99; Kirkland and Kennedy, *Historic Camden,* 2: 260; Salley, ed., *JS,* Feb. 16, 1782.

108. The quotes are from Rowland Rugeley in 1819, in Faux, *Memorable Days in America,* 62.

109. Petition from Henry Rugeley, *JHR,* Jan. 30, 1783; *SCG,* March 27, 1784; Henry Rugeley to Mother, Oct. 2, 1784, X311.127, Rugeley, ed., *Rugeley Papers,* 45; Henry Rugeley to John Chesnut, Oct. 9, 1782, NGP/CL, 69: 44.

"Scoofs" is, of course, a variation of "scoffelite," the term Whigs originally employed to identify the followers of Joseph Coffel, the former Moderator who later emerged as a British supporter in the western backcountry. It was also used to designate those backcountry Tories who fled to East Florida after 1775. By the close of the Revolutionary War, "scoffelite" had become a pejorative term by which to designate and malign Loyalists in general. Klein, *Unification of a Slave State,* 95–96, 99–100.

110. Edward M. Boykin to Lyman Draper, Oct. 7, 1872, DMC/SP, 17vv, 229; CLG/CS, Vol. 16, July 15, 1768, 437; Vol. 23, Jan. 10, 1771, 30; Vol. 25, May 15, 1772, 443; Vol. 25, May 21, 1772, 495; Vol. 27, Dec. 1, 1772, 432; John Witherspoon to John Adamson, CBPR, P-4, Mar. 9, 1775, 486. Adamson's tract included the lands originally granted to Daniel Bready, John Hudson, and Michael Branham. The property was known as "The Adamson Place" or "The Retreat." Kirkland and Kennedy, *Historic Camden,* 1: 290, 130.

111. Clark, *Loyalists in the Southern Campaign,* 1: 147; Edgar, *Partisans and Redcoats,* 58–59, 79–86; John Bratton to Edward M. Boykin, Apr. 18, 1876, quoted in Kirkland and Kennedy, *Historic Camden,* 1: 281–284; Statement of Rev. Samuel H. Hay, Sept. 30, 1872, DMC/SP 17 w 231. In addition to Lt. John Adamson of the Camden Loyalist militia, a Lt. William Adamson of the New York Volunteers accompanied Capt. Huck's command. Badly wounded, William Adamson died later that year at Camden. John Adamson, although badly bruised, survived. Contemporary sources point to the New York Adamson as the defender of Martha Bratton, but her son William Bratton identified him as the Camden militiaman. Michael C. Scoggins, "Will the Real Captain Adamson Please Stand Up?," *York County Magazine,* August 2008. See also Scoggins, *The Day It Rained Militia: Huck's Defeat and the Revolution in the South Carolina Backcountry, May–July, 1780* (Charleston, S.C.: History Press, 2005), Ch. 6.

112. Cornwallis to Rawdon, July 26, 1780, CP 30/11/78, 48; Kirkland and Kennedy, *Historic Camden,* 1: 288–289.

113. "Petitions from John Adamson and a Number of Inhabitants," *JHR,* Jan. 28, 1783; Edward M. Boykin to Lyman Draper, Oct. 7, 1872, DMC/SP, 17vv, 229; Kirkland and Kennedy, *Historic Camden,* 1: 286–287.

114. Clark, ed., *Loyalists in the Southern Campaign,* 1: 149; Kirkland and Kennedy, *Historic Camden,* 1: 86, 286, 288, 289; *JHR,* Feb. 23, 1784; Mar. 14, 1784.

115. Cornwallis vouched for Cary's loyalty but attributed his difficulties to his reluctance to assume command and the unreliability of his militiamen. He recognized that they were "guilty of plundering, as the sole object of the militia is to break up, as they call it, their neighbours of the opposite party." Cornwallis to Balfour, Sept. 3, 1780, CP 30/11/80, 1–4.

116. Joshua Dinkins's family was known to have "suffered at Cary's hands." Lyman Draper, Notes of Interview with M. S. Taylor, 1871, DMC/SP, 16vv, 26–27. Clark, *Loyalists in the Southern Campaign,* 1: 492–497, 500; Lambert, "A Loyalist Odyssey," 169–172.

117. CBPR, Vol. W-5, June 30, 1783, 188; Vol. M-5, 155, July 3, 1783, 29; Vol. V-3, Oct. 11, 1785, 93. For the Carys' travels and travails, see Lambert, "Loyalist Odyssey," 173–181.

118. A list of confiscated property is included in Appendix 3, Losses of American Loyalists, GOD, 1784–1789; Edward Countryman, *The American Revolution* (New York: Hill and Wang, 1985), 157. Details of Charles and George Ogilvie's suits may be found in William Cumine to Edward Penman, Sept. 12, 1784, William Cumine to Thomas Bee, June 13, 1784, CMMP, 12/33/28, and GOD. For their claims see Peter Wilson Coldham, ed., *American Loyalist Claims, Vol. 1, Abstracted from the Public Record Office, Audit Office Series 13, Bundles 1–35 & 37* (Washington, D.C.: National Genaeological Society, 1980), 201–202, 371. Charles Ogilvie, "Petition," *JHR*, Jan. 30, 1783; "Report on Petition," *JHR*, Mar. 8, 1783.

119. George Ogilvie of Auchires, His Family-Losses in America, His Removal to Aberdeen, GOD. H. F. Waters, "South Carolina Gleanings in England," *South Carolina Historical Magazine* 6 (1905): 118; Charles Ogilvie, St. Mary le Bone, 8 Feb., 1788, Middlesex Coroners, "Coroner's Inquests into Suspicious Deaths" (hereafter CO/IC), 1st May 1781–31st Dec. 1799, http://www.londonlives.org/browse.jsp?id+LMCOIC65101_n2413-1&div'LMCOIC6510.

120. Kirkland and Kennedy, *Historic Camden,* 1: 65; 97–98; 129; Clark, ed., *Loyalists in the Southern Campaign,* 1: 113; Jones, ed., "Journal of Alexander Chesney," 114; Lambert, *South Carolina Loyalists,* 220; SCLC, Vol. 54, 449.

121. Kirkland and Kennedy, *Historic Camden,* 1: 283, 289; PGA, Item 8, Nov. 10, 1795; Item 25, Nov. 29, 1804; Committee Reports, Legislative Papers, 1782–1866 (hereafter CR), S165005, Item 104, Dec. 2, 1795, South Carolina Department of Archives and History, Columbia.

122. Clark, ed., *Loyalists in the Southern Campaign,* 1: 111, 114, 127, 144; SCLC, Vol. 54, 449; Vol. 56, 303–309.

123. Edward M. Boykin to Lyman Draper, Oct. 7, 1872, DMC/SP, 17vv, 231; Lambert, *South Carolina Loyalists,* 299–300.

124. Francis Tidwell served initially as a lieutenant in Capt. John Land's company in Col. Richard Richardson's militia regiment in 1778, but he later changed sides to become a captain in the Fairfield Regiment of Loyalist militia. William T. Graves, "A Return of Captain John Land's Company, Dec. 1778, Who Marched the 7th Inst. Under the Command of Major Joseph Brown and Now in Camp Near Monck's Corner, Dec'r. 1778," Southern Campaign American Revolution Pension Statements and Rosters, http:www.revwarapps.org/b11.pdf, 2009; J. D. Lewis, "The American Revolution in South Carolina," http://www.Carolina.com/SC/Revolution/patriots_sc_capt_francis_tidwell. html, 2009. His murder was reported in *RG,* Apr. 13, 1782. Oral tradition arising from the incident at Cary's Fort described Dinkins as "a chunky, plucky little man whose family had suffered at Cary's hands, [who chased] Cary around a tree at the fort, with his gun cocked to get a shot at the Tory leader, when Col. Thomas Taylor came up and ordered him to desist." Notes Taken on a Trip of 1871 by Lyman Draper, Interview with Maj. M. S. Taylor of DeSoto Parish, La., DMC/SP, 16vv, 26–27. Although imprisoned, Samuel Dinkins was apparently moving freely within Camden by the spring of 1781. He was also one of the signers of the petition to relieve John Adamson from penalty under the Confiscation Act. Kirkland and Kennedy, *Historic Camden,* 1: 141, 287; Plantation Journal, Mar. 28, 1781, SMP. For Willis Whitaker's service in the militia, see Kirkland and Kennedy, *Historic Camden,* 1: 396. The other signers of the petition were Willis's uncle William Whitiker, John McKinnie, Roger Gibson, John King, Narbeth Carter, Charles Lewis, and Arthur Brown Ross. Willis Whitaker was elected to two terms in the state legislature, and Brown was appointed a justice of the county court: Kirkland and Kennedy, *Historic Camden,* 1: 342, 396–397, Joan A. Inabinet and L. Glen Inabinet, *A History of Kershaw County, South Carolina* (Columbia: University of South Carolina Press, 2011), 88, 104; Kirkland and Kennedy, *Historic Camden,* 2: 44, 402.

125. As early as 1778 William Ancrum complained to the merchants Panton, Forbes & Co. in Pensacola that three Negroes had been stolen from his plantation in the Wateree Valley. He suspected the McGirts, who had been active in the area: WAALB, May 9, 1778. McGirt's postwar activities in Spanish East Florida made him perhaps the most notorious outlaw in the province. Captured in 1785, he, along with his family, was released to the Bahamas the following year. He returned in 1788, was captured and again released, and moved north to the St. Mary's River area. Wanted by authorities in both Florida and Georgia, McGirt was among the captives taken by American troops in engaged in suppressing a

border rebellion in 1795. Released for a third time, he vanished into the Indian country. Late in life he returned to South Carolina in ill health and spent the remainder of his life there. Helen Hornbeck Tanner, *Zespedes in East Florida, 1784–1790* (Coral Gables, Fla.: University of Miami Press, 1963; reprint ed., Jacksonville: University of North Florida Press, 1989), 38, 45, 46, 225; Kirkland and Kennedy, *Historic Camden,* 1: 104, 115, 123–124, 299–300, 303–304; Wilbur H. Siebert, *Loyalists in East Florida, 1774–1785,* Vol. 2 (Deland: Florida State Historical Society, 1929), 328–330; *SCG,* July 7, 1799, Apr. 3, 1784,

126. Kirkland and Kennedy, *Historic Camden,* 1: 396–397; Ames, "Cantey Family," 126–127, 245–247; N. Louise Bailey, Mary L. Morgan, and Carolyn R. Taylor, eds., *Biographical Directory of the South Carolina Senate,* Vol. 1 (Columbia: University of South Carolina Press, 1986), 270–271.

127. Kirkland and Kennedy, *Historic Camden,* 1: 301–302, 304–305; Boykin, *History of the Boykin Family,* 19.

Chapter 11. "To Promote and Enjoy the Blessings of Peace"

1. Edward M. Boykin, *History of the Boykin Family, from Their First Settlement in Virginia 1685, and in South Carolina, Georgia, and Alabama, to the Present Time* (Camden, S.C.: Colin MacRae, 1876), 7.

2. William Boykin, Samuel's father, purchased two tracts totaling four hundred acres in Fredericksburg Township in the spring of 1756. Ann Sinnixon to William Boykin, CBPR, Vol. RR, Mar. 26, 1756, 375; Thomas Moon and Mary Moon to William Boykin, CBPR, Vol. RR, May 21 1756, 369. William Boykin died in early 1760, as indicated by his will dated Feb. 4 and proved the following day. Caroline T. Moore, comp. and ed., *Abstracts of the Wills of the State of South Carolina, 1760–1784,* Vol. 1 (Columbia, S.C.: R. L. Bryan, 1964–1969), 269. As the eldest male heir, he presumably assumed management of the family upon reaching his maturity. Thomas J. Kirkland and Robert M. Kennedy, *Historic Camden, Vol. 1: Colonial and Revolutionary* (Columbia, S.C.: The State Co., 1905), 346. By the time of the Revolution, he had added several tracts to his landholdings and acquired at least 664 slaves. CBPR, Vol. C-4, Aug. 12, 1772, 67; Vol. R-5, Aug. 29, 1778, 211; Maxwell Brown, *The South Carolina Regulators* (Cambridge, M: Belknap Press of Harvard University Press, 1963), 145. His rising status in backcountry society was reflected in his membership in the Committee of the Continental Association from Saxe Gotha District. Kirkland and Kennedy, *Historic Camden,* 1: 110, 124. He was appointed by the Provincial Congress to protect debtors in that district and became tax collector for Saxe Gotha and parts adjacent in 1778. *SCG,* Jan. 30, 1775; *SC&AGG,* Apr. 1778. For Boykin's activities as a Regulator, see Boykin, *History of the Boykin Family,* 7–9, and Brown, *South Carolina Regulators,* 347. During the Revolution he was commissioned a captain in the militia and commanded the company of Catawba Indians. Kirkland and Kennedy, *Historic Camden,* 1: 118–119; Wilmot G. DeSaussure, *The Names . . . of the Officers Who Served in the South Carolina Regiments of the Continental Establishment; [and] . . . in the Militia* (Columbia: Presbyterian Printing House for the State Society of the Cincinnati of South Carolina, 1886). Samuel Boykin was appointed a justice of the peace for Camden District in 1776 and for Claremont County (which encompassed the region southeast of Camden from 1785 to 1791) in 1787. *SC&AGG,* May 8, 1776; *JHR,* May 28, 1787. In addition to managing his own properties, he also superintended William Ancrum's Redbank plantation in 1780. William Ancrum to John Chesnut, Nov. 27, 1780, NGP/CL, 11: 25. Following the war, he entered into the mercantile partnership of Chesnut, Boykin & Co.: JRCCP, Box 110B, Item 10A, Feb. 20, 1784, South Carolina Department of Archives and History, Columbia. In 1788 Samuel Boykin was elected a delegate to the state convention held for the purpose of ratifying the federal constitution. Brown, *South Carolina Regulators,* 121. In 1791 he was appointed one of three county court judges for the newly formed Kershaw County, *JHR,* Feb. 18, 1791, and in May he was a member of the committee formed to welcome President George Washington to Camden during his Southern Tour. Kirkland and Kennedy, *Historic Camden,* 1: 309, 327.

3. The original account of Samuel Boykin's final adventure and demise is from Boykin, *History of the Boykin Family,* 10. His death was reported in the [Charleston] *City Gazette & Daily Advertiser* on Jan. 9, 1792.

4. Nathaniel Greene to Gen. Robert Howe, Dec. 29, 1780, "Revolutionary War Letters," *South Carolina Historical Magazine* 38 (1937): 76–77.

5. Keith Krawczynski, ed., "William Drayton's Journal of a 1784 Tour of the South Carolina Backcountry," *South Carolina Historical Magazine* 97 (1996): 203.

6. Joseph Kershaw to Nathaniel Greene, Dec. 11, 1782, NGP/CL, 72: 61.

7. David Ramsey, *The History of the Revolution of South Carolina from a British Province to an Independent State.* 2 vols. (Trenton, N.J.: Isaac Collins, 1785), Vol. 2, 371–372. The impact of the recent war on the tenuous nature of the long-term credit on which South Carolina's economy rested was noted by contemporary observers such as Timothy Ford: "Diary of Timothy Ford, 1785–1786, with Notes by Joseph W. Barnwell," *South Carolina Historical Magazine* 13 (1912): 201–202; Rachel N. Klein, *Unification of a Slave State: The Rise of the Planter Class in the South Carolina Backcountry, 1760–1808* (Chapel Hill: University of North Carolina Press for the Institute of Early American History and Culture, 1990), 114–115, 125–126. Thomas Bee, a knowledgeable contemporary source, reported that the production of rice and indigo, South Carolina's principal exports prior to the Revolution, had been cut in half by war losses. Alexander Moore, "Thomas Bee's Notes on the State of South Carolina," *Journal of the Early Republic* 7 (1987): 120–121.

8. Robert A. Becker, "Salus Populi Suprema Lex: Public Peace and South Carolina Debtor Relief Laws, 1783–1788," *South Carolina Historical Magazine* 80: 66–67.

9. W. Hardy Wickwar, *300 Years of Development Administration in South Carolina* (Columbia: Bureau of Government Research and Service, University of South Carolina), 68.

10. A lawyer by profession, John Faucheraud Grimke was perhaps South Carolina's most eminent jurist in the postwar period. He was born December 16, 1752, the son of the Charleston jeweler John Paul Grimke and his wife, Mary Faucheraud. Prior to the American Revolution he studied law in London, and upon his return to South Carolina at the beginning of hostilities he received a commission as a captain of artillery. Later he was elected deputy adjutant general of South Carolina with the rank of colonel. He was taken prisoner at the capture of Charleston in May 1780; although paroled, he was confined but later released and eventually joined Gen. Greene's army. After the war, he returned to the law and was elected a judge in 1783. He served as speaker of the state House of Representatives from 1785 to 1786 and was a member of the convention to adopt the federal Constitution in 1788. The following year he became senior associate judge of the Court of Sessions and Common Pleas, virtually the Chief Justice of South Carolina, and held this position until his death on August 9, 1819. Henry A. M. Smith, "Goose Creek," *South Carolina Historical Magazine* 29 (1928): 190; Jeanne A. Calhoun, Martha A. Zierden, and Elizabeth A. Paysinger, "The Geographic Spread of Charleston's Merchant Community," *South Carolina Historical Magazine* 29: 202; "Order Book of John Faucheraud Grimke, August 1778–May 1780," *South Carolina Historical Magazine* 13 (1912): 42–43.

11. Robert A. Becker, ed., "John F. Grimke's Eyewitness Account of the Camden Court Riot, April 27–28, 1785," *South Carolina Historical Magazine* 83 (1982): 209–213.

12. The role of the debt crisis in unifying the interests of backcountry planters with those of the coastal region follows arguments advanced by Rachel N. Klein, who contended that the unity among the state's commercial elites was instrumental in containing regional conflict in the postrevolutionary period, a factor critical to the integration of the backcountry during that formative time. Klein, *Unification of a Slave State,* 127–135. Rice exports from South Carolina quadrupled from 24,224 barrels in 1782 to 100,000 barrels in 1790. John Drayton, *A View of South Carolina, as Respects Her Natural and Civil Concerns* (Charleston, S.C.: W. P. Young; reprint ed., Spartanburg, S.C.: The Reprint Co., 1972), 173.

13. Klein, *Unification of a Slave State,* 116–118.

14. The *Royal Gazette* reported the appointments in its Nov. 3, 1781 edition, noting that "most of the persons appointed Ordinaries are commanders of parties of Rebel Militia"; Kirkland and Kennedy, *Historic Camden,* 1: 286; *JHR,* Jan. 24, 1782; Jan. 30, 1783; Jan. 31, 1784; J. S. Salley, ed., *JS,* Feb. 26, 1782, 142–143; *RG,* Mar. 13, 1782.

15. Joan A. Inabinet and L. Glen Inabinet, *A History of Kershaw County, South Carolina* (Columbia: University of South Carolina Press, 2011), 87. In the winter of 1783 the legislature appointed Henry Hampton ordinary and Alexander Moore sheriff of Camden District: *JHR,* Feb. 5, Feb. 10, 1783.

16. Adele Stanton Edwards, ed., *Journals of the Privy Council, 1783–1789* (hereafter *JPrC*) (Columbia: University of South Carolina Press, 2011), May 28, Oct. 22, 1783; Apr. 7, Apr. 21, 1784, 62, 85, 97–98, 99–100.

17. In one of several similar petitions, residents from the District Between Broad and Catawba Rivers asserted "that the state of the backcountry is truly distressing for want of the due administration" and "recommend the immediate establishment of the County Courts." *JHR*, Jan. 27, 1785. The bill establishing the county courts was introduced shortly thereafter and ratified two months later. *JHR*, Jan. 29, Mar. 24, 1785.

18. "Amendment to the Bill for Dividing the Ste into Counties," *JHR*, Feb. 21, 1785. James and Margaret Ingram operated a plantation on a tract of nearly a thousand acres in the vicinity of Hanging Rock Creek. Their residence was situated on the Catawba Path, now the principal wagon road paralleling the Wateree, at a point centrally located in the region served by the court. CPB, Vol. 17, Nov. 4, 1772, 269; SPB/ChS, Vol. 5, Aug. 2–3, 1784, 137–138; Inabinet and Inabinet, *History of Kershaw County*, 88; Terry W. Lipscomb, *South Carolina in 1791: George Washington's Southern Tour* (Columbia: South Carolina Department of Department of Archives and History and History, 1993), 74–77. Among the public buildings dispersed in the new counties was a jail constructed by Henry Hampton upon Thomas Sumter's request "at the Waxhaws." A justice in Fairfield County, Hampton sought without success to have the legislature reimburse him for his efforts. *JHR*, Feb. 15, 1785.

19. "Unanimous Petition from a Large Body of People Making a Part of the Inhabitants of Lancaster, Fairfield, Richland, and Claremont Counties, in the First of Which the Town of Camden is Included," *JHR*, Mar. 1, 1787. The Grand Jury of Camden District reiterated the difficulty of access, declaring, "If courts sit at such a distance from the inhabitants, as to make it almost impossible for them to attend, and so expensive as to deter suitors having just cause from seeking redress, the citizen is deprived legally of one of his most valuable privileges. "Judge's Charge to the Grand Jury of Camden District, Dec. 1, 1790," Grand Jury Presentments (hereafter GJP), S165010, South Carolina Department of Archives and History, Columbia.

20. "Petition from the Inhabitants of Camden," *JHR*, Mar. 1, 1787, notation; Feb. 4, 11, 19, 1791; Dec. 21, 1792.

21. Klein, *Unification of a Slave State*, 135–142. At least two unsuccessful petitions were filed by inhabitants of Camden District to abolish or suspend courts in Claremont, Clarendon, and Lancaster Counties. *JHR*, Jan. 29, Feb. 3, 10, Mar. 3, 1789.

22. *JHR*, Feb. 18, 29, 1788; GJP, Dec. 1, 1790; *JHR*, Jan. 27, 1791.

23. Jo Anne McCormick, "The Quakers of Colonial South Carolina, 1670–1807" (Ph.D. diss., University of South Carolina, 1985), 171–172; Kenneth L. Carroll, "The Irish Quaker Community at Camden," *South Carolina Historical Quarterly* 77 (1976): 82.

24. The Presbyterian church was rebuilt at the foot of Church Street, on the same site as the building dismantled during the occupation. Thomas J. Kirkland and Robert M. Kennedy, *Historic Camden, Vol. 2: Nineteenth Century* (Columbia, S.C.: State Printing Co., 1926), 2: 292–293.

25. The Baptist church was completed in 1809 and stood on the on the northwest corner of market and York Streets. Kirkland and Kennedy, *Historic Camden*, 2: 277–278.

26. The Methodists erected their church in 1798 on the south side of King Street. Richard J. Hooker, ed., *The Carolina Backcountry on the Eve of the Revolution: The Journal and Other Writings of Charles Woodmason, Anglican Itinerant* (Chapel Hill: University of North Carolina Press, 1953), 20; Inabinet, *Lyttleton Street United Methodist Church*, 4–7, 13; Elizabeth Williams Thornton, "Items from the Reminiscences of Mrs. Phinehas Thornton, Dec.11, 1856," Elizabeth Thornton Papers (hereafter ETP), South Caroliniana Library, University of South Carolina, Columbia.

27. Meetinghouses existed at Flat Rock Creek and Beaver Creek north of Camden and farther downriver at Swift Creek, as well as on Twenty-five Mile Creek on the west side of the Wateree. Congregations are known to have met in the vicinity of Hanging Rock as well as at Singleton's Creek and Beaver Creek. Inabinet and Inabinet, *History of Kershaw County*, 87.

28. The Episcopal Church began regular services in 1830 and dedicated a church on the west side of Broad Street south of DeKalb two years later. Kirkland and Kennedy, *Historic Camden*, 2: 280–283;

John Wesley Brinsfield, *Religion and Politics in Colonia South Carolina* (Easley, S.C.: Southern Historical Press, 1983), 133.

29. Klein, *Unification of a Slave State,* 143; "Petition from the Inhabitants of the District Between Broad and Catawba Rivers," *JHR,* Jan. 27, 1785; "Petition from Inhabitants of the Lower Part of Camden District," *JHR,* Oct. 5, 1785.

30. John Hammond Moore, *Columbia and Richland County: A South Carolina Community, 1740–1990* (Columbia: University of South Carolina Press, 1993), 41–48; *JHR,* Feb. 22, Mar. 14, Mar. 22, 1786; Mar. 23, Mar. 28, 1787; Jan. 23, Mar. 2, 1789.

31. Klein, *Unification of a Slave State,* 146–148; *JHR,* Mar. 2, 1789; Wickwar, *Development Administration,* 77. Columbia now housed offices associated with the secretary of state, the commissioners of the Treasury, the auditor general, the surveyor general, and the attorney general. As a concession to lowcountry interests, principal government agencies continued to maintain offices in Charleston. Moore, *Columbia and Richland County,* 50. The emergence of livestock, wheat, and tobacco as principal crops in South Carolina during the postwar period paralleled the experience in other former British North American colonies. See Robert D. Mitchell, "Agricultural Change and the American Revolution: A Virginia Case Study," *Agricultural History* 47 (1973), 131–132.

32. Ramsey, *History of South Carolina,* 2: 217; Drayton, *View of South Carolina,* 135–139; Judith J. Schulz: "The Rise and Decline of Camden as South Carolina's Major Trading Center, 1751–1829: A Historical Geographic Study" (M.A. thesis, University of South Carolina, 1972), 38, 42; D. Huger Bacot, "The South Carolina Middle Country at the End of the End of the Eighteenth Century," *South Atlantic Quarterly* 23 (1924): 53–54.

33. For Duncan McRa see Council of Safety, Commissions, Feb. 20, 1776, quoted in Alexander Gregg, *History of the Old Cheraws* (Columbia, S.C.: The State Co., 1867; reprint ed., Greenville, S.C.: Southern Historical Press, 1991), 245, 290; Kirkland and Kennedy, *Historic Camden,* 1: 289, 352, 368, 388; Kirkland and Kennedy, *Historic Camden,* 2: 11. Chesnut, Boykin & Co. existed as early as October 1786, CMMP, 12/33/31, and the partnership of Chesnut & Co. was named in a suit two years later, JR, Box 110B, Item 10A, Feb. 20, 1784. The agreement naming Boykin, McRa, and Cantey as managers of Chesnut's property is contained in CMMP, 12/33/38. Thomas Broom was born the son of Robert Broom and Frances Jacobs on May 4, 1760, in St. Anne's Parish, Cecil Co., Md. Broom served as a private and later sergeant in Lt. Col. Henry (Light Horse Harry) Lee's Legion cavalry during Greene's 1781 campaign in South Carolina, when Lee passed through Camden and observed the town's potential as well as its currently devastated condition. Henry Lee, *Memoirs of the War in the Southern Department of the United States* (New York: University Publishing Co., 1869; reprint ed., New York: Arno Press, 1969), 345–354; Ramsey, *History of South Carolina,* 2: 216–217. An account of the Sanders Creek mill is contained in CMMP, 12/34/16. McRa & Cantey acquired the large mill tract from James Kershaw. Called the "Indian Camp," it was purported to be the site of the Catawba village occupied in 1760–1761. JKD, June 15, 24, 1798; Kirkland and Kennedy, *Historic Camden,* 1: 388. The description of McRa's mill was purportedly written by Camden resident William M. Shannon, "Rides about Camden, 1873," in *Rides about Camden, 1853 & 1873,* ed. Harvey S. Teal (Columbia, S.C.: McDonald Letter Shop, 1961), 21. Drayton, *View of South Carolina,* 211.

34. For land preferences, see Kenneth E. Lewis and Frank J. Krist Jr., "Settlement Expansion in Fredericksburg Township, South Carolina, 1740–1770," Vol. VI, Report submitted to the Savannah River Archaeological Research Program, South Carolina Institute of Archaeology and Anthropology, University of South Carolina (1997), 3. The locations of English's lands and mills and Chesnut's mill are shown in SPB/ChS, Vol. 21, Nov. 14, 1787, 178, and CMMP, 12/34/30, May 3, 1806. A list of mills in the boundaries of present-day Kershaw County appears in Inabinet and Inabinet, *History of Kershaw County,* 103.

35. Robert Mills, *Statistics of South Carolina* (Charleston, S.C.: Hurlbut and Lloyd, 1856; reprint ed., Spartanburg, S.C.: The Reprint Co., 1972), 588; Drayton, *View of South Carolina,* 137–138. John Chesnut to Thomas English, Jan. 24, 1798, CMMP, 12/34/17. Records of Chesnut's deliveries of corn

for the years 1790–1795 reveal that he sold more than fourteen thousand bushels to various buyers. CMMP, 12/33/37; 12/33/38; 12/34/1;12/34/4; 12/34/7; 12/34/9; 12/34/10.

36. Drayton, *View of South Carolina,* 135–136; *SCG,* Nov. 10, 1766. For accounts of tobacco, see Chesnut, Boykin & Co. Account with Zachariah Cantey & Co. 1786–1788, CMMP, 12/33/31; Jasper Sutton account with Zachariah Cantey, 1787, CMMP, 12/33/34; and McRa and Cantey Account Book, Camden, S.C., 1792–1799 (hereafter MCAB), South Caroliniana Library, University of South Carolina, Columbia. JKD, Jan. 18, 1796; Ramsey, *History of South Carolina,* 2: 312. Cooper, *Statutes at Large,* Vol. 5, no. 1456, 1789.

37. Drayton, *View of South Carolina,* 227. The chart on p. 176 shows that the production of indigo expanded rapidly following the war, rising from 618 pounds in 1782 to a peak of 839,666 pounds in 1792. The decade-long war with France, which began the following year, abruptly cut off European markets, and exports of indigo declined precipitously. A. & W. Tunno account with John Chesnut, CMMP, 12/34/2. Henry Rugeley to Matthew Rugeley, Feb. 1, 1793; Jan. 11, 1794, Helen Hoskins Rugeley, ed., *Rugeley Papers: Blue-Blooded Brits in Reduced Circumstances* (Austin, Tex.: By the Author, 1997), X311.144, 63, X311.148, 64. Settlers on the Pee Dee also planted indigo into the 1790s: George Lloyd Johnson Jr., *The Frontier in the Colonial South, South Carolina Backcountry, 1736–1800* (Westport, Conn.: Greenwood Press, 1997), 167. The Rev. Evan Pugh grew indigo at Cashawy regularly from1783 to 1790 and probably as late as 1795. Horace Fraser Rudisill, ed., *The Diaries of Evan Pugh (1762–1801)* (Florence, S.C.: St. David's Society, 1993), 230, 303, 353, 362, and the store at Chatham received payment for a consignment of indigo as late as 1794. Kershaw & Co. account with William Ancrum, CMMP, 12/34/6.

38. Bacot, "South Carolina Middle Country," 54.

39. Specialized heavy, flat-bottomed vessels designed for transporting a variety of cargoes, including heavy, bulky goods such as cotton, tobacco, and bricks, in the shallow waters of the coastal rivers. Developed in the early eighteenth century, these boats were ideal for operating in shoal waters and loading from river banks where piers were absent. Archaeologists have recovered the partially intact remains of such a craft from Brown's Ferry on the Black River in Georgetown County. This wreck has provided valuable details relating to the construction of these distinctive river craft. J. Richard Steffy, "The Thirteenth Colonies: English Settlers and Seafarers," in *Ships and Shipwrecks of the Americas: A History Based on Underwater Archaeology,* ed. George F. Bass (New York: Thames and Hudson, 1996), 119–125.

40. Interest in inland navigation is evidenced by the South Carolina legislature's appropriation of funds to clear the major rivers, including the Wateree, as early as 1784. *JHR,* Mar. 26, 1784; Feb. 19, 1785. Efforts to open the Catawba River soon followed. *JHR,* Mar. 18, 1786; Feb. 6, 1788. Kirkland and Kennedy, *Historic Camden,* 2: 36.

41. Bacot, "South Carolina Middle Country," 54; John Chesnut, Corn Sales Accounts, May 1790–Mar. 1794; CMMP, 12/33/38, 12/34/3; James Kershaw Diary, JKP, Jan. 27, 1800; Mar. 5, 1802.

42. South Carolina's decision to improve its waterways to facilitate the transport of bulk agricultural commodities from its interior followed a larger trend of canal construction in the United States that began during the closing decades of the eighteenth century. Plans involved opening navigation on the Saluda-Broad-Congaree-Catawba-Wateree-Santee River system as well as the Pee Dee and its tributaries to the north. Although the Santee Canal Company was incorporated in 1786, construction of the canal began only in 1793. Containing eleven locks to raise and lower vessels, the canal stretched twenty-one and a half miles between the Santee and Cooper Rivers. The first boat passed over its length in May 1800. Robert J. Kapsch, *Historic Canals & Waterways of South Carolina* (Columbia: University of South Carolina Press, 2010), 6–8, 17–19, 34–41.

43. Caroline E. MacGill, *History of Transportation in the United States before 1860* (Washington, D.C.: Carnegie Institution of Washington, 1917; reprint ed., Gloucester, Mass.: Peter Smith, 1948), 276–279; Julian J. Petty, *The Growth and Distribution of Population in South Carolina* (Columbia: South Carolina State Planning Board, 1943; reprint ed., Spartanburg, S.C.: The Reprint Co., 1975), 73–74;

Charles F. Kovacik and John J. Winberry, *South Carolina: A Geography* (Boulder, Colo.: Westview Press, 1987), 94–95; David Kohn and Bess Glen, eds., *Internal Improvements in South Carolina, 1817–1828* (Washington, D.C.: By the Authors, 1938), op cit. The canal projects, begun in the 1790s, focused on the rivers of the Santee drainage. By the time of their completion in the 1820s, the Wateree, Catawba, Congaree, Saluda, and Broad Rivers were open to navigatiion. In 1797 John Chesnut constructed a boat specifically for passing through the Santee Canal. This boat was capable of carrying nine hundred bushels of corn, two hundred barrels of flour, or thirty-five hogsheads of tobacco. His boats were delivering cargoes directly to Charleston wharves by 1805. Kirkland and Kennedy, *Historic Camden,* 2: 36; Macbeth, Henry & Co. to John Chesnut, Jan. 15, 1805, CMMP, 12/34/29; Ramsey, *History of South Carolina,* 2: 294.

44. The boatbuilder may have been John Kirkpatrick, a Scotsman who had become a successful merchant in Camden in the 1790s. Kirkland and Kennedy, *Historic Camden,* 1: 408n; 2: 36; 388–389. For Cato, see, James Kershaw Diary, JKP, Sept. 20, 1797; Aug. 24, 1799; Aug. 11, 1800. Named boats included *Peggy, Venture, Harpoon, and Oeconomy,* owned by James Kershaw, James Kershaw Diary, JKP, July 7, 1797; Jan. 18, 1798; Apr. 27, 1801; Jan. 6, 1811; *Sally,* owned by John Adamson, James Kershaw Diary, JKP, Apr. 26, 1800; *Peggy,* owned by Zachariah Cantey, James Kershaw Diary, JKP, Nov. 5, 1800; and *La Belle Catherine,* owned by Isaac DuBose and named after his fiancée. Kirkpatrick built *Poly Brisbane* and an unnamed "canal boat" for Daniel Carpenter: James Kershaw Diary, JKP, Sept. 14, 1797. The other unnamed boats were owned by Zebulon Rudolph and McRa & Cantey. James Kershaw Diary, JKP, Jan. 14, 1802; Mar. 5, 1802.

45. Henry Laurens stressed the importance of frequent and regular mail service to business negotiations and their relevance to successful trade. Henry Laurens to Samuel Groube, Apr. 4, 1772, Philip M. Hamer et al., eds., *The Papers of Henry Laurens* (hereafter *HLP*), Vol. 8 (Columbia: University of South Carolina Press, 1968–1990), 245–246. By 1774 official mail routes from the northern colonies passed through South Carolina and extended as far south as St. Augustine in East Florida and a regular route connected Charleston and Georgetown. *SC&AGG,* Aug. 27, 1770; Mar. 12, 1771; Frank H. Norton, ed., *Journal Kept by Hugh Finley, Surveyor of the Post Roads on the Continent of North America, during His Survey of the Post Office between Falmouth and Casco Bay in the Province of Massachusetts, and Savannah in Georgia* (Brooklyn, N.Y.: Frank H. Norton, 1867), 55. This route was maintained by the General Post Office of the United States after independence was declared: *GSSC,* Nov. 25, 1778.

46. Harvey S. Teal and Robert J. Stets, *South Carolina Postal History and Illustrated Catalog of Postmarks, 1760–1860* (Lake Oswego, Ore.: Raven Press, 1989), 16–17, 23–26. Mail delivery to Camden was delayed for a month in 1794 after the carrier fell ill on the road and in 1794 when the carrier was injured in a fall from his horse. As the volume of mail in Camden exceeded "four horse loads," a carriage was sent to bring the mail to Charleston. The vagaries of overland travel supported private mail delivery in Camden as late as 1816. In that year private mail routes were established from Camden to Sumterville and to Beaver Creek. Kirkland and Kennedy, *Historic Camden,* 2: 36, 37.

47. The wealth of these individuals is reflected by the fact that they constituted four of the five largest slaveowners in Kershaw District in1800: U.S. Census Office, Population, South Carolina, 1800. MacBeth, Henry & Co. to John Chesnut, Feb. 23, 1803, CMMP, 12/34/26. Charges for Shipping, 1810, CMMP, 12/34/35. Even later on, John Chesnut's factor could proclaim, "We have . . . been a good deal in the flour way, and have cleared off every barrel on hand from the Camden mills." Kirkpatrick & Douglas to John Chesnut, CMMP, Feb. 14, 1815.

48. At mid-century, some contemporary observers estimated that the total returns on invested capital were as high as 33 percent. Robert M. Weir, *Colonial South Carolina: A History* (New York: KTO Press, 1983; reprint ed., Columbia: University of South Carolina Press, 1997), 216–217; Peter Coclanis, *The Shadow of a Dream: Economic Life and Death in the South Carolina Low Country, 1670–1920* (New York: Oxford University Press, 1989), 121–125.

49. For discussions of the transition of frontier farmers into a planter elite and the motives for and form of their transformation, see Eugene D. Genovese, *The World the Slaveholders Made: Two Essays in Interpretation* (New York: Pantheon Books, 1969), 140–144. The social and political power of the

planter elite derived not only from their wealth but also from their freedom from farm labor, which allowed them to involve themselves in a variety of other activities. Klein, *Unification of a Slave State,* 7–8. Contemporary sources acknowledged the potential profitability of planting, but cautioned that success depended on frugality and a continual reinvestment of profits in order to build an operation of a scale sufficient to free the owner of the necessity of day-to-day management. An American, *American Husbandry,* Vol. 1 (London: J. Brew, 1775), 424–425.

50. Weir, *Colonial South Carolina,*163; Klein, *Unification of a Slave State,* 179–182.

51. Estimates of the individual landholdings are based on grants, purchases, and other transactions recorded in PL; CBP; CLG; CLG/CS; CBPR; SPB/ChS; and State Plat Books, Columbia Series (hereafter SPB/ColS), S213192, South Carolina Department of Archives and History, Columbia.

52. Larry Schweikart, "Southern Banks and Economic Growth in the Antebellum Period: A Reassessment," *Journal of Southern History* 53 (1987): 19–23; Howard Bodenhorn, *State Banking in Early America* (New York: Oxford University Press, 2003), 45–46, 223–224; Benjamin J. Klebaner, "State-Chartered American Commercial Banks, 1781–1801," *Business History Review* 53 (1979): 534–536; Douglass C. North, *The Economic Growth of the United States, 1790–1860* (New York: W. W. Norton, 1966), 46; Bray Hammond, *Banks and Politics in America: From the Revolution to the Civil War* (Princeton, N.J.: Princeton University Press, 1957), 114–115, 126–127, 164, 168; Curtis P. Nettels, *The Emergence of a National Economy, 1775–1815, Vol. 2: The Economic History of the United States* (New York: Holt, Rinehart and Winston, 1962), 297.

53. Walter Edgar, *South Carolina: A History* (Columbia: University of South Carolina Press, 1998), 270–271; Inabinet and Inabinet, *History of Kershaw County,* 113–114. To encourage the expansion of cotton growing in South Carolina, the state purchased the patent for Whitney's gin in 1801, allowing its manufacture and use by others. Despite complications, this transaction was completed by 1804. D. Huger Bacot, "South Carolina and the Whitney Cotton Gin," *South Carolina Historical Magazine* 19 (1918): 151–152; William A. Schaper, "Sectionalism and Representation in South Carolina, a Sociological Study," *Annual Report of the American Historical Association for the Year 1900,* vol. 1 (Washington, D.C.: Government Printing Office, 1901), 388–389. The botanist Francois André Michaux commented in 1806 on the rise of cotton and its replacement of tobacco as an export crop: Michaux, "Lowcountry and Upcountry South Carolina as Seen by a Famous Botanist, 1802–1803," in *South Carolina, The Grand Tour, 1780–1865,* ed. Thomas D. Clark (Columbia: University of South Carolina Press, 1973), 42. He also noted the impact of the Whitney cotton gin.

54. Henry Rugeley to Matthew Rugeley, July 17, 1790, X311.136, Rugeley, ed., *Rugeley Papers,* 53–54.

55. The quotes are from the account of traveler Robert Gilmore, who also noted the impacrt of the Whitney gin. "Excerpts from a Journal of Robert Gilmore, 1806–1807," in *Five Visitors to Kershaw County, 1806–1832,* ed. Harvey S. Teal (Camden, S.C.: Kershaw County Historical Society, 1997), n.p. John Chesnut's accounts reveal that he was shipping baled cotton as early as 1803. CMMP, 12/34/26. John Chesnut was the largest slaveholder in Kershaw County in 1800, owning 180 enslaved persons. Ten years later he had increased his holdings to 234 slaves. Zachariah Cantey and Duncan McRa were among the five largest resident slaveholders in both years. The other planters were Burwell Boykin, brother of Samuel, and Isaac DuBose, in 1800 and Boykin and John Adamson, the forgiven Loyalist, in 1810. Kershaw County Historical Society, *Second Federal Census, Population, 1800, South Carolina, Kershaw* County (Camden, S.C.: Kershaw County Historical Society, 1970); Kershaw County Historical Society, *Third Federal Census, Population, 1810, South Carolina, Kershaw* County (Camden, S.C.: Kershaw County Historical Society, 1972).

56. J. Maxwell Green, "Bermuda (alias Somers Islands), Historical Sketch." *Bulletin of the American Geographical Society* 33 (1901): 231; Wilfred Brenton Kerr, *Bermuda and the American Revolution: 1760–1783* (Princeton, N.J.: Princeton University Press, 1936), 53–54; George C. Rogers Jr., "The Papers of James Grant of Ballindalloch Castle, Scotland," *South Carolina Historical Review* 77 (1976): 151. During the time of Kershaw's exile in Bermuda, its governor stressed the prevalence of illegal trade with the rebellious colonies, citing the island's dependence on American foodstuffs. George Bruere to Cornwallis, Nov. 27, 1780, CP 30/11/4, 219–220. Henry Tucker and his kinsmen and partners Daniel

and Robert were descendants of the original immigrant to Bermuda, St. George Tucker, founder of one of the island's leading families. Henry followed a political career. He married Frances Bruere, the daughter of Bermuda's sitting governor, in 1770 and was appointed colonial treasurer. Subsequently he served on the Council and was colony secretary, provost marshal, and president of the Council. The family also had connections in the mainland colonies. Henry's oldest brother, Thomas Tudor, studied medicine in Charleston and settled there, while his youngest brother, St. George, emigrated in 1771 to Virginia, where he practiced law, served as a militia colonel in the Revolution, and later became a prominent judge. Henry's partners, the merchants Richard and John Jennings, had also been active in the contraband trade with the American colonies and, with Henry Tucker, had participated in the clandestine shipment of gunpowder to the rebels from Bermuda in1775. The last partner was George Bascome, described as a clever lawyer from St. George. Kerr, *Bermuda and the American Revolution,* 14–17, 37–38, 43n, 48, 53–58; M. Jarvis, *Bermuda's Architectural Heritage, St. George's* (Hamilton: Bermuda National Trust, 1998), 90.

57. Kirkland and Kennedy, *Historic Camden,* 1: 378; Joseph Kershaw to John Rutledge, Feb. 24, 1784, in ibid., 379; James Kershaw to Messrs. Kershaw, July 26, 1783, in Peter G. D. Kershaw, "A Kershaw Family, 1670–1970," p. 67, Port Charlotte, Fla., 1974 (photocopied), 78. Indents paid to Joseph Kershaw totaled £4,077.6.6. SEIRC, Book F, Nos. 214–219, 231–233; Nos. 221–223, 233–234; No. 224–225, 234; No. 226–229, 234–235; No. 230, 236; Book V, No. 348, 146; Book W, No. 348, 146; No. 529, 274; Joseph Kershaw, AA, Reel 83, Frame 152, File 4259. Debts totaling £12,210.3.2 3/4 appear in "List of Judgements Entered Up in Charleston Against Joseph Kershaw before June 1791," CMMP, 12/33/40.

58. Joseph Kershaw to Richard Jennings, Henry Tucker, John Jennings, James Tucker, Daniel Tucker, Robert Tucker, George Bascome, and James Hall, CBMC, Vol. T-5, May 5, 1786113–117, 120–122; Joseph Kershaw to John Jennings, CBMC, Vol. T-5, 117–120. Joseph Kershaw to John Bonner, KCRCC/C, Vol. Vol. M-5, Feb. 23, 1784, 267; Joseph Kershaw to Isaac Alexander, CBMC, Vol. Q-5, Jan. 27, 1784, 453; Joseph Kershaw to Richard Furman, CBMC, Vol. S-5, Nov. 30, 1784, 95; Joseph Kershaw to J. Cooke, CBMC, Vol. Z-5, Mar. 13, 1786, 353; Joseph Kershaw to Aaron Loocock, LCRCC/C, Vol. B, May 6, 1786, 8; Joseph Kershaw to Edward Neufville, CBMC, Vol. Z-5, Mar. 13, 1786, 353. The store site was sold in 1798.

59. For sales of these properties, see, LCRCC/C, Vol. B, May 6, 1786, 1, and LCRCC/C, Vol. B, May 9, 1786, 8. Kirkland and Kennedy, *Historic Camden,* 2: 15. James Kershaw rented the brewhouse to George Broom for a annual fee, JKD, Feb. 12, 1793, and sold the "brewing implements" to William Mayrant the following year: Aug. 14, 1794. The brewhouse square was not sold until seven years after Loocock's death in 1794, Estate of Aaron Loocock to Lewis Ciples, KCRCC/C, Vol. C., 1801, 190, and the store site remained in Ancrum's possession nearly as long. William Ancrum to Gayeton Aiguier, KCRCC/C, Vol. BB, May 28, 1798, 220. Date ranges derived from an analysis of ceramics recovered from the sites of these buildings indicate that the store property was in use until 1810 and the brewhouse until 1815. Kenneth E. Lewis, *Camden: Historical Archaeology in the South Carolina Backcountry* (Belmont, Calif.: Thomson Wadsworth, 2006), 109–114.

60. Walter B. Edgar and N. Louise Bailey, *Biographical Directory of the South Carolina House of Representatives, Vol. 2: The Commons House of Assembly, 1692–1775* (Columbia: University of South Carolina Press, 1977), 376–377; *JHR,* Feb. 14, 1784; Kirkland and Kennedy, *Historic Camden,* 1: 35, 308–309.

61. Letter of Attorney, Feb. 12, 1794, CMMP, 12/34/31; Mabel L. Webber, ed., "Marriage and Death Notices from the *City Gazette," South Carolina Historical Magazine* 21 (1920): 121. "Estate Sale of Property of Col. Joseph Kershaw, Broadside Advertisement, 28 Apr. 1794," CMMP, 12/34/31. Edward Neufville vs. James Kershaw, Suit, Kershaw County, Records of the Clerk of Court, Pleadings and Judgements (hereafter KCRCC/P&J), Book F, 1791–1801, Apr. 1801, 445–454,; William Ancrum to John Chesnut, May 13, 1805, CMMP, 12/34/29. A suit filed in 1816 by John and Richard Jennings, heirs to Jennings, Tucker & Co., against Kershaw's surviving heirs accused John and Mary Kershaw and a sister, Sarah Kershaw Perkins, together with James Kershaw's widow, Lydia Ann, with conspiring to circumvent the firm's original claim against the estate. The disposition of Joseph Kershaw's lands and a list of those remaining in 1819 appear in or attached to Joseph Kershaw, Will, Kershaw County,

Records of the Probate Judge, Estates (hereafter KCRPJ/E), Apt. 37, Pkg. 1354, Est. Bk. C, Sept. 21, 1815, 59. Upon his death in 1815, James Kershaw left all of his real and personal estate to his wife, Lydia Ann Kershaw. James Kershaw, Will, KCRPJ/E, Apt. 37, Pkg. 1351, Est. Bk. G, Mar. 8, 1816, 113. Details of Jennings, Tucker & Co.'s claims against the Kershaw family may be found in James Tucker et al., vs. Joseph Kershaw et al., Suit, Kershaw County, Court of Equity (hereafter KCCE), Roll 112, Apt. F, Mar. 8, 1816; "Camden District Equity Journal," *South Carolina Magazine of Ancestral Research* 14 (1986), no. 1, 47; no. 2, 93, 96, 97, 98. For the subsequent ownership of the Great White House, see Kirkland and Kennedy, *Historic Camden,* 1: 278. The Camden Orphan Society acquired the property for its private school in 1805 and used the mansion for an orphan house and society meeting rooms. Camden Orphan Society, Records, June 22, July 4, 1805, Sept. 11, 1811, South Caroliniana Library, University of South Carolina, Columbia. For subsequent ownership of the Hermitage and Camden mills tracts, see John Chesnut, Will, KCRPJ/E, Apt. 130, Pkg. 5119, Estate Bk. A1, Apr. 1818, 477, and plats of these properties, CMMP, 12/34/19, n. d.; 12/34/20, n. d.; and 12/34/31, 1807.

62. For the subsequent history of the Kershaw family, see Kirkland and Kennedy, *Historic Camden,* 1: 380–381; 2: 180–185, 260, 335.

63. Joseph Kershaw to William Henry Harrington, Sept. 25, 1781, in Walter Clark, ed., *The State Records of North Carolina, Vol. 15: 1780–81* (Goldsboro, N.C.: Nash Bros., 1898), 644–645. The management of the Pee Dee plantations were overseen by Holden Wade, a resident of Chatham and a member of the St. David's vestry who removed the "books, papers, etc." upriver for safekeeping during the occupation. Gregg, *History of the Old Cheraws,* 180–181; Holden Wade to John Chesnut, Jan. 5, 1782, NGP/CL, 51: 50. Ely Kershaw's will, proved Mar. 23, 1783, directed that his estate be sold and the proceeds divided among his sons, John and Ely II, at age 21 and his daughter, Rebecca, upon her marriage. The lack of reference to his wife, Mary Cantey Kershaw, implies that she was no longer living when the will was filed on Aug. 1, 1780. Caroline T. Moore, comp. and ed., *Abstracts of the Wills of the State of South Carolina, 1783–1800* (Columbia: R. L. Bryan Co., 1974), 7–8.

64. Advertisement, Nov. 18, 1786, CMMP, 12/33/31; Robert Welsh to John Chesnut, Feb. 19, 1790, CMMP, 12/33/37; Duncan McRa and Daniel Weeks, Memorandum of Agreement, Feb. 18, 1791, CMMP, 12/33/39; John Chesnut to George Mitchell, July 27, 1791. CMMP, 12/33/40; Daniel Sturgis, Oath, Dec. 23, 1791, CMMP, 12/33/40; George Mitchell to John Chesnut, Jan. 9, 1792, CMMP, 12/33/40; Daniel Hicks, Receipt, Feb. 16, 1793, CMMP, 12/34/16.

65. William Ancrum to John Chesnut, Nov. 19, 1788, CMMP, 12/33/33; Archibald Brown to John Chesnut, June 20, 1789, CMMP, 12/33/35; CMMP, 12/34/17; Archibald Brown and John Chesnut, Memorandum, May 6, 1789, CMMP, 12/33/35; Account of Sales of Ely Kershaw's Lots in Camden, Sept. 1, 1794, and May 7, 1798, CMMP, 12/34/7; William Ancrum to John Chesnut, Mar. 9, 1798, CMMP, 12/34/17; William Ancrum to Froneau & Paine, Apr. 14, 1798, CMMP,12/34/18; William Ancrum to John Chesnut, Sept. 17, 1799; William Ancrum, Receipts, Jan. 1, Apr. 4, 1800,CMMP, 12/34/21.

66. Ely Kershaw's indents for Revolutionary War services totaled at least £1,214.0.9. Adele Stanton Edwards, ed., *Journals of the Privy Council, 1783–1789* (hereafter *JPrC*) (Columbia: University of South Carolina Press, 1971), 88; John Chesnut as executor of Ely Kershaw estate, SEIRC, Book E, No. 115, p. 185. With Joseph Kershaw, John Chesnut settled a large suit with Nicholas Eveleigh for the value of 123 slaves and oversaw the settlement of outstanding debts with the mercantile firms of Greenwood & Higginson. William Greenwood, Receipt, May 22, 1800, CMMP, 12/34/22; as well as to William Ancrum, Receipts for Payments on Kershaw & Co.'s Debts, May 11, 1805, CMMP, 12/34/29; and William Blalock, Receipt for Debt of Ely Kershaw Estate, May 23, 1807, CMMP, 12/34/32.

67. A native of North Carolina, Joseph Brevard served in the Continental army as a lieutenant and after the Revolution settled in Camden. He practiced law with William Falconer of Chesterfield and served as sheriff of Camden District from 1789 to 1791. He was admitted to the bar in 1792 and elected to the twelfth and thirteenth General Assemblies (1796–1799) from Kershaw County. He served in the South Carolina Senate from Kershaw and Lancaster District for the fourteenth General Assembly (1800–1801) and was later elected U.S. Representative in the Sixteenth Congress (1819–1821). He owned Nettleton plantation and Antrim plantation on the Wateree River and other acreage on the Wateree

River, Twenty-five Mile Creek, and Great Lynches Creek, as well as a townhouse in Camden. Brevard died Oct. 11, 1821, and was buried in Camden. Kirkland and Kennedy, *Historic Camden,* 1: 321–326, 386; N. Louise Bailey, Mary L. Morgan, and Carolyn R. Taylor, eds., *Biographical Directory of the South Carolina Senate,* Vol. 1 (Columbia: University of South Carolina Press, 1986), 183–184.

68. Ira Berlin, *Many Thousands Gone: The First Two Centuries of Slavery in North America* (Cambridge, Mass.: Belknap Press of Harvard University Press, 1998), 307–308; *JHR,* Mar. 17, 1787; Jan. 23, 1788; Nov. 2, 1788.

69. Joyce E. Chaplin, "Creating a Cotton South in Georgia and South Carolina, 1760–1815," *Journal of Southern History* 57 (1991): 172–173; Louis Cecil Gray, *A History of Agriculture in the Southern United States to 1860,* 2 vols. (Washington, D.C.: Carnegie Institution of Washington, 1933; reprint ed., Gloucester, Mass.: Peter Smith, 1958), Vol. 2, 279–280; Berlin, *Many Thousands Gone,* 314.

70. In 1800 the General Assembly abolished the larger judicial districts and redefined the individual counties as judicial districts. As a result, the old counties became districts and were referred as such after this date. Kovacik and Winberry, *South Carolina: A Geography,* 7. Population statistics are based on those in Petty, *Growth and Distribution of Population,* Appendix B, 216–217, and Appendix F, 226–227.

71. Kershaw County Historical Society, *Second Federal Census, Population,1800, Kershaw County;* Kershaw County Historical Society, *Third Federal Census, Population, 1810, Kershaw County;* Kershaw County Historical Society, *Fourth Federal Census, Population, 1820, South Carolina, Kershaw County* (Camden, S.C.: Kershaw County Historical Society, 1973); Kershaw County Historical Society, *Fifth Federal Census, Population, 1830, South Carolina, Kershaw County* (Camden, S.C.: Kershaw County Historical Society, 1994); Harvey S. Teal, ed., *Old Times in Camden: Pen Pictures of the Past, by William M. Shannon* (Camden, S.C.: Kershaw County Historical Society, 1996), 29–30. Following the war John Adamson turned from mercantile activities to successfully develop his plantation, The Retreat, situated on the Wateree north of Camden. Actively involved in town society, he died in 1816, "leaving a large fortune." Kirkland and Kennedy, *Historic Camden,* 1: 263, 290, Edward M. Boykin to Lyman Draper, Oct. 7, 1872, DMC/SP, 17vv, 231.

72. The estimated loss of slaves was reported by the Revolutionary general and postwar governor William Moultrie. Berlin, *Many Thousands Gone,* 296–301; John Hope Franklin and Loren Schweninger, *Runaway Slaves: Rebels on the Plantation* (Oxford: Oxford University Press, 1999), 86–89; *SC&AGG,* Dec. 27, 1780; John Buchanan, *The Road to Guilford Courthouse: The American Revolution in the South* (New York: John Wiley, 1997), 391; Bobby G. Moss and Michael C. Scoggins, *African-American Loyalists in the Southern Campaign of the American Revolution* (Blacksburg, S.C.: Scotia-Hibernia Press, 2005), v–vii; William Moultrie, *Memoirs of the American Revolution, as Far as It Relates to the States of North Carolina, South Carolina, and Georgia,* Vol. 2 (New York: David Longworth, 1802), 351–352.

73. George Galphin to Henry Laurens, Dec. 29, 1778, Hamer et al., eds., *HLP,* 15: 20. Adam Fowler Brisbane's account is contained in Mary Brisbane vs. Isaac Alexander and Margaret Alexander, Defendant's Answer to Bill of Complaint, United District of Lancaster, Sumter, Richland, and Kershaw/ Records of the Court of Equity (UDLSRK/RCE), Roll 40, Apt. F, May 26, 1801, 36–52.

74. William Ancrum, Petition, *JHR,* Mar. 1, 1785. James Cary to Joshua English, Nov. 15, 1780, in Kirkland and Kennedy, *Historic Camden,* 1: 105. Solomon and Flora from Joseph Kershaw's estate, together with Isaac, who belonged to his brother, and Derry, from John Chesnut's plantation, joined the Engineer's Department of British Army in 1780. *RG,* Mar. 14, 1781. During the occupation, Samuel Mathis, Joseph's brother-in-law, reported that he had recovered several Kershaw family slaves, Jin, Caesar, and Punch, who had fled to the military hospital in Camden. SMJ, Mar. 1, 4, 1781. Several unnamed slaves belonging to Kershaw had been taken into exile to Jamaica by James Cary. PGA, Item 66, Dec. 1, 1802; CR, Item 62, Dec. 14, 1802.

75. The slaves named were included in the will of John Chesnut, KCRPJ/E, Apt. 130, Pkg. 5119, Est. Bk. A1, Apr. 1818, 477; Kershaw County Historical Society, *Third Federal Census, Manufacturing, 1810, South Carolina, Kershaw County* (Camden, S.C.: Kershaw County Historical Society, 1974), 1–3; Duncan McRa, Will, WT, Kershaw County, Reel 15, Frame 345, Est. Pkt. Apt. 51, Pkg. 1804, Dec. 1824.

76. Robert William Fogel and Stanley L. Engerman, *Time on the Cross: The Economics of American Negro Slavery* (Boston: Little, Brown, 1974), 55–57. Although a slave, Guinea Cato became legendary because of his exploits during the Revolution. His steadfast support of the Whig cause and his loyalty as a "faithful" servant drew the attention of early chroniclers, who portrayed him as a model of ideal behavior. Joseph Johnson, *Traditions and Reminiscences Chiefly of the American Revolution in the South* (Charleston, S.C.: Walker & James, 1851), 468. References to Cato's assignments reveal a more prosaic picture of his existence. As a trustworthy skilled worker who possessed management abilities, he served as both supervisor and craftsman, but his employment always remained subject to the needs of his owner. James Kershaw Diary, JKP, Sept. 20, 1798; Aug. 24, 1799; Sept. 11, 1799; Oct. 7, 1799; Aug. 11 and 16, 1800; Aug. 12, 20, 1801; and Memo to Joseph English, Nov. 10, 1801. Kirkpatrick was a well-known boat builder in Camden. Kirkland and Kennedy, *Historic Camden,* 1: 408n. A Revolutionary War veteran, Benjamin Carter operated a tannery northeast of Camden, producing fine leathers and moroccos. Ibid., 359. Daniel Brown was a graduate of Harvard College and came to Camden to open a law office with his brother in 1786. Ibid., 2: 227n, 252, 259. Joseph English was the brother of Joshua English, the Loyalist militia captain, whose daughter Sarah married James Kershaw. Geoff and Tom's arrival, like Geoff's disappearance "in ye night" two weeks later, was noted in James Kershaw Diary, JKP, Apr. 12, 1798; Nov. 1, 1808; Nov. 16, 1808.

77. Because they were perhaps their owners' most valuable, slaves were not freed in large numbers; however, the wills of planters often specified that favored slaves were to be freed. John Chesnut freed Teena, who had nursed his daughter during a long-term illness, and her children and provided her with an annual stipend. He also manumitted two mulatto children, Edward and Juliana Burke, upon reaching maturity and specified they should be trained "in useful occupations." John Chesnut, Will, KCRPJ/E, Apt. 13, Pkg. 5119, Est. Bk. A 1, 477, Apr. 1818. Samuel Mathis assigned Sylvia and Pat to his grandson Samuel M. Green with instructions that they be set free. Samuel Mathis, Will, KCRPJ/E, Est. Pkt. Apt. 44, Pkg. 1547, WT, Reel 15, Frame 150, Dec. 19, 1823.

78. Berlin, *Many Thousands Gone,* 319–321; Kershaw County Historical Society, *Census, Population, 1800.*

79. Bonds Conway purchased his freedom with the assistance of Zachariah Cantey, who paid his owner with funds provided by Conway. At the time of his death in 1843, he owned the block bordered by King, Market, York, and Lyttleton Streets in Camden and several houses situated on this property. Bonds Conway, Will, KCRPJ/E/Apt. 17, Pkg. 556, Est. Bk. A, Feb. 14, 1843, 49. In addition to Conway, Inabinet and Inabinet, *History of Kershaw County,* 44, 622n 7, identified Ned Harris, Buck Jakobs, Tom Martin, Jim Pemberton, Tom Pemberton, Scipio Stanley, David Sweat, John Webb, and Jim Wickham as members of Camden's free black community.

80. Berlin, *Many Thousands Gone,* 322–323.

81. Woodmason noted that "Free Negroes and Mullatoes . . . greatly abound here, . . . who have taken Refuge in these Parts from the No. Colonies." Hooker, ed., *Carolina Backcountry,* 23, 25, 277. The Harris, Griffin, and Jeffers families have been well documented in works concerning the Revolutionary War: Moss and Scoggins, *African-American Patriots in the Southern Campaign,* 109–110; Michael C. Scoggins, "'Voluntarily Enlisted as a Soldier in the Revolution': A Case Study of Free African-Americans in the South Carolina Continental and State Troops during the Revolutionary War," Research paper, Cultural & Heritage Museums (York, S.C., 2008); Paul Heinegg, *Free African Americans of North Carolina and Virginia* (Baltimore, Md.: Genealogical Pub. Co., 1994), 362.

82. For Miller Sam, see Moss and Scoggins, *African-American Patriots in the Southern Campaign,* 207. The signers of the "Petition of . . . Inhabitants of Camden District . . . Who Come Under the Description of Free Negroes, Mulattoes, and Mustizoes," *JHR,* Dec. 3, 1793, bore ten surnames, including Anderson, Bird, Coal, Going, Harris, Jones, Morriss, Shampaign, Shandley, and Woodward. Inabinet and Inabinet, *History of Kershaw County,* 625, n. 33. A similar petition, filed in 1804 by twenty women attests to at least eight additional free black families in Richland District: Wilson, Rawlinson, Seveat, Jacobs, Holley, Bolton, and Portia. Petitions of Sundry Females of Colour Pray & to be Exempt from Taxation, PGA, Item 1885, n.d.; Scoggins, "Voluntarily Enlisted as a Soldier," 5n.

83. Kenneth E. Lewis, "The Tinworker's Widow: Gender and the Formation of the Archaeological Record in the South Carolina Backcountry," in *Shared Spaces and Divided Places: Material Dimensions of Gender Relations and the American Historical Landscape,* ed. Deborah L. Rotman and Ellen-Rose Savulis (Knoxville: University of Tennessee Press, 2003), 388–90; Lewis, *Camden: Historical Archaeology,* 145–146. In 1800 the Kershaws collectively possessed sixty-three bondsmen and women. Kershaw County Historical Society,*Census, Population, 1800.*

84. A company of Catawbas had fought the British under Samuel Boykin's command at Sullivan's Island in 1776, and they sustained casualties in action against the Cherokees that year. Its warriors fought at Hanging Rock and elsewhere. Catawba warriors served under Lee and Pickens, and a Catawba militia company saw action with Sumter until the close of hostilities. Douglas Summers Brown, *The Catawba Indians: The People of the River* (Columbia: University of South Carolina Press, 1968), 259–263, 267–270; Steven G. Baker, "The Working Draft of: The Historic Catawba Peoples: Exploratory Perspectives in Ethnohistory and Archaeology" (Columbia: Office of Research, University of South Carolina, 1975),141–143. Drayton, *View of South Carolina.,* 98–99; William Johnson, *Sketches of the Life and Correspondence of Nathanael Greene,* Vol. 1 (Charleston, S.C.: A. E. Miller, 1822; reprint ed., New York: DeCapo Press, 1978), 500–501; Samuel C. Williams, ed., "General Richard Winn's Notes—1780," *South Carolina Historical Magazine* 43 (1942): 7. The Catawbas who served under Capt. Thomas Drennan are listed in Pay Bill, June 21, 1783, Company of Catawba Indians, AA, Reel 77, Frame 43, File 3931A. Those serving with Gen. Thomas Sumter are also listed in Draper's Notes, DMC/SP, 20vv, 216–220. Advanced British units advancing into the Waxhaws noted the Catawbas' absence and their abandonment of crops and property. Aware of the Indians' tie to the rebel cause and the presence of American leaders among them, their commander anticipated the need to "utterly destroy" their settlement if they showed any signs of hostility. Francis Rawdon to Charles Cornwallis, June 11, 1780, CP 30/11/2, 125; George Turnbull to Charles Cornwallis, June 15, 1780, CP 30/11/2, 158. "A Petition to the Legislature of the State of South Carolina from the Catawba Indians," Feb. 13, 1784, JBKP, noted the appropriation of cattle by the American militia and sheep by the British army. Their hogs had either been destroyed or driven wild.

85. *JHR,* Feb. 6, 1782; *JS,* Feb. 7, 1782. The legislature appropriated a total of £299.15.8 sterling to the Catawbas "for 58 days of service by 35 men under different commands." *JHR,* Report of Committee to Consider Provision for Catawba Indians, Feb. 24, 1784; Samuel Mathis & Co., Invoice of Goods Distributed to the Catawba Indians, 23d May, 1784, to be made up in Hoes, Axes & Gunflints and to the Widows of Willis & Peters, Killed in the Service, JBKP; Message from Gov. William Moultrie, *JHR,* Feb. 17, 1785. James H. Merrell, *The Indians' New World: Catawbas and Their Neighbors from European Contact through Removal* (Chapel Hill: University of North Carolina Press, 1989), 218–221.

86. "Petition to the Legislature," Feb. 13, 1784; "Petition of the Catawba Nation of Indians . . . Respecting the Enclosed in a Letter from Colonel Kershaw," *JHR,* Mar. 10, 1786; Joseph Kershaw to Gov. William Moultrie, Apr. 24, 1786, NGP/CL, 85: 31. Tribal members continued to maintain ties with the Kershaw family following his death, as witnessed by a visit of "the Indians" to his son James as late as 1801. James Kershaw Diary, JKP, Dec. 3, 1801.

87. Baker, "Historic Catawba Peoples," 146–147; Brett H. Riggs, "Temporal Trends in Native Ceramic Traditions of the Lower Catawba River Valley," *Southeastern Archaeology* 29 (2010): 37. The quote is from Winslow C. Watson, ed., *Men and Times of the Revolution; or, Memoirs of Elkanah Watson* (New York: Dana, 1856), 258. For accounts of the Catawbas, see J. F. D. Smyth, *A Tour of the United States of America, Containing an Account of the Present Situation of That Country,* Vol. 1 (London: G. Robinson, 1784), 196–197; Robert Mills to Sarah Mather, 1804 in Mills, "Letters from Robert Mills," *South Carolina Historical Magazine* 39 (1938): 111. Merrell, "Indians' New World," 562–564.

88. During the period of British rule, the King's Proclamation of 1763 prohibited the issuance of survey warrants or patents on any lands reserved to Indians or the purchase of such lands, and, after independence, the federal Trade and Intercourse Act of 1790 forbade the purchase, grant, lease, or other conveyance of lands belonging to Indian tribes or nations. The State of South Carolina, with the

support of the Catawba Nation, passed legislation allowing and regulating the leasing of Catawba lands, resulting in nearly all reservation lands being leased by 1830. This set the stage for the signing of the Treaty of Nation Ford in 1840, by which the Catawbas ceded their lands to the state in return for the promise of a smaller tract. After two years of wandering homeless, they were resettled on a 630-acre tract within the old reservation's boundaries. The Catawbas continued to occupy this land, and it became the basis for subsequent territorial claims. Mark Ulmer, "Tribal Property: Defining the Parameters of the Federal Trust Relationship under the Non-Intercourse Act: Catawba Indian Tribe vs. South Carolina," *American Law Review* 12 (1984): 109–110, 116–118. An 1808 act of the South Carolina legislature attempted to regulate leasing through a superintendent, but dissatisfaction with the terms of the leases and the superintendent's inability to enforce their conditions led the Catawbas to petition for stricter controls. "Petitions of Chiefs and Headmen of the Catawba Nation Of Indians in York District," PGA, Item 6, Nov. 30, 1810; Item 28, Nov. 27, 1811; Item 5, n.d., 1815.

In addition to the reservation lands, individual Catawbas acquired property in their own right. Peter Harris, who had soldiered with both Georgia and South Carolina troops during the Revolution, received three bounty land grants totaling two hundred acres in Chester County for his service. Peter Harris, AA, Reel 67, Frame 454, File 3368A; Michael C. Scoggins, "Biographies of Third South Carolina Continental Regiment Soldiers in Painting," *Southern Campaigns of the American Revolution* 3, no. 12 (2006): 32–33.

89. Steven G. Baker, "Colono-Indian Pottery from Cambridge, South Carolina, with Comments on the Historic Catawba Pottery Trade," *South Carolina Institute of Archaeology and Anthropology, Notebook* 4, no. 1 (1972): 13–15; R. P. Stephen Davis and Brett H. Riggs, "An Introduction to the Catawba Project," *North Carolina Archaeology* 53 (2004): 4–5, 9–13, 26; Brett H. Riggs et al., "Catawba Pottery in the Post-Revolutionary Era: A View from the Source," *North Carolina Archaeology* 55 (2006): 60–88; Riggs, "Temporal Trends in Native Ceramic Traditions," 36–40.

90. As Greene's army neared Camden from the north, Guilford Dudley witnessed "Logtown then in flames, and the houses crumbling down, the enemy having, upon our approach, withdrawn their pickets and applied the torch to that appendage to the village of Camden." Guilford Dudley, RWP-BLWAF, R 234, Application W 8681. The classic description of the British destruction that left Camden "little more than a heap of rubbish" is from Nathaniel Greene to Samuel Huntington, May 14, 1781, Conrad, ed., *PNG,* 8: 250. Archaeological investigations at Camden, on the other hand, have shown that the destruction was confined to specific areas. Although buildings were damaged, much of the town remained intact following the British army's departure. Kenneth E. Lewis, "'Little Better Than a Heap of Rubbish': History. Legend, and the Archaeological Record at Camden," *South Carolina Historical Magazine* 114 (2013): 246–248.

91. Joseph Lee Boyle, ed., "The Revolutionary War Diaries of Captain Walter Finney," *South Carolina Historical Magazine* 98 (1997): 134.

92. Smyth, *Tour of the United States of America,,* 202; Krawczynski, ed., "William Drayton's Journal," 202.

93. David Humphreys to George Washington, W. W. Abbot and Dorothy Twohig, eds., *The Papers of George Washington: Presidential Series, 1788–1791,* Vol. 4 (Charlottesville: University Press of Virginia, 1987–1999), 171; Arnold Roschen Letter quoted in G. D. Bernheim, *History of the German Settlements and the Lutheran Church in North and South Carolina* (Philadelphia: The Lutheran Book Store, 1872; reprint ed., Spartanburg, S.C.: The Reprint Co., 1972), 320; Winslow C. Watson, ed., *Men and Times of the Revolution; or, Memoirs of Elkanah Watson* (New York: Dana, 1856), 259.

94. William Loughton Smith, "Journal of William Loughton Smith, 1790–1791," *Proceedings of the Massachusetts Historical Society,* 3rd ser., 51 (1917–1918): 75; Jedediah Morse, *American Gazetteer* (Boston: S. Hall, and Thomas & Andrews, 1797); Drayton, *View of South Carolina,* 211. In December 1797 the Methodist bishop Thomas Coke found Camden a "tolerable town" and agreed with Drayton's estimate of "about two hundred houses." Albert M. Shipp, *The History of Methodism in South Carolina.* (Nashville, Tenn.: Southern Methodist Publishing House, 1884), 284–285.

95. Morse, *American Gazetteer;* Drayton, *View of South Carolina,* 211.

96. Harvey S. Teal, ed., *Old Times in Camden: Pen Pictures of the Past, by William M. Shannon* (Camden, S.C.: Kershaw County Historical Society, 1996), 27; Kirkland and Kennedy, *Historic Camden,* 1: 278–279; "Two Ancient Landmarks," *Scribner's Monthly* 9 (1875): 618; Margaret Maxwell Martin, "Rides about Camden, 1853," 19; Donald Jackson and Dorothy Twohig, eds., *The Diaries of George Washington,* Vol. 6 (Charlottesville: University Press of Virginia, 1976), 148; Lucy Carpenter to William Blanding, Nov. 23, 1848; Feb. 23, 1849, William Blanding Papers (hereafter WBP), South Caroliniana Library, University of South Carolina, Columbia. For the use of the Kershaw mansion by spectators at military reviews, see "Fourth of July and Other Days in Old Camden," *Camden Chronicle,* 1912.

97. Sarah Thompson Alexander, "Camden Fifty Years Ago," South Caroliniana Library, University of South Carolina, Columbia; "Items from the Reminiscences of Mrs. Phineas Thornton, Dec. 11, 1856," ETP. James Kershaw, Plat of Lower Camden, Kirkland Papers, Box 1–12, South Caroliniana Library, University of South Carolina, Columbia. Reference to the "Red House" appeared in and advertisement in the *Charleston Morning Post and Advertiser,* Aug. 4, 1786, quoted in Kirkland and Kennedy, *Historic Camden,* 2: 262–263. Joseph Kershaw's 1788 will referred to a "School House Lot" on Market Street. A "Red House Lot" lay just to the north, and a "Red Store Lot" was immediately to the west on Broad Street. Joseph Kershaw, Will, KCRPJ/E, Apt. 37, Pkg. 1354, Est. Bk. C, Sept. 21, 1815, 59. The similarity of these names to that of the boarding school implies that they refer to the same building. The brewhouse still stood when the executors of Aaron Loocock's estate sold the block of sixteen lots to Lewis Ciples on May 26, 1801, and when, two years later, on Sept. 5, 1803, he transferred the property to Sarah English. KCRCC/C, Book C, p. 190, Book D, 133. The Blue House was built after the Revolution. It was the residence of Dr. Isaac Alexander and lay on a tract acquired by his wife, Margaret Brisbane Smith, in 1788, a year prior to their marriage. Adam Fowler Brisbane to Margaret Smith, CBMC, Vol. Y-5, Aug. 25, 1788, Brent Holcomb, ed., *Kershaw County, South Carolina, Minutes of the County Court, 1791–1799* (Easley, S.C.: By the Author, 1986), 21. For the Presbyterian Church, see Kirkland and Kennedy, *Historic Camden,* 2: 292. The presence of the market house was mentioned in a property transfer from James Kershaw to Richard Lloyd Champion: KCRCC/C, Book B, 107.

98. Kenneth E. Lewis, *Camden: A Frontier Town in Eighteenth Century South Carolina,* Anthropological Studies 2 (Columbia: South Carolina Institute of Archaeology and Anthropology, 1976), 44, 106; Lewis, "The Tinworker's Widow," 86–103; Lewis, *Camden: Historical Archaeology,* 119–120, 127, 130–133, 168.

John Dinkins acquired the lots on which the tavern stood from the estate of Aaron Loocock in 1795, but his family apparently had operated the establishment for several years. KCRCC/C, Book A, 182 The legislature rented its ballroom in 1791 for the use of the circuit court, and three years later Camden residents entertained Edmond C. Genêt of the new French republic there during his visit to South Carolina. *JHR,* Dec. 16, 1791; Kirkland and Kennedy, *Historic Camden,* 1: 319; Klein, *Unification of a Slave State,* 206. Thomas Dinkins owned the lots on which his house stood on the west side of Broad Street as late as February 1806: KCRCC/C, Book E, 362. Gayeton Aiguier acquired the Kershaw store property from William Ancrum on May 28, 1798: KCRCC/C, Book BB, 220. Ancrum had purchased the tract previously from Joseph Kershaw: LCRCC/C, Book B, 11. Joseph Kershaw sold the brewhouse block to Aaron Loocock on Apr. 6, 1786: LCRCC/C, Book 10, 10. The family, however, appears to have had use of the property during the following decade. James Kershaw rented the brewhouse to George Brown in 1793 and sold the "brewing implements" the following year. James Kershaw Diary, JKPD, Feb. 12, 1793; Aug. 14, 1794. The date ranges of the occupations of all these buildings are based on an analysis of the ceramic artifacts recovered. Lewis, *Camden: Historical Archaeology,* 114.

99. Kirkland and Kennedy, *Historic Camden,* 1: 15–17; Schulz, "Rise and Decline of Camden," 46–47; Lipscomb, *South Carolina in 1791,* 71–72. The Extended Plan of Camden was created by legislative act in conformity with the report of a commission that consisted of James Kershaw, John Kershaw, William Lang, James Chesnut, and Samuel Mathis. Cooper, ed., *Statutes at Large,* Vol. 5, Act No. 1702, 1798.

100. For a comprehensive list of Camden businesses in the 1790s, 1800s, and 1810s, see Schulz, "Rise and Fall of Camden," Appendices F, G, and H, 109–113.

101. By late 1792 the jail had apparently fallen into such disrepair that the Camden District Grand Jury found it "very inadequate in point of strength & that in its present state it is impossible to secure some culprits." GJP, Nov. 21, 1792. Thirteen years later the Kershaw District grand jury reported that the jail was again in "ruinous" condition, "having been greatly injured by lightning." GJP, April 1805; Kirkland and Kennedy, *Historic Camden,* 2: 254.

102. *JHR,* Feb. 7, 23, 25, Nov. 3, 1788; Jan. 27, Mar. 6, 1789; Feb. 19, 1791. Camden was divided into four wards arranged from south to north in May 1792: Kirkland and Kennedy, *Historic Camden,* 1: 15, 30.

103. Daniel C. Littlefield. *Rice and Slaves: Ethnicity and the Slave Trade in Colonial South Carolina,* (Baton Rouge: Louisiana State University Press, 1981) 159–160. A 1792 store account from Camden revealed that half of the Revolutionary War veterans trading there had immigrated from outside the state. Joyce E. Chaplin, "Creating a Cotton South in Georgia and South Carolina, 1760–1815," *Journal of Southern History* 57 (1991): 185–186.

104. Pierre Jumelle was a native of the parish of La Petite Rivier de l'Artibonite, Saint Domingue. Francois Villepigue, who was born in France, emigrated to the island with his family in 1786. He was killed in 1800, and his widow and sons subsequently fled. They arrived in Charleston and made their way to Camden in 1807. *KCCSP,* 27; Robert MacMillan Kennedy, *De Mortuis: Concerning Those That Lie in the Old Burial Grounds in and about Camden, S.C.* (Columbia: The State Co., 1935), 19; Kirkland and Kennedy, *Historic Camden,* 2: 344, 439.

105. Teal, ed., "Old Times in Camden,1873," 24–25, 27; Kirkland and Kennedy, *Historic Camden,* 2: 23, 224, 388–389; 418, 436–438; Kennedy, *De Mortius,* 14; Inabinet and Inabinet, *History of Kershaw County,* 107; Jeannie Heyward Jervey Register, "Marriage and Death Notices from the *City Gazette,*" *South Carolina Historical Magazine* 26 (1925): 167; Elizabeth Heyward Jervey, "Marriage and Death Notices from the *Charleston Courier,*" *South Carolina Historical Magazine* 30 (1929): 122.

106. Charles Reznikoff and Uriah Z. Engelman, *The Jews of Charleston: A History of an American Jewish Community* (Philadelphia: Jewish Publication Society of America, 1950), 3–9, 11–18; James William Hagy, *This Happy Land: The Jews of Colonial and Antebellum Charleston* (Tuscaloosa: University of Alabama Press, 1993), 12–14, 24–32, 57–60.

107. Reznikoff and Engelman, *The Jews of Charleston,* 49, 50, 53; Barnett A. Elzas, *The Jews of South Carolina, from the Earliest Times to the Present Day* (Philadelphia: J. B. Lippincott, 1905), 244; Hagy, *This Happy Land,* 21, 24, 116, 177–179, 359, 363, 395; J. Hampton Hoch, *The History of Pharmacy in South Carolina* (Charleston, S.C.: South Carolina Pharmaceutical Association, 1951), 74; Kirkland and Kennedy, *Historic Camden,* 2: 407, 447; Samuel Levy, Will, KCRPJ/E, Book C, Apt. 40, Pkg. 1444, Jan. 12, 1801, 313. Joseph Kershaw, Will, KCRPJ/E, Apt. 37, Pkg. 1354, Est. Bk. C, Sept. 21, 1815, 59.

108. Kirkland and Kennedy, *Historic Camden,* 1: 321–322, 343, 393; ibid., 2: 100–103, 259; Kennedy, *De Mortius,* 13–14; Teal, ed., *Old Times in Camden,* 30; Elizabeth Heyward Jervey, "Death Notices from the *City Gazette* and *Daily Advertiser,*" *South Carolina Historical Magazine* 33 (1932): 301.

109. Kirkland and Kennedy, *Historic Camden,* 1: 362–364; ibid., 2: 293; Kennedy, *De Mortius,* 14, 20–22; Mabel L. Webber, "Marriage and Death Notices from the *City Gazette,*" *South Carolina Historical Magazine* 24 (1923): 34.

110. Kirkland and Kennedy, *Historic Camden,* 1: 352–353; ibid., 2: 344; Isaac Alexander and Margaret Alexander vs. exia. A. F. Brisbane, Complaint, UDLSRK/RCE, Roll 40, Apt. F, Oct. 10, 1798, 36–52.

111. Kirkland and Kennedy, *Historic Camden,* 1: 393, 322, 343; E. Haviland Hillman, "The Brisbanes," *South Carolina Historical Magazine* 14 (1913): 128; Kennedy, *De Mortius,* 14; Kirkland and Kennedy, *Historic Camden,* 1: 365.

112. Klein, *Unification of a Slave State,* 239–246, 257–266, 276–282; Schulz, "Rise and Decline of Camden," 38; Lacy K. Ford, *Origins of Southern Radicalism: The South Carolina Upcountry, 1800–1860* (New York: Oxford, 1988), 32–34; Kirkland and Kennedy, *Historic Camden,* 1: 15; 2, 263–264; Inabinet and Inabinet, *History of Kershaw County,* 109, 116–121.

113. Frank Lawrence Owsley, *Plain Folk of the Old South* (Chicago: Quadrangle Books, 1949), 134–135; Orville Vernon Burton, *In My Father's House Are Many Mansions: Family and Community in Edgefield, South Carolina* (Chapel Hill: University of North Carolina Press, 1985), 104, 117.

Chapter 12. "A New Generation and a New Town"

1. Lacy K. Ford, *Origins of Southern Radicalism: The South Carolina Upcountry, 1800–1860* (New York: Oxford, 1988), 49–51, 52, has argued that the form of republicanism espoused by residents of the interior incorporated an ideology that might more accurately be called "country-republican," emphasizing political ideals of the Revolutionary era that stressed the link between the concept of independence and the ability to control one's own household affairs, especially those relating to economy. Personal independence without restriction became the essence of freedom that was secure only when it rested on a proper economic foundation. This belief favored a political economy based on the idea that widespread ownership of productive property freed men from dependence on others and protected them from manipulation by demagogues and capitalists. Such a political economy prevailed in the antebellum backcountry to the extent that the bulk of the free population consisted of land or property owners whose control of wealth met the minimum economic standard for personal independence. Ownership of slaves was an important factor in amassing the wealth upon which independence rested, and its presence separated the ideology of country-republicanism from the free-labor ideology of the Republican party. Rachel N. Klein, *Unification of a Slave State: The Rise of the Planter Class in the South Carolina Backcountry, 1760–1808* (Chapel Hill: University of North Carolina Press for the Institute of Early American History and Culture, 1990), 303–305, summarizes the argument for political unification in South Carolina. For discussions of the tensions resulting from inequalities in the antebellum economy see Edward Pessen, "How Different from Each Other Were the Antebellum North and South?," *American Historical Review* 85 (1980): 1146–1147; Stanley L. Engerman, "A Reconsideration of Southern Economic Growth," *Agricultural History* 49 (1975): 354–357; Douglass C. North, *The Economic Growth of the United States, 1790–1860* (New York: W. W. Norton & Co., 1966), 122–134. Contemporary arguments relating to the defense of slavery are summarized in Drew Gilpin Faust, "A Southern Stewardship: The Intellectual and the Proslavery Argument," *American Quarterly* 31 (1979): 74–80: Eugene D. Genovese, *The World the Slaveholders Made: Two Essays in Interpretation* (New York: Pantheon Books, 1969), 118–150, 1850.

2. Phinehas Thornton to Clarissa Martin, Dec. 20, 1850, letter in author's possession.

3. Sarah Thompson Alexander, "Camden Fifty Years Ago," [1850], KP, Box 2–23, South Caroliniana Library, University of South Carolina, Columbia. Sarah Thompson Alexander was the second wife of Dr. Isaac Alexander, a Revolutionary War surgeon from North Carolina. Captured at the Battle of Camden, he attended the wounded, including Gen. DeKalb. He returned to settle in Camden in 1784 and built the Blue House on the west side of Broad Street before 1788. He practiced medicine in Camden until his death in 1812. During this time he also served the public in various capacities, including county legislator in 1786, intendant of Camden in 1794 and 1807, judge of the Kershaw County Court from 1794 to 1799, trustee of South Carolina College, and elder of the Bethesda Presbyterian Church. He married Margaret Brisbane Smith, half sister of planter Adam Fowler Brisbane, about 1788. Following her death in 1806, he married Sarah Thompson, a niece of Phinehas Thornton. Thomas J. Kirkland and Robert M. Kennedy, *Historic Camden, Vol. 1: Colonial and Revolutionary* (Columbia, S.C.: The State Co., 1905), 35, 191, 342–343; ibid., *Vol. 2: Nineteenth Century* (Columbia, S.C.: State Printing Co., 1926), 2, 18, 293, 349; Joseph Ioor Waring, *History of Medicine in South Carolina, 1670–1825* (Columbia: South Carolina Medical Association, 1963), 341, 377; Elizabeth Heyward Jervey, "Marriage and Death Notices from the *City Gazette*," *South Carolina Historical Magazine* 31 (1930): 163; Jervey, "Marriage and Death Notices from the *City Gazette* and *Daily Advertiser*," *South Carolina Historical Magazine* 37 (1936): 85–86. For the impact of railroad transportation and the development of the initial early railroad connection to Camden and the establishment of banks there, see Kirkland and Kennedy, *Historic Camden*, 2: 40–41, 42–43, and Lacy K. Ford, "Yeoman Farmers in the South Carolina Upcountry: Changing Production Patterns in the Late Antebellum Era," *Agricultural History* 60, no. 4 (1986): 30.

4. Phinehas Thornton to Clarissa Martin, Dec. 20, 1850; Ford, *Origins of Southern Radicalism*, 37–38; Peter Coclanis, *The Shadow of a Dream: Economic Life and Death in the South Carolina Low*

Country, 1670–1920 (New York: Oxford University Press, 1989), 132–137; Walter Edgar, *South Carolina: A History* (Columbia: University of South Carolina Press, 1998), 273–275, 330–339; Kirkland and Kennedy, *Historic Camden,* 2: 83–90.

5. Ford, "Yeoman Farmers in the South Carolina Upcountry," 32–36.

6. Hugh Swinton Legaré, *Writings of Hugh Swinton Legaré . . . Consisting of a Diary of Brussels, and Journeys of the Rhine; Extracts from His Private and Diplomatic Correspondence: Orations and Speeches: and Contributions to the New-York and Southern Reviews* (Charleston,S.C.: Brges & James, 1846), 221, and *Camden Journal,* Feb. 22, 1834, July 25, Nov. 20, 1835, quoted in Julian J. Petty, *The Growth and Distribution of Population in South Carolina* (Columbia: South Carolina State Planning Board, 1943; reprint ed., Spartanburg, S.C.: The Reprint Co., 1975), 141–142, and in Joan A. Inabinet and L. Glen Inabinet, *A History of Kershaw County, South Carolina* (Columbia: University of South Carolina Press, 2011), 147. Farm making on the frontier required access to the capital resources needed to acquire and improve the land, a factor that favored immigrants who had achieved previous success and possessed the entrepreneurial motivation to invest their resources in a new endeavor. Stephen I. Thompson, *Pioneer Colonization: A Cross-Cultural View,* Addison-Wesley Modules in Anthropology 33 (Reading, Mass.: Addison-Wesley, 1973), 8–9; Kenneth E. Lewis, *West to Far Michigan: Settling the Lower Peninsula, 1815–1860* (East Lansing: Michigan State University Press, 2002), 103–109. The migration of younger family members, who had access to the capital, slaves, and other resources necessary to place western lands into large-scale production, proved a viable strategy for established planting families that sought to expand their operations. Robert William Fogel and Stanley L. Engerman, *Time on the Cross: The Economics of American Negro Slavery* (Boston: Little, Brown, 1974), 44. Frank Lawrence Owsley, *Plain Folk of the Old South* (Chicago: Quadrangle Books, 1949), 24, 134–135, argued that the desire to acquire public lands in the West was the most common motive among small farmers who saw abundance of cheap land and an expanding market for agricultural produce as a key to economic security and well-being.

7. Kirkland and Kennedy, *Historic Camden,* 1: 369; 352; 393; 349; 301–304, 357; 374–375; Inabinet and Inabinet, *History of Kershaw County,* 148.

8. Petty, *Growth and Distribution of Population,* 226–227.

9. Samuel Wyly and others had petitioned for a fair at Pine Tree Hill as early as 1765; however the Assembly denied their request. "Petition from Settler Living at or Near Pine Tree Hill," *JCHA,* Mar. 20, 1765. Nine years later, the legislature approved a similar petition by the partners of Kershaw & Co.: *SCG,* Mar. 30, 1765; Kirkland and Kennedy, *Historic Camden,* 1: 12–13. *JHR,* Mar. 16, 1783; "Petition from Charles Mason, Evander McIver, Thomas Powe and William Dewit," *JHR,* Mar. 5, Mar. 9, 1785; "Petition of John Winn, Richard Winn and John Vanderbuilt," *JHR,* Feb. 21, Mar. 8, 1785. Not all petitions for fairs were successful. An effort to create a fair at Chatham, on the Wateree opposite Camden, failed to win approaval of the legislature. "Petition of Joseph Kershaw, John Chesnut and William Kershaw," Mar. 1, 1785.

10. Caroline E. MacGill, *History of Transportation in the United States before 1860* (Washington, D.C.: Carnegie Institution of Washington, 1917; reprint ed., Gloucester, Mass.: Peter Smith, 1948), 422–427. Built between 1820 and 1829, the State Road precipitated the construction of feeder routes and bridges over rivers to connect with it. The road saw especially heavy use between Columbia and Charleston. Roads and railroads soon drew traffic away from the canals on the Wateree, and by 1838 the Wateree/Catawba navigation system had been abandoned. Robert J. Kapsch, *Historic Canals & Waterways of South Carolina* (Columbia: University of South Carolina Press, 2010), 18–19, 116–117, 134–141. Recognized as the key to developing agricultural resources throughout the interior, railroads attracted investment capital in the late 1840s and expanded rapidly in subsequent years. A branch of the South Carolina Railroad extended east out of Columbia and crossed the low, swampy lands along the Wateree on a four-mile-long trestle. It then proceeded north along the river's eastern bank, reaching Camden on Nov. 1, 1848. Kirkland and Kennedy, *Historic Camden,* 1: 40–41; Ford, *Origins of Southern Radicalism,* 219–221.

11. Even before the railroad arrived, Columbia had surpassed of Camden in size. The capital had five hundred houses in 1826, whereas Camden had only three hundred. Robert Mills, *Statistics of South*

Carolina (Charleston, S.C.: Hurlbut and Lloyd, 1856; reprint ed., Spartanburg, S.C.: The Reprint Co., 1972), 590. John Hammond Moore, *Columbia and Richland County: A South Carolina Community, 1740–1990* (Columbia: University of South Carolina Press, 1993), 136–137.

12. Wesley Everett Rich, *The History of the United States Post Office to the Year 1829* (Cambridge, Mass.: Harvard University Press, 1924), 68–71. The postal system played a key role in integrating society and the economy in antebellum America. Communication depended heavily on the mail. In addition to bringing individuals tidings from family and friends, the mail service offered agricultural and business enterprises vital communications and exchange services. Letters and printed matter carried news of politics, agricultural innovations, and marketing trends. Indeed, the marked increase in letters sent after 1800 was largely a result of the growth in the use of the mail for conducting business affairs over long distances. The information and materials the mail carried linked the country's new settlements and maintained connections with older settled areas. Wayne E. Fuller, *The American Mail: Enlarger of the Common Life* (Chicago: University of Chicago Press: 1972), 88; Richard R. John, *Spreading the News: The American Postal System from Franklin to Morse* (Cambridge, Mass.: Harvard University Press, 1995), 148.

13. Harvey S. Teal and Robert J. Stets, *South Carolina Postal History and Illustrated Catalog of Postmarks, 1760–1860* (Lake Oswego, Ore.: Raven Press, 1989),, 16–18, 23–33, 81.

14. The courthouse was a two-storied building constructed to a fully-developed temple plan originally fronted by an Ionic portico. Modified in 1847, the building remains standing. John M. Bryan, *America's First Architect: Robert Mills* (New York: Princeton Architectural Press, 2001) 156–160; Kirkland and Kennedy, *Historic Camden,* 2: 257.

15. James Kershaw to Richard Lloyd Champion KCRCC/C, Book B, p. 107; PGA, Item 69, Nov. 12, 1812; Cooper and McCord, ed., *Statutes at Large,* Vol. 5, Act No. 2023, 1839; *Camden Gazette,* Apr. 6, 1816.

16. Kirkland and Kennedy, *Historic Camden,* 2: 42; Edgar, *South Carolina,* 284; Ford, *Origins of Southern Radicalism,* 242; Bodenhorn, *State Banking,*224.

17. See for e.g., "The Need for Education, Sermon Book IV, 1770," in Hooker, ed., *Carolina Backcountry,* 118–119; "Statement of Chief Justice Gordon and Justice Murray Following Their Return from the Camden Circuit," *SCG,* Dec. 10, 1772; "Presentment of Cheraws Grand Jury," *SCG,* Dec. 27, 1773; J. H. Easterby, "The South Carolina Education Bill of 1770," *South Carolina Historical Magazine,* 48 (1947), 103;

18. Apparently no formal schools existed in Camden before the Revolution, although Charles Woodmason attempted unsuccessfully to organize a free school for "poor children" during his residence there. Journal, Oct. 5, Dec. 21, 1766, in Hooker, *Carolina Backcountry,* 7, 11. A boarding school for young ladies apparently operated before 1786 at the "Red House," situated in on Broad Street just north of the old square. Joseph Kershaw's 1788 will mentioned a "School House Lot"situated on Market Street east of the "Red Store Lot," perhaps a reference to the same institution. Kirkland and Kennedy, *Historic Camden,* 2: 262–263. The presence of literate native residents, such as Samuel Mathis, implies that some children at Pine Tree Hill/Camden received a rudimentary education; however, parents with the financial wherewithal who desired formal schooling for their children were obliged to send them elsewhere to attend classes. Joseph Kershaw sent his eldest sons James and John to England for their education when they were aged eight and seven respectively, enrolling them at Rishworth School near his family home in Yorkshire. Later they attended Richmond Academy in Surry before returning to South Carolina in 1784. Whiteley, "Joseph Kershaw of Baitingsgate," 4; Joseph Kershaw to Henry Laurens, Jan. 5, 1780, Hamer et al., *HLP,* 15: 221; Kirkland and Kennedy, *Historic Camden,* 1: 276.

The General Assembly incorporated the Camden Orphan Society in 1788 for the purpose of erecting school buildings and promoting the schooling of "poor orphans and other poor children in distress." Although the society sponsored the education of four orphans annually, other students paid tuition. The school opened in 1791 and in 1805 enlarged its curriculum to become an academy and operated at various locations in Camden, including the Kershaw mansion from 1805 to 1822. *JHR,* Feb. 27, 1788; Kirkland and Kennedy, *Historic Camden,* 2: 263–269; Inabinet and Inabinet, *History of Kershaw*

County, 109, 137–138. For discussions of other private and specialty school in Camden, see, Kirkland and Kennedy, *Historic Camden,* 2: 271–276, and Inabinet and Inabinet, *History of Kershaw County,* 138–141.

In addition to the Camden Orphan Society, successful academies, like the Willington Academy in Abbeville District and the Columbia Academy in the capital, arose in every district in the state. In the eastern Backcountry, two additional academies, Mt. Zion at Winnsboro, organized in 1777 and St. David's at Society Hill founded the following year, stood out as institutions that educated regional elites throughout the antebellum period. In 1801, the legislature incorporated South Carolina College as the pinnacle of the state's educational system, locating the new institution at Columbia. Edgar, *South Carolina,* 298; Moore, *Columbia and Richland County,* 69–70, 100–102. Kirkland and Kennedy, *Historic Camden,* 2: 263.

19. Ibid., 278, 283, 288–289, 292–295; Inabinet, *Lyttleton Street United Methodist Church,* 60–61.

20. The Intendant was the head of Camden's town council, which also included four wardens, all of whom were elected annually. Kirkland and Kennedy, *Historic Camden,* 1: 15. Mills, *Statistics,* 586; Simms, *Geography of South Carolina,* 88. William M. Shannon's descriptive accounts of Camden in 1873 and 1776 mention Kershaw's founding role: Shannon, "Rides about Camden, 1873," in *Rides about Camden, 1853 & 1873,* ed. Harvey S. Teal (Columbia: SC: McDonald Letter Shop, 1961), 21; Harvey S. Teal, ed, *Old Times in Camden: Pen Pictures of the Past, by William M. Shannon* (Camden, S.C.: Kershaw County Historical Society, 1996), 3–4, as does another contemporary sketch of the town. W. S. Alexander and John W. Corbett, *A Descriptive Sketch of Camden, S.C.* (Charleston, S.C.: Walker, Evans & Cogswell, 1888; reprint ed., Camden, S.C.: Kershaw County Historical Society, 1996), 7.

Kershaw's mansion remained an attraction throughout the antebellum period. Anne Royall, *Mrs. Royall's Southern Tour, or Second Series of the Black Book, Vol. 2* (Washington, DC: By the Author, 1831), 41, visited the mansion in 1830 in her travels. Nearly two decades later, Lucy Carpenter remarked that it was the house left standing to mark the site of the old town. Lucy Carpenter to William Blanding, Nov. 23, 1848, WBP. By then it had become "a dilapidated building . . . tenantless and forsaken": Margaret Maxwell Martin, "Rides about Camden, 1853," in *Rides about Camden,* ed. Harvey S. Teal (Columbia, S.C.: McDonald Letter Shop, 1961), 19. An mid-nineteenth century resident recalled visiting the abandoned house as a boy. His description mentioned the fence, the caretakers living in the yard, and his frightening ascent into a building inhabited by a "bat, owls and of course, ghosts." The mansion and its historical importance were sufficient for an anonymous author to present it and its associations to a national audience a decade after its destruction. "Two Ancient Landmarks," *Scribner's Monthly* 9 (1875): 618. Long vacant, the Kershaw mansion was used as a storehouse for foodstuffs by the Confederate government during the winter of 1865. When federal troops under Gen. Oliver Howard reached Camden in late February, they destroyed provisions stored there, including many public buildings. Kirkland and Kennedy, *Historic Camden,* 2: 164–167, present conflicting accounts. One states that the house was destroyed by the Confederate commissary to keep the enemy from capturing the supplies it contained, while the other contends that Union troops burned it to deny the contents to Confederates. The fire apparently cooked and preserved meat and other consumables in the ashes of the structure, providing food for a local population left destitute by the invading army.

21. All historical sources dealing with the Revolution in the southern states mention Camden as the site of two major battles significant to the outcome of the war. Joseph Kershaw's role in the Revolution appeared as early as 1794 with the publication of Stedman's account of the British occupation of Camden: Charles Stedman, *History of the American War* (London: J. Murray, 1794), 193–194n. His earlier participation in the 1775 Drayton-Tennent-Hart mission was chronicled in John Drayton's *Memoirs of the American Revolution, from the Commencement to the Year 1776, Vol. 1* (Charleston, S.C.: A. E. Miller, 1821), 324, 364–365, 368, 376; and William Moultrie's 1802 two-volume work, *Memoirs of the American Revolution, as Far as It Relates to the States of North Carolina, South Carolina, and Georgia,* Vol. 1 (New York: David Longworth, 1802), 125, 129, discussed his participation in the Purrysburg expedition of 1779. Joseph Johnson's *Traditions and Reminiscences Chiefly of the American Revolution in the South* (Charleston, S.C.: Walker & James, 1851), 463–469, included extensive discussions of the Kershaw brothers as well as the fate of Joseph's family and the occupation of his mansion in Camden. Both

British commanders at Camden, Earl Cornwallis and Lord Rawdon, went on to distinguished military careers untainted by the American War. Despite the humiliation of his surrender at Yorktown, Virginia, in the fall of 1781, Cornwallis was received at home as a hero. Appointed governor general and commander in chief of Bengal in 1786, he successfully used his military abilities to expand British power in India. Upon his return in 1793, he became Marquess Cornwallis and was appointed Lord Lieutenant of Ireland five years later. He returned to India as governor general in 1805 but died shortly after his arrival. John Buchanan, *The Road to Guilford Courthouse: The American Revolution in the South* (New York: John Wiley, 1997), 389–390. Rawdon was promoted to general in 1803, and later he too became governor general of Bengal, where he served from 1813 to 1822. Alan Valentine, *British Establishment, 1760–1784: An Eighteenth Century Biographical Dictionary* (Norman: University of Oklahoma Press, 1970), Vol. 2, 732.

22. As intendant of Camden and chairman of the reception committee to welcome George Washington to the town, Joseph Kershaw delivered the welcoming address to the first president on Mar. 25, 1791. It is perhaps noteworthy that the dinner and reception for Washington were held at the home of John Chesnut in Camden. Kirkland and Kennedy, *Historic Camden,* 1: 308–312. Lafayette's visit in 1825 occurred long after Kershaw's death in 1791; nevertheless, the marquis initially planned to honor the family with a stop at the home of Sarah Kershaw Perkins, Joseph's daughter, during his visit. Ibid., 2: 66n.

23. Priscilla Ann Trantham Oliver, *Living in Camden: Scenes since* Historic Camden (Camden, S.C.: Kershaw County Historical Society, 1995), 6–13.

24. Martin, "Rides about Camden, 1853," 8.

25. Ibid., 10.

Bibliography

Primary Sources

MANUSCRIPT SOURCES

Historic Camden Foundation, Camden, S.C.

Benjamin Ingraham Diary, excerpt
Kershaw & Company, Charleston Store Account Book, 1778–1779, KCCSAB
Unidentified Camden Account Book, 1779–1780, UCAB

Great Britain, Public Records Office

British Headquarters (Sir Guy Carleton) Papers, 1747 (1777)–1783, GCP
Cornwallis Papers, 1738–1805, CP

Kershaw County, Camden, S.C.

Court of Equity, Suits, KCCE
Records of the Clerk of Court, Conveyances, KCRCC/C
Records of the Clerk of Court, Pleadings and Judgements, KCRCC/PJ
Records of the Probate Judge, Estates, KCRPJ/E
United District of Lancaster, Sumter, Richland, and Kershaw, Records of the Court of Equity, UDLSRK/RCE

Lancaster County, Lancaster, S.C.

Records of the Clerk of Court, Conveyances, LCRCC/C

Massachusetts Historical Society, Cambridge, Mass.

Benjamin Lincoln Papers, microfilm, BLP

National Archives, Washington, D.C.

Horatio Gates Letters/Papers of the Continental Congress, HGL/PCC
Nathanael Greene Papers, Papers of the Continental Congress, NGP
Papers of the Continental Congress, 1774–1789, PCC
Revolutionary War Pension and Bounty Land Warrant Application Files, RWPBLWAF

South Carolina Department of Archives and History, Columbia, S.C.

Audited Accounts of Claims Growing Out of the Revolution, S108092, 1778–1804
Colonial Land Grants, Copy Series, S213019, 1773–1788, CLG/CS
Colonial Plat Books, S213184, 1731–1775, CPB
Conveyance Book, Public Register, S372001, 1719–1776, CBPR
Conveyance Book, Register of Mesne Conveyance, S363001, 1776–1785, CBMC

Committee Reports, Legislative Papers, 1782–1866, S165005, 1782–1866, CR
Copies of Plats and Plans, S213187, 1728–1800, CPP
Grand Jury Presentments, S165010, 1783–1877, GJP
Inventories of Estates, 1736–1776, IE
Journal of the Commons House of Assembly, JCHA
Journal of the House of Representatives, JHR
Judgement Rolls, Court of Common Pleas, S136002, 1703–1790, JRCCP
Memorial Books, S111001, 1731–1778, MB
Miscellaneous Papers (Main Series), S213003, 1741–1843, MR
Petitions to the General Assembly, S165015, 1782–1866, PGA
Records of the Secretary of State, Wills, 1732–1776, RSS/W
Robert W. Gibbes Collection of Revolutionary War Manuscripts, S213089, 1773–1820, RWGRWM
South Carolina Loyalist Claims, SCLC
State Plat Books, Columbia Series, S213192, 1796–1868, SPB/ColS
State Plat Books, Charleston Series, S213190, 1784–1860, SPB/ChS
Township Grants, S213016, 1736–1761, TSG
Will Transcripts, S108093, 1782-ca. 1855, WT

South Carolina Historical Society, Charleston, S.C.

Chesnut-Miller-Manning Papers, 1741–1888, CMMP
Ely Kershaw Account Book, 1769–1774, EKAB

South Carolina Institute of Archaeology and Anthropology,
University of South Carolina, Columbia, S.C.

Site Survey Record

South Caroliniana Library, University of South Carolina, Columbia, S.C.

Camden Orphan Society Records, 1786–1812
Elizabeth Williams Thornton, Reminiscences, Dec. 11, 1836, Elizabeth Williams Thornton Papers, ETP
Estate Sale of Col. Joseph Kershaw, Broadside Advertisement, Apr. 28, 1794
George Ogilvie Diary, 17841789, GOD
Thomas J. Kirkland Papers, KP
James Kershaw Papers, 1786–1825, JKP
Williams-Chesnut-Manning Families Papers
Joseph Brevard Kershaw, Notes on Equity, JBKNE, Joseph Brevard Kershaw Papers, 1766–1931, JBKP
Matthew Singleton Papers, 1773–1783, MSP
Thomas J. Kirkland Papers
Henry Rugeley Ledger, 1776–1790, HRL
Sarah Thompson Alexander, "Camden Fifty Years Ago"
McRa & Cantey Account Book, 1792–1799, MCAB
Samuel Mathis Papers, 1781–1901, SMP
William Ancrum Account Book and Letterbook, 1757–1782, WAALB
William Blanding Papers, 1827–1920, WBP

Southern Historical Collections, University of North Carolina, Chapel Hill, N.C.

Henry William Harrington Papers, 1748–1809, HWHP
Kershaw-Chesnut Papers, 1751–1832, Preston Davie Collection, 1751–1832, KCP/PDC
Preston Davie Collection, PDC

State Historical Society of Wisconsin, Madison, Wis.

Draper Manuscript Collection, Sumter Papers, 4vv, microfilm, DMC/SP
Joseph Kershaw Account Books, 1774–1775, JKAB

West Yorkshire Archive Service, Wakefield, Yorkshire, England

Yorkshire Parish Records
West Yorkshire, England, Baptisms, Marriages and Burials, 1512–1812, WYEBMB

William L. Clements Library, University of Michigan, Ann Arbor, Mich.

MacKenzie Papers, MP
Henry Clinton Papers, HCP
Jethro Sumner Papers, 1780–1781, JSP
Nathanael Greene Papers, NGP/CL
Stub Entries to Indents of Revolutionary Claims, SEIRC
William Henry Lyttelton Papers, WHLP

MAPS

Accurate Survey of the Town of Camden. Copies of Plats and Plans, Vol. 1, p. 7. South Carolina Archives, Columbia [ca. 1798].

Cook, James. A Map of the Province of South Carolina. Map 81 x 78 cm., scale ca. 1:600,00. London, 1773.

DeBrahm, William. A Map of South Carolina and a Part of Georgia. Col. map on 2 sheets, each 69 x 122 cm., scale 1:316,800. London: T. Jefferys, 1757.

Faden, William. A Map of South Carolina and a Part of Georgia. Col. map on 4 sheets, 136 x 123 cm., scale ca. 1:320,000. London, 1780.

Heard, John. Plan of the Town of Camden, Craven County, South Carolina. Copies of Plats and Plans, Vol. 1, p. 7. South Carolina Archives, Columbia [1771].

Hunter, George. The Charecke Nation by Col. Herbert's Map & My Own Observations. Map 42 x 66 cm., scales vary. 1730. Geography and Map Division, Library of Congress, Washington, D.C.

Kershaw, James. Plat of Lower Camden. Map 49 x 32 cm.,scale varies. 1811. Kirkland Papers, Box 1-12, South Caroliniana Library, University of South Carolina, Columbia.

Mouzon, Henry. An Accurate Map of North and South Carolina, with Their Indian Frontiers. Col. Map on 2 sheets, each 50 x 142 cm., scale ca. 1:530,000. London: Robert Sayer and J. Bennett., 1775.

Myer, William E. The Trail System of the Southeastern United States in the Early Colonial Period. Col. Map 33 x 39 cm., scale 1:1,267,200. In "Indian Trails of the Southeast," *Annual Report of the Bureau of American Ethnology* 42 (1928): 727–857.

St. Julian, James de. Plat of the Town of Fredericksburg on Wateree River, Feb. 2, 1734. Copies of Plats and Plans, Vol. 1, p. 47. South Carolina Archives, Columbia.

NEWSPAPERS

Camden [S.C.] Chronicle, 1891–2008
Camden [S.C.] Gazette, 1816–1822
Camden [S.C.] Journal, 1826–1859
City Gazette & Daily Advertiser (Charleston), 1792
Gazette of the State of South Carolina (Charleston), 1777–1780
Evening Courier (Halifax, U.K.), 2007
Pennsylvania Gazette (Philadelphia), 1728–1800
Royal Gazette., (Charleston), 1781–1782
South Carolina and American General Gazette (Charleston), 1764–1781

South Carolina Gazette (Charleston), 1732–1775
South Carolina Gazette and Country Journal (Charleston), 1765–1775
The Southern Home (Charlotte, N.C.), 1870–1881

PUBLISHED PRIMARY SOURCES

Abbot, W. W., and Dorothy Twohig, eds. *The Papers of George Washington: Presidential Series, 1788–1791.* 8 vols. Charlottesville: University Press of Virginia, 1987–1999.

Alexander, W. S., and John W. Corbett. *A Descriptive Sketch of Camden, S.C.* Charleston, S.C.: Walker, Evans & Cogswell, 1888; reprint ed., Camden, S.C.: Kershaw County Historical Society, 1996.

An American. *American Husbandry, Containing an Account of the Soil, Climate, Production, and Agriculture, of the British Colonies in North America and the West Indies, Vol. 1.* London: J. Brew, 1775.

Ashe, Thomas. "Carolina; or a Description of the Present State of that Country (1682)." In *Narratives of Early Carolina, 1650–1708.* Edited by Alexander S. Salley Jr., 135–160. New York: Charles Scribner's Sons, 1911.

Aspinall, A., ed. *The Correspondence of George, Prince of Wales, 1770–1812.* 8 vols. London: Cassell, 1963–1971.

Baxley, Charles B., ed. "Annotated Pension of Richard Clinton." *Southern Campaigns of the American Revolution* 2, no. 3 (2005): 14–15.

Becker, Robert A., ed. "John F. Grimke's Eyewitness Account of the Camden Court Riot, April 27–28, 1785." *South Carolina Historical Magazine* 83 (1982): 209–213.

Boyle, Joseph Lee, ed., "The Revolutionary War Diaries of Captain Walter Finney." *South Carolina Historical Magazine* 98 (1997): 126–152.

Bull, William. "Governor William Bull's Representation of the Colony, 1770." In *The South Carolina Scene: Contemporary Views, 1697–1774.* Edited by H. Roy Merrens, 253–270. Columbia: University of South Carolina Press, 1977.

"Camden District Equity Journal." *South Carolina Magazine of Ancestral Research* 14 (1986), no. 1, 47; no. 2, 93, 96, 98.

Catesby, Mark. "Mark Catesby's *Natural History,* 1731–47." In *The South Carolina Scene: Contemporary Views, 1697–1774.* Edited by H. Roy Merrens, 87–109. Columbia: University of South Carolina Press, 1977.

Chalmers, Lionel. *An Account of the Weather and Diseases of South Carolina.* 2 vols. London: Edward and Charles Dilly, 1776.

———. "A Sketch of the Climate, Water, and Soil in South Carolina, . . . Written in 1776." *The American Museum or Universal Magazine* 3 (1788): 316–334.

Cheves, Langdon, ed. *The Shaftesbury Papers and Other Records Relating to Carolina and the First Settlement on the Ashley River Prior to 1676.* Charleston, S.C.: South Carolina Historical Society, 1897; reprint ed., Charleston: Tempus, 2000.

Clark, Walter. *The State Records of North Carolina, Vol. 15: 1780–81.* Goldsboro, N.C.: Nash Bros., 1898.

Coldham, Peter Wilson, ed. *American Loyalist Claims, Vol. 1: Abstracted from the Public Record Office, Audit Office Series 13, Bundles 1–35 & 37.* Washington, D.C.: National Genealogical Society, 1980.

"Colonel Robert Gray's Observations on the War in Carolina." *South Carolina Historical Magazine* 11 (1910): 139–159.

Conrad, Dennis M., ed. *The Papers of Nathanael Greene, Vol. 9: 11 July, 1781–2 December 1781.* Chapel Hill: University of North Carolina Press for the Rhode Island Historical Society, 1997.

Cooper, Thomas, and David J. McCord, eds. *The Statutes at Large of South Carolina.* 10 vols. Columbia, S.C.: A. S. Johnson, 1836–1841.

Davis, Charles, ed. "The Journal of William Moultrie While a Commissioner on the North and South Carolina Boundary Survey, 1772." *Journal of Southern History* 8 (1942): 549–555.

DeSaussure, Wilmot G. *The Names, as Far as Can Be Ascertained, of the Officers Who Served in the South Carolina Regiments on the Continental Establishment, . . . in the Militia; of What Troops ere Upon the*

Continental Establishment; and of What Militia Organizations Served. Columbia: Presbyterian Publishing House for the State Society of the Cincinnati of South Carolina, 1886.

"A Description of South Carolina (1761)." In *Historical Collections of South Carolina.* Edited by B. R. Carroll, 193–272. New York: Harper & Bros., 1836.

DeVorsey, Louis, Jr., ed. *DeBraham's Report of the General Survey in the Southern District of North America.* Columbia: University of South Carolina Press, 1971.

Drayton, John. *Memoirs of the American Revolution, From Its Commencement to the Year 1776, Inclusive; As Relating the State of South Carolina, Vol. 1.* Charleston, S.C.: A. E. Miller, 1821.

———. *A View of South Carolina, as Respects Her Natural and Civil Concerns.* Charleston, S.C.: W. P. Young; reprint ed., Spartanburg, S.C.: The Reprint Co., 1972.

Dudley, Guilford. "A Sketch of the Military Services Performed by Guilford Dudley, Then of the Town of Halifax, North Carolina, during the Revolutionary War." *Southern Literary Messenger* 11 (1845): 144–148, 231–235, 281–287, 370–375.

Edwards, Adele Stanton, ed. *Journals of the Privy Council, 1783–1789.* Columbia: University of South Carolina Press for the South Carolina Department of Archives and History, 1971.

Egle, William Henry, ed. "Journal of Lieut. William McDowell, of the First Penna. Regiment, in the Southern Campaign, 1781–1782." *Pennsylvania Archives,* 2nd ser., 15 (1893): 295–340.

Faux, W. "Memorable Days in America: Being a Journal of a Tour to the United States (1823)." In *Five Visitors to Kershaw District, 1806–1832.* Edited by Harvey S. Teal, 54–70. Camden, S.C.: Kershaw County Historical Society, Preserve Pamphlet #7, 1996.

Ford, Timothy. "Diary of Timothy Ford, 1785–1786, with Notes by Joseph W. Barnwell." *South Carolina Historical Magazine* 13 (1912): 181–204.

Fries, Adelaide L., Kenneth G. Hamilton, Douglas L. Rights, and Minnie J. Smith, eds. *Records of the Moravians in North Carolina.* 11 vols. Raleigh: North Carolina Historical Commission, 1922–1969.

Garden, Alexander. "Letter from a Scientist, 1757." In *The Colonial South Carolina Scene: Contemporary Views, 1697–1774.* Edited by H. Roy Merrens, 206–216. Columbia: University of South Carolina Press, 1977.

"A Gentleman's Account of His Travels, 1733–34." In *The Colonial South Carolina Scene: Contemporary Views, 1697–1774.* Edited by H. Roy Merrens, 110–121. Columbia: University of South Carolina Press, 1977.

Gibbes, R. W., ed. *Documentary History of the American Revolution.* Columbia, S.C.: Banner Steam-Power Press, 1853.

Gilmore, Robert. "Robert Gilmore's Journal." In *Five Visitors to Kershaw District, 1806–1832.* Edited by Harvey S. Teal, n.p. Camden, S.C.: Kershaw County Historical Society, Preserve Pamphlet #7, 1996.

Glen, James. "Governor James Glen's Valuation, 1751." In *The Colonial South Carolina Scene: Contemporary Views, 1697–1774.* Edited by H. Roy Merrens, 175–188. Columbia: University of South Carolina Press, 1977.

Graves, William T., ed. and annot. "Reverend Oliver Hart's Diary of the Journey to the Backcountry." *Southern Campaigns of the American Revolution* 2, no. 4 (2005): 26–31.

———. "A Return of Capt. John Land's Company of the Upper Battalion of Col. Richardson's Regiment, Who Marched the 7th Inst. under the Command of Major Joseph Brown and Now in Camp Near Monck's Corner, Dec'r. 1778." Southern Campaign American Revolution Pension Statements and Rosters. http:www.revwarapps.org/b11.pdf (accessed Oct. 22, 2012).

Gray, Robert. "Colonel Robert Gray's Observations on the War in Carolina." *South Carolina Historical Magazine* 11 (1910): 138–159.

Griffiths, Thomas. "A Journey of the Voyage to South Carolina in the Year 1767." In *The Colonial South Carolina Scene: Contemporary Views, 1697–1774.* Edited by H. Roy Merrens, 240–247. Columbia: University of South Carolina Press, 1977.

Hamer, Phillip, George C. Rogers Jr., David R. Chesnutt, C. James Taylor, and Peggy J. Clark, eds. *The Papers of Henry Laurens.* 15 vols. to date. Columbia: University of South Carolina Press, 1968.

Harper, Francis, ed. *The Travels of William Bartram, Naturalist's Edition.* New Haven: Yale University Press, 1958.

Hemphill, William E., and Wylma A. Waites, eds. *Extracts from the Journals of the Provincial Congresses of South Carolina, 1775–1776.* Columbia: South Carolina Department of Archives and History, 1960.

Hemphill, William W., Wylma A. Waites, and R. Nicholas Olsberg, eds. *Journals of the General Assembly and the House of Representatives, 1776–1780.* Columbia: University of South Carolina Press, 1970.

Henderson, Archibald, ed. *Washington's Southern Tour, 1791.* Boston: Houghton Mifflin, 1923.

Heyward, Thomas. "An Address to the Public, from the South Carolina Society for Promoting and Improving Agriculture and Other Rural Concerns." *The American Museum or Universal Magazine* 5 (1789): 41–42.

Hilton, William. "A Relation of a Discovery Lately Made Off the Coast of Florida, 1664." In *Narratives of Early Carolina, 1650–1708.* Edited by Alexander S. Salley Jr., 31–62. New York: Charles Scribner's Sons, 1911.

Holcomb, Brent H., ed. *St. David's Parish, South Carolina, Minutes of the Vestry, 1768–1832, Parish Register, 1819–1824.* Easley, S.C.: Southern Historical Press, 1979.

———, ed. *Kershaw County, South Carolina, Minutes of the County Court, 1791–1799.* Easley, S.C.: By the Author, 1986.

———, ed. *Petitions for Land from the South Carolina Council Journals, Vols. I–VI: 1734–1770.* Columbia, S.C.: SCMAR, 1996–1999.

Hooker, Richard J., ed. *The Carolina Backcountry on the Eve of the Revolution: The Journal and Other Writings of Charles Woodmason, Anglican Itinerant.* Chapel Hill: University of North Carolina Press, 1953.

"Inscriptions from the 'Chapel of Ease' of St. James Church Goose Creek, Situated Near Mt. Holly, S.C." *South Carolina Historical Magazine* 13 (1912): 64–69.

Jackson, Donald, and Dorothy Twohig, eds., *The Diaries of George Washington.* 6 vols. Charlottesville:, University Press of Virginia, 1976.

Jenkins, J[ames]. *Experience, Labours, and Sufferings of Rev. Thomas Jenkins of the South Carolina Conference.* Columbia, S.C.: By the Author, 1842.

Jervey, Elizabeth Heyward, ed. "Marriage and Death Notices from the *Charleston Courier. South Carolina Historical Magazine* 30 (1929): 117–124.

———, ed. "Marriage and Death Notices from the *City Gazette. South Carolina Historical Magazine* 31 (1930): 158–169.

———, ed. "Marriage and Death Notices from the *City Gazette and Daily Advertiser." South Carolina Historical Magazine,* 33 (1932): 299–305 and 37 (1936): 84–89.

Jervey, Ellen Heyward, ed. "Items from a South Carolina Almanac [1793]." *South Carolina Historical Magazine* 32 (1931): 73–80.

Johnson, Joseph. *Traditions and Reminiscences Chiefly of the American Revolution in the South.* Charleston: Walker & James, 1851.

[Johnson, Robert]. "A Governor Answers a Questionnaire, 1719/20." In *The Colonial South Carolina Scene: Contemporary Views, 1697–1774.* Edited by H. Roy Merrens, 56–66. Columbia: University of South Carolina Press, 1977.

Johnson, William. *Sketches of the Life and Correspondence of Nathanael Greene.* 2 vols. Charleston: A. E. Miller, 1822; reprint ed., New York: DeCapo Press, 1978.

Jones, E. Alfred, ed. "The Journal of Alfred Chesney, a South Carolina Loyalist in the Revolution and After." *Ohio State University Bulletin.* 26, no. 4 (1921): whole vol.

Jones, George Fenwick, ed. and trans. "Commissary [George Philip] von Reck's Report on Georgia [1734]." *Georgia Historical Quarterly* 47 (1963) 95–110.

———, ed. and trans. "Von Reck's Second Report form Georgia." *William and Mary Quarterly,* 3rd ser., 22 (1965): 319–333.

Journal of the General Assembly of South Carolina, March 26, 1776–April 11, 1776, September 17, 1776–October 20, 1776. Columbia, S.C.: The State Co. for the South Carolina Historical Commission, 1906, 1909.

Kershaw County Historical Society. *First Federal Census, Population, 1798, South Carolina, Camden District.* Camden, S.C.: Kershaw County Historical Society, 1969.

———. *Second Federal Census, Population, 1800, South Carolina, Kershaw County.* Camden, S.C.: Kershaw County Historical Society, 1970.

———. *Third Federal Census, Population, 1810, South Carolina, Kershaw County.* Camden, S.C.: Kershaw County Historical Society, 1972.

———. *Fourth Federal Census, Population, 1820, South Carolina, Kershaw County.* Camden, S.C.: Kershaw County Historical Society, 1973.

———. *Third Federal Census, Manufacturing, 1810, South Carolina, Kershaw County.* Camden, S.C.: Kershaw County Historical Society, 1974.

———. *Fifth Federal Census, Population, 1830, South Carolina, Kershaw County.* Camden, S.C.: Kershaw County Historical Society, 1994.

Krawczynski, Keith, ed. "William Drayton's Journal of a 1784 Tour of the South Carolina Backcountry." *South Carolina Historical Magazine* (1996): 182–205.

Lamb, Roger. *An Original and Authentic Journal of Occurrences during the Late American War, from Its Commencement to the Year 1783.* Dublin: Wilkinson & Courtney, 1809.

Lawson, John. *A New Voyage to Carolina.* Edited by Hugh Talmage Lefler. Chapel Hill: University of North Carolina Press, 1967.

Lee, Henry. *Memoirs of the War in the Southern Department of the United States.* Edited by Robert E. Lee. New York: University Publishing Co., 1869; reprint ed., New York: Arno Press, 1969.

Legaré, Hugh Swinton. *Writings of Hugh Swinton Lagaré . . . Consisting of a Diary of Brussels, and Journey of the Rhine; Extracts from His Private and Diplomatic Correspondence; Orations and Speeches; and Contributions to the New-York and Southern Reviews.* Charleston: Burges & James, 1846.

Loewald, Klaus G., Beverly Starika, and Paul S. Taylor, eds. "Johann Martin Bolzius Answers a Questionnaire on Carolina and Georgia, Parts I and II." *William and Mary Quarterly,* 3rd ser., 3, 14 (1957), 218–261; 15 (1958), 228–252.

Martin, Margaret Maxwell. "Rides about Camden, 1853." In *Rides about Camden, 1853 & 1873.* Edited by Harvey S. Teal, 1–19. Columbia, S.C.: McDonald Letter Shop, 1961.

Mathews, Maurice. "A Contemporary View of Carolina in 1680." *South Carolina Historical Magazine* 55 (1954): 153–159.

Michaux, Francois. "Lowcountry and Upcountry South Carolina as Seen by a Famous Botanist, 1802–03." In *South Carolina, the Grand Tour, 1780–1865.* Edited by Thomas D. Clark, 31–48. Columbia, University of South Carolina Press, 1973.

Middlesex Coroners. "Coroner's Inquests into Suspicious Deaths, CO/IC, 1st May 1781–31st Dec. 1799." http://www.londonlives.org/browse.jsp?id+LMCOIC65101_n2413-l&div'LMCOIC6510 (accessed June 15, 2010).

Mills, Rob ert. "Letters from Robert Mills." *South Carolina Historical Magazine* 39 (1938): 110–124.

———. *Statistics of South Carolina.* Charleston, S.C.: Hurlbut and Lloyd, 1826; reprint ed., Spartanburg, S.C.: The Reprint Co., 1972.

———. *Atlas of the State of South Carolina, 1825.* Introduction by Gene Waddell. Greenville, S.C: Southern Historical Press, 1980.

Moore, Caroline T., comp. and ed. *Abstracts of the Wills of the State of South Carolina, 1740–1760.* Columbia, S.C.: R. L. Bryan, 1964.

———, comp. and ed. *Abstracts of the Wills of the State of South Carolina, 1760–1784.* Columbia, S.C.: R. L. Bryan, 1969.

———, comp. and ed. *Abstracts of the Wills of the State of South Carolina, 1783–1800.* Columbia, S.C.: R. L. Bryan, 1974.

Moore, John Hammond, ed. "Jared Sparks Visits South Carolina." *South Carolina Historical Magazine* 72 (1971): 150–160.

Morse, Jedidiah. *The American Gazetteer.* Boston: S. Hall and Thomas & Andrews, 1797.

Moultrie, William. *Memoirs of the American Revolution, So Far as It Relates to the States of North Carolina, South Carolina, and Georgia.* 2 vols. New York: David Longworth, 1802.

McDowell, William L., Jr., ed. *Documents Relating to Indian Affairs, May 21, 1750–August 7, 1754.* Columbia: South Carolina Archives, 1958.

———, ed. *Documents Relating to Indian Affairs, 1754–1765.* Columbia: South Carolina Archives, 1970.

[Nairne, Thomas]. "A Letter from South Carolina (1710)." In *Settling a New World: Two Colonial South Carolina Promotional Pamphlets.* Edited by Jack P. Greene, 33–76. Columbia: University of South Carolina Press, 1989.

[Norris, John]. "A Description or True Relation of South Carolina (1712)." In *Settling a New World: Two Colonial South Carolina Promotional Pamphlets.* Edited by Jack P. Greene, 77–147. Columbia: University of South Carolina Press, 1989.

North Carolina Magazine. 1 (Jul. 20, 1764): 55.

Norton, Frank H., ed. *Journal Kept by Hugh Finley, Surveyor of the Post Roads on the Continent of North America, during His Survey of the Post Offices between Falmouth and Casco Bay in the Province of Massachusetts and Savannah in Georgia; Begun the 13th Septr 1773 and Ended 26th June 1774.* Brooklyn, N.Y.: Fran H. Norton, 1867.

O'Donnell, James H., ed. "A Loyalist View of the Drayton-Tennent-Hart Mission to the Upcountry." *South Carolina Historical Magazine* 67 (1966): 15–28.

[Ogilvie, George]. *Carolina; or, The Planter, Written in 1776.* London: By the Author, 1790.

"Order Book of John Faucheraud Grimke, August 1778–May 1780." *South Carolina Historical Magazine* 13 (1912): 42–55.

"Papers of the First Council of Safety of the Revolutionary Party in South Carolina, June–November, 1775." *South Carolina Historical Magazine* 2 (1901): 167–193; 3 (1902): 69–85.

Purry, Peter. "A Description of the Province of South Carolina (1731)." In *Historical Collections of South Carolina.* Edited by B. R. Carroll, 125–140. New York: Harper & Bros., 1836.

Ramsey, David. *The History of the Revolution of South Carolina from a British Province to an Independent State.* 2 vols. Trenton, N.J.: Isaac Collins, 1785.

———. *The History of South Carolina, From Its First Settlement in 1670, to the Year 1808.* 2 vols. Charleston, S.C.: David Longworth, 1809.

"Records Kept by Colonel Isaac Hayne." *South Carolina Historical Magazine* 10 (1909): 145–170; 11 (1910): 92–106.

Register, Jeannie Heyward, ed. "Marriage and Death Notices from the *City Gazette. South Carolina Historical Magazine* 26 (1925): 45–58, 162–171, 228–236.

"Revolutionary War Letters." *South Carolina Historical Magazine* 38 (1937): 76–77.

Robbins, Walter L., ed. and trans. "John Tobler's Description of South Carolina (1753)." *South Carolina Historical Magazine* 71 (1970): 141–161.

Ross, Charles, ed. *Correspondence of Charles, First Marquis Cornwallis.* 3 vols. London: John Murray, 1859.

Royall, Anne. *Mrs. Royal's Southern Tour, or, Second Series of the Black Book.* Washington, D.C.: By the Author, 1831.

Rudisill, Horace Fraser, ed. *The Diaries of Evan Pugh (1762–1801).* Florence, S.C.: St. David's Society, 1993.

Rugeley, Helen Hoskins, ed. *Rugeley Papers: Blue-Blooded Brits in Reduced Circumstances.* Austin, Tex.: By the Author, 1997.

———, ed. *Rugeleys in America, Vol. II: English & American Ancestors.* Austin, Tex.: Rugeley Family Association, 1997.

Saberton, Ian. *The Cornwallis Papers: The Campaigns of 1780 and 1781 in the Southern Theatre of the American Revolutionary War.* East Sussex: Naval & Military Press, 2010.

Salley, A. S., ed. *Col. Hill's Memoirs of the Revolution.* Columbia: Historical Commission of South Carolina, 1921.

———, ed. "Diary of William Dillwyn During a Visit to Charles Town in 1772." *South Carolina Historical Magazine* 36 (1935): 1–6, 29–35, 73–78.

———, ed. "Journal of General Peter Horry." *South Carolina Historical Magazine* 38 (1937): 49–53, 81–86, 116–119, 39 (1938): 46–49, 96–99, 125–128, 157–159.

———, ed. *Journal of the Senate of the State of South Carolina, January 8, 1782–February 26, 1782.* Columbia: The State Co. for the South Carolina Historical Commission, 1941.

Sandford, Robert. "A Relation of a Voyage on the Coast of the Province of Carolina, 1666." In *Narratives of Early Carolina, 1650–1708.* Edited by Alexander S. Salley Jr., 75–108. New York: Charles Scribner's Sons, 1911.

Scott, Edwin J. *Random Recollections of Long Life, 1806–1876.* Columbia, S.C.: C. A. Calvo, 1884.

Seymour, William. "Journal of the Southern Expedition, 1780–1783, by William Seymour, Sergeant Major of the Delaware Regiment." *Pennsylvania Magazine of History and Biography* 7 (1883): 286–298, 377–394.

Shannon, William M. "Rides about Camden, 1873." In *Rides about Camden, 1853 & 1873.* Edited by Harvey S. Teal, 19–25. Columbia, S.C.: McDonald Letter Shop., 1961.

Shaw, John Robert. *A Narrative of the Life & Travels of John Robert Shaw, the Well-Digger, Now Resident of Lexington, Kentucky.* Lexington, Ky.: Daniel Bradford, 1807.

"A Short Description of the Province of South Carolina (1763)." In *Historical Collections of South Carolina.* Edited by B. R. Carroll, 463–536. New York: Harper & Bros., 1836.

Simms, William Gilmore. *The Geography of South Carolina.* Charleston: Babcock, 1843.

Simons, Robert Bentham. "Regimental Book of Captain James Bentham, 1778–1800." *South Carolina Historical Magazine* 54 (1953): 37–47.

Smith, Sam B., and Harriett Chapell Owsley, eds. *The Papers of Andrew Jackson, Vol. 1: 1770–1803.* Knoxville: University of Tennessee Press, 1980.

Smith, William Loughton. "Journal of William Loughton Smith, 1790–1791." *Proceedings of the Massachusetts Historical Society,* 3rd ser., 51 (1917–1918): 20–88.

Smyth, J. F. D. *A Tour of the United States of America, Containing an Account of the Present State of That Country, Vol. I.* London: G. Robinson,1784.

Starr, Raymond, ed. "Letters from John Lewis Gervais to Henry Laurens, 1777–1778." *South Carolina Historical Magazine* 66 (1965): 15–37.

Stedman, Charles. *History of the American War.* London: J. Murray, 1794.

Tarleton, Banastre. *A History of the Campaigns of 1780 and 1781, in the Southern Provinces of North America.* London: T. Cadell, 1787; reprint ed., Spartanburg, S.C.: The Reprint Co., 1967.

Teal, Harvey S., ed. *Old Times in Camden: Pen Pictures of the Past by William M. Shannon.* Preserves Pamphlet # 6. Camden, S.C.: Kershaw County Historical Society, 1996.

Thornton, Phinehas. *The Southern Gardener and Receipt Book.* 2nd ed. Introduction by Shirley Abbott. Newark, N.J.: A. L. Dennis for the Author, 1845; reprint ed., Birmingham, Ala.: Oxmoor House, 1984.

Tobler, John. *The South Carolina Almanack for 1755.* Germantown, Pa.: Christopher Sower for Jacob Viart, CharlestonS.C.

———. *The Charles Town Directory for 1782.* Charleston: R. Wells & Son, 1782; reprint ed., Charleston: Historical Commission of Charleston, 1951.

Waters, H. F., ed. "South Carolina Gleanings in England." *South Carolina Historical Magazine* 6 (1905): 117–125.

Watson, Winslow C., ed. *Men and Times of the Revolution; or Memoirs of Elkanah Watson.* New York: Dana, 1856.

Webber, Mabel L., ed. "Death Notices from the *South Carolina and American General Gazette,* and Its Continuation the *Royal Gazette:* May 1766–June 1782." *South Carolina Historical Magazine* 17 (1916): 46–50.

———, ed. "Marriage and Death Notices from the *City Gazette.*" *South Carolina Historical Magazine* 21 (1920): 153–160; 24 (1923): 30–39.

Willcox, William B., ed. *The American Rebellion: Sir Henry Clinton's Narrative of His Campaigns, 1775–1782, with an Appendix of Original Documents.* New Haven: Yale University Press, 1954.

Williams, Samuel Cole, ed. *Adair's History of the American Indians (1775).* Johnson City, Tenn.: Watauga Press, 1950.

———, ed. "General Richard Winn's Notes–1780." *South Carolina Historical Magazine* 43 (1942): 201–212; 44 (1943): 1–10.

Willson, Samuel. "An Account of the Province of Carolina." In *Historical Collections of South Carolina.* Edited by B. R. Carroll, 19–36. New York: Harper & Bros., 1836.

Withington, Lothrop, ed. "South Carolina Gleanings in England." *South Carolina Historical Magazine* 8 (1907): 211–219.

Woodward, Henry. "A Faithful Relation of My Westo Voyage, 1674." In *Narratives of Early Carolina, 1650–1708.* Edited by Alexander S. Salley Jr., 125–134. New York: Charles Scribner's Sons, 1911.

A Young Gentleman. "A Young Gentleman's Account of His Travels, 1733–34." In *The South Carolina Scene: Contemporary Views, 1697–1774.* Edited by H. Roy Merrens, 253–270. Columbia: University of South Carolina Press, 1977.

Secondary Sources

ARTICLES

Adams, Richard N. "On the Relation between Plantation and "Creole Cultures." In *Plantation Systems of the New World,* pp. 73–79. Social Science Monographs VII. Washington, D.C.: Pan American Union, 1959.

Allen, J. "Hydraulic Engineering." In *A History of Technology, Vol. V: The Late Nineteenth Century, c. 1850 to 1900,* pp. 522–551. Edited by Charles Singer, E. J. Holmyard, A. R. Hall, and Trevor I. Williams. New York: Oxford University Press, 1958.

Ames, Joseph S. "Cantey Family," *South Carolina Historical Magazine* 11 (1910): 203–258.

Anderson, David G., and Glen T. Hanson. "Early Archaic Settlement in the Southeastern United States: A Case Study from the Savannah River Valley." *American Antiquity* 53 (1988): 262–288.

Anderson, David G., David A. Stahle, and Malcolm Cleaveland. "Paleoclimate and the Potential Food Reserves of Mississippian Societies: A Case Study from the Savannah River Valley." *American Antiquity* 60 (1995): 258–286.

Anthony, Ronald W. "Colono Wares." In *Home Upriver: Rural Life on Daniel's Island, Berkeley County, South Carolina, Vol. 1,* pp. 7-22–7-51. Edited by Martha Zierden, Lesley Drucker, and Jeanne Calhoun. Columbia: South Carolina Department of Highways and Public Transportation, 1986.

———. "Tangible Interaction: Evidence from Stobo Plantation." In *Another's Country: Archaeological and Historical Perspectives on Cultural Interactions in the Southern Colonies,* pp. 45–64. Edited by J. W. Joseph and Martha Zierden. Tuscaloosa: University of Alabama Press, 2002.

Aptheker, Herbert. "Maroons within the Present Limits of the United States." In *Maroon Societies: Rebel Communities in the Americas,* pp. 151–167. Edited by Richard Prince. Garden City, N.Y.: Anchor Books, 1973.

Arensberg, Conrad M. "American Communities." *American Anthropologist* 57 (1955): 1143–1162.

———. "The Community as Object and Sample." *American Anthropologist* 63 (1961): 241–264.

Bacot, D. Huger. "South Carolina and the Whitney Cotton Gin." *South Carolina Historical Magazine* 19 (1918): 151–152.

———. "The South Carolina Up Country at the End of the Eighteenth Century." *American Historical Review* 28 (1922–23): 682–698.

———. "The South Carolina Middle Country at the End of the Eighteenth Century." *South Atlantic Quarterly* 23 (1924): 50–60.

Baker, Steven G. "Colono-Indian Pottery from Cambridge, South Carolina, with Comments on the Historic Catawba Pottery Trade." *South Carolina Institute of Archaeology and Anthropology, Notebook* 4, no. 1 (1972): 3–30.

Baldwin, Robert E. "Patterns of Development in Newly Settled Regions." *Manchester School of Social and Economic Studies* 24 (1956): 161–179.

Barr, William B. "Childsbury Towne and Ashley River Ferry Town: Elements of Control in the Economic Landscape of Colonial South Carolina." In *Underwater Archaeology Proceedings from the Society for Historical Archaeology Conference,* pp. 88–93. Edited by Paul Forsythe Johnson. Pleasant Hill, Calif.: Society for Historical Archaeology, 1994.

Baxter, W. T. "Accounting in Colonial America." In *Studies in the History of Accounting,* pp. 272–287. Edited by A. C. Littleton and B. S. Yamey. London: Sweet & Maxwell, 1956.

Beck, Robin A., Jr., James A. Brown, Douglas J. Bolender, and Timothy K. Earle. "Eventful Archaeology: The Place of Space in Structural Transformation." *Current Anthropology* 48 (2007): 833–860.

Becker, Robert A. "Salus Populi Suprema Lex: Public Peace and South Carolina Debtor Relief Laws, 1783–1788." *South Carolina Historical Magazine* 80 (1979): 65–75.

Beeman, Richard R. "The Political Response to Social Conflict in the Southern Backcountry: A Comparative View of Virginia and the Carolinas during the Revolution." In *The Southern Backcountry During the Revolution,* pp. 213–239. Edited by Thad W. Tate and Peter Albert. Charlottesville: University Press of Virginia for the United States Capital Historical Society, 1985.

Bieder, Robert E. "Kinship as a Factor in Migration." *Journal of Marriage and Family* 35 (1973): 429–439.

Blanton, Richard E., Gary W. Feinman, Stephen A. Kowalewski, and Peter N. Peregrine. "Agency, Ideology, and Power in Archaeological Theory." *Current Anthropology* 37 (1996): 1–14.

Blouet, Brian W. "Factors Influencing the Evolution of Settlement Patterns." In *Man, Settlement, and Urbanism,* pp. 3–15. Edited by Peter J. Ucko, Ruth Tringham, and G. W. Dimbleby. London: Gerald Duckworth, 1972.

Brocklebank, Giles. "Royds Family Pedigree, from the Work of Sir Clement Royds (1910)." http://www.fitzwalter.com/afh/Royds/roydspl.html (accessed Mar. 15, 2010).

Brumfiel, Elizabeth. "Distinguished Lecture in Archaeology: Breaking and Entering the Ecosystem-Gender, Class, and Faction Steal the Show." *American Anthropologist* 94 (1992): 551–567.

Bushman, Richard Lyman. "Markets and Composite Farms in Early America." *William and Mary Quarterly,* 3rd ser., 55 (1998): 351–374.

Calhoun, Jeanne A., Martha A. Zierden, and Elizabeth A. Paysinger. "The Geographic Spread of Charleston's Merchant Community." *South Carolina Historical Magazine* 86 (1985): 182–220.

Carney, Judith Ann. "From Hands to Tutors: African Expertise in the South Carolina Rice Economy." *Agricultural History* 67 (1993): 1–30.

———. "Landscapes of Technology Transfer: Rice Cultivation and African Continuities." *Technology and Culture* 37 (1996): 5–35.

Carroll, Kenneth L. "The Irish Quaker Community at Camden." *South Carolina Historical Magazine* 77 (1976): 69–83.

Carson, Cary, Norman F. Barka, William M. Kelso, Gary Wheeler Stone, and Dell Upton. "Impermanent Architecture in the Southern American Colonies." In *Material Life in America, 1600–1860,* pp. 113–158. Edited by Robert Blair St. George. Boston: Northeastern University Press, 1988.

Casagrande, Joseph B., Stephen I. Thompson, and Philip D. Young. "Colonization as Research Frontier: The Ecuadorian Case." In *Process and Pattern in Culture: Essays in Honor of Julian H. Steward,* pp. 281–325. Edited by Robert A. Manners. Chicago: Aldine, 1964.

Cerny, Philip G. "Globalization and Other Stories: The Search for a New Paradigm for International Relations." *International Relations* 51 (1996): 617–637.

Chaplin, Joyce E. "Creating a Cotton South in Georgia and South Carolina, 1760–1815." *Journal of Southern History* 57 (1991): 171–200.

Clark, Andrew Hill. "Suggestions for the Geographical Study of Agricultural Change in the United States, 1790–1840." *Agricultural History* 46 (1972): 155–172.

Cobb, Charles R., and Chester B. DePratter. "Multi-Sited Research on Colonowares and the Paradox of Globalization." *American Anthropologist* 114 (2012): 446–461.

Coclanis, Peter. "Rice Prices in the 1820s and the Evolution of the South Carolina Economy." *Journal of Southern History* 48 (1982): 531–544.

———. "Bitter Harvest: The South Carolina Lowcountry in Historical Perspective." *Journal of Economic History* 45 (1985): 251–259.

Coe, Joffre L. "The Formative Cultures of the Carolina Piedmont." *Transactions of the American Philosophical Society,* new ser., 54, 1964.

Cole, B. J. "Reply to D. Gordon." *American Naturalist* 137 (1991): 262–263.

Coon, David L. "Eliza Lucas Pinckney and the Introduction of Indigo Culture in South Carolina." *Journal of Southern History* 42 (1976): 68–76.

Crass, David Colin, and Bruce Penner. "The Struggle for the South Carolina Frontier: History and Archaeology at New Windsor Township." *South Carolina Antiquities* 24 (1992): 37–56.

Crumley, Carole L. "Heterarchy and the Analysis of Complex Societies." *Archaeological Papers of the American Anthropological Association* 6, issue 1 (1995): 1–5.

Davis, R. P. Stephen, Jr., and Brett H. Riggs. "An Introduction to the Catawba Project." *North Carolina Archaeology* 53 (2004): 1–41.

Davis-Floyd, Robbie. "Rituals." In *International Encyclopedia of the Social Sciences,* Vol. 7, pp. 259–264. Edited by William A. Darity. Detroit: Macmillan Reference USA, 2008.

Dederer, John Morgan. "Making Bricks without Straw: Nathanael Greene's Southern Campaigns and Mao Tse-Tung's Mobile War." *Military Affairs* 47 (1983): 115–121.

DePratter, Chester. "The Kingdom of Cofitacheque." In *The Forgotten Centuries: Indians and Europeans in the American South, 1521–1704,* pp. 197–226. Edited by Charles Hudson and Carmen Cheves Tesser. Athens: University of Georgia Press, 1994.

DePratter, Chester, and Chris Judge. "Wateree River." In *Lamar Archaeology: Mississippian Chiefdoms in the Deep South,* pp. 56–58. Edited by Mark Williams and Gary Shapiro. Tuscaloosa: University of Alabama Press, 1990.

Dobbs, G. Rebecca. "Frontier Settlement and'Initial Conditions: The Case of the North Carolina Piedmont and the Indian Trading Path." *Historical Geography* 37 (2009): 114–137.

Dornan, Jennifer L. "Agency in Archaeology: Past, Present, and Future Directions." *Journal of Archaeological Method and Theory* 9 (2002): 303–329.

Driver, Leonie, Malcolm Hislop, Stephen Litherland, and Eleanor Ramsey. "The North Service Range, Ashton Hall, Birmingham: Excavation and Recording." *Post-Medieval Archaeology* 42, pt. 1 (2008): 104–129.

Duff, Meaghan N. "Creating a Plantation Province: Proprietary Land Policies and Early Settlement Patterns." In *Money, Trade, and Power: The Evolution of South Carolina's Plantation Society,* pp. 1–25. Edited by Jack P. Greene, Rosemary Brana-Shute, and Randy J. Sparks. Columbia: University of South Carolina Press, 2001.

Dunbar, Gary S. "Colonial South Carolina Cowpens." *Agricultural History* 35 (1961): 125–131.

Duncan, James, and Nancy Duncan. " (Re) Reading the Landscape." *Environmental Planning: Society and Space* 6 (1988): 117–126.

Dunn, Richard S. "The English Sugar Islands and the Founding of South Carolina." *South Carolina Historical Magazine* 72 (1971): 81–93.

Earle, Carville V. "A Staple Interpretation of Slavery and Free Labor." *Geographical Review* 68 (1978): 51–65.

Earle, Carville V., and Ronald Hoffman. "Staple Crops and Urban Development in the Eighteenth Century South." *Perspectives in American History* 10 (1976): 7–80.

Easterby, J. H. "The St. Thomas Hunting Club, 1785–1801." *South Carolina Historical Magazine* 46 (1945): 123–131, 209–213.

———. "The South Carolina Education Bill of 1770." *South Carolina Historical Magazine* 48 (1947): 95–111.

Egan, Geoff. "Post-Medieval Britain and Ireland in 1988." *Post-Medieval Archaeology* 23: 25–67.

Egnal, Marc. "The Economic Development of the Thirteen Continental Colonies, 1720–1775." *William and Mary Quarterly*, 3rd ser., 32 (1975): 191–222.

Egnal, Marc, and Joseph A. Ernst. "An Economic Interpretation of the American Revolution." *William and Mary Quarterly*, 3rd ser., 29 (1972): 3–32.

Eisenstadt, S. N. "Multiple Modernities," *Daedalus* 129 (2000), 1–29.

Engerman, Stanley L. "A Reconsideration of Southern Economic Growth." *Agricultural History* 49 (1975): 343–361.

Epstein, S. R. "Regional Fairs, Institutional Innovation, and Economic Growth in Late Medieval Europe." *Economic History Review*, 2nd ser., 47 (1994): 459–482.

Ernst, Joseph A., and H. Roy Merrens. "'Camden's Turrets Pierce the Skies': The Urban Process in the Southern Colonies during the Eighteenth Century." *William and Mary Quarterly*, 3rd ser., 30 (1973): 549–574.

———. "The South Carolina Economy of the Middle Eighteenth Century: A View from Philadelphia." *West Georgia College Studies in the Social Sciences* 12 (1973): 16–29.

Fairlie, Susan. "Dyestuffs in the Eighteenth Century." *Economic History Review*, 2nd ser., 17 (1965): 488–510.

Faragher, John Mack. "Open-Country Community: Sugar Creek, Illinois, 1820–1850." In *The Countryside in the Age of Capitalist Transition: Essays in the Social History of Rural America*, pp. 233–258. Edited by Steven Hahn and Jonathan Prude. Chapel Hill: University of North Carolina Press, 1985.

Farrell, Joseph, and Suzanne Scotchmer. "Partnerships." *Quarterly Journal of Economics* 103 (1988): 279–297.

Faust, Drew Gilpin. "A Southern Stewardship: The Intellectual and the Proslavery Argument." *American Quarterly* 31 (1979): 63–80.

Feiss, Carl. "Early American Public Squares." In *Town and Square: From the Agora to the Village Green*, pp. 237–255. Edited by Paul Zucker. Cambridge, Mass.: MIT Press, 1970.

Ferguson, Clyde. "Functions of the Partisan Militia in the South during the American Revolution." In *The Revolutionary War in the South: Power, Conflict, and Leadership*, pp. 239–258. Edited by W. Robert Higgins. Durham, N.C.: Duke University Press, 1979.

Ferguson, Leland G., ed. "Archaeological Investigations at the Mulberry Site." *South Carolina Institute of Archaeology and Anthropology, Notebook* 6, nos. 3–4 (1974): whole volume.

———. "An Archaeological-Historical Analysis of Fort Watson, December 1780–April 1781." In *Research Strategies in Historical Archaeology*, pp. 41–71. Edited by Stanley South. New York: Academic Press, 1977.

———. "Lowland Plantations, the Catawba Nation, and River Burnished Pottery." In *Studies in South Carolina Archaeology: Essays in Honor of Robert L. Stephenson*, pp. 185–191. Edited by Albert C. Goodyear III and Glen T. Hanson. Anthropological Studies 9. Columbia: South Carolina Institute of Archaeology and Anthropology, 1989.

Fewkes, Vladimir. "Catawba Pottery-Making with Notes on Pamunkey Pottery-Making, Cherokee Pottery-Making, and Coiling." *Proceedings of the American Philosophical Society* 88 (1944): 69–124.

Flannery, Kent V. "The Cultural Evolution of Civilizations." *Annual Review of Ecology and Systematics* 3 (1972): 399–426.

Flatres, P. "Hamlet and Village," In *Man and His Habitat: Essays Presented to Emyr Estyn Evans*, pp. 165–185. Edited by R. H. Buchanan, Emrys Jones, and Desmond McCourt. New York: Barnes and Noble, 1971.

Forbes, R. J. "Power to 1850." In *A History of Technology, Vol. IV: The Industrial Revolution, ca. 1750 to ca. 1850*, pp. 148–167. Edited by Charles Singer, E. J. Holmyard, A. R. Hall, and Trevor I. Williams. New York: Oxford University Press, 1958.

Ford, Lacy K. "Yeoman Farmers in the South Carolina Upcountry: Changing Production Patterns in the Late Antebellum Era." *Agricultural History* 60 (1986): 17–37.

Forte, Maximilian C. "Globalization and World Systems Analysis: Toward New Paradigms of a Geo-Historical Social Anthropology (A Research Review)." *Review* 21 (1998), 29–99.

Fox, H. S. A. "Going to Town in Thirteenth-Century England." In *Man Made the Land: Essay in English Historical Geography,* 69–78. Edited by Alan H. R. Baker and J. B. Harley. Newton Abbot, Devon: David & Charles, 1973.

Friedmann, Harriet. "World Market, State, and Family Farm: Social Bases of Household Production in the Era of Wage Labor." *Comparative Studies in Science and History* 20 (1978): 545–586.

———. "Simple Commodity Production and Wage Labor in the American Plains." *Journal of Peasant Studies* 6 (1979): 71–100.

———. "Household Production and the National Economy: Concepts for the Analysis of Agrarian Formations." *Journal of Peasant Studies* 7 (1980): 158–184.

Friis, Herman R. "A Series of Population Maps of the Colonies of the United States," Mimeographed Publication Series, No. 3. New York: American Geographical Society, 1940.

Garner, B. J. "Models of Urban Geography and Settlement Location." In *Models in Geography,* pp. 303–360. Edited by Richard J. Chorley and Peter Haggett. London: Methuen, 1967.

Gill, Harold B., Jr. "Wheat Culture in Colonial Virginia." *Agricultural History* 52 (1978): 380–393.

Gills, Barry K., and Andre G. Frank. "5000 Years of World Systems History: The Culmination of Accumulation." In *Core/Periphery Relations in Pre-Capitalist Worlds,* pp. 67–112. Edited by Christopher K. Chase-Dutton and Thomas D. Hall. Boulder, Colo.: Westview, 1991.

Goebel, Ted, Michael R. Waters, and Dennis H. O'Rourke. "The Late Pleistocene Dispersal of Humans in the Americas." *Science* 319, no. 5869 (2008): 1497–1502.

Goodyear, Albert C., III. "The 2010 Activities of the Southeastern Paleoindian Survey." *South Carolina Institute of Archaeology and Anthropology, Legacy* 15, no. 1 (2011): 8–15.

Goodyear, Albert C., III, James L. Michie, and Tommy Charles. "The Earliest Carolinians." In *Studies in South Carolina Archaeology: Essays in Honor of Robert L. Stephenson,* pp. 19–52. Edited by Albert C. Goodyear III and Glen T. Hanson. Anthropological Studies 9. Columbia: South Carolina Institute of Archaeology and Anthropology, 1989.

Graves, William T. "The South Carolina Whig Militia: 1775–1781, An Overview." *Southern Campaigns of the American Revolution* 2, no. 5 (2005): 7–11.

Greaves, Ida C. "Plantations in the World Economy." In *Plantation Systems of the New World,* pp. 13–25. Social Science Monographs 7. Washington, D.C.: Pan American Union, 1959.

Green, J. Maxwell. "Bermuda (alias Somers Islands), Historical Sketch." *Bulletin of the American Geographical Society* 33 (1901): 220–242.

Greene, Jack P. "The Role of the Lower House of Assembly in Eighteenth Century Politics." *Journal of Southern History* 27 (1961): 451–474.

———. "Colonial South Carolina and the Caribbean Connection." *South Carolina Historical Magazine* 88 (1887): 192–210.

Greene, Jack P., and J. R. Pole. "Reconsidering British-American Colonial History: An Introduction." In *Colonial British America: Essays on the New History of the Early Modern Era,* pp. 1–17. Edited by Jack P. Greene and J. R. Pole. Baltimore: Johns Hopkins University Press, 1984.

Greven, Philip J., Jr. "The Average Size of Families and Households in the Province of Massachusetts in 1762 and in the United States in 1790: An Overview." In *Household and Family in Past Time,* pp. 545–560. Edited by Peter Laslett and Richard Wall. Cambridge: Cambridge University Press, 1972.

Griffin, James B. "Eastern North American Archaeology: A Summary." *Science* 156, no. 3772 (1967): 175–191.

Groover, Mark D. "Evidence for Folkways and Cultural Exchange in the Eighteenth Century South Carolina Backcountry." *Historical Archaeology* 28, no. 1 (1994): 41–64.

Groover, Mark D., and Richard D. Brooks. "The Catherine Brown Cowpen and Thomas Howell Site: Material Characteristics of Cattle Raisers in the South Carolina Backcountry." *Southeastern Archaeology* 22 (2003): 92–111.

Grove, David. "The Function and Future of Urban Centres." In *Man, Settlement, and Urbanism,* pp. 539–565. Edited by Ruth Tringham and G. W. Dimbleby. London: Gerald Duckworth, 1972.

Handlin, Oscar. "Peasant Origins." In *Tribal and Peasant Societies: Readings in Economic Anthropology,* pp. 456–478. Edited by George Dalton. Garden City, N.Y.: Natural History Press, 1967.

Hardy, Stephen G. "Colonial South Carolina's Rice Industry and the Atlantic Economy." In *Money, Trade, and Power: The Evolution of South Carolina's Plantation Society,* pp. 108–140. Edited by Jack P. Greene, Rosemary Brana-Shute, and Randy J. Sparks. Columbia: University of South Carolina Press, 2001.

Harrington, M. R. "Catawba Potters and Their Work." *American Anthropologist* 10 (1908): 399–407.

Harris, Lorene B., Thomas J. Blumer, and Brett H. Riggs. "Glimpses of a Nearby Nation: The Making of Catawba Pottery with Georgia Harris and Edith Brown." *Southern Culture* (Winter 2008): 102–111.

Henretta, James A. "Families and Farms: *Mentalité* in Pre-Industrial America." *William and Mary Quarterly,* 3rd ser., 35 (1978): 3–32.

———. "The Transition to Capitalism in America." In *The Origins of American Capitalism: Collected Essays,* pp. 218–238. Edited by James A. Henretta. Boston: Northeastern University Press, 1991.

Hilliard, Sam B. "The Tidewater Rice Plantation: An Ingenious Adaptation to Nature." *Geoscience and Man* 12 (1975): 57–66.

———. "Antebellum Tidewater Rice Culture in South Carolina and Georgia." In *European Settlement and Development in North America: Essays on Geographic Change in Honor of Andrew Hill Clark,* pp. 97–115. Edited by James B. Gibson. Toronto: University of Toronto Press, 1978.

Hillman, E. Haviland. "The Brisbanes." *South Carolina Historical Magazine* 14 (1913): 115–133, 175–197.

Hodgen, Margaret T. "Fairs of Elizabethan England." *Economic Geography* 18 (1942): 389–400.

Hofstra, Warren R., and Robert D. Mitchell. "Town and Country in Backcountry Virginia: Winchester and the Shenandoah Valley, 1730–1800." *Journal of Southern History* 59 (1993): 619–646.

Hudson, Charles M. "Elements of Southeastern Indian Religion." *Iconography of Religions* 10 (1984): 11.

Hudson, Charles, Robin A. Beck Jr., Chester B. DePratter, Robbie Ethridge, and John E. Worth. "On Interpreting Cofitachequi." *Ethnohistory* 55 (2008): 465–490.

Hurst, D. Gillian. "Post-Medieval Britain in 1966." *Post-Medieval Archaeology* 1 (1967): 107–121.

Jellison, Richard M. "Antecedents of the South Carolina Currency Acts of 1736 and 1746." *William and Mary Quarterly,* 3rd ser., 16 (1959): 556–567.

Jennings, Jesse D., and Charles H. Fairbanks. "Pottery Type Descriptions." *Southeastern Archaeological Conference Newsletter* 1, no. 2 (1939): 2, 4.

Johnson, George Lloyd, Jr. "The Welsh in the Carolinas in the Eighteenth Century." *North American Journal of Welsh Studies* 4 (2004): 12–19.

Johnson, Michael P. "Runaway Slaves and Slave Communities in South Carolina, 1799–1830." *William and Mary Quarterly,* 3rd ser., 38 (1981): 418–441.

Jordan, Louis. "South Carolina Currency, June 1, 1775." Colonial Currency, a Project of the Robert H. Gore, Jr. Numismatic Endowment, University of Notre Dame, Department of Special Collections. http:www.coins.nd.edu/ColCurrency/CurrencyText/SC-06-01-75b.html (accessed Sept. 23, 2009)

Joseph, J. W., and Martha Zierden. "Cultural Diversity in the Southern Colonies." In *Another's Country: Archaeological and Historical Perspectives in the Southern Backcountry,* pp. 1–12. Edited by J. W. Joseph and Martha Zierden. Tuscaloosa: University of Alabama Press, 2002.

Kearney, Michael. "The Local and the Global: The Anthropology of Globalization and Transnationalism." *Annual Review of Anthropology* 24 (1995): 547–565.

———. "Peasantry," In *International Encyclopedia of the Social Sciences,* Vol. 6, pp. 195–196. Edited by William A. Darity. Detroit: Macmillan Reference USA, 2008.

Keller, Kenneth W. "The Outlook of Rhinelanders on the Virginia Frontier." In *Diversity and Accommodation: Essays on the Cultural Composition of the Virginia Frontier,* pp. 99–133. Edited by Michael J. Puglisi. Knoxville: University of Tennessee Press, 1992.

Kendrick, N. "Josiah Wedgwood: An Eighteenth Century Entrepreneur in Salesmanship and Marketing Techniques." *Economic History Review,* new ser., 12 (1960): 408–433.

Kennedy, Michael V. "'Cash for Turnips': Agricultural Production for Local Markets in Colonial Pennsylvania." *Agricultural History* 74 (2000): 587–608.

King, Adam. "Leadership Strategies and the Nature of Mississippian Chiefdoms in Northern Geogia." In *Leadership and Polity in Mississippian Society,* pp. 73–90. Edited by Brian M. Butler and Paul D. Welch. Occasional Paper 33. Carbondale: Southern Illinois University, Center for Archaeological Investigations, 2006.

Klebaner, Benjamin J. "State-Chartered American Commercial Banks, 1781–1801." *Business History Review* 53 (1979): 529–538.

Klein, Rachel. "Frontier Planters and the American Revolution: The South Carolina Backcountry, 1775–1782." In *An Uncivil War: The Southern Backcountry during the American Revolution,* pp. 37–69. Edited by Ronald Hoffman, Thad W. Tate, and Peter J. Albert. Charlottesville: University Press of Virginia for the United States Capital Historical Society, 1985.

Kovacik, Charles F. "Health Conditions and Town Growth in Colonial and Antebellum South Carolina." *Social Science and Medicine* 12 (1978): 131–136.

Kulikoff, Allan. "Households and Markets: Toward a New Synthesis of American Agrarian History." *William and Mary Quarterly,* 3rd ser., 50 (1993): 342–355.

Lambert, Robert S. "A Loyalist Odyssey: James and Mary Cary in Exile, 1783–1804." *South Carolina Historical Magazine* 79 (1978): 167–181.

Lange, Frederick W., and Jerome S. Handler. "The Ethnohistorical Approach to Slavery." In *The Archaeology of Slavery and Plantation Life,* pp. 15–32. Edited by Theresa A. Singleton. Orlando, Fla.: Academic Press, 1985.

Lansing, Stephen. "Complex Adaptive Systems." *Annual Review of Anthropology* 32 (2003): 183–204.

Laslett, Peter. "The Comparative Study of the Household and Family." *Journal of Social History* 4 (1970): 75–87.

———. "Introduction: The History of the Family." In *Household and Family in Past Time,* pp. 1–89. Edited by Peter Laslett and Richard Wall. Cambridge: Cambridge University Press, 1972.

Lavier, Harry S. "Rethinking the Social Role of the Militia: Community-Building in Antebellum Kentucky." *Journal of Southern History* 68 (2002): 777–816.

Lemon, James T. "Household Composition in Eighteenth Century America and Its Relationship to Production and Trade: The Situation among Farmers in Southeastern Pennsylvania." *Agricultural History* 41 (1967): 59–70.

Lewis, G. J. "Rural Communities." In *Progress in Geography,* pp. 149–172. Edited by Michael Pacione. London: Croom Helm, 1983.

Lewis, J. D. "Capt. Francis Tidwell." The American Revolution in South Carolina. http//:www.Carolina.com/SC/Revolution/patriots_sc_capt_francis_tidwell.html (accessed Feb. 18, 2011).

Lewis, Kenneth E. "The Camden Jail and Market Site: A Report of Preliminary Investigations." *South Carolina Institute of Archaeology and Anthropology, Notebook* 16 (1984): whole volume.

———. "Economic Development in the South Carolina Backcountry: A View from Camden." In *The Southern Colonial Backcountry: Interdisciplinary Perspectives on Frontier Communities,* pp. 87–107. Edited by David Colin Crass, Steven D. Smith, Martha A. Zierden, and Richard D. Brooks. Knoxville: University of Tennessee Press, 1998.

———. "The Tinworker's Widow: Gender and the Formation of the Archaeological Record in the South Carolina Backcountry." In *Shared Spaces and Divided Places: Material Dimensions of Gender Relations and the American Historical Landscape,* pp. 86–103. Edited by Deborah L. Rotman and Ellen-Ross Savulis. Knoxville: University of Tennessee Press, 2003.

———. "Little Better Than a Heap of Rubbish: History, Legend, and the Archaeological Record at Camden." *South Carolina Historical Magazine* 114 (2013): 231–248.

Lewis, Peirce F. "Axioms for Reading the Landscape, Some Guides to the American Scene." In *The Interpretation of Ordinary Landscapes,* pp. 11–32. Edited by D. W. Meinig. New York: Oxford University Press, 1979.

Little, Thomas J. "Adding to the Church Such as Shall be Saved: The Growth and Influence of Evangelicalism in Colonial South Carolina, 1740–1775." In *Money, Trade, and Power: The Evolution of South Carolina's Plantation Society,* pp. 363–382. Edited by Jack P. Greene, Rosemary Brana-Shute, and Randy J. Sparks. Columbia: University of South Carolina Press, 2001.

Littlefield, Daniel C. "The Slave Trade to Colonial South Carolina: A Profile." *South Carolina Historical Magazine* 91 (1990): 68–99.

Lloyd, Richard W. "Inscriptions from Cemeteries in and Near Camden." *South Carolina Historical Magazine* 25 (1924): 47–55.

Lowenthal, David. "Geography, Experience, and Imagination: Towards a Geographical Epistemology." *Annals of the Association of American Geographers* 51 (1961): 241–260.

Lowie, Robert H. "Religion in American Life." *American Anthropologist* 65 (1963): 532–542.

Lurie, Nancy Oestreich. "Indian Cultural Adjustment to European Civilization." In *Seventeenth Century America,* pp. 33–60. Edited by James Morton Smith. Chapel Hill: University of North Carolina Press, 1959.

Malinowski, Bronislaw. "The Group and Individual in Functional Analysis." *American Journal of Sociology* 44 (1939): 938–964.

Mancall, Peter C., Joshua L. Rosenbloom, and Thomas Weiss. "Indians in the Economy of Eighteenth Century South Carolina." In *The Atlantic Economy during the Seventeenth and Eighteenth Centuries: Organization, Operation, Practice, and Personnel,* pp. 297–322. Edited by Peter A. Coclanis. Columbia: University of South Carolina Press, 2005.

McKendrick, N. "Josiah Wedgwood: An Eighteenth-Century Entrepreneur in Salesmanship and Marketing Techniques." *Economic History* 12 (1960): 408–433.

McWilliams, James E. "Brewing Beer in Massachusetts Bay, 1640–1690." *New England Quarterly* 71 (1998): 543–569.

Meaders, Daniel E. "South Carolina Fugitives as Viewed through Local Colonial Newspapers with Emphasis on Runaway Notices, 1732–1801." *Journal on Negro History* 60 (1975): 288–319.

Meinig, D. W. "The Beholding Eye, Ten Versions of the Same Scene." In *The Interpretation of Ordinary Landscapes,* pp. 33–48. Edited by D. W. Meinig. New York: Oxford University Press, 1979.

Menard, Russell R. "What Ever Happened to Early American Population History?" *William and Mary Quarterly,* 3rd ser., 50 (1993): 356–366.

———. "Financing the Lowcountry Economic Boom: Capital and Growth in Early South Carolina." *William and Mary Quarterly,* 3rd ser., 51 (1994): 659–676.

Meroney, Geraldine M. "William Bull's First Exile from South Carolina, 1777–1781." *South Carolina Historical Magazine* 80 (1979): 91–104.

Merrell, James H. "'Minding the Business of the Nation': Hagler as Catawba Leader." *Ethnohistory* 33 (1986): 55–70.

Merrens, H. Roy, and George D. Terry. "Dying in Paradise: Malaria, Mortality, and the Perceptual Environment in Colonial South Carolina." *Journal of Southern History* 50 (1984): 533–550.

Merrill, Michael. "Cash Is Good to Eat: Self-Sufficiency and Change in the Rural Economy of the United States." *Radical History Review* 3 (1977): 42–71.

Miller, George L. "Marketing Ceramics in North America: An Introduction." *Winterthur Portfolio* 19, no. 1 (1984), 1–5.

Mitchell, Robert D. "The Commercial Nature of Frontier Settlement in the Shenandoah Valley." *Proceedings of the Association of American Geographers* 1 (1969): 109–113.

———. "The Shenandoah Valley Frontier." *Annals of the Association of American Geographers* 62 (1972): 461–486.

———. "Agricultural Change and the American Revolution: A Virginia Case Study." *Agricultural History* 47 (1973): 119–132.

———. "The Settlement Fabric of the Shenandoah Valley, 1790–1860: Pattern, Process, and Structure." In *After the Backcountry: Rural Life in the Great Valley of Virginia, 1800–1900*, pp. 34–47. Edited by Kenneth E. Coons and Warren R. Hofstra. Knoxville: University of Tennessee Press, 2000.

Moore, Alexander. "Thomas Bee's Notes on the State of South Carolina." *Journal of the Early Republic* 7 (1987): 115–122.

Moore, Peter N. "Local Origins of Allegiance in Revolutionary South Carolina: The Waxhaws as a Case Study." *South Carolina Historical Magazine* 107 (2006): 26–41.

Muller, Edward K. "Regional Urbanization and Selective Growth of Towns in North American Regions." *Journal of Historical Geography* 3(1977): 21–40.

Nash, R. C. "South Carolina and the Atlantic Economy in the Later Seventeenth and Eighteenth Centuries." *Economic History Review* 45 (1992): 677–702.

Nobles, Gregory. "Breaking into the Backcountry: New Approaches to the Early American Frontier: 1750–1800." *William and Mary Quarterly*, 3rd ser., 46 (1989): 641–670.

———. "The Rise of Merchants in Rural Market Towns: A Case Study of Eighteenth Century Northampton, Massachusetts." *Journal of Interdisciplinary History* 24 (1990): 5–23.

———. "Straight Lines and Stability: Mapping the Political Order of the Anglo-American Frontier." *Journal of American History* 80 (1993): 9–35.

Noël Hume, Ivor. "An Indian Ware of the Colonial Period." *Quarterly Bulletin of the Archaeological Society of Virginia* 17, no. 1 (1962): 2–14.

North, Douglass C. "Agriculture and Regional Economic Growth." *Journal of Farm Economics* 41 (1959): 943–951.

———. "Institutions." *Journal of Economic Perspectives* 5 (1991): 97–112.

Olson, Gary D. "Loyalists and the American Revolution: Thomas Brown and the South Carolina Backcountry." *South Carolina Historical Magazine* 68 (1967): 201–209.

Ortner, Sherry. "Theory in Anthropology since the Sixties." *Comparative Studies in Science and History* 26 (1984): 126–166.

Otto, John Solomon. "The Origins of Cattle Ranching in Colonial South Carolina, 1670–1715." *South Carolina Historical Magazine* 87 (1986): 117–124.

———. "Livestock-Raising in Early Colonial South Carolina, 1670–1700." *Agricultural History* 61 (1987): 13–24.

Padilla, Elena. "Colonization and Development of Plantations." In *Plantation Systems of the New World.* Social Science Monographs 7, pp. 26–37. Washington, D.C.: Pan American Union, 1959.

Peebles, Christopher, and Susan M. Kus. "Some Archaeological Correlates of Ranked Societies." *American Antiquity* 42 (1977): 421–448.

Pessen, Edward. "How Different from Each Other Were the Antebellum North and South?" *American Historical Review* 85 (1980): 1119–1149.

Piker, Joshua. "Colonists and Creeks: Rethinking the Pre-Revolutionary Southern Backcountry." *Journal of Southern History* 70 (2004): 503–540.

Pirenne, Henri. "Aspects of Medieval European Economy." In *Tribal and Peasant Societies: Readings in Economic Anthropology*, pp. 418–440. Edited by George Dalton. Garden City, N.Y.: Natural History Press, 1967.

Ponsford, Michael. "Post-Medieval Britain and Ireland in 2002." *Post-Medieval Archaeology* 37 (2002): 221–375.

Potter, Jim. "Demographic Development and Family Structure." In *Colonial British America: Essays in the New History of the Early Modern Era*, pp. 123–156. Edited by Jack P. Greene and J. R. Pole. Baltimore: Johns Hopkins University Press, 1984.

Price, Edward T. "The Central Courthouse Square in the American County Seat." *Geographical Review* 58 (1968): 29–60.

Price, Jacob M. "Economic Function and the Growth of American Port Towns in the Eighteenth Century." *Perspectives in American History* 8 (1974): 123–186.

Prunty, Merle, Jr. "The Renaissance of the Southern Plantation." *Geographical Review* 45 (1955): 459–491.

Pugh, Robert C. "The Revolutionary Militia in the Southern Campaign." *William and Mary Quarterly,* 3rd ser., 14 (1957): 154–175.

Ramsey, William L. "'All & Singular Slaves:' A Demographic Profile of Indian Slavery in Colonial South Carolina." In *Money, Trade, and Power: The Evolution of South Carolina's Plantation Society,* pp. 166–186. Edited by Jack P. Greene, Rosemary Brana-Shute, and Randy J. Sparks. Columbia: University of South Carolina Press, 2001.

Rauschenberg, Bradford L. "John Bartlam, Who Established 'New Pottworks in South Carolina' and Became the First Successful Creamware Potter in America." *Journal of Early Southern Decorative Arts* 17 (1991): 1–66.

Riggs, Brett H. "Temporal Trends in Native Ceramic Traditions of the Lower Catawba River Valley." *Southeastern Archaeology* 29 (2010): 31–43.

Riggs, Brett H., R. P. Stephen Davis Jr., and Mark Plane. "Catawba Pottery in the Post-Revolutionary Era: A View from the Source." *North Carolina Archaeology* 55 (2006): 60–88.

Robertson, Roland. "Globalization: Time-Space and Homogeneity." In *Global Modernities.* Edited by Miles Featherstone, Scott Lash, and Roland Robertson. London: Sage, 1995.

Rogers, George C., Jr. "The Papers of James Grant of Ballindalloch Castle, Scotland." *South Carolina Historical Magazine* 77 (1976): 145–160.

Roseberry, William. "Political Economy." *Annual Review of Anthropology* 17 (1988): 161–185.

Rothenberg, Winifred B. "The Market and Massachusetts Farmers, 1750–1855." *Journal of Economic History* 42 (1981): 283–314.

Rothstein, Morton. "Antebellum Wheat and Cotton Exports: A Contrast in Marketing Organization and Economic Development." *Agricultural History* 40 (1966): 91–100.

Salt, George W. "A Comment on the Use of the Term Emergent Properties." *American Naturalist* 113 (1979): 145–148.

Samford, Patricia. "The Archaeology of African-American Slavery and Material Culture." *William and Mary Quarterly,* 3rd ser., 53 (1996): 87–114.

Sauer, Carl Ortwin. "The Morphology of Landscape (1925)." In *Land and Life: A Selection from the Writings of Carl Ortwin Sauer,* pp. 351–379. Edited by John Leighly. Berkeley: University of California Press, 1963.

Schaper, William A. "Sectionalism and Representation in South Carolina: A Sociological Study." *Annual Report of the American Historical Association for the Year 1900,* Vol. 1, pp. 237–463. Washington, D.C.: Government Printing Office, 1901.

Schlebecker, John T. "Stockmen and Drovers during the Revolution." *Proceedings of the Pioneer America Society* 2 (1973): 4–15.

Schlumbohm, Jurgen. "From Peasant Society to Class Society: Some Aspects of Family and Class in a Northwest German Protoindustrial Parish, Seventeenth –Nineteenth Centuries." *Journal of Family History* 17 (1992): 183–199.

Schreg, Ranier. "Panamanian Coarse Handmade Earthernware—A Melting Pot of African, American, and European Traditions?" *Post-Medieval Archaeology* 44, pt. 1 (2010): 135–164.

Schulz, Judith J. "The Hinterland of Revolutionary Camden, South Carolina." *Southeastern Geographer* 16 (1976): 91–97.

Schweikart, Larry. "Southern Banks and Economic Growth in the Antebellum Period: A Reassessment." *Journal of Southern History* 53 (1987): 19–36.

Scoggins, Michael C. "Biographies of Third South Carolina Continental Regiment Soldiers in Painting." *Southern Campaigns of the American Revolution* 3, no. 1 (2006): 32–35.

———. "Will the Real Captain Adamson Please Stand Up?" *York County Magazine,* Aug. 2008.

Scott, Kenneth. "Sufferers in the Charleston Fire of 1740." *South Carolina Historical Magazine* 64 (1963): 203–211.

Shammas, Carole. "How Self-Sufficient Was Early America?" *Journal of Interdisciplinary History* 13 (1982): 247–272.

Sharrer, G. Terry. "Indigo in Carolina, 1671–1796." *South Carolina Historical Magazine* 72 (1971): 94–103.

Shy, John W. "A New Look at Colonial Militia." *William and Mary Quarterly*, 3rd ser., 20 (1963): 176–185.

———. "The American Revolution: The Military Conflict Considered as a Revolutionary War. In *Essays on the American Revolution*, pp. 121–156. Edited by Stephen G. Kurtz and James H. Hutson. Chapel Hill: University of North Carolina Press, 1973.

Siener, William H. "Charles Yates, the Grain Trade, and Economic Development in Fredericksburg, Virginia, 1750–1810." *Virginia Magazine of History and Biography* 93 (1985): 404–426.

Simmons, J. Susanne Schramm. "August County's Other Pioneers: The African American Presence in Frontier Augusta County." In *Diversity and Accommodation: Essays on the Cultural Composition of the Virginia Frontier*, pp. 159–171. Edited by Michael J. Puglisi. Knoxville: University of Tennessee Press, 1997.

Simoneau, Daniel. "The Intendant's Palace Site: New Insight into Its Physical Evolution and Initial Occupation." *Post-Medieval Archaeology* 43, pt. 1 (2009): 171–182.

Singleton, Theresa A., and Mark Bograd. "Looking for the Colono in Colonoware." In *Lines That Divide: Historical Archaeologies of Race, Class, and Gender*, pp. 3–21. Edited by James Delle, Stephen A. Mrozowski, and Robert Paynter. Knoxville: University of Tennessee Press, 2000.

Smith, Bruce D. "Variation in Mississippian Settlement Patterns." In *Mississippian Settlement Patterns*, pp. 479–503. Edited by Bruce D. Smith. New York: Academic Press, 1978.

Smith, Carol A. "Beyond Dependency Theory: National and Regional Patterns of Underdevelopment in Guatemala." *American Ethnologist* 5 (1978): 574–617.

———. "Forms of Production in Practice: Fresh Approaches to Simple Commodity Production." *Journal of Peasant Studies* 11 (1984): 201–221.

Smith, Henry A. M. "Some Forgotten Towns in Lower South Carolina." *South Carolina Historical Magazine* 14 (1913): 198–208.

———. "The Baronies of South Carolina, XVI, Quenby and the Eastern Branch of Cooper River." *South Carolina Historical Magazine* 18 (1917): 24–26.

———. "The Ashley River: Its Seats and Settlements." *South Carolina Historical Magazine* 19 (1919): 36.

———. "The Upper Ashley: And the Mutations of Families." *South Carolina Historical Magazine* 20 (1919): 151–198.

———. "Goose Creek." *South Carolina Historical Magazine* 29 (1928): 167–192.

South, Stanley. "The Ceramic Forms of the Potter Gottfried Aust at Bethabara, North Carolina, 1755–1771." *Conference on Historic Site Archaeology Papers, 1965–1966* 1 (1967): 35–52.

———. "Excavating the Fortified Area of the 1670 Site of Charles Towne, South Carolina." *Conference on Historic Site Archaeology Papers, 1969* 4 (1971): 37–60.

———. "Exploratory Archaeology at Holmes' Fort, the Blockhouse, and Jail." *Conference on Historic Site Archaeology Papers, 1970* 5 (1971): 35–50.

———. "Evolution and Horizon as Revealed in Ceramic Analysis in Historical Archaeology." *Conference on Historic Site Archaeology Papers, 1971* 6 (1972): 71–116.

———. "John Bartlam's Porcelain at Cain Hoy, 1765–1770." In *Ceramics in America*, pp. 196–202. Edited by Robert Hunter. Milwaukee: Chipstone Foundation, 2007.

South, Stanley, and Michael O. Hartley. "Deep Water and High Ground: Seventeenth Century Settlement Patterns on the Carolina Coast." In *Structure and Process in Southeastern Archaeology*, pp. 263–286. Edited by Roy S. Dickens Jr. and H. Trawick Ward. Tuscaloosa: University of Alabama Press, 1985.

Spaulding, Phinizy. "South Carolina and Georgia: The Early Days." *South Carolina Historical Magazine*, 69 (1968): 83–96.

Speck, Frank G. "Chapters on the Ethnology of the Powhattan Tribes of Virginia." *Indian Notes and Monographs* 1 (1928): 394–418.

———. "Siouan Tribes of the Carolinas Known from Catawba, Tutelo, and Documentary Sources." *American Anthropologist* 37 (1935): 201–225.

Steffy, J. Richard. "The Thirteen Colonies: English Settlers and Seafarers." In *Ships and Shipwrecks in the Americas: A History Based on Underwater Archaeology,* pp. 107–128. Edited by George F. Bass. New York: Thames and Hudson, 1996.

Stewart, Mart A. "'Whether Wast, Deodand, or Stray:' Cattle, Culture, and the Environment in Early Georgia." *Agricultural History* 65 (1991): 1–28.

Stine, Linda France, Melanie Cabeck, and Mark D. Groover. "Blue Beads as African American Cultural Symbols." *Historical Archaeology* 30, no. 3 (1996): 49–75.

Stowers, A. "Watermills, c. 1500–c. 1850." *A History of Technology, Vol. IV: The Industrial Revolution, c. 1750 to c. 1850,* pp. 199–213. Edited by Charles Singer, E. J. Holmyard, A. R. Hall, and Trevor I. Williams. New York: Oxford University Press, 1958.

Stranraer-Mull, Gerald. "A Parish History of the Churches in Ellon and Cruden Bay." http://freespace.virgin.net/gerald.stranraer-mull/parish/history.htm (accessed Sept. 15, 2011)

Strickland, Robert N. "Camden Revolutionary War Fortifications (38KE1): 1969–70 Excavations." *South Carolina Institute of Archaeology and Anthropology, Notebook* 3, no. 3 (1971): 55–71.

Strickon, Arnold. "The Euro-American Ranching Complex." In *Man, Culture, and Animals: The Role of Animals in Human Ecological Adjustments,* pp. 229–258. Edited by Anthony Leeds and Andrew P. Vayda. Publication 78. Washington, D.C.: American Association for the Advancement of Science, 1965.

Stumpf, Stuart O. "South Carolina Importers of General Merchandise, 1735–1765." *South Carolina Historical Magazine* 84 (1983): 1–10.

Sweezy, Paul M., and Harry Magdoff. "Capitalism and the Distribution of Income and Wealth." *Monthly Review* 39, no. 5 (1987): 1–16.

Taaffe, Edward J., Richard L. Morrill, and Peter R. Gould. "Transportation Expansion in Underdeveloped Countries: A Comparative Analysis." *Geographical Review* 53 (1963): 503–529.

Ter Braake, Alex L. "Trans-Atlantic Mail in Colonial and Revolutionary Days." In *The Posted Letter in Colonial and Revolutionary America, 1728–1970,* Part 1, F, pp. 1–56. Edited by Alex L. Ter Braake. (State College, Pa.: American Philatelic Research Library, 1975.

Ter Braake, Alex L., and Nicholas J. Johnson. "The Early Letter Post of Charleston, S.C." In *The Posted Letter in Colonial and Revolutionary America, 1728–1970,* Part 1, N, pp. 1–16. Edited by Alex L. Ter Braake. State College, Pa.: American Philatelic Research Library, 1975.

Thauer, Theodore. "The Quaker Party in Pennsylvania, 1755–1765." *Pennsylvania Magazine of History and Biography* 71 (1947): 19–43.

Thompson, Stephen I. "Religious Conversion and Religious Zeal in an Overseas Enclave: The Case of the Japanese in Bolivia." *Anthropological Quarterly* 41 (1968): 201–208.

Thorp, Daniel B. "Doing Business in the Backcountry: Retail Trade in Colonial Rowan County, North Carolina." *William and Mary Quarterly,* 3rd ser., 48 (1991): 387–408.

———. "Taverns and Communities: The Case of Rowan County, North Carolina." In *The Southern Colonial Backcountry: Interdisciplinary Perspectives on Frontier Communities,* pp. 76–86. Edited by David Colin Crass, Steven D. Smith, Martha Zierden, and Richard D. Brooks. Knoxville: University of Tennessee Press, 1998.

Tiebout, Charles M. "Exports and Regional Economic Growth." *Journal of Political Economy* 64 (1956): 160–164.

Trigger, Bruce G. "The Determination of Settlement Patterns." In *Settlement Archaeology,* pp. 53–78. Edited by K. C. Chang. Palo Alto, Calif.: National Press, 1968.

Trinkley, Michael B. "An Archaeological Overview of the South Carolina Woodland Period: It's the Same Old Riddle." In *Studies in South Carolina Archaeology: Essays in Honor of Robert L. Stephenson,* pp. 73–90. Edited by Albert C. Goodyear and Glen T. Hanson. Anthropological Studies 9. Columbia: South Carolina Institute of Archaeology and Anthropology, 1989.

Turner, Frederick Jackson. "The Significance of the Frontier in American History." *Annual Report of the American Historical Association for the Year 1893*, pp. 199–227. Washington, D.C.: Government Printing Office, 1894.

"Two Ancient Landmarks." *Scribner's Monthly* 9 (1875): 615–618.

Ulmer, Mark. "Tribal Property: Defining the Parameters of the Federal Trust Relationship under the Non-Intercourse Act: Catawba Nation vs. South Carolina." *American Law Review* 12 (1984): 101–145.

Usner, Daniel H., Jr. "The Frontier Exchange in the Eighteenth Century." *William and Mary Quarterly*, 3rd ser. (1987): 166–192.

Van Ruymbeke, Bertrand. "The Huguenots of Proprietary South Carolina: Patterns of Migration and Integration." In *Money, Trade, and Power: The Evolution of South Carolina's Plantation Society*, pp. 26–48. Edited by Jack P. Greene, Rosemary Branna-Shute, and Randy J. Sparks. Columbia: University of South Carolina Press, 2001.

Wallerstein, Immanuel. "The Rise and Future Demise of the World Capitalist System: Concepts for Comparative Analysis." *Comparative Studies in Society and History* 16 (1974): 387–415.

———. "The Modern World System and Evolution." *Journal of World Systems Research*, 1 (1995): 1–15.

Wantanabe, John M. "Ritual Economy and the Negotiation of Autarky and Interdependence in a Ritual Mode of Production." In *Mesoamerican Ritual Economy: Archaeological and Ethnological Perspectives*, pp. 301–322. Edited by E. Christian Wells and Karla L. Davis-Salazar. Denver: University Press of Colorado, 2007.

Watson, Alan D. "The Quitrent System in Royal South Carolina." *William and Mary Quarterly*, 3rd ser., 33 (1976): 183–211.

———. "Household Size and Composition in Pre-Revolutionary North Carolina." *Mississippi Quarterly* 31 (1978): 551–569.

Watts, W. A. "The Late Quaternary Vegetation History of the Southeastern United States." *Annual Review of Ecological Systematics* 11 (1980): 387–409.

———. "Late Quaternary Vegetation of White Pond, South Carolina." *Quaternary Research* 13 (1980): 192–194.

Weir, Robert M. "The Harmony We Were Famous For: An Interpretation of Pre-Revolutionary South Carolina Politics." *William and Mary Quarterly*, 3rd ser., 26 (1969): 473–501.

———. "Who Shall Rule at Home: The American Revolution as a Crisis of Legitimacy for the Colonial Elite." *Journal of Interdisciplinary History* 6 (1976): 679–700.

———. "'The Violent Spirit,' the Reestablishment of Order, and the Continuity of Leadership in Post-Revolutionary South Carolina." In *An Uncivil War: The Southern Backcountry during the American Revolution*, pp. 70–98. Edited by Ronald Hoffman, Thad W. Tate, and Peter J. Albert. Charlottesville: University Press of Virginia for the United States Capital Historical Society, 1985.

Wells, Robert V. "Household Size and Composition in the British Colonies in America, 1675–1775." *Journal of Interdisciplinary History* 4 (1974): 543–570.

———. "The Population of England's Colonies in America: Old English or New Americans." *Population Studies* 46 (1992): 85–102.

Whebell, C.F.J. "Corridors: A Theory of Urban Systems." *Annals of the Association of American Geographers* 59 (1969): 1–26.

Winberry, John J. "Reputation of Carolina Indigo." *South Carolina Historical Magazine* 80 (1979): 242–250.

Wolf, Eric R. "Types of Latin American Peasantry: A Preliminary Discussion." *American Anthropologist* 57 (1955): 452–471.

———. "Specific Aspects of Plantation Systems in the New World." In *Plantation Systems of the New World*, pp. 136–147. Pan American Union, Social Science Monographs VII. Washington, D.C.: Pan American Union, 1959.

———. "Distinguished Lecture: Facing Old Insights, New Questions." *American Anthropologist* 92 (1990): 586–596.

———. "Incorporation and Identity in the Making of the Modern World." In *Pathways of Power: Building an Anthropology of the Modern World,* pp. 353–369. Edited by Eric E. Wolf with Sydel Silverman. Berkeley: University of California Press, 2001.

Wolf, Eric R., and Sidney W. Mintz. "Haciendas and Plantations in Middle America and the Antilles." *Social and Economic Studies* 6 (1957): 380–412.

Woods, Michael. "The Culture of Credit in Colonial Charleston." *South Carolina Historical Magazine* 99 (1998): 258–380.

Zierden, Martha. "Frontier Society in South Carolina: An Example from Willtown (1690–1800)." In *Another's Country: Archaeological and Historical Perspectives on Cultural Interactions in the Southern Colonies,* pp. 181–197. Edited by J. W. Joseph and Martha Zierden. Tuscaloosa: University of Alabama Press, 2002.

BOOKS AND MONOGRAPHS

Ackerman, Robert K. *South Carolina Land Policies.* Columbia: University of South Carolina Press, 1977.

Aldrich, Samuel R. and Earl R. Leng. *Modern Corn Production.* Cincinnati: The Farm Quarterly, 1965.

Allen, H. C. *Bush and Backwoods: A Comparison of the Frontier in Australia and the United States.* East Lansing: Michigan State University Press, 1959.

Anderson, David G. *The Savannah River Chiefdoms: Political Change in the Prehistoric Southeast.* Tuscaloosa: University of Alabama Press, 1994.

Anderson, Fred. *A People's Army: Massachusetts Soldiers and Society in the Seven Year's War.* Chapel Hill: University of North Carolina Press, 1984.

———. *Crucible of War: The Seven Years' War and the Fate of British North America: 1754–1766.* New York: Vintage Books, 2000.

Bailey, N. Louise, Mary L. Morgan, and Carolyn R. Taylor. *Biographical Directory of the South Carolina Senate, 1776–1985.* 3 vols. Columbia: University of South Carolina Press, 1986.

Barry, John M. *Natural Vegetation of South Carolina.* Columbia: University of South Carolina Press, 1980.

Bennett, Richard, and John Elton. *History of Corn Milling, Vol. II: Watermills and Windmills.* New York: Burt Franklin, 1898.

Berlin, Ira. *Many Thousands Gone: The First Two Centuries of Slavery in North America.* Cambridge, Mass.: Belknap Press of Harvard University Press, 1998.

Bernheim, G. D. *History of the German Settlements and of the Lutheran Church in North and South Carolina.* Philadelphia: Lutheran Book Store, 1872; reprint ed., Spartanburg, S.C.: The Reprint Co., 1972.

Berry, Brian J. L. *Geography of Market Centers and Retail Distribution.* Englewood Cliffs, N.J.: Prentice Hall, 1967.

Bivins, John F., Jr. *The Moravian Potters of North Carolina.* Chapel Hill: University of North Carolina Press, 1973.

Bodenhorn, Howard. *State Banking in Early America.* New York: Oxford University Press, 2003.

Booraem, Hendrik. *Young Hickory: The Making of Andrew Jackson.* Dallas: Taylor Trade Publishing, 2001.

Borick, Carl P. *Relieve Us of This Burthen: American Prisoners of War in the Revolutionary South, 1780–1782.* Columbia: University of South Carolina Press, 2012.

Bouch, C. M. L., and G. P. Jones. *A Short Social History of the Lake Counties, 1500–1830.* Manchester, UK: Manchester University Press, 1961.

Bourdieu, Pierre. *Outline of Theory and Practice.* New York: Cambridge University Press, 1977.

Boykin, Edward M. *History of the Boykin Family, from Their First Settlement in Virginia in 1685, and in South Carolina, Georgia, and Alabama, to the Present Time.* Camden, S.C.: Colin MacRae, 1876.

Braudel, Fernand. *Civilization and Capitalism, 15th–18th Century, Vol. 2: The Wheels of Commerce.* Translated by Siân Reynolds. New York: Harper & Row, 1979.

———. *Civilization and Capitalism, 15th–18th Century, Vol. 3: The Perspective of the World.* Translated by Siân Reynolds. New York: Harper & Row, 1984.

———. *The Identity of France, Vol. 1: History and Environment.* Translated by Siân Reynolds. New York: Harper & Row, 1988.

Braun, E. Lucy. *Deciduous Forests of Eastern North America.* Philadelphia: Blakiston, 1950.

Bridenbaugh, Carl. *Vexed and Troubled Englishmen, 1590–1642.* New York: Oxford University Press, 1968.

Brinsfield, John Wesley. *Religion and Politics in Colonial South Carolina.* Easley, S.C.: Southern Historical Press, 1983.

Brooks, Richard D., Mark D. Groover, and S. C. Smith. *Living on the Edge: The Archaeology of Cattle Raisers in the South Carolina Backcountry.* Savannah River Research Papers 10. Columbia: South Carolina Institute of Archaeology and Anthropology, 2000.

Brown, Douglas Summers. *The Catawba Indians: People of the River.* Columbia: University of South Carolina Press, 1968.

Brown, Richard Maxwell. *The South Carolina Regulators.* Cambridge, Mass.: Belknap Press of the Harvard University Press, 1963.

Brunson, Charlotte Boykin Salmond. *Kershaw County Cousins.* Columbia, S.C.: R. L. Bryan, 1978.

Bryan, John M. *America's First Architect: Robert Mills.* New York: Princeton Architectural Press, 2001.

Buchanan, John. *The Road to Guilford Courthouse: The American Revolution in the South.* New York: John Wiley, 1997.

Burton, Orville Vernon. *In My Father's House Are Many Mansions: Family and Community in Edgefield, South Carolina.* Chapel Hill: University of North Carolina Press, 1985.

Butler, Jon. *Becoming America: The Revolution before 1776.* Cambridge, Mass.: Harvard University Press, 2000.

Carney, Judith Ann. *Black Rice: The Origins of Cultivation in the Americas.* Cambridge, Mass.: Harvard University Press, 2001.

Carson, Thomas, ed. *Gale Encyclopedia of U.S. Economic History,* Vol. 2. Detroit: Gale Group, 1999.

Cathey, Cornelius Oliver. *Agricultural Developments in North Carolina, 1783–1860.* James Sooprunt Studies in History and Political Science, Vol. 38. Chapel Hill: University of North Carolina Press, 1956.

Chapple, Eliot D., and Carleton S. Coon. *Principles of Anthropology.* New York: Henry Holt, 1942.

Chatfield, Michael. *A History of Accounting Thought.* New York: Robert E. Krieger, 1977.

Clark, Christopher. *The Roots of Rural Capitalism: Western Massachusetts, 1780–1860.* Ithaca, N.Y.: Cornell University Press, 1990.

Clark, Murtie June. *Loyalists in the Southern Campaign of the Revolutionary War.* 3 vols. Baltimore: Genealogical Publishing Co., 1981.

Clowse, Converse D. *Economic Beginnings in Colonial South Carolina.* Columbia: University of South Carolina Press, 1971.

Coclanis, Peter. *The Shadow of a Dream: Economic Life and Death in the South Carolina Lowcountry, 1670–1920.* New York: Oxford University Press, 1989.

Coleman, Kenneth. *Colonial Georgia: A History.* New York: Charles Scribner's Sons, 1976.

Cook, H. T. *The Hard Labor Section.* Greenville, S.C.: By the Author, 1936.

Countryman, Edward. *The American Revolution.* New York: Hill and Wang, 1985.

Crane, Verner W. *The Southern Frontier, 1670–1732.* Ann Arbor: University of Michigan Press, 1929; Ann Arbor Paperbacks, 1956.

Cronen, William. *Changes in the Land: Indians, Colonists, and the Ecology of New England.* New York: Hill and Wang, 1982.

———. *Nature's Metropolis: Chicago and the Great West.* New York: W. W. Norton, 1991.

Dalcho, Frederick. *An Historical Account of the Protestant Episcopal Church in South Carolina, from the First Settlement to the War of the Revolution.* Charleston, S.C.: E. Thayer, 1820.

Davies, K. G. *The North Atlantic World in the Seventeenth Century.* Minneapolis: University of Minnesota Press, 1974.

Davis, David Brian. *The Problem of Slavery in Western Culture.* Ithaca, N.Y.: Cornell University Press, 1966.

Davis, R. P. Stephen, Jr., Brett H. Riggs, and David Cranford. *Archaeology at Ayers Town: An Early Federal Period Community in the Catawba Nation.* Research Laboratories of Archaeology, Research Report No. 37, University of North Carolina, 2014. http://www.rla.unc.edu/Publications/pdf/Resrep37/ (accessed June 8, 2014).

Dederer, John Morgan. *War in America to 1775: Before Yankee Doodle.* New York: New York University Press, 1990.

Demos, John. *A Little Community: Family Life in Plymouth Colony.* New York: Oxford University Press, 1970.

De Vries, Jan. *The Economy of Europe in an Age of Crisis, 1600–1750.* Cambridge: Cambridge University Press, 1976.

Dickson, R. J. *Ulster Emigration to Colonial America, 1718–1775.* Belfast: Ulster Historical Foundation, 1966.

Duby, Georges. *Rural Economy and Country Life in the Medieval West.* London: Edward Arnold, 1968.

Duffy, Christopher. *Fire & Stone: The Science of Fortress Warfare, 1660–1860.* Newton Abbot, Devon, UK: David & Charles, 1975.

Duncan, Louis C. *Medical Men in the American Revolution, 1775–1783.* Carlisle Barracks, Pa.: Medical Field Service School, 1931.

Durkheim, Emile. *The Elementary Forms of Religious Life.* Translated by Joseph Ward Swain. New York: Free Pree, 1965.

Earle, Timothy. *Chiefdoms, Power, Economy, and Ideology.* New York: Cambridge University Press, 1991.

———. *Bronze Age Economics: The Beginnings of Political Economies.* Boulder, Colo.: Westview Press, 2002.

Edgar, Walter. *South Carolina: A History.* Columbia: University of South Carolina Press, 1998.

———. *Partisans and Redcoats: The Southern Conflict That Turned the Tide of the American Revolution.* New York: William Morrow, 2001.

Edgar, Walter B., and N. Louise Bailey. *Biographical Directory of the South Carolina House of Representatives, Vol. 2: The Commons House of Assembly, 1692–1775.* Columbia: University of South Carolina Press, 1977.

Elzas, Barnett A. *The Jews of South Carolina, from the Earliest Times to the Present Day.* Philadelphia: J. B. Lippincott, 1905.

Faragher, John Mack. *Sugar Creek, Life on the Illinois Prairie.* New Haven: Yale University Press, 1986.

Fenn, Elizabeth A. *Pox Americana: The Great Smallpox Epidemic of 1775–82.* New York: Hill and Wang, 2001.

Ferguson, Leland G. *Uncommon Ground: Archaeology and Early African America, 1650–1800.* Washington, D.C.: Smithsonian Institution Press, 1992.

Fischer, David Hackett. *Albion's Seed: Four British Folkways in America.* New York: Oxford University Press, 1989.

Flandrin, Jean-Louis. *Families in Former Times: Kinship, Household, and Sexuality.* New York: Cambridge University Press, 1979.

Flynn, Jean Martin. *The Militia in Antebellum South Carolina Society.* Spartanburg, S.C.: The Rrprint Co., 1991.

Fogel, Robert William, and Stanley L. Engerman. *Time of the Cross: The Economics of American Negro Slavery.* Boston: Little, Brown, 1974.

Ford, Lacy K., Jr. *Origins of Southern Radicalism: The South Carolina Upcountry, 1800–1860.* New York: Oxford University Press, 1988.

Franklin, John Hope, and Loren Schweninger. *Runaway Slaves: Rebels on the Plantation.* New York: Oxford University Press, 1999.

Fried, Morton H. *The Evolution of Political Society: An Essay in Political Anthropology.* New York: Random House, 1967.

Frothingham, E. H., and R. M. Nelson. *South Carolina Forest Resources and Industries.* U.S. Department of Agriculture, Miscellaneous Publication No. 552. Washington, DC: Government Printing Office, 1944.

Fuller, Wayne E. *The American Mail: Enlarger of the Common Life.* Chicago: University of Chicago Press, 1972.

Gallay, Alan. *The Indian Slave Trade: The Rise of the English Empire in the American South, 1670–1717.* New Haven: Yale University Press, 2002.

Galpin, C. J. *The Social Anatomy of an Agricultural Community.* AES Research Bulletin no. 34. University of Wisconsin–Madison, 1915.

Genovese, Eugene D. *The World the Slaveholders Made: Two Essays in Interpretation.* New York: Pantheon Books, 1969.

Giddens, Anthony. *Central Problems in Social Theory: Action, Structures, and Contradiction in Social Analysis.* Berkeley: University of California Press, 1979.

Gordon, John W. *South Carolina and the American Revolution: A Battlefield History.* Columbia: University of South Carolina Press, 2003.

Gray, H. Peter. *A Generalized Theory of International Trade.* New York: Holmes and Meier, 1976.

Gray, Louis Cecil. *A History of Agriculture in the Southern United States to 1860.* 2 vols. Washington, D.C.: Carnegie Institution of Washington, 1933; reprint ed., Gloucester, Mass.: Peter Smith, 1958.

Green, Edwin L. *A History of Richland County, South Carolina, Vol. 1: 1732–1805.* Columbia, S.C.: R. L. Bryan, 1932; reprint ed., Greenville, S.C.: Southern Historical Press, 1996.

Gregg, Alexander. *History of the Old Cheraws.* Columbia: The State Co., 1867; reprint ed., Greenville, S.C.: Southern Historical Press, 1991.

Hadden, Sally E. *Slave Patrols: Law and Violence in Virginia and the Carolinas.* Cambridge, Mass.: Harvard University Press, 2001.

Hagy, James William. *This Happy Land: The Jews of Colonial and Antebellum Charleston.* Tuscaloosa: University of Alabama Press, 1993.

Hammond, Bray. *Banks and Politics in America: From the Revolution to the Civil War.* Princeton, N.J.: Princeton University Press, 1957.

Handler, Jerome S., and Frederick W. Lange. *Plantation Slavery in Barbados: An Archaeological and Historical Investigation.* Cambridge, Mass.: Harvard University Press, 1978.

Hardeman, Nicholas P. *Shucks, Shocks, and Hominy Blocks: Corn as a Way of Life in Pioneer America.* Baton Rouge: Louisiana State University Press, 1981.

Hart, John Fraser. *The Look of the Land.* Englewood Cliffs, N.J.: Prentice Hall, 1975.

Heinegg, Paul. *Free African Americans of North Carolina and Virginia.* Baltimore: Genealogical Publishing Co., 1994.

Henretta, James A. *The Evolution of American Society, 1700–1815: An Interdisciplinary Analysis.* Lexington, Mass.: Heath and Co., 1973.

Herskovits, Melville J. *Man and His Works: The Science of Cultural Anthropology.* New York: Alfred A. Knopf, 1948.

Heyrman, Christine Leigh. *Southern Cross: The Beginnings of the Bible Belt.* New York: Alfred A. Knopf, 1997.

Hibbert, Christopher. *Redcoats and Rebels: The American Revolution through British Eyes.* New York: Avon Books, 1990.

Hirsch, Arthur Henry. *The Huguenots of Colonial South Carolina.* Durham, N.C.: Duke University Press, 1928; reprint ed., Columbia: University of South Carolina Press, 1999.

Hoch, J. Hampton. *The History of Pharmacy in South Carolina.* Charleston, S.C.: South Carolina Pharmaceutical Association, 1951.

Holschlag, Stephanie L., and Michael J. Rodeffer. *Ninety Six: Siegeworks Opposite Star Redoubt.* Ninety Six, S.C.: Ninety Six Historic Site, 1976.

———. *Ninety Six: Exploratory Excavations in the Village.* Ninety Six, S.C.: Star Fort Historical Commission, 1977.

Holschlag, Stephanie L., Michael J. Rodeffer, and Marvin L. Cann. *Ninety Six: The Jail.* Ninety Six, SC: Star Fort Historical Commission, 1978.

Honigman, John J. *Personality and Culture.* New York: Harper & Bros., 1954.

Hudson, Charles M. *The Catawba Nation.* Athens: University of Georgia Press, 1970.

———. *The Southeastern Indians.* Knoxville: University of Tennessee Press, 1976.

———. *The Juan Pardo Expedition: Exploration of the Carolinas and Tennessee, 1556–1568.* Athens: University of Georgia Press, 1990.

Hunt, Charles B. *Physiography of the United States.* San Francisco: W. H. Freeman, 1967.

Inabinet, Joan A. *Lyttleton Street United Methodist Church of Camden, S.C.: A History.* Camden, S.C.: Pine Tree Publishing Co., 2003.

Inabinet, Joan A., and L. Glen Inabinet. *A History of Kershaw County, South Carolina.* Columbia: University of South Carolina Press, 2011.

Jakle, John A. *Images of the Ohio Valley: A Historical Geography of Travel, 1740–1860.* New York: Oxford University Press, 1977.

Jarvis, M. *Bermuda's Architectural Heritage: St. George's.* Hamilton: Bermuda National Trust, 1998.

John, Richard R. *Spreading the News: The American Postal System from Franklin to Morse.* Cambridge, Mass.: Harvard University Press, 1995.

Johnson, George Lloyd, Jr. *The Frontier in the Colonial South: South Carolina Backcountry, 1736–1800.* Westport, Conn.: Greenwood Press, 1997.

Jones, Daniel P. *The Economic & Social Transformation of Rural Rhode Island, 1780–1850.* Boston: Northeastern University Press, 1992.

Jordan, Terry G. *North American Cattle Ranching Frontiers: Origin, Diffusion, and Differentiation.* Albuquerque: University of New Mexico Press, 1993.

Jordan, Terry G., and Matti Kaups. *The American Backwoods Frontier: An Ethnic and Ecological Interpretation.* Baltimore: Johns Hopkins University Press, 1989.

Joyner, Charles. *Down by the Riverside: A South Carolina Slave Community.* Chicago: University of Illinois Press, 1984.

Kapsch, Robert J. *Historic Canals and Waterways of South Carolina.* Columbia: University of South Carolina Press, 2010.

Kelso, William M. *Kingsmill Plantations, 1619–1800: Archaeology of Country Life in Colonial Virginia.* Orlando, Fla.: Academic Press, 1984.

Kendall, Hugh P. *Beeston Hirst and Thrum Hall in Soyland: The Royde Family.* Halifax, UK: Halifax Antiquarian Society, 1915.

Kennedy, Robert McMillan. *De Mortuis: Concerning Those That Lie in the Old Burial Grounds in and about Camden, S.C.* Columbia, S.C.: The State Co., 1935.

Kerr, Wilfred Brenton. *Bermuda and the American Revolution, 1760–1783.* Princeton, N.J.: Princeton University Press, 1936.

Kershaw County Cemetery Survey Project. *Kershaw County, South Carolina, Cemetery Survey, Vol. 3.* Camden, S.C.: Kershaw County Historical Society, 1991.

Kershaw County Historical Society. *A Guide to Historic Sites in Camden, South Carolina.* Camden, S.C.: Kershaw County Historical Society, 1992.

Kirkland, Thomas J., and Robert M. Kennedy. *Historic Camden, Vol. 1: Colonial and Revolutionary.* Columbia, S.C.: The State Printing Co., 1905.

———. *Historic Camden, Vol. 2: Nineteenth Century.* Columbia, S.C.: The State Printing Co., 1926.

Klein, Rachel N. *Unification of a Slave State: The Rise of the Planter Class in the South Carolina Backcountry, 170–1808.* Chapel Hill: University of North Carolina Press for the Institute of Early American History and Culture, 1990.

Kohn, David, and Bess Glen, eds. *Internal Improvements in South Carolina, 1817–1828.* Washington, D.C.: By the Author, 1938.

Kovacik, Charles F., and John J. Winberry. *South Carolina: A Geography.* Boulder, Colo.: Westview Press, 1987.

Kroeber, Alfred. *Anthropology*. New York: Harcourt Brace, 1948.

Kuchler, A. W. *Potential Natural Vegetation of the Coterminous United States*. American Special Publication 36. New York: American Geographical Society, 1964.

Kulikoff, Allan. *Tobacco and Slaves: The Development of Southern Cultures in the Chesapeake*. Chapel Hill: University of North Carolina Press, 1986.

———. *The Agrarian Origins of American Capitalism*. Charlottesville: University Press of Virginia, 1992.

———. *From English Peasants to Colonial American Farmers*. Chapel Hill: University of North Carolina Press, 2000.

Lambert, Robert Stansbury. *South Carolina Loyalists in the American Revolution*. Columbia: University of South Carolina Press, 1987.

Landers, H. L. *The Battle of Camden, South Carolina, August 16, 1780*. Washington, D.C.: Government Printing Office, 1929.

Laslett, Peter. *The World We Have Lost: England before the Industrial Age*. New York: Charles Scribner's Sons, 1971.

Laurie, Pete, and David Chamberlain. *The South Carolina Aquarium Guide to Aquatic Habitats of South Carolina*. Columbia: University of South Carolina Press, 2003.

Legg, James B., Steven D. Smith, and Tomara S. Wilson. *Understanding Camden: The Revolutionary War Battle of Camden as Revealed through Historical, Archaeological, and Private Collections Analysis*. Columbia: South Carolina Institute of Archaeology and Anthropology, 2005.

Lewis, Kenneth E. *Archaeological Investigations at the Kershaw House, Camden (38KE1), Kershaw County, South Carolina*. Research Manuscript Series 78. Columbia: South Carolina Institute of Archaeology and Anthropology, 1975.

———. *Camden: A Frontier Town in Eighteenth Century South Carolina*. Anthropological Studies 2. Columbia: South Carolina Institute of Archaeology and Anthropology, 1976.

———. *A Functional Study of the Kershaw House Site in Camden, South Carolina*. Research Manuscript Series 110. Columbia: South Carolina Institute of Archaeology and Anthropology, 1977.

———. *An Archaeological Survey of Long Bluff State Park, Darlington County, South Carolina*. Research Manuscript Series 129. Columbia: South Carolina Institute of Archaeology and Anthropology, 1978.

———. *The American Frontier: A Archaeological Study of Pattern and Process*. Orlando, Fla.: Academic Press, 1984.

———. *West to Far Michigan: Settling the Lower Peninsula, 1815–1860*. East Lansing: Michigan State University Press, 2002.

———. *Camden: Historical Archaeology in the South Carolina Backcountry*. Belmont, Calif.: Thomson-Wadsworth, 2006.

Leyburn, James G. *Frontier Folkways*. New Haven: Yale University Press, 1935.

Lipscomb, Terry W. *South Carolina in 1791: George Washington's Southern Tour*. Columbia: South Carolina Department of Archives and History, 1993.

Littlefield, Daniel. *Rice and Slaves: Ethnicity and the Slave Trade in Colonial South Carolina*. Urbana: University of Illinois Press, 1981.

Logan, John H. *A History of the Upper Country of South Carolina, Vol. 1*. Charleston, S.C.: S. G. Courtnay, 1859.

Lossing, Benjamin. *Pictorial Field Book of the American Revolution*. 2 vols. New York: Harper & Bros., 1860.

Lowie, Robert H. *Social Organization*. New York: Holt, Rinehart, 1948.

Lumpkin, Henry. *From Savannah to Yorktown: The American Revolution in the South*. Columbia: University of South Carolina Press, 1981.

MacGill, Caroline E. *History of Transportation in the United States before 1860*. Washington, D.C.: Carnegie Institute of Washington, 1917; reprint ed., Forge Village, Mass.: Peter Smith, 1948.

Marx, Karl. *Capital: A Critique of Political Economy*. Edited by Paul Eden and translated by Paul Cedar. New York: E. P. Dutton, 1930.

Mason, Roger D. *Euro-American Settlement Systems in the Central Salt River Valley of Northeast Missouri.* Publications in Archaeology No. 2. Columbia: University of Missouri–Columbia, American Archaeology Division.

McCusker, John J. *Money and Exchange in Europe and America, 1600–1775: A Handbook.* Chapel Hill: University of North Carolina Press, 1978.

McCusker, John J., and Russell R. Menard. *The Economy of British America, 1607–1789.* Chapel Hill: University of North Carolina Press for the Institute of Early American History and Culture, 1985.

Meinig, D. W. *The Shaping of America: A Geographical Perspective on 500 Years of History, Vol. 1: Atlantic America, 1492–1800.* New Haven: Yale University Press, 1986.

Meriwether, Robert L. *The Expansion of South Carolina, 1729–1765.* Kingsport, Tenn.: Southern Publishers, 1940.

Merrell, James H. *The Indians' New World: Catawbas and Their Neighbors from European Contact through Removal.* Chapel Hill: University of North Carolina Press, 1989.

Merrens, H. Roy. *Colonial North Carolina in the Eighteenth Century: A Study in Historical Geography.* Chapel Hill: University of North Carolina Press, 1964.

Michie, James L. *The Discovery of Old Fort Congaree.* Research Manuscript Series 208. Columbia: South Carolina Institute of Archaeology and Anthropology, 1989.

Migliazzo, Arlin C. *To Make This Land Our Own: Community, Identity, and Cultural Adaptation in Purrysburg Township, South Carolina, 1732–1865.* Columbia: University of South Carolina Press, 2007.

Milhous, Evelyn Perry. *History of the Milhous Family in South Carolina.* Miami: By the Author, 1944.

Milling, Chapman. *Red Carolinians.* Chapel Hill: University of North Carolina Press, 1940.

Mitchell, Cleaveland J., Jr. *Soil Survey of Kershaw County Area, South Carolina.* U.S. Department of Agriculture, Soil Conservation Service, in Cooperation with the South Carolina Experiment Station and the South Carolina Land Resources Conservation Commission. Washington, D.C.: Government Printing Office, 1989.

Mitchell, Robert D. *Commercialism and Frontier: Perspectives on the Early Shenandoah Valley.* Charlottesville: University Press of Virginia, 1977.

Mooney, James. *The Siouan Tribes of the East.* Smithsonian Institution, Bureau of American Ethnology, Bulletin 22. Washington, D.C.: Government Printing Office, 1894.

Moore, Caroline T., comp. and ed. *Abstracts of the Wills of Charleston District, South Carolina, and Other Wills Recorded in the District, 1783–1800.* Columbia, S.C.: R. L. Bryan, 1974.

Moore, Christopher. *The Loyalists: Revolution, Exile, Settlement.* Toronto: McClelland & Stewart, 1994.

Moore, David. *Catawba Valley Mississippian: Ceramics, Chronology, and Catawba Indians.* Tuscaloosa: University of Alabama Press, 2002.

Moore, John Hammond. *Columbia and Richland County: A South Carolina Community, 1740–1990.* Columbia: University of South Carolina Press, 1993.

Moore, Peter. *World of Toil and Strife: Community Transformation in Backcountry South Carolina, 1750–1805.* Columbia: University of South Carolina Press, 2007.

Morton, Ronald. *Soil Survey of Chesterfield County Area, South Carolina.* U.S. Department of Agriculture, Soil Conservation Service, in Cooperation with the South Carolina Agricultural Experiment Station and the South Carolina Department of Natural Resources. Washington, D.C.: Government Printing Office, 1995.

Moss, Bobby G., and Michael Scoggins. *African-American Patriots in the Southern Campaign of the American Revolution.* Blacksburg, S.C.: Scotia-Hibernia Press, 2004.

———. *African-American Loyalists in the Southern Campaign of the American Revolution.* Blacksburg, S.C.: Scotia-Hibernia Press, 2005.

Nelson, Lowry. *Rural Sociology.* New York: American Book Co., 1952.

Nelson, William H. *The American Tory.* Boston: Basic Books, 1961.

Nettels, Curtis P. *The Economic History of the United States, Vol. 2: The Emergence of a National Economy, 1775–1815.* New York: Holt, Rinehart and Winston, 1962.

Netting, R. M., R. R. Wilk, and E. J. Arnould, eds. *Households, Historical and Comparative Studies of the Domestic Group.* Berkeley: University of California Press, 1984.

Newton, Milton B., Jr. *Louisiana House Types: A Field Guide.* Mélanges, No. 2. Baton Rouge: Louisiana State University, 1971.

Noël Hume, Ivor. *A Guide to Artifacts of Colonial America.* New York: Alfred A. Knopf, 1970.

North, Douglass C. *The Economic Growth of the United States, 1790–1860.* New York: W. W. Norton, 1966.

Oliver, Priscilla Ann Trantham. *Living in Camden: Scenes since Historic Camden.* Camden, S.C.: Kershaw County Historical Society, 1995.

Opler, Morris E. *An Apache Life-Way: The Economic, Social, and Religious Institutions of the Chiricahua Apache.* Chicago: University of Chicago Press, 1941.

Overstreet, William C., and Henry Bell III. *The Crystalline Rocks of South Carolina.* U.S. Department of the Interior, Geological Survey, Bulletin 1183. Washington, D.C.: Government Printing Office, 1965.

Owsley, Frank Lawrence. *Plain Folk of the Old South.* Chicago: Quadrangle Books, 1949.

Pan American Union. *Plantation Systems of the New World.* Pan American Union, Research Monographs VII. Washington, D.C.: Pan American Union, 1959.

Perkins, Edwin J. *The Economy of Colonial America.* New York: Columbia University Press, 1980.

Peterson, Harold L. *Round Shot and Rammers: An Introduction to Muzzle-Loading Land Artillery in the United States.* New York: Bonanza Books, 1969.

Petty, Julian J. *The Growth and Distribution of Population in South Carolina.* Columbia: South Carolina State Planning Board, 1943; reprint ed., Spartanburg, S.C.: The Reprint Co., 1973.

Phillips, Kevin. *The Cousins' Wars: Religion, Politics, and the Triumph of Anglo-America.* New York: Basic Books, 1999.

Plumb, J. H. *England in the Eighteenth Century.* Baltimore: Penguin, 1972.

Polanyi, Karl. *The Great Transformation: The Political and Economic Origins of Our Time.* Boston: Beacon Press, 1957.

Postan, M. M. *The Medieval Economy and Society: An Economic History of Britain, 1100–1500.* Berkeley: University of California Press, 1972.

Price, Jacob M. *Capital and Credit in British Overseas Trade: The View from the Chesapeake, 1700–1776.* Cambridge, Mass.: Harvard University Press, 1980.

Prucha, Francis Paul. *The Great Father: The United States Government and the American Indians.* 2 vols. Lincoln: University of Nebraska Press, 1984.

Quattlebaum, Paul. *The Land Called Chicora.* Gainesville: University of Florida Press, 1956.

Redfield, Robert. *Peasant Society and Culture.* Chicago: University of Chicago Press, 1956.

Reiss, Oscar. *Medicine and the American Revolution: How Diseases and Their Treatments Affected the Colonial Army.* Jefferson, N.C.: McFarland, 1998.

Reps, John W. *The Making of Urban America: A History of City Planning in the United States.* Princeton, N.J.: Princeton University Press, 1965.

———. *Tidewater Towns: City Planning in Colonial Virginia and Maryland.* Charlottesville: University Press of Virginia for the Colonial Williamsburg Foundation, 1972.

Reznikoff, Charles, and Uriah Z. Engelman. *The Jews of Charleston: A History of an American Jewish Community.* Philadelphia: Jewish Publication Society of America, 1950.

Rich, Everett Wesley. *The History of the Post Office to the Year 1829.* Cambridge, Mass.: Harvard University Press, 1924.

Rogers, George C., Jr. *Charleston in the Age of the Pinckneys.* Norman: University of Oklahoma Press, 1969.

———. *The History of Georgetown County, South Carolina.* Columbia: University of South Carolina Press, 1970.

Rorabaugh, W. J. *The Alcoholic Republic: An American Tradition.* New York: Oxford University Press, 1979.

Sabean, David Warren. *Property, Production, and family in Neckorhausen, Germany, 1700–1870.* Cambridge: Cambridge University Press, 1990.

Sachs, William S., and Ari Hoogenbloom. *The Enterprising Colonials: Society on the Eve of the Revolution.* Chicago: Argonaut, 1965.
Sahlins, Marshall. *Tribesmen.* Englewood Cliffs, N.J.: Prentice Hall, 1968.
———. *Stone Age Economics.* New York: Aldine, 1972.
Samford, Patricia M. *Subfloor Pits and the Archaeology of Slavery in Colonial America.* Tuscaloosa: University of Alabama Press, 2007.
Santee-Wateree Planning Council. *Land Use Sketch Plan, Santee-Wateree Planning District.* Columbia: Santee-Wateree Planning Council, 1972.
Sassaman, Kenneth E., and David G. Anderson. *Middle and Late Archaeological Records of South Carolina: A Synthesis for Research and Resource Management.* Columbia: Council of South Carolina Professional Archaeologists, 1994.
Scoggins, Michael C. *The Day It Rained Militia: Huck's Defeat and the Revolution in the South Carolina Backcountry, May–July 1780.* Charleston: History Press, 2005.
Sellers, Charles. *The Market Revolution in Jacksonian America, 1815–1846.* New York: Oxford University Press, 1991.
Sellers, Leila. *Charleston Business on the Eve of the American Revolution.* Chapel Hill: University of North Carolina Press, 1934.
Service, Elman R. *Primitive Social Organization: An Evolutionary Perspective.* New York: Random House, 1962.
Seward, Rudy Ray. *The American Family: A Demographic History.* Beverley Hills, Calif.: Sage, 1978.
Shipp, Albert M. *The History of Methodism in South Carolina.* Nashville, Tenn.: Southern Methodist Publishing House, 1884.
Sider, Gerald M. *Culture and Class in Anthropology and History: A Newfoundland Illustration.* Paris: Cambridge University Press, 1991.
Siebert, Wilbur H. *Loyalists in Est Florida, 1774–1785.* 2 vols. Deland: Florida Historical Society, 1929.
Sirmans, M. Eugene. *Colonial South Carolina, A Political History, 1663–1763.* Williamsburg, Va.: For the Institute of Early American History by the University of North Carolina Press, 1966.
Smith, Alice R. Huger, and D. E. Huger Smith. *The Dwelling Houses of Charleston, South Carolina.* Philadelphia: J. B. Lippincott, 1917.
Smith, M. G. *Corporations and Society: The Social Anthropology of Collective Action.* Chicago: Aldine, 1974.
Smith, Page. *As a City upon a Hill: The Town in American History.* New York: Alfred A. Knopf, 1966.
Smith, Steven D., James B. Legg, Tamara S. Wilson, and Jonathan Leader. *"Obstinate and Strong": The History and Archaeology of the Siege of Fort Motte.* Columbia: South Carolina Institute of Archaeology and Anthropology, 2007.
Smith, T. Lynn. *The Sociology of Rural Life.* New York: Harper & Bros., 1940.
Smith, Warren B. *White Servitude in Colonial South Carolina.* Columbia: University of South Carolina Press, 1961.
Snowden, Yates. *History of South Carolina.* 5 vols. New York: Lewis Publishing Co., 1920.
South, Stanley. *Method and Theory in Historical Archaeology.* New York: Academic Press, 1977.
———. *The Search for John Bartlam at Cain Hoy: America's First Creamware Potter.* Research Manuscript Series 219. Columbia: South Carolina Institute of Archaeology and Anthropology, 1993
———. *Historical Archaeology in Wachovia: Excavating Eighteenth Century Bethabara and Moravian Pottery.* New York: Kluwer/Plenum, 1999.
———. *Archaeological Pathways to Historical Site Development.* New York: Kluwer, 2002.
———. *Ninety Six Fortification Search: Ninety Six National Historic Site.* Research Manuscript Series 232. Columbia: South Carolina Institute of Archaeology and Anthropology, 2006.
Squire, Ephraim, and Edwin H. Davis. *Ancient Monuments of the Mississippi Valley.* Smithsonian Contributions to Knowledge, Vol. 1. Washington, D.C.: Smithsonian Institution, 1848.
Stamp, L. Dudley. *Britain's Structure and Scenery.* London: Collins, 1946.
Steffen, Jerome O. *Comparative Frontiers: A Proposal for Studying the American West.* Norman: University of Oklahoma Press, 1980.

Stilgoe, John R. *Common Landscape of America, 1580 to 1845*. New Haven: Yale University Press, 1982.

Stoner, Michael J., and Stanley South. *Exploring 1670 Charles Towne, 38CH1 A/B: Final Archaeological Report.* Research Manuscript Series 230. Columbia: South Carolina Institute of Archaeology and Anthropology, 2001.

Storck, John, and Walter Doewin Teague. *Flour for Man's Bread.* London: Oxford University Press, 1952.

Swanton, John R. *Early History of the Creek Indians and Their Neighbors.* Smithsonian Institution, Bureau of American Ethnology, Bulletin 73. Washington, D.C.: Government Printing Office, 1922.

Tanner, Helen Hornbeck. *Zespedes in East Florida, 1784–1790.* Coral Gables, Fla.: University of Miami Press, 1963; reprint ed., Jacksonville: University of North Florida Press, 1989.

Teal, Harvey S., and Robert J. Stets. *South Carolina Postal History and Illustrated Catalog of Postmarks, 1760–1860.* Lake Oswego, Ore.: Raven Press, 1989.

Thompson, Stephen I. *Pioneer Colonization: A Cross-Cultural View.* Addison-Wesley Modules in Anthropology 33. Reading, Mass.: Addison-Wesley, 1973.

Thorp, Daniel B. *The Moravian Community in Colonial North Carolina: Pluralism on the Southern Frontier.* Knoxville: University of Tennessee Press, 1989.

Trotter, Elinor. *Seventeenth Century Life in the County Parish.* London: Frank Cass, 1968.

U.S. Army Corps of Engineers. *Provisional Reconnaissance Inventory of the Charleston District.* Office of the Chief of Engineers, Engineer Agency for Resources Inventories. Washington, D.C.: Government Printing Office, 1972.

Urban, Mark. *Fusiliers: The Saga of a British Redcoat Regiment in the American Revolution.* New York: Walker, 2007.

Usner, Daniel H., Jr. *Indians, Settlers, and Slaves in a Frontier Exchange Economy: The Lower Mississippi Valley before 1783.* Chapel Hill: University of North Carolina Press for the Institute of Early American History and Culture, 1992.

Valentine, Alan. *The British Establishment, 1760–1784: An Eighteenth Century Biographical Dictionary.* Norman: University of Oklahoma Press, 1970.

Ver Steeg, Clarence L. *Origins of a Southern Mosaic.* Athens: University of Georgia Press, 1975.

Vlach, John Michael. *Back of the Big House: The Architecture of Plantation Slavery.* Chapel Hill: University of North Carolina Press, 1993.

Waddell, Gene. *Indians of the South Carolina Lowcountry, 1562–1751.* Spartanburg, S.C.: The Reprint Co. for the Southern Studies Program, University of South Carolina, 1980.

Walker, Williston. *A History of the Christian Church.* Rev. ed. New York: Charles Scribner's Sons, 1959.

Wallerstein, Immanuel. *The Modern World System: Capitalist Agriculture and the Origins of the European World Economy in the Sixteenth Century.* New York: Academic Press, 1974.

———. *The Modern World System II: Mercantilism and the Consolidation of the European World Economy, 1600–1750.* New York: Academic Press, 1980.

Walton, Gary M., and James E. Shepherd. *The Economic Rise of Early America.* London: Cambridge University Press, 1979.

Warhus, Mark. *Another America: Native American Maps and the History of Our Land.* New York: St. Matin's Press, 1997.

Waring, Joseph Ioor. *A History of Medicine in South Carolina, 1670–1825.* Columbia: South Carolina Medical Association, 1963.

Waterhouse, Richard. *A New World Gentry: The Making of Merchant and Planter Class in South Carolina, 1670–1770.* Charleston, SC: The History Press, 2005.

Weatherill, Lorna. *The Growth of the Pottery Industry in England, 1660–1815.* New York: Garland, 1986.

Weber, Max. *Economy and Society.* Edited by Guenter Roth and Claus Wittlich, translated by Ephraim Fischoff. Berkeley: University of California Press, 1978.

Weigley, Russell F. *The Partisan War: The South Carolina Campaign of 1780–1782.* Columbia: University of South Carolina Press, 1970.

Weir, Robert M. *Colonial South Carolina: A History.* New York: KTO Press, 1983; reprint ed., Columbia: University of South Carolina Press, 1997.

White, Richard. *The Roots of Dependency: Subsistence, Environment, and Social Change among the Choctaws, Pawnees, and Navajos.* Lincoln: University of Nebraska Press, 1983.

White, William B., Jr. *The Ross-Chesnut-Sutton Family of South Carolina.* Franklin, N.C.: Genealogical Publishing Services, 2002.

Wickwar, W. Hardy. *300 Years of Development Administration in South Carolina.* Columbia: Bureau of Government Research, University of South Carolina, 1970.

Wilbur, C. Keith. *Revolutionary Medicine.* Old Saybrook, Conn.: Globe Pequot Press, 1980.

Wilkie, Laurie, and Paul Farnsworth. *Sampling Many Pots: An Archaeology of Memory and Tradition at a Bahamian Plantation.* Gainesville: University Press of Florida, 2005.

Wittkowsky, George H., and J. L. Moseley. *Kershaw County: Economic and Social.* Columbia: Department of Rural Social Science, University of South Carolina, 1923.

Wolf, Eric R. *Peasants.* Englewood Cliffs, N.J.: Prentice Hall, 1966.

———. *Peasant Wars of the Twentieth Century.* New York: Harper & Row, 1969.

———. *Europe and the People without History.* Berkeley: University of California Press, 1982.

Wolf, Stephanie Grauman. *As Varied as Their Land: The Everyday Lives of Eighteenth-Century Americans.* New York: HarperCollins, 1993.

Wood, Kenneth A. *Post Dates: A Chronology of Intriguing Events in the Mails and Philately.* Albany, Ore.: Van Dahl, 1985.

Wood, Peter H. *Black Majority: Negroes in Colonial South Carolina from 1670 through the Stono Rebellion.* New York: Alfred A. Knopf, 1974.

Zimiles, Martha, and Murray Zimiles. *Early American Mills.* New York: Bramhall House, 1973.

UNPUBLISHED WORKS

Baker, Steven G. "Cofitacheque: Fair Province of Carolina." Master's thesis, University of South Carolina, 1975.

———. "The Working Draft of: The Catawba Peoples: Exploratory Perspectives in Ethnohistory and Archaeology." Report to Duke Power Company and Other Sponsors of Institutional Grant J-100. Columbia: Office of Research, University of South Carolina, 1975.

Borders, Dale Ray. "The Effect of Kinship on Settlement Patterns on the Southwest Michigan Frontier." Ph.D. dissertation, Michigan State University, 2003.

Brooks, Richard D. "Cattle Ranching in Colonial South Carolina: A Case Study in History and Archaeology of the Lazarus/Catherina Brown Cowpen." Master's thesis, University of South Carolina, 1988.

Cable, John S. "'Cultural Background.' In Archaeological Recovery at Sites 38SU45, 38SU133, and 38SU145, with Results of Test Excavations Conducted at 38SU136, 38SU137, and 38SU141, Poinsett Electronic Combat Range, Sumter County, South Carolina." U.S. Air Force Air Combat Command Series, Report of Investigations 7. Plano, Tex.: Geo-Marine, Inc., 1998.

Calmes, Alan. "Report of Excavations at the Revolutionary War Period Fortifications of Camden, South Carolina." Report to Camden District Heritage Foundation, Camden, S.C., 1968.

Daniels, Martha. "Mulberry Plantation's Family." Paper presented to the South Carolina Genealogical Society, Columbia, S.C., July 11, 2014.

Hughes, Kaylene. "Populating the Back Country: The Demographic and Social Characteristics of the Colonial South Carolina Frontier, 1730–1760." Ph.D. dissertation, Florida State University, 1985.

Kershaw, Peter G. D. "A Kershaw Family: 1670–1970." Port Charlotte, Fla., 1974. Photocopy in author's possession.

Lewis, Kenneth E. "Report of Archaeological Work at the Southwest Redoubt and the Presbyterian Cemetery." Report to Camden Historical Commission, Camden, S.C., 1983.

———. "Archaeological Investigations in Southwestern Camden: Report of the 1996–1998 Project." Report to Camden Historical Commission, Camden, S.C., 1999.

Lewis, Kenneth E., and Frank J. Krist Jr. "Settlement Expansion in Fredericksburg Township, South Carolina, 1740–1770." Report to Savannah River Archaeological Program, South Carolina Institute of Archaeology and Anthropology, Columbia, 1997.

McCormick, Jo Ann. "The Camden Backcountry Judicial Precinct, 1769–1790." Master's thesis, University of South Carolina, 1975.

———. "The Quakers of Colonial South Carolina, 1670–1807." Ph.D. dissertation, University of South Carolina, 1984.

Richardson, Katherine H. "The Impact of the Township System on the Backcountry of South Carolina: From Garrison Towns to 'Traditional' Towns." Paper presented at the Southern Colonial Backcountry Conference, Columbia, S.C., Oct. 15, 1993.

Scoggins, Michael C. "'Voluntarily Enlisted as a Soldier in the Revolution': A Case Study of Free African-Americans in the South Carolina Continental and State Troops during the Revolutionary War." Research paper, Cultural & Heritage Museums, York, S.C., 2008.

Strickland, Robert N. "Archaeological Excavations at Camden, 1971–1973." Report to Camden Historical Commission, Camden, S.C., 1976.

Terry, George D. "'Champaign Country': A Social History of an Eighteenth Century Low Country Parish in South Carolina, St. Johns Berkeley." Ph.D. dissertation, University of South Carolina, 1981.

Thornton, Phinehas. Letter to Clarissa Martin, Dec. 20, 1850. Letter in author's possession.

Trinkley, Michael, and Natalie Adams. "Archaeological Survey of the Santee-Cooper Lugoff-Allied Signal Transmission Line, Kershaw County, South Carolina." Chicora Foundation, Research Contribution 65, Columbia, S.C., 1991.

Whiteley, Hazel M. "Joseph Kershaw of Baitingsgate: Transcribed from Original Sources." Rippon-den, UK: 2001. Photocopy in author's possession.

Index